Vol. 11 *The Doctrine of the Saints' Perseverance Explained and Confirmed.*

Vol. 12 *Vindiciae Evangelicae: or, the Mystery of the Gospel Vindicated.*
Of the Death of Christ, and of Justification.
A Review of the Annotations of Grotius.

Vol. 13 *The Duty of Pastors and People Distinguished.*
Eshcol: a Cluster of the Fruit of Canaan.
Of Schism; in Three Books.
Nonconformity Vindicated.
Tracts on the Power of the Magistrate, Indulgence, Toleration, etc.

Vol. 14 *Animadversions on 'Fiat Lux'.*
Vindication of Animadversions.
The Church of Rome no safe Guide.
On Union among Protestants.
The State and Fate of Protestantism.

Vol. 15 *Discourse concerning Liturgies.*
Discourse concerning Evangelical Love, Church Peace, and Unity.
Inquiry concerning Evangelical Churches.
Answer to Dr Stillingfleet on the unreasonableness of Separation.
Instruction in the Worship of God.

Vol. 16 *The Nature of a Gospel Church.*
Tracts on Excommunication, Church Censures, Baptism, etc.
On the Divine Original of the Scriptures.
Posthumous Sermons.
Indices.

DIVISION 4 : EXPOSITORY

Vol. 17 *Concerning the Epistle to the Hebrews.*
Concerning the Messiah.
Concerning the Jewish Church.

Vol. 18 *The Sacerdotal Office of Christ.*
A Day of Sacred Rest.
Summary of Observations on Hebrews.

Vol. 19 *Exposition of Hebrews, 1–3:6.*

Vol. 20 *Exposition of Hebrews, 3:7–5:14.*

Vol. 21 *Exposition of Hebrews, 6:1–7:28.*

Vol. 22 *Exposition of Hebrews, 8:1–10:39.*

Vol. 23 *Exposition of Hebrews, 11:1–13:25.*

The Works of John Owen

VOLUME IX

The Works of JOHN OWEN

EDITED BY

William H. Goold

VOLUME IX

The Banner of Truth Trust

This Edition of
THE WORKS OF JOHN OWEN
first published by Johnstone & Hunter, 1850-53

Reprinted by
THE BANNER OF TRUTH TRUST
3 Murrayfield Road, Edinburgh EH12 6EL, UK
P.O. Box 621, Carlisle, PA 17013, USA

VOLUME IX

1965

Second printing 1976
Third printing 1982
Fourth printing 1990
Fifth printing 1998
Sixth printing 2009
Seventh printing 2017
Eighth printing 2021

THIS VOLUME ISBN–13: 978 0 85151 065 1
16-VOLUME SET ISBN-13: 978 0 85151 392 8

*

Printed in the USA by
Versa Press, Inc.,
East Peoria, IL

CONTENTS OF VOL. IX.

PART I.—A SERMON PUBLISHED 1690.

Page

PREFATORY NOTE BY THE EDITOR 2

SERMON.

SEASONABLE WORDS FOR ENGLISH PROTESTANTS.

SERMON.—"For Israel hath not been forsaken, nor Judah of his God, of the LORD of hosts; though their land was filled with sin against the Holy One of Israel."—JER. li. 5 3

PART II.—SERMONS PUBLISHED 1721.

PREFATORY NOTE BY THE EDITOR 18

SERMONS I., II.

THE STRENGTH OF FAITH.

SERMONS.—"He staggered not at the promise of God through unbelief; but was strong in faith, giving glory to God."—ROM. iv. 20 19

SERMONS III., IV.

THE NATURE AND BEAUTY OF GOSPEL WORSHIP.

SERMONS.—"For through him we both have access by one Spirit unto the Father."—EPH. ii. 18 53

SERMONS V.–IX.

OF WALKING HUMBLY WITH GOD.

SERMONS.—"And to walk humbly with thy God."—MIC. vi. 8 84

SERMONS X.–XIII.

PROVIDENTIAL CHANGES, AN ARGUMENT FOR UNIVERSAL HOLINESS.

Page

SERMONS.—"Seeing then that all these things shall be dissolved, what manner of persons ought ye to be in all holy conversation and godliness?"—2 PET. iii. 11 131

SERMONS XIV., XV.

THE SIN AND JUDGMENT OF SPIRITUAL BARRENNESS.

SERMONS.—"But the miry places thereof, and the marshes thereof, shall not be healed; they shall be given to salt."—EZEK. xlvii. 11 179

SERMON XVI.

HUMAN POWER DEFEATED.

SERMON.—"The stout-hearted are spoiled, they have slept their sleep; and none of the men of might have found their hands."—Ps. lxxvi. 5 197

SERMONS XVII., XVIII.

THE DIVINE POWER OF THE GOSPEL.

SERMONS.—"For I am not ashamed of the gospel of Christ: for it is the power of God unto salvation to every one that believeth; to the Jew first, and also to the Greek."—ROM. i. 16 217

SERMONS XIX., XX.

GOD THE SAINTS' ROCK.

SERMONS.—"From the end of the earth will I cry unto thee, when my heart is overwhelmed: lead me to the Rock that is higher than I."—Ps. lxi. 2 . . 237

SERMON XXI.

GOSPEL CHARITY.

SERMON.—"And above all these things put on charity, which is the bond of perfectness."—COL. iii. 14 256

SERMON XXII.

CHRIST'S PASTORAL CARE.

SERMON.—"Feed thy people with thy rod, the flock of thine heritage, which dwell solitarily in the wood, in the midst of Carmel: let them feed in Bashan and Gilead, as in the days of old."—MIC. vii. 14 271

SERMON XXIII.

A CHRISTIAN, GOD'S TEMPLE.

SERMON.—"For ye are the temple of the living God; as God hath said, I will dwell in them, and walk in them; and I will be their God, and they shall be my people. Wherefore come out from among them and be ye separate, saith the Lord, and touch not the unclean thing; and I will receive you, and will be a Father unto you, and ye shall be my sons and daughters, saith the Lord Almighty."—2 COR. vi. 16–18. 285

SERMON XXIV.

GOD'S WITHDRAWING HIS PRESENCE, THE CORRECTION OF HIS CHURCH.

Page

SERMON.—"O LORD, why hast thou made us to err from thy ways, and hardened our heart from thy fear? Return for thy servants' sake, the tribes of thine inheritance."—ISA. lxiii. 17 296

SERMON XXV.

THE BEAUTY AND STRENGTH OF ZION.

SERMON.—"Walk about Zion, and go round about her: tell the towers thereof. Mark ye well her bulwarks, consider her palaces; that ye may tell it to the generation following. For this God is our God for ever and ever; he will be our guide even unto death."—PS. xlviii. 12–14 307

SERMON XXVI.

PERILOUS TIMES.

SERMON.—"This know also, that in the last days perilous times shall come."—2 TIM. iii. 1 320

SERMONS XXVII. XXIX.

THE CHRISTIAN'S WORK OF DYING DAILY.

SERMONS.—"I protest by your rejoicing which I have in Christ Jesus our Lord, I die daily."—1 COR. xv. 31 334

SERMON XXX.

THE EVIL AND DANGER OF OFFENCES.

SERMON.—"Woe unto the world because of offences! for it must needs be that offences come; but woe to that man by whom the offence cometh!"—MATT. xviii. 7 352

SEVERAL PRACTICAL CASES OF CONSCIENCE RESOLVED.

PREFATORY NOTE BY THE EDITOR 358

DISCOURSE I.

QUESTION.—What conviction of a state of sin, and of the guilt of sin, is necessary to cause a soul sincerely to look after Christ? 359

DISCOURSE II.

QUESTION.—Seeing the act of closing with Christ is secret and hidden, and the special times and seasons of our conversion unto God are unknown unto most, what are the most certain evidences and pledges that we have cordially and sincerely received Christ, and returned unto God? 362

DISCOURSE III.

Page

QUESTION.—What concern have we in the sins of the day wherein we live? . 365

DISCOURSE IV.

QUESTION.—How may we recover from a decay of the principle of grace? . . 368

DISCOURSE V.

QUESTION.—How we may make our application unto Christ; not in general, but under what notion and apprehension of the person of Christ? 373

DISCOURSE VI.

QUESTION.—How may we make our addresses to Christ for the exercise of grace; that is, that we may have grace strengthened, and be ready for all exercise? or, How may we make application to Christ, that we may receive grace from him to recover from decays? 376

DISCOURSE VII.

QUESTION.—When our own faith is weakened as to the hearing of our prayers,—when we ourselves are hindered within ourselves from believing the answer of our prayers, have no ground to expect we should be heard, or no ground to believe we are heard,—what are those things that greatly weaken our faith as to the answer of our prayers; that though we continue to pray, yet our faith is weakened as to the hearing of our prayers? and what are the grounds that weaken men's faith in such a state? 379

DISCOURSE VIII.

QUESTION.—When may any one sin, lust, or corruption, be esteemed habitually prevalent? 381

DISCOURSE IX.

QUESTION.—Whether lust or corruption, habitually prevalent, be consistent with the truth of grace? 386

DISCOURSE X.

QUESTION.—What shall a person do who finds himself under the power of a prevailing corruption, sin, or temptation? 390

DISCOURSE XI.

QUESTION.—What is our duty with respect to dark and difficult dispensations of God's providence in the world? 392

DISCOURSE XII.

QUESTION.—How we are to prepare for the coming of Christ? 398

DISCOURSE XIII.

Page

On the contest between Christ and Antichrist 401

DISCOURSE XIV.

QUESTION.—What is the duty of believers under divine warnings? . . . 403

PART III.—SERMONS PUBLISHED 1756.

PREFATORY NOTE BY THE EDITOR 408

SERMONS I., II.

THE EVERLASTING COVENANT, THE BELIEVER'S SUPPORT UNDER DISTRESS.

SERMONS.—"Although my house be not so with God; yet he hath made with me an everlasting covenant, ordered in all things, and sure: for this is all my salvation, and all my desire, although he make it not to grow."—2 SAM. xxiii. 5 . 409

SERMON III.

THE MINISTRY THE GIFT OF CHRIST.

SERMON.—"Wherefore he saith, When he ascended up on high, he led captivity captive, and gave gifts unto men."—EPH. iv. 8 431

SERMON IV.

MINISTERIAL ENDOWMENTS THE WORK OF THE SPIRIT.

SERMON.—"But all these worketh that one and the self-same Spirit, dividing to every man severally as he will."—1 COR. xii. 11 441

SERMON V.

THE DUTY OF A PASTOR.

SERMON.—"And I will give you pastors according to my heart, which shall feed you with knowledge and understanding."—JER. iii. 15 452

SERMONS VI.–IX.

THE EXCELLENCY OF CHRIST.

SERMONS.—*To the chief Musician upon Shoshannim, for the sons of Korah, Maschil, A Song of loves.*

"My heart is inditing a good matter: I speak of the things which I have made touching the King; my tongue is the pen of a ready writer. Thou art fairer than the children of men; grace is poured into thy lips: therefore God hath blessed thee for ever. Gird thy sword upon thy thigh, O most mighty, with thy glory and thy majesty."—Ps. xlv. 1–3 462

SERMON X.

THE USE AND ADVANTAGE OF FAITH IN A TIME OF PUBLIC CALAMITY.

Page
SERMON.—"The just shall live by his faith."—HAB. ii. 4 490

SERMON XI.

THE USE OF FAITH UNDER REPROACHES AND PERSECUTIONS.

SERMON.—"The just shall live by his faith."—HAB. ii. 4 498

SERMON XII.

THE USE OF FAITH, IF POPERY SHOULD RETURN UPON US.

SERMON.—"The just shall live by his faith."—HAB. ii. 4 505

SERMON XIII.

THE USE OF FAITH IN A TIME OF GENERAL DECLENSION IN RELIGION.

SERMON.—"The just shall live by his faith."—HAB. ii. 4 510

PART IV.—SERMONS PUBLISHED 1760.

PREFATORY NOTE BY THE EDITOR 518
Epistle Dedicatory 519
Preface 520

DISCOURSE I.

DISCOURSE.—"For he hath made him to be sin for us, who knew no sin; that we might be made the righteousness of God in him."—2 COR. v. 21 . . 521

DISCOURSES II., III.

DISCOURSES.—"The cup of blessing which we bless, is it not the communion of the blood of Christ? The bread which we break, is it not the communion of the body of Christ?"—1 COR. x. 16 523

DISCOURSE IV.

DISCOURSE.—"As often as ye eat this bread, and drink this cup, ye do show the Lord's death till he come."—1 COR. xi. 26 538

DISCOURSES V., VI.

DISCOURSES.—"But let a man examine himself, and so let him eat of that bread, and drink of that cup."—1 COR. xi. 28 544

DISCOURSE VII.

Page

DISCOURSE.—"He said, ... Take, eat."—1 COR. xi. 24 563

DISCOURSE VIII.

DISCOURSE.—"Christ also hath once suffered for sins, the just for the unjust, that he might bring us to God; being put to death in the flesh, but quickened by the Spirit."—1 PET. iii. 18 566

DISCOURSE IX.

DISCOURSE.—"They worshipped him; but some doubted."—MATT. xxviii. 17 . 569

DISCOURSE X.

DISCOURSE.—"Teaching them to observe all things whatsoever I have commanded you: and, lo, I am with you alway, even unto the end of the world."—MATT. xxviii. 20 571

DISCOURSE XI.

DISCOURSE.—"He shall see of the travail of his soul, and shall be satisfied."—ISA. liii. 11 576

DISCOURSE XII.

DISCOURSE.—"That I may know him, and the power of his resurrection, and the fellowship of his sufferings, being made conformable unto his death."—PHIL. iii. 10 579

DISCOURSES XIII., XIV.

DISCOURSES.—"For I have received of the Lord that which also I delivered unto you, That the Lord Jesus, the same night in which he was betrayed, took bread: and, when he had given thanks, he brake it, and said, Take, eat; this is my body, which is broken for you: this do in remembrance of me. After the same manner also he took the cup, when he had supped, saying, This cup is the new testament in my blood: this do ye, as oft as ye drink it, in remembrance of me. For as often as ye eat this bread, and drink this cup, ye do show the Lord's death till he come."—1 COR. xi. 23-26 582

DISCOURSES XV., XVI.

DISCOURSES.—"And I, if I be lifted up from the earth, will draw all men unto me."—JOHN xii. 32 592

DISCOURSE XVII.

DISCOURSE.—"And Aaron shall lay both his hands upon the head of the live goat, and confess over him all the iniquities of the children of Israel, and all their transgressions in all their sins, putting them upon the head of the goat," etc.—LEV xvi. 21 597

DISCOURSES XVIII., XIX.

Page

DISCOURSES.—" I am crucified with Christ: nevertheless I live; yet not I, but Christ liveth in me: and the life which I now live in the flesh I live by the faith of the Son of God, who loved me, and gave himself for me."—GAL. ii. 20 600

DISCOURSE XX.

DISCOURSE.—" The love of God is shed abroad in our hearts by the Holy Ghost, which is given unto us."—ROM. v. 5 606

DISCOURSE XXI.

DISCOURSE.—" And to know the love of Christ, which passeth knowledge."—EPH. iii. 19 609

DISCOURSE XXII.

DISCOURSE.—" And lo a voice from heaven, saying, This is my beloved Son, in whom I am well pleased."—MATT. iii. 17 612

DISCOURSE XXIII.

DISCOURSE.—" As often as ye eat this bread, and drink this cup," etc.—1 COR. xi. 26 615

DISCOURSE XXIV.

DISCOURSE.—" Always bearing about in the body the dying of the Lord Jesus."—2 COR. iv. 10 618

DISCOURSE XXV.

DISCOURSE.—" Except ye eat the flesh of the Son of man, and drink his blood, ye have no life in you."—JOHN vi. 53 620

POSTHUMOUS SERMONS.

PART I.

A SERMON PUBLISHED

M.DC.XC.

PREFATORY NOTE.

The following is the first of Owen's posthumous Sermons. It was preached on the occasion of a fast, December 22, 1681; and was published separately, in 1690, with the subjoined quaint preface by Daniel Burgess. The latter was the son of an excellent Nonconformist minister, Daniel Burgess, who was ejected from Collinburn, Wiltshire, under the Bartholomew Act, 1662. The son was a somewhat eccentric but celebrated and much-respected preacher in London,—a kind of Latimer among the Nonconformists of his time. He died in 1713, and his funeral sermon was preached by Matthew Henry:—

"To the Reader,—Upon the desire of some interested in the publication of this sermon, I have perused it, and do communicate these my thoughts concerning it.

"There appear unto me in it those two things, which do above all others commend any sermon, or any other book,—namely, most weighty and seasonable argument, with very judicious and methodical management.

"If I am able to judge, the management speaks *arma virumque*, the man and his furniture; and it is, like its great author, well known to this age, and like to be so unto future ones by his writings, in more than one language. There is a favour due unto all posthumous pieces,—of which sort this is; but there is little need that this piece seems to have of it.

"As for its argument, it is very salvation; and that not merely personal or domestical, but national. This, if any thing, will be acknowledged momentous; and now, if ever, it must be acknowledged seasonable;—now, in this our day, 'known only to the Lord;'—nay, now, that it is neither day nor night, as the prophet speaks;—now, that city and country are crying, 'Watchman, what of the night? watchman, what of the night?'—now, that the three frightful signs of approaching night are so upon us; I mean, shadows growing long, labourers going apace home, and wild beasts going boldly abroad. 'Quis talia fando temperet à lachrymis?'

"In a word, here is that which will sufficiently recommend itself to all serious readers. It is the complaint of many, that our booksellers' shops are become heaps of dry sand, in which many a rich stone is lost: but it is known to all, that diamonds will be found out by their own lustre; and I make no great question but so this sermon will be. That it may be so, and may go much abroad, and do good wherever it comes, is the prayer of

"Thy servant in Christ Jesus,

"D. Burgess."

"*From my house in Bridges Street, in Covent Garden, Aug. 7, 1690.*"

POSTHUMOUS SERMONS.

SERMON.

SEASONABLE WORDS FOR ENGLISH PROTESTANTS.

"For Israel hath not been forsaken, nor Judah of his God, of the LORD of hosts; though their land was filled with sin against the Holy One of Israel."—JER. li. 5.

THIS chapter and the foregoing are an eminent prophecy and prediction of the destruction of Babylon and of the land of the Chaldeans,—of the metropolitical city of the empire and of the nation itself. There is a double occasion for the inserting of these words. The first is, to declare the grounds and reasons why God would bring that destruction upon Babylon, and upon the land of the Chaldeans. The words of verse 4 are, "The slain shall fall in the land of the Chaldeans, and they that are thrust through in her streets." Why so? "For," saith he, "Israel hath not been forsaken." The reason why God will destroy the empire of Babylon is, because he will remember Israel, and what they have done against him. This lies in store for another Babylon, in God's appointed time. The second reason is, that it may be for the comfort, for the supportment of Israel and Judah under that distress which was then befalling them, upon the entrance of this Babylon in the land of the Chaldeans. "Notwithstanding all," saith he, "yet 'Israel is not forsaken, nor Judah of his God.'"

We are called this day to join our cries with the nation in the behalf of the land of our nativity. And though it hath been, as most of you know, my constant course, on such solemn days as these are, to treat in particular about our own sins, our own decays, our own means of recovery; yet, upon this occasion, I shall, as God shall help me, from these words, represent unto you the state of the nation wherein we live, and the only way and means for our deliverance from universal destruction. To declare our interest herein, some things must be observed concerning this Babylon, whose destruction is so solemnly prophesied of in this and the foregoing chapter; and I must observe three things concerning it:—

First. That *Babylon was the original of apostasy from the natural worship of God unto idolatry in the whole world.* There was great iniquity before the flood, but no mention of any idolatry. There was a natural worship of God throughout the world that was not corrupted with idolatry. There is no mention of it until the building of Babel; there it began. The tower which they built they turned into a temple of Belus, whom they had made a god, and laid his image in the top of it. There was the original. You shall see immediately how we are concerned. There was the original of apostasy from natural worship unto idolatry.

Secondly. Their *idolatry.* The idolatry that there began consisted in image-worship, in the worshipping of graven images; which was their idolatry that they set up with respect unto men departed, whom they worshipped by them. Four times in this prophecy doth God say he will "take vengeance on their graven images." And from Isa xl. to the end of xlvi. you have a description of the idolatry of Babylon,—that it all consisted in making carved idols and graven images. The rest of the world, especially of the eastern nations, fell into the worshipping of the *sun,* which they called Baal, and Moloch, and Chemosh,—all names of the sun; and the worship of the *moon,* which they called Ashtaroth and the queen of heaven; but the idolatry of Babylon was by graven images and idols.

Thirdly. *They were,* so far as appears upon record, *the first state in the world that ever persecuted for religion,* that oppressed the true worshippers of God, as such; as being "mad upon their idols," as the prophet saith they were,—they were inflamed upon them. They were the first that oppressed the church because of its worshipping of God, and destroyed that worship among them. Hence the church prays in this chapter, "The vengeance of the LORD and of his temple be upon Babylon:"—not only the vengeance of the Lord for destroying of his people, but the vengeance of his temple, for destroying of his worship, be upon Babylon,—"shall Zion say." "Others have afflicted me," saith he in the same chapter; "but this Nebuchadnezzar, king of Babylon, hath broken my bones." They were the great oppressors of the church.

Upon these three accounts (which is that I would observe), the name of Babylon, and all that is spoken of it in the Old Testament, is transferred to the apostate Church of Rome in the New, and all applied unto it, in the Book of the Revelation; and that upon this great analogy, which I shall now briefly show:—

Why doth God call the apostate state of the church, under the New Testament, "Babylon, Babylon the Mystery?" For these three reasons:—

First. As old Babylon was the rise and spring of apostasy from natural worship in the world unto idolatry, so this new Babylon was the rise and spring of apostasy from evangelical worship in the world unto idolatry. Mark the analogy. Hence she is called "The mother of harlots;" that is, she that had brought forth all the idolatrous churches and worship that were in the world. Did Babylon begin to apostatize into idolatry from natural worship? so Rome began to apostatize into idolatry from spiritual, evangelical worship. Therefore the Holy Ghost calls her Babylon.

Secondly. The peculiar idolatry of Babylon consisted in image-worship,—the worshipping of men departed under images made to their likeness. And the peculiar idolatry of Rome consists in image-worship,—the worshipping of saints departed; which is a great part of their idolatry. And therein they are Babylon also.

Thirdly. As Babylon was the spring of all persecution against, and oppression of, the church of God under the Old Testament, so Rome hath been the spring of all persecution and oppression of the church of God, since the apostasy, under the New Testament.

On these accounts hath the Holy Ghost, in infinite wisdom, transferred over the name, and state, and other things spoken of Babylon from the old unto the new.

I have mentioned this, that you may see the interest of England in this text of Scripture. So far as the truth of religion is owned in this nation, so far as there is a testimony given against idolatry, we are to God as Israel and Judah, though the land be filled with sin. At the time of this prophecy, Israel and Judah were in danger of present destruction and desolation from the old Babylon; and if we do not mock God in all we do, we are under apprehensions that England, and the church of God in England, is under danger of the same desolation and destruction from new Babylon, upon the same account and principle. If we do not mock God, this is that we profess at this day. Wherefore the parallel runs thus far equal. Such as was Babylon of old, such is that at present; such as was the danger of Israel and Judah from them at that day, such is the danger of England from the new at this present. This is spoken in general.

For the opening of the words, observe these three things:—

First. That there is in them a *reduplication of the names or titles of God.* He is in this verse called by the name of "The LORD of hosts," and by the name of "The Holy One of Israel." Where there are such reduplications of the name of God or any of his titles, the Holy Ghost would have us take notice that it is a matter of great importance whereof he speaks.

Secondly. *There is a distribution and application of these names of God unto distinct occasions, suitable unto them.*

1. There is in it mentioned an intimation of a surprisal with some protection or deliverance. Whom shall it be done by? "The LORD

of hosts," saith he, " the LORD his God." And he doth not in vain add immediately, "The LORD of hosts," that title of God,—he who hath the host above and the host below in his sovereign disposal. God's host above are all the holy angels, and all the heavenly bodies in their influences. The stars in their courses fought against Sisera; and he hath lately hung forth among us a flag or ensign of his host above, intimating that he is arising in his indignation, as "the LORD of hosts," and hath hung forth an ensign before his coming, full of dread and terror. And he is " the LORD of hosts" here below, of all men and of all creatures, disposing of them as seems good unto him. The prophet adds this name of God, because of the unspeakable greatness of the thing he mentions; namely, that Israel should not be forsaken, nor Judah, while the land was so filled with sin, and the whole interest of Babylon so coming upon them.

2. The other title of God is, "The Holy One of Israel." This is applied peculiarly unto their sin: " The land is filled with sin against the Holy One of Israel." It is the greatest, it is the highest aggravation of sin, that it is against the holiness of God, " who is a God of purer eyes than to behold iniquity." So hath the wisdom of the Holy Ghost applied these two distinct titles of God unto the two distinct considerations of the people;—first, of their protection, that he is " The LORD of hosts ;" secondly, as of their sin, that he is " The Holy One of Israel."

Thirdly. The third thing is this:—That *in this woful state there is yet an intimation made of a covenant-interest of Judah in God, and that God did yet own them as his in covenant:* " Israel hath not been forsaken, nor Judah of his God." Brethren! no man, I think, hath less of faith than I,—no man doth more despond; but if I could see these two things in concurrence, "His God," and "The LORD of hosts," (that is, sovereign grace, according to his covenant; and sovereign power, according to his providence,)—there is ground for any man's faith to build upon: "His God, the LORD of hosts." Nothing but sovereign grace and sovereign power can preserve a people, when their land is full of sin against the Holy One of Israel, and destruction seems to encompass them, from the interest of Babylon.

I shall speak yet a little more particularly. You may consider in the words,—

1. That which is mentioned in the last place;—*the state of the people* at this time: "Their land was filled with sin against the Holy One of Israel."

2. An intimation of approaching, deserved destruction on that account: " Though the land;"—it is in that condition that it ought to look for nothing but destruction.

3. A strange and wonderful surprisal, notwithstanding this, in sove-

reign grace and power: "Israel hath not been forsaken, nor Judah of his God, the LORD of hosts."

What I shall speak to is this:—

When a land is filled with sin against the Lord, let men's hopes and expectations be what they will, they are in danger of utter destruction, and cannot be saved but by the actings of sovereign grace and power.

I shall for the handling hereof (at least I design to) do these three things:—I. Show when a land is filled with sin against the Holy One of Israel. II. Gather up what evidences we have that England is not yet utterly forsaken of God. III. Manifest what is indispensably required of us, that we may not be given up unto that utter desolation and destruction that lieth at the door.

I do believe that I am not in my thoughts far from your case,—far from the case of the nation. I do not search for things to speak to; I shall speak only those that are compliant with the common reason and understanding of all sober persons.

I. There are three ways whereby a land may be said to be filled with sin:—

1. When the sins of a land or nation are come to the full, to the utmost measure that God hath allotted to them in his patience. There is such an allotment of patience to every nation under heaven, and when it comes to its appointed issue, no means under heaven can defer or delay their destruction one day. Thus saith God before the flood, "The land is filled with sin, the whole earth with violence;—a flood shall take them away." The cry of Sodom and Gomorrah came up to God; they had filled up their measure;—God sent fire and brimstone to destroy them. "You shall not yet go into Canaan." Why? "The iniquity of the Amorites is not yet full." There is a time appointed, wherein the iniquity of the Amorites shall come up to its full measure, beyond which their destruction shall not be delayed. This was not now the case of Israel and Judah. It proved afterward to be their case, as the apostle describes it, 1 Thess. ii. 15, 16, "Who both killed the Lord Jesus and their own prophets, and have persecuted us; and they please not God, and are contrary to all men; forbidding us to speak to the Gentiles, that they might be saved, to fill up their sins alway: for the wrath is come upon them to the uttermost." How come? They have filled their measure, reached to their bounds;—"wrath is come upon them to the uttermost." I hope, I pray, that this is not, that this may not be, the state of England;—that our land is not so filled with sin, as that God's decree of absolute and universal desolation should be gone forth against us.

2. A land may be said to be filled with sin, when it is come to that degree and measure, as that God will not pass it by without some severe, desolating judgment. He will not utterly forsake it, he will

not utterly destroy it; but let all mankind do what they will, he will not pass it by without some severe, desolating judgment. Such was their case even at this time;—you may see in 2 Chron. xxxvi. 16, "But they mocked the messengers of God, and despised his words, and misused his prophets, until the wrath of the LORD arose against his people, till there was no remedy." It was impossible that the judgment of God should be turned away from them. In this state God saith, "Pray not for this people; my heart shall not be toward them," (until he had brought his judgment upon them;)—"though Moses and Samuel stood before me, I will not hear them."[1] Ay, but what if reformation come in? "Nay, nay," saith he, "it is determined against them;—reformation shall not save them." See 2 Kings xxiii. 25, 26, where there is an account given of the greatest reformation that ever was wrought in Judah, by Josiah. So it is said, "Like unto him was there no king before him, that turned to the LORD with all his heart, and with all his soul, and with all his might, according to all the law of Moses; neither after him arose there any like him," —having reformed the whole nation. Then, sure, all will be well. See the next words, "Notwithstanding the LORD turned not from the fierceness of his great wrath, wherewith his anger was kindled against Judah. . . . . And the LORD said, I will remove Judah also out of my sight." There is a time and season when God, although he will not utterly destroy and forsake a nation for ever, yet he will not pass them by, until he hath brought a severe, destructive scourge upon them. Whether this be the state of England at this day, or no, God only knows, and of mankind not one. Whether we are come to that state wherein there is no remedy, wherein nothing we do shall prevent desolating judgments, I say, God only knows, and of men not one.

3. A land is filled with sin, when it is come to such a degree and measure, as that there is no rule of the word, nor any prognostic from Providence, nor any conjecture from the state of things, that can give any determination what will be the issue. Judgment is deserved; and there is nothing remains but to look upon the balance as it is held in the hand of sovereignty: which way it will turn God only knows. The decree is not yet gone forth. In this your state, God doth not say, "Pray not for this people;" God doth not say, "Though you reform, I will not turn from the fierceness of my wrath:" but God saith, "Who knows if God will return and leave a blessing? who knows if God will be entreated, and have mercy?" He leaves it upon the absolute pleasure of sovereignty, to give us encouragement to wait upon him. Because I take this—yea, and I take it in the best of my hopes—to be that wherein we are concerned, pray take these two things along with you, before I go to show it in particular:—The first

[1] [See Jer. vii. 16, xi. 14, xv. 1.]

is, that, in this state, if God gives time and space, there is encouragement enough left to make our applications to him for the removal of impending judgments. Methinks sometimes I see by faith the Lord high lift up upon his throne, and his train filling the temple with his glory, and holding the balance of this nation in his hand, and [that he] can turn it to mercy or judgment, as seems good unto him. While it is so,—while though the woman be put into the ephah, yet the talent of lead is not laid upon her, [Zech. v. 7,]—there is time for intercession, yet time for the interposition of God. And, secondly, I say,—and do you take it as you see good, but I will tell you my persuasion,—that if there be not a compliance with the calls of God unto this nation, upon this suspension and arrest of judgment that we are under, we shall as certainly perish as if we were in either of the two former conditions. If the Chaldeans were all wounded men, —if there was no hope, no strength, no relief, in the papal cause,— they shall rise up and smite, as in the day wherein "Shalman spoiled Beth-arbel," and "the mother was dashed in pieces upon her children," Hos. x. 14;—unless there be a compliance with the calls of God in the days wherein we live.

Let us, then, a little, as God will give strength, inquire when a nation is so filled with sin against the Holy One of Israel as certainly to put the balance into the hands of sovereignty, and to take off all rules and prognostics (which, with great grief, I have heard sometimes insisted upon), and reduce us merely to the hand of sovereignty. When is it that a land is so filled with sin?

(1.) A land is so filled with sin, when all sorts of provoking sins do abound in it;—when there is no exception to be put into the indictment;—when there is no provoking sin that can be thought on that is not in the nation. For if there be but one provoking sin absolutely excluded, there is room for mercy to dwell. Who now shall plead for England? who shall put in an exception for England into this indictment? Oh, poor England! among all thy lovers thou hast not one to plead for thee this day! From the height of profaneness and atheism, through the filthiness of sensuality and uncleanness, down to the lowest oppression and cheating, the land is filled with all sorts of sin. If there be any that can put in an exception as to any provoking sin that is not among us, let them stand forth and plead the cause of this nation. I profess my mouth is stopped. "The land is filled with sin against the Holy One of Israel." It is to no purpose to enumerate our sins,—the roll is too long to be read at this time; and I am sorry it hath been cut, and thrown into the fire, when it hath been spoken of, contemned, and despised, as Jeremiah's was by Jehoiakim. But so it is.

(2.) A land is so filled with sin against the Holy One of Israel, when all sorts of persons in a land are guilty of provoking sins. Pray, mistake me not; I do not say all persons of all sorts. God forbid. If it had been so, we had long since been like unto Sodom and Gomorrah. "If the Lord of hosts had not left us a small remnant, we should have been as Sodom, and we should have been like unto Gomorrah," Isa. i. 9. But, whereas there are many sorts of persons,—rulers, and them that are ruled; high and low, rich and poor; in court, in city, in country; I say, all sorts of persons have been guilty of these provoking sins,—we, and our princes, as Daniel speaks, and our rulers, and the people, the inhabitants of the land of all sorts,—who shall plead here for England? who shall bring forth a sort of persons? Nay, it is not so in the throne;—nay, it is not so at court;—nay, it is not so among the clergy;—nay, it is not so in the city;—nay, it is not so in the country;—it is not so with the rich; it is not so with the poor. Let any one that can, bring in a plea for this poor nation, that we may not conclude the land is filled with sin against the Holy One of Israel.

But you will say, "Here lies an exception: There are many persons, many churches, free from these flagitious and provoking sins;—there is a sort of persons, churches, and professors, who walk in the fear of God, and are free from all these sins: and, therefore, it doth not extend to all sorts."

Brethren, you know my mind full well in this matter. I have been for these three last years upon all occasions inculcating it upon you. I acknowledge, the churches in this nation are not guilty of those sins whereby God is provoked against the nation to bring on national judgments; but I do say, that churches and professors in this nation are guilty of those sins for which Christ will bring correcting judgments upon churches and professors: so that we are all in the same way and bottom, though not all upon the same account. The land is filled with sin. How are your thoughts concerned in these things, brethren? I confess to you I speak my heart, my conscience, as in the presence of God, and as that which you are concerned to consider.

I have given you two evidences that this land is so filled with sin against the Holy One of Israel. I will give you two more.

(3.) When the sins of a land have upon them the greatest aggravations that national sins are capable of. What are they? They are plain:—they are against warnings, and against mercies; all sorts of sins in all sorts of persons, against all sorts of warnings and against all sorts of mercies. God hath not left this land without warnings in heaven above, and in earth beneath. Was there no warning given us in the wasting, *desolating plague?*[1] no warning in the consuming,

[1] The plague in 1665, which cut off 68,596 of the population, according to the London bills of mortality.

raging fire?[1] no warning in the *bloody war*[2] that ensued thereon? no warning in all the *prodigious appearances* in heaven above that we have had?—none in that[3] which at present hangs over us, as an ensign of God's supernal host? I acknowledge there hath been, I fear, a weakness in one kind of warning,—by the public dispensation of the word. But God hath not left himself without witness: he hath multiplied warnings, and they have not been complied withal. Have they, brethren? "Were they at all afraid," saith Jeremiah, "when the roll was read? or, did they rend their clothes?" Jer. xxxvi. 24. No, not at all. Have these warnings of God been complied withal? Hath the voice of God in them been heard? Hath the nation been afraid? Have they rent their clothes and returned to the Lord? They have not. We yet continue, God help us! in a state of sin against warnings. And as for mercies,—the mercies of peace and plenty have been the food of lust, of covetousness and sensuality, and have pampered us in wantonness, to the rending and tearing one another.

(4.) When, in the secret workings of God's providence, there is an inclination in a sinful people unto a compliance with them [those] from whom their destruction is like to proceed, it is a sign that God is withdrawn from them, and that the land is so filled with sin. When Israel was to be destroyed by the Assyrian, when Israel saw his sickness, he sent to the king of Assyria, applied himself to the king of Assyria, by whom he was to be destroyed, Hos. v. 13. When Judah saw his sickness, all his inclinations and applications were unto the Babylonians and Chaldeans, by whom he was to be destroyed. The prophet Ezekiel hath a whole chapter to tell you of the fondness of that people upon the Babylonians before their destruction. Ezek. xxiii., "They were all like princes and mighty men, and thou wast in love with them, and committedst adultery with them;" that is, partookest and compliedst with their idolatry. When it is so, it is evident that God is greatly withdrawn from such a people, and that they are nigh unto their desolation.

What shall we plead for England in this matter? Is it not known what wretched and vile compliances we have had with a neighbour nation, the French,—following their manners, imitating their customs,

[1] The fire which destroyed a large part of London in 1666.

[2] Most probably the war with the Dutch, which had begun in 1665, and in the course of which the Dutch fleet sailed up the Thames, and destroyed the ships of war at Chatham.

[3] Probably the celebrated comet of 1680–81, known by the name of Halley's comet. The observations made by Halley and Flamsteed on this body are partly the basis, on which Newton, from the theory of gravitation, proved the orbit of comets. It was visible for a considerable time, and shone with great brilliance. Some knowledge of the facts alluded to is needed, to appreciate the force and pertinence of Owen's appeals; though, in the progress of science, a different inference would now be drawn from such celestial phenomena as the comet and the meteor.—ED.

promoting their interest, advancing their reputation, when every man almost among us talked of nothing but that we should be destroyed by the French?—an eminent token of the hand of God upon us, and that the land is so filled with sin against the Holy One of Israel. Nay, go farther;—whence is it (for we bear ourselves herein not only upon the truth of the thing itself, but also upon the proclamation inviting us upon this day), whence is it that we fear the judgments of God? whence do we fear desolation, confusion, destruction upon this nation,—to our religion, to our liberties, to our lives? Is it not from the papal interest? There is it stated by our rulers, and in the thoughts of all sober persons. And had we been wise, we might have seen it many years ago. But what have we been doing for some ages? Deserting our principles, forsaking the foundation we stood upon against the Papacy, foregoing those avowed principles of the first reformers, pleading for compliance, pleading for a possibility of reconciliation,—avowing them to be a true church. And, in one word, if the power of the protestant religion had not been preserved in the body of the people, it had, by some, been long ago given up to the papal interest, and this working effectually among us at a time when we were in dread (all that were wise and considerative) that there would from thence arise the desolation and destruction of this church.

I have given you these evidences that this land of ours is so filled with sin against the Holy One of Israel;—and if they can answer it, and disprove it, no man shall more rejoice in it than myself.

I should, in the next place, show the danger that land is in when things lie in this equal balance. For, I pray, observe, I have not given these things to prove the land hath filled up its measure of iniquity, and must certainly be destroyed; I have not given them to prove absolutely that there is a decreed judgment that cannot be diverted,—that there is no remedy,—that, notwithstanding reformation, God will say, "I will not turn away the fierceness of mine anger;" —but I have given them only to prove, that we are in that state and condition wherein there is no certain rule of the word, no indication of Providence, no rational consideration of the state of things that can give us any security of protection or deliverance; but that we are absolutely resolved upon sovereign grace and mercy: and without relief from thence, I shall only say, as to the proof of the proposition, what the prophet saith, Isa. xxxiv. 16, "Seek ye out of the book of the LORD, and read: no one of these things shall fail."

To omit all the considerations and all the proof I intended, that sovereign grace and mercy must be our relief, if ever we be relieved, I proceed unto the second thing; which is,—

II. To give in evidences that England is not yet utterly forsaken of the Lord its God, the Lord of hosts, though the land be thus filled with sin. So that there is ground of encouragement yet remaining to apply ourselves to God. And, in truth, I will tell you the best I can think of:—

1. *The large and wonderful discovery of the horrible plot, of the horrible Popish plot,*[1] *laid for the ruin, destruction, and desolation of the nation, is an evidence that England is not yet, I say, utterly forsaken of the Lord its God.* It was not discovered by our rulers, from whom it was hid. It was not discovered by the severe indagation and watchfulness of ministers of state from foreign intelligence,—the usual way of discovering such plots. It was not discovered by persons of authority and interest, to warrant the discovery. It was not so in a time when the nation was awake, and looked about them, and were jealous of such things; but in the deepest security. It hath admitted,—it hath met with all the endeavours of hell and men for the covering of it; yet, through the conduct of the holy providence of God, it hath broke forth to that discovery, as that it is publicly proclaimed to all the nation. I say, with the wife of Manoah, "If God would have destroyed us, he would not have showed us this thing." If he had utterly forsaken us, he would have left us to have been swallowed up, when we should not have had leisure to have cried, Alas! To me, I say, it is an evidence that England is not yet utterly forsaken.

2. *That God hath stirred up some, at least, of the nobles and our rulers to follow on this discovery, to bring it forth to light, and to pursue them to condign punishment who were the contrivers, authors, abettors, and carriers on of that bloody design.* I will not speak one word or syllable to their dishonour or disrespect who deserve both honour and respect from us: but this I will say, that if I know them, or any thing of them, this is not from themselves; this is from the clothing of the Spirit of God, and anointing to this very work, and is not from themselves, nor their own principles, nor their own inclinations, but the hand of God in them and upon them. Add hereunto the strange and wonderful quiet disposure of the magistracy of this city into the hand of persons prudent, diligent, and watchful, whom we have reason to pray for, and bless God for. And it is

[1] The allusion is to the Popish Plot which Titus Oates was thought to have discovered. He was a clergyman of infamous character. Expelled from his benefice in the Church of England, he had entered the Jesuit college of St Omer. Thence he returned to England, and in 1678 lodged information before Sir Edmondsbury Godfrey that the Roman Catholics were busy with a scheme for burning London, landing a French army in Ireland, and assassinating the king. Sir E. Godfrey, who, as justice of the peace, had received the depositions of Oates, was shortly afterwards found dead in a field near London; and it was evident that he had been murdered. Papers were found on Edward Coleman, a Roman Catholic emissary, which afforded some corroboration to the story of Oates. These facts secured universal credit at the time for the allegations of Oates. The importance which Dr Owen attaches to this plot must evidently be understood in the light of the prevailing and universal impression among British Protestants at the time when the sermon was delivered.—Ed.

strengthened by the stirring up of a spirit in the common people unto an unheard-of heat and earnestness in bearing witness and testimony against Popery and all their abominations, in such a manner as hath not fallen out in any nation under heaven; and this acted above and beyond their spirits and principles. These things, to me, are some evidences that England is not yet utterly forsaken of the Lord its God, though the land be full of sin.

3. I could instance in the *embroilments of foreign nations abroad.* At this time they are all quiet; but who is there that doth not know that they all stand as it were on the tiptoe, looking who shall first begin to cut throats and kill men? Even all the nations in Europe are in this posture at this day. Though they are quiet this cold weather, yet, "Who shall begin first? who shall make the attack? and who shall defend?" is the talk of all Europe,—whereby some of them may have been hindered from a public contributing to the ruin of this poor nation.

4. It is an evidence that England is not yet forsaken, in that *a secret, efficacious influence of divine Providence hath preserved the body politic of the nation in its being and union, when all the ligaments of law and mutual trust have been broken.* There hath been such a dissolution of mutual trust, and all ordinary ligaments of the politic union of a nation, that if God had not powerfully grasped the whole in his hand, we had long since been in confusion, and every man's sword had been in the side of his brother and his neighbour. But to this day we are preserved in peace, by a secret, influential power of divine wisdom and providence,—whose footsteps I would adore more and more; which is so much the more excellent, in that it is not visible, and by outward force, but merely upon the minds of men. This is, to me, another evidence that England is not yet forsaken of its God, the Lord of hosts.

5. My last is this,—*That after God hath, by so many ways and so many means, declared unto us his displeasure against our sin, having declared the sentence in his word, yet he hath visibly granted an arrest of judgment.* "The sentence shall not be put in execution," saith God, "while I give this people a time, and space, and season of repentance and reformation." Alas! if God had utterly forsaken us, he would have taken us off in the midst of our security; evil would have risen, and we should have known the morning of it; destruction would presently have overtaken us. But now God hath given us various calls, various warnings, and leaves us a space, as yet, to see what we will do, and what will become of us. "I will give them a trial," saith God; "the decree shall not yet go forth,—judgment shall not yet come forth to execution; I will give them a space for repentance." And this consideration hath a double corroboration of this blessed space and season God hath given us, for to apply ourselves so far to his call as to remove his judgments that are impending over us.

(1.) The first is, that he *hath reserved a remnant among us that do make use of this space and season to apply themselves unto the throne of grace, and to cry mightily for mercy.* God hath not taken his Holy Spirit from us. God hath not said, by any open work or secret intimation of providence, "Pray no more for this people; my heart shall not be toward them." He hath not said so; and, therefore, there are yet among us precious souls who do lift up prayers to God night and day, not only for themselves and families, not only for the church of God, but for this poor land of our nativity, that, if it were the will of God, we may not see it soaked in blood;—that God would not come forth to destroy it with a curse;—that God would pity, and spare, and have mercy upon it;—that he would not make it an "Aceldama,"—a field of blood. There are many cries to God to this purpose. So that there are some by whom this space and season God hath given us is made use of.

(2.) It hath strength from this, that *there is an invitation and encouragement given to the whole nation to join together in their cries to God this day for the same end and purpose.* I confess to you (give me leave to speak it), I am afraid the body of the nation, considering their conduct in this sort of duty, will make no great work of it, towards the averting of judgments in such a day as this is. And I am afraid, also, that the approaching carnival, or time of feasting, will quickly blot out all impressions that ought to be in the minds of men from such a day as this is. This is all I can say,—God is publicly acknowledged; and what influence that may have in a farther suspension of judgment, till the nation be better prepared to seek unto him, I know not.

Methinks these are evidences (to me they are) that England is not yet utterly forsaken of the Lord its God:—The miraculous discovery of the plot for our destruction;—the pursuit of it by some of our rulers, and the body of the nation;—the embroilment of foreign nations in their own concerns;—the preservation of the political interest and body, when all the ligaments of law, and love, and trust were dissolved;—the space and season that God gives us (that we are not immediately hurried into blood and confusion), attended with a spirit of prayer in some of God's own people, and with a public acknowledgment of God in this day in the nation.

III. I should now proceed to my last thing,—to show you, that in this state, wherein a land is so filled with sin as absolutely to put the determination of all things into the hand of sovereignty, and where yet there remains some evidences that God hath not utterly forsaken us, what is required of us, what is expected from us, that may be a means to turn away the wrath and displeasure of God from this poor land and nation.

I should have spoken to the following things:—

1. That whatsoever be the language of God's calls, unless there be a general compliance with them, this land cannot be saved.

2. I should have shown you, that all the diligence, and the courage, and the watchfulness of the rulers, shall not be able to preserve us from that destruction which we have deserved;—unless something else be done ere long, their hearts will faint, and their hands fail, and their thoughts be divided. For that alone will not do.

3. Prayer will not do in this case; though that be necessary and required, it will not do it. God doth not cry to us merely that we should cry to him. "Why criest thou?" said God to Joshua; "there is an accursed thing. Why dost thou lie upon thy face, and cry, and pray, when judgment is coming upon you? There is an accursed thing got among you." It is so with us.

4. To speak very plain in a plain case;—the state of this nation is such, let our expectation and our hopes be what they will, and prognostics be multiplied, God can multiply upon another hand;—the case of this nation is such, that without repentance evidenced, and universal reformation sincerely endeavoured, England cannot be saved,—will not be saved;—God will forsake it,—destruction from the Lord will overtake us.

5. I should have told you, also, what I judge indispensably necessary, that any such reformation may be obtained in this nation; as,—

(1.) That there be, *through the providence of God, provided another manner of administration of the word throughout the nation than at present there is; which is the only means of conviction, and conversion unto God.* Signs, and wonders, and judgments, terrify;—it is the word that must reform, and turn to God. And if the state of things continue so, that some who are able and wise for the work are forbid, and others, that engross all to themselves, are either unable or negligent in it,—I have no great hopes of seeing reformation in this land.

(2.) *Unless the generality of magistrates be better principled for, and better instructed in, their office, than as yet they seem to be, a reformation will not be carried through this nation.* And,—

(3.) Which is the principal,—*That those who have been examples in sinning, and in drawing others to sin, become examples in repenting, and reforming, and turning to God.*

(4.) Lastly, That the *whole nation be stirred up, and do not faint in the pursuit of it.*

I have scarce been able to speak the heads of these things unto you. I wish I had strength to speak all that is in my thoughts and heart upon this matter unto this whole nation; for hereon, and not on any thing else, depends the deliverance and safety of it.

POSTHUMOUS SERMONS.

PART II.

SERMONS PUBLISHED

M.DCC.XXI.

PREFATORY NOTE.

UNDER the second division of the Posthumous Sermons of Owen are included all the previously unpublished discourses which appeared in the folio edition of his Sermons and Tracts, 1721. The editors of that volume state, after alluding to his sermons formerly printed,—"With these are printed a considerable number of sermons and other tracts never before published, which we do assure the public are genuine,—a great part of them having been transcribed from his own copies, and the rest taken from his mouth by a gentleman of honour and known integrity."

The gentleman referred to was Sir John Hartopp. Dr Isaac Watts, on the death of that baronet, preached a well-known and beautiful sermon on "The Happiness of Separate Spirits." "When I name Sir John Hartopp," said the preacher, "all that knew him will agree that I name a gentleman, a scholar, and a Christian." In the course of the tribute he pays to the memory of the deceased, he alludes to the cordial friendship that long subsisted between Sir John and "that great and venerable man, Dr Owen;" and mentions that he had supplied Asty with important information for his brief memoir of our author. Sir John Hartopp deserved the warm eulogy of Dr Watts. He was a good man, and the friend of good men. He was thrice elected Member of Parliament for Leicestershire, at the time when the attempt was made to exclude the Duke of York from the crown. He attended the ministry of Owen in London, and was in the habit of taking notes in short-hand of his sermons, which he afterwards transcribed in full. From these manuscripts most of the posthumous sermons of our author have been derived. He died in 1722, after the publication of the folio edition of Owen's Sermons; and his name, therefore, is a voucher for the genuineness of all the discourses contained in this division.

Two discourses on "The Strength of Faith" are here given first, because connected with one on the same text in the preceding volume,—vol. viii. p. 207. The discourses which bear no date follow. The subsequent discourses in this division are arranged according to the years in which it has been ascertained that they were preached.—ED.

POSTHUMOUS SERMONS.

SERMON I.

THE STRENGTH OF FAITH.

"He staggered not at the promise of God through unbelief; but was strong in faith, giving glory to God.—ROM. iv. 20.

IN this chapter the apostle singleth out a signal example, to make good the conclusion which, by sundry convincing demonstrations, he had proved in the foregoing chapter; namely, that the justification of a sinner could by no means be brought about nor accomplished but by the righteousness of faith in Christ. This, I say, in the example of Abraham, and from the testimonies given concerning him, and the way whereby he was justified before God, the apostle proves from the beginning of the chapter to the end of verse 17. From thence to the end of verse 22 he describes that faith of Abraham whereby he obtained acceptation with God; that in all things he might propose him as an example and an encouragement unto us.

Among the many excellencies which are given in, in the description of this faith of his, arising from its cause, object, matter, and manner, not now to be insisted on, this is none of the least which is mentioned in my text, "He staggered not."

There is a μείωσις in the words, wherein, by a negation, the contrary to what is denied is strongly asserted: "He staggered not by unbelief;" that is, he was steadfast in believing, or, as it is expounded in the close of the verse, "he was strong in faith."

The words may yield us these two observations:—

Observation 1. All staggering at the promises of God is through unbelief.

Saith the apostle, "He staggered not through unbelief." Men are apt to pretend many other reasons, and do use other pleas; but the truth is, all our staggering is through unbelief. But this proposition from these words I have long since, in another way, proved, evinced, and applied.[1]

[1] See the sermon on this text, vol. viii. p. 207.

There is another proposition lies in the text, and that I shall now apply myself unto, which is this:—

Obs. 2. Steadfastness in believing the promises is exceeding acceptable unto God.

In treating upon this subject, I shall do these two things:—I. Explain the terms of the proposition. II. Give the proof of it.

I. As to the former of these,—

1. There is the object concerning which the affirmation is laid down: "The promises," the promises of God. The promises of God are the declaration of the purposes of his grace towards his elect, according to the tenor of the covenant. That pointed unto in my text was the old great promise of Christ, which contains in it all others; because "in him all the promises of God are yea and amen," 2 Cor. i. 20. So that although I shall speak nothing but what will be true with reference to every promise of God whatever, yet I shall bear a chief respect to the promises that exhibit Christ and the free grace of God in him unto sinners;—steadfastness in believing these promises.

2. There is the act that is exercised about this object; and that is, *believing*. It is steadfastness in believing we speak of.

I shall not make it my design to insist much on the nature of faith, and to debate the differences that are among men about it. Only so much must be spoken concerning it as may give us an acquaintance with that whereof we are treating.

How many have been the disputes of men about the nature of faith—the subject, proper object, formal reason of it—all know. And how little the church of God is beholding to men, who have made it their business to involve things of general duty, and absolute necessity unto all believers, in intricate disputes,—men that will duly weigh it may easily know. By some men's too much understanding, others are brought to understand nothing at all. He that would have the things of his own spiritual experience and daily duty made unintelligible to him, let him consider them as stated in men's philosophical disputes about them. Thus, some place faith in one distinct faculty of the soul, some in another, and some say there are no such things as distinct faculties in the soul. Some place it in both the chief,—the understanding and the will; and some say, it is impossible that one habit should have its residence in two faculties.

For my part, my intention principally is, to speak to such as God chooseth,—the poor and foolish of the world. And the means whereby he will bring them to himself are not, I am sure, above that understanding which the Son of God hath given them, 1 John v. 20. And whereas the general way, in treating of faith, is, for the most part, to use strictness of expression, that so it may be delivered in a philosophical exactness; the constant way of the Holy Ghost is, by metaphorical expressions, accommodations of it to things of sense and daily usage in the meanest, to give a relish and perception of it to all that are interested in it. And so shall I labour to speak, that every one that doth believe may know what it is to believe.

Only observe this, by the way,—that I speak of believing and of faith in respect of that end, and to that purpose only, in reference whereunto Paul here treats of it; that is, in respect of justification and our acceptation with God. I say, then,—

(1.) That faith, or *believing*, in this restrained sense, doth not consist solely in the assent of the mind to the truth of the promises, or of any promise. When one affirms any thing to us, and we say we believe him,—that is, that the thing he speaks is true,—then there is this assent of the mind. Without this there is no faith. But this alone is not the faith we speak of. This alone and solitary the devils have, and cannot choose but have it, James ii. 19. They believe that which makes them tremble, on the authority of God who revealeth it.

But you will say, "The devil believes only the threats of God,—that which makes him tremble; and so his belief is not a general assent, but partial;—and is thereby distinguished from our assent; which is to all that God hath revealed, and especially the promises."

I answer, The devil believes the promises no less than he doth the threats of God; that is, that they are true, and shall be accomplished. It is part of his misery, that he cannot but believe them. And the promises of God are as much suited to make him tremble as his threatenings. The first promise to us was couched in a threatening to him, Gen. iii. 15. And there is no promise wherein a threatening to him is not couched. Every word concerning Christ, or grace by him, speaks his downfall and ruin. Indeed, his destruction lies more in promises than threats. Promises are what weakens him daily, and gives him a continual foretaste of his approaching destruction.

On this consideration it is evident, that believing, or faith, cannot be solely an assent to the truth of these promises upon the fidelity of the promiser; but this it is also, or originally. Hence it is called, "the receiving the testimony of God," and, therein, "setting to our seal that God is true," John iii. 33. But yet, I think there is somewhat more in receiving of the testimony of God, and setting our seal to it (agreeing, as in contracts, that so it is, and so it shall be), than the bare assent of the mind to the truth of the promises; although, in ordinary speech, to receive a man's testimony, is no more than to believe [that] what he saith, of that concerning which he speaks, is true. But there seems, moreover, in the annexed expression of "setting to our seal," that that is included which he speaks of to Job, chap. v. 27, "Hear it, and know it for thy good." There is a receiving of it for ourselves, in those expressions; which adds much to a bare assent. I say, then, this assent is of faith, though it be not faith. And in saying it is not justifying faith, we do not deny it, but affirm it to be faith in general. The addition of a peculiar assent destroys not the nature of a thing. Now, faith in general is such an assent as hath been described.

(2.) It is not in the sole consent of the will to close with the promise, as containing that which is good and suitable. There is the matter of the promise to be considered in believing, as well as the promise itself. Christ, with his righteousness and benefits, is, as it were, tendered unto us therein. Whence, by believing we are said to accept of, to "receive the atonement," Rom. v. 11. Now, to consent that the matter of the promise—that which is exhibited in the word of it—is good and desirable, and [that it is] so to us, and to choose it on that account, is required to believing also; and it is properly the receiving of Christ, John i. 12. But yet it is not only precisely and exclusively this. Sarah's faith, Heb. xi. 11, is described by this, that she "judged him faithful who had promised." And this is of the nature of faith, as was said before, the judging him faithful that promiseth, and assenting to the truth of his promises on that account. Now, the first of these may be without the second,—our assent may be without the consent of the will; but the latter cannot be without the former. But yet, there is such an assent as will certainly produce this choice also.

(3.) I suppose I need not say, it doth not entirely consist in the good-liking of the affections, and embracing the things promised. The stony ground received the word presently, and with joy, Matt. xiii. 20. It is said, verse 5, that the seed sprung up immediately, because it had not depth of earth. Where men have warm affections, but not thoroughly-prepared minds and hearts, they presently run away with the word, and profess great matters from it; but where it is laid in deep, it is longer commonly before it appears. When a man receives the word only in the affections, the first touch of them cannot be hid; instantly he will be speaking of it, melt under it, and declare how he is affected with it: "Oh, this sermon hath done me good indeed!" But yet this is not faith, when it is alone. They receive the word with joy, but have not root in themselves, verses 20, 21. When Christ promised "the bread of life,"—that is, himself,—John vi., how many were instantly affected with it, and carried out to strong desires of it! "Lord," say they, "evermore give us this bread," verse 34. They like it, they desire it, at that season; their affections are taken with it: but yet they were but πρόσκαιροι, "temporary," not true believers; for after a season "they went back, and walked no more with Christ," verse 66. Those "who have a taste of the heavenly gift," Heb. vi. 4, do you not think they like the taste, and are affected with it? There are, indeed, innumerable deceits in this business. I might show on how many false and corrupt accounts, on what sandy foundations, many men's affections may be exceedingly taken with the word of promise, preached or considered; so that there is no concluding of believing to lie in any such thing. When affections go before believing, they are little worth; but when they follow it, they are exceeding acceptable and precious in the sight of God.

(4.) It is not solely "fiducia,"—a *trust*, affiance, or confidence. There is a twofold fiducial trust;—one whereby we trust in Christ for the forgiveness of sin; which you may call adherence. It is such a cleaving to Christ, as that we trust in him for the forgiveness of sins, and acceptation with God. And so much as we trust, so much we adhere, and no more. There is also a trust that our sins are forgiven us; we trust or rest upon it. Now, it cannot be that either of these should be faith entirely, and that the whole of it should be included in them. There is something more in believing than in trusting; and something more in trusting than is absolutely necessary to preserve the entire notion of believing: for we may believe that wherein we do not trust. But yet this I grant, that where there is believing in Christ, there will be trusting in him, more or less. And when faith is increased to some good height, strength, and steadfastness, it is mainly taken up in trust and confidence, John xiv. 1. So to believe as to free our hearts from trouble and disquietment, upon any account whatever, is to trust properly; and that doubting, and staggering, and fear, which in Scripture we find condemned as opposite to faith, are indeed directly opposite to this fiduciary reposing our souls on Christ. So the apostle describes his faith or believing, 2 Tim. i. 12. So to believe as to be persuaded that God is able to keep what we commit to him, is to put our trust in him.

(5.) Having spoken thus much of these particulars, waiving all the arbitrary determinations of the schools, and exactness of words, as to philosophical rules and terms, I shall give you such a general description of faith, or believing, as may answer in some measure the proper and metaphorical expressions of it in the Scriptures; where it is termed, *looking* or *seeing*, *hearing*, *tasting*, *resting*, *rolling* ourselves, *flying for refuge*, *trusting*, and the like.

[1.] There must be, what I spake of in the first place, an assent to the whole truth of the promises of God, upon this ground and bottom,—that he is able and faithful to accomplish them. This certainly is in, if it be not all, our *receiving the testimony* or witness of God, John iii. 33. Sarah, of whom we spake before, received the testimony of God. How did she do it? She "judged him faithful who had promised," Heb. xi. 11. This God proposes to us in the first place. Eternal life is promised by God, who cannot lie, Tit. i. 2; that is, who is so faithful, as that it is utterly impossible he should deceive any. So Heb. vi. 17, 18, "Wherein God, willing more abundantly to show unto the heirs of promise the immutability of his counsel, confirmed it by an oath; that by two immutable things, in which it was impossible for God to lie, we might have a strong consolation, who have fled for refuge to lay hold upon the hope set before us." The design of God is, that we may receive encouragement in our flying for refuge to the hope set before us,—that is, in believing. What doth he propose to this end? Why, his own faithfulness and immutability, on the account of the engagement of his word and oath. Abraham's faith spoken of, Rom. iv., compriseth this,—yea, is commended from it, verse 21.

The Scripture, indeed, mentions sundry properties of God, on the credit whereof, if I may so speak, our souls are to assent to the truth of his promises, and to acquiesce therein. Two especially are usually named:—

1*st*. His power: "He is able." So Rom. iv. 21, xi. 23.

2*dly*. His faithfulness: as in the places before mentioned, and sundry others.

The sum is, that on the account of God's faithfulness and power, this we are to do, if we will believe;—we are to assent to the truth of his promises, and the certainty of their accomplishment. If this be not done, it is in vain to go forward. Let, then, those who intend any advantage by what shall afterward be spoken, stay here a little, and consider how they have laid this foundation. Many there are who never come to any stability all their days, and yet are never able to fix on any certain cause of their shaking and staggering. The foundation was laid disorderly. This first closing with the faithfulness and power of God in the promises, was never distinctly acted over in and by their souls. And if the foundation be weak, let the building be never so glorious, it will totter, if not fall. Look, then, to this beginning of your confidence, that this fail you not. And when all other holds fail, this will support you from utter sinking, if at any time you are reduced to that condition that you have nothing else.

[2.] Over and above this, faith, in the Scripture, is expressed (and we find it by experience) to be the will's consent unto, and acceptance of, the Lord Jesus Christ as mediator,—he that accomplished his work as the only way of going to the Father, as the sole and sufficient cause of our acceptation with him, as our only righteousness before him.

It hath been said, that faith is the receiving of Christ as a priest, and a lord, to be saved by him, and ruled by him. This sounds excellent well. Who is so vile that, endeavouring to believe, is not willing to be ruled by Christ, as well as saved by him? A faith that would not have Christ to be Lord to rule us, is that faith alone which James rejects. He that would be saved by Christ, and not ruled by him, shall not be saved by him at all. We are to receive a whole Christ, not by halves;—in regard of all his offices, not one or another.

This sounds well, makes a fair show, and there is, in some regard, truth in what is spoken; but "Latet anguis in herba,"—Let men explain themselves, and it is this: The receiving of Christ as a king, is the yielding obedience to him. But that subjection is not a fruit of the faith whereby we are justified, but an essential part of it; so that there is no difference between faith and works or obedience, in the business of justification, both being alike a condition of it.

When I lately read one saying, "That this was one principle that the Church of England went on, in the Reformation, that faith and works have the same consideration in the business of justification," I could not but stand amazed, and conclude that either he or I had been asleep ever since we were born; or that there were two Churches of England,—one that I never knew, and another that he never knew; or else that prejudice is powerful, and makes men confident. Is that the doctrine of the Church of England, as they call it? When, where, by whom was it taught, but by Papists and Socinians, until within a very few years, in England? What place hath it in confessions, homilies, liturgies, controversy writers, or any else of repute for learning and religion in England? But this is no place for contest.

Others at length mince the matter, and say, that faith and works have the same respects to our justification that shall be public and solemn at the last day, at the day of judgment. And is this all that they have intended? How they will justify themselves at the day of judgment for troubling the peace of the saints of God, and shaking the great fundamental articles of the Reformation, I know not; but it is no news, for men loving novelties to dispute themselves they know not whither, and to recoil or retire unhandsomely.

It is true, then, we acknowledge, that faith receives Christ as a lord, as a king; and it is no true faith that will not, doth not do so, and put the soul upon all that obedience which he, as the captain of our salvation, requires at our hands. But faith, as it justifies (in its concurrence, whatever it be, thereunto), closeth with Christ for righteousness and acceptation with God only. And, give me leave to say, it is in that act no less exclusive of good works than of sin. It closeth with Christ in and for that, on the account whereof he is our righteousness, and for and by which we are justified.

But you will say, "This makes you Solifidians;[1] and are you not justly so accounted?"

I say, So was Paul a Solifidian, whose epistles will confute all the

[1] A name derived from two Latin words, signifying *faith alone*.—Ed.

formalists and self-justiciaries in the world. We are Solifidians as to justification:—Christ, grace, and faith are all. We are not Solifidians as to salvation nor gospel conversation, nor the declaration of the efficacy of our believing. Such Solifidians as exclude every thing from an influence in our justification but our acceptation by the grace of God, on faith's receiving of Christ for righteousness and salvation, were all the apostles of Jesus Christ. Such Solifidians as exclude or deny the necessity of works and gospel obedience to him that is justified,—or that say, a true and justifying faith may consist without holiness, works, and obedience,—are condemned by all the apostles, and James in particular.

This, then, I say, is required to faith, or believing,—that we thus receive Christ. John i. 11, "His own received him not." The not receiving of Christ for such purposes as he is sent unto us by the Father, is properly unbelief; and therefore, as it follows, the so receiving him is properly faith, or believing, verse 12. Thus, in preaching the gospel, we are said to make a tender or proffer of Christ, as the Scripture doth, Rev. xxii. 17. Now, that which answers a tender or proffer, is the acceptance of it. So that the soul's willing acceptance of the Lord Jesus Christ for our righteousness before God, being tendered to us in the promises of the gospel for that end and purpose, from the love of the Father, is the main of that believing which is so acceptable unto God.

[3.] Add hereunto that which I cannot say is absolutely of the nature of faith, but in some degree or other (secret or more known to the soul) a necessary concomitant of it; and that is, the soul's resting and quieting itself, and satisfying its affections, in its interest in and enjoyment of a sweet, desirable Saviour. This is called, "cleaving unto the LORD," Josh. xxiii. 8,—the fixing and fastening our affections on God, as ours in covenant. This is the soul's resting in God, its affiance and trusting in him.

And in these three things, which are intelligible to the meanest soul, and written evidently in the words of the Scripture, and in the experience of those who have to do with God in Christ, do I place the believing which is so acceptable to God.

3. There is, next, the qualification of this believing, as laid down in the proposition; and that is, steadfastness,—steadfastness in believing. This is included in the negative. It is said of Abraham that "he staggered not;" that is, he was steadfast. To clear this up a little, take these few observations:—

(1.) Faith, or believing, consists in such an habitual frame of heart, and such actings of the soul, as are capable of degrees of straitening or enlargement, of strength and weakness. Hence there is mention in the Scripture of great faith, "O woman, great is thy faith;" and of little faith, "O ye of little faith;"—of strong faith, Abraham "was strong in faith;" and of weak faith, or being weak in faith, "him that is weak in the faith receive;"—of faith with doubting, "O ye of little faith, why did ye doubt?" and of faith excluding doubting, "Being strong in faith, he staggered" or "doubted not."

(2.) That faith in every respect is equal as unto sincerity, and differs only in degrees; yea, it is equal in respect of the main effects and advance of it,—in justification, perseverance, and salvation. A little faith is no less faith than a great faith; yea, a little faith will carry a man as safely to heaven, though not so comfortably, nor so fruitfully, as a great faith. Now,—

(3.) Steadfastness respects those different degrees of faith. It is not of the nature of faith, but bespeaks such a degree of it as is acceptable to God that we should have, and every way advantageous to ourselves. It is mentioned by Peter, 2 Epist. iii. 17, "Beware lest ye fall from your own steadfastness," or decline from that stability in believing which you have attained; and by Paul, Col. ii. 5. So that,—

(4.) There may be a true faith, that yet may have many troublesome, perplexing doubtings accompanying it, many sinful staggerings and waverings attending it; and yet not be overthrown, but continue true faith still. Men may be true believers, and yet not strong believers. A child that eats milk hath as truly the nature of a man, as he that, being grown up, lives on strong meat. Now, steadfastness denotes stability in believing, in respect of the three things before mentioned, and by it faith is denominated strong and effectual. And it argues,—

[1.] A well-grounded, firm, unshaken assent to the truth of the promises; and so it is opposed to wavering, James i. 5, 6.

[2.] A resolved, clear consent to receive and close with Christ, as tendered in the promise, for life; and so it is opposed to doubting,—that is, troublesome, disquieting, perplexing doubts.

[3.] The settled acquiescence of the soul in the choice made and the close consented unto; and so it is opposed to abiding trouble, John xiv. 1.

This steadfastness in believing doth not exclude all temptations from without. When we say a tree is firmly rooted, we do not say that the wind never blows upon it. The house that is built on the rock is not free from assaults and storms. The Captain of our salvation, the beginner and ender of our faith, was tempted; and we shall be so, if we follow him. Nor doth it exclude all doubting from within. So long as we have flesh, though faith be steadfast, we shall have unbelief; and that bitter root will bring forth some fruit, more or less, according as Satan gets advantage to water it. But it excludes a falling under temptation, and consequently that trouble and disquietness which ensues thereon: as likewise abiding perplexing doubts, which make us stagger to and fro between hope and fear, questioning whether we close with Christ or not,—have any interest in the promise or not; and is attended with disconsolation and dejectedness of spirit, with real uncertainty of the event.

This, then, is that which I intend by *steadfastness in believing,*—the establishment of our hearts in the receiving of Christ, as tendered by the love of the Father, to the peace and settlement of our souls and consciences. And that our hearts should be thus fixed, settled, and established,—that we should live in the sense and power of it,—is, I say, exceeding acceptable unto God.

There is a twofold evil and miscarriage among us, in the great foundation business of closing with Christ in the promise. Some spend all their days in much darkness and disconsolateness,—disputing it to and fro in their own thoughts, whether their portion and interest lie therein or not. They are off and on, living and dying, hoping and fearing, and commonly fear most when they have best hold,—for that is the nature of doubting. When they are quite cast down, then they set themselves a-work to get up; and when they are up to any comfortable persuasion, instantly they fear that all is not well and right,—it is not so with them as it should be: and thus they stagger to and fro all their lives, to the grief of the Spirit of God, and the discomfort of their own souls.

Others, beginning a serious closing with Christ, upon abiding grounds, and finding it a work of difficulty and tediousness to flesh and blood, relapse into generals, inquire no more, but take it for granted that as much is done as they can accomplish; and so grow formal and secure.

To obviate both these evils, I shall confirm the proposition laid down; but before I proceed to that, I shall draw some corollaries that arise from what hath been spoken in the explication of the proposition already insisted on:—

Corollary 1. *Though a little weak faith, where steadfastness is wanting, will carry a man to Christ in heaven, yet it will never carry him comfortably nor pleasantly thither.*

He who hath but a weak faith shall be put to many desperate plunges; every blast of temptation shall cast him down from his consolation, if not turn him aside from his obedience. At best, he is like a man bound in a chain on the top of a high tower; though he cannot fall, yet he cannot but fear. However, it will have a good issue.

Corol. 2. *The least true faith will do its work safely, though not so sweetly.*

True faith in the least degree, gives the soul a share in the first resurrection. It is of the vital principle which we receive when we are quickened. Now, be it never so weak a life we have, yet it is a life that shall never fail. It is of the seed of God, which abideth,—incorruptible seed, that dieth not. A believer is spirit,—is quickened from the dead; be he never so young, never so sick, never so weak, he is still alive, and the second death shall have no power over him. A little faith gives a whole Christ. He that hath the least faith hath as true an interest, though not so clear an interest, in the righteousness of Christ as the most steadfast believer. Others may be more holy than he, but not one in the world is more righteous than he; for he is righteous with the righteousness of Christ. He cannot but be low in sanctification, for a little faith will bring forth but little or low obedience; if the root be weak, the fruit will not be great. But he is beneath none in justification. The most imperfect faith will give present justification, because it interests the soul in a present Christ. The lowest degree of true faith gives the highest completeness of righteousness, Col. ii. 10. You, who have but a weak faith, have yet a strong Christ. So that, though all the world should set itself against your little faith, it should not prevail. Sin cannot do it; Satan cannot do it;—hell cannot do it. Though you take but weak and faint hold on Christ, he takes sure, strong, and unconquerable hold on you. Have you not often wondered, that this spark of heavenly fire should be kept alive in the midst of the sea? It is everlasting; a spark that cannot be quenched,—a drop of that fountain that can never be wholly dried up. Jesus Christ takes special care of them that are weak in faith, Isa. xl. 11. On what account soever they are sick, and weak, and unable, this good Shepherd takes care of them. He shall rule, and they shall abide, Mic. v. 4.

Corol. 3. There may be faith, a little faith, where there wants steadfastness, and [where there] is much doubting.

Steadfastness is an eminent qualification, that all attain not to; so that there may be faith where there is doubting, though I do not say there must be. Doubtings in themselves are opposite to believing. They are, if I may so say, unbelieving. A man can hardly believe all his days, and never doubt; but a man may doubt all his days, and never believe. If I see a field overgrown with thistles and weeds, I can say, There may be corn there; but yet the thistles and weeds are not corn. I speak this, because some have no better bottom for their quiet, than that they have been disquieted,—that they have doubted. Doubting may be where faith is; but we cannot conclude that where there is doubting, there is faith; for it may rise against presumption and security as well as against believing. Yet observe, there is a twofold doubting:—

(1.) Of the end. Men question what will become of them in the close; they fluctuate about what will be their latter end. Did not

Balaam do so when he cried, "Let me die the death of the righteous, and let my latter end be like his"? That wretched man was tossed up and down between hopes and fears. This is common to the vilest person in the world. It is but the shaking of their security, if they be alone.

(2.) About the means. The soul doubts whether it loves Christ, and whether Christ loves it or not. This is far more genuine than the former. It discovers, at least, that such a soul is convinced of the excellency and usefulness of Christ, and that it hath a valuation for him; yea, perhaps this may be jealousy from fervency of love sometimes, and not always from weakness of faith. But, however, with these doubtings, faith, at least a little faith, may consist. So was it with the poor man who cried out, "Lord, I believe; help thou mine unbelief." There is believing and unbelieving, faith and doubting, both at work at the same time in the same person,—Jacob and Esau struggling in the same womb.

Use. Let not men from their doubting conclude to their believing. He that satisfies himself that his field hath corn because it hath thistles, may come short of a harvest. If thy fears be more about the end than the means,—more about future happiness than present communion with God,—thou canst scarce have a clearer argument of a false, corrupt frame of heart. Some flatter themselves with this, that they have doubted and trembled; but now they thank God they are quiet and at rest. How they came to be so, they cannot tell; only, whereas they were disquieted and troubled, now all is well with them. How many of this sort have I known, who, whilst convictions have been warm upon them, have had many perplexing thoughts about their state and condition; after a while, their convictions have worn off, and their doubtings thence arising departed, and they have sunk down into a cold, lifeless frame! This is a miserable bottom of quiet. If there were no way of casting out doubts and fears but by believing, this were somewhat; but presumption and security will do it also, at least for a season.

But these things fall in only by the way, in reference to what was spoken before.

II. I proceed now to confirm the proposition laid down, according to the explanation given of it before:—

1. And this I shall do first from Scripture testimonies:—

(1.) Take the text itself: "He was strong in faith, giving glory to God." All that God requires of any of the sons of men is, his glory;—that he will not give unto another, Isa. xlii. 8. Let God have his glory, and we may take freely whatever we will;—take Christ, take grace, take heaven,—take all. The great glory which he will give to us, consists in giving him his glory, and beholding of it. Now, if this be the great thing, the only thing, that God requires at our hands,—if this be the all which he hath reserved to himself, that he be glorified as God, as our God,—he that gives him that, gives him what is acceptable to him. Thus Abraham pleased God by being strong or steadfast in believing. He was strong in faith, and gave glory to God.

The glory of God is spoken of in various senses in the Scripture:—

[1.] The Hebrew word כָּבוֹד, signifies "pondus," or "weight;" whereunto the apostle alludes when he speaks of "an eternal weight of glory," 2 Cor. iv. 17. This is the glory of the thing itself. It likewise signifies splendour, or brightness, where the apostle, in like manner, speaks of "the brightness of glory," Heb. i. 3; which is the greatness and excellency of beauty in all perfections. In this sense, the infinite excellency of God, in his inconceivable perfections, raised up in such brightness as utterly exceeds all our apprehensions, is called his "glory." And so he is "The God of glory," Acts vii. 2, or, the most glorious God; and our Saviour is called "The Lord of glory," 1 Cor. ii. 8, in the same sense. In this respect we can give no glory to God; we can add nothing to his excellencies, nor the infinite, inconceivable brightness of them, by any thing we do.

[2.] Glory relates not only to the thing itself that is glorious, but to the estimation and opinion we have of it,—that is, δόξα; when that which is in itself glorious is esteemed so. The philosopher saith, "Gloria est frequens de aliquo fama cum laude;" or, "Consentiens laus bonorum, incorrupta vox bene judicantium de excellenti virtute." And, in this respect, that which is infinitely glorious in itself, may be more or less glorious in its manifestation and the estimation of it. So glory is not any of God's excellencies or perfections; but it is the esteem and manifestation of them amongst and unto others.

This God declares to be his glory, Exod. xxxiii. 19. Moses desires to see the "glory" of God. This God calls his "face;" that is, the glory of God in itself. "This," saith God, "thou canst not see: 'Thou canst not see my face,'—or, the brightness of my essential glory, the splendour of my excellencies and perfections." Well, what then? shall he have no acquaintance with it? After this God places him in a rock, and tells him, there he will show him his glory. And this he doth under the name of his "back parts;" that is, he will declare to him wherein and how his glory is manifested. Now, this Rock that followed them was Christ, 1 Cor. x. 4. The Lord places Moses in that rock to show him his glory; intimating that there is no glimpse of it to be obtained but only by them who are placed in Christ Jesus. Now, what is this glory of God which he thus showed to Moses? That he declares, Exod. xxxiv. 6;—causing his majesty, or some visible signs of his presence, "to pass before him," he proclaims the name of God, with many gracious properties of his nature and blessedness.

As if he should say, "Moses, wouldst thou see my glory? This is it, that I may be known to be 'the LORD, the LORD God, merciful and gracious;'—let me be known to be this, and thus, and this is the glory I aim at from the sons of men."

See, now, how steadfastness in believing gives glory to God. It advanceth and magnifieth all these properties of God, and gives all his attributes their due exaltation. An excellent estimation of them is included in it. Might I here descend to particulars, I could manifest that there is not any property of God, whereby he hath made himself known to us, but steadfastness in believing gives it the glory which in some measure is due unto it; and that all doubting arises from our calling some divine attribute into question. It were easy to show how this gives God the glory of his faithfulness, truth, power, righteousness, grace, mercy, goodness, love, patience, and whatever else God hath revealed himself to be.

This, then, is the force of this first testimony: If the glory of God be all that he requires at our hands, and this steadfastness in believing gives him this glory, and this alone doth so, it must needs be acceptable unto him.

(2.) A testimony of the same importance[1] is Heb. vi. 17, 18. "The heirs of the promise," those to whom it is made (the great promise of Christ), are believers; these are said here, "to fly for refuge," καταφυγόντες, "the fliers with speed." The expression is evidently metaphorical. The allusion, say some, is taken from those who ran in a race for a prize. This, they say, the word κρατῆσαι that follows, (which signifies "to take fast hold on") doth import. Men that run in a race, when they attain the end, seize on, and lay fast hold of the prize.

Our translators, by rendering the word "flying for refuge," manifest that they had respect to the manslayers flying to the city of refuge under the Old Testament: and this way go sundry interpreters. And I am inclined to this acceptation of the metaphor upon a double account:—

[1.] Because I think the apostle would more willingly allude to a Hebrew custom, writing to the Hebrews touching an institution of God, and that directly typical of the matter he had in hand, than to a custom of the Greeks and Romans in their races, which hath not so much light in it, as to the business in hand, as the other.

[2.] Because the design of the place doth evidently hold out a flying from something, as well as a flying to something; in which regard it is said, that there is "consolation" provided for them; namely, in their deliverance from the evil which they feared and fled from. Now, in a race there is indeed a prize proposed, but there is no evil

[1] *Importance* sometimes occurs in the writings of Owen, under a signification attached to it by some old English writers, and according to which it is equivalent to *import, meaning, signification.*—ED.

avoided. It was otherwise with him that fled for refuge; for as he had a city of safety before him, so he had the avenger of blood behind him; and he fled with speed and diligence to the one, that he might avoid the other. Now, these cities of refuge were provided for the manslayer, who, having slain a man at unawares, and being thereby surprised with an apprehension of danger—it being lawful for the avenger of blood to slay him—fled with all his strength to one of those cities, where he was to enjoy immunity and safety.

Thus a poor sinner, finding himself in a condition of guilt, surprised with a sense of it, seeing death and destruction ready to seize upon him, flies with all his strength to the bosom of the Lord Jesus,—the only city of refuge from the avenging justice of God and curse of the law. Now, this *flying* to the bosom of Christ,—the hope set before us for relief and safety,—is believing. It is here called *flying* by the Holy Ghost, to express the nature of it to the spiritual sense of believers. What, now; doth he declare himself to be affected with their "flying for refuge,"—that is, their believing? Why, he hath taken all means possible to show himself abundantly willing to receive them. He hath engaged his word and promise, that they may not in the least doubt or stagger, but know that he is ready to receive them, and give them "strong consolation." And what is this consolation? Whence may it appear to arise? Whence did consolation arise to him who, having slain a man at unawares, should fly to a city of refuge? Must it not be from hence,—the gates of the city would certainly be open to him, that he should find protection there, and be safe-guarded from the revenger? Whence, then, must be our strong consolation, if we thus fly for refuge by believing? Must it not be from hence, that God is freely ready to receive us,—that he will in no wise shut us out, but that we shall be welcome to him; and with the more speed we come, the more welcome we shall be? This he convinces us of, by the engagement of his word and oath to that purpose. And what farther testimony would we have that our believing is acceptable to him?

It is said, Heb. x. 38, "If any man draw back, my soul [the Lord's] shall have no pleasure in him." What is it to draw back? It is to decline from his steadfastness of believing. So the apostle interprets it, verse 39, "We are not of them who draw back unto perdition; but of them that believe." Drawing back is opposed to believing. In these drawers-back that come not up to steadfastness in believing, nor labour so to do, the Lord's "soul hath no pleasure;"—that is, he exceedingly abhors and abominates them; which is the force of that expression. His delight is in those who are steadfast in adhering to the promises; in them his soul takes pleasure.

When the Jews treated with our Saviour about salvation, they ask him, "What shall we do, that we might work the work of God?" John vi. 28,—that work of God by which they might come to be accepted with him; which is the cry of all convinced persons. Our Saviour's answer is, verse 29, "This is the work of God, that ye believe." "Will ye know the great work, wherein God is so delighted?" "It is this," saith he, "that ye 'believe,' and be steadfast therein."

Hence, also, are many exhortations that are given us by the Holy Ghost to come up hereunto; as Heb. xii. 12; Isa. xxxv. But I shall not farther insist on testimonies, which exceedingly abound to this purpose. The farther demonstrations of the point ensue:—

2. The next shall consist in the farther improvement of the first testimony concerning the glory of God, arising from our being steadfast in believing.

This is granted by all, that God's ultimate end in all things he doth himself, and in all that he requires us to do, is his own glory. It cannot be otherwise, if he be the first, only independent being, and prime cause of all things, and their chiefest good. God having, then, placed his glory in that which cannot be attained and brought about without believing, in answer to his present constitution of things, it must needs be acceptable to him; as is a suitable means to a designed end to any one's acting in wisdom and righteousness.

Bear in mind, I pray, what it is that I mean by believing. Though the word be general and large, yet in my intendment it is restrained to the particulars insisted on,—namely, the constant establishment of our souls in receiving the Lord Jesus, tendered unto us in the truth and from the love of the Father, for the pardon of sins, and acceptation of our persons before God. This, I say, according to God's constitution of things in the covenant of grace, is necessary to bring about that end of glory to himself which he aims at. Hence he sums up his whole design to be "the praise of his glorious grace," Eph. i. 6.

In Prov. xxv. 2, if I mistake not, this is clearly asserted, "It is the glory of God to conceal a thing," or "to cover a matter." I told you before what is the glory of God. It is not the splendour and majesty of his infinite and excellent perfections, which arise not from any thing he doth, but from what he is; but it is the exaltation, manifestation, and essence of those excellencies. When God is received, believed, known to be such as he declares himself,—therein is he glorified; that is his glory. This glory, saith the Holy Ghost, arises from the covering a matter.

What matter is this? It is not the glory of God to cover every matter, all things whatever; yea, it is his glory to "bring to light the hidden things of darkness." The manifestation of his own works "declares his glory," Ps. xix. 1. So doth the manifestation of the good works of his people, Matt. v. 16. It is, then, things of some peculiar kind that are here intended. The following opposition discovers this, " The honour of kings is to search out a matter." What matter is it that it is the glory of the king to find out? Is it not faults and offences against the law? Is it not the glory of magistrates to find out transgressions, that the transgressors may be punished? This is the glory of the magistrate, to inquire, find out, and punish offences, transgressions of the law. It is, then, in answer hereunto, a sinful thing, sin itself, that is the matter or thing which it is the glory of God to cover. But what is it to cover a sinful matter? It is that which is opposed to the magistrate's finding it out;—what that is, we have a full description in Job xxix. 16, 17, "The cause I knew not, I searched out, and I brake the jaws of the wicked." It is to make judicial inquisition after, to find out hidden transgressions, that the offenders may be brought to condign punishment; so that God's concealing a matter is his not searching, with an intention of punishment, into sins and sinners, to make them naked to the stroke of the law. It is his hiding of sin from the condemning power of the law.

The word here used is the same with that of David, Ps. xxxii. 1, " Blessed is the man whose sin is covered." And in sundry other places is it used to the same purpose; which is expressed, Mic. vii. 19, by " casting all our sins into the bottom of the sea." That which is so disposed of is utterly covered from the sight of men. So doth God express the covering of the sins of his people, as to their not appearance to their condemnation,—they shall be " cast into the bottom of the sea." Hence are our sins, in the New Testament, said ἀφίεναι, which we translate "forgiven," and "to forgive;" and ἄφεσις, " forgiveness," in twenty places. The word signifies properly to " remove" or "dismiss" one; ἁμαρτήματα ἀφίεναι, is "peccata missa facere,"—"to send or remove away our sins out of sight;" the same in substance with that which is here called "to cover." And so is the word used in another business, Matt. xxiii. 23, Ἀφήκατε τὰ βαρύτερα τοῦ νόμου,— " You have omitted the weightier things of the law;" that is, you have laid them aside, as it were, out of sight, taking no care of them. Now, the bottom of all these expressions of *removing*, *hiding*, *covering*, and *concealing* sin, which gives life and significancy to them, making them import forgiveness of sin, is the allusion that is in them to the mercy-seat under the law. The making and use of it we have, Exod. xxv. 17, 18. It was a plate of pure gold, lying on the ark, called כַּפֹּרֶת, or " a covering." In the ark was the law, written on tables of stone. Over the mercy-seat, between the cherubims, was the oracle representing the presence of God. By which the Holy Ghost does signify, that the mercy-seat was to cover the law, and the condemning power of it, as it were, from the eye of God's justice, that we be not consumed. Hence is God said to cover sin, because by the mercy-seat he hides that which is the strength and power of sin, as to its guilt and tendency unto punishment. The apostle calls this "mercy-seat," τὸ ἱλαστήριον, Heb. ix. 5. That word is used but once more in the New Testament, and then Christ is called so, Rom. iii. 25, or ὃν προέθετο ὁ Θεὸς ἱλαστήριον,—"whom God hath proposed as a mercy-seat." Christ alone is that mercy-seat by whom sin, and the law from whence sin hath its rigour, is hidden. And from that typical institution is that expression in the Old Testament, "Hide me under thy wings,"—the wings of the cherubims, where the mercy-seat was; that is, in the bosom of Christ.

Now, saith the Holy Ghost, thus to hide, to cover, to pardon sin by Christ, is the glory of God, wherein he will be exalted and admired, and for which he will be praised. Give him this, and you give him his great aim and design. Let him be believed in, trusted on, as God in Christ pardoning iniquity, transgression, and sin,—so reconciling the world to himself, and manifesting his glorious properties therein,—and he hath his end.

Should I now proceed to show what God hath done, what he doth, and will do, to set up his glory, it would make it evident, indeed, that he aimed at it. His eternal electing love lies at the bottom of this design. This is the tendency of it,—that God may be glorified in the forgiveness of sin. The sending of his Son,—a mystery of wisdom, goodness, and righteousness past finding out,—with all that, by his authority and commission, he did, suffered, and doth, was, that his name might be glorified in this thing. Hath the new covenant of grace any other end? Did not God on purpose propose, make, and establish that covenant in the blood of his Son; that whereas he had, by his works of creation and providence, by the old covenant and law, given glory to himself in other respects, he might by this glorify himself in the hiding of iniquity? The dispensation of the Spirit for the conversion of sinners, with all the mighty works ensuing thereupon, is to the same and no other purpose. Wherefore doth God exercise patience, forbearance, long-suffering towards us,—such as he will be admired for to eternity,—such as our souls stand amazed to think of? It is only that he may bring about this glory of his,—the covering of iniquity and pardoning of sin.

Now, what is it that on our part is required, that this great design of God for his glory may be accomplished in and towards us? Is it not our believing, and steadfastness therein? I need not stay to manifest it; nor yet give farther light or strength to our inference from what hath been spoken,—namely, that if these things are so, then our believing and steadfastness therein is exceeding acceptable to God.

3. For the last demonstration of the point, I shall add the consideration of one particular that God useth in the pursuit of his glory,

before mentioned; and that is, his institution and command of preaching the gospel to all nations, and the great care he hath taken to provide instruments for the propagation of it, and promulgation therein of the word of his grace, Matt. xxviii. 19, "Go preach the gospel to 'all nations;'—'to every creature,'" Mark xvi. 15. What is this gospel, which he will have preached and declared? Is it any thing but a declaration of his mind and will concerning his gracious acceptation of believing, and steadfastness therein? This God declares of his purpose, his eternal, unchangeable will,—that there is, by his appointment, an infallible, an inviolable connection between believing on Jesus Christ, the receiving of him, and the everlasting fruition of himself. This he declares to all; but his purpose to bestow faith effectually relates only to some: they "believe who are ordained to eternal life." But this purpose of his will—that believing in Christ shall have the end mentioned, righteousness and salvation in the enjoyment of himself—concerns all alike. Now, to what end hath the Lord taken care that this gospel shall be so preached and declared, and that to the consummation of the world, but that indeed our believing is acceptable to him?

But I shall desist from the pursuit of this demonstration, wherein so many things offer themselves to consideration, as that the naming of them must needs detain me longer from my principal aim than I am willing.

SERMON II.

THE use of the point insisted on is, to encourage to the duty so commended and exalted; or, it contains motives unto steadfastness in believing the promises. Amongst the many that are usually insisted on to this purpose, I shall choose out some few that seem to be most effectual thereunto:—

Use 1. We shall begin with the consideration of God himself, even the Father; and that declaration of his love, kindness, tenderness, readiness, and willingness to receive poor believers, which he hath made of himself in Christ Jesus. According as our apprehensions are of him, and his heart towards us, so will the settlement of our souls in cleaving to him by believing be. We are, amongst men, free and easy with them whom we know to be of a kind, loving, compassionate disposition; but full of doubts, fears, and jealousies, when we have to deal with those who are morose, peevish, and froward. Entertaining hard thoughts of God, ends perpetually in contrivances to fly and keep at a distance from him, and to employ ourselves about any thing in the world rather than to be treating and conversing with him. What delight can any one take in him whom he conceives to be always furious, wrathful, ready to destroy? or, what comfortable expectation can any one have from such a one? Consider, then, in some particulars, what God declares of himself, and try, in the exercising of your thoughts thereon, whether it be not effectual to engage your hearts to steadfastness in believing the promises, and closing with the Son of his love tendered in them:—

(1.) He gives us his name for our support, Isa. l. 10. He speaks to poor, dejected, bewildered, fainting sinners: "Give not over; let not go your hold; though you be in darkness to all other means of support and consolation, yet 'trust in the name of the LORD.' And," saith he, "in case you do so, this 'name shall be a strong tower unto you,'" Prov. xviii. 10. And what this name of God, which is such a stay and safe defence, is, is declared at large, Exod. xxxiv. 6, 7. This name of his, is that glory which he promised to show to Moses, chap. xxxiii. To be known by this name is that great glory of God which he aims to be exalted in; yea, and God is so fully known by his name, and the whole of the obedience he requireth of us is so ordered and disposed in the revelation thereof, that when our Saviour had made him and his whole will known from his bosom, he sums up his whole work in this, "I have manifested thy name unto the men which thou gavest me out of the world," John xvii. 6. The manifestation of the name of God to the elect was the great work of Christ on the earth, as he was the prophet and teacher of his church. He declared the name of God,—his gracious, loving, tender nature,—his blessed properties, that were fit to encourage poor creatures to come to him, and to trust in him. This, then, is his name with whom we have to do in this matter;—the name he hath given himself for us to know him and call him by,—that we may deal with him as such, as his name bespeaks him to be. He is gracious, loving, ready to pity, help, receive us; delighting in our good, rejoicing in our approach to him. This he hath proclaimed of himself,—this his only Son hath revealed him to be. He is not called Apollyon, a destroyer; but, the Saviour of men. Who would not venture on him, in and by the way which himself hath appointed and approved?

(2.) As is his name, so is his nature. Saith he of himself, Isa. xxvii. 4, "Fury is not in me." He speaks with reference to his church, to believers, of whom we are speaking. There is no such thing as that anger and wrath in God in reference to thee whereof thou art afraid. Hast thou had hard thoughts of him? Hast thou nothing but entertained affrighting reports concerning him, as though he were a devouring fire and endless burnings? "Be not," saith he, "mistaken; 'fury is not in me.'" He hath not one wrathful, revengeful thought towards thee. No; take hold of his strength, and you shall have peace, verse 5. Nay, he is " love," 1 John iv. 8, 16;—of an infinitely loving and tender nature,—all love. There is nothing in him that is inconsistent with love itself. We see how a little love, that is but a weak affection in the nature of a man, will carry a tender father towards a child. How did it melt, soften, reconcile the father of the prodigal in the parable! " O my son Absalom! would God I had died for thee!" saith David, a poor father in distress for the death of a rebellious child. How will a child bear himself above dread and terror, under many miscarriages, upon the account of the love of a tender father! What, then, shall we say or think of Him who is love in the abstract,—whose nature is love? May we not conclude that certainly he " is merciful and gracious, slow to anger, and plenteous in mercy," as the psalmist speaks? Ps. ciii. 8. According as we are, by degrees, led into an acquaintance with God in his properties (for we are led into it by degrees and steps, not being able at once to bear all the glory which he is pleased here to shine upon us with), so are we amazed with his several excellencies. Experience of any property of God as engaged in Christ, and exercising itself for our good, is greatly conquering to the soul; but none so much as this,—his being love, and ready to forgive on that account. Such is the frame of the church, Mic. vii. 18, " Who is a God like unto thee, that pardoneth iniquity, and passeth by transgression?" Can it enter into the heart of man? O who is like to him! Is it possible he should be thus to sinners! This discovery overwhelms the soul, and strengthens it in faith and trust in him.

There is a general compassion in God, by which he proceeds in the dispensation of his providence, that is too hard for the apprehensions of men when they come to be concerned in it. Poor Jonah was angry that he was so merciful, chap. iv. 2, " I knew that thou wast not one for me to deal with: thou art so gracious and merciful, slow to anger, of such kindness, and repentest thee of the evil, that it is not for me, with any credit or reputation, to be engaged and employed in thy work and service." And if God be thus full of compassion to the world, which to-day is, and to-morrow shall be cast into the fire, is he not much more loving and tender unto you, " O ye of little faith?" Suit, then, the thoughts of your hearts, in your dealing with God, to this revelation which he hath made of his own nature. He is good,—love and kindness itself; fury is not in him,—he is ready to forgive, accept, embrace. And,—

(3.) According to his name and nature, so are his dealings with us, and his actings towards us. From him who is so called, so disposed, we may expect that what he doth in a suitableness thereunto he will do with great readiness and cheerfulness, that so he may answer his name, and express his nature. "How, then, will he show and manifest these things?" See Isa. lv. 7, He will have mercy: he is love,—he will have mercy; yea, "he will abundantly pardon." "But how will he do it?" Verse 8, Alas! you cannot think how: his thoughts are not as your thoughts. You have poor, low, mean thoughts of God's way of pardoning; you can by no means reach to it, or comprehend it: raise your apprehensions to the utmost, yet you come not near it. Verse 9, "As the heavens are higher than the earth, so are my ways higher than your ways, and my thoughts than your thoughts." "But doth not God, then, pardon as we do?—come hardly to it, through many persuasions, and at length do it ἑκὼν ἀέκοντί γε θυμῷ,—'with an unwilling kind of willingness,' that ingenuous spirits had almost as willingly have our wrath as our pardon?" No such thing. What he doth, he doth with his whole heart, and his whole soul, Jer. xxxii. 41; and rejoices in the doing of it, Zeph. iii. 17. He will have mercy, he will abundantly pardon; he will do it with his whole soul; he will rejoice in his so doing, and rest in his love. I know not what we can desire more, to assure us of free acceptance with him. You will say, perhaps, that this is but sometimes; and it is well if we can come nigh him in that season. Nay, but he is acting herein suitably to his name and nature; his whole soul and his whole heart is in it: and therefore he will take a course for the accomplishing of it. Isa. xxx. 18, He will wait to be gracious. His heart is set upon it, and he will take advantage to accomplish his desire and design. And if our stubbornness and folly be such as to be ready to wear out his patience,—to make him weary, as he complains, Isa. xliii. 24, and to cause him to serve beyond the limits of his patience,—he will be exalted, take to himself his great power for the removal of our stubbornness, that he may be merciful unto us. One way or other he will accomplish the desire of his heart, the design of his grace.

For the farther clearing of this truth, take along with you these few considerations of God's dealing with us, and his condescension therein, that he may act suitably to his own nature and name:—

[1.] His comparing himself to creatures of the most tender and boundless affection, Isa. xlix. 15, 16. This is as high as we can go. The affection of a mother to a sucking child, the child of her womb, is the utmost instance that we can give of love, tenderness, and affection. "This," says God, "you cannot think, you ought not to imagine, that a tender, loving mother, should not have compassion on 'a sucking child, the son of her womb.' Things will act according to their natures,—even tigers love their own offspring; and shall 'a woman forget her sucking child?' But yet," saith God, "raise up your apprehensions to this, take it for granted that she may do so,—which yet, without offering violence to nature, cannot be imagined,—'yet I will not forget you;'—this will not reach my love, my affection." Were we as secure of the love of God to us, as we are of the love of a good, gracious mother to her sucking child, whom we see embracing of it, and rejoicing over it all the day long, we would think our estate very comfortable and secure. But, alas! what is this to the love of God to the meanest saint on the earth! What is a drop to the ocean! what is a little dying, decaying affection, to an infiniteness, an eternity of love! See the working of this love in God, Hos. xi. 8, 9; Jer. xxxi. 20.

[2.] His condescension to entreat us that it may be so,—that he may exercise pity, pardon, goodness, kindness, mercy towards us. He is so full, that he is, as it were, pained until he can get us to himself, that he may communicate of his love unto us. "We pray you," says the apostle, "in Christ's stead, as if God by us did beseech you." What to do? what is he so earnest about? what would God have of us? Some great thing, some difficult service assuredly. "No," says he, "but, 'be reconciled to God,'" 2 Cor. v. 20. Says God, "O ye sons of men, 'why will ye die?' I beseech you, be friends with me; let us agree;—accept of the atonement. I have love for you; take mercy, take pardon; do not destroy your own souls." "This is the rest wherewith ye may cause the weary to rest; and this is the refreshing," Isa. xxviii. 12. Remember how the Scripture abounds with exhortations and entreaties to this purpose.

[3.] In condescension to our weakness, he hath added his oath to this purpose. Will we not yet believe him? will we not yet venture upon him? Are we afraid that if we put ourselves upon him, into his hand, he will kill us, we shall die? He gives us this last possible relief against such misgiving thoughts. "Swear unto me that I shall not die, is the utmost that any one requires, when, with the greatest ground of mistrust, he gives up himself to him that is mightier than he. "Now, 'as I live, saith the LORD,' I would not the death of a sinner," Ezek. xxxiii. 11. Methinks this should put an end to all strife. We have his promise and oath, Heb. vi. 18, and what would we have more? He is of an infinite loving and tender nature; he entreats us to come to him, and swears we shall not suffer by our so doing. Innumerable other instances of the like kind might be given, to evidence the actings of God towards us to be suitable to his name and nature, before insisted on.

Now the end aimed at, as you know, in these considerations, is, by them to encourage our hearts in the belief of the promises. It is God with whom therein we have to do. The things we receive by our believing are excellent, desirable, what alone we want, and which will do us good to eternity. The difficulties of believing arise from our unworthiness, and the terror of him with whom we have to do.

To disentangle our souls from under the power of such fears and considerations, this, in the first place, is proposed,—the tender, gracious, loving nature of Him with whom herein we have to do. Fill your hearts, then, with such thoughts of God as these; exercise your minds with such apprehensions of him. The psalmist tells you what will be the issue of it, Ps. ix. 10, "They that know thy name will put their trust in thee;"—establishment in believing will ensue. If we know the name of God, as by himself revealed,—know the love and kindness wrapped up therein,—we cannot but trust him. Let us be always thinking of God, with a clear persuasion that so it is; that he is gracious, loving, ready to receive us, delighting, rejoicing to embrace us, to do us good, to give us mercy and glory,—whatever he hath promised in Christ; and it will exceedingly tend to the establishment of our hearts.

But now, concerning the things that have been spoken, great caution is to be used. It is not a general notion of the nature of God that I have been insisting on; but the goodness and love of God to his in Christ Jesus. Wherefore, farther, to clear this whole business, and that a sure foundation may be laid of this great thing, I desire to add the following observations:—

1*st.* I acknowledge that all that can be said, by all or any of the sons of men, concerning the goodness, loveliness, kindness of God in his own blessed nature, is inconceivably, infinitely below what it is in itself. What a little portion is it that we all know of his goodness! Though we have all his works and his whole word to teach us, yet, as we have no affections large enough to entertain it, so no faculty to receive or apprehend it. Admiration—which is the soul's "nonplus," its doing it knows not what, the winding of it up until it stands still, ready to break—is all that we can arrive unto in the consideration hereof. His excellencies and perfections in this kind are sufficient, superabundant, for the engagement of the love and obedience of all rational creatures; and when they can go no farther, they may, with the psalmist, call in all their fellow-creatures to the work. Nor can any man exercise himself in a more noble contemplation than that of the beauty and loveliness of God. "How great is his goodness! how great is his beauty!" They who have nothing but horrid, harsh apprehensions of the nature of God,—that he is insupportably severe and wrathful,—know him not. To have thoughts of him as cruel and sanguinary; to make use of his greatness and infinite excellencies only to frighten, terrify, and destroy the work of his hands, who is good, and doth good,—who made all things good, in beauty and order, and who loves all the things he hath made,—who hath filled all that we see or can think on with the fruits of his goodness,—is unreasonable, unjust, and wicked. Consider God and his works together as he made them, and in the order by him assigned to them; —there is nothing in his nature towards you but kindness, benignity, goodness, power (exerted to continue to you the goodness first imparted), grace, and bounty, in daily, continual additions of more.

But, alas! they are sinners of whom we speak. It is true, in God, as he is by nature, there is an abundant excellency and beauty, a ravishing goodness and love, for the endearing of his creatures. As he made them, they could desire no more: the not loving him above all for his loveliness, for the suitableness of his excellencies to bind their hearts to him as their chiefest and only good, was the sin of some of them; but now the whole state of things is changed, upon a supposition of the entrance of sin. God, indeed, is not changed;—his excellencies and perfections are the same from eternity to eternity: but the creature is changed; and what was desirable and amiable before to him, ceases to be so to him, though it continue to be so in itself. He who, whilst he stood in the law of his creation, had boldness with God,—was neither afraid nor ashamed,—after he had sinned, trembled at the hearing of his voice; yea, endeavoured to part with him for ever, and to hide himself from him. What property of God was more endearing to his creatures than his holiness? How is he glorious, lovely, desirable above all, to them who abide in his image and likeness! But as for sinners, they cannot serve him, because of his holiness, Josh. xxiv. 19. In the revelation of God to sinners, together with the discovery of the excellencies before mentioned,—of his goodness, kindness, graciousness,—there is also a vision given of his justice, wrath, anger, severity, and indignation, against sin. These unconquerably interpose between the sinner and all emanations and fruits of goodness and love. Whence, instead of being endeared to God, their contrivance is that of Micah vi. 6, 7; and upon a conviction of the successlessness of any such attempts, they cry out, "Who among us shall dwell with everlasting burnings?" Isa. xxxiii. 14. A desire to avoid him to all eternity is all that a sinner's most choice consideration of God, in his own essential excellencies, can lead him to. For who will set the thorns in battle against him? who will bring the stubble that is fully dry to a consuming fire? And therefore it is that those who propose general grace, from a natural goodness in God, as a ground of consolation to sinners, when they come to answer that objection, "Yea, but God is just, as well as merciful," do, with many good words, take away with one hand just as much as they give with the other. "Apprehend," say they, "God's gracious nature; he is good to all; trust upon it: believe not them that say otherwise." But he is just also, and will not let any sin go unpunished; and therefore cannot but punish sin according to its demerit. Where is now the consolation spoken of? Wherefore observe,—

2dly. That since the entrance of sin, there is no apprehension—I mean for sinners—of a goodness, love, and kindness in God, as flowing from his natural properties, but upon an account of the interposition of his sovereign will and pleasure. It is most false which by some is said,—that special grace flows from that which they call general grace, and special mercy from general mercy. There is a whole nest of mistakes in that conception. God's sovereign, distinguishing will is the fountain of all special grace and mercy. "I will," saith he, "cause all my glory to pass before thee;" and, "I will have mercy on whom I will have mercy," Exod. xxxiii. 19; Rom. ix. 15. Here is the fountain of mercy, even the will of God. He is of a merciful and gracious nature; but dispenses mercy and grace by his sovereign will. It is electing love that is at the bottom of all special grace, all special kindness; whence the election obtains, when the rest are hardened, Rom. xi. 7 [margin]. He blesseth us with spiritual blessings, according as he hath chosen us, Eph. i. 3, 4. God having made all things good, and imparted of the fruits of his goodness to them, might, without the least injury to, or restraint of, his own goodness, have given over all them who sinned, and came short of his glory, to an everlasting separation from him. That he deals otherwise with any of them, is not from any propensity in his nature and goodness towards their relief; but from his sovereign, wise, gracious will, wherein he most freely purposed in himself to do them good by Christ, Eph. i. 9.

This I say, then, all considerations of the goodness and mercifulness of the nature of God, and of general grace on that account, are so balanced in the soul of a sinner by those of his justice and severity,—so weakened by the experience all men have of the not exerting those properties effectually for the good of all that are pretended to have a right thereunto,—that they are no ground, as so considered, of consolation to sinners. And if any one should venture to draw nigh unto God on the account of such general grace, he would meet the sword of justice before he would lay hold upon Him. So that,—

3dly. Where there is mention in the Scripture made of the goodness of God, by which he reveals himself to be love, to be gracious and tender, it is not upon the general account of his perfections considered in himself, but on the new and special account of the free engagement of his attributes in Christ with regard to his elect. Such expressions, as far as they have a spiritual tendency, and are not restrained to the law of providence, belong to the covenant of grace, and God manifested in Christ. And this is that which is intended by our divines, who say that it is not naturally from the goodness of God that he doth good to sinners, but from his gracious will; for were it not for that, all communications of the other unto sinners would be everlastingly shut up.

This, then, is that which we are to close withal,—the gracious nature of God, even the Father, as manifested in Christ, on the ground of the atonement made for sin. This is he whom the poor, weak believer hath to do withal. This is he who invites us to the acceptation of Christ in the promises,—he with whom we have principally to do in all this affair. He is love,—ready, willing to receive and embrace those who come to him by Christ. Be convinced of his good-will and kindness, his patience to us-ward, and we cannot but be established in closing with his faithfulness in his promises.

4thly. Observe who it is of whom I am speaking. It is believers, those who are interested in God by Christ. Let others, then (such as are not so), take heed lest they abuse and wrest the doctrine of the grace of God to their own destruction. I know nothing is more common with men of vain and light spirits, formalists, yea, and open presumptuous sinners, than to say and think, "God is merciful; there is yet good hopes on that account. He made not men to damn them; and whatever preachers say, it will, at least it may, be well with us at last." But, poor creatures! even this God of whom we have been speaking, "is a consuming fire;—a God of purer eyes than to behold iniquity;"—a God that will not let the least sin go unpunished. And the greater is his love, his goodness, his condescension to those who come in unto him upon his own terms by Christ; the greater will be his wrath and indignation against those who refuse his tender of love in his own way, and yet "add drunkenness to thirst, and say they shall have peace, though they walk in the imaginations of their own hearts."

Use 2. Let a second motive be taken from the excellencies of the Lord Jesus Christ, whom, by believing, we do close with and receive. Now, the excellencies of his person are such, as not only may engage us to come to him to attain them, but they are all suited to encourage us in our coming,—to support us, and make us steadfast in our believing.[1]

Use 3. We may likewise to the same purpose consider the promises of God, wherein both his love and the excellency and suitableness of the Lord Jesus Christ are signally and eminently expressed. Many things to very good purpose are usually spoken of the promises;—their nature, stability, preciousness, efficacy, centring all in one covenant, their confirmation in Christ, are usually insisted on; being those in particular which the soul in believing closes withal. I shall at present pitch on these two things:—(1.) The infinite condescension the Lord useth in them for the obviating [of] all the objections and fears of our unbelieving hearts. (2.) The manifestation of

[1] Upon this head, in its several branches, see his book, "Of Communion with God," part ii., chap. iii., digression 1, in the Doctrinal Division of his works, vol. ii.

his wisdom and love, in suiting them to the most pressing wants, troubles, disquietments, and fears of our souls, [so] that we must needs see his intendment in them to do us good.

(1.) The first of these might be evinced by sundry sorts of instances. I shall insist on one only,—and that is, the unexpected relief that is laid up in them for us, exhibiting grace and mercy when any thing in the world might rather be looked for. This, with the use of it, I shall manifest by an induction of some particular promises which are generally known to all:—

Isa. xliii. 22–26. Here are persons guilty of sundry sinful follies. The Lord chargeth them home upon their consciences, to their trouble and disquietment; he makes them go with wounds and blows upon that account. They had neglected his worship, and not called on his name. And whereas they could not utterly cast off all performance of duties, yet what they did abide in the performance of was exceeding burdensome to them; they were weary of it,—yea, weary of God therein, and of all spiritual communion and converse with him:—"Thou hast been weary of me." Their convictions compelled them to do God some service; but it was, as we say, a death to them;—they were weary of it; and most things, either as to the matter or manner that God required, they utterly neglected What, then, says God of himself in reference to this state of theirs? "Notwithstanding all my patience, thou hast made me weary of thee; like one that hath a hard service, that cannot abide in it. It is a bondage," says God, "for me to have any thing to do with thee." Suppose we now a poor soul, fully convinced that thus is the state and condition with him,—so powerful is his unbelief and corruption, that he is weary of God and his ways: it may be he would faintly have it otherwise, and therefore binds himself to the performance of duties, if so be that God thereby may be flattered;—but withal, because of his innumerable follies, God also is weary of him, that he can bear the bondage of him no longer; he is "weary of serving." What can such a one conclude with himself, but that everlasting separation from God will be the close of this dispensation? He is weary of God, and God is weary of him; surely, then, they must part, and that for ever. What remedy is there, or can there be? Poor soul! lie down in darkness.

But see, now, what God says in this case, and what an unexpected condescension there is in the word of promise. Is it, Be gone? Take a bill of divorce? Take thine own course, and I will take mine against thee? No; says God, "This is an estate and condition whereof I am weary, and thou art weary;—I am weary of thy multiplying the guilt of sin; thou art wearied in serving the power of thy sin. I will put an end to this state of things; we will have peace again between us. I will blot out thy sins, and remember thine iniquities no more. I, even I, will do it." He redoubles the word passionately, emphatically, to call to mind who he is with whom in this condition we have to do: "'I, even I,'—who am God, and not man; I,—whose thoughts are not as your thoughts; I,—who am great in mercy, and who will abundantly pardon;—I will do it."

Yea, but saith the poor convinced soul, "I know no reason why thou shouldst do so,—I cannot believe it; for I know not upon what account I should be so dealt withal." Says God, "I know full well that there is nothing in thee upon the account whereof I should thus deal with thee; there is nothing in thee, but for what thou deservest to be everlastingly cut off; but quiet thy heart, I will do it for my own sake I have deeper engagements on my own account for this than thou canst look into."

Doubtless, such a word as this, coming in when God and the soul are at the point of giving over and parting fellowship,—when the soul is ready to do so indeed, and hath great cause to think that God will be first therein,—then, contrary to all expectation, and above all hopes, —must needs constrain it to cry out, as Thomas, upon sight of the wounds of Christ, "My Lord and my God." Let the soul that cannot get itself unto any steadfastness in closing with Christ in the promises—that staggers, and is tossed to and fro between hopes and fears, being filled with a sense of sin and unworthiness,—dwell a while upon the consideration of this unexpected surprisal, and give up itself to the power of it.

Isa. lvii. 17, 18, gives me another instance to the same purpose. This seems to be the description of a man totally rejected of God. The most dejected sinner can hardly make a more deplorable description of his condition, though ready enough to speak all the evil of himself that he can think of. Let us see how things are disposed. There is an iniquity found in him and upon him, that the soul of God abhors. In this evil there is a continuance, until God manifest himself to take notice of it, and to be provoked with it: "I was wroth," saith God [according to the sense of the text quoted], "and took a course to let him know so. I laid my hand upon him, and smote him in some outward dispensation, that he could not but take notice that I was wroth. Upon this smiting it may be he begins to seek and pray, but I am not found of him; I hid me,—I let him pray, but took no notice of him, but hid myself in wrath. Surely this will do, he will now leave his iniquity and return to me. Nay," saith God, "he grows worse than ever; neglecting my smiting, hiding, wrath, he goes on frowardly in the ways of his own heart."

God had appointed in the law, that when a son was rebellious against his parents, and grown incorrigible therein, he should be "stoned with stones." What shall be done, then, with this person, who is thus incorrigible under the hand of God? Says God, "'I have seen his ways,'—it will not be better. Shall I destroy him, consume him, make him as Admah and Zeboim? Ah! 'my bowels are turned in me; my repentings are kindled together: I will heal him.' If he goes on thus, and no outward means will do him good, he must perish; but 'I will heal him.' He wounded his soul; I also wounded him in the blows I gave him when I was wroth. Is he not 'my dear son? . . . . . Since I spake against him, I do earnestly remember him still: therefore my bowels are troubled for him; I will surely have mercy upon him,'" Jer. xxxi. 20. He shall have wine and oil, grace and pardon, for all his wounds. But, alas! he is not able to go one step in God's ways, he is so wonted to his own. "Leave that to me," saith God; "'I will lead him;' I will give him strength, guidance, and direction to go in my way. 'I will lead him, yea, and give him comfort' also."

Now, if any one cannot in some measure bring his condition within the verge and compass of this promise, it is hard with him indeed. And as I know the necessity of that duty, and usefulness of searching our hearts for the fruits of the Spirit in us, whereby we are made meet for communion with God,—which are all evidences of our acceptance with God, and pardon of sin thereon; so, I dare say, these are promises that will sufficiently warrant a perplexed soul to close with Christ, as tendered from the love of the Father, even when it can find in itself no other qualifications or conditions, but only such as render it every way unworthy to be accepted. We do not say to a poor, naked, hungry, harbourless man, "Go, get thee clothes, get thee food, get thee a habitation, and then I will give thee an alms: no, but, "Because thou wantest all these, therefore I will give thee an alms." "Because thou art poor, blind, polluted, guilty, sinful, I will give thee mercy," says God.

Yea, but at least a man's sense of his state and condition, with his acknowledgment of it, is needful to precede his closing with the promise. It is so as to his receiving of it,—this oftentimes being the fruit and work of the promise as given itself. But as to the tender of the promise, and Christ in the promise, unto us, it is not so. When did God give the great promise of Christ to Adam? was it when he was sorrowing, repenting, qualifying his soul? No; but when he was flying, hiding, and had no thoughts but of separation from God. God calls him forth, and at once tells him what he had deserved, pronounces the curse, and gives him the blessing. "I raised thee up," saith Christ, "under the apple-tree; there thy mother brought thee forth," Cant. viii. 5. From the very place of sin Christ raiseth up the soul. So Isa. xlvi. 12, "Hearken to me, ye stout-hearted, that are far from righteousness." Here are two notable qualifications, stout-heartedness, and remoteness from righteousness. What saith God to them? Verse 13, He discourses to them of mercy and salvation; and, chap. lv. 1, "Buy," saith he, "wine and milk." "Yea, but I have nothing to buy withal, and these things require a price." Indeed, so they do; but take them "without money, and without price." "But he calls on them only who are 'thirsty.'" True; but it is a thirst of indigency and total want, not a thirst of spiritual desires; for in whomsoever that is, they have already tasted of this wine and milk, and are blessed, Matt. v. Nay, we may go one step farther. Prov. ix. 4, 5, Christ invites them to his bread and wine who have no heart [חֲסַר־לֵב]. This, commonly, is the last objection that an unbelieving heart makes against itself,—it hath no mind to Christ. Indeed he hath no heart for Christ. "But yet," saith Christ, "thou shalt not thus go off,—I will not admit of this excuse; you that have no heart, 'turn in hither.'"

Now, I say, this obviating of all objections by unexpected appearances of love, mercy, and compassion in the promises, is a strong inducement unto steadfastness in believing. When a soul shall find that God takes for granted that all is true which it can charge itself withal; that its sin, folly, unbelief, heartlessness, is so as he apprehends it, and unconceivably worse than he can think; that he takes for granted all the aggravations of his sins, that lie so dismally in his eye,—his backsliding, frowardness, greatness of sin, impotency, coldness at the present, not answering in affection to the convictions that are upon him; and notwithstanding all this, yet [says,] "Come, let us agree; accept of peace, close with Christ, receive him from my love,"—surely it cannot but in some measure engage it into a rest and acquiescence in the word of promise.

(2.) The second part of this motive is taken from the suitableness of the promises to every real distress and cause of staggering whatever. My meaning is, that whereas we are exercised with great variety of doubts and fears, of pressures and perplexities, God hath tempered his love and mercy in Christ, as prepared in the promises, unto every one of these wants and straits whatever. Had God only declared himself to us as God almighty, God all-sufficient, he might justly require and expect that we should act faith on him in every condition. But, moreover, he hath, as it were, drawn out his own all-sufficiency in Christ into numberless streams, flowing in upon all our particular wants, distresses, and temptations whatever. When God gave manna in the wilderness, it was to be gathered and ground in mills, or beat in mortars, and fried in pans, before it could be eaten, Numb. xi. 8; but the bread which came from heaven, the manna in the promises, is already ground, beaten, baked, ready for every one's hunger. It is useful, if you have a well about your house, whither you may repair to draw water; but when you have several pipes from a fountain, that convey water to every room, for every particular business, you are greatly to blame if your occasions are not supplied. We have not only a well of salvation to draw water from, but also innumerable streams flowing from that well into every empty vessel.

I shall give one or two instances of this kind:—

Isa. xxxii. 2: Here are four pressures and troubles mentioned, whereunto we may be exposed:—[1.] The *wind;* [2.] A *tempest;* [3.] *Dearth;* [4.] *Weariness.* And unto all these is the man in the promise—the Lord Jesus Christ, the King that "reigns in righteousness," verse 1—suited as a supply in them, or against them.

[1.] The first proposed evil is the *wind;*—and in respect hereof Christ is a "hiding-place." He that was ready to be cast from the top of a rock with a strong wind, would desire nothing more than a hiding-place until the strong blast were over. When fierce winds have driven a vessel at sea from all its anchors, so that it hath nothing to keep it from splitting on the next rock whereunto it is driven, a safe harbour, a hiding-place, is the great desire and expectation of the poor creatures that are in it. Our Saviour tells us what this wind is, Matt. vii. 25. The wind that blows upon and casts down false professors to the ground, is the wind of strong and urging temptations. Is this the condition of the soul? [do] strong temptations beat upon it, which are ready to hurry it down into sin and folly,—that it hath no rest from them, one blast immediately succeeding another,—that the soul begins to faint, to be weary, give over, and say, "I shall perish; I cannot hold out to the end?" Is this thy condition? See the Lord Christ suited unto it, and the relief that is in him in this promise,—he is "a hiding-place." Saith he, "These temptations seek thy life; but with me thou shalt be safe." Fly to his bosom, retreat into his arms, expect relief by faith from him, and thou shalt be safe.

[2.] There is a *tempest;*—in reference whereunto Christ is here said to be "a covert." A tempest, in the Scripture, represents the wrath of God for sin. "He breaketh me," saith Job, "with a tempest," chap. ix. 17, when he lay under a sense of the displeasure and indignation of God. He threatens to rain upon the wicked "an horrible tempest," Ps. xi. 6. A tempest is a violent mixture of wind, rain, hail, thunder, darkness, and the like. Those who have been at sea will tell you what a tempest means. Such was that in Egypt, Exod. ix. 23. There was thunder and hail, and fire running upon the ground; fire or dreadful lightning, mingled with hail, verse 24. What did men now do, upon the apprehension of this tempest? They made their servants and cattle flee into the houses, verse 20; got them into safe covert, that they might not be destroyed;—and they were safe, accordingly.

Suppose a poor creature to be under this tempest, full of sad and dreadful thoughts and apprehensions of the wrath of God; behind, before, round about, he can see nothing but hailstones and coals of fire; heaven is dark and dismal over him; he hath not seen sun, moon, or stars, in many days,—not one glimpse of light from above, or hopes of an end. "I shall perish; the earth shakes under me; the pit is opening for me. Is there no hope?" Why, see how Christ is suited in this distress also. He is "a covert" from this tempest; get into him, and thou shalt be safe. He hath borne all this storm, as far as thou art concerned; abide with him, and not one hurtful drop shall fall upon thee,—not one hair of thy head shall be singed with this fire. Hast thou fears? hast thou a sense of the wrath of God for sin? dost thou fear it will one day fall upon thee, and be thy portion? Behold a covert, a sure defence, is here provided.

[3.] There is *drought*, causing barrenness, making the heart as a dry place, as a heath or a parched wilderness;—in reference whereunto Christ is a river of water, abundantly, plentifully flowing for its refreshment. Drought in the Scripture denotes almost all manner of evil, it being the great, distressing punishment of those countries. When God threatens sinners, he says they "shall be like the heath in the desert, and shall not see when good" (or water) "cometh; but shall inhabit the parched places in the wilderness," Jer. xvii. 6; he shall be left to barrenness and want of all refreshment. And David complains, in his great distress, that his "moisture was turned into the drought of summer," Ps. xxxii. 4.

Two things are evidently in this drought,—want of grace or moisture, to make the soul fruitful; and want of rain or consolation, to make it joyful. Barrenness and sorrow, or disconsolation, are in this dry place. Let us, then, suppose this condition also. Doth the soul find itself like the parched ground? It hath no moisture to enable it to bring forth fruit, but is dry, sapless; all the fruits of the Spirit seem to be withered;—faith, love, zeal, delight in God, not one of them flourishes; yea, it thinks they are quite dead; it hath no showers, not any drop of consolation, no refreshment, but pines away under barrenness and sorrow. What would now best suit such a condition? Why, turn in a stream of water upon this parched ground. Let there be springs in this thirsty place, let "water break out in the wilderness, and streams in the desert," as Isa. xxxv. 6, and how will all things be changed! Those things that hung their heads, and had no beauty, will flourish again; and the things that are ready to die will be revived. Why, in this condition Jesus Christ will be water, and that in abundance,—rivers of water, that there shall be no want. He will, by his Spirit, give supplies of grace to make the soul fruitful; he will give in consolation to make it joyful.

[4.] There is *weariness;*—and in respect hereof Christ is said to be "*the shadow of a great rock.*" Weariness of travel and labour, through heat and drought, is insupportable. He that is to travel in a thirsty land, dry and hungry, the sun beating on his head, will be ready, with Jonah in such a condition, to wish he were dead, to be freed of his misery. Oh, how welcome will "the shadow of a great rock" be to such a poor creature! If Jonah rejoiced in "the shade of a gourd," how much better is "the shadow of a great rock!" Many a poor soul, exercised with temptations, hindered in duties, scorched with a sense of sin, is weary in his journeying towards Canaan, in his course of obedience; and thinks with himself, it were better for him even to die than to live, having no hopes to come to his journey's end. Let now this poor soul lie down and repose himself a little under the shadow and safe-guarding protection of this Rock of ages, the Lord Jesus Christ,—how will his strength and resolution come to him again!

Thus, I say, is Christ in the promises peculiarly suited to all the several distresses that we may at any time fall into. I might multiply instances to this purpose; but this one may suffice to make good the consideration proposed, for the encouraging of us to believe, from the suiting of the grace in the promises to all our wants.

Two things, then, may hence be deducted:—

1*st.* The willingness of God that we should be established in believing. To what end should the Lord thus obviate all objections that can possibly arise in a misgiving heart, and accommodate grace in Christ to all perplexities and troubles we at any time lie under, were he not willing we should lay hold on that grace, own it, accept it, and give him the praise of it? If I should go to a poor man, and tell him, "Thou art poor, but see, here are riches; thou art naked, but here is clothing; thou art hungry and thirsty, here is food and refreshment; thou art wounded, but I have the most precious balm in the world:"—if I have no intent to have him partake of these riches, food, raiment, medicine, do not I egregiously mock and deride the man's misery and sorrow? Will a wise or good man do thus? Though many will deafen their ears to the cries of the poor, yet who almost is so desperately wicked as to delight himself in sporting at their misery, and increasing their sorrow? And shall we think that the God of heaven, "the Father of mercy, and God of all consolation," who is all goodness, sweetness, and truth (as hath been declared), when he doth so suit and temper his fulness to our wants, and suits his grace in Christ to all our fears and troubles for their removal, doth it to increase our misery, and mock our calamity? I speak of the heirs of promise, to whom they are made and do belong. Is it not time for you to leave disputing and questioning the sincerity and faithfulness of God in all these engagements? What farther, what greater security can we expect or desire? So that,—

2dly. All unbelief must needs be at length totally resolved into the stubbornness of the will. "Ye will not come unto me," saith our Saviour, "that ye may have life." When all a man's objections are prevented and answered,—when all his wants are suited,—when a ground is laid that all his fears may be removed, and yet he keeps off and closes not,—what can it be but a mere perverseness of will that rules him? Doth not such an one say, "Let the Lord do what he will, say what he can, though my mouth be stopped, that I have nothing whorewith to wrangle or contend any more, yet I will not believe"? Let this, then, be another motive or encouragement, which, added to what was spoken before concerning God, even the Father, and the Lord Jesus Christ, is all I shall insist upon.

SERMON III.

THE NATURE AND BEAUTY OF GOSPEL WORSHIP.

"For through him we both have access by one Spirit unto the Father."
EPH. ii. 18.

IN the foregoing verses the apostle makes mention of a double reconciliation, wrought by the blood of the cross,—the one, of the Jews and Gentiles unto God; the other, of the same persons one to another. There were two things in the law:—First, Worship instituted under it; Secondly, The curse annexed unto it. The first of these being appropriated to the Jews, with an exclusion of the Gentiles, was the cause of unspeakable enmity and hatred between them. The latter, or the curse, falling upon both, was a cause of enmity between God and both of them. The Lord Jesus Christ, in his death removing both these, wrought and effected the twofold reconciliation mentioned. First, He brake down "the middle wall of partition between us," verse 14, and so "made both one;" that is, "between us,"—the Jews and Gentiles. He hath taken away all cause of difference that should hinder us to be one in him. And how hath he done this? By taking away "the law of commandments contained in ordinances," verse 15;—that is, by abolishing that way of worship which was the Jews' privilege and burden, from which the Gentiles were excluded; so breaking down that wall of partition. Secondly, By the cross at his death he slew the enmity, or took away the curse of the law; so reconciling both Jews and Gentiles unto God; as verse 16. By bearing the curse of the law, he reconciled both unto God;—by taking away and abolishing the worship of the law, he took away all grounds of difference amongst them.

Upon this reconciliation ensueth a twofold advantage or privilege; —an access into the favour of God, who before was at enmity with them; and a new and more glorious way of approaching unto God in his worship than that about which they were before at difference among themselves.

The first of these is mentioned, Rom. v. 2. And that which is there called, an "access into this grace wherein we stand," may in the text be called, an "access unto the Father;" that is, the favour and acceptance with God which we do enjoy. Thus our access unto God is our sense of acceptance with him upon the reconciliation made for us by Jesus Christ. But this seems not to me to be the special intendment of the text; for that access unto God here mentioned seems to be the effect of the reconciliation of the Jews and Gentiles among themselves, by the abolishing of the ceremonial worship;—a new and more glorious way of worship being now provided for them both in common, is there expressed. Before the reconciliation made, one party alone had the privilege of the carnal worship then instituted; but now both parties have in common such a way of worship, wherein they have immediate access unto God;—in which the apostle asserts the beauty and glory of the gospel worship of Jews and Gentiles above that which, enjoyed by the Jews, was a matter of separation and division between them. And this appears to be the intendment of the words from verse 17. That which is here asserted, is not an immediate effect of the reconciliation made by the blood of Christ on the cross, but of his preaching peace unto, and calling both Jews and Gentiles,—gathering them unto himself, and so to the worship of God. Being called by the word of peace, both the one and the other, as to our worship, we have this access.

And the following words, to the end of the chapter, do make it yet more plain and evident. Sundry things doth the apostle, upon the account of this their access unto God, speak of the Gentiles.

First, Negatively,—that they are no more "strangers and foreigners," verse 19; that is, that they are not so in respect of the worship of God, as in that state and condition wherein they were before their calling, through a participation of the reconciliation made by the blood of Christ. The apostle had declared, verses 11, 12, they were the uncircumcision, aliens, foreigners; that is, men who had no share in, nor admittance unto, the solemn worship of God, which was empaled in the commonwealth of Israel. "But now," says he, "ye are so no more;"

that is, you have a portion and interest in that worship wherewith God is well pleased.

Secondly, Positively, the apostle affirms two things of them:—first, That they are "fellow-citizens with the saints, and of the household of God," verse 19; secondly, That they were built up to be "an holy temple," or "an habitation to God," verses 20–22. Both which relate to the solemn worship of God under the gospel. The first asserts them to be now members of the church;—the latter, that by and among them God was worshipped with that divine service which came in the room of that which was appointed in the temple, now by Christ removed and taken away.

This being the design of the Holy Ghost in this place, I shall present it in this one proposition unto you:—

That *it is an eminent effect and fruit of our reconciliation unto God and among ourselves, by the blood of Christ, that believers enjoy the privileges of the excellent, glorious, spiritual worship of God in Christ, revealed and required in the gospel.*

I shall, in the prosecution of this subject,—I. Briefly prove that we obtain this privilege as a fruit, and upon the account of the reconciliation made by the blood of Christ. II. Show that the worship of the gospel is indeed so beautiful, glorious, and excellent, that the enjoyment of it is an eminent privilege: which I shall principally manifest from the text; and, in so doing, open the several parts of it.

I. That believers enjoy this privilege as a fruit and effect of the death and blood of Jesus Christ, I shall confirm only with one or two places of Scripture, Heb. ix. 8, compared with chap. x. 19–22. Whilst the first tabernacle was standing, before Christ by his death had removed it, and the worship that accompanied it,—which was the partition-wall mentioned that he brake down,—there was no immediate admission unto God;—the way into the holiest not made with hands, which we now make use of in the gospel worship, was not yet laid open, but the worshippers were kept at a great distance, making their application unto God by outward, carnal ordinances. The tabernacle being removed, now a way is made, and an entrance is given to the worshippers, into the holiest, in their worship. How is that obtained? by what means? Chap. x. 19–22, It is "by the blood of Jesus Christ,"—by the rending of his flesh. This privilege of entering into the holiest, which is a true expressing of all gospel worship, could no otherwise be obtained for nor granted unto believers, but by the blood of Christ. We "enter into the holiest by the blood of Jesus," by which he prepared, perfected, or "consecrated for us a new and living way" into it. Peter also gives us the same account of the rise of this privilege, 1 Epist. ii. 4, 5. That which is ascribed unto believers is, that they offer up "spiritual sacrifices, acceptable unto God by Jesus Christ." That is the worship whereof we speak. To fit them for, and enable them hereunto, they are "made a spiritual house, a holy priesthood;"—they are both the temple wherein God dwells by his Spirit, and they are the priests that offer acceptable sacrifices unto him. By what means, then, do they attain this honour? By their "coming unto Christ," and that as he was "disallowed of men, and chosen of God." Herein the apostle includes the whole mystery of his death and blood-shedding, wherein he was most openly rejected of men, and most eminently owned of God in his accomplishment of the work of reconciliation.

I shall not farther confirm the first part of the proposition, but proceed to evidence,—

II. That the worship of God under the gospel is so excellent, beautiful, and glorious, that it may well be esteemed a privilege, purchased by the blood of Christ, which no man can truly and really be made partaker of but by virtue of an interest in the reconciliation by him wrought. For "through him we have an access by one Spirit unto God."

This, as I said, I shall evince two ways:—FIRST, *Absolutely*. SECONDLY, *Comparatively*, in reference unto any other way of worship whatever.

And the FIRST I shall do from the text.

It is a principle deeply fixed in the minds of men, yea, ingrafted into them by nature, that the worship of God ought to be orderly, comely, beautiful, and glorious. Hence men in all ages, who have thought it incumbent on them to imagine, find out, and frame the worship of God, or any thing thereunto belonging, have made it constantly their design to fix on things, either in themselves or in the manner of their performance (to their judgment), beautiful, orderly, comely, and glorious. And, indeed, that worship may be well suspected not to be according to the mind of God, which comes short in these properties of order and beauty, comeliness and glory. I shall add unto this only this reasonable assertion, which no man can well deny,—viz., that what is so in his worship and service, God himself is the most proper judge. If, then, we evince not that spiritual gospel worship, in its own naked simplicity, without any other external adventitious helper or countenance, is most orderly, comely, beautiful, and glorious (the Holy Ghost in the Scripture being judge), we shall be content to seek for these things where else, as it is pretended, they may be found. To this end,—

1. The first thing in general observable from these words is, that in the spiritual worship of the gospel the whole blessed Trinity, and each person therein distinctly, do in that economy and dispensation wherein they act severally and peculiarly in the work of our redemp-

tion, afford distinct communion with themselves unto the souls of the worshippers. So are they all here distinctly mentioned: "Through him" (that is, Jesus Christ, the Son of God) "we have access by one Spirit" (that good and holy Spirit the Holy Ghost) unto God, that is the Father;" for so is that name to be taken ὑποστατικῶς, "personally," when it is mentioned in distinction from the Son and Spirit. There is no act, part, or duty of gospel worship, wherein the worshippers have not this distinct communion with each person in the blessed Trinity. The particulars shall be afterward spoken unto.

This is the general order of gospel worship, the great rubric of our service. Here in general lieth its decency, that it respects the mediation of the Son, through whom we have access, and the supplies and assistance of the Spirit, and a regard unto God as a Father. He that fails in any one of these, he breaks all order in gospel worship. If either we come not unto it by Jesus Christ, or perform it not in the strength of the Holy Ghost, or in it go not unto God as a Father, we transgress all the rules of this worship. This is the great canon, which if it be neglected, there is no decency in whatever else is done in this way. And this, in general, is the glory of it. Worship is certainly an act of the soul, Matt. xxii. 37. The body hath its share by concomitancy and subserviency to the direction of the mind. The acts of the mind and soul receive their advancements and glory from the object about which they are conversant. Now that, in this gospel worship, is God himself in his Son and Holy Ghost, and none else. Acting faith on Christ for admission; and on the Holy Ghost for his assistance (so going on in his strength); and on God, even the Father, for acceptance,—is the work of the soul in this worship. That it hath any thing more glorious to be conversant about, I am as yet to learn. But these things will be handled apart afterward. This, in general, is the order and glory of that worship of which we speak.

2. The same is evident from the general nature of it,—that it is an access unto God. "Through him we have an access to God." There are two things herein that set forth the excellency, order, and glory of it:—(1.) It brings an access; (2.) The manner of that access, intimated in the word here used; it is προσαγωγή.

(1.) It is an access, an approach, a drawing nigh unto God; so the apostle calls it a "drawing near," Heb. x. 22, "Let us draw near with a true heart;" that is, unto God, in "the holiest," verse 19. In the first giving out of the law, and instituting the legal worship, the people were commanded to keep at a distance; and they were not, on pain of death, so much as to touch the mount where the presence of God was, Exod. xix. 12. And, accordingly, they stood afar off, whilst Moses drew near to the thick darkness where God was, chap. xx. 21. So, not only when the high priest went into the most holy place once a-year with blood (of which afterward), but when the priests in their courses went into the holy place to burn incense daily, the people were kept without, as Luke i. 10. But this gospel worship is our access or drawing nigh to God; no interposition of vails, or any other carnal ordinance whatever. All is made open, and a new and living way of access given unto us, Heb. x. 20. And what, in general, can be added to set forth the glory of this worship, to a soul that knows what it is to draw nigh to God, I know not. The heathens of old derided the Egyptians, who, through many stately edifices, and with most pompous ceremonies, brought their worshippers to the image of an ape. I say no more; but let them look to it, how they will acquit themselves who frame much of their worship in a ceremonious access to an altar or an image. The plea of referring unto God at the last hath been common to all idolaters, of what sort soever, from the foundation of the world.

(2.) It is a προσαγωγή that we have in this worship;—a manuduction unto God, in order, and with much glory. It is such an access as men have to the presence of a king, when they are handed in by some favourite or great person. This, in this worship, is done by Christ. He takes the worshippers by the hand, and leads them into the presence of God; there presenting them (as we shall see), saying, "Behold I and the children which God hath given me," Heb. ii. 13. This is the access of believers; thus do they enter into the presence of God. Some, it may be, will be ready to say, that a man may be ashamed to speak such great things as these of poor worms, who have neither order in their way, nor eloquence in their words, nor comeliness in their worship. Let such men know that they must yet hear greater things of them: and it is meet, indeed, they should be in all things conformable unto Christ; and, therefore, have neither form, nor comeliness, nor beauty in themselves, their way, or their worship, to the eyes of the world, as Isa. liii. 2. And "the world knows not them" and their ways, because "it knew not him" nor his ways, 1 John iii. 1. But if God may be allowed to judge in his own matters, the spiritual worship of the saints is glorious, since in it they have such an access, such a manuduction unto God.

3. From the immediate object of this worship; and that is God. We have an access to God. It is, as I said, the Father who is here peculiarly intended. God, as God,—he who is the beginning and end of all, whose nature is attended with infinite perfection,—he from whom a sovereignty over all doth proceed,—is the formal object of all divine and religious worship. Hence, divine worship respects, as its object, each person of the blessed Trinity equally, not as this or that person, but as this or that person is God; that is the formal reason of all divine worship. But yet, as the second person is con-

sidered as vested with his office of mediation, and the Holy Ghost as the comforter and sanctifier of his saints; so God the Father is in a peculiar manner the object of our faith, and love, and worship. So Peter tells us, 1 Epist. i. 21, that through Christ we "believe in God, that raised him up from the dead, and gave him glory." Christ being considered as mediator, God that raised him from the dead—that is, the Father—is regarded as the ultimate object of our worship; though worshipping him who is the Father as God, the other persons are in the same nature worshipped. This whole matter is declared, Gal. iv. 6 (which I cannot now particularly open), with this explanation, that in our access unto God, Christ being considered as the mediator, and the Holy Ghost as our comforter, advocate, and assister, the saints have a peculiar respect unto the person of the Father.

There are two things that hence arise, evidencing the order, decency, and glory of gospel worship:—(1.) That we have in it a direct and immediate access unto God; (2.) That we have access unto God as the Father of our Lord Jesus Christ, and ours in him.

(1.) This is no small part of the glory of this worship, that our access is unto *God himself*. When outward worship was in its height and glory, the access of the worshippers immediately was but unto some visible sign and pledge of God's presence. Such was the temple itself; such was the ark and the mercy-seat. So Paul, describing the tabernacle and temple worshippers, Heb. x. 1, calls them προσερχομένους, "the comers unto sacrifices." There was, as it were, a stop put upon their access, in the visible representations of God's majesty and presence to which they did approach. But now, in this spiritual worship of the gospel, the saints have direct and immediate access unto God, "the way into the holiest," not made with hands, being laid open unto them all. And where they are enjoined the use of any outward signs, as in the sacraments, it is not, as it were, to stop them there from entering into heaven, but to help them forward in their entrance; as all know who are acquainted with their true nature and use. I do not say that any of the worship of old was limited in the sensible pledge and tokens of God's presence; but only that the spirit of the worshippers was kept in subjection, so as to approach unto God only as he exhibited himself to their faith in those signs, and not immediately, as we do under the gospel.

(2.) We have in this spiritual worship of the gospel access unto God *as a Father*. I showed, in the opening of the words, that God is distinctly proposed here as the Father of our Lord Jesus Christ, and in him our God and Father. Hence are we said to come "to the throne of grace," Heb. iv. 16; that is, unto God as he is gloriously exalted in the dispensation of grace, in kindness, love, mercy, —in a word, as a Father. God on the throne of grace, and God as a

Father, is all one consideration; for, as a Father, he is all love, grace, and mercy to his children in Christ. When God came of old to institute his worship in giving of the law, he did it with the dreadful and terrible representation of his majesty, that the people chose not to come near, but went and "stood afar off, and said unto Moses, Speak thou with us, and we will hear: but let not God speak with us, lest we die," Exod. xx. 18, 19. And by this dreadful representation of the majesty of God, as the object of that worship, were they kept in fear and bondage all their days. But now are the saints encouraged to make their approach unto God as a Father; the glory whereof the apostle excellently expresseth, Rom. viii. 14, 15. That fear and bondage wherein men were kept under the law is now removed, and in the place thereof a spirit of children, with reverent boldness going to their father, is given unto us. This, I say, adds to the glory, beauty, and excellency of gospel worship. There is not the meanest believer but, with his most broken prayers and supplications, hath an immediate access unto God, and that as a Father; nor the most despised church of saints on the earth but it comes with its worship into the glorious presence of God himself. And this I shall add, by the way,—that men's attempting to worship God who are not interested in this privilege of access unto him, is the ground of all the superstitious idolatry that is in the world. I shall instance in two things, which are the springs of all others:—

[1.] Having not experience of the excellency of this privilege, nor being satisfied with the use of it, men have turned aside to the worship of saints and angels in heaven. This is the very substance of all the reasons that the Papists plead in the justification of that superstition: "To have access to God! It is too great a boldness to come to him immediately; and so it becomes us humbly to make use of the favourites of the court of heaven, of saints and angels, to desire them to entreat with God for us." Now, not to speak of their unacquaintedness with the mediation of Christ herein, which is plain infidelity, what is this but directly saying, "We understand nothing of gospel worship (wherein believers by Christ have a direct 'access with boldness' to God himself); and therefore it is that we had rather fix on this 'voluntary humility,' as the apostle calls it, Col. ii. 18, than venture on this access unto God"? This, I say, is the reasoning of men unacquainted with this part of the glory of gospel worship.

[2.] Hence are they forced to invent outward, visible pledges and signs of God's presence, as they imagine, to which they may have access; seeing they are unacquainted with that which is directly unto God himself. Hence images and pictures, altars and the *east*, must be regarded in worship; with which they can have an immediate conversation,—have an access in their thoughts to them, and, as they think, by them unto God. And on the same account must the sacraments be changed, and that which was appointed to assist us in our entrance unto God be made a god, that men may have an easy access unto him. Carnal men, that know nothing of the other, whose souls are not at all moulded or affected by any pure act of faith, are here stirred by their senses, and act by them in their worship. And this is the ground wherein all their pompous rites, invented by men in the worship of God, do grow;—even a design and engine to afford carnally-minded men somewhat to be conversant about in their worship, who have no principle to enable them to use this privilege of approaching unto God himself. It is true, they will say it is God alone whom they worship, and whom they intend to draw nigh unto; but I must needs say, that if they knew what it were to do so immediately by Christ, they would be satisfied therewith, and not seek such outward helps in their way as they do.

4. It appears from the principal procuring cause and means of this our access to God; which is Jesus Christ,—through him we have this access. This is a new spring of beauty and glory, which we must consider in the particulars of it. That access which the people of God had to the outward pledge of his presence, was by their high priest; and that not in his own person, but barely in his representation of them; and that but once a year: but in the worship of the gospel, the saints have an access through Christ unto God himself in their own persons, and that continually. Now, we have this access through Christ upon many accounts:—

(1.) Because he hath purchased and procured this favour for us, that we should so approach unto God, and find acceptance with him. We are "accepted in the Beloved," Eph. i. 6. I must not stay to show how, by paying a ransom for us, and "bearing our iniquities," he hath answered the law, removed the curse, reconciled us to God, pacified his anger, satisfied justice, procured for us eternal redemption; all which belongs to his procuring for us this favour of acceptance with God. The apostle gives us the sum of it, Heb. ii. 17, He hath, as a high priest, "made reconciliation for the sins of the people;" on the account whereof they have an "access by faith into this grace," Rom. v. 1, 2. In this sense have we our access unto God through Christ. He hath purchased it for us. It is no small portion of the price of his blood. Nothing else could procure it;—not all the wealth of the world, not all the worth of angels in heaven: none could do it but himself. Go into the most pompous, stately place of outward worship upon the earth,—consider all the wealth and glory of its structure and ornaments; it is an easy thing for a wise man to guess what it all cost, and what is the charge of it. However, none so foolish, but can tell you it is all the price of money; it was bought with "silver and gold," and "corruptible things;" it is the "thick clay:" and he that hath most money may render that kind of worship most beauteous and glorious. But now the gospel worship of believers is the price of the "blood of the Son of God." Access to God for sinners could no other way be obtained. Let men, as the prophet speaks, "lavish gold out of their bags" (Isa. xlvi. 6) upon their idols; their self-invented worship shall come as short, in true glory and beauty, of the meanest prayers of poor saints, as the purchase of corruptible things doth of the fruit of the blood and death of the Son of God, 1 Pet. i. 18, 19.

(2.) We have this access from Christ, inasmuch as he hath opened, prepared, and dedicated a way for us to enter into the presence of God. Favour being procured, a way of entrance is also to be provided; otherwise poor souls might say, "There is water, indeed, in the well; but the well is deep, and we have not wherewith to draw. There is an acceptance purchased for us in the presence of God; but by what way shall we come unto him?" I say, he hath provided for us also a way whereby we may enter, Heb. x. 19, 20,—"By a new and living way." The way into the holiest, of old, was through the vail that hung always before; which the apostle calls "the second vail," chap. ix. 3. The form and use thereof you have, Exod. xxvi. 31, 32, etc. Through this vail the high priest entered into the holy place. Instead hereof, for an entrance into the presence of God in the holy place not made with hands, Christ hath provided and dedicated a "new and living way" for us. This way is himself; as he telleth Thomas, John xiv. 6, "I am the way." It is by him alone that any can obtain an access unto God. But as to our constant approach in worship, there is a peculiar respect had unto his suffering for us in the flesh. We enter "by his blood," and "through his flesh." How is that? As men being to go to some great potentate or general in an army have, it may be, some word or token which they show, declare, or make use of, if by any they are hindered in their address,—so it is with believers. The law would stop them in their access to God; so would sin and Satan: but their being "sprinkled with the blood of Christ" is the token that lays all open unto them, and removes all obstacles out of the way;—and when they come into the presence of God, it is the suffering of Christ in the flesh that they insist on as to their acceptation with him. They go to God through him, in his name, "making mention of his righteousness," death, and bloodshedding, pleading for acceptance on his account. This is their "new and living way" of going unto God;—this path they tread, this entrance they use; and no man can obtain an access unto God but by an interest herein. I wonder not at all that men who know not this way—who have no share, nor ever took one step in it—do fix on any kind of worship whatever, rather than once make trial what it is to place the glory of their worship in an access unto God, seeing they have no interest in this way, without which all attempts after it would be altogether fruitless and vain. Now, this adds to the order, and increaseth the glory and beauty, of the spiritual worship of the gospel. Go to the mass-book and the rubric of it;—you will see how many instructions and directions they give priests about the way of going into their sanctum and to their altars;—how they must bow and bend themselves, sometimes one way sometimes another; sometimes kneel, sometimes stand; sometimes go backwards, sometimes forward. This is their way to the breaden god; this they call order, and beauty, and glory; and with such like things are poor, simple sots deluded, and carnal wretches, enemies to Christ and his Spirit, blinded to their eternal ruin. Surely, methinks, this way of gospel access to God is far more comely and glorious:—it is in and by Christ,—a way dedicated by himself on purpose; it is sprinkled with his blood; it is opened by his suffering in the flesh, and abides "new and living" for ever. Were not blindness come on men to the utmost,—were it not evident that they can see nothing afar off,—that they are wholly carnal and unspiritual, "savouring not the things of God,"—it were impossible that they should reject these pearls of the gospel for the husks of swine, such things as they shall never be able to vie with the old heathen in. This only may be said in their excuse, that they cast away and reject what they had no share in, for that which is most properly their own.

(3.) We have this access through Christ, in that he is entered before us into the presence of God, to make way for our access unto him, and our acceptance with him. So the apostle, Heb. iv. 14, "We have a great high priest, that is passed into the heavens, Jesus the Son of God." He is gone already into the presence of God to that purpose. The same apostle tells us, chap. vi. 19, 20, "Let us look to 'that within the vail, whither Jesus the forerunner is for us entered,'"—πρόδρομος ὑπὲρ ἡμῶν εἰσῆλθεν. The words are better rendered, "The forerunner for us is entered." He is a forerunner for us,—one that is gone into the presence of God to declare that all his saints are coming to him, coming into his presence with their solemn worship and oblations;—he is entered into heaven himself, to carry, as it were, tidings, and make way for the entrance of his saints. This is no small encouragement to follow him: he is gone before for us, and is in continual expectation of the coming of them whose forerunner he is; as is the manner of those who take that office. And this also adds to the glory of gospel worship, with them to whom Christ is precious and honourable: with them by whom he is despised, it is no wonder if his ways be so also. This belongs also to the rubric, and adds to the order of gospel worship. It is an access to God, even the Father, in the holy place not made with hands, on the account of the atonement made, and favour and acceptance purchased, by Jesus Christ, being sprinkled with his blood, and following him, as one that is gone before to provide admittance for us. Here is order and beauty too, if we have either faith or eyes to apprehend or perceive what is so.

(4.) We have this access through Christ, as he is "the high priest over the house of God." This the apostle at large declares, and much insists upon, in the Epistle to the Hebrews. One or two places shall suffice to instance in. Chap. iv. 14–16: The inference which the apostle makes from this consideration, that Christ is our high priest entered into heaven, is, that we should draw nigh unto the throne of grace; and, because he is such a holy priest as he there describes, that we should draw nigh with boldness, or spiritual confidence of our acceptance with God. And this the apostle manageth at large throughout that epistle;—that notwithstanding all the outward glory and splendour of the legal worship, yet that which is appointed in the gospel is far to be preferred before it, inasmuch as the High Priest of this is unspeakably above the high priest by whom that was principally administered. And again, chap. x. 21, 22, the encouragement to draw nigh to God is taken from this, that we have a "high priest over the house of God." And it is also considerable, what the Holy Ghost requireth in them who should come nigh to worship God under the guidance and conduct of this blessed and merciful high priest. Is it that they have such vestments and ornaments in their admission? No; but faith, and sanctification, and holiness, are the three great qualifications of these worshippers. "Let us draw nigh," saith he, "in full assurance of faith," etc., "and our bodies washed with pure water;"—that is, purified with the blood of Christ, typified in the water of baptism; or else, it may be, effectually cleansed in soul and body by the Holy Ghost, who is frequently compared to water in the work of purifying and sanctifying the souls of believers.

Upon this general head I might make a long stand, to evidence the beauty, order, and glory of the spiritual worship of God, in that it is our access to God through Christ, "as the great high priest over the house of God." This, indeed, is so great, that the apostle makes it the sum of his whole dispute about the excellency of the gospel, and our coming to God thereby, Heb. viii. 1, 2. "This is," saith he, "upon the matter, the sum of all: Those with whom we have to do, they had a high priest, in whom, and the administration by him performed, consisted the glory of all their worship. We also," saith he, "have a high priest no less than they had; but herein there is no comparison between them and us, that we have such a high priest,"—whom he describes;—first, from his own dignity, honour, and glory; he is "set on the right hand of the Majesty of heaven;"—secondly, from his office or ministry,—namely, that he ministers not in a tabernacle, such as was that of Moses, and Solomon's temple, but in heaven itself, the place of the glorious presence and immediate manifestation of God's glory;—which he calls "the tabernacle which the Lord pitched;" that is, which he appointed for the place of worship to his saints under the ministry of Christ, their high priest. And though other places are necessary here on earth for their assemblies, as they are men clothed with flesh and infirmities, yet there is none pitched, appointed, or consecrated for the holy and solemn acceptance of their service, but heaven itself; where the High Priest is always ready to administer it before God. And as to the assemblies here below, all places are now alike. And what can be more glorious than this,—namely, that the whole spiritual worship of the gospel, performed here on earth by the saints, is administered in heaven by such a holy Priest, who is at the right hand of the throne of the majesty of God! and yet under his conduct we have by faith an entrance into the presence of God.

Go to, now, you by whom the spiritual worship of the gospel is despised; [you] that—unless it be adorned, as you say (or rather defiled), with the rites and ceremonies of your own invention—think there is no order, comeliness, or beauty in it! set yourselves to find out whatever pleaseth your imaginations; borrow this of the Jews, that of the Pagans, all of the Papists that you think conducing to that end and purpose; lavish gold out of the bag for the beautifying of it;—will it compare with this glory of the worship of the gospel, that is all carried on under the conduct and administration of this glorious High Priest? It may be they will say that they have that too, and that ornaments do not hinder but that they have also their worship attended with that glory relating to the holy Priest. But do they think so indeed? and do they no more value it than it seems they do? Why are they not contented with it, but they must find out many inventions of their own to help to set it off? Surely it is impossible that men, thoroughly convinced of its spiritual excellency, should fall into that fond conceit of making additions of their own unto it. Nor do they seem rightly to weigh that the holy God doth, all along, oppose this spiritual excellency of gospel worship to the outward splendour of rites and ordinances, instituted by himself for a time; so that what men seek to make up in these things doth but absolutely derogate from the other; and all will one day know, whether it be for want of excellency in the spiritual administration of the gospel worship, under and by the glorious High Priest, or for want of minds enlightened to discern it, and hearts quickened to experience it, that some do lay all the weight of the beauty of gospel worship on matters that they either find out themselves, or borrow from others who were confessedly blind as to all spiritual communion with God in Christ. But if any man list to contend, "we have no such custom, neither the church of God;" only I hope it will not be accounted a crime, that any please themselves and are contented with that glory and beauty, in their worshipping of God, which is given unto it from hence, that they have in it an access to God by Jesus Christ, as the great high priest of their profession and service. However, I am sure this is, and may well be, an unspeakable encouragement and comfort in the duty of drawing nigh unto God, to all the saints, whether in their persons, families, or assemblies,—that Jesus Christ is the great high priest that admits them to the presence of God; who is the minister of that heavenly tabernacle where God is worshipped by them. If we are but able, as the apostle speaks, to look to the things that are not seen, 2 Cor. iv. 18,—that is, with eyes of faith,—we shall find that glory that will give us rest and satisfaction; and for others, we may pray, as Elisha for his servant, that the Lord would open their eyes, and they would quickly see the naked, poor places of the saints' assemblies not only attended with horses and chariots of fire, but also Christ walking in the midst of them, in the glory wherewith he is described, Rev. i. 13–16; which surely their painted or carved images will be found to come short of. And if the Lord Jesus Christ be pleased, in his unspeakable love, to call his churches and ministers his "glory," as he doth, 2 Cor. viii. 23, surely these may be contented to make him their only glory. To which purpose we may observe,—

[1.] Our Saviour Christ warns us of some who thought to be heard for their heathenish "vain repetitions" and "much babbling," Matt. vi. 7. I will not make application of it unto any; but this I say, that men will not be a little mistaken, if they think to be heard for any carnal self-invented furtherance of their devotion. But here lies the joy and confidence of the poor saints,—they have a merciful High Priest over the house of God, by whom they are encouraged to draw nigh with boldness to the throne of grace. He takes them by the hand, and leads them into the presence of God; where, through his means, they obtain a favourable acceptance.

[2.] Nor need they be solicitous about their outward estate and condition. This was the misery of the Jews of old,—that when they were driven from Jerusalem, and carried into captivity, they were deprived of all the solemn worship of God; they had no high priest, no sacrifice, no altar, tabernacle, or solemn assemblies,—which were all tied to that place. Hence we find how bitterly David complains, when, by the persecution of Saul, he was for a season driven from the place of God's holy and solemn worship: he saw not the glorious ornaments of the high priest, nor the beautiful structure of the tabernacle, nor the order of the Levites and priests in worship. It is now otherwise with the people of God, be they never so poor, and destitute of all outward accommodations. Are their assemblies in the mountains, in the caves and dens of the earth?—Christ, according to his promise, is in the midst of them as their high priest, and they have in their worship all the order, glory, and beauty (I mean, observing gospel rules) that in any place under heaven they can enjoy and be made partakers of. All depends on the presence of Christ, and their access to God by him; and he is excluded from no place, but thinks any place adorned sufficiently for him which his saints are met in or driven unto. Let the hands that hang down be lifted up, and feeble knees be strengthened;—whatever their outward, distressed condition may be, here is order, beauty, and glory, in the worship of God, above all that the world can pretend unto!

[3.] Here lies encouragement to them upon a spiritual account, as to the state of things between God and their own souls. They have discoveries made unto them of the glory, majesty, and holiness of God. They know that he is "a consuming fire;"—they have visions of his excellencies, which the world is not acquainted with. They are also sensible of their own poverty, wretchedness, sin, weakness, —how unfit, how unable to approach unto him, or to have to do with him in his holy worship;—they are ashamed of their own prayers and supplications, and could oftentimes, when they are gone through, wish them undone again, considering how unanswerable they are to the greatness and holiness of God. In this condition there is a plentiful relief tendered to faith from the consideration of this High Priest. That this may be more evident, and that the beauty and glory of gospel worship may be by them farther discovered, I shall particularly insist on some parts of it:—

First. Our High Priest bears and takes away all the sinfulness and failings that are in or do accompany the holy worship of his saints. The world is apt to despise the worship of the saints, as mean and contemptible,—unmeet for the majesty of God. This puts them on the inventing of what they suppose more glorious and beautiful, though God abhors it. But the saints themselves know that of their defects, wants, and failings in their worship, that the world know not of, and how unfit it is and unsuited to the holy majesty of God, with whom they have to do. They know how the bitter root of unbelief in their hearts springs up and defiles them and their duties;—how effectually vanity works in their minds, and a secret loathness in their wills, in their best duties and most solemn acts of worship; besides innumerable other sinful distempers, that oftentimes get ground and place in their hearts. These, they know, are the things that, in and of themselves, are enough to defile, pollute, and render abominable all their worship; yea, and if God should "mark what is amiss," the guilt of their holy worship is enough to make both it and them that perform it to be for ever rejected. But now, here is their relief; here beauty, glory, and order, is recovered to their worship;—Christ, as their high priest, takes away all the evil, filth, and iniquity of their holy things, that they may be presented pure, and holy, and glorious before God. So did Aaron typically of old, Exod. xxviii. 38. Thus doth Christ, our high priest, really answer for all that is amiss. All failings, all miscarriages in his saints, them he takes on his own score; and what is from his Spirit, that enters into the presence of the holy God. So, Eph. v. 25–27, he presents it to himself, and by him it is presented unto God. By this means doth the Lord Christ preserve the glory and beauty of gospel worship, notwithstanding all the defects, and failings, and defilements, that, from the weakness and sins of his saints, do seem to cleave unto it.

Secondly. This is not enough. Besides the weakness, sinfulness, and imperfections that attend their duties, for which they may be justly rejected, there is not any thing of worth in them for which they may be accepted;—nothing that should yield a sweet savour unto God. Wherefore Christ, as the high priest by whom all believers have their access unto God, takes their duties and prayers, and adds incense unto them, that they may have a sweet savour in heaven, Rev. viii. 3. The altar is the place for the priests offering their sacrifices of prayers; and our altar is in heaven: other men may appoint theirs elsewhere. The Lord Christ, the high priest in the temple of God in heaven, and in the holy place not made with hands, is the angel that stands at the altar before the Lord,—the golden altar of incense before the throne;—not the altar for sacrifice, which he hath finished already, but only the altar of incense or intercession, remains. On this golden altar are the prayers of all saints offered. But how came they to be acceptable unto the Lord? Why, this high priest hath much incense, a bottomless store and treasure of righteousness that he adds unto them; which is the only sweet perfume in the presence of the Lord. This makes all their worship glorious indeed. Christ, the high priest, takes away the iniquity and failings of them, he adds his own righteousness unto it; and so in his own person offers it on the golden altar (that is, his own self) before the throne of God continually.

Now, as this tends exceedingly to the consolation of believers, so it stains the glory of all the outward pompous worship that some are so delighted in. For believers, what can more tend to their comfort and encouragement, than that the Lord Christ takes their poor weak prayers, which themselves are oftentimes ashamed of and humbled for, and are ready to cry out against themselves by reason of them; and what by taking away the evil of them, what by adding the incense of his own righteousness, makes them acceptable at the throne of grace! They little know what beauty and glory those very duties which they perform and are troubled at are clothed withal: and for the beauty and glory of gospel worship, in comparison of all the self-invented rites of men, how will one thought of faith about this administration of Christ in heaven with the prayers of the saints, cast contempt and shame upon them! What is all their gaudy preparation, in comparison of the high priest of the saints offering up their prayers on the golden altar before the throne of God! This is order, comeliness, and beauty.

Thirdly. Christ, as the high priest of the saints, presents both their persons and their duties in the presence of and before the Lord. This is that which was signified of old in the high priest's precious stones set in gold on his breast and shoulders, with the names of the children of Israel in them, Exod. xxviii. 21. Christ, our high priest, is entered into the holy place for us, and there presents all his saints and their worship before the Lord, being " not ashamed to call them brethren," and saying of them, " Behold I and the children which the Lord hath given me."

And this is the fourth thing in the words, manifesting the excellency and glory of gospel worship, taken from the principal procuring cause:—It is an access to God, *through Christ.*

SERMON IV

5. THIS also adds greatly to the glory and excellency of evangelical worship, that we have in it an access unto God, " in one Spirit," or " by one Spirit."

I shall show in brief,—(1.) How we have it " by the Spirit;" (2.) How " in one," or " by one Spirit."

(1.) That by the Spirit the Holy Ghost is here intended, is not questioned by any. He is that " one Spirit" who works in these things, and " divideth to every one as he pleaseth," 1 Cor. xii. 11. I shall not here handle the whole work of the Holy Ghost in and upon the souls of the saints, in and for the performance of all the duties of worship wherein they draw nigh unto God by Christ and obtain communion with him, as absolutely considered; but only so far as his work renders the worship we speak of beautiful and comely; which is the matter we have in hand. And that I shall do in some few considerations:—

[1.] The Lord Jesus Christ hath promised to send his Spirit to believers, to enable them, both for matter and manner, in the performance of every duty required in the word, Isa. lix. 21. He will give his word and Spirit. The promise of the one and the other is of equal extent and latitude. Whatever God proposeth in his word to be believed, or requireth to be done,—that he gives his Spirit to enable to believe and do accordingly. There is neither promise nor precept, but the Spirit is given to enable believers to answer the mind of God in them; nor is the Spirit given to enable unto any duty, but what is in the word required. The Spirit and the word, in their several places, have an equal latitude; the one as a *moral rule*, the other as a *real principle of efficiency*. Hence they who require duties which the word enjoins not, have need of other assistances than what the Spirit of grace will afford them; and those who pretend to be led by the Spirit beyond the bounds of the word, had need provide themselves of another gospel. Now, with promises hereof doth the gospel abound. He shall " lead us into all truth;"—he shall " teach us all things;"—he shall " abide with us for ever." Having given his disciples precepts for their whole duty to God and himself, he promiseth them his Spirit to abide with them, to enable them for the accomplishment of them.

[2.] There are *three* things that are needful for the right performance of gospel worship:—1*st*. *Light* and *knowledge*, that we may be acquainted with the mind and will of God in it,—what it is that he accepteth and approveth, and is appointed by him; that we may know "how to choose the good and refuse the evil,"—like the sheep of Christ, hearing his voice and following him, not hearkening to the voice of a stranger. 2*dly*. *Grace* in the heart, so that there may be, in this access unto God, a true, real, spiritual, saving communion, obtained with him in those acts of faith, love, delight, and obedience, which he requireth; without which it is in any thing " impossible to please God." 3*dly*. *Ability* for the performance of the duties that God requireth in his worship, in such a manner as he may be glorified, and those who are called to his worship edified in their most holy faith. Where these three concur, there the worship of God is performed in a due manner, according to his own mind and will; and so, consequently, is excellent, beautiful, and glorious,—God himself being judge. Now, all these do believers receive by and from the Spirit of Christ; and, consequently, have by him their access to the Father; that is, are enabled unto, and carried on in, the worship which God requireth at their hands.

1*st*. It is he who enables them to discover the mind of God, and his will concerning his worship, that they may embrace what he hath appointed, and refuse the thing whereof he will say at the last day, "Who hath required this at your hand?" He is promised to "lead them into all truth," as the Spirit of truth, John xvi. 13; and is the blessed "unction" that teacheth them all things, 1 John ii. 27,—all things for the glory of God, and their own consolation. It is he that speaks the word, which sounds in the ears, "This is the way; walk in it." And when Paul prays for the guidance of the saints, he doth it by praying that God would give them the "Spirit of wisdom and revelation" in Christ, Eph. i. 17. Now, this he doth two ways:—

(1*st.*) By causing them diligently to attend unto the word, the voice of Christ, for their direction, and to that only. This is the great work of the Spirit. So John xvi. 13, it is said, "He shall not speak of himself; but whatsoever he shall hear, that shall he speak;"—that is, he shall reveal and declare nothing but what is the mind of Christ manifested in the word; and that he shall call men to attend unto. "To the law and to the testimony" (to the word),—that is his constant voice. If men turn to any other teaching, they go out of the compass of his commission,—that direction which the Father began from heaven, "This is my beloved Son; hear him." He is the only master and teacher that the Spirit carries all believers unto. He still cries, "Hear him; attend unto him speaking in the word." It is true, in point of practice, according to the rule for the remedying of scandals and disorders, we are commanded to "hear the church," or obey the wholesome directions of it, and to walk according to the gospel; but as to the worship of God, both as to the matter and rules in the appointment of it, we are called continually by the Spirit to hear Christ always;—and that spirit is not of Christ which sends us to any else.

(2*dly.*) By revealing the mind of Christ unto us in the word. This is his work, which he undertakes and performs. I confess that, notwithstanding the assistance that he is ready to give unto them, there are many mistakes, even amongst the saints themselves, in their apprehensions in and about the worship of God. They are many times careless in attending to his directions; negligent in praying for his assistance; slight and overly in the use of the means by him appointed for the discovery of truths; regardless of dispossessing their minds of prejudices and temptations, hindering them in the discovery of the mind of God. It is, therefore, no wonder they are left to be corrected under their own mistakes and miscarriages. But this hinders not but that the Spirit may be said to give the knowledge of the worship of God in the word unto believers; and that because it is not, nor can be, profitably and savingly attained any other way. As "no man can say that Jesus is the Lord, but by the Spirit,"—so no man can know the way of God's house and worship but by the Spirit;—and we see by experience, that those that despise his assistance, rather trust to themselves and other men for the worship of God than to the word. This he does, ordinarily, in the use of means,—at least so far, that though in some particulars there may be amongst them mistakes, yet not usually such but that their performances are accepted of God in Christ. And in those things wherein they are at any time "otherwise minded" than according to truth, if they continue waiting, that also shall be revealed unto them from the word by the Spirit. The worship of God is not of man's finding out, but of his designation who is "the wisdom of God." It is not taught by human wisdom, nor is it attainable by human industry; but by the wisdom and revelation of the Spirit of God. It is every way divine and heavenly in its rise, in its discovery; and so becoming the greatness and holiness of God. For what doth please God, God himself is the sole judge. If any thing else set up itself in competition with it, for beauty and glory, it will be found to be engaged in a very unequal contest at the last day.

2dly. Believers have this access by the Spirit, inasmuch as he enables them to approach unto God in a spiritual manner, *with grace in their hearts,* as he is the Spirit of grace and supplication. This is one special end for which the Spirit is promised unto believers,—namely, that he may be in them "a Spirit of grace and supplication," enabling them to draw nigh unto God in a gracious and acceptable manner, Zech. xii. 10, 11. And this is one part of the work that he doth perform, when he is bestowed on them according to the promise. Rom. viii. 26, 27: Let men do their best and utmost, they know not so much as what they ought to pray for; but the Spirit of Christ alone enables them to the whole work. If all the men in the world should lay their heads together to compose one prayer for the use of any one saint but for one day, they were not able to do it so as that it should answer his wants and conditions; nor can any man do it for himself, without the help and assistance of the Spirit, whose proper work this is.

It were a long work, to show what the Holy Ghost, as a Spirit of grace in the hearts of believers, doth to this end, that they may have, in their access unto God, a saving, spiritual communion with him in Christ; wherein, indeed, consists the chiefest head of all the glory and beauty that is in the worship of God. Should I handle it, I must insist upon all these particulars:—

(1*st.*) That the Holy Spirit discovers their wants unto them, their state and condition, with all the spiritual concernments of their souls; with which, without his effectual working, no man can come to a saving acquaintance spiritually. Men may think it an easy thing to know what they want; but he that knows the difficulty of obedience, the deceitfulness of the heart, the wiles of Satan, the crafts and sleights of indwelling sin, will not think so, but will grant that it is alone to be discovered by the Spirit of grace.

(*2dly.*) It is he alone which really affecteth the heart and soul with their wants, when they are discovered unto us. We are of ourselves dull and stupid in spiritual things; and when matters of the most inexpressible concernment are proposed, we can pass them by without being affected in any proportion to their weight and importance. The Holy Ghost deeply affects the heart with its spiritual concernments, works sorrow, fear, desire, answerable to the wants that are discerned, making " intercession with sighs and groans that cannot be uttered."

(*3dly.*) It is he alone that can reveal the saving relief and supplies that God hath provided in the promises of the gospel for all the wants of the saints; so enabling them to make their supplications according to the mind of God. It is not the consideration of the letter of the promises that will discover savingly unto us the glorious relief that is provided in them for our wants; but it is revealed unto the saints effectually by the Spirit, as provided by the love of the Father, and purchased by the blood of the Son, and stored up for us in the covenant of grace, that we may make our requests for our portions according to the will of God.

(*4thly.*) It is the Holy Ghost that works in believers faith, love, delight, fervency, watchfulness, perseverance,—all those graces that give the soul communion with God in his worship,—and in Christ renders their prayers effectual. He doth this radically, by begetting, creating, ingenerating them in the hearts of believers, in the first infusion of the new, spiritual, vital principle with which they are endued when they are born of him; as also by acting, exciting, and stirring them up in every duty of the worship of God that they are called unto; so enabling them to act according to the mind of God.

By these hath the soul spiritual communion with God in the duties of his worship; and these, with sundry other things, should be handled, if we aimed to set out the work of the Spirit in the worship of the gospel as he is a Spirit of grace and supplication. But the mentioning of them in general is sufficient for the end proposed,—namely, to discover the beauty and the glory of the worship that is thus carried on. Herein lies that which all the beauty of the world fades before, and becomes as a thing of nought,—which brings all the outward pomp of ceremonious worship into contempt;—I mean the glory and excellency that lies in the spiritual communion of the soul with God, by the grace of the Holy Ghost, in that heavenly intercourse which is between God and his saints in their worship, by this means. The Holy Ghost is essentially God himself, blessed for ever in his own person. He comes upon the hearts of the elect, and communicates of his own grace unto them. These graces he enables them to act, exert, and put forth in their worship of God. These God delights in, as coming from himself, as of his own workmanship in us;—he seeth a return of himself to himself, of his grace to his glory: and by these do the saints approach into his presence, speak to him, treat with him, and hear from him. It is the language of faith and love alone, and the like graces of his Spirit, that God hears in his worship. Other voices, cries, and noises he regards not; yea, at least, if not some of them in themselves, yet all of them when these are wanting, are an abomination unto him. However, this is the beauty and the glory of the worship of the gospel,—the beauty and glory that God sees in it. Where this work of the Spirit of God is in his worship, there faith, love, delight, and fervency are in a saving and spiritual manner exercised. He is an atheist, who will deny that they are acceptable to God,—that this worship is glorious, beautiful, and comely: and he is no better, who thinks that any outward solemnity can render worship so, when these are wanting. So that they are the things on which the whole doth turn.

3dly. As always from the foundation of the world, so in the New Testament, the solemn worship of God is to be performed in the assemblies of his saints and people. Now, where the same worship is to be performed by many, the very law of nature and reason requireth that some one or more, according as there is necessity, should go before the rest of the assembly in the worship which they have to perform, and be as the hand, or mouth, or eyes to the whole body or assembly. And so, also, hath our Lord ordained,—namely, that in all the public and solemn worship of gospel assemblies, there should be some appointed to go before them in the performance of the duties of the worship that he requireth of them, be they what they will. Now, as the things themselves, wherein these persons are to minister before the Lord in their assemblies, are all of them prescribed by God himself; so, as to the manner of their performance, there are these two marks or guides to direct the whole:—first, it must be so performed as to tend to the *glory* of God; and, secondly, to the *edification* of the assembly itself. It would be too long for me to show you what is required to this one thing, that the worship of God be carried on in the assembly to the edification of the saints; which is, that all the ordinances of God may have their proper work in them, and effects towards them, for the increase of their faith and graces, and carrying them on in their course of obedience and communion with God. The consideration of this work made the apostle say, Πρὸς ταῦτα τίς ἱκανός; In a word, so far as possible it may be done, their state and condition is to be spread before the Lord in prayer, according as they experience it in their own souls,—their desires to be drawn forth and expressed,—their pleas for mercy and grace to be managed, with the like ends of prayer; their condition to be suited, in instruction, consolation, and exhortation, and the like, in preaching the word. So of all other ordinances; they are to be managed and administered so as may best tend to the edification of the assembly. Now, this is supposed by the third benefit that the saints receive by the Spirit, as to their approach unto God: he gives gifts and abilities, spiritual gifts unto them whom he calleth unto this work of going before the assemblies in the worship of God, that they may perform all things to the glory of God and the edification of the body. I shall not so much as once mention the supplies that are invented and found out by men for this end and purpose. There is not a soul that hath the least communion with God, but knows their emptiness and utter insufficiency for that which they pretend unto.

Now, that the Holy Ghost furnisheth men with gifts for this end and purpose, we have abundant testimonies in the Scripture; and, blessed be God, we have evidence of it abundantly in and from those who are endued with them, 1 Cor. xii. 4, 7, 8, 11. The design of the apostle in that chapter is to treat of the worship of God, as it is to be carried on and performed in the gospel assemblies of saints; of which he gives an instance in the Church of Corinth. For the right performance hereof, he lays down, in the first verse, that spiritual gifts are bestowed. Being to treat of the public worship of God, he begins with spiritual gifts, whereby men are enabled thereunto. The author of all those gifts, he informs us in the fourth verse, is the Holy Ghost; he is sent by Christ to this very end and purpose, to bestow them on his churches. The end of the collation, he informs us, is the profit and edification of the whole body, verse 7. Every one that receives them, doth it to this purpose,—that he may use them to the good and benefit of the whole. To this end are they bestowed in great variety, as verse 8,—that by them the use of the body may be supplied, and church edification may be carried on. And having thus showed their nature, end, and distribution, he again asserts their author to be the Holy Ghost, verse 11. And we have direction, upon this foundation, given for the exercise and use of those gifts, in sundry places; as 1 Pet. iv. 10, 11.

This then, also, as to the more solemn and public worship of God, is performed by that Spirit in whom we have an access unto the Father:—he gives spiritual gifts unto men, enabling them to perform it in a holy, evangelical manner, so as God may be glorified, and the assemblies of the saints edified, in the administration of all ordinances, according to what they are appointed unto. He enables men to pray, so as that the souls of the saints may be drawn forth thereby unto communion with God, according unto all their wants and desires;—he enables them to preach or speak as the "oracles of God," so as that the saints may receive instruction suitable to their condition, as to all the ends of the good word of God, whose dispensation is committed unto them;—he enables men to administer the seals of the covenant so, that the faith of the saints may be excited and stirred up to act and exert itself in a way suitable to the nature of each ordinance. And all those gifts are bestowed on men on purpose for the good and edification of others; they are never exercised in a due manner, but they have a farther reach and efficacy in and upon the souls of the saints, than he that is intrusted with them was able to take a prospect of. He little knows how many of his words and expressions are, in the infinite wisdom of the Holy Ghost, suited in an unspeakable variety to the conditions of his saints;—here one, there another, is wrought upon, affected, humbled, melted, lifted up, rejoiced by them; the Holy Ghost making them effectual to the ends for which he hath given out the gifts from whence they do proceed. I might mention sundry other advantages which we have that belong to our access unto God by one Spirit; but because it were endless to enumerate all particulars, and they may be reduced to some one of these general heads, I shall mention no more of them. This, then, is the first evidence that we have in the words, given unto the glory, beauty, and excellency of gospel worship: In it we have an access unto the Father in the Spirit; which relates unto the things before mentioned, or rather touched on. Here is order: The Spirit reveals the mind of God as to the worship that is acceptable unto him;—he furnishes the souls of the saints with all those graces whereby and wherein they have communion with God in his worship;—he gives gifts unto some, enabling them to go before the assemblies in the worship of God, according to his mind, and unto their edification. Blessed order, that the gates of hell shall not prevail against! Order, proceeding from the God of order;—his own project and appointment! Here is beauty, decency, loveliness. It is all the work of the glorious and holy Spirit, which is like himself,—holy, glorious, and beautiful; and to set up any thing of any man's finding out in competition with it, is that which the Lord's soul abhors.

(2.) As the saints in the gospel have access unto God *in the Spirit*, so they have all their access *in one Spirit;* and this is the spring of all the uniformity which God requires. So the apostle tells us, that, as to the gifts themselves, there are diversities of them, and difference in them, 1 Cor. xii. 4–6. But where, then, is uniformity? If one man have better and greater gifts than another;—one man be more eminent in one kind, another in another;—one excelling in prayer, another in prophesying and preaching,—what confusion must this needs breed! Where is, then, any uniformity in all this? The apostle answereth, verse 11. Here lies the uniformity of gospel worship,—that though the gifts bestowed on men for the public performance of it be various, and there is great diversity among them, yet it is *one Spirit* that bestows them all among them, and that in the order before mentioned. One and the same Spirit discovers the will and worship of God to them all;—one and the same Spirit works the same graces for their kind in the hearts of them all;—one and the same Spirit bestows the gifts that are necessary for the carrying on of gospel worship in the public assemblies to them who are called to that work. And what if he be pleased to give out his gifts in some variously, as to particulars, "dividing to every one severally, as he will?" yet this hindereth not but that, as to the saints mentioned, they all approach unto God by one Spirit; and so have uniformity in their worship throughout the world. This is a *catholic uniformity;* when whatever is invented by men under that name reaches but to the next hedge, and, as might be easily proved and evinced, is the greatest principle of deformity and disorder in the world. This, then, is the uniformity of gospel worship:—all the saints, everywhere, have their access in it unto God in one Spirit, who worketh alike in the general in them all, though he gives out diversities of gifts, serving to the edification of the whole.

And these are the evidences that are directly and "in terminis" given to the proposition of the beauty, excellency, order, and uniformity, of gospel worship in the text, as we consider it absolutely in itself. Before I come to consider its glory comparatively, in reference to the outward solemn worship of the temple of old, I shall add but one consideration more, which is necessary for the preventing of some objections, as well as for the farther clearing of the truth insisted on; and that is taken from the place where spiritual worship is performed. Much of the beauty and glory of the old worship, according to carnal ordinances, consisted in the excellency of the place wherein it was performed;—first, the tabernacle of Moses; then the temple of Solomon, of whose glory and beauty we shall speak afterward. Answerable hereunto, do some imagine there must be a beauty in the place where men assemble for gospel worship; which they labour to paint and adorn accordingly. But they "err, not knowing the Scriptures." There is nothing spoken of the place and seat of gospel worship, but it is referred to one of these three heads,—all which render it glorious:—

1. It is performed in heaven. Though they who perform it are on earth, yet they do it, by faith, in heaven. The apostle saith that believers, in their worship, do "enter into the holiest;" which he exhorts them to draw nigh unto, Heb. x. 19, 22. What is the "holiest," whereinto they enter with their worship? It is that whereinto Jesus Christ is entered as their forerunner, Heb. vi. 20. It is into heaven itself, chap. ix. 24. You will say, "How can these things be, that men

should enter into heaven while they are here below?" I say, Are men "masters in Israel," and ask this question? They who have an access unto the immediate presence of God, and to the throne of grace, enter into heaven itself. And this adds to the glory we treat of. What poor low thoughts have men of God and his ways, who think there lies an acceptable glory and beauty in a little paint and varnish! Heaven itself, the place of God's glorious residence, where he is attended with all his holy angels, is the state [place?] of this worship. Hence is that glorious description given of it, Rev. iv. throughout; where it is expressly said to be "in heaven," though it is only the worship of the church that is described. It were easy from hence to manifest the glory we have spoken of, in the several parts of it. But I do but point out the heads of things.

2. The second thing mentioned, in reference to the place of this worship, is the persons of the saints; these are said to be the "temple of the Lord," 1 Cor. vi. 19, "Your body is the temple of the Holy Ghost, which is in you, which ye have of God." Chap. iii. 16, "Know ye not" (verse 17) "the temple of God is holy?" God hath now no material temple; but he hath chosen this spiritual one,—the hearts and souls of his saints: and beautiful temples they are, being washed with the blood of Christ, beautified with the graces of the Spirit, adorned for communion with him; hence "the King's daughter" is said to be "all glorious within," Ps. xlv. Whatever men may think, God, that knoweth his own graces in the hearts of his, and in whose eyes nothing is beautiful or of price but grace, knows and judges that this place of his worship, this temple that he hath chosen, is full of beauty and glory. Let who will be judge, that pretends to be a Christian, whether is more beautiful in the sight of God,—"a living stone," adorned with all the graces of the Spirit, a heart full of the grace of Christ,—or a dead stone cut out of the quarries, though graven into the similitude of a man?

3. The assemblies of the saints are spoken of as God's temple, and the seat and place of public, solemn, gospel worship, Eph. ii. 21, 22. Here are many living stones framed into an holy house in the Lord, an habitation for God by his Spirit. God dwells here. As he dwelt in the temple of old, by some outward, carnal pledges of his presence; so, in the assemblies of his saints, which are his habitation, he dwells unspeakably in a more glorious manner by his Spirit. Here, according to his promise, is his habitation. Now, the saints' assemblies, according to the order of the gospel, are "a building fitly framed together:" as the tabernacle and temple were of old in their outward structure, whereby they were raised; so they in their spiritual union in and under Christ their head. And they are a temple, a holy temple, —holy with the "holiness of truth," as the apostle speaks, chap. iv. 24;

—not a typical, relative, but a real holiness, and such as the Lord's soul delighteth in. I know some can see no beauty in the assemblies of the saints, unless there be an outward beauty and splendour in the fabric and building wherein they convene. But that is not at all the thing in question, what some men can see, or cannot see. Christ himself had unto some "no form nor comeliness that he should be desired;"—no more have his saints, his ways, his worship. That is not it which we inquire after; but what is beautiful, comely, and of price in the eyes and judgment of God. Neither is that the matter in question, whether these or those are saints of God, or no? But only, whether an assembly of saints, as such, which are the temple of God, and being called together according to the order of the gospel, be not a glorious seat of worship? God saith it is so; and if men say otherwise, those that are not enchanted with what I shall not name, will easily know what to give credit to.

SECONDLY.[1] Proceed we now, in the next place, to set forth the glory and beauty of this worship of the gospel *comparatively*, with reference to the solemn outward worship which, by God's own appointment, was used under the Old Testament; which, as we shall show, was far more excellent on many accounts than any thing of the like kind,—that is, as to outward splendour and beauty,—that was ever found out by men. And I shall do this the more willingly, because the Holy Ghost doth so much and so frequently—and that not without many great and weighty causes—insist upon it in the New Testament, having intimated it beforehand in many places of the Old. To the right understanding of what is gospel, and delivered in Scripture on this account, some things are previously to be considered:—

1. As the whole worship of the old church, so the whole manner of it, with all its rites, ceremonies, and ornaments, both in the tabernacle and temple, were of God's own appointment. There was not the least part of the fabric wherein his worship was celebrated, nor any ornament of it,—not one rite or ceremony that did attend it,—but it was all of it wholly of God's own designation and command. This is known and confessed. Moses made all things "according to the pattern showed him in the mount;" and at the finishing of the whole work, it is in one chapter ten [eight?] times repeated, that he did as the Lord commanded him, Exod. xl. Now, surely this gave it a beauty, order, and glory incomparably above whatever the wisest of the sons of men are able to invent. "Let the potsherd contend with the potsherds of the earth; but woe unto him that contends with his Maker!" The worship of the pope and his invention may possibly outdo the beauty and order of the worship of the Turk and his invention; but I hope they will not compare with God, nor make themselves equal with

[1] See the division as announced, p. 56.

him. But why should I say I hope it, when the contrary is evident? For doth he not undertake to assign new rules of his own in the worship of God? and doth he not therein make himself equal with God, whose prerogative it is to be the only lawgiver to his people's consciences, and the only prescriber of his own worship? But this I may yet hope, that men will not nakedly aver, that what is of their appointment is equal unto, and comparable with, what God appoints. Take their institutions and God's together, and the former, surely, will have great disadvantage in respect of the authors. This, in general, I suppose, will be granted, though men be very apt practically to make void the commands of God by their traditions and institutions, laying more weight upon some one of them than on all the commands of Jesus Christ.

" But, it may be, though God appointed that worship of old, and all the concernments of it, he intended not to make that beautiful and glorious, but plain and homely; so that it doth not follow that it is beautiful and excellent because it was by him appointed." Answer, Though we may well and safely abide by this general proposition, that what God hath appointed in his own worship is therefore beautiful and glorious, excellent, orderly, and comely, because he hath appointed it; yet I add,—

2. That it was God's intendment to make, appoint, and dispose of all things so, that the solemnity of his worship might be very beautiful and glorious. He appoints the high priest's garments to be made expressly "for glory and for beauty," Exod. xxviii. 2,—such as might be specious and goodly to look upon; and speaking of the church-state, when he had formed and fashioned it by his institution, he saith, her renown went forth among the heathen for beauty, for it was perfect through the comeliness he had put upon her, Ezek. xvi. 14. There was in her ways of worship a renowned beauty, a perfect comeliness; whence, saith the prophet, " A glorious high throne from the beginning is the place of our sanctuary," Jer. xvii. 12. But I shall not need to multiply testimonies to this purpose. Who knows not what things are spoken of the tabernacle, the temple, and all the worship belonging to them, everywhere in the Scripture? As God appointed, so it came to pass;—it was the most beautiful solemnity that ever the sun shone upon. Mosaical worship, I say, as celebrated in Solomon's temple, outdid all the glory and splendour that ever the world, in any place, in any age from the foundation of it, ever enjoyed. Should all the princes of Europe lay their treasures together, they were not able to build a fabric of that charge, magnificence, and glory, as was Solomon's temple. It were endless to go over particulars. The garments of the high priest were such as rendered him so awful and glorious, that Alexander the Great, that famous conqueror

of the east, fell down before him with a prostrate reverence. The order of the house, and all the worship in it,—who can fix his mind upon it without admiration! How glorious was it when the house of Solomon stood in its greatest order and beauty, all overlaid with gold,—thousands of priests and Levites ministering in their orders, with all the most solemn musical instruments that David found out, and the great congregation assembled of hundreds of thousands, all singing praises to God! Let any man in his thoughts a little compare the greatest, most solemn, pompous, and costly worship that any of the sons of men have in these latter days invented and brought into the Christian Church, with this of the Judaical, and he shall quickly find that it holds no proportion with it,—that it is all a toy, a thing of nought in comparison of it. Take the Cathedral of Peter in Rome: bring in the pope and all his cardinals in all their vestments, habiliments, and ornaments; fill their choir with the best singers they can get; set out and adorn their images and pictures to the utmost that their treasures and superstition will reach to;—then compare it to Solomon's Temple and the worship thereof; and,—without the help of the consideration that the one was from heaven, the other is of men,—the very nature of the things themselves will manifest how vain the present pretences are to glory and beauty. How much more may this be spoken of such underling pretenders as some are!

These things being premised, we say now, that, notwithstanding this whole worship, and all the concernments of it, was appointed by God himself; notwithstanding it was designed by him to be beautiful and glorious, and that indeed it was the very top of what external beauty and splendour could reach unto;—yet that it was no way comparable to the beauty and glory of this spiritual worship of the New Testament; yea, had no glory in comparison of it. This, then, I shall briefly demonstrate:—(1.) In general; and then, (2.) By an induction of some particular instances.

For the former, I need go no farther than that place where the apostle doth expressly handle this comparison, viz., 2 Cor. iii. 7–10. He doth here on set purpose compare the ministration of the law in the letter, with all its outward legal worship, rites, and ceremonies, with the administration of the gospel in the Spirit, and the worship of God attending thereon. And first, he acknowledgeth that the old ministration was very glorious; which he either gives an instance of, or proves it by that of Moses' face shining when he came down from the mount, when he had received the law, and the pattern of all that worship which he was to appoint unto that church. It seems that God left that shining on the face of Moses—which was such that the people could not bear the brightness of it—to testify how glorious that was about which he had received revelation; so that, indeed, saith the apostle, "That ministration was glorious, very glorious,—yea, glory in the abstract," verse 9. Nothing was there ever in the world to be compared with it. We will, then, compare it now with the ministration of the Spirit, and the worship of God under the gospel. It may be he will say, "It is not all out so glorious, indeed." Nay, but he goes farther, and tells us that this doth so excel in glory, comeliness, and excellency, that, in respect unto it, the other had *no glory* at all. What, then, may be said of any thing invented by men in the worship of God for glory and beauty? I dare not say what the apostle saith of that which God himself appointed,—that it hath any glory and beauty in itself. But yet, suppose it hath so; let men esteem it as glorious and beautiful as they can possibly fancy it to be,—yet, unless the same vail be on their minds in reading the Gospel which is on the Jews' in reading Moses, they cannot but see and acknowledge that it hath no glory in comparison of that spiritual worship which we have described.

Some particular instances will make the general comparison more evident. I shall only name these three, which—being the principal spring of all the beauty, glory, and order of the worship of old—are peculiarly considered by the apostle to this very purpose, in the Epistle to the Hebrews, where he sets out the excellency of the evangelical administrations of the covenant and worship of God above and beyond the legal:—

1. The first of these was the temple, the seat of all the solemn outward worship of the old church. The beauty and glory of it were in part spoken to before; nor shall I insist on any particular description of it. It may suffice, that it was the principal state [place] of the beauty and order of the Judaical worship, and which rendered all exceeding glorious;—so far, that the people idolized it, and put their trust in it;—that upon the account of it they should be assuredly preserved, notwithstanding their presumptuous sins: and, indeed, it had such blessings and promises annexed unto it, that if there were at this day any place or house in the world that had the like, I should desire to be among the first that should enter into a pilgrimage of going to it, though it were as far beyond Jerusalem as it is thither. But yet, notwithstanding all this, Solomon himself, in his prayer at the dedication of that house, 1 Kings viii. 27, seems to intimate that there was some check upon his spirit, considering the unanswerableness of the house to the great majesty of God. It was a house on the earth,—a house that he did build with his hands; intimating that he looked farther to a more glorious house than that. And what is it, if it be compared with the temple of gospel worship? Whatever is called the temple now of the people of God, is as much beyond that of old as spiritual things are beyond carnal, as heavenly beyond earthly, as

eternal beyond temporal. First, In some sense the body of Christ is our temple, as himself called it, speaking of the temple of his body as being prefigured by it,—as having the fulness of the Godhead dwelling in him, typified by the presence of God in the old temple, and being the centre wherein all his people meet with their worship of God, as those of old did in the temple. And surely there is no comparison, for beauty and excellency, between the house that Solomon built and the Son of God, " who is the brightness of his glory, and the express image of his person." Again, The persons and the assemblies of the saints, as I showed before, are a temple to God under the gospel. They are his body, Eph. i. 23; and his house, Heb. iii. 6. Nor is the old temple, made of wood and stones, gold and silver, to be compared with this living house, washed with the blood of Christ, adorned with the real graces of the Spirit, and garnished with all the choice jewels of God's eternal love. They are God's delight, " the first-fruits of the creature" to him, the spouse of Christ,—through his graces altogether lovely. The Lord Jesus sees more beauty and glory in the weakest assemblies of his saints, coming together in his name, and acted and guided in his worship and ways by his Spirit, than ever was in all the worship of Solomon's temple when it was in its glory. Thirdly, Heaven itself, the holy place not made with hands, is also the saints' temple under the gospel. Believers have in their worship an open way into the holiest made for them by Christ, who entered into it as the forerunner, Heb. vi. 20; opening it to them, also giving admission into it, chap. x. 19–21. And how exceedingly doth this exalt the excellency of the spiritual worship of the gospel! What was the glory of Solomon's temple to the glory of the meanest star in heaven! How much less was it, then, in comparison of the glorious presence of God in the highest heavens, whither believers enter with all their worship, even where Christ sits at the right hand of God!

2. The second spring of the beauty of the old worship—which was, indeed, the hinge upon which the whole turned—was the priesthood of Aaron, with all the administrations committed to his charge. The pomp, state, and ceremonies, that the Papists have invented in their outward worship, or that heap which they have, in several parcels, borrowed of the Heathen and Jews, is a toy in comparison of the magnificence of the Aaronical administrations. The high priest under the gospel is Christ alone. Now, I shall spare the pains of comparing these together;—partly, because it will be by all confessed that Christ is incomparably more excellent and glorious; and partly, because the apostle, on set purpose, handles this comparison in sundry instances in the Epistle to the Hebrews; where any one may run and read it, it being the main subject-matter of that most excellent epistle.

3. The order, glory, number, significancy, of their sacrifices, was another part of their glory. And, indeed, he that shall seriously consider that one solemn anniversary sacrifice of expiation and atonement, which is instituted, Lev. xvi., will quickly see that there was very much glory and solemnity in the outward ceremony of it. "But now," saith the apostle, "*we have a better sacrifice,*" Heb. ix. 23. We have him who is the high priest, and altar, and sacrifice,—all himself; of worth, value, glory, beauty,—upon the account of his own person, the efficacy of his oblation, the real effect of it,—more than a whole creation, if it might have been all offered up at one sacrifice. This is the standing sacrifice of the saints, offered "once for all;"—as effectual now any day as if offered every day: and other sacrifices, properly so called, they have none. I might mention other particulars; but I suppose, through the grace of our Lord Jesus Christ, we have in some measure manifested the excellency, beauty, order, and uniformity, of the spiritual worship of the gospel; and that both absolutely in itself, and in comparison with any other way of worship whatever. From all which it will be easily made to appear, that this may well be reckoned among the unspeakable privileges that are purchased for us by the death of Christ;—which was the thing first proposed to consideration.

SERMON V.

OF WALKING HUMBLY WITH GOD.

"And to walk humbly with thy God."—MIC. vi. 8.

THE beginning of this chapter contains a most pathetical expostulation of God, by the prophet, with his people, about their sins and unworthy walking before him. Having, with an apostrophe to the mountains and hills, verses 1, 2, stirred up their attention, and raised them to the consideration of his plea with them in verses 3–5, he emphatically presses them with the mercies he had of old bestowed upon them, with the patience and love toward them which he showed and exercised in his dealings with them.

The conviction being effectual to awaken them, and fill them with a sense of their horrible ingratitude and rebellions, verses 6, 7, they begin to make inquiry, according as is the custom of persons under the power of conviction, what course they shall take to avoid the wrath of God, which they could not but acknowledge was due to them. And here, as God speaks, Hos. vii. 1, when he would heal them, their iniquity and wickedness is discovered more and more; they discover the wretched principles whereon they were acted, in all that they had to do with God.

Indeed convictions, on what account soever, made effectual upon the soul, draw out its inward principles; which are not otherwise to be discovered. Many there are who have, in notion, received the doctrine of free justification by the blood of Christ, whom, while they are secure in their ways, without trouble or distress, it is impossible to persuade that they do not live and act upon that principle, and walk before God in the strength of it. Let any great conviction, from the word or by any imminent or pressing danger, befall these men,—then their hearts are laid open,—then all their hopes are in their repentance, amendment of life, performance of duties in a better manner; and the iniquity of their self-righteousness is discovered.

Thus was it with these Jews. Their sins being charged home upon them by the prophet, so that they are not able to stand under their weight and burden, he now discovers the bottom of all their principles in dealing with God; and that is this, that having provoked him, something they must do whereby to appease him and atone his anger.

In their contrivance to this purpose, they fix on two general heads. First, They propose things which God himself had appointed, verses 6, 7;—secondly, Things of their own finding out, which they supposed might have a farther and better efficacy to the end aimed at than any thing appointed of God himself, verse 7.

First. They look to sacrifices and burnt offerings for help;—they consider whether by them, and on their account, they may not come before the Lord, and bow themselves before the high God; that is, perform such a worship for which they may be acquitted from the guilt of their sins.

Sacrifices were a part of the worship of God appointed by himself, and acceptable to him when offered in faith, according to his mind; yet we find God frequently rejecting them in the Old Testament, whilst yet their institution was in force, and themselves good in their kind. Now, this rejection of them was not absolute, but with respect to somewhat that vitiated the service in them. Among these, two were most eminent:—

1. When they were rested in, as the matter and cause of their justification and acceptation with God, beyond their typical virtue.

2. When they were relied on to countenance men in the neglect of moral duties, or to continue in any way of sin.

Both these evils attended this appeal of the Jews unto their sacrifices. They did it first to please God, or appease God,—that on their account they might be freed from the guilt of sin, and be accepted:

and then to countenance themselves in their immoralities and wickedness; as is evident from the prophet's reply, verse 7, calling them from their vain confidence in sacrifices, to justice, judgment, mercy, and humble walking with God. But,—

Secondly, They find this will not do; conscience will not be satisfied nor peace be obtained by any performance of these ordinary duties, though they should engage in them in an extraordinary manner; no, though they could bring thousands of rams, and ten thousand rivers of oil. Though men attempt never so vigorously, in never so extraordinary a manner, to quiet their souls, terrified with the guilt of sin, by any duties whatever, it will not do,—the work will not be accomplished; therefore they will make farther attempts. If nothing that God hath appointed will reach the end they aim at, because they were never appointed by him for that end, they will invent or use some way of their own that may appear to be of more efficacy than the other: "Shall I give my first-born for my transgression?"

The rise and occasion of such sacrifices as here are mentioned,—the sacrificing of men, of men's sacrificing their own children; the use of such sacrifices throughout the world, among all nations; the craft and cruelty of Satan in imposing them on poor, sinful, guilty creatures, with the advantages which he had so to do,—I have elsewhere declared. For the present, I shall only observe two things in the state and condition of convinced persons, when pressed with their sins, and a sense of the guilt of them, who are ignorant of the righteousness of God in Christ:—

1. They have a better opinion of their own ways and endeavours, for the pleasing of God and quieting their consciences, than of any thing of God's institution, or the way by him appointed for that end. This is the height that they rise to, when they have fixed on what is most glorious in their own eyes. Tell a Papist who is convinced of sin, of the blood of Christ,—it is folly to him. Penances, satisfaction, purgatory, intercession of the church in the mass, have much more desirableness in them:—these Eliabs must wear the crown. The case is the same with innumerable poor souls at present, who hope to find more relief in their own duties and amendment of life than in the blood of Christ, as to the appeasing of God and obtaining of peace.

2. There is nothing so horrid, desperate, irksome, or wicked, that convinced persons will not engage to do under their pressure on the account of the guilt of sin. They will burn their children in the fire, whilst the cries of their conscience outcry the lamentation of their miserable infants: which, as it argues the desperate blindness that is in man by nature, choosing such abominations rather than that way which is the wisdom of God; so also the terrors that possess poor souls convinced of sin, that are unacquainted with the only remedy.

This being the state and condition of these poor creatures, the prophet discovers to them their mistake and desperate folly in the verse of my text.

Two things are contained in this verse;—the one is implied, the other expressed in words:—

First. Here is something implied; and that is, a reproof of the error and mistake of the Jews. They thought sacrifices were appointed for the appeasing of God by their performance of them; and that this was their business in their worship,—by their duty in performance of them, to make satisfaction for the guilt of sin. This the prophet calls them from, telling them that is not their business, their duty: God hath provided another way to make reconciliation and atonement; it is a thing above their power. Their business is to walk with God in holiness; for the matter of atonement, that lies on another hand. "He hath showed thee, O man, what he requireth of thee:" he expects not satisfaction at thy hands, but obedience on the account of peace made.

Secondly. What is expressed is this,—that God prefers moral worship, in the way of obedience, to all sacrifices whatever; according to the determination afterward approved by our Saviour, Mark xii. 33, "What doth the LORD require of thee?"

Now, this moral obedience he refers to three heads:—Doing justly; loving mercy; and walking humbly with God.

How the two first are comprehensive of our whole duty in respect of men, containing in them the sum and substance of the second table, I shall not stay to declare.

It is the third head that I have fixed on, which peculiarly regards the first table and the moral duties thereof.

Concerning this I shall do these three things:—I. I shall show what it is to walk with God. II. What it is to walk humbly with God. III. Prove this proposition: Humble walking with God, as our God in covenant, is the great duty and most valuable concernment of believers.

I. As to our walking with God, some things are required to it, and some things are required in it:—

1. Some things are required to it; as,—

(1.) Peace and agreement. Amos iii. 3, "Can two walk together, except they be agreed?" And he tells us, that walking with God, when there is no peace with him, is like walking in a forest where and when the lion roareth, verse 8,—when a man can have no thoughts but what are full of expectation of his immediately being torn asunder and devoured. So God threateneth to deal with them that pretend to walk with him, and yet are not at peace with him, Ps. l. 22, "Now consider this, ye that forget God, lest I tear you in pieces, and there be none to deliver." Who are these? Those to whom he speaks, verse 16, "But unto the wicked, God saith:" the exceptive "but," distinguishes them from those of whom he spoke before, verse 5, who had made a covenant with him by sacrifice, and so obtained peace in the blood of Christ. When Cain and Abel went into the field together, and were not agreed, the issue was, that the one slew the other. When Joram met Jehu in the field, he cried, "Is it peace?" and finding by his answer that they were not agreed, he instantly flew, and cried out for his life. "'Agree,' saith our Saviour, 'with thine adversary whiles thou art in the way,' lest the issue be sad to thee."

You know at what enmity God and man do stand, whilst he is in the state of nature. They are alienated from God by wicked works, —are enemies; and their carnal mind is enmity to him, Rom. viii. 7; and his wrath abideth on them, John iii. 36;—they are children of his wrath, Eph. ii. 3. Were I to pursue this head in particulars, I could manifest from the rise and first breach, from the consideration of the parties at variance, the various ways of managing of it, and its issue, that this is the saddest enmity that can possibly be apprehended. You know, also, what our peace and agreement with God is, and whence it doth arise. Christ is "our peace," Eph. ii. 14. He hath made an end of the difference about sin, Dan. ix. 24. He hath made peace for us with God; and by our interest in him, we, who were afar off, are made nigh, and obtain peace, Rom. v. 1; Eph. ii. 14, 15.

This, then, I say, in the first place, is required to our walking with God,—that we are at peace with him, and agreement in the blood of Christ;—that we are by faith actually interested in the atonement; —that our persons are accepted, as the foundation of the acceptation of our duties. Without this, every attempt for walking with God in obedience, or the performance of any duties, is,—

[1.] Fruitless. All that men do is lost. "The sacrifice of the wicked is an abomination;" their holy things are dung, which God will remove. In all their duties they labour in the fire; not any of their works shall turn to their eternal account. God looks on all their duties as the gifts of enemies, that are selfish, deceitful, and, of all things, to be abhorred. Such men may have their reward in this life; but as to what they aim at, their pains are lost, their hearing is lost, their alms are lost,—all is fruitless.

[2.] Presumptuous. They put themselves upon the company of God, who hates them, and is hated by them. Ps. l. 16, "But unto the wicked saith God" (this is God's language to them in their duties), "Thou bold, presumptuous rebel, what hast thou to do to take my name in thy mouth? Why dost thou howl thus before me, and offer swine's blood in my presence? How camest thou hither, not having a wedding garment? I hate thy most solemn oblations." Indeed, it will be found at the issue, that intolerable presumption lies at the bottom of all unregenerate men's attempts to walk with God. They count it a slight thing to do so;—they deal with him as one that took very little notice how he is dealt withal.

This, I say, is the first thing required to our walking with God,—that we be at peace and agreement with him in the blood of Christ. And, as the psalmist says, "Consider this, ye that know not God," who have not made a covenant with him, in and by the sacrifice of his Son. You meet him in the field,—you put yourselves upon his company,—you pretend to walk with him in these duties, and those other, which custom, education, conviction, or self-righteousness, puts you upon;—in every one of them you provoke him to his face to destroy you. You seem to flatter him that you are agreed, when he declares that you are at enmity. Let a man deal thus with his ruler:—conspire against his crown and dignity, attempt his death, despise his authority, reproach his reputation; and then, when he is proclaimed rebel and traitor, and condemned to die, let him come into his presence, as in former days, and deal with him as a good subject,—offer him gifts and presents;—shall he think to escape? Will he not be seized on, and delivered over to punishment?

Every man, in his natural estate, is a rebel against God. Thou hast rejected his authority, conspired his ruin, the ruin of his kingdom,—art proclaimed by him a traitor and rebel,—art sentenced to eternal death: is it for thee now to meet him,—to go and flatter him with thy mouth, and fawn upon him in thy other duties? Will he not remember thy rebellions, despise thy offerings, command thee out of his presence into bonds and prison,—abhor thy gifts? What canst thou else expect at his hands? This is the best and utmost of their condition, in their obedience, who are not interested in Christ; and the more earnest and zealous you are, the more ready in the performance of duties, the more do you put yourselves on him and his company who hates you upon the justest grounds in the world, and is ready to destroy you.

(2.) The second previous thing is, oneness of design. For persons occasionally to fall into the company of one another, and so to pass on together for a little season, doth not suffice for them to be said to walk together. Oneness of aim and design is required to it.

The aim of God, in general, is his own glory; he makes all things for himself, Prov. xvi. 4; Rev. iv. 11;—in particular, as to the business of our walking with him, it is the praise of his glorious grace, Eph. i. 6.

Now, in this aim of God to exalt his glorious grace, two things are considerable:—First, That all which is to be looked for at the hand of God, is upon the account of mere grace and mercy, Tit. iii. 4, 5. God aims at the exalting of his glory in this,—that he may be known, believed, magnified, as a God pardoning iniquity and sin. And, secondly, That the enjoyment of himself, in this way of mercy and grace, is that great reward of him that walks with him. So God tells Abraham, when he calls him to walk before him, "I am thy shield, and thy exceeding great reward," Gen. xv. 1. The enjoyment of God in covenant, and the good things therein freely promised and bestowed by him, is the exceeding great reward of them that walk with God. This also, then, is required of him that will walk with God,—that he hath the same design in his so doing as God hath;—that he aims in all his obedience at the glory of God's grace; and the enjoyment of him as his exceeding great reward.

Now, according to what was before said of the design of God, this may be referred unto three heads:—

[1.] In general:—that the design of the person be the glory of God. "Whatever we do," saith the apostle (that is, in our worship of God, and walking with him), "let all be done to his glory." Men who, in their obedience, have base, low, unworthy ends, walk as contrary to God in their obedience as in their sins. Some serve him for custom; some for an increase of corn, wine, or oil, or the satisfying of some low earthly end; some aim at self and reputation. All is lost;—it is not walking with God, but warring against him.

[2.] To exalt the glory of God's grace. This is one part of the ministry of the gospel,—that in obedience we should seek to exalt the glory of grace. The first natural tendency of obedience was, to exalt the glory of God's justice. The new covenant hath put another end upon our obedience: it is to exalt free grace;—grace given in Christ, enabling us to obey; grace accepting our obedience, being unworthy; grace constituting this way of walking with God; and grace crowning its performance.

[3.] Aiming at the enjoyment of God, as our reward. And this cuts off the obedience of many from being a walking with God. They perform duties, indeed; but what sincerity is there in their aims for the glory of God? Is it almost once taken into their thoughts? Is not the satisfaction of conscience, the escape of hell and wrath, the sole aim they have in their obedience? Is it of concernment to them that the glory of God be exalted? Do they care, indeed, what becomes of his name or ways, so they may be saved? Especially, how little is the glory of his grace aimed at! Men are destroyed by a self-righteousness, and have nothing of a gospel obedience in them. Look on the praying and preaching of some men: is it not evident that they walk not with God therein, seek not his glory, have no zeal for it, no care for his name; but rest in the discharge of the duty itself?

(3.) That a man may walk with another, it is required that he have a living principle in him, to enable him thereunto. Dead men cannot walk; or if they do, acted by any thing but their own vital principle and essential form, they are a terror to their companions,—not a comfort in their communion. For a dead carcase, or a trunk, to be moved up and down, is not walking. Hence this is everywhere laid down as the principle of our obedience,—that we "who were dead are quickened;" that "the law of the Spirit of life makes us free from the law of sin and death," Rom. viii. 2. That we may walk with God, a principle of a new life is required; that we may have power for it, and be pressed to it from that which is within us. Had not a man rather walk alone, than have a dead carcase, taken out of a grave, and acted by an external force and power, to accompany him?

This, I say, is a third consideration. The matter of our walking with God consists, as shall be showed, in our obedience,—in our performance of duties required. In this, we are all more or less engaged; yea, so far, that perhaps it is hard to discover who walks fastest, and with most appearance of strength and vigour. But, alas! how many dead souls have we walking amongst us!

[1.] Are there none who are utter strangers to a new spiritual life —a life from above, hid with Christ in God, a life of God—that mock almost at these things; at least, that can give no account of any such life in them;—that think it strange it should be required of them that they should give any account of this life, or of being begotten again by the Spirit; yea, that make it a most ridiculous thing? "What, then, is it they will yet plead for themselves? Why do they not walk with God? Is not their conversation good and blameless? Who can charge them with any thing? Do they not perform the duties required of them?" But, friend, would it be acceptable to thee to have a dead man taken out of his grave, and carried along with thee in thy way? All thy services, thy company, is no other to God; he smells nothing but a noisome steam from thy presence with him: thy hearing, praying, duties, meditations,—they are on this account all an abomination to him. Tell me not of thy conversation. If it be from a pure conscience (that is, a conscience purified in the blood of Christ), and faith unfeigned, which is the life, or a fruit of it, whereof we are speaking,—it is glorious and commendable; if from other principles, the Lord abhors it.

[2.] Are there none who are acted, in their obedience and duties, not from inward principles, and spiritualized faculties, but merely from outward considerations, and external impressions? The apostle tells us how believers "grow," and "go on to perfection," Eph.

iv. 16; Col. i. 19. Christ is the head; from him, by the Spirit, into every joint and sinew is derived an influence of life, that the body may thereby and therewith go on towards perfection. How is it with sundry others? They are set upon their feet by custom or conviction: one joint is supplied by repute, another by fear and shame, a third by self-righteousness, a fourth by the lash of conscience; and so they are driven on by a mere external impress. And these are the principles of the obedience of many. By such things as these are they acted in their walking with God. Do you suppose you shall be accepted, or that peace will be your latter end? I fear many that hear me this day may be in this condition. Pardon me if I am jealous with a godly jealousy. What means else that hatred of the power of godliness, that darkness in the mystery of the gospel, that cursed formality, that enmity to the Spirit of God,—that hatred of reformation, that is found amongst us?

Use. If there be so many things required to walking with God, to fit men for it; and many who do strive to walk with him are yet lost from a defect of them, in the midst of their obedience and performance of duties,—what will become of them, where shall they appear, who never once attempted to walk with him,—who are wrought upon by no considerations to make it their business so to do? I speak not only of those amongst us, young and old, whose pride, folly, idleness, debauchery, profaneness, hatred of the ways of God, testify to their faces, to all the world, to the shame and danger of the places wherein they live, that they are servants to sin, and walk contrary to God,—who also will walk contrary unto them, until they are no more. I speak not, I say, of such as these, who are judged of all; nor yet only of those who are kept to outward observances merely on the account of the discipline of the place, and the hopes which they have laid up in it for their outward good, with such other carnal aims;—but of some also who ought to be leaders of others, and examples to that flock that is amongst us. What endeavours to walk with God are found upon them, or seen in their ways? Vanity, pride in themselves, families, and relations, yea, scoffing at religion and the ways of God, are the examples some give. I wish worldliness, selfishness, hardness, and straitness of bowels, with open vanity, do not eat up all humble walking with God, as to the power of it, in others.

The vanity of the highest profession, without this humble walking, which is another deceit, shall be afterward spoken unto.

For the present, let me speak to them of whom I have spoken somewhat already. If many shall cry, "Lord, Lord," and not be heard; if "many shall strive to enter," and shall not; what will be their lot and portion? Poor creatures! you know not the condition of your souls; you cry "Peace, and sudden destruction is at hand."

Take heed, lest the multitude of sermons and exhortations you have, make you not, like the men that dwell by the falls of mills, deaf with their continual noise. God sends his messengers sometimes to make men deaf, Isa. vi. 10. If that be your portion, it will be sad with you. Give me leave to ask you two or three questions, and I have done:—

1. Do you not please yourselves, some of you, in your ways, and that with contempt of others? Do you not think they are fools, or envious, or hypocrites, or factious, that reprove you; and scorn them in your hearts? Do you not rather love, honour, imitate, such as never pressed you (nor will) to this business of a new life,—to walk with God; and so suppose the times ruined, since this new-fangled preaching came up amongst you;—desiring to hear things finely spoken, and fopperies of men ignorant of God and themselves? Or,—

2. Do you not relieve yourselves, with the help of profligate souls, that you will be better,—you will repent when the season is better suited for it, and your present condition is changed? Or,—

3. Do not some of you labour to put far from you all thoughts of these things? "Amici, dum vivimus, vivamus;"—"It will be well enough with us, though we add drunkenness to thirst." Do not, I say, one or all of these rotten, corrupted principles lie at the bottom of your loose walking with God? Take heed, I beseech you, lest the Lord tear you in pieces!

SERMON VI.

Having told you what things are previously required to our walking with God,—

2. Our next inquiry is, as to the matter or thing itself;—what it is to walk with God.

The expression itself is very frequent in Scripture, both as to the examples of them that did so, and as to precepts for others so to do.

It is said of Enoch, that he "walked with God," Gen. v. 24. And "Noah walked with God," Gen. vi. 9. Hezekiah "walked before God," Isa. xxxviii. 3. Abraham is commanded to walk with God, Gen. xvii. 1; yea, and the same thing is almost a hundred times in the Scriptures, with some little variation, so expressed. Sometimes we are said to "walk with God;" sometimes to "walk before him;" sometimes to "follow after him," to "follow hard after him;" sometimes "to walk in his ways;"—all to the same purpose.

The expression, you know, is metaphorical; by an allusion taken from things natural, spiritual things are expressed therein.

Not to press the metaphor beyond its principal intention, nor to insist on all particulars wherein any thing of allusion may be found, nor yet insist on the proof of that which is owned and acknowledged, —walking with God, in general, consisteth in the performance of that obedience, for matter and manner, which God, in the covenant of grace, requires at our hands.

I shall only manifest unto you some few of the chief concernments of this obedience, which give life and significancy to the metaphor, and so pass on:—

(1.) That our obedience be walking with God, it is required that we be in covenant with him, and that the obedience be required in the tenor of that covenant.

This, as to the matter of it, was spoken to before, under the head of what was required to this walking with God,—namely, that we have peace and agreement with him. Here it is formally considered—from that expression, "with God"—as the spring and rule of our obedience. Therefore this expression is comprehensive of the whole duty of the covenant on our part. As, Gen. xvii. 1, "I am God Almighty," or "All-sufficient,"—that is, unto thee I will be so,—as this is comprehensive of the whole of the covenant on the part of God,—that he will be unto us an all-sufficient God; so the words that follow are comprehensive of the whole of our duty,—"Walk before me;" which are exegetically explained in the next words, "and be thou perfect." The covenant,—the agreement that is between God and us in Christ, wherein he promises to be our God, and we give up ourselves to be his people,—is the bottom and spring of that obedience which is walking with God; that is, at an agreement with him, in covenant with him,—with whom, out of covenant, we have no commerce.

(2.) It is an obedience according to the tenor of that covenant wherein we are agreed with God. Walking with God according to the tenor of the covenant of works was, "Do this, and live." The state is now changed. The rule now is that of Gen. xvii. 1, "'Be thou perfect,' or upright, 'before me,' in all the obedience I require at thy hands."

Now, there are sundry things required to our walking with God in obedience, so that it may answer the tenor of the covenant wherein we are agreed.

[1.] That it proceed from faith in God, by Christ the mediator. Faith in God, in general, is, and must be, the principle of all obedience, in what covenant soever, Heb. xi. 6; but faith in God, through Christ the mediator, is the principle of that obedience which, according to the tenor of the new covenant, is accepted. Hence it is called

"The obedience of faith," Rom. i. 5; that is, of faith in God by Christ, as the foregoing and following words evince. His blood is the blood of this covenant, Heb. ix. 15, x. 29. The covenant itself is confirmed and ratified thereby; and by the blood of that covenant do we receive what we receive from God, Zech. ix. 11. Hence, whenever God makes mention of the covenant to Abraham, and stirs him up to the obedience that is required in it, he still mentions the "seed;" "which is Christ," saith the apostle, Gal. iii. 16. As it is said, in general, that "he that comes to God must believe that he is;" so, in particular, as to the new covenant, Christ says of himself, "I am the way:" there is no going to the Father but by him, John xiv. 6. They who have believed in God, must be careful to maintain good works, Tit. iii. 8; that is, they who have believed in God through Christ. If, in our obedience, we walk with God according to the tenor of the new covenant, that obedience ariseth from justifying faith; that is, faith in God through Christ.

[2.] That it be perfect; that is, that the person be perfect or upright therein: "Walk before me, and be thou perfect," Gen. xvii. 1. It was said of Noah, that he was "perfect in his generations," Gen. vi. 9; as it is also said of many others. David bids us "mark the perfect man," Ps. xxxvii. 37; that is, the man that walketh with God according to the tenor of the new covenant. And our Saviour, calling for this obedience, commands us to "be perfect, as our heavenly Father is perfect," Matt. v. 48.

Now there is a twofold perfection:—

1*st*. There is a τελείωσις,—a consummation in righteousness. So it is said of the law, that it "made nothing perfect," Heb. vii. 19, or brought nothing to perfect righteousness. And the sacrifices made not the comers unto God by them perfect, Heb. x. 1. They could not τελειῶσαι, consummate the work of righteousness, which was aimed at. In this sense we are said to be perfect, "complete" in Christ, Col. ii. 10; and, as it is said in another case, Ezek. xvi. 14, our beauty is "perfect" through his comeliness. This is the perfection of justification; whereof we speak not.

2*dly*. There is a perfection within us. Now this also is twofold:— A complete perfection of enjoyment; and a perfection of tendency towards enjoyment:—

(1*st*.) In respect of the first, Paul says he was not made perfect, Phil. iii. 12; and tells us where and by whom it is obtained, Heb. xii. 23, "The spirits of just men made perfect." Just men are not thus made perfect until their spirits be brought into the presence of God. This perfection is the aim of Christ's redemption, Eph. v. 25, 26; and of all their obedience, Eph. iv. 14. But this is not the perfection which the covenant requires, but which it tends and brings to, whilst by the promise of it we are carried on in the work of "perfecting holiness in the fear of God," 2 Cor. vii. 1. See Job ix. 20.

(*2dly.*) There is also a perfection of tendency to this end. So Noah is said to be perfect, and Job perfect; and God commands Abraham to be perfect; and David describes the happy condition of the perfect man. Concerning this, observe,—

[1*st.*] There is no word in the Scripture whereby this perfection, and being perfect, is expressed, that in its use is restrained to such an absolute perfection as should admit of no mixture of failing or defect. The word used concerning Noah, and in the terms of the covenant to Abraham, is תָּמִים, of תָּם, from תָּמַם; which hath various significations. When spoken in the abstract, as תָּם is often used, it signifies "simplicity of manners," without craft; which, in the New Testament, is *ἀκακία* [*ἄκακος*, Rom. xvi. 18]. So Jacob is said to be אִישׁ תָּם, Gen. xxv. 27, which we have rendered, "a plain man;" that is, plain-hearted, without guile,—as Christ speaks of Nathanael. Of this sense of the word you have a notable example, 1 Kings xxii. 34, where the man that slew Ahab is said to draw a bow לְתֻמּוֹ, "in his simplicity," which we have rendered, "at a venture;" that is, without any pernicious design in particular. So, Job ix. 21, תָּם is opposed to רָשָׁע; that is, to him that is "unquiet, malicious," and "perverse." Such a man in the New Testament is said to be *ἀνέγκλητος* and *ἄμωμος*,—that is, "one that cannot be justly blamed," or reproved, "for dealing perversely." Many other instances might be given. The word יָשָׁר, which we have commonly rendered "upright," is used also to this purpose; but it is so known that this word in its use in the Scripture goes no farther than "integrity," nor reaches to an absolute perfection, that I shall not need to insist on it.

The words used in the New Testament are chiefly *τέλειος* and *ἄρτιος*, neither of which in their use is restrained to this perfection. Hence James saith, he is *τέλειος*, who bridles his tongue, chap. iii. 2. The word is but once used positively of any man in an indefinite sense; and that is, 1 Cor. ii. 6, where it evidently denotes only men of some growth in the knowledge of the mystery of the gospel. But I shall not farther pursue the words.

[*2dly.*] Two things are contained in this perfection of obedience that is required in our walking with God in the new covenant. The first whereof regards our obedience; the second, the persons obeying.

1*st.* The perfection that respects the obedience itself, or our objective perfection, is that of parts, or the whole of the will and counsel of God as to our obedience. The law or will of God concerning our obedience is perfect; it hath an integrity in it; and we must have respect to all the parts of it that are revealed to us. So David, "I have a respect unto all thy commandments," Ps. cxix. 6. See James ii. 10.

2dly. Subjective perfection, in respect of the person obeying, is his sincerity and freedom from guile,—the uprightness of his heart in his obedience. And this is that which is mainly intended in that expression of being " perfect,"—being upright, without guile, hypocrisy, false or selfish ends,—in singleness and simplicity of heart doing the whole will of God.

This, then, I say, is that perfection of obedience which makes it walking with God. Whatever comes short of this,—if the heart be not upright, without guile, free from hypocrisy and self-ends,—if the obedience be not universal, it is not walking with God. This is a perfection in a tendency to that which is complete; which Paul wished for the Corinthians, 2 Cor. xiii. 9; and which he exhorted the Hebrews to, chap. vi. 1. If we fail in this, or come short of this perfection, by any guile of our hearts, by voluntary retaining any sweet morsel under our tongue, by keeping a knee for Baal, or a bow for Rimmon,—we walk not with God. It is sad to think how many lose all they do or have wrought by coming short in this perfection. One vile lust or other,—love of the world, pride, ambition, idleness, hard-heartedness,—may lose all, spoil all; and men walk contrary to God when they think they walk most with him.

(3.) That our obedience may be walking with God, it is required that it be a constant, progressive motion towards a mark before us. Walking is a constant progress. He that is walking towards a place that he hath in his eye may stumble sometimes, yea, perhaps, and fall also; but yet, whilst his design and endeavour lies towards the place aimed at,—whilst he lies not still when he falls, but gets up again and presses forward,—he is still, from the chief aim of his acting, said to walk that way. But now, let this man sit down, or lie down in the way, you cannot say he is walking; much less can you say that he is walking that way, if he walk quite contrary. So is it in that obedience which is walking with God. " I press forward," saith the apostle, " to the mark," Phil. iii. 14; " I follow after it," chap. iii. 12. And he bids us " so run that we may obtain." There is a constant pressing forwards required in our obedience. Saith David, " I follow hard after God." The enjoyment of God in Christ is the mark before us; our walking is a constant pressing towards it. To fall into, yea, perhaps, fall under, a temptation, hinders not but that a man may still be said to be walking, though he makes no great speed, and though he defiles himself by his fall. It is not every omission of a duty, it is not every commission of sin, that utterly cuts off in the performance of the duty; but to sit down and give over,—to engage in a way, a course of sin,—this is that which is called walking contrary to God, not with him.

(4.) Walking with God, is to walk always as under the eye of God.

Hence it is called "walking before him," before his face, in his sight. The performance of all duties of obedience as under the eye of God, is required unto this walking with him.

Now, there are two ways whereby a man may do all things as under the eye of God:—

[1.] By a general apprehension of God's omniscience and presence, as "all things are open and naked before him," Heb. iv. 12; on this consideration, that he knows all things,—that his understanding is infinite,—that nothing can be hid from him,—that there is no flying out of his presence, Ps. cxxxix. 7, nor hiding from him, the darkness being light to him. Men may have a general persuasion that they are under the eye of God: and this is in the thoughts of all;—I do not say actually, but in respect of the principle of it that lies in them; which, if it may freely act itself, will make them know it and consider it, Ps. xciv. 9; Job xxiv. 23; Prov. xv. 3.

[2.] There is a performance of obedience under the eye of God, as one that is peculiarly concerned in that obedience. God says to David, Ps. xxxii. 8, "'I will guide thee with mine eye.' The consideration of mine eye being upon thee, shall instruct thee, or teach thee in the way which thou shalt go. Mine eye is on thee, as concerned in thy ways and obedience." This is to walk before God,—to consider him as looking on us, as one deeply concerned in all our ways, walking, and obedience.

Now, we consider the Lord as thus concerned, as one from whom we receive,—1*st*, *Direction; 2dly, Protection; 3dly, Examination and trial.*

1*st*. *Direction*. So before,—"I will guide thee with mine eye." Consideration of the eye of God on us, sends us to him for counsel and direction in the whole course of our obedience. If a child walk in any way with his father looking on him, if he be at a loss at any time which way he ought to go, will he not inquire of him who knows, who looks on him in all his ways? Are we at any loss in our way? know we not what to do, or how to steer our course?—[Let us] look to Him whose eye is upon us, and we shall have direction, Prov. xxii. 12.

2*dly*. *Protection* in our walking in our obedience: Ps. xxxiv. 15, His eyes are so upon them, that his ears are open to them, to give them protection and deliverance: so fully, 2 Chron. xvi. 9. This is one end why the eyes of God are upon his and their ways,—that he may show himself strong in their behalf. "I have seen it," he lays at the bottom of all their deliverance.

3*dly*. For *trial and examination:* Ps. xi. 4, 5, His eyes are upon us, for to search and try if there be, as David speaks, any way of wickedness in us. This use he makes of the consideration of the omnipresence and omniscience of God, Ps. cxxxix. 7–18. Having set forth God's intimate knowledge of and acquaintance with him, and all his ways, verses 23, 24, he makes use of it, by appealing to him about his integrity in his obedience. So saith Job to God, "Hast thou eyes of flesh? or seest thou as man seeth?" chap. x. 4; that is, thou dost not. And what is this spoken in reference unto? Even his trying the paths and obedience of the sons of men, verse 6. When our Saviour comes to try, examine, and search the obedience of his churches, he is said to have "eyes of fire," Rev. i. 14. And, in pursuit of it, he still tells his churches, "I know thy works;"—or, "I have not found thee perfect; I have something against thee:"—all arguing a trial and examination of their obedience.

This, I say, is to walk before God, or under his eye,—to consider him looking on us peculiarly, as one concerned in our ways, walking, and obedience; that we may constantly take counsel of him, fly to him for protection, and consider that he weighs and tries all our ways and works, whether they are perfect according to the tenor of the covenant of grace.

Now, there are two things that will certainly follow this consideration of our walking with God, being under his eye and control:—

(1*st.*) Reverential thoughts of him. This God, who is a consuming fire, is nigh to us; his eyes are always on us. "Let us," saith the apostle, "have grace, whereby we may serve him acceptably," Heb. xii. 28, 29. If men order their deportment and carriage, at least, unto a reverential appearance before their rulers or governors, who see only their outside, shall we not have a regard of Him who always hath his eye upon us, searches our hearts, and tries our reins,—the most secret reserve of our souls? But of this afterward.

(2*dly.*) Self-abasement under a sense of our great vileness, and the imperfection of all our services. But both these belong properly to the next consideration,—of what it is to walk humbly with God.

(5.) Our walking with God in our obedience, argues complacency and delight therein, and that we are bound unto God in his ways with the cords of love. He that goes unwillingly, by compulsion, with another, when every step is wearisome and burdensome to him, and his whole heart desires to be discharged of his company, can very improperly be said to walk with him, and no farther than as the mere motion of the body may be so expressed. The Lord walketh with us, and he rejoiceth over us, and in us, Zeph. iii. 17; as also he expresseth his delight in the particular service that we yield unto him, Cant. ii. 14. So also saith the Son and Wisdom of God, Prov. viii. 31; his joy and his delight is in the obedience of the sons of men. Hence are those longing expressions of God after the obedience of his people, "'O that there were such an heart in thee, that thou wouldst fear me! Turn ye, turn ye; when shall it once be!' What have you seen in me, that you are gone away?" And our Saviour, the husband of the church, carries this to the greatest height imaginable, Cant. iv. 9–16. He speaks as one transported by a delight not to be borne, which he receives from the love and obedience of his spouse,—comparing it with things of the highest natural delight, and preferring them far before them.

Now, surely, if God hath this delight in us in our walking before him, is it not expected that our delight should be in him in our obedience? It suits not my present business to go over the testimonies of Scripture, wherein either we are required to delight in the Lord, or have the example of the saints, who did so to the height proposed to us; or to insist on the nature of the delight I speak of. Job makes it a sure mark of a hypocrite, that he "will not," notwithstanding all his obedience, "delight himself in the Almighty," Job xxvii. 10. Only take notice that there is a twofold delight in this matter:—[1.] A delight in the obedience itself, and the duties of it; [2.] A delight in God in that obedience.

[1.] There may be a delight in the duties of obedience, upon some foreign respect, when there is no delight in God in them. A man may delight to go along with another in the way, on the account of some pleasantness in the way, or other occasions which he hath to draw him that way, though he hath no delight at all in the company of him with whom he walks. God tells us of a hypocritical people, that sought him daily, and delighted to know his ways, and took delight in approaching to God, Isa. lviii. 2. And it is said of some, that Ezekiel's ministry was to them as "a cheerful song of one that had a pleasant voice;" wherefore they came and heard and attended on it, when their hearts went after their sins, Ezek. xxxiii. 31, 32. There may be something in the administration of the ordinances of God, in the person administering, in the things administered, which may take the minds of hypocrites, so that they may run after them, and attend to them with great delight and greediness. John "was a burning and a shining light," saith our Saviour to the wicked Jews; and "they were willing for a season to rejoice" (or delight) "in his light," John v. 35. How many have we seen running after sermons, pressing with the multitude, finding sweetness and contentment in the word, who yet have nothing but novelty, or the ability of the preacher, or some outward consideration, for the bottom of their delight!

[2.] There is a delight in God in our obedience,—"Delight thyself in the LORD," saith the psalmist, Ps. xxxvii. 4;—and a delight in obedience and duties, because it is his will, and his ways. When a person aims in every duty to meet with God, to have converse with him, to communicate his soul to him, and to receive refreshment from him; when on this account our duties and all our ways of obedience are sweet and pleasant to us;—then do we in them walk with God. Let not men think, who perform duties with a bondage-frame of spirit; to whom they are weariness and burdensome, but that they dare not omit them; who never examine their hearts whether they meet with God in their duties, or have any delight in so doing;—let them not think, I say, whatever they do, that at all they walk with God.

I shall not insist on more particulars.

Use 1. Of direction. Know that it is a great thing to walk with God as we ought. We heard before how many things were required to render it acceptable; now, some of the things that it consists in. Who, almost, hath prepared his heart to walk with God as he ought? who considers whether his walking be such as it ought to be? Believe me, friends, a formal performance of duties, in a course or a round, from one day, one week to another, both in private and public, may possibly come exceeding short of this walking with God. Men content themselves with a very slight and formal course. So they pray morning and evening; so they take part with some of the people of God against open profane persons; so they keep themselves from such sins as would wound a natural conscience,—all is well with them. Be not deceived, walking with God must have,—

(1.) All the strength and vigour of the soul laid out in it. "Thou shalt love the LORD thy God with all thy heart." The soul and heart of a man is to be in the work; his design and contrivance about it; his contending in it. Form and a course will not do it.

(2.) It is to have the perfection of the new covenant in universality, and sincerity attending it. It is not the doing of this or that thing, but the doing of all things by Christ commanded; not a loving of friends only, but of enemies; not a denial of the ways of ungodly men only, but a denial of self and the world; not a doing hurt to none only, but a doing good to all; not a hatred to evil men's ways only, but a love to their persons; not praying and hearing only,—but giving alms, communicating, showing mercy, exercising loving-kindness in the earth; not a mortification of pride and vanity only, especially if as to others in any outward appearance,—but of envy, wrath, discontent. In a word, it is "perfecting holiness in the fear of the Lord" that is required. If men professing religion, who are almost devoured by world, or flesh, or envy, or faction, or idleness, or uselessness in their generation, would but lay their hearts to the rules we have considered, they would find they had but little cause to hug themselves in their ways and walking.

I might here go over all the particulars that have been insisted on, and try our obedience by them. But,—

Use 2. For others, I shall only ask over the heads of what have been delivered. Would you be thought to walk with God?—

(1.) What evidence have you that you are in covenant with him? that your covenant with hell and death is broken, and that you are taken into the bond of the covenant of grace? What account can you give to God, others, or your own souls, of this your covenant state and condition? How many are at a loss as to this foundation of all walking with God!

(2.) Is your obedience from faith? What evidence have you thereof? Go over all the causes, effects, and adjuncts of a justifying faith, and try whether you have this principle of all acceptable obedience. How hath it been wrought in you? What work of the Spirit have you had upon you? What have been your conviction, humiliation, and conversion? When, how, by what means wrought? Are your hearts purified by it, and are you by it baptized into one Spirit with the people of God? or are you still enemies to them?

(3.) Is your walking universal and perfect, according to the tenor of the covenant? Have you no sweet morsel under your tongue, no beloved lust that is indulged to, that you cannot as yet thoroughly part with? no allowed reserve for sin?

(4.) Do you delight in God in that obedience you yield? or are his ways a burden unto you, that you are scarce able to bear them, —weary of private prayer, of Sabbaths, of all the worship of God? I leave these things with your consciences.

SERMON VII.

WHAT it is to walk with God hath been declared.

II. What is added thereunto of duty, in this qualification, comes nextly to be considered.

Amongst the many eminent qualifications of the obedience of believers, we shall find, in the issue, this to stand in the forefront, among the chiefest (the words in the original are, וְהַצְנֵעַ לֶכֶת): To "humble thyself in walking," or, to "walk with God."

A man would think that it is such an honour and advancement, that a poor sinful creature should be taken into the company of the great God, to walk with him, that he had need be exhorted to take upon him great thoughts of himself, that he may be prepared for it. "Is it a light matter," says David, "to be son-in-law to a king?" "Is it a light matter to walk with God? How had the heart of a man need to be lifted up, which hath such apprehensions of its condition!" The matter is quite otherwise. He that would have his heart exalted up to God, must bring it down in itself. There is a pride in every man's heart by nature, lifting him up, and swelling him until he is too high and big for God to walk with.

Now, whereas there are two things in our walking with God considerable:—first, The inward power of it; and, secondly, The outward privilege of it, in an orderly admittance to the duties of it;—the former alone is that which edifieth us in this duty; the latter puffeth up. These Jews here, and their successors the Pharisees, having the privilege of performing the outward duty of walking with God, were, as Capernaum, lifted up unto heaven; and, trusting in themselves that they were righteous, they despised others;—of all men, therefore, they were most abhorred of God. This is that which the Holy Ghost beats them from,—resting in the privilege to come up to the power. God tells us of the prince of Tyrus, that he set his heart as the heart of God, Ezek. xxviii. 6;—he would be on even terms with him, independent, the author of his own good, fearless. So, in some measure, is the heart of every man by nature; which, indeed, is not to be like God, but the devil.

To prevent this evil, I shall inquire, what it is that is here required of us, under these two heads:—1. What it is in reference whereunto we are to humble ourselves in walking with God; 2. How we are to do it:—

1. There are two things that we are to humble ourselves unto in our walking with God:—(1.) The law of his grace? (2.) The law of his providence:—

(1.) In all our walking with God, we are to humble ourselves in bowing to the law and rule of his grace; which is the way that he hath revealed wherein he will walk with sinners. The apostle tells us of the Jews in sundry places, that they had a mind to walk with God; they had "a zeal for God." So he had himself in his Pharisaism, Phil. iii. 6. He "was zealous towards God," Acts xxii. 3; and so were the Jews, Rom. x. 2, "I bear them record, they have a zeal of God." And they followed after righteousness, "the law of righteousness," chap. ix. 31; they took pains to "establish their righteousness," chap. x. 3. What can be more required to walking with God than a zeal for him,—for his laws and ways, and a diligent endeavour to attain a righteousness before him? How few do we see attain thus much! What repute have they in the world that do so? But yet, saith the apostle, they did not attain to walk with God, nor the righteousness they sought after, chap. ix. 31. But what is the reason of it? Why, in their attempt to walk with God, they did not bow themselves to the law of his grace. So chap. x. 3; they went about to establish their own righteousness, and did not submit themselves to the righteousness of God. What righteousness is that? Why, "the righteousness of faith," according to the law of grace, Rom. i. 17. "They sought it not by faith, but as it were by the works of the law," chap. ix. 32. And the ground of all this is discovered, verse 33. Behold, here are two effects of Christ towards several persons: some stumble at him, and so are not able to walk on with God. Who are they? He tells you, verse 32. Some are not ashamed. Who are they? They that believe, and so submit to the law of God's grace. It is evident, then, that men may labour to walk with God, and yet stumble and fall, for want of this humbling themselves to the law of his grace.

Let us see, then, how that may be done, and what is required thereunto. It is, then, required,—

[1.] That the bottom of all a man's obedience lie in this,—that in himself he is a lost, undone creature, an object of wrath, and that whatever he have of God in any kind, he must have it in a way of mere mercy and grace. To this apprehension of himself must proud man, that would fain have something of his own, humble himself. God abhors every one that he sees coming towards him on any other account. Our Saviour Christ lets men know what they are, and what they must be, if they will come to God by him. "I came," saith he, "to save that which was lost," Matt. xviii. 11. "I came not to call the righteous, but sinners to repentance," Matt. ix. 13. Verse 12, "The whole have no need of a physician, but they that are sick." "I came into the world," says he, "that they that are blind may see, and that they which see might be made blind," John ix. 39. This is the sum: "If you intend to have any thing to do with God by me, know yourselves to be lost sinners, blind, sick,—dead; so that whatever you have, you must have it in a way of mere grace."

And how was this direction followed by Paul? Will you see the foundation of his obedience? You have it, 1 Tim. i. 13–15, "I was thus and thus: I am the chief of sinners; 'but I obtained mercy.' It is mere mercy and grace upon the account whereof I have any thing from God:"—which principle he improves to the height, Phil. iii. 7–9, "All loss, all dung; Christ is all in all." This the proud Pharisees could not submit unto. It is the subject of much of their disputes with our Saviour. To be lost, blind, nothing,—they could not endure to hear. Were they not children of Abraham? Did they not do so and so? To tell them that they are lost and nothing, is but to speak out of envy. And on this rock do thousands split themselves, in the days wherein we live. When they are overpowered by any conviction to an apprehension of a necessity of walking with God (as more or less, at one time or other, by one means or other, most men are), they then set themselves on the performance of the duties they have neglected, and of the obedience which they think acceptable, abiding in that course whilst their conviction abides; but never humbling themselves to this part of the law of God's grace,—to be vile, miserable, lost, cursed, hopeless in themselves;—never making thorough work of it. They lay the foundation of their obedience in a quagmire, whose bottom should have been digged into; and stumble at the stumbling-stone, in their first attempt to walk with God.

Now, there are two evils attending the mere performance of this duty, which utterly disappoint all men's attempts for walking with God:—

1*st.* That men without it will go forth, somewhat, at least, in their own strength, to walk with God. "Why," say the Pharisees, "can we do nothing? 'Are we blind also?'" Acting in the power of self will cleave to such a one, so as not to be separated; it will steal upon him in every duty he goes about. Now, nothing is more universally opposite to the whole nature of gospel obedience than this, that a man should perform the least of it in his own strength, without an actual influence of life and power from God in Christ. "Without me," says Christ, "ye can do nothing," John xv. 5. All that is done without strength from him, is nothing. God works in us "to will and to do of his good pleasure," Phil. ii. 13. Whatever a man doth, which God works not in him, which he receives not strength for from Christ, is all lost, all perishing. Now, our fetching in of strength from Christ for every duty, is founded wholly in that subjection to the law of grace whereof we speak.

2*dly.* His obedience will build him up in that state wherein he is, or edify him towards hell and destruction:—of which more afterward.

[2.] The second thing that we are to humble ourselves unto in the law of grace is, a firm persuasion, exerting itself effectually in all our obedience, that there is not a righteousness to be obtained before God by the performance of any duties or obedience of ours whatever. That this lies in the law of the grace of God, the apostle disputes at large, Rom. iv. 13–15, "If," saith he, "righteousness be by the law,"—that is, by our obedience to God according to the law,—"then faith and the promise serve to no purpose;" there is an inconsistency between the law of grace (that is, of faith and the promise) and the obtaining of a righteousness before God by our obedience. So Gal. ii. 21, "If righteousness were by the law, then Christ is dead in vain." "You would walk with God according to his mind; you would please him in Jesus Christ. What do you do? You strive to perform the duties required at your hand, that on their account you may be accepted as righteous with God. I tell you," saith the apostle, "if this be the state of things, 'Christ is dead in vain:' if this be a righteousness before God to be obtained by any thing you can do, the gospel is to no purpose."

And this, also, is the proud heart of man to humble himself to, if he will walk with God;—he must obey, he must perform duties, he must be holy, he must abstain from every sin; and that, all, under a quick, living, energetical persuasion, that by these things a righteousness before God is not to be obtained. This is to influence all your duties, to steer you in your whole course of obedience, and to accompany you in every act of it. How few are influenced with this persuasion in their walking with God! Do not most men proceed on other practical principles? Is not their great reserve for their appearance before God hewed out of their own obedience? God knows they walk not with him.

[3.] In the midst of all our obedience which is our own, we must believe and accept of a righteousness which is not our own, nor at all wrought or procured by us; of which we have no assurance that there is any such thing, but by the faith we have in the promise of God: and thereupon, renouncing all that is in or of ourselves, we must merely and solely rest on that for righteousness and acceptance with God. This the apostle affirms his heart to be humbled unto, Phil. iii. 7–9, the place before mentioned. He reckons up all his own duties,—is encompassed with them,—sees them lying in great abundance on every hand; every one of them offering its assistance, perhaps painting its face, and crying that it is "gain;" but saith the apostle, "'You are all loss and dung;' I look for another righteousness than any you can give me."

Man sees and knows his own duty, his own righteousness and walking with God; he seeth what it costs and stands him in; he knows what pains he hath taken about it; what waiting, fasting, labouring, praying it hath cost him; how he hath cut himself short of his natural desires, and mortified his flesh in abstinence from sin. These are the things of a man, wrought in him, performed by him; and the spirit of a man knows them; and they will promise fair to the heart of a man that hath been sincere in them, for any end and purpose that he shall use them. But now, for the righteousness of Christ,—that is without him; he seeth it not, experiences it not; the spirit that is within him knows nothing of it; he hath no acquaintance with it, but merely as it is revealed and proposed in the promises, wherein yet it is nowhere said to him, in particular, that it is his, and was provided for him, but only that it is so, to and for believers. Now, for a man to cast away that which he hath seen, for that which he hath not seen; to refuse that which promises to give him a fair entertainment and supportment in the presence of God, and which he is sure is his own, and cannot be taken from him, for that which he must venture on upon the word of promise, against ten thousand doubts, and fears, and temptations that it belongs not to him;—this requires humbling of the soul before God; and this the heart of a man is not easily brought unto. Every man must make a venture for his future state and condition. The question only is, upon what he shall venture it? Our own obedience is at hand, and promises fairly to give assistance and help: for a man, therefore, wholly to cast it aside upon the naked promise of God to receive him in Christ, is a thing that the heart of man must be humbled unto. There is nothing in a man that will not dispute against this captivity of itself: innumerable proud reasonings and imaginations are set up against it; and when the mind and discursive, notional part of the soul is overpowered with the truth, yet the practical principle of the will and the affections will exceedingly tumultuate against it. But this is the law of God's grace, which must be submitted unto, if we will walk with him;—the most holy, wise, and zealous, who have yielded the most constant obedience unto God,—whose good works and godly conversation have shone as lights in the world,—must cast down all these crowns at the foot of Jesus, renounce all for him, and the righteousness that he hath wrought out for us. All must be sold for the pearl;—all parted with for Christ. In the strictest course of exactest obedience in us, we are to look for a righteousness wholly without us.

[4.] We must humble ourselves to place our obedience on a new foot of account, and yet to pursue it with no less diligence than if it stood upon the old. Eph. ii. 8–10, "By grace are ye saved through faith; and that not of yourselves: it is the gift of God: not of works, lest any man should boast. For we are his workmanship, created in Christ Jesus unto good works, which God hath before ordained that we should walk in them." "If not of works, then what need of works any more? The first end appointed to our obedience was, that we might be saved. This end, it seems, is taken away: our works and duties are excluded from any efficiency in compassing of that end; for if it be of works, 'then grace is no more grace,' Gal. ii. 21. Then let us lay all works and obedience aside, and sin, that grace may abound." That many did, that many do, make this use of the grace of God, is most evident; so turning it into lasciviousness. "But," saith the apostle, "there is more to be said about works than so. Their legal end is changed, and the old foundation they stood upon is taken away. But there is a new constitution making them necessary,—a new obligation, requiring them no less exactly of us than the former did, before it was disannulled." So Eph. ii. 10, "'We are his workmanship, created in Christ Jesus unto good works.' God saving us by grace, hath, on that account, appointed that we should walk in obedience. There is this difference:—before, I was to perform good works because I was to be saved by them; now, because I am saved without them." God saving us in Christ, by grace, hath appointed that we shall perform that in a way of acknowledgment of our free salvation, which before we were to do to be saved. Though works left no room at all for grace, yet grace leaves room for works, though not the same they had before grace came. This, then, are we to humble ourselves to,—to be as diligent in good works, and all duties of obedience, because we are saved without them, as we could be to be saved by them. He that walks with God must humble his soul to place all his obedience on this foot of account. He hath saved us freely; only let our conversation be as beseemeth the gospel. How this principle is effectual in believers, as to the crucifying of all sin, Paul declares, Rom. vi. 14, " Sin shall not have dominion over you: for ye are not under the law, but under grace." The argument to carnal reason would lie quite contrary. " If we are not under the law,—that is, the condemning power of the law,—then let sin have its dominion, power, sway. Did not the law forbid sin, under pain of damnation?—' Cursed is every one that continueth not,' etc. Did not the law command obedience with the promise of salvation?—' The man that doth the things of it shall live therein.' If, then, the law be taken away from having power over us to these ends and purposes, as to forbid sin with terror of damnation, and command obedience for righteousness and salvation, what need we perform the one or avoid the other?" " Why, upon this account," saith the apostle, " that we are under grace; which, with new ends, and on new motives and considerations, requires the one and forbids the other."

Have we now, or do we constantly humble ourselves to this part of the law of God's grace,—that we build up and establish our obedience on grace, and not on the law; on motives of love, not fear; from what God hath done for us in Christ, rather than from what we expect,—because " eternal life is the gift of God, through Jesus Christ our Lord?"

[5.] We are to humble ourselves to this,—that we address ourselves to the performance of the greatest duties, being fully persuaded that we have no strength for the least. This is that which lies so cross to flesh and blood, that our souls must be humbled to it if ever we are brought to it; and yet without this there is no walking with God. There are great and mighty duties to be performed in our walking with God in a way of gospel obedience: there is cutting off right hands, plucking out right eyes; denying, yea, comparatively, hating father, mother, and all relations; dying for Christ, laying down our lives for the brethren; crucifying the flesh, cutting short all earthly desires, keeping the body in subjection, bearing the cross, self-denial, and the like;—which, when they come to be put in practice, will be found to be great and mighty duties. This is required in the law of grace,—that we undertake and go through with these all our days, with a full assurance and persuasion that we have not strength of ourselves, or in ourselves, to perform the least of them. "We are not sufficient of ourselves," saith the apostle, 2 Cor. iii. 5. We cannot think a good thought. Without Christ we can do nothing, John xv. 5. This, to a carnal heart, looks like making of brick without straw. "A hard saying it is, who can bear it?" May not men sit down and say, "Why doth he yet complain? Is he not austere, reaping where he hath not sown? Are his ways equal?" Yea, most equal, righteous, and gracious; for this is the design of his thus dealing with us, that upon our addressing ourselves to any duty, we should look to him from whom are all our supplies, and thereby receive strength for what we have to do. How unable was Peter to walk upon the water! Yet, when Christ bids him come, he ventures in the midst of the sea; and with the command hath strength communicated to support him. God may call us to do or suffer what he pleases, so that his call have an efficacy with it to communicate strength for the performance of what he calls us to, Phil. i. 29.

This, I say, are we to humble ourselves unto,—not only in the general to reckon that the duties that are required of us are not proportioned to the strength residing in us, but to the supply laid up for us in Christ; but also to lie under such an actual conclusion in every particular duty that we address ourselves to. This, in civil and natural things, were the greatest madness in the world; nor is it needful that you should add any farther discouragement to a man from attempting any thing, than to convince him that he hath no strength or ability to perform or go through with it. Once persuade him of that, and there is an end of all endeavours; for who will wear out himself about that which it is impossible he should attain? It is otherwise in spirituals: God may require any thing of us that there is strength laid up in Christ for, enough to enable us to perform it; and we may by faith attempt any duty, though never so great, if there be grace to be obtained for it from Christ. Hence is that enumeration of the great things done by believers through faith,—utterly beyond their own strength and power, Heb. xi. 33, 34, "Out of weakness were made strong." When they entered upon the duty, they were weakness itself; but in the performance of it grew strong, by the supply that was administered. So we are said to come to Christ to "find grace to help in time of need," Heb. iv. 16,—when we need it, as going about that which we have no might nor power for.

This is the way to walk with God,—to be ready and willing to undergo any duty, though never so much above or beyond our strength, so we can see that in Christ there is a supply. The truth is, he that shall consider what God requires of believers, would think them to have a stock of spiritual strength like that of Samson's, since they are to fight with principalities and powers, contend against the world, and self, and what not; and he that shall look upon them will quickly see their weakness and inability. Here lies the mystery of it,—the duties required of them are proportioned to the grace laid up for them in Christ,—not to what they are at any time themselves intrusted withal.

[6.] This, also, is another thing we are to humble ourselves unto,—to be contented to have the sharpest afflictions accompanying and attending the strictest obedience. Men walking closely with God, may perhaps have some secret reserves for freedom from trouble in this life: hence they are apt to think strange of a fiery trial, 1 Pet. iv. 12; and therefore, when it comes upon them, they are troubled, perplexed, and know not what it means; especially if they see others prospering, and at rest in the land, who know not God. Their estates are ruined, names blasted, bodies afflicted with violent diseases, children taken away, or turning profligate and rebellious, life in danger every hour,—perhaps killed all the day long: hereupon they are ready to cry, with Hezekiah, Isa. xxxviii. 3, "LORD, remember;" or to contend about the business, as Job did, being troubled that he was disappointed in his expectation of dying in his nest. But this frame is utterly contrary to the law of the grace of God; which is, that the children that he receives are to be chastised, Heb. xii. 6; that they are to undergo whatever chastening he will call them to: for, having made the Captain of their salvation perfect through all manner of sufferings, he will make his conformable to him. This, I say, is part of the law of the grace of God, that in the choicest obedience we willingly undergo the greatest afflictions. The management of this principle between God and Job were worth while to consider; for although he disputed long, yet God left him not until he brought him to own it, and to submit unto it with all his heart. This will farther appear in our second head, about submitting to the law of the providence of God. The truth is, to help our poor weak hearts in this business, to prevent all sinful repinings, disputes, and the like, he hath laid in such provision of principles as may render the receiving of it sweet and easy to us; as,—

1*st.* That he doth not correct us for his pleasure, but that he may make us partakers of his holiness: so that we are not in heaviness unless it be needful for us; which we may rest upon, when we neither see the cause nor the particular of our visitation;—then, on this account we may rest on his sovereign will and wisdom.

2*dly.* That he will make all things work together for our good.

This takes the poison out of every cup we are to drink, yea, all the bitterness of it. We have concernments that lie above all that here we can undergo or suffer; and if all work for our advantage and improvement, why should they not be welcome to us?

3dly. That conformity and likeness to Jesus Christ is hereby to be attained; and sundry other principles there are given out, to prevail with our hearts to submit and humble our souls to this part of the law of God's grace: which is a thing that the devil never thought Job would have done, and was therefore restless until it was put to the trial; but he was disappointed and conquered, and his condemnation aggravated.

And this is the first thing required of us,—namely, that we humble ourselves to the law of the grace of God.

Use 1. Let us now take some brief account of ourselves, whether we do so or no. We perform duties, and so seem to walk with God; but,—

(1.) Is the bottom of our obedience a deep apprehension and a full conviction of our own vileness and nothingness,—of our being the chief of sinners, lost and undone; so that we always lie at the foot of sovereign grace and mercy? Is it so? Then, when, how, by what means, was this apprehension brought upon us? I intend not a general notion that we are sinners; but a particular apprehension of our lost, undone condition, with suitable affections thereunto. Do we cry to the Lord out of the depths? or is the end of our obedience to keep ourselves out of such a condition? I am afraid many amongst us, could we, or themselves, by any means dive into the depths of their hearts, would be found to yield their obedience unto God merely on the account of keeping them out of the condition which they must be brought unto before they can yield any acceptable obedience to him. If we think at all to walk with God, let us be clear in this, that such a sense and apprehension of ourselves lies at the bottom of it,—"Of sinners I am chief."

(2.) Doth this always abide in our thoughts, and upon our spirits, —that, by all we have done, do, or can do, we cannot obtain righteousness to stand in the presence of God; so that in the secret reserves of our hearts we place none of our righteousness on that account? Can we be content to suffer loss in all our obedience, as to an end of righteousness? and do we appear before God simply on another head, as if there were no such thing as our own obedience in the world? Herein, indeed, lies the great mystery of gospel obedience,—that we pursue it with all our strength and might, with all the vigour of our souls, and labour to abound in it, like the angels in theirs,—perfecting holiness in the fear of the Lord; and yet, in point of the acceptation of our persons, to have no more regard unto it than if we had yielded no more obedience than the thief on the cross.

(3.) Do we, then, humble ourselves to accept of the righteousness that God in Christ hath provided for us? It is a common working of the heart of them whom God is drawing to himself;—they dare not close with the promise, they dare not accept of Christ and his righteousness,—it would be presumption in them. And the answer is common,—that indeed this is not fear and humility, but pride. Men know not how to humble themselves to a righteousness purely without them, on the testimony of God: the heart is not willing to it; we would willingly establish our own righteousness, and not submit to the righteousness of God. But how is it with our souls? Are we clear in this great point, or no? If we are not, we are at best shuffling with God;—we walk not with him. He admits none into his company, but expressly on the terms of taking this righteousness that he hath provided; and his soul loathes them that would tender him any thing in the room thereof, as men engaged to set up their wisdom and righteousness against his. But I must conclude.

Use 2. If all these things are required to our walking with God, where shall they appear, what shall be their lot and portion, who take no thought about these things? Some we see visibly to walk contrary to him, having no regard to him at all, nor considering their latter end. Others have some checks of conscience,—that think to cure these distempers and eruptions of sin with a loose cry of "God be merciful to them." Some go a little farther,—to take care of the performance of duties; but they seek not God in a due manner, and he will make a breach upon them. The Lord awaken them all before it be too late!

SERMON VIII.

WHAT it is to humble ourselves to the law of God's grace, you have heard.

(2.) I come now to show what it is to humble ourselves to the law of his providence.

By the law of providence, I intend, God's sovereign disposal of all the concernments of men in this world, in the variety, order, and manner which he pleaseth, according to the rule and infinite reason of his own goodness, wisdom, righteousness, and truth.

[1.] To evince what it is to humble ourselves to this law, some general observations must be given. And,—

1*st*. There is, and ever was, somewhat, very much, in God's providential administration of the things of this world, and the concernments of the sons of men therein, which the most improved reason of men cannot reach unto, and which is contrary to all that is in us, as merely men;—of judgment, affections, or what else soever we are acted by.

"Thy judgments," saith David unto God, "are far above out of his sight," Ps. x. 5; that is, of the man he is speaking of: he is not able to see the ground and reason, the order and beauty of them. And Ps. xxxvi. 6, "Thy righteousness is like a great mountain, and thy judgments are a great deep;" that is, as the sea, which none can look into the bottom of, nor know what is done in the caverns thereof. So that there is a height in the judgments of God not to be measured, and a depth not to be fathomed. Men cannot look into his ways. So also Ps. lxxvii. 19, "Thy way is in the sea, and thy path in the great waters, and thy footsteps are not known." Men must be content to stand at the shore, and admire at the works of God; but as to the beauty and excellency of them, they cannot search them out. To this purpose discourseth Zophar, in Job xi. 7–12. It is of the excellency and perfection of God in his works of providence that he is speaking; in the consideration of whose unsearchableness, he closes with that of verse 12, "Vain man would know the secrets of the counsels of God, the reason of his ways; but, in his attempts after it, he is as an ass, as a wild ass, as the colt of a wild ass;"—than which nothing could be spoken with more contempt, to abase the pride of a poor creature.

The ways of God are, we know, all perfect. He is our rock; and his work is perfect: nothing can be added to them, nor taken from them; yea, they are all comely and beautiful in their season. There is not any thing comes out from him, but it is from wonderful counsel; and all his ways will at length be found to praise him. But, as Job speaks, chap. ix. 11, we perceive it not,—we take no notice of it; for who hath known his mind, or been his counsellor? Rom. xi. 33, 34.

Hence, not only the heathen were entangled in the consideration of the works of providence,—some, upon it, turning Atheists; most, ascribing all things to blind, uncertain *chance* and *contingency;* and others (very few) labouring to set a lustre upon what they could not understand,—but we have the people of God themselves disputing with him about the equality of his ways; bringing arguments against it, and contending against his wisdom in them: "Ye say, The way of the LORD is not equal," Ezek. xviii. 25. And again are they at it, chap. xxxiii. 20, "Yet ye say, The way of the LORD is not equal." Yea, not only the common people, but the choicest of God's servants, under the Old Testament, were exceedingly exercised with this, that they could not oftentimes see the beauty and excellency, nor understand the reason or order, of God's dispensations; which I might prove at large, in the instances of Job, David, Heman, Jeremiah, Habakkuk, and others. Yea, there was nothing that God was more put to, in dealing with his people of old, than to justify the righteousness and perfections of his providential dispensations against their unjust, unbelieving complaints and manners.

This, then, being the condition of God's providential dispensations in general,—that there is much in them, not only above us, and unsearchable to us, as to the reason and beauty of his ways, but also contrary to all that is in us of reason, judgment, or affections; there is surely need of humbling our souls to the law of this providence, if we intend to walk with him. Neither is there any other way to come to an agreement with him, or to quiet our hearts from repining.

2dly. There are four things in God's providential disposing of the things and concernments of men in the world that require this humbling of ourselves to him, as being no way able to grapple with him:—(*1st.*) Visible confusion; (*2dly.*) Unspeakable variety; (*3dly.*) Sudden alterations; (*4thly.*) Deep distresses.

(*1st.*) Visible confusion,—like that mentioned, Isa. viii. 22. He that takes a view of the general state of things in the world, will see nothing but trouble, darkness, and anguish; "yea, darkness cover the earth, and gross darkness the people." The oppression of tyrants, wasting of nations, destruction of men and beasts, fury and desolations, make up the things of the past and present ages;—the greatest and choicest parts of the earth, in the meantime, inhabited by them that know not God,—that hate him, that fill and replenish the world with habitations of cruelty, sporting themselves in mischief, like the leviathan in the sea. In respect hereof, God is said to make "darkness his secret place" and his pavilion, Ps. xviii. 11; and to "dwell in the thick darkness," 2 Chron. vi. 1;—and to wait for the issue of this dispensation, to humble themselves to the law of it, is the patience and wisdom of the saints. See Hab. ii. 1.

(*2dly.*) Unspeakable variety. Not to insist on particulars, the case of the saints throughout the world is the only instance I shall mention, and that on a twofold account:—

[*1st.*] Compared among themselves, in what unspeakable variety are they dealt withal! some under persecution always,—some always at peace; some in dungeons and prisons,—some at liberty in their own houses; the saints of one nation under great oppression for many ages,—of another, in quietness; in the same places some poor, in great distress, put hard to it for daily bread all their lives,—others abounding in all things; some full of various afflictions, going softly and mourning all their days,—others spared, and scarce touched with the rod at all;—and yet, commonly, the advantage of holiness and close walking with God lying on the distressed side. How doth God deal, also, with families in respect of grace, while he takes one whole family into covenant, and leaves out another whole family, whose heads and springs are no less holy? He comes into a house, and takes one, and leaves another;—takes a despised outcast, and leaves a darling. Of them, also, some are wise, endowed with great gifts and abilities;—others weak to contempt and reproach. Who can, now, with an eye of reason, look upon them, and say they are all the children of one Father, and that he loves them all alike? Should you come into a great house, and see some children in scarlet, having all things needful, others hewing wood and drawing water,—you would conclude that they are not all children, but some children, some slaves: but when it shall be told you that they are all one man's children; and that the hewers of wood, that live on the bread and water of affliction, and go in tattered rags, are as dear to him as the other; and that he intends to leave them as good an inheritance as any of the rest;—if you intend not to question the wisdom and goodness of the father of the family, you must resolve to submit to his authority with a quiet subjection of mind. So is it in the great family of God; nothing will quiet our souls, but humbling ourselves to the law of his providence.

[2*dly.*] Comparing them with others was the hard case of old; the pleading whereof by Job, David, Jeremiah, and Habakkuk, is so known, that I shall not need farther to insist upon it.

I shall not farther manifest this from the variety which is in the dispensations of God towards the men of the world, which the wisest of men can reduce to no rule of righteousness, as things pass among us. Solomon acquaints us with it, Eccles. ix. 11. Things are disposed of according to no rule that we may fix our expectations on; which ruined the reason of that mirror of mankind, in a natural condition, Marcus Brutus, and made him cry out, Ὦ τλῆμον ἀρετή.

(3*dly.*) Sudden alterations. As in the case of Job, God takes a man whom he hath blessed with choice of blessings, in the midst of a course of obedience and close walking with himself, when he expected to die in his nest, and to see good all his days;—ruins him in a moment; blasts his name, that he who was esteemed a choice saint, shall not be able to deliver himself from the common esteem of a hypocrite; slays his children; takes away his rest, health, and every thing that is desirable to him. This amazes the soul; it knows not what God is doing, nor why he pleads with it in so much bitterness. A man that either is, or may fall into such a condition, will find that he will never be able to walk with God in it, without humbling himself to the law of his providence.

(4*thly.*) Great, deep, and abiding distresses have the same effects with sudden alterations;—of which more afterwards.

And these are, in general, some of the things in God's providential disposal of the things of men in this world, that are too hard and wonderful for flesh and blood; wherein his paths are in the deep; which are contrary to all rules of procedure that he hath given us to judge by, who are to judge of things but once, he being to call all things to a second account.

[2.] Having given these two observations, I return to what I first proposed,—namely, the duty of humbling ourselves to the law of the providence of God, so far as it concerns us in particular.

I do not intend merely that men, in general, should be content with the dealings of God in the world; but that we should humble our hearts to him in what falls to be our share therein, though it come under any one or more of the heads of difficulty before mentioned. Our lots are various in this world: how they may be farther different before we go out of it we know not. Some are in one condition,—some in another. That we envy not one another, nor any in the world; that we repine not at God, nor charge him foolishly,—is that I aim at;—a thing sufficiently necessary in these days, wherein good men are too little able to bear their own condition, if in any thing it differs from [that of] others.

The next thing, then, is, to consider how and wherein we are to humble ourselves to the law of the providence of God. There are things on this account which our souls are to be humbled unto:—

First. His sovereignty. May he not do what he will with his own? This is so argued out in Job that I shall need to go no farther for the confirmation of it. See chap. xxxiii. 8–13. The words are the sum of what was, or was apprehended to be, the complaint of Job,—that in the midst of his innocency and course of obedience, God dealt hardly with him, and brought him into great distresses. What is the reply hereunto? Verse 12, "Behold, in this thou art not just." It is a most unequal thing for any man to make any such complaints. Whether Job did so or not, may be disputed; but for any one to do so, is certainly most unjust. But on what ground is that asserted? See the words following: "'God is greater than man; why strivest thou with him?' It is to no purpose to contend with him that is mightier than thou. And it is likewise unjust to do it with him, who is infinitely and incomparably so, upon the account of his absolute dominion and sovereignty. 'For,' saith he, 'He giveth no account of his matters.' He disposeth of all things as he will, and as he pleaseth." This is pursued to the utmost, chap. xxxiv. 18, 19. Men will not be forward openly to revile or repine against their governors; and what shall be said of God, who is infinitely exalted above them? Hence you have the conclusion of the whole matter, verses 31–33.

This, I say, is the first thing that we are to humble ourselves unto. Let us lay our mouths in the dust, and ourselves on the ground, and say, " It is the Lord; I will be silent, because he hath done it. He is of one mind, and who can turn him? He doth whatever he pleaseth. Am not I in his hand as clay in the hand of the potter? May he not make what kind of vessel he pleases? When I was not, he brought me out of nothing by his word. What I am, or have, is merely of his pleasure. Oh, let my heart and thoughts be full of deep subjection to his supreme dominion and uncontrollable sovereignty over me!" This quieted Aaron in his great distress; and David in his, 2 Sam. xv. 25, 26; and Job in his. It is pleaded by the Lord, Jer. x., Rom. ix. 11, and innumerable other places. If we intend to walk with God, we must humble ourselves to this, and therein we shall find rest.

Second. His wisdom. He is wise also, as he speaks in derision of men's pretending to be so; indeed, God is only wise. Now, he hath undertaken to make "all things work together for good to them that love him," Rom. viii. 28;—that we shall not be in heaviness unless it be needful, 1 Pet. i. 6. In many dispensations of his providence we are at a loss,—we cannot measure them by that rule. We see not how this state or condition can be good for the church in general, or us in particular. We suppose it would be more for his glory, and our advantage, if things were otherwise disposed. Innumerable are the reasonings of the hearts of the sons of men on this account; we know not the thoughts of our own souls herein, how vile they are. God will have us humble ourselves to his wisdom in all his dispensations, and to captivate our understandings thereunto. So Isa. xl. 27, 28. This is that which our hearts are to rest in, when ready to repine,—there is no end of his understanding; he sees all things, in all their causes, effects, circumstances,—in their utmost reach, tendency, and correspondency. We walk in a shade, and know nothing of what is before us. The day will come when we shall see one thing set against another, and infinite wisdom shining out in them all; that all things were done in number, weight, and measure; that nothing could have been otherwise than it is disposed of, without the abridgment of the glory of God and the good of his church. Yea, I dare say, that there is no saint of God, that is distressed by any dispensation of providence, but that, if he will seriously and impartially consider his own state and condition, the frame of his heart, his temptations, and ways, with so much of the aims and ends of the Lord as will assuredly be discovered to faith and prayer, but he will have some rays and beams of infinite wisdom shining in it, tempered with love, goodness, and faithfulness. But whether for the present we have this light or not, or are left unto darkness, this is the haven and rest of our tossed souls, the ark and bosom of our peace,—to humble our souls to the infinite wisdom of God in all his procedure; and on that account quietly to commit all things to his management.

Third. His righteousness. Though God will have us acquiesce in his sovereignty, when we can see nothing else, yet he will have us know that all his ways are equal and righteous. The holy God will do no iniquity. That he is righteous in all his ways, and holy in all his works, is pleaded as much as any thing that he hath discovered of himself: "Shall not the Judge of all the earth do right?" Is God unjust who inflicteth vengeance? God forbid. The righteousness of God—all which springeth from, and is reduced to, the universal rectitude of his nature, in respect of the works that he doth—is manifold. It is that which is called "Justitia regiminis,"—his righteousness in rule or government, in the dispensation of rewards and punishments, —that I am speaking of. Now, because we are not able to discern it in many particulars of his proceedings, to help us in humbling our souls unto it, take these considerations:—

First. That God judgeth not as man judgeth. Man judgeth according to the seeing of the eye, and the hearing of the ear; but God searcheth the heart. Little do we know what is in the heart of men; —what transactions there are or have been between God and them, which, if they were drawn forth, as they shall be one day, the righteousness of God in his procedure would shine as the sun. Rest on this,—we know much less of the matter on the account whereof God judgeth, than we do of the rule whereby he judges. Most things are to him otherwise than to us.

Secondly. God is the great Judge of all the world,—not of this or that particular place; and so disposeth of all as may tend to the good of the whole, and his glory in the universality of things. Our thoughts are bounded—much more our observation and knowledge—within a very narrow compass. That may seem deformed unto us which, when it lies under an eye that at once hath a prospect of the whole, is full of beauty and order. He that was able to see at once but some one small part of a goodly statue, might think it a deformed piece; when he that sees it altogether is assured of its due proportion and comeliness. All things in all places, of the ages past and to come, lie at once naked before God; and he disposes of them so as that, in their contexture and answer one to another, they shall be full of order;— which is properly righteousness.

Thirdly. God judges here, not by any final, determinate sentence, but in a way of preparation to a judgment to come. This unties all knots, and solves all difficulties whatever. This makes righteous and beautiful the deepest distresses of the godly, and the highest advancements of wicked men. And there let our souls rest themselves in quietness, Acts xvii.

Fourthly. His goodness, kindness, love, tenderness. Our souls must submit themselves to believe all these to be in all God's dispensations. I shall but name that one place wherein the apostle disputes for it, Heb. xii. 1–6; and add that wherewith Hosea closes his declaration of God's various dispensations and dealings with his people, chap. xiv. 9.

This, now, it is to humble our souls to the law of God's providence in all his dispensations,—to fall down before his sovereignty, wisdom, righteousness, goodness, love, and mercy. And without this frame of heart, there is no walking with God; unless we intend to come into his presence to quarrel with him,—which will not be for our advantage.

This was Paul's frame, Phil. iv. 11, "I have *learned* it," saith he; "it is not in me by nature, but I have now learned it by faith, I have humbled my soul to it," (ἐν οἷς εἰμι,)—"in the things, state, condition, good or bad, high or low, at liberty or in prison, respected or despised, in health or sickness, living or dying," (ἐν οἷς εἰμι,) "therein to bow myself to the law of the good providence of God; which is contentment." So was it also with David. Ps. cxxxi. 1: He did not exercise himself, or trouble himself, about the ways and works of God that were too high and too hard for him. How, then, did he behave himself? Verse 2: Something in his heart would have been inquiring after those things; but he quieted himself, and humbled his soul to the law of the providence of God, which hath that comfortable issue mentioned, verse 3,—an exhortation not to dispute the ways of God, but to hope and trust in him, on the account mentioned before. This is also the advice that James gives to believers of all sorts, chap. i. 9, 10. Let every one rejoice in the dispensations of God, willingly bowing their hearts to it.

This is a popular argument, of daily use. Should I insist on the reasons of it,—its consequence, effects, and advantage; its necessity, if we desire that God should have any glory, or our own souls any peace; the perfect conquest that will be obtained by it over the evil of every condition; and stretch it in application to the saddest particular cases imaginable (for all which the Scripture abounds in directions),—I should go too far out of my way.

This, then, I say, is the second thing we are to humble ourselves unto.

2. My other inquiry remains,—namely, how or by what means we are thus to humble ourselves to the law of grace and providence?

I shall but name one or two of the principal graces, in the exercise whereof this may be performed:—

(1.) Let faith have its work. There are, among others, two things that faith will do, and is suited to do, that lie in a tendency hereunto:—

[1.] It empties the soul of self. This is the proper work of faith,—to discover the utter emptiness, insufficiency, nothingness that is in man unto any spiritual end or purpose whatever. So Eph. ii. 8, 9. Faith itself is of God, not of ourselves; and it teaches us to be all by grace, and not by any work of ours. If we will be any thing in ourselves, faith tells us then it is nothing to us; for it only fills them that are empty, and makes them all by grace who are nothing by self. While faith is at work, it will fill the soul with such thoughts as these: " I am nothing; a poor worm at God's disposal; lost, if not found by Christ;—have done, can do, nothing on the account whereof I should be accepted with God: surely God is to be, in all things, submitted to; and the way of his mere grace accepted." So Rom. iii. 27. This is the proper work of faith,—to exclude and shut out boasting in ourselves; that is, to render us to ourselves such as have nothing at all to glory or rejoice in in ourselves, that God may be all in all. Now, this working of faith will keep the heart in a readiness to subject itself unto God in all things, both in the law of his grace and providence.

[2.] Faith will actually bring the soul to the foot of God, and give it up universally to his disposal. What did the faith of Abraham do when it obeyed the call of God? Isa. xli. 2. It brought him to the foot of God. God called him, to be at his disposal universally, by faith to come to it, following him, he knew not for what, nor whither. "Leave thy father's house and kindred;"—he disputes it not. " Cast out Ishmael, whom thou lovest;"—he is gone. " Sacrifice thine only Isaac;"—he goes about it. He was brought by faith to the foot of God, and stood at his disposal for all things. This is the proper nature of faith,—to bring a man to that condition. So was it with David, 2 Sam. xv. 26. This faith will do. Will God have me to suffer in my name, estate, family? " It is the LORD," saith faith. Will he have me to be poor, despised in the world,—of little or no use at all to him or his people? " Who," saith faith, " shall say to him, What doest thou?" In any state and condition, faith will find out arguments to keep the soul always at God's disposal.

(2.) Constant, abiding reverence of God will help the soul in this universal resignation, and humbling of itself. Now, this reverence of God is an awful spiritual regard of the majesty of God, as he is pleased to concern himself in us, and in our walking before him, on the account of his holiness, greatness, omniscience, omnipresence, and the like. So Heb. xii. 28, 29; Ps. lxxxix. 7, viii. 9.

Now, this reverence of God ariseth from three things, as is evident from the description of it:—

[1.] The infinite excellency and majesty of God and his great name. This is the apostle's motive, Heb. xii. 29, iv. 13. So Deut. xxviii. 58. The excellency of God in itself, is not only such as makes wicked men and hypocrites to tremble, whenever the thoughts of it seize on them, Isa. xxxiii. 14, but also it hath filled the saints themselves with dread and terror, Hab. iii. 16. Nor is there any bearing the rays of his excellency, but as they are shadowed in Christ, by whom we have boldness to approach unto him.

[2.] The infinite, inconceivable distance wherein we stand from him. Thence is that direction of the wise man to a due regard of God at all times, Eccles. v. 2: He is in heaven, whence he manifests his glorious excellency in a poor worm creeping on the mire and clay of the earth. So did Abraham, Gen. xviii. 27. What an inconceivable distance is there between the glorious majesty of God, and a little dust which the wind blows away and it is gone!

[3.] That this inconceivably glorious God is pleased, of his own grace, to condescend to concern himself in us poor worms, and our services, which he stands in no need of, Isa. lvii. 15. His eye is upon us,—his heart is towards us. This makes David break into that admiration, 1 Chron. xvii. 16; and should do so to us.

Now, what are the advantages of keeping alive a reverence of God in our hearts; how many ways it effectually conduces to enable us to humble our souls to the law of his grace and providence; what an issue it will put to all the reasonings of our hearts to the contrary,—I cannot stay to declare. And the improvement of these two graces, faith and reverence, is all that I shall at present recommend unto you for the end and purpose under consideration.

But I come, in the next place, to that part of this whole discourse which was at first principally intended.

SERMON IX.

We have at large considered the nature of this duty.

III. Let us now proceed to prove the proposition at first laid down, and shut up the whole; viz.,—

Humble walking with God is the great duty and most valuable concernment of believers.

"What doth the Lord thy God require of thee?" This is sufficiently asserted in the words of the text itself, which being so emphatically proposed, stand not in need of any farther confirmation by testimony; but because this is a business the Scripture doth much abound in, I shall subjoin a single proof upon each part of the proposition,—that it is both our great duty and most valuable concernment.

For the former, take that parallel place of Deut. x. 12, 13. That which is summarily expressed in my text by walking humbly with God, is here more at large described, with the same preface, "What doth the LORD thy God require of thee?" It gives us both the root and fruit; the root, in fear and love; the fruit, in walking in God's ways and keeping his commandments. The perfection of both is, to fear and love the Lord with all the heart and all the soul, and to walk in all his ways. This is the great thing that God requires of professors.

A place of the same importance, as to the excellency of this concernment of believers, which is the second consideration of it, you have in the answer of the scribe, commended by our Saviour, Mark xii. 33; as if he should say, in these days, "This is better than all your preaching, all your hearing, all your private meetings, all your conferences, all your fastings." Whole burnt-offerings and sacrifices were then the instituted worship of God, appointed by him, and acceptable to him, as are the things which I now repeated. But all these outward things may be counterfeited,—hypocrites may perform the outward work of them, as they then offered sacrifice; but walking humbly with God cannot: nor are they, in the best of men, of any value, but as they are parts and fruits of humble walking. If in and under the performance of them there be, as there may be, a proud, unmortified heart,—not subdued to the law of the Spirit of life,—not humbled in all things to walk with God; both they and their performance are abhorred of God. So that, though these things ought to be done, yet our great concernment lies, as to the main, in humble walking: "Only let your conversation be as becometh the gospel."

This is the import of the expression at the beginning of the verse,—"What doth the LORD thy God require of thee?" Thou mayest cast about in thy thoughts to other things, wherein either thyself may be more delighted, or, as thou supposest, may be more acceptable to God. Be not mistaken; this is the great thing that he requires of thee,—to walk humbly with him.

The grounds of it are:—

1. Every man is most concerned in that which is his great end; the bringing about of that is of most importance to him; the great exercise of his thoughts is,—whether he shall succeed as to this or not. The chief end of believers is, the glory of God. This, I say, is so, or ought to be so. For this purpose they were made, redeemed to this purpose, and purchased to be a peculiar people. Now, the Scripture everywhere teaches, that the great means of our glorifying God, is by our humble walking with him, according as it was before described. John xv. 8, "Herein is my Father glorified, that ye bear much fruit." You may have many thoughts that God is glorified by

works of miracles, and the like, amazing and dazzling the eyes of the world. Be it so; but in the most eminent manner, it is by your bearing fruit. You know the general rule that our Saviour gives his followers, Matt. v. 16. It is from our good works that men give glory to God. Which advice is again renewed by the Holy Ghost, 1 Pet. ii. 12.

Now, there are sundry ways whereby glory redounds to God by believers' humble walking with him:—(1.) It gives him the glory of the doctrine of grace. (2.) It gives him the glory of the power of his grace. (3.) It gives him the glory of the law of his grace,—that he is a king obeyed. (4.) It gives him the glory of his justice. (5.) It gives him the glory of his kingdom;—first, in its order and beauty; secondly, in multiplying his subjects:—

(1.) It gives God the glory of the doctrine of grace, or of the doctrine of the gospel; which is therefore called "The glorious gospel of God," because it so brings glory to him. Walking according to this rule, we adorn the doctrine of the gospel in all things. So the apostle tells us, Tit. ii. 11, 12: "This is that which this grace teacheth us; the substance is, to walk humbly with God." And when men professing it walk answerable to it, it is rendered glorious. When the world shall see that these are the fruits which that doctrine produceth, they must needs magnify it. The pride, folly, and wickedness of professors, hath been the greatest obstacle that ever the gospel received in this world. Nor will it, by any endeavours whatever, be advanced, until there be more conformity unto it in them who make the greatest profession of it. Then is the word glorified, when it hath a free course and progress, 2 Thess. iii. 1; which it will not have without the humble walking of professors. What eminent gifts are poured out in the days wherein we live! what light is bestowed! what pains in preaching! how is the dispensation of the word multiplied!—yet how little ground is got by it! how few converted! The word hath a free course in preaching, but is not glorified in acceptable obedience. Is it not high time for professors and preachers to look at home, whether the obstacle lie not in ourselves? Do we not fortify the world against the doctrine we profess, by the fruits of it they see in ourselves, and our own ways? Do they not say of us, "These are our new lights and professors; proud, selfish, worldly, unrighteous; negligent of the ordinances themselves profess to magnify; useless in their places and generations;—falling into the very same path which they condemn in others"? Perhaps they may deal falsely and maliciously in these things; but is it not high time for us to examine ourselves, lest, abounding in preaching and talking, we have forgot to walk humbly with God;—and so, not glorifying the gospel, have hindered the free course of its work and efficacy?

(2.) Humble walking with God gives him the glory of the power of his grace,—his converting, sanctifying grace. When the world shall see a poor, proud, selfish, rebellious, froward, perhaps dissolute and debauched creature, made gentle, meek, humble, self-denying, sober, useful,—they cannot but inquire after the secret and hidden virtue and power which principled such a change. This is given as the glory of the grace that was to be administered under the gospel, —that it should change the nature of the vilest men;—that it should take away cruelty from the wolf, and violence from the leopard, rage from the lion, and poison from the asp,—making them gentle and useful as the kid and the calf, the cow and the ox, Isa. xi. 6–9. It is not in our nature to humble ourselves to walk with God; we have an opposition to it and all parts of it: no angels or men can persuade us to it. Our carnal mind is enmity to him, not subject to his law,—nor can be. To have our souls humbled, brought to the foot of God, made always ready, willing, obedient, turned in their whole course, changed in all their ways and principles;—this glorifies the grace of God which is dispensed in Christ; by which alone it is that the work is wrought. When men make profession to have received converting and renewing grace from God, and so separate themselves from the men of the world on that account, yet live as they do, or worse, so that their ways and walking are contemptible to all;—it is the greatest reproach imaginable to that work of grace which they make profession of.

(3.) This gives God the glory of his law, whereby he requires this obedience at our hands. The obedience of them that are subject to it, sets forth the glory of the wisdom, goodness, and power of the lawgiver in that law. But this may be referred to the first head.

(4.) It gives him the glory of his justice, even in this world. There are two sorts of people in the world; the children of God, and others. Temptations lie on both, in reference to each other. The children of God are often disturbed by the outward prosperity of the wicked: the men of the world, at the public claim which they [the children of God] make in the privilege of God's love and protection: "Why they rather than others,—than we?" For the first, we know upon what principle they are to satisfy themselves. For the latter, this gives God the glory of his justice, when those whom he owns in this world, who expect a crown of reward from him, do walk humbly with him. So the apostle, 2 Thess. i. 4, 5, "Your patience and faith in tribulation," saith he to the saints, "is a manifest token of the righteous judgment of God, that ye may be counted worthy of his kingdom." Their patient and humble walking will be an evidence to convince even the world of the righteous justice of God, in rewarding of them and rejecting of itself. Though eternal life be the gift of God, and chiefly respects the praise of his glorious grace in Jesus Christ, yet God intending to bestow it on us in a way of reward, he will therein visibly glorify his justice also. Now, this gives a foretaste of it unto men, when they shall see those whom he will reward to walk humbly with him; wherein it may appear that his ways are equal, and his judgment righteous; or, as the apostle speaks, "according to truth."

(5.) It gives him the glory of his kingdom, in being an effectual means for the increase of the number of his subjects, and so the propagation of it in the world.

Now, if on all these, and on sundry other considerations, God be glorified in a humble walking with him, beyond any thing else in this world; this humble walking must certainly be the great and incomparable concernment of all them whose chief end is the advancement of the glory of God.

2. It is our great concernment, because God is greatly delighted in it; it is well-pleasing to him. The humble walking of professors is the great delight of the soul of God,—all that he hath in this world to delight in. If this be our aim, if this be our great interest,—that we may please God, that he may delight in us, and rejoice over us; this is the way whereby it is to be done, Isa. lvii. 15, "As I dwell," saith God, "in the high and holy place,—delight to abide in the heavens, where I manifest my glory; so I dwell with the humble and contrite spirit with delight and joy." Men in an opposition to this frame, be they what they will else in outward profession, are proud men. Nothing takes away pride in the sight of God but this humble walking with him. Now, "the proud he knoweth afar off," Ps. cxxxviii. 6; he takes notice of them with scorn and indignation; they are to him an abominable thing. It is three times solemnly asserted in the Scriptures, that God resisteth the proud, or scorneth the scorner, and giveth grace to the humble and lowly, Prov. iii. 34; James iv. 6; 1 Pet. v. 5. God scorns, abominates, resists, and sets himself against such men; but he gives grace or favour to the lowly, to the humble. This is admirably set out, Isa. lxvi. 1–3. He deals there with a professing people,—men that in all they did, said, "Let the LORD be glorified," verse 5. These men, aiming at acceptance with him, and to have him delight in them, pretended principally two things:—

(1.) The glory of the temple,—that high and holy house that was built to his own name. Says God, as to this, "Do you think that I have any need of it, or any delight in it, as it is such a goodly and glorious fabric in your eyes? The heaven is my throne," saith he, "and the earth my footstool; my hands have made all these things,—what need have I of the house you have built, or what delight in it?"

(2.) They pleaded his worship and service; the duties they performed therein,—their sacrifices and oblations,—praying, hearing.

"Alas!" saith God, "all these things I abhor." And so he compares them to the things which his soul did most hate, and which he had most severely forbid, verse 3. But if God will take delight in none of these things,—if neither temple nor ordinances, worship nor duty of religion, will prevail,—what is it that he delights in? Saith the Lord, "'To this man will I look;' I will rejoice over him, and rest in my love." Let now the proud Pharisee come and boast his righteousness, his duties, his worship, and performances;—the eye of God is on the poor creature behind the door, that is crying, "God be merciful to me, a sinner;" that is, giving himself up to sovereign mercy, and following after him upon that account. We have got a holiness that puffeth up, that in some hath little other fruit but "Stand from me; I am holier than thou." God delights not in it. It is a hard thing to excel in humble walking; it [*i. e.*, to excel, distinction] is easier obtained by other ways; but God delights not in them.

3. It is our great concernment, because this makes us alone eminently conformable to Jesus Christ. When the church is raised up to an expectation of his coming, she is bid to look for him as one "meek and lowly," Zech. ix. 9. And when he calls men to a conformity to his example, this he proposes to them. "Learn of me," saith he, Matt. xi. 29. What shall we learn of him? what doth he propose to our imitation?—that we should work miracles? walk on the sea? open blind eyes? raise the dead? speak as never man spake? "No," saith he; "this is not your concernment; but 'learn of me, for I am meek and lowly in heart, and you shall find rest for your souls.'" "Let this mind be in you," saith the apostle, "that was in Jesus Christ," Phil. ii. 5. What mind was this? He describes it in the next verse,—in his humbling, emptying himself, making himself poor, nothing, that he might do the will of God; coming to his foot, waiting for his command, doing his will cheerfully and readily. "Let," saith he, "this mind be in you, to be like Christ in this." I might go over all the contents of humble walking with God, and show the excellency of Jesus Christ in them, and how our conformity to Christ doth principally consist therein; but I must hasten.

4. I might farther evince it, by an induction of the promises that are made unto humble walking with God. But this would be a long work, to insist on the most considerable particulars; so that I shall wholly omit it.

5. It will appear so by comparing it with any thing else wherein men may suppose their interest and concernment to lie:—

(1.) Some men (I speak of professors) live as though their great concernments were in heaping up to themselves the things of this world. Their hearts are devoured with cares about them, and their thoughts taken up with them. This I shall not so much as compare with humble walking with God; nor make it my business—from the vanity, uncertainty, uselessness as to any eternal end, unsatisfactoriness, attendings of fear, care, and love—to manifest their great incompetency once to come into consideration in this inquiry, as to what is the great concernment of a professor.

(2.) There are others whose designs lie after greatness, high places, esteem in the world,—to be somebody in their days; outrunning the providence and call of God to that end; and who make this their business and interest, without farther consideration. But we may say the same of these as of the former,—their way is folly, though they that follow them should praise their sayings.

(3.) There are those whose aim is to be learned indeed, and so accounted. This they make their work; on this they set up their rest; this takes up their time and strength. If this succeed, all is well;—they have their hearts' desire. The beauty of this also is fully sullied, and the vanity of it hath been discovered by many, and the shame of its nakedness made to appear. Is this thy great concernment? Dost thou waste thy time and spirit about it? Is this the bosom of thy rest? Hast thou here laid up thy glory? and dost thou aim at this as thy end? Poor creature! thou snuffest up the empty wind. All this while God may abhor thee; and thy learning will never swell to such a greatness as that the door of hell will not be wide enough to receive thee. The vanity, vexation, dreadfulness, emptiness, of this concernment may be easily discovered.

Nay, put all these together; suppose thou hadst high places, learning, and an answerable repute and credit to them all, that thou hadst on these heads all that thy heart can desire, and more than ever man had before thee,—would it all give rest to thy soul? Canst thou not look through it all? Why, then, dost thou spend thy strength for a thing of nought? Why is the flower of thy spirit laid out about these things, that indeed are not, or are as a thing of nought? But,—

(4.) Some men's great concernment seems to lie in a profession of religion. So they may attain to that, and therewithal a name to live, it doth suffice. Whether this humble walking with God, in any of the causes or effects of it, be found on them, they are not solicitous. That men may not rest here, give me leave to offer two or three considerations:—

[1.] All that they do may be counterfeited; and so, wherein is its excellency? It may be done by him who hath not the least of God or Christ in him. Hypocrites may hear much, pray often, speak of God and the things of God, perform all duties of religion, excel in gifts and parts, be forward in profession to a great repute,—and yet be hypocrites still.

[2.] All this hath been done by them who have perished. Many who are now in hell have done all these things, and went down to the pit with the burden of their profession and duties at their back. I could reckon up instances. And let me but try this foundation, which safely I may,—namely, that whatever excellencies have been found in hypocrites and perishing souls, may all meet in one, and yet he be an hypocrite still,—and I shall merit easily the best [repute] of mere profession. Take the zeal of Jehu, the hearing of Herod, the praying of the Pharisee, the fasting of the Jews, Isa. lviii., the joy of the stony ground, and you may dress up a perishing soul to a proportion of profession beyond what the most of us attain unto.

[3.] It is useless in the world. I shall freely say, Take away this humble walking, and all profession is a thing of nought; it doth no good at all in the world. Is it for the advantage of mankind, that a man should have credit and repute in religion, and cannot give an instance scarce that any man, high or low, rich or poor, hath been the better for him in the world? that they who should do good to all, do good to none at all? Is this being fruitful in the gospel? is this studying the good works that are profitable to all?—is this doing good to mankind in the places wherein we are?

[4.] This is the readiest way for a man to deceive himself to eternity. He that would go down to the pit in peace, let him keep up duties in his family and closet; let him hear as often as he can have an opportunity; let him speak often of good things; let him leave the company of profane and ignorant men, until he have obtained a great repute for religion; let him preach and labour to make others better than he is himself; and, in the meantime, neglect to humble his heart to walk with God in a manifest holiness and usefulness, and he will not fail of his end.

Let me not be mistaken. God forbid I should countenance profane men in their contempt of the ways of God, and the reproaches of hypocrisy that they are ready to cast upon the best of the saints of God; I say, God forbid. Nor let me be interpreted in the least to plead for men who satisfy themselves in a righteousness without these things,—whom I look upon as men ignorant wholly of the mystery of God and the Father, and of Christ, and evidently uninterested in the covenant of grace. No; this is all I aim at,—I would not have professors flatter themselves in a vain, empty profession, when the fruits they bear of envy, hatred, pride, folly, proclaim that their hearts are not humbled to walk with God. Will, then, these, or any of these things, stand in competition with that which we propose for the great concernment of souls? Doubtless, in comparison of it, they are all a thing of nought.

Use 1. Is humble walking with God our great concernment? Let us make it our business and our work to bring our hearts unto it all our days. What do we, running out of the way all the day long, spending our strength for that which is not bread? My business is not,—whether I be rich or poor, wise or unwise, learned or ignorant; whether I shall live or die; whether there shall be peace or war with the nations; whether my house shall flourish or wither; whether my gifts be many or few, great or small, whether I have good repute or bad repute in the world;—but only, whether I walk humbly with God or not. As it is with me in this respect, so is my present condition,—so will be my future acceptation. I have tired myself about many things;—this one is necessary. What doth the Lord my God require of me, but this? What doth Christ call for, but this? What doth the whole sanctifying work of the Holy Ghost tend to, but that I may walk humbly with God?

Give me leave to name a motive or two unto it:—

(1.) In humble walking with God we shall find peace in every condition. "Learn of me; for I am meek and lowly: and ye shall find rest unto your souls." "Let war come on the nation,—I shall have peace. Let a consumption come on my estate,—I shall have peace. Let nearest relations be taken away,—I shall have peace." The soul that sets up its rest, and makes it its great concernment to walk humbly with God, is brought to his foot, bent to his will, is ready for his disposal; and whatever God does in the world with himself, his, or others, he hath peace and quietness in it. His own will is gone, the will of God is his choice; his great concernment lies not in any thing that can perish, that can be lost.

(2.) We shall also find comfort. Mephi-bosheth cried, "Let all go, seeing the king is come in peace; which was all that I desired." When a man shall see, in the worst state and condition, that his great concernment is safe; that though all is lost, God, who is all, is not lost; that this can never be taken from him;—it fills his heart with delight. Is he in prosperity? he fears not the loss of that which he most values. Is he in adversity? yet he can walk with God still; which is his all. He can therefore glory in tribulations, rejoice in afflictions;—his treasure, his concernment is secure.

(3.) This alone will make us useful in our generation, and fruitful in the knowledge of our Lord and Saviour Jesus Christ. On this depends all the glory we bring to God, and all the good we do to men.

Let us, then, make this our business,—aim at it; and, in the strength of Christ, we shall have peace in it.

Use 2. To humble us all, that we have spent so much of our time and days in and about things wherein we are indeed so little concerned, let us a little bring our ways and affairs to the balance of the sanctuary. One hath risen early, gone to bed late, and worn out himself to increase knowledge and learning. What is it, when we have done?—an engine in the hand of Satan to puff us up with pride and folly; a diversion from the knowledge of Christ, full of vexation of spirit. How many other things have entangled us! What weight have we laid upon them! How have we put a value upon that profession, which hath been a shame rather than an honour to the gospel! The Lord forgive us our folly, in spending ourselves in and about things wherein we are so little concerned; and help us, that our mistake be not at last found out to be fatal! Could we seriously take a view of our ways and time, and see how much of it we have spent in and about things that indeed will, in the issue, do us no good; it would certainly fill our souls with a great deal of shame and confusion.

Use 3. As to them who seem not at all to be concerned in this business, who never made it their design in their lives to walk with God in the way that hath been spoken to; let me tell such,—

(1.) It is more than probable that they may be apt to take advantage at what hath been spoken against empty professors and profession; to triumph in their thoughts against them all, and say, "Such, indeed, they are, and no better." If so, it is possible that this discourse, through the just judgment of God, may tend to their farther hardening in their sin,—pride and folly. What is the Lord's intendment towards you, I know not. It is my duty to warn you of it. Some that are professors may fail of the mark of our high calling; but you that are none, can never attain it: but take heed that this be not the issue of this dispensation of the word towards you. I had rather never speak more in this place, than speak any one word with an intention to give you an advantage against professors. If you take it, it will be your ruin.

(2.) Consider this,—if the righteous be scarcely saved, where will you, and such as you, bitter scoffers, neglecters of ordinances, haters of the power of godliness and the purity of religion, appear? You whose pride and folly, or whose formality, lukewarmness, and superstition, whose company and society, whose ways and daily walking, proclaim you to be wholly strangers to this concernment of believers,—I say, what will be your lot and portion?

(3.) Consider how useless you are in this world. You bring no glory to God, but dishonour; and whereas by any outward acts you may suppose you do good sometimes to men, know that you do more hurt every day than you do good all your lives. How many are by you ensnared into hell! how many hardened! how many destroyed, by living in formality or profaneness!

SERMON X.

PROVIDENTIAL CHANGES, AN ARGUMENT FOR UNIVERSAL HOLINESS.

"Seeing then that all these things shall be dissolved, what manner of persons ought ye to be in all holy conversation and godliness?"—2 PET. iii. 11.

THAT this second epistle was written unto the same persons to whom the former was directed, the apostle himself informs us, chap. iii. 1. Who they were to whom the first was directed, he declares fully, 1 Epist. i. 1, 2, "Peter, an apostle of Jesus Christ, to the strangers scattered throughout Pontus, Galatia," &c.

"Strangers" are taken two ways: First, In a large, general, and spiritual sense. So all believers are said to be strangers and pilgrims in this world, because they are not of the world, but they look for another country, another city, another house, whose framer and builder is God. Secondly, In a proper, natural sense, for those who abide or dwell in a land that is not their own, wherein they have not right of inheritance with the natives and citizens of it. In this sense the patriarchs were strangers in the land of Canaan before it came to be the possession of their posterity; and the children of Israel were strangers four hundred years in the land of Egypt.

Now, though the persons to whom the apostle wrote were strangers in the first sense,—pilgrims, whose conversation and country was in heaven,—yet they were no more so than all other believers in the world; so that there was no just cause of saluting them peculiarly under that style and title, were there not some other special reason of that appellation. They were, therefore, also strangers in the latter sense;—persons who had no inheritance in the place of their abode, that were not the free and privileged natives of the country where they dwelt and inhabited; that is, they were Jews scattered abroad in those parts of the world.

The people of Israel in those days were under various distributions and appellations. First, They were the natives of Jerusalem, and the parts adjacent; and these were in the gospel peculiarly called Jews. You have it often mentioned, that in our Saviour's discourse with them, the Jews answered so and so; that is, the natives of Jerusalem, and places adjoining. Secondly, Those who inhabited the sea-coasts of the country, whom the others much despised, and called them, from the place of their habitation, as if they had been men of another nation, "Galileans." Thirdly, Those who lived in several dispersions, up and down the world, among other nations. Of these there were two chief sorts:—1. Those who lived in some parts of

Europe, in Asia the less, also at Alexandria, and other Greek colonies. These are in the Scripture sometimes called Greeks, Acts xvii.; and elsewhere commonly termed Hellenists; because they used the Greek language, and the Greek Bible then in use. 2. Those who lived in the greater Asia, in and about Babylon; as also in the countries here enumerated by the apostle:—the Jews converted to the faith, that lived scatteredly up and down in those parts of Asia.

Peter being in a special manner designed by the Holy Ghost the apostle of the Circumcision, and being now at Babylon in the discharge of his apostolical office and duty, 1 Epist. v. 13; and being now nigh unto death, which he also knew, 2 Epist. i. 14; and not perhaps having time to pass through and personally visit these scattered believers,—he wrote unto them these two epistles, partly about the main and important truths of the gospel, and partly about their own particular and immediate concernment as to the temptations and afflictions wherewith they were exercised.

It is evident, from sundry places in the New Testament, what extreme oppositions the believing Jews met withal, all the world over, from their own countrymen, with and among whom they lived. They in the meantime, no doubt, warned them of the wrath of Christ against them for their cursed unbelief and persecutions; particularly letting them know, that Christ would come in vengeance ere long, according as he had threatened, to the ruin of his enemies. And because the persecuting Jews, all the world over, upbraided the believers with the temple and the holy city, Jerusalem, their worship and service instituted of God, which they had defiled; they were given to know, that even all these things also should be destroyed, for their rejection of the Son of God. After some continuance of time, the threatening denounced being not yet accomplished,—as is the manner of profane persons and hardened sinners, Eccles. viii. 11,—they began to mock and scoff, as if they were all but the vain pretences, or loose, causeless fears of the Christians. That this was the state with them, or shortly would be, the apostle declares in this chapter, verses 3, 4. Because things continued in the old state, without alteration, and judgment was not speedily executed, they scoffed at all the threats about the coming of the Lord that had been denounced against them.

Hereupon the apostle undertakes these three things:—

First. He convinces the scoffers of folly by an instance of the like presumption in persons not unlike them, and the dealings of God in a case of the same nature.

Secondly. He instructs believers in the truth of what they had before been told concerning the coming of Christ, and the destruction of ungodly men.

Thirdly. He informs them in the due use and improvement that ought practically to be made of the certainty of this threatening of the coming of Christ.

For the first, he minds them, as I said, of the old world, verses 5, 6. Before the destruction of that world, God sent " Noah, a preacher of righteousness," who, both in word and deed, effectually admonished men of the judgment of God that was ready to come upon them; but they scoffed at his preaching and practice, in building the ark, and persisted in their security. " Now," saith he, " this they willingly are ignorant of;"—it is through the obstinacy and stubbornness of their will, they do not consider it; for otherwise they had the Scripture, and knew the story. There is no ignorance like that where men's obstinacy and hardness in sin keeps them from a due improvement of what they ought to have improved to its proper purpose. They are to this day willingly ignorant of the flood, who live securely in sin under the denunciation of the judgments of God against sin.

I shall only observe, by the way, not to look into the difficulties of these verses, that I be not too long detained from my principal intendment,—that the apostle makes a distribution of the world into heaven and earth, and saith, they " were destroyed with water, and perished." We know that neither the fabric or substance of the one or other was destroyed, but only men that lived on the earth; and the apostle tells us, verse 5, of *the heavens and earth that were then*, and were destroyed by water, distinct from *the heavens and the earth that were now*, and were to be consumed by fire: and yet, as to the visible fabric of heaven and earth, they were the same both before the flood and in the apostle's time, and continue so to this day; when yet it is certain that the heavens and earth whereof he speaks were to be destroyed and consumed by fire in that generation. We must, then, for the clearing our foundation, a little consider what the apostle intends by " the heavens and the earth" in these two places:—

1. It is certain, that what the apostle intends by the " world," with its heavens and earth, verses 5, 6, which was destroyed by water; the same, or somewhat of that kind, he intends by " the heavens and the earth" that were to be consumed and destroyed by fire, verse 7. Otherwise there would be no coherence in the apostle's discourse, nor any kind of argument, but a mere fallacy of words.

2. It is certain, that by the flood, the world, or the fabric of heaven and earth, was not destroyed, but only the inhabitants of the world; and therefore the destruction intimated to succeed by fire, is not of the substance of the heavens and the earth, which shall not be consumed until the last day, but of persons or men living in the world.

3. Then we must consider in what sense men living in the world are said to be the " world," and the " heavens and earth" of it. I shall

only insist on one instance to this purpose, among many that may be produced, Isa. li. 15, 16. The time when the work here mentioned, of planting the heavens, and laying the foundation of the earth, was performed by God, was when he "divided the sea," verse 15, and gave the law, verse 16, and said to Zion, "Thou art my people;"—that is, when he took the children of Israel out of Egypt, and formed them in the wilderness into a church and state. Then he planted the heavens, and laid the foundation of the earth,—made the new world; that is, brought forth order, and government, and beauty, from the confusion wherein before they were. This is the planting of the heavens, and laying the foundation of the earth in the world. And hence it is, that when mention is made of the destruction of a state and government, it is in that language that seems to set forth the end of the world. So Isa. xxxiv. 4; which is yet but the destruction of the state of Edom. The like also is affirmed of the Roman empire, Rev. vi. 14; which the Jews constantly affirm to be intended by Edom in the prophets. And in our Saviour Christ's prediction of the destruction of Jerusalem, Matt. xxiv., he sets it out by expressions of the same importance. It is evident, then, that, in the prophetical idiom and manner of speech, by "heavens" and "earth," the civil and religious state and combination of men in the world, and the men of them, are often understood. So were the heavens and earth that world which then was destroyed by the flood.

4. On this foundation I affirm, that the heavens and earth here intended in this prophecy of Peter, the coming of the Lord, the day of judgment and perdition of ungodly men, mentioned in the destruction of that heaven and earth, do all of them relate, not to the last and final judgment of the world, but to that utter desolation and destruction that was to be made of the Judaical church and state; for which I shall offer these two reasons, of many that might be insisted on from the text:—

(1.) Because whatever is here mentioned was to have its peculiar influence on the men of that generation. He speaks of that wherein both the profane scoffers and those scoffed at were concerned, and that as Jews;—some of them believing, others opposing the faith. Now, there was no particular concernment of that generation in that sin, nor in that scoffing, as to the day of judgment in general; but there was a peculiar relief for the one and a peculiar dread for the other at hand, in the destruction of the Jewish nation; and, besides, an ample testimony, both to the one and the other, of the power and dominion of the Lord Jesus Christ;—which was the thing in question between them.

(2.) Peter tells them, that, after the destruction and judgment that he speaks of, verse 13, "We, according to his promise, look for new heavens and a new earth," etc. They had this expectation. But what is that promise? where may we find it? Why, we have it in the very words and letter, Isa. lxv. 17. Now, when shall this be that God will create these "new heavens and new earth, wherein dwelleth righteousness?" Saith Peter, "It shall be after the coming of the Lord, after that judgment and destruction of ungodly men, who obey not the gospel, that I foretell." But now it is evident, from this place of Isaiah, with chap. lxvi. 21, 22, that this is a prophecy of gospel times only; and that the planting of these new heavens is nothing but the creation of gospel ordinances, to endure for ever. The same thing is so expressed, Heb. xii. 26–28.

This being, then, the design of the place, I shall not insist longer on the context, but briefly open the words proposed, and fix upon the truth contained in them:—

First, There is the foundation of the apostle's inference and exhortation, Τούτων οὖν πάντων λυομένων.—"Seeing that I have evinced that all these things, however precious they seem, or what value soever any put upon them, shall be dissolved,—that is, destroyed; and that in that dreadful and fearful manner before mentioned,—in a way of judgment, wrath, and vengeance, by fire and sword;—let others mock at the threats of Christ's coming,—he will come, he will not tarry; and then the heavens and earth that God himself planted,—the sun, moon, and stars of the Judaical polity and church,—the whole old world of worship and worshippers, that stand out in their obstinacy against the Lord Christ,—shall be sensibly dissolved and destroyed. This, we know, shall be the end of these things, and that shortly."

There is no outward constitution nor frame of things, in governments or nations, but it is subject to a dissolution, and may receive it, and that in a way of judgment. If any might plead exemption, *that*, on many accounts, of which the apostle was discoursing in prophetical terms (for it was not yet time to speak it openly to all) might interpose for its share. But that also, though of God's creation, yet standing in the way of, and in opposition to, the interest of Christ, —that also shall be dissolved. And certainly there is no greater folly in the world, than for a mere human creation, a mere product of the sayings and the wisdom of men, to pretend for eternity, or any duration beyond the coincidence of its usefulness to the great ends that Christ hath to accomplish in the world. But this is not my business.

Secondly, There is the apostle's inference from, or exhortation on this supposition, expressed emphatically by way of interrogation: "What manner?" Now, herein two things are included:—

1. The evidence of the inference. It follows necessarily, unavoidably; every one must needs make this conclusion,—so that he leaves it to themselves to determine whose concernment it is. So the apostle

Paul, in another case, Heb. x. 29, leaves it to themselves to determine, as a case clear, plain, unquestionable. So here: and this is a most effectual way of insinuating an inference and conclusion, when the parties themselves who are pressed with it are made judges of its necessary consequence. "Judge ye whether holiness becomes not all them who are like to be concerned in such providential alterations."

2. The extent and perfection of the duty, in its universality and compass, is, in this manner of expression, strongly insinuated: "What manner of persons?"—that is, "Such as, indeed, it is not easy to express what attainments in this kind we ought, on this account, to press after." This apostle useth the same kind of expression to set forth the greatness and height of what he would deliver to the thoughts of men, 1 Pet. iv. 17, 18. There is in this kind of expression somewhat more insinuated to the mind than we know how to clothe with any words whatever.

Two things seem principally to be intended:—

(1.) That even the saints themselves, in such cases, ought to be other manner of men than usually they are, under ordinary dispensations of providence. Mistake not: our old measures will not serve; another manner of progress than as yet we have made is expected from us; it is not ordinary holiness and godliness that is expected from us under extraordinary calls from God and Christ.

(2.) That our endeavours to be godly and holy ought to be boundless and endless. No less is included in this apostrophe, "What manner of persons ought we to be!"—not resting in what we have attained, nor what may seem sufficient to keep our heads above water, —but an endless and boundless pressing on. Alas! it will hardly enter into our hearts to think what manner of men we ought to be.

Thirdly. For the matter of this exhortation and inference from the former principle, couched in this interrogation,—it is, "All holy conversation and godliness." The word "all" is not in the original; but both the other words are in the plural number,—"In holy conversations and godlinesses." Now, these expressions being not proper in our language, the translators have supplied the emphasis and force of them by the addition of the word "all." And there is no just cause of quarrel with them for so doing;—only, in the original the words are more weighty and emphatical than that supply doth readily reach unto. That which is principally intended is, that all the concernments whatever of holiness and godliness are couched in the words. So that two things are in them:—

1. The two general parts of that universal duty that we owe to God; and they are these:—(1.) Holiness of conversation; which is comprehensive of all holiness and righteousness, both in principle and practice; for no conversation is holy but what comes from a holy heart,

and is carried on to that great and holy end,—the glory of God. (2.) Godliness, or the worship of God according to the appointment and institution of Christ. This is the proper importance[1] of εὐσέβεια, as distinct from holiness of conversation,—a due adherence to, and observance of, the instituted worship of God.

2. The extent and compass of them both, and their degrees. It is not in this or that part of conversation,—to be holy in one thing and loose in another,—to be holy in one capacity, and vain in another,—to be godly as a private person, and ungodly or selfish as a magistrate; nor is it to observe one part of worship, and despise another: but in all concernments of conversation, in all parts of worship, doth this duty lie,—"In all holy conversation and godliness."

Fourthly. There is the relation that we ought to bear to the universality of holiness and godliness. We ought to be "in" them;—δεῖ ὑπάρχειν ὑμᾶς,—"You ought to be, to exist, in them." In these things is your life. They are not to be followed now and then, as your leisure will serve; but in all that you do you ought to be still in these, as in the clothes that you wear,—the garment that is on you. Be what you will, or where you will, or employed as you are called, yet still you ought to be in holiness and godliness. And what persons you ought to be in them, or how, hath been declared.

Observation. Great providential alterations or destructions made upon the account of Christ and his church, call for eminency of universal holiness and godliness in all believers.

I esteem it my duty to speak somewhat to this proposition, as containing the direction of our great duty in this day. That we have had many providential alterations amongst us, is known to all. What light I have about their relation to Christ and his church, I shall make bold to communicate when I come to the application of the truth in hand, and thereby make way for the pressing of the duty of the text on ourselves in particular. For the present, I confess I am ashamed and astonished at the deportment of many who are professors in these days. They see and talk of the alterations and dissolutions that God is pleased to make;—but what is the improvement that is made hereof? Many take advantage to vent their lusts and passions,—some one way, some another: one rejoicing at the ruin of another, as if that were his duty; others repining at the exaltation of another, as if that were their duty; some contriving one form of outward constitutions, others for another. (I speak of private persons.) But who almost looks to that which is the special call of God under such dispensations? Let us, then, I pray you, take a little view of our duty, and the grounds of it; and who knows but that the Lord may by it enlarge and fix our hearts to the love and prosecution of it?

[1] See note, p. 32 of this volume.

The two great providential alterations and dissolutions that have been and shall be made on the account of Christ and his church, to which all lesser are either consequent or do lie in a tendency, are that, first, of the *Judaical* church and state, whereof I have spoken; and, secondly, that of the *Antichristian* state and worship, whereunto all the shakings of these nations seem to tend, in the wisdom of God, although we are not able to discern their influence thereunto:—

1. Now, for the first of these, we may consider it in its coming as foretold, and as accomplished:—

(1.) As it was foretold and threatened by Christ. How were believers cautioned to be ready for it with eminent holiness and watchfulness therein! So Luke xxi. 34, 36, "Take heed to yourselves; watch, therefore." Why so? "Christ is coming," verse 27. When? "Why, in this generation," verse 32. What to do? "Why, to dissolve heaven and earth," verse 25; to "dissolve the Jewish church and state. Watch, therefore; give all diligence." So also Matt. xxiv. 42. "Watch, therefore." Oh! on this account what manner of persons ought we to be!

(2.) As accomplished. See what use the apostle upon it directs believers unto, Heb. xii. 26–28. This is the use, this the call of Providence, in all these mighty alterations: "Let us have grace,"—strive for it. The nature of the works of God call aloud for an eminent frame of holiness, and close adherence unto God in his worship. I could show how both the duties of my text are here expressed; but I need not.

2. So is it also in reference to that other great work of God in the world relating to Christ and his church, which is the ocean of providence whereinto all the rivulets of lesser alterations do run; I mean, the destruction of Antichrist and his Babylonish kingdom.

What a frame shall be in the saints on the close of that work, the Holy Ghost declares at large, Rev. xix.,—all rejoicing and spiritual communion with God! and whilst the work is on the wheel, those whom God will own in it he sets his mark on as holy, called, and chosen.

The grounds hereof are,—

1. Because in every such providential alteration or dissolution of things on the account of Christ and his church, there is a peculiar coming of Christ himself. He cometh into the world for the work he hath to do; he cometh among his own to fulfil his pleasure among them. Hence such works are called "his coming;" and "the coming of his day." Thus James exhorts these very Jews to whom Peter here writes, with reference to the same things, James v. 7–9, "Be patient unto the coming of the Lord." But how could that generation extend their patience to the day of judgment? "Nay," saith he,

"that is not the work I design, but his coming to take vengeance on his stubborn adversaries;" which he saith, verse 8, "'draweth nigh,' is even at hand; yea, Christ, 'the judge, standeth before the door,'" verse 9, "ready to enter;"—which also he did within a few years. So upon or in the destruction of Jerusalem (the same work), Luke xxi. 27, the Son of man is said to "come in a cloud, with power and great glory;"—and they that escape in that desolation are said to "stand before the Son of man," verse 36. So, in the ruin and destruction of the Roman empire, on the account of their persecution, it is said that "the day of the wrath of the Lamb was come," Rev. vi. 16, 17.

In all such dispensations, then, there is a peculiar coming of Christ, a peculiar drawing nigh of him, to deal with all sorts of persons in a special manner. Though he be oftentimes encompassed with many clouds, and with much darkness, yet he is present, exerting his authority, power, wisdom, righteousness, and grace in an eminent manner. It is with him as it is with God in other works, Job ix. 11; though all "see him not, perceive him not," yet "he goeth by," and "passeth on." The lusts, prejudices, corruptions, selfishness, injustice, oppressions of men,—the darkness, unbelief, fears, carnal wisdom, of the saints themselves,—the depth, compass, height, unsearchableness, of the path of the wisdom of Christ himself,—keep us in the dark as to his presence in this and that particular; but yet in such dispensations he is come, and passeth on towards the accomplishment of his work, though we perceive it not. Now, "what manner of persons ought we to be in all holy conversation and godliness," to meet this great King of saints at his coming? What preparation ought there to be! what solemnity of universal holiness for his entertainment! He is in such dispensations continually nigh us, whether we take notice of it or not.

I say, then, if there be a special coming and a special meeting of Christ in such dispensations, I suppose I may leave the inference unto all holy conversation and godliness, with the apostle, to the breasts and judgment of them that are concerned. Are we in this work to meet the Lord Jesus? What manner of persons ought we to be!

It may be observed, that Christ puts very great weight on the present frame and course which he finds men in at his coming. Matt. xxiv. 46, "Blessed is that servant, whom his Lord when he cometh shall find so doing." He annexes blessedness to the frame and course he finds men in at his coming; and [commends him that] waiteth for that hour, verse 42. Be not asleep when the thief comes to break up the house; take heed that that day take you not unprovided,—that you be not overtaken in the midst of the cares of this world. And he complains that when he comes he shall not "find faith on the earth," Luke xviii. 8.

But you will say, "Is this enough, then, that we look to be found in all godliness and holiness at his coming? May we indulge ourselves and our lusts at other seasons, so we be sure to be then provided? Is not the command of duty equal and universal as to all times and seasons? or is it pointed only unto such dispensations?"

Ans. 1. The inference for preparedness for the coming of Christ is to universal holiness, at all seasons; and that upon the account of the uncertainty of it. This our Saviour presseth again and again. "You know not at all when it will be, nor how,—no, not in the least; you believe it not when it is come: 'I shall not find faith of it on the earth,'" saith Christ. "Men will not take notice of it, nor acknowledge it, nor own it, as my coming; wherefore you have no way to be prepared for it, but by universal, perpetual watchfulness."

Ans. 2. The exhortation lies not unto holiness and godliness in general, but as to the degrees of it,—what manner of men we ought to be in them. It is not a godly conversation at an ordinary rate, that may find acceptance at another time, which will suffice to meet Christ at his coming; and that on sundry accounts, afterward to be mentioned. I shall at present only treat of some grounds of it from his own person who cometh, and whom we are to meet; and speak of the work he hath to do in his coming afterward:—

(1.) On the account of his personal excellencies and holiness. Consider how he is described when he comes to walk among his churches, Rev. i. 13–17: He is full of beauty and glory. When Isaiah saw him, chap. vi., he cries out, "I am undone, I am a man of unclean lips;" because of the dread and terror of his holiness. And Peter also, "Depart from me, Lord; for I am a sinful man." They were not able to bear the thoughts of his glorious holiness so nigh to them. When the holy God of old was to come down among the people at the giving of the law, all the people were to sanctify themselves, and to wash their clothes, Exod. xix. 10, 11. And order was still taken that no unclean thing might be in the camp, because of the presence of the holy God, though but in a type and resemblance. Whether we observe it or no, if there be any dissolving dispensations among us that relate to Christ or his church, there is a Holy One in the midst of us; or there will be, when any such dispensations shall pass over us. And to think to have to do in the works and ways wherein he hath to do, with hearts unlike and unsuitable unto him, to act our lusts and follies immediately under the eye of his holiness, to set our defiled hands to his pure and holy hands,—his soul will abhor it. This is a boldness which he will revenge,—that we should bring our neglect and lusts into his holy presence. Christ is in every corner,—in every turn of our affairs; and it is incumbent on us to consider how it is fit for us to behave ourselves in his special presence.

(2.) Upon the account of his authority. He who thus comes is the King of saints, and he comes as the King of saints,—he comes to exert his regal power and authority, to give a testimony to it in the world. So Isa. lxiii. 1–4: He shows his glory, his might, his kingdom, and authority in this work. So Rev. xix. 12: When he comes to destroy his antichristian enemies, he hath many crowns on his head; he exerciseth his regal power and authority. What is the duty of saints when their King is so nigh them, when he is come into the midst of them,—whilst he puts forth the greatness of his power round about them? Will it become them to be neglective of him? to be each man in the pursuit of his own lusts, and ways, and works, in the presence of their King? Holiness and godliness hath a due regard to the authority of Christ. Wherever there is a due subjection of soul unto Christ, all holy conversation and godliness will ensue. To be neglective in or of any part of holy conversation,—to be careless of any part of worship, under the special eye of the Lord of our lives and our worship, is not to be borne with.

(3.) On the account of the present care, kindness, and love, that he is exerting in all such dispensations towards his. It is a time of care and love. The way of his working out the designs of his heart are, indeed, ofttimes dark and hid, and his own do not see so clearly how things lie in a tendency to the event and fruits of love; but so it is;—Christ comes not but with a design of love and pity towards his,—with his heart full of compassion for them. Now, what this calls for at their hands, seeing their holiness and worship is all that his soul is delighted in, is evident unto all.

Put, now, these things together:—Every such dispensation is a coming of Christ;—the coming of Christ, as it is trying in itself, so it is the coming of the holy King of saints in his love and pity towards them; yea, be the dispensation what it will, never so sharp and severe unto them, yet it is in love and compassion to their souls;—their work is to meet this their holy King in the works of his love and power: and "what manner of persons ought we to be?"

SERMON XI.

2. THE second ground is, because every such day is a lesser day of judgment,—a forerunner, pledge, and evidence of that great day of the Lord which is to come. God's great and signal judgments in the world are to be looked on as pledges of the final judgment at the last

day. So Jude tells us that, in the destruction of Sodom and Gomorrah, " God set forth an example of them that shall suffer the vengeance of eternal fire," verse 7. And Peter calls the time of the destruction of the Judaical church and state expressly " the day of judgment and perdition of ungodly men," 2 Epist. iii. 7. So to the full is the destruction of the Roman persecuting state expressed, Dan. vii. 9, 10, 14. The solemnity of the work and whole procedure bespeaks a great day, a day of judgment; it is so, and a representation of that which is to come. And the like also is set forth, chap. xii. 1–3; and the same description have we of the like day of Christ, Mal. iv. 1.

Every such day, I say, then, is a lesser day of judgment, wherein much judging-work is accomplished. This Daniel tells us, chap. xii. 10,—it is a trying, a purifying, a teaching, a hardening, a bleeding time. There are great works that are done upon the souls and consciences of men by Christ in such a day, as well as outwardly; and all in a way of judgment. To let pass, then, the outward, visible effects of his wrath and power, of his wisdom and righteousness, I shall consider some few of the more secret judiciary acts that the Lord Christ usually exerts in such a day:—

(1.) He pleads with all flesh that are concerned in the alterations and desolations he makes. God puts this as one act of his in judgment, that he pleads with men, Ezek. xxxviii. 22. In his judgments he pleads with and against men about their sins. And in that great representation of the day of judgment, Joel iii. 2, God is said to " plead with all nations." Now, I say, in general, Christ in such a day pleads with all men concerned. His providences have a voice, and that a contending, pleading voice. Unless men are utterly blinded and hardened (as, indeed, the most are), they cannot but hear him, in his great and mighty works, contending with them about their sin and unbelief,—representing to them his righteous judgment to come. Though men now cast off things, on this account and that; and, being filled with their lusts, passions, fury, revenge, or ease, sensuality and worldliness, think these things concern them not; yet the day will come wherein they shall know, that the Lord Christ in his mighty works was pleading even with them also, and that in a way of judgment about their sin and folly.

(2.) In such a day Christ judges and determines the profession of many a false hypocrite, who hath deceived the church and people of God. One great work of the last day shall be the discovery of hypocrites: it is thence principally called, " The day wherein the secrets of all hearts shall be revealed." Many a fair pretender in the world shall be found to have been an enemy of Christ and the gospel. So is the day of Christ's coming in the flesh represented, Mal. iii. 1, 2. All were high in their professions of desiring his coming, and of delighting in him; but when he came, what was the issue? How few endured the trial! The false, hypocritical, selfish hearts, who had treasured up the hopes of great things to themselves, being discovered by the trials and temptations wherewith his coming was attended, themselves were utterly cast off from their profession into open enmity to God and his Son. So dealeth the Lord Christ in and under the dispensations whereof we speak, to this day. What by the fury of their own lusts, what by the temptations which lie in their way, what by the advantages they meet withal for the exercise of their vile affections, their hypocrisy is discovered, and themselves cast out of their profession. Notable effects of this acting of Christ as a judge have we seen in the dispensation that is passing over us. Some he hath judged by the sentence and judgment of his churches. How many false wretches have been cast out of churches, that have withered under their judgment, and returned no more! Some who have not walked in the order of his churches by him appointed, he hath judged by the world itself;—suffered their sin and folly so to break forth, that the world itself hath cast them out from the number of professors, and owned them as its own. Some have been judged as to their profession of him by strong temptations; that is, their lusts, ambition, selfishness, which have carried them into ways and compliances wherein they have been compelled to desert, and almost renounce all their former profession. Some have been tried and judged by the errors and abominations of the times, and turned aside from the simplicity of the gospel. Now, though there have been, and are, these and many other ways and means of casting men out of and from the profession that they have made, some good, some bad, some in themselves of a mere passive nature, and indifferent; yet they all proceed from Christ in a judiciary way,—they are acts of his in his day of judgment;—and O that England might not yet be farther filled with instances and examples of this kind!

(3.) He doth exercise his judgment in blinding and hardening of wicked men; yet they shall not see nor perceive what he is doing, but shall have advantages to do wickedly, and prejudices to blind them therein. So expressly, Dan. xii. 10, "They shall do wickedly, and they shall not understand." There are two parts of his judgment in such a day, about and against them. *First*, His giving of them up to their own lusts, to do wickedly: "They shall do wickedly." Wicked they are, and they shall act accordingly; they shall do it in such a day to the purpose, Rev. xvi. 10, 11. Christ will providentially suffer occasions, advantages, provocations, to lie before them, so that they shall do wickedly to the purpose; they shall have daily fresh occasions to curse, repine, blaspheme, oppose Christ and his interest, or to seek themselves, and the satisfaction of their lusts, which at other times they shall not be able to do. Be they in what condition they will, high or low, exalted or depressed, in power or out of it, they shall in such a season do wickedly, according as their advantages and provocations are. And for men to be given up to their own hearts' lusts, is the next door to the judgment of the great day, when men shall be given up to sin, self, and Satan, unto eternity. *Secondly,* He blinds them: "None of the wicked shall understand." Strange! Who seems so wise and so crafty as they? Who do understand the times, and their advantages in them, more than they? Who more prudent for the management of affairs than they? But the truth is, none of them, no, not one of them, shall, or do, or can understand; that is, they understand not the work of Christ, the business and design that he hath in hand, nor what is the true and proper interest of them who are concerned in these dispensations. There are many ways whereby Christ exerts this blinding and infatuating efficacy of his providence towards wicked men in such a day of judgment, that they shall not understand or know that he is at all concerned in the works that are in the world.

Sometimes the very things that he doth are such, and so contrary to the prejudicate opinions of men, that they can never understand that they are things which he will own. How many have been kept from understanding any thing of Christ in the world, in the days wherein we live, from their inveterate prejudices on the account of old superstitions, and forms of government which have been removed! They will rather die than believe that Christ hath any hand in these things: "They shall not understand."

Sometimes the persons by whom he doth them, keep them from understanding. "Shall these men save us?"—these whom they look upon as the offscouring of the earth. "Sure, if Christ had any work to do in the world, he would make use of other manner of instruments for the accomplishing of them." They are no less offended with the persons that do them than the things that are done. Christ worketh all this, that they should not understand.

Sometimes the manner of doing what he hath to do [keeps them from understanding,]—the darkness wherewith it is attended, the strange process that he makes,—sometimes weak, sometimes foolish, sometimes disorderly to the reasoning of flesh and blood, though all beautiful in itself, and in relation to him.

And sometimes Christ sends a spirit of giddiness into the midst of them, that they shall err and wander in all their ways, and not see nor discern the things that are before them: "None of the wicked shall understand."

By these, and many such ways as these, doth Christ in these days of his coming exercise judgment on ungodly men;—not to mention the outward destruction, desolation, and perdition, which usually in such seasons he brings upon them.

(4.) He exerciseth judgment at such a time even among the saints themselves. Ps. lxxxii. 1: He is judging in the great congregation. So Ps. l. 4–8: All this solemnity of proceeding is for the judgment of his own people; and his judging of them is in a plea about their obedience and failing therein. The sum of this his dealing with them is expressed, Rev. iii. 9.

We may, then, consider,—[1.] What it is that Christ pleadeth with his own people about his coming; [2.] What are the ways and means whereby he doth so:—

[1.] There are sundry things on the account whereof Christ at his coming pleads with his saints. One or more of them:—

1*st*. On the account of some secret lusts that have defiled them, and which they have either indulged themselves in, or not so vigorously opposed as their loyalty unto Christ required. Times of peace and outward prosperity are usually times wherein, through manifold temptations, even the saints themselves are apt to sully their consciences, and to have breaches made upon their integrity; sometimes in things they do know, and sometimes in things they do not know, nor take notice of. Instances may be given in abundance of such things. In this condition Christ deals with them, as Isa. iv. 4. There is blood and filth upon them; the spirit of judgment and burning must be set at work; which, as it principally aims at the internal efficacy of the Spirit in the cleansing of sin, so it respects a time of providential alterations and trials, wherein that work is effectually exerted. Christ in these dispensations speaks secretly to the consciences of his saints, and minds them of this and that folly and miscarriage, and deals with them about it. He asks them if things be not so and so with them?—if they have not thus and thus defiled themselves?—whether these hearts are fit to converse with him? and leaves not until their dross and tin be consumed.

2*dly*. On the account of some way or ways wherein they may have been unadvisedly, or through temptation, or want of seeking counsel aright from him, engaged. They may be got, in their employments, in their callings, in the work that lies before them in this world, into ways and paths wherein Christ is not pleased they should make any progress. What through leaning to their own understandings, what through an inclination of saying "A confederacy" to them to whom the people say "A confederacy," what through the common mistakes in the days wherein they live, even the saints may be engaged in ways that are not according to the mind and will of Christ. Now, in such a day of Christ's coming, though he spares the souls of his saints and forgives them, yet he "takes vengeance of their inventions," Ps. xcix. 8.

He will cast down all their idols, and destroy and consume every false way wherein they were. One is, it may be, in a way of superstition and false worship; another in a way of pride and ambition; another in a way of giving countenance to the men of the world, and things wherein God delights not;—Christ will take vengeance of all these their inventions in the day of his coming. He acts as "a refiner's fire," and as "fullers' soap."

3dly. On the account of inordinate cleaving unto the shaken, passing things of the world. This is a peculiar controversy that Christ hath with his, upon the account of adherence to the passing world; and it is a thing wherein, when he comes, too many will be found faulty. I might also insist on their unbelief, and other particulars. But,—

[2.] The ways and means whereby Christ judgeth and pleadeth with his own, on these accounts, are also various:—

1*st.* He doth it by the afflictions, trials, and troubles, that he exerciseth them with at his coming. The use of the furnace is to take away dross; and the issue of afflictions and trials, to take away sin:—this is their fruit. So, Dan. xii. 1, the time of Christ's coming shall be a day of trouble, such as never was. And what shall be the issue? Verse 10, "Many shall be purified, and made white, and tried." Their trials and troubles, their great tribulations, shall be purifying and cleansing. Though the design of Christ in the issue, at the appointed season, be the peace and deliverance of his saints; yet, in the carrying on of his work, great trials and tribulations may befall them all; and many may fall in the way, and perish as to the outward man. Hence, Dan. xii. 13, there is an appointed time of rest, and it will be a blessed thing for them that shall be preserved unto it; but whilst those days and seasons are coming to their period, there is often "a time of great trouble," verse 1. And "the power of the holy people may be scattered," verse 7, and many afflictions and trials may befall them. Now, by these doth Christ plead with his, for the consumption of their lusts, and the destruction of their inventions,—for the purging and purifying of them. All our trials, pressures, troubles, disappointments, in such a day, are the actings of Christ to this end and purpose. The influences that affliction hath unto these ends are commonly spoken unto.

2*dly.* He doth it by pouring out of his Spirit in a singular manner, for this end and purpose, so to plead with, judge, and cleanse his saints. It is in the administration of his Spirit that at his coming "he sits as a refiner and purifier of silver," Mal. iii. 1–3; and we see what work he accomplishes thereby. The Holy Ghost, who is the great pleader for the saints, and in them, doth at such a time effectually plead with them, by convictions, persuasions, arguings, application of the word, motions, strivings, and the like. Hence those who are unrefined at such a season are said in a peculiar manner "to vex," to grieve "the Holy Spirit" of God, Isa. lxiii. 10. His design upon them is a design of love; and to be rejected, resisted, opposed, in his actings and motions,—this grieves and vexes him. Men know not what they do, in neglecting the actings of the Holy Ghost; which are peculiarly suited to providential dispensations. When God is great in the world in the works of his providence,—in alterations, dissolutions, shakings, changings, removals,—and sends his Spirit to move and work in the hearts of men, answerably to his mind and will in these dispensations, so that there is a harmony in the voice of God without and within, both speaking aloud and clearly; then to neglect the workings of the Spirit brings men into that condition complained of, Ezek. xxiv. 13, "Because I have purged thee, and thou wast not purged, thou shalt not be purged any more."

It may be observed, that at such seasons when Christ hath any great and signal work to bring forth in the world, he doth by his Spirit deal with the hearts and consciences of the most wicked and vile men; which, when the secrets of all hearts shall be discovered at the last day, will exceedingly exalt the glory of his wisdom, patience, goodness, holiness, and righteousness. So did he with them before the flood; as is evident from Gen. vi. 3. When an utter destruction was to come, he saith, his Spirit shall strive with them no more;—that is, about their sin and rebellion. That this Spirit was the Spirit of Christ, and that the work of dealing with these ungodly men was the work of Christ, and that it was a fruit of long-suffering, Peter declares, 1 Epist. iii. 18–20. And if he deals thus with a perishing world, by a work that perisheth also,—how much more doth he it in an effectual work upon the hearts of his own! It is the Spirit that speaks to the churches in all their trials, Rev. ii. iii.

By this means, I say, then, Christ pleads with his saints; secretly and powerfully judging their lusts, corruptions, failings,—consuming and burning them up. He first, by frequent motions and instructions, gives them no rest in any unequal path; then discovers to them the beauty of holiness, the excellency of the love of Christ, the vanity and folly of every thing that hath interrupted their communion with him; and so fills them with godly sorrow, renunciation of sin, and cleaving unto God;—which is the very promise that we have, Ezek. vi. 10.

3dly. As he doth it by the inward, private, effectual operation of his Spirit, so he doth it by the effusion of his light and gifts in the dispensation of the word. Christ seldom brings any great alteration upon the world, but together with it, or to prepare for it, he causeth much effectual light to break forth in the dispensation of his word.

Before the first destruction of Jerusalem by the Babylonians, how he dealt with them he declares, 2 Chron. xxxvi. 15, "And the LORD God of their fathers sent to them by his messengers, rising up betimes, and sending; because he had compassion on his people, and on his dwelling-place." And before the final dissolution of the heavens and earth of that church and state, he preached to them himself in the flesh. A glorious light! Before the ruin of the antichristian world, he sends the angel with the everlasting gospel, and his two witnesses to hold forth the light of the gospel; and we must witness to this his way and wisdom in our generation. Now, though there are many rebels against light, and many whose lusts are enraged by the breaking forth of truth in its beauty and lustre; and many that, being dazzled with it, do run out of its paths into ways of error and folly, and none of the wicked do understand; yet, among the saints, the more light the more holiness,—for their light is transforming. This, then, is another means whereby, in such a day, Christ consumes the lusts and judges the inordinate walking of his own,—even by the light which in an eminent manner he sends forth in the dispensation of the word.

Now, if the time and season whereof we speak be such a day of judgment, wherein Christ thus pleads with all men, and with his own in an especial manner, I think the inference unto eminency in universal holiness may be left upon the thoughts and minds of all that are concerned. Especially from these considerations doth the inference lie strong unto the ensuing particulars, in the ways of holiness and godliness:—*First*, Of self-searching and self judging in reference to our state and condition. Dreadful are the actings of Christ in such a day on the souls and consciences (ofttimes on the names and lives) of corrupt, unsound professors;—in part I declared them before. If any now should be found in such a condition, his day of judgment is come, his sealing to destruction. This the apostle calls to in such a dispensation, 1 Cor. xi. 31, 32. Self-judging, as to our state and condition, ways and practices, is a great principle of holy conversation and godliness. When Christ comes to judge, we ought surely to judge ourselves; and abounding in that work is a great means of preservation from the temptations of the days whereunto we are exposed. *Secondly*, Of weanedness from the world and the things thereof. Christ's coming puts vanity on all these passing things. This is surely contained in the text, "Seeing that these things shall be dissolved, what manner of persons," etc. At best they are vain and passing, uncertain things; in such a dispensation as is spoken of, they are all obnoxious to dissolution, and many of them certainly to be removed and taken away. And why should the heart of any one be set upon them? why should we not fix our souls on things more profitable, more durable? It is no small matter to meet the Lord Christ at his coming, Mal. iii. 1–3. They were all full of desires of the coming of Christ; they sought after him: "The Lord whom ye seek." They delighted in the thoughts of him: "Whom ye delight in." Well, he came, according to their desires; he whom they sought was found. And what was the issue? Why, very few of them could abide the day of his coming, or stand when he appeared. He had a work to do they could not away with. They desired his coming,—they desired the day of the Lord; but, as the prophet says, Amos v. 18, "Woe unto them! to what end have they desired it?—it was darkness to them, not light." That was the coming of Christ in person to his temple. It is not otherwise in any of his other comings in providential dispensations. Many men long for it, delight in it,—it is our duty so to do; but what is the issue? One is hardened in sin and lust;—another is lifted up, as though himself were something, when he is nothing;—a third stumbles at the coming itself, and falls: "Woe unto them! the day of the LORD is darkness unto them, and not light."

I proceed now to the *use*. But to make way for the due improvement of the apostle's exhortation unto us, some previous considerations must be laid down:—

First. It is known to all the world that we have had great providential alterations and dissolutions in these nations. He must be a stranger, not in England only, but in Europe, almost in the whole world, that knows it not. Our heavens and our earth, our sea and our dry land, have been not only shaken, but removed also. The heavens of ancient and glorious fabric, both civil and ecclesiastical, have been taken down by fire and sword, and the fervent heat of God's displeasure. It is needless for me to declare what destructions, what dissolutions, what unparalleled alterations we have had in these nations. Persons, things, forms of government of old established, and newly-framed constitutions, we have seen all obnoxious to change or ruin.

Secondly. It is no less certain that we may say, concerning all these things, "Come and see what God hath wrought." And as to these desolations of nations, ruin of families, alterations of governments, we may say of them all, as the psalmist, Ps. xlvi. 8, "Come, behold the works of the LORD, what desolations he hath made in the earth." It is his work; he hath done it himself. There is no evil in the city, and the Lord hath not done it, Amos iii. 6. Have there been any exaltations of men, recoveries from depression, relief of the oppressed, establishments of new frames and order of things?—it hath been all from him, Dan. ii. 21, iv. 32. Indeed, the days wherein we live are full of practical atheism. Some, out of mere stoutness of heart and innate unbelief, will take no notice of God in all these things. Ps. x. 4, "The wicked, through the pride of his countenance, will not seek after God: God is not in all his thoughts." As things have been, so they suppose they are, and will be; but as to the consideration of him who disposeth of all as seems good unto him, they are strangers unto it. Some have had their lusts enraged, and themselves so provoked and disappointed, that, flying upon the instruments which God hath used, they have been filled with prejudice, and utterly blinded as to any discovery of the ways or work of God in these revolutions. Some have been utterly cast down in their thoughts, because they have not been able to discover the righteousness, beauty, and order, of the ways of God; his footsteps having been in the deep, while his paths have not been known. And some, having found an open door for the satisfaction of their lusts,—pride, covetousness, ambition, love of the world, reputation, vain-glory, and uncleanness,—have been so greedily engaged in the pursuit of them, that they have taken little or no notice of the hand of God in these things. And others are at a stand, like the Philistine priests and diviners, 1 Sam. vi. 9. They know not whether all this hath been from the hand of God, or whether some chance hath befallen us. I shall not need to mention those in Isa. xlvii. 13,—"astrologers, star-gazers, and monthly prognosticators," who have endeavoured also to divert the thoughts of unbelieving, foolish men, from a due consideration of the Author of all our revolutions. To all which I shall answer in general in the words of Hannah, 1 Sam. ii. 3–9, "God hath done all these things." And men that will not take notice of him and his proceedings, shall at length be forced so to do, Isa. xxvi. 11.

These things being premised, one principal inquiry, which must be the bottom and foundation of the ensuing directions, is, whether it may appear that these providential alterations and dissolutions have related to Christ and his interest in the world in an especial manner?

That we may yet a little farther clear our way, you may farther observe, what I intend, by relating unto Christ and his church in an especial manner:—

1. Whereas the Lord Christ is, by the appointment of the Father, made "heir of all things," Heb. i. 2, and "hath all judgment committed unto him," over all flesh, in all the world,—which include his right to send his gospel into what nation and place he pleaseth;—so all the alterations that are in the world, all things relate to him, and do lie in a remote tendency to the advancement of his glory. He will work out his own glorious ends from all the breakings of all the nations in the world; even where the interest of his gospel seems outwardly to be very little, or nothing at all. But it is not in this

sense that we make our inquiry; for so there would be nothing peculiar in the works that have been among us.

2. Things may relate unto Christ and his church upon the account of special promise. Christ hath a special and peculiar concernment in providential dissolutions when they so relate to him; and that appears in these things:—

(1.) When the judgments that are exercised in such a dispensation flow from provocations given unto the Lord Christ, upon the account of his church. So Isa. xxxiv. 8. All the dissolutions mentioned of the heavens and the earth, verse 4, were on Zion's account, and the controversy that Christ had with Idumea about her. So, chap. lxiii. 4, the day of vengeance is the year of the redeemed. Whence, in such a day, the saints themselves are stirred up to take notice that the desolations wrought in the earth are on their account, Jer. li. 35; and so it is fully expressed in the ruin of antichristian Babylon, in the Revelation. Where, then, there is a peculiar relation of any dissolving providence unto Christ and his church, the judgments exerted in and under it regard the vengeance of the church, and proceed from the provocations of Christ on that account.

(2.) Some promises made unto Christ concerning his inheritance,—some promises of Christ unto his church,—are, in such a day, brought forth unto accomplishment. The promises of Christ to the church are of two sorts:—First, General, essential to the new covenant; and these belong equally to all saints, of all ages, in all places,—not to one more than another. Every saint hath an equal right and interest in the essential promises of the covenant with any other saint whatever; there is no difference, but one God, Lord, and Father of all, is good unto them all alike. And, secondly, There are promises which are peculiarly suited to the several states and conditions into which the visible kingdom of Christ is, in his wisdom, to be brought in several ages. Such are the promises of the calling of the Jews,—of the destruction of Antichrist,—of the increase of light in the latter days,—of the peace, rest, and prosperity of the church in some times or ages, after trials and tribulation. Now, they are the promises of this latter sort that relate unto providential dispensations.

Having premised these things, I shall now briefly offer some grounds of hope, that such have been the alterations and dissolutions wherein we have been exercised in this generation:—

FIRST. Because very many of the saints of God have obtained real, evident, soul-refreshing communion with Christ in and about these things, on this foundation, that the things on the wheel amongst us have had a peculiar relation unto him. There is nothing of more certainty to the souls of any, than what they have real, spiritual experience of. When the things about which they are conversant lie only in notion, and are rationally discoursed or debated, much deceit may lie under all; but when things between God and the soul come to be realized by practical experience, they give a never-failing certainty of themselves. Now, by holding communion about these things with Christ, I understand the exercise of faith, love, hope, expectation, delight, on and in Christ, on the one hand; and the receiving relief, supportment, consolation, joy, patience, perseverance, on the other;—from both which, holiness, faithfulness, and thankfulness have proceeded and been increased. Now, this communion with Christ, in and about the works of his providence amongst us, very many of the saints have obtained; and, which is the height and complement of it, died in the clear visions of Christ in such communion. Now there are two things that offer sufficient security against any deceit or mistake in this thing:—

1. The goodness, care, and faithfulness of God towards his own; which will not suffer us to fear that he would lead all his people into such a temptation wherein, in their chiefest communion (as they apprehended) with himself, they should feed on the wind and delusion. If the foundation of all this intercourse with God was false, and not according to his mind, then so was the whole superstructure. Now, that God for many years should lead his people into a way of prayer, faith, hope, thankfulness, and yet all false and an abominable thing, because all leaning on a false ground and supposition; none that consider his goodness and tender pity towards his own, with the delight of his soul in their worship and ways, can once imagine. It is true, men may be zealously engaged in ways and acts of worship, and *that* all their lives, wherein they think they do God good service; and yet both they and their service be abominated by him for ever. But men cannot do so in faith, love, obedience, thankfulness; which alone we speak of. At least, he will not suffer his saints to do so; of whom alone we speak. We have, then, the tender mercies and faithfulness of God to assure us in this case.

2. The self-evidencing efficacy of faith in spiritual experiences strengthens their persuasion. Many, doubtless, may persuade themselves that they have communion with God, and yet feed upon ashes, and a deceived heart turns them aside. The principle of such a delusion I shall not now lay open. But when it is indeed obtained by faith, it is always accompanied with a soul-quieting, refreshing evidence; for faith in its operation will evince itself to the soul where it is. I do not say it always doth so. It may be so clouded with darkness of mind, so overpowered by temptations, that in its most spiritual and genuine acting, it may be hid from the soul wherein it is,—which we find to be the condition of many a gracious soul; but in itself it clears up its own actings. Things that have a self-evidencing power,

may be hindered from exerting it; but when they do exert it, it is evident. Put a candle under a bushel, it cannot be seen; but take away the hinderance, and it manifests itself. It is so in faith, and its actings. They may be so clouded to the soul itself in which they act, that it may not be able to attain any comforting evidence of it. But take away the bushel,—fear, prejudices, temptations, corrupt reasonings,—and it will assure the soul of itself and its working. Neither is its working more evident than its fruit, or the product of its operations in the soul; it brings forth love, rest, peace, all with a spiritual sense upon the heart and spirit. Now, these have been in this thing so evident in the souls of the saints, that they have bespoken that faith which cannot deceive nor be deceived.

The bottom, then, of the communion which the saints had with Christ in this work, and have, must either be faith or fancy. If faith, then the communion was and is real, and the work true that it is built upon. That it was not, that it is not, the fancy or imagination of a deluded heart, may appear from these considerations:—

(1.) From its extent. We know it possessed the minds of the universality of believers in this nation, who were not, nor are at this day, combined in our political interest, but are wofully divided among themselves; yet have all had, more or less, this persuasion of the work relating unto Christ. Now, that this should be any corrupt imagination, seems to me impossible. I speak not of outward actions and proceedings; for so, I know, whole nations may politically combine in evil,—though I will not believe that ever the generality of the saints of Christ shall do so. But I speak of the frame of their hearts and spirits as to communion with Christ in faith and love; whereunto no outward reasonings or interests could influence them in the least: "Digitus Dei est hoc."

(2.) It appears from the permanency and flourishing of this principle in straits and difficulties. A corrupt imagination, be it never so strong and vigorous in its season, and whilst its food is administered to it, in the temptation it lives upon, yet, in trials great and pressing, it sinks and withers; or, if the difficulty continue, for the most part—unless where it falls on some natures of an unconquerable pertinacy—utterly vanisheth. But now, this principle of the saints' communion with Christ about the work of our generation was never more active, vigorous, and flourishing, did never more evidence itself to be of a divine extract, than in the greatest straits and difficulties,—in the mouth and entrance of the greatest deaths. Then did it commonly rise up to its greatest heights and assurance. Our temptations, whether Christ be in this work or no, have, for the most part, befallen us since we had deliverance from pressing, bloody troubles. And I think I may say, that there are very many saints in these nations who can truly say, that the best and the most comfortable days that ever they saw in their lives, were those wherein they were exercised with the greatest fears, dangers, and troubles; and that upon the account of the strengthening of this principle of communion with Christ. And in very many hath it been tried out to the death, when corrupt fancies were of little worth.

(3.) It appears from the fruits of this persuasion. Every corrupt imagination and fancy is of the flesh; and the works of the flesh are manifest. Whatever it may do in conjunction with convictions, and for a season, yet in itself, and in a course, it will bring forth no fruit but what tends to the satisfaction of the flesh. But now, the principle under consideration did bring forth fruits unto God, in godliness and righteousness.

But you will say, "Do we not see what fruit it hath brought forth? Is not the land full of the steam of the lusts of men engaged in the work of this age? Can hell itself afford a worse savour than is sent forth by many of them?"

Answer 1. Very many who have been engaged never pretended to ought of this principle, but followed professedly on carnal (at best, rational and human) accounts solely. Now, these being men of the world, and being fallen into days of notable temptations, no wonder if their lusts work and tumultuate, and that to purpose. The principle is not to suffer for their miscarriages who renounce it.

Ans. 2. There was a mixed multitude which in this business went up with the people of God, who pretended to this principle indeed, and talked and spake of the interest of Christ; but, knowing nothing of the power of it, when these men were brought into the wilderness, and there met with provocations on the one hand and temptations on the other, they fell a lusting: and, indeed, they have pursued and acted their lusts to purpose also; which have been, indeed, the more abominable, in that some of them have still the impudence to pretend this principle of faith as to the interest of Christ, which teacheth no such things, nor produceth any such fruits as they abound withal.

Ans. 3. Many who have really the power of this principle in them, have yet been overpowered by temptations, and have brought forth fruits directly opposite unto that obedience, and holiness, and self-denial, which the principle spoken of tends unto. This, for the most part, hath fallen out since deliverance came in; and so the vigour of faith, raised by daily exercise, was much decayed. None, therefore, of these things can be charged on the principle itself, whose natural, genuine effects we have experienced to be such as no corrupt fancy or imagination could produce.

Many other reasons of this nature might be insisted on; but this is my first ground.

SECONDLY. Because in this much work hath been really done for Christ. Whatever have been the designs of any or all of the sons of men, Christ hath done so much for himself, as I can from thence with confidence conclude that the whole hath related unto him. Indeed, in the work he doth, his interest ofttimes lies very much in the dark, yea, is utterly hid from the instruments he employs. Little did the Medes and Persians think, in the destruction of Babylon, that they were executing the vengeance of Zion, and [avenging] the blood of Jerusalem, a poor city ruined sixty or seventy years before. And when the Romans destroyed Jerusalem, little did they think whose work they had in hand. And whatever instruments thought or intended, Christ hath done notable work for himself. The destruction of false worship as established by a law, the casting down of combinations for persecution, are no small works. I say, much work hath been done for Christ. There was a generation of men that were risen to a strange height in the contempt of the Spirit and ways of Christ,—combined in a resolution to oppose and persecute all the appearance of him, either by light or holiness, in his saints; setting up an outside, formal worship, in opposition unto the spiritual worship of the gospel. And upon the account of the light and truth which he began to command forth in those days, an unspeakable aggravation attended their guilt;—in the pursuit of whose design some were imprisoned, some banished into the ends of the earth, some beggared, many ruined and given up to death itself. Now, what work hath Christ made in these days on the men of that generation? what vengeance hath he taken on them? This is certain, not to insist on particulars, that whatever new sort or combination of men may rise up in their spirit and design, and whatever success they may obtain, yet the generality of the men of that provocation, at least the heads and rulers of it, are already sealed up under the indignation of the Lord Jesus, and the vengeance he takes for Zion. I shall not insist on more particulars. The wasting and destruction of the most eminent persecutors of the saints; the ruin and destruction of civil and ecclesiastical fabrics and combinations of men designing the opposing and persecuting of the Spirit of Christ; the removal of all that false worship under the pretence whereof they persecuted all the spiritual appearances of Christ,—hath been all work done for him.

THIRDLY. The breaking forth of much glorious gospel light under this dispensation evinces its relation unto Christ. Look upon the like outward work at any other time in the world. What is the issue of war, blood, confusion? Is it not darkness, ignorance, blindness, barrenness? Hath it not been so in other places of the world? But now, in the coming forth of Christ, though he hath a sword in one hand, yet he hath the sun in the other; though he cause darkness in the destruction and desolation that attend his vengeance, yet he gives light and faith to his saints, Mal. iv. 1, 2. Christ never comes for vengeance only; his chief design is love. Love brings forth light, and that which reveals him more to his saints, and which endears his saints more to him. But I have manifested before that he brings light with him; and he hath done so in this dispensation. Light as to the mysteries of the gospel,—light as to the riches of his grace,—light as to the way of his worship, of his ordinances and institutions,—hath broken out amongst us;—as Dan. xii. 4. It is such a day he speaks of.

I know how obnoxious this observation is to a sad objection:—"Call you these days of light and knowledge? Say you that truth hath shined forth or been diffused? Is it increased or more scattered abroad? Is not the contrary true?"

Ans. It cannot be denied but that many grievous and enormous abominations have been broached in these times, under the name and pretence of light and truth. But is that singular to these days? hath it not been so upon every appearance of Christ? As the light hath been, so hath been the pretence of it in error and darkness. No sooner was Christ come in the flesh, but instantly there were many false Christs: "Lo, here is Christ," and, "There is Christ," was common language in those days; as, "This is the only way," and "That is the only way," is now;—and yet the true Christ was in the world. And whatever light at any time comes forth, some mock;—false light about the same thing immediately breaks forth. So was it in the first spreading of the gospel, so in the late Reformation, and so in our days; and this is no evidence against the coming of Christ, but rather for it. For,—

1. Satan pours out this flood of abominations on purpose to bring an ill report upon the truth and light that is sent out by Christ. The great prejudice against truth in the world is, that it is new. "He seems to be a setter forth of strange" (or new) "gods," say they of Paul, because he preached Jesus and the resurrection. To increase this prejudice, the devil, with it or after it, sends forth his darkness; which, first, enables the world to load the truth itself with reproaches, whilst it comes accompanied with such follies as though it also were of the number; secondly, it disables weak friends to find out and close with the truth amidst so many false pretenders. Where much false money is abroad in the world, every man cannot discern and receive only that which is good. Much less will men always keep safe when they are so unstable and uncertain, as they are for the most part, about choosing of truth.

2. God permits it so to be,—

(1.) For the trial of careless professors. There must be heresies, that the approved may be tried. Most men are apt to content themselves with a lazy profession. They will hold to the truth whilst nothing appears but truth. Let error come with the same pretences and advantage,—they are for that also. Now, God delights to judge such persons even in this world, to manifest that they are not of the truth,—that they never received it in the love thereof. And he sifts and tries the elect by it; and that for many advantages not now to be insisted on. As, first, That they may experiment the efficacy of truth; secondly, His power in their preservation; thirdly, That they may hold truth upon firm and abiding grounds.

(2.) God permits it, to set a greater lustre and esteem upon truth. Truth, when it is sought after, when it is contended for, when it is experimented in its power and efficacy, is rendered glorious and beautiful; and all these, with innumerable other advantages, it hath by the competition that is set up against it by error. When men keep to the truth, by the power of God and the sense of its sweetness and usefulness to their own souls, and shall see some by their errors turned aside to one abomination, some to another,—some made to wither by them and under them,—they discern the excellency of the truth they embrace. So that, notwithstanding this exception, the observation stands good.

FOURTHLY. It appears from the general nature of the dispensation itself, which clearly answers the predictions that are of the great works to be accomplished in the latter days, upon the account of Christ and his church. This is a general head, whose particulars I shall not enter into. They cannot be managed without a consideration of all at least of the most principal prophecies of the last times, and of the kingdom of Christ, as to its enlargement, beauty, and glory in them;—too large a task for me to enter upon at present.

And these are some of the grounds on which I am persuaded that the alterations and providential dissolutions of these days have related unto and do lie in a subserviency to the interest of Christ and his church, whatever be the issue of the individual persons who have been engaged therein.

Come we now to the *uses.*

SERMON XII.

Use 1. OF trial or examination.

Hath Christ for many years now been in an especial manner come amongst us? Do these alterations relate to him and his interest, and so require universal holiness and godliness? Let us, then, in the first place, see whether, in their several stations, the men of this generation have walked answerable to such a dispensation. Christ, indeed, hath done his work; but have we done ours? He hath destroyed many of his enemies, judged false professors, hardened and blinded the wicked world, sent out his Spirit to plead with his people, and taken vengeance on their inventions; he hath given out plentiful measures of truth and light: but now the whole inquiry is, Whether all or any of us have answered the mind of Christ in these dispensations, and prepared ourselves to meet him as becometh his greatness and holiness?

For the generality of the people of the nation, Christ hath been pleading with them about their unbelief, worldliness, atheism, and contempt of the gospel. And what hath been the issue? Alas! he that was filthy is filthy still; he that was profane is so still; swearers, drunkards, and other vicious persons, are so still. Where is that man in a thousand in the nation that takes notice of any peculiar plea of Christ with him about his sin in any of these dispensations? One cries out of one party of men, another curses another party,—a third is angry with God himself; but as to the call of Christ in his mighty appearances, who almost takes any notice of it? The abominable pride, folly, vanity, luxury, that are found in this city, testify to their faces that the voice of Wisdom is not heard in the cry of fools. And whereas Christ's peculiar controversy with this nation hath been about the contempt of the gospel, is there any ground got upon the generality of men? is any reformation wrought on this account among them? nay, may we not say freely, that there is a greater spirit of hatred, enmity, and opposition to Christ and the gospel risen up in the nation than ever before? Light hath provoked and enraged them, so that they hate the gospel more than ever. How mad are the generality of the people on and after their idols,—their old superstitious ways of worship, which Christ hath witnessed against! What an enmity against the very doctrine of the gospel! what a combination in all places is there against the reforming dispensation of it! And is this any good omen of a comfortable issue of this dispensation? Is not Christ ready to say of such a people, "Why should you be smitten any more? you will revolt more and more?" and to swear in his wrath that they shall not enter into his rest? Nay, may he not justly take his gospel from us, and give it to a people that will bring forth fruit? O England! that in this thy day thou hadst known the things of thy peace! I fear they will be hidden from thee. The temptations of the day, the divisions of thy teachers, with other their miscarriages, and thine own lusts, have deceived thee,—and, without mercy, insuperable mercy, will ruin thee. Shall this shame be thy glory,—that Christ hath not conquered thee,—that thou hast hardened thyself against him?

But passing them, let us inquire, whether the mind of Christ hath, in these dispensations, been answered in a due manner by the saints themselves?—have they made it their business to meet him "in all holy conversation and godliness?" Indeed, to me the contrary appears, upon these considerations:—(1.) Their great differences among themselves about lesser things; (2.) Their little difference from the world in great things; (3.) The general miscarriage of them all in things prejudicial to the progress of the gospel; (4.) The particular deviation of some into ways of scandal and offence; (5.) The backsliding of most if not of all of them.

(1.) Consider their great differences among themselves about lesser things. I cannot insist on the weight that is laid by our Saviour on the union of his disciples, with the condescension and love which he requires of them to that purpose,—the motives and exhortations given by the Holy Ghost unto them on that account,—the provision of principles and means made in the gospel for it,—the necessity of it to the promotion of the interest of Christ in the world,—the benefit and advantage of it to the saints themselves,—the testimony given by it to the power of Christ and truth of his word,—the blasphemies and woful, soul-ruining offences that ensue on the contrary frame,—the weakening of faith, hinderance of prayer, quenching of zeal, strengthening of the men of the world, that attend the neglect of it;—I must not, I say, insist on these things; but see John xvii. 21–23, and Phil. ii. 1 3, of a hundred places that might be mentioned. How little the mind of Christ, and his expectation at his coming, hath been answered by his saints in this particular, is evident unto all.

[1.] Who is there, almost, who, having got any private opinion, true or false, wherein he differs from all or any of his brethren, who is not ready to proclaim it, without due regard to scandal and division, and even to quarrel with and divide from all that will not think as he thinks, and speak as he speaks? Now, the pride, self-fulness, vanity of mind, unlikeness to Christ, folly, want of faith and love, that is in such a frame, can never be expressed, nor sufficiently lamented. Christ abhors such a frame of spirit as he doth the pollution of the world.

[2.] Neither is this all; but men will lay more weight on their mint and cummin, on the lesser things wherein they differ from their brethren,—spend more time about them, write more books of them, labour more in their prosecution,—than they will do in and about the weighty things of law and gospel;—all which will appear at length to have been but the laying of hay and stubble on the foundation that must be consumed.

[3.] And farther;—men fall to judging and censuring each other as to their interest in Christ, or their eternal condition. By what rule?—the everlasting gospel?—the covenant of grace? No; but of the disciples: "Master, they follow not with us." They that believe not our opinion, we are apt to think believe not in Jesus Christ; and because we delight not in them, that Christ does not delight in them. This digs up the roots of love, weakens prayer, increases evil surmises (which are of the works of the flesh), genders strife and contempt;—things that the soul of Christ abhors.

[4.] The abomination of this wickedness ends not here; persecution, banishment, the blood of one another, hath on this account lain in the hearts and minds of some of the saints themselves. Not only have expressions to that purpose broken out from particular men, but it is to be feared that designs for it have been managed by parties and combinations. And are they not ready to dress up one another with such names and titles as may fit them for ruin? Sectaries, heretics, schismatics, on the one side;—priests, antichristian dogs, on the other: and all this while Christ is in the midst of us! And doth this answer the expectation of Christ? is this a preparation to meet him "in all holy conversation and godliness?" Can we render ourselves more unlike him, more unmeet for communion with him? Are not saints ready to join with the world against saints?—to take the vilest men into their bosom that will close with them in defaming, deriding, or, it may be, destroying their brethren? Doth Christ look for this usage in the house of his friends?

(2.) Consider their little difference from the world in great things. The great separation that Christ requires and commands of his saints is, from the world. He died to redeem them from it and out of it,—to deliver them from the present evil world,—the ways, works, fellowship, and ends of it; so providing that, in all holy conversation, his people should dwell alone, and not be reckoned among the nations.

Now, there are five things wherein Christ calls for his own to be differenced from the world and the men thereof:—[1.] In spirit; [2.] In principle; [3.] In conversation; [4.] In ends; [5.] In worship.

[1.] In spirit. He tells us everywhere, that it is one Spirit that is in his,—another that is in the world. 1 John iv. 4, "Greater is he that is in you, than he that is in the world." "There is a 'he' in you, and a 'he' in the world; and they are different and opposite. There is dwelling in you the Spirit of truth, which the world cannot receive, nor doth it know him," John xiv. 17. And when his disciples began to act in the power of a carnal spirit, he tells them they knew not what spirit they were of.

[2.] In principle. The principle that Christ requires in his saints is faith, working by love, and guided by that wisdom which is from above. 1 Tim. i. 5: Here are the saints' principles (I mean, should be so) of all their operations. A pure heart, and love, which is the end of all faith, is their great principle. This cleanses the conscience, and so sets them on work;—by this they take in strength for operation from Christ, without whom they can do nothing, John xv. 5. By this they receive light and guidance from Christ, and that wisdom which is from above, enabling them to order their affairs with discretion, James iii. 17, 18. Now, the principle that is in the world is self,—self acted and guided by carnal wisdom; which is sensual and devilish; on the account whereof they despise the principle and actings of the saints, Ps. xiv. 6.

[3.] In conversation. He hath redeemed us from a vain conversation, 1 Pet. i. 18. There is a peculiar emphasis put upon a conversation that becomes the gospel. There is a twofold conversation;—one that becometh the world and the men of the world; another that becometh the gospel and the profession thereof. That these be kept unmixed is the great exhortation of the apostle, Rom. xii. 2. And if you would know wherein a worldly conversation consists, the apostle telleth us, 1 John ii. 16. A conversation wherein any of these things bear sway, is a conversation of this world. That all holiness, all manner of holiness, universal holiness and godliness, is in the gospel conversation, to which the saints are called, shall be afterward spoken unto.

[4.] In ends. There is a double end of men's working and acting in this world:—1*st*. General, which regulates the course of their lives and conversations; 2*dly*. Particular, which regulates their particular actings and works: and in both these are the saints and the world differenced:—

1*st*. The general end of the saints is the glory of God. This lies in their eye, in their design,—how God may be glorified by them, his name exalted, his interest promoted; this way the bent of their minds and spirits tends. The general end of the men of the world is self; all is resolved into self. Whatever they do or act in public or private, whatever their pretence be, yet self is their end;—self-admiration, self-ostentation, self-satisfaction,—all centres in self. Sometimes, indeed, they may perform things that seem to be of a public tendency,—for the good of mankind, the good of nations, yea, it may be, the good of the church; so that it is hard for themselves to discover, or for others to charge them, it may be, that they act for self: but there are these two things that will evince men to make self their general end and aim, even then when they act for public ends:—

(1*st*.) This is a rule that will not fail men:—whatever in public actings is not done with a single eye for the glory of God, is done for self. These two divide all the general ends of men; and where one is not enthroned, the other is. Now, though some men may so far proceed in public actings, that it may not be evident wherein their self-interest lies,—though that also be but seldom,—yet, if they do not eye the glory of God with a single eye in these their actings, it is all for self;—and so it will be found at the last day. Now, how few will be left not turning into self on this rule, now [that] pretences run so high of public aims, might be easily evinced. It were no hard matter to discover how, in things of a public tendency, men make some fleshly imagination or other the god they worship;—so *that* be enthroned, they are little solicitous about the glory of God himself.

(*2dly.*) The difference of these ends even in public actings may be seen from the ways, means, and frame of spirit in which they are carried on. Let men pretend what they will to public ends, yet if they press after them with a proud, carnal, wrathful, envious spirit, by the ways, wisdom, and in the spirit of the world, without faith and submission to God, it is self and not God that is their aim. And this also might be improved to strip men of glorying in their public designs, were that my present business. Jehu's spirit spoiled his work.

2dly. There is a particular end that regulates the public actings of men. This in the saints is their doing the work of their generation; that, as Noah, they may walk with God in their generation. This is their integrity as to the special course of their lives, and their particular employment,—how they may fulfil the work of their generation. The special end of the men of the world is the satisfaction of one particular lust or other. "Will this increase my wealth, my power, my carnal interest in this world, my reputation for wisdom and ability, or give me advantage to grow in this or that corrupt end in particular?" This is the secret inquiry of their deceived hearts; this influences and regulates all their particular actings.

[5.] As to their separation in worship, I shall only point to that one place, and leave it, 2 Cor. vi. 14–18, and chap. vii. 1, which belongs to that discourse.

Now, I wish I had a more difficult task in hand,—I wish it were harder for me to manage any principle of conviction that we have not been prepared to meet Christ in his coming, from this consideration of our little difference from the world in these great things of principle, spirit, walking, ends, and worship. For,—

What a fleshly, wrathful, carnal, worldly spirit hath discovered itself in many professors; nay, in the most!—how little of the humble, lowly, meek, loving spirit of Christ! Many think it their glory to be unlike Christ in the spirit of their minds,—high, heady, self-full, proud, revengeful. What little difference between them and the men of the world! How like to one another! What oneness is found in them! Is this to learn Christ? to put on Christ? Is this the image of Christ that manifests itself in most professors? Nor,—

Are they at a distance from the world as to the principle of their walking and working. Do they walk by faith, and work by faith? are they guided by the wisdom that is from above? make they God their refuge? or are any men more dipped into a principle of carnal wisdom than most professors are? To seek counsel of God, to take the law of their proceedings at his mouth, to look up to him for guidance and direction, to derive strength from the Lord Christ by believing for the work of their employments,—in how few are these things found! Their own wisdom, their own counsel, their own contrivance, their own abilities, shall do their work. Carnal policy and fleshly wisdom are their net and drag.

Moreover, what is our conversation? How like the world in our persons, in our families, in our spirits, callings,—in whatever the world may properly call its own! Professors have justled the men of the world out of the possession of the ways of the world. How few are found walking in a world-condemning conversation! a gospel-glorifying conversation! a fruitful, holy conversation! We are known from the world by word more than by deed; which is not the way that James directs us unto.

I might go through with the rest of the considerations mentioned, and manifest that there is another evil found amongst us; for as we have great differences among ourselves about little things, so we have little difference from the world in those which are great and weighty.

(3.) Consider the general miscarriage almost of all professors in things prejudicial to the advancement of the gospel. The pretence whereof we have served ourselves all along, hath been, of the furtherance, propagation, and advancement of the gospel. Our Lord Christ hath sent out light, and given opportunities suitable unto such a design;—never greater advantages nor greater opportunities from the foundation of the world. If ever they be required at the hands of this generation, they will be found to have been so. Whence, then, hath it been that the work hath not gone on and prospered? why doth it yet stick? Hath it not been from the woful miscarriage of those who were looked on as the means and instruments of carrying it on? Have there been a few saints in a place? It is odds [but] that they have been at variance among themselves, and made sport for the vain multitude by their divisions; or they have walked frowardly, provokingly, uselessly, worldly, [so] that their pretence for the gospel hath been despised because of their persons. Have they, as men concerned in the honour of Christ and the gospel, as men enjoying the blessed principle of his Spirit, laboured to be useful, fruitful,—to do good to all, to be meek, lowly, self-denying, charitable, abounding in good works, patient towards opposers, not reviling again, not returning evil for evil, bearing, suffering, committing all to Christ? Alas! how few are there who have so walked! Could some see believers making it their business to be like Christ in the world,—to deny themselves as he did,—to do good to all as he did,—to be patient under persecution and reproaches as he was,—to be tender, pitiful, merciful, like him,—to abide in faith and prayer as he did; what might we not expect, as to the advancement of the gospel amongst us? We complain of cold preaching among ministers, of dead and dull attendance in hearers, of contempt of the word in the most, whereby the power of the gospel is kept within narrow bounds. But the truth is, the prejudices that have been raised by the miscarriages of professors have had a greater influence unto that evil event than any of the rest. And hath this been to meet Christ in his coming?

(4.) Of the like nature are the scandalous offences of many. I shall not insist on the scandalous apostasies of many professors, who, some by one great sin, some by another, are fallen off from the profession of the gospel. I wish that too many other instances might not be found among them that remain. Are there not some proud unto scandal, or sensual unto scandal, or covetous unto scandal, or negligent of their families and relations unto scandal, or conformable to the ways, customs, and fashions of the world unto scandal? I wish no such things might be found among us.

(5.) Add hereunto the general backsliding, or going back from God, that is amongst professors. We scarce seem to be the same generation of men that we were fifteen or sixteen years ago:—some have utterly lost their principle. Zeal for God, reformation, purity of ordinances, interest of Christ in his saints, are things to be despised, things that have no concernment in our condition and affairs; as though we had no more need of Christ or his interest amongst us: and in the best, is not a fresh spirit of our present engagement almost lost?

But why should I insist farther on these things? Are not the things that have been spoken sufficient for a rebuke, or a conviction at least, that the professing people of Christ have not walked as though they had a just respect to his coming, or his peculiar presence amongst them? May we not justly fear, that our multiplied provocations may at length prevail with him to withdraw, to put a stop to his work that is upon the wheel; not only to leave us to manifold entanglements in the carrying of it on, but also utterly to forsake it,—to cast down the tower, and pluck up the hedge that he hath made about his vineyard, and leave it to be laid waste? He must have a heart like the flint in the rock of stone, that doth not tremble at it. But complaints will not be our relief. That which is incumbent on us, if yet there may be hope, is our answering the exhortation in my text. If, then, any sense do fall upon our spirits that Christ is come amongst us in a peculiar manner, in the providential alterations and dissolutions that have been among us; and that we have not hitherto demeaned ourselves as becometh them who are called to meet him, and to walk with him in such ways and paths as his amongst us have been;—then, I say, let us apply ourselves in our next use to the exhortation that lies before us,—to all manner of "holy conversation."

Use 2. Of exhortation. That, I say, then, which we are now to attend unto, is the exhortation that is included in this expression, "What manner of persons ought we to be?" To further the efficacy of this exhortation, give me leave to premise some few things:—

First. There are general reasons of holiness and godliness, and there are special motives unto them. I am not now dealing upon the general reasons of holiness on the account of the covenant of grace; and so shall not press it on those considerations upon believers as such. But I speak of it in reference unto the peculiar motive mentioned in the text,—namely, the providential dissolution of temporal concernments; and so speak to believers as men interested therein,—as persons whom Christ hath a special regard unto in these his dispensations. It is one thing to say, "What manner of persons ought ye to be, whom God hath loved with an everlasting love, whom Christ hath washed in his own blood,—who have received the Spirit of Christ?" and another to say, "Ye that are loved with an everlasting love, are washed in the blood of Christ, and made partakers of the Holy Ghost, seeing that Christ is come amongst us to the dissolution of the great things of the nations, what manner of persons ought ye to be?" That is it in a peculiar pressing unto holiness on the account of the motive that is intended.

Secondly. There is a holiness and godliness that is required universally, at all times, in all places and seasons, and in all persons whatever, by the gospel; and there is a peculiar improvement of that holiness and godliness at some seasons, and in some persons, that is not required at other times, and of other persons. Christ hath work for all the grace of his people in this world; and, according as opportunities for that work are presented unto them, they ought to stir up their grace for it. In the times of Christ's coming, he hath great work to do for and by the holiness and godliness of his people. A great testimony is to be given to himself thereby; his work is much to be promoted by it; the world to be convinced, condemned; his judgments against them justified in the sight of all;—and much more hath Christ to do with the holiness of his people at such a season. Now, it is this peculiar improvement of covenant, gospel holiness that is required; not only that holiness that is indispensably incumbent on us by the virtue of the covenant, but that heightening and improvement of it which the season wherein we live, and the work that Christ hath to do, do require of us.

These things being premised, let us now proceed to the management of our exhortation; and observe,—

(1.) That the apostle calls us to a consideration how this work may be effected: "What manner of persons ought ye to be?" Consider with yourselves the equity of the matter, the greatness of the motive, and the ways whereby it may be answered. The business is not now to be left at an ordinary rate, nor unto private meditations; it is to be made a matter of solemn consideration and design; it is to be managed with advice and counsel: consider, I say, "what manner of persons." It is not about holiness in general that I speak; but about that holiness which becomes us in such a season. This, then, is the first part of this exhortation,—that as to the improvement of holiness answerable to the season of this coming of Christ, we would carry it on by design, by counsel, by deliberate consideration; not only labouring to be holy ourselves, but to promote the work of holiness, the eminency, the activity, the usefulness of it, in one another,—in all believers,—so far as our prayers, exhortations, and examples, can reach. This the apostle pleads for on the same account, Heb. iii. 13; and chap. x. 23, 24, to the same purpose. And we have the practice of it, Mal. iii. 16. It was such a time and season as that we treat of, Christ was coming to his temple, verses 1–3. The earth was full of wickedness and contempt of him. What do the saints do? Do they content themselves with their ordinary measures? Do they keep all close to themselves? No; they confer, advise, consult, and that frequently, how, wherein, whereby, the expectation of their coming Lord may be answered. The reasons, arguments, way of carrying on such a counsel and design, the apostle declares, Rom. xiii. 11–14, "The time requires it, the duty is urgent, temptations are many, failings have been great,—the Lord is nigh at hand." Let, then, believers enter together into this plot, this design; draw as many as they can into it; promote it by all ways and means possible. Let them get together; make this their aim, their design,—engage in it as the duty of their day, of their time and season. This would be a plot that the men of the world would have more just cause to fear than ever they had of any, and yet dare not question, disturb, or interrupt;—a design that would blow up their contrivance, disappoint their counsel, ruin their interest,—shake heaven and earth. Let every one contribute the best of his counsel, the best of his grace, the best of his interest in heaven, the utmost of his self-denial, to the carrying of it on. Methinks we have dwelt long enough upon others' failings,—fruitless, selfish designs; the world is full of the noise, the steam, the filth of them. Oh, that the stream of our endeavours might now be another way! Oh, that God would stir up some that might stand up and cry, "Who is for God? who is on our side for holiness now?" If ministers at their meetings, if Christians at theirs, would make this their business; if all would agree to sacrifice their lusts, their self-love, their by-opinions to this work,—what glory would redound to Christ! what salvation would be wrought in the earth! Why do any of us lie complaining? Let us up and be doing; there is no doubt, no question to be made. This is that which Christ lengthens his controversy with us about, that he will bring us to, or ruin us and destroy us as to this world. Ministers meet. What do they? Pray a while, and spend their time in and about differences, controversies,—how they may do this or that, which I shall not name. Christians meet, and pray, and go away as they came. Lusts are not sacrificed; faults are not confessed to one another; exhortations mutual are not used;—no ground is got for holiness or godliness, but things remain as they did, or rather grow worse and worse every day: at best, profession rises, and the power of religion falls and decreases.

I heartily wish professors would be persuaded to come together to advise, to consult for God,—for the glory of Christ and the gospel, and for their own interest in this thing;—to consider what are the pressing temptations of the days wherein we live; what are the corruptions and lusts that are apt to be provoked and excited by these temptations, or by the state of things amongst us; what duties seem to be neglected; and what are the common, visible failings and scandal of professors, wherein themselves, through party, or neglect, or selfishness, have been wanting: and to advise and pray for the remedying of all these evils. I wish they would seriously stir up and exhort one another to contend mightily for the crucifying of all their secret lusts and bosom sins,—for heart-purity and likeness to Christ in all things; that they would incite others, and draw all they can into their society and combination in all parts of the nation. In particular, let not us of this place stand still, expecting when others will begin the work. The meaner, poorer, worse we are, the more incumbent is it on us to rise and be doing. The water is moved, teaching [healing?] is in it, and we strive not who shall enter first, but rather stand striving, contesting with others, to put them before us!

This is the first direction:—Let us make the matter of holiness and godliness suited to the coming of Christ a business of design, counsel, and common engagement; whereunto every one may contribute of the store which from God he hath received. Blessed will be those servants whom their Master, when he cometh, shall find so doing!

SERMON XIII.

I SHALL now add some cautions as to the pursuit of the first direction:—

[1.] Take heed of a degeneration into self-righteousness. Intendments of holiness have more than once been ruined by Satan through this deceit; they have set out upon conviction, and ended in Pharisaism. Now, this hath been done many ways:—

1*st.* Some, really convinced of the vanity of an empty profession, and of boasting of saintship upon the account of faith and light without holiness and godliness,—which was the way of many when James and John wrote their epistles,—fall to dispute and contend (as well they may) for the absolute necessity of holiness and strict obedience, of fruitfulness and good works. But Satan here gets advantage upon men's natural spirits, their heats, and contentions, and insinuates an inherent righteousness, upon the account whereof we should, under one pretence or other, expect acceptation with God as to the justification of our persons. So he prevailed upon the Galatians. The way is narrow and strait that lies between the indispensable necessity of holiness, and its influence into our righteousness. Because no faith will justify us before God, but that also which will justify itself by fruitfulness before men, a great mistake arises, as though what it doth for its own justification were to be reckoned unto ours. Many in our days have gone off from the mystery of the gospel on this account.

2*dly.* It prevails from a secret self-pleasing, that is apt to grow on the minds of men from a singularity in the performance of duties. This is that which the Heart-searcher aims to prevent in his command, that " when we have done all, we should say we are unprofitable servants;" that is, in the secrets of our hearts to sit down in a sense of our own worthlessness. And here lies another great practical difficulty,—namely, to have the rejoicing of a good conscience in our integrity and constancy in duties, without a reflection upon something of self, that the soul may please itself and rest in. Nehemiah fixes on the medium, chap. xiii. 22. He had in the sight of God the testimony of his conscience concerning the service he had done for the house of God; but as to the rest, he winds up all in mercy, pardon, and grace. " God, I thank thee I am not as other men," is apt to creep into the heart in a strict course of duties. And this self-pleasing is the very root of self-righteousness; which, as it may defile the saints themselves, so it will destroy those who only in the strength of their convictions go forth after a holiness and righteousness: for it quickly produceth the deadly, poisonous effect of spiritual pride; which is the greatest assimilation to the nature of the devil that the nature of man is capable of.

3dly. Our own holiness hath an advantage upon spiritual sense against the righteousness of Christ. The righteousness of Christ is utterly a strange thing to the best of unbelievers; and this puts them by all means upon the setting up of their own, Rom. x. 3. And believers themselves know it only by faith, Rom. i. 17; which is "of things not seen." But what we are ourselves, what we do, what we aim at, and in what manner, this we have a near sense of. And holiness is apt to insinuate itself into the conscience with a beauty that is none of its own, to proffer itself to the soul's embraces instead of Jesus Christ. Its native beauty consists in its answering the will of God, conforming the soul to the likeness of Christ, and being useful in the world, in a covenant of mere mercy. From its presence, and the sense we have of it, the heart is apt to put a varnish and false beauty upon it, as to the relief of conscience upon the account of justification. As it was of old with the children of Israel, when Moses was in the mount, and not seen, nor had they any visible pledge of the presence of God, instantly they turned their gold into a calf that would be always present with them;—being in the dark as to the righteousness of Christ, which is, as it were, absent from them, men set up their own holiness in the stead of it; which, though of itself it be of God, yet turned into self-righteousness is but a calf,—an idol, that cannot save them.

This is my first caution. But that we may make the better improvement of it, as unto present practice, I shall add some evidences of the prevalency, or at least contending, of self-righteousness for an interest in the soul, under a pretence of duty and holiness; as,—

(1*st.*) When, under a design of holiness, there is an increase of a bondage-frame of spirit;—when the mind begins to be enslaved to the duties which it doth itself perform;—when that amplitude, freedom, and largeness of mind which is in a gracious frame of heart decays, and a servile bondage-frame grows in the room of it, so that the soul doth what it doth under this notion, that it dare not do otherwise. "Where the Spirit of the Lord is, there is liberty," 2 Cor. iii. 17. Those that come to Christ, he makes free, John viii. 36;—there is freedom and spiritual largeness of heart unto obedience and duty. A will unto duty, enlarged, dilated, and sweetened by love, delight, joy, complacency in the matter of obedience, is the freedom we speak of. This frame, I confess, is not always alike prevalent in gracious souls. They may have things ready to die; sin within, temptations without, desertion from God,—all of them together, each of them, may disturb this harmony, and bring them for a time, it may be a long time, under an indisposition unto such a frame;—but this is for the most part predominant. When such a frame decays, or is not, all endeavours, pains, attempts, severities in duties, do all relate to the law,—to bondage; and consequently lead to self-righteousness, fear, subjection of conscience to duties,—not [to] God in Christ in the duty; fluctuating of peace according to performances. The soul, in its strictest course, had need fear a snare.

(*2dly.*) Increasing in form, and withering in power. Forms are of three sorts:—[1*st.*] Those of institution; [*2dly.*] Moral; [*3dly.*] Arbitrary, in conversation.

[1*st.*] There are forms and ways of worship, whereof some are, and all pretend to be, of Christ's institution. Let us at present take it for granted that they are all what they are apprehended to be,—namely, from Christ. For a man to grow high, earnest, zealous, in and about them,—to be strict and severe in contending for them, and yet find no spiritual refreshment in them, or communion with God, nor to grow in faith and love by them, is to dwell on the confines of self-righteousness, if not hypocrisy. This was the very sin of the Jews about their institutions, so much condemned in the Scripture. None use instituted ways or forms of worship profitably, but such as find communion with God in them, or are seriously humbled because they do not.

[*2dly.*] The outward form of moral duties, that depend not merely on institution, is the same. Such are praying, preaching, hearing. Abounding in them, without a suitable increase in grace, power, liberty, love, meekness, lowliness of mind, argues, though under the highest light to the contrary, a real mixture of self.

[*3dly.*] There are also outward forms in conversation that are used to the same purpose. We have had some who have changed their outward form in a few years as often as Laban changed Jacob's wages. What shape they will next turn themselves into, I know not. This is not going from strength to strength, and increasing in life and power, but from one shape to another. And as their word and prophecy is directly proportioned and answerable, in its outward appearance, to the administration of the Old Testament, and not at all to the spiritual dispensation of the New; so it may be feared that, in the principle of their obedience, they lie under a legal bondage and self-righteousness, which hath utterly spoiled that which, perhaps, in its first design, set out for mortification and holiness.

(*3dly.*) Where self-righteousness is getting ground, these two, bondage and form, at length bring forth burdensomeness and wearisomeness. This God charges on such justiciaries, Isa. xliii. 22, "Thou hast been weary of me." The ways and worship of God grow very grievous and burdensome to such a soul. He is a stranger to that of the apostle, "His commandments are not grievous;" and that of our

Saviour himself, "My yoke is easy, and my burden is light." The easiness of the yoke of Christ ariseth from the assistance that is given to him that bears it by the Holy Ghost, as also the connaturalness that is wrought in the heart to all the duties of it. Both these accompany a gospel frame. But when a soul is deserted of these, the yoke grows heavy, and galleth him; but yet he must go on. This is from self-righteousness. Let this, then, be our first caution.

[2.] Take heed of monastic uselessness. I am persuaded monkery came into the world not only with a glorious pretence, but also with a sincere intention. Men weary of the ways, weary of the lusts and sin of the world, designing personal holiness, left their stations, and withdrew themselves into retirement. David was almost gone with this design, Ps. lv. 6, "O that I had wings!" and Jeremiah, chap. ix. 2, "O that I had a lodging in the wilderness!" Whose heart hath not been exercised with reasonings of this kind, "Oh, that we could be freed from the incumbrances and provocations of this world; what manner of persons might we be in all holy conversation and godliness?" But consider,—

1*st.* What success this design prosecuted hath had in others. How quickly did it degenerate into wretched superstition, and was thereon blasted and rejected of God!

2*dly.* God can suffer temptation to pursue us into a wilderness, that shall more obstruct us in the progress of holiness than all the difficulties we meet withal in this world. It is not of what kind our temptations are, but what assistance we are to expect under them, that we are to look after.

3*dly.* Not our communion [our intercourse with men], but God's work, is to be considered. God hath work to do in this world; and to desert it because of its difficulties and entanglements, is to cast off his authority. Universal holiness is required of us, that we may do the will of God in our generation, Gen. vi. 9. It is not enough that we be just, that we be righteous, and walk with God in holiness; but we must also serve our generation, as David did before he fell asleep. God hath a work to do; and not to help him, is to oppose him.

[3.] Take heed of laying a design for holiness in a subserviency unto any carnal interest,—of crying, with Jehu, "Come see my zeal for the LORD of hosts,"—thereby to do our own work and compass our own ends. The great scandal that hath befallen the days wherein we live, and which hath hardened the spirits of many against all the ways of God, is, that religion, godliness, zeal, holiness, have been made a cloak for carnal and secular ends. What of this hath been really given, and what hath been taken on false imaginations, the last day will discover. In the meantime this is certain, that there is a corruption in the heart of man, rising up to such a visible prostitution of the whole profession of religion,—which of all things must be carefully avoided.

And this is the grand exhortation that I shall insist on: Let it be our design to promote generation-holiness in ourselves and others, with the cautions insisted on.

(2.) That which in the next place is considerable, is the proposing of the ingredients that lie in the motive to holiness, here expressed by the apostle, "Seeing that these things shall be dissolved." As,—

[1.] It will be a furtherance of holiness, to take off our hearts from an esteem and valuation of all things that are so obnoxious to dissolution. An estimation or valuation of earthly things is on all accounts the greatest hinderance to the promotion of holiness. Earthly-mindedness, pride of spirit, elation above our brethren, self-estimation, carnal confidence, contempt of the wisdom and grace of others, aptness to wrath and anger,—some or all of these always accompany such a frame.

The apostle also makes this an effectual means of the improvement of holiness,—that the mind be taken off from the delightful contemplation of visible things, 2 Cor. iv. 18. Things will work towards "a weight of glory," (in which words the apostle alludes to the Hebrew word כָּבוֹד, "glory," which comes from a root signifying to "weigh," or "to be heavy;" that being the only weighty thing, and all others light and of no moment;)—this way, I say, things will work, whilst our minds are taken off from things that are seen. The mind's valuation of them is as great an obstruction to the growth of holiness as any thing whatever that can beset us in our pilgrimage. Now, what can give a greater allay to the warmth of our thoughts and minds, than their continual obnoxiousness to dissolution and change? This the apostle makes his argument everywhere. "They are temporal things," saith he, "things that abide not, things obnoxious to change and ruin. The world passeth away, and the figure of it. Wilt thou set thine heart upon that which is not?" And there lies the force of the inference under consideration: "Seeing that these things shall be dissolved,"—and it may be in a way of judgment, in a dreadful, fearful manner,—how is it incumbent on us to fix our hearts on more durable things, to choose the better part, the better portion! What advantage can it be to enlarge our hearts to the love of the things that are upon the wing?—to cleave to parting things with our affections?—to grow in our desires after that which withdraws itself from us continually? Let us, then, consider how many duties have been omitted,—how many temptations have been offered and objected to us,—how many spiritual frames of heart prevented or expelled,—how much looseness and vanity of mind introduced,—how much self-confidence promoted,—by an over-valuation of these things; and we shall then see what influence a watching against it may have to the furtherance of a design of holiness.

[2.] It will be so, to take off our care about them. This also is a worm that lies at the root of obedience, and is of itself able to wither it, if not removed. Our Lord Jesus Christ, giving us instruction how we should be prepared for the coming of such a day as that whereof we are speaking, charges us, among other things, to take heed that we " be not overcharged with the cares of this life," Luke xxi. 34. Indeed, there is nothing so opposite to that peculiar holiness and godliness that is required of us, in and under great providential dissolutions, as this of care about perishing things. The special holiness that we press after is a due mixture of faith, love, self-denial, fruitfulness,—all working in a peculiar and eminent manner. Now, to every one of these is this care a canker and a gangrene, fitted to eat out and devour the life and spirit of them. The very nature of faith consists in a universal casting of our care on God, 1 Pet. v. 7, " Cast all your care on him." All our care about temporal, spiritual, eternal things, let us cast all this on God,—our whole burden. This is believing, this is faith: and what is more opposite unto it than this care and solicitousness of the soul about the obtaining or retaining of these things? Resignation, acquiescency, rest,—all which are acts or effects of faith,—are devoured by it. Trust in God, affiance, delight in his will,—[it] ruins them all. How can a soul glorify God in believing in a difficult season, that is overlaid with this distemper. Nothing is more diametrically opposite thereunto.

Love enlarges the heart to Christ, and every thing of Christ: valuation, delight, satisfaction, accompany it. It makes the heart free, noble, ready for service, compassionate,—zealous. Nothing is more called for in such a day: and the decay of faith, in the trials and temptations of such a season, is called the " waxing cold of love;" as the fruit decays when the root is consumed. To think of glorifying God in the days wherein we live, without hearts warmed, enlarged, made tender, compassionate, by gospel love, is to think to fly without wings, or to walk without feet. What day, almost, what business, wherein our love is not put to the trial, in all the properties of it! Whether it can bear and forbear; whether it can pity and relieve; whether it can hope all things, and believe all things; whether it can exercise itself towards friends and towards enemies; whether it can give allowance for men's weakness and temptations; whether it can value Christ above all, and rejoice in him in the loss of all, and many the like things, is it continually tried withal. Now, nothing so contracts and withers the heart, as to all these things, as the cares of this world do. Whatever is selfish, fearful, unbelieving, is inwrapped in them. They sometimes pine, wither, and render useless, the whole man;—always drink up the spirit, and deprive it of any communion with God in any thing it hath to do.

The same may be said concerning self-denial and fruitfulness; which in an eminent manner Christ now calls upon us for. Love, care, and fear, about the things that shall be dissolved, unframes the soul for them.

On these considerations, and the like which might be added, may this direction be improved, and no small obstacle unto a course of universal holiness and godliness be taken away. Is the power, are the riches, the pleasures of the world valuable?—Alas! they are all passing away; it is but yet a little while, and their place shall know them no more. Yet, could we take off our hearts from an undue valuation of these things, and care about them, half our work were done.

(3.) That which remains, for the closing of our discourse on this subject, is to give some few motives unto the duty proposed; and I shall only mention three generals:—[1.] Relating unto ourselves; [2.] Unto others; [3.] Unto Christ himself.

[1.] As to ourselves;—this alone will maintain peace and quiet in our souls, in and under those dissolutions of things that we are to be exercised with. We know what desolations, what ruin of families, what destruction of all outward enjoyments in many, they have already in these nations been attended with; and we know not how soon, nor by what ways or means, the bitterest part of the cup, as to outward pressures and calamities, may become our portion. We have seen somewhat of the beginning of the work of Christ;—where he will cease, what he hath yet farther to do, we know not. Our concernment, then, certainly was never greater than it is at this day, to keep up peace and rest within. If there should be a confederacy of outward and inward trouble, who can stand before it? A wounded body, a wounded (it may be ruined) estate, and a wounded spirit all together, who can bear? This is that alone which the world cannot take from us; which is not obnoxious to sword, fire, plots, conspiracies,—nothing without us,—even the peace that is left us, left to our own keeping, through the Holy Ghost, by Jesus Christ. It is not committed to parliaments, to armies, to rulers, to keep for us: it is committed to our own souls to keep, through the Holy Ghost; and no man can take it from us. Again: as it is valuable on this account, that it cannot be taken from us; so on this also, that it will countervail and support us under the loss of all that can. Peace in God, rest in sole retirement, quietness, and security of mind on spiritual, gospel accounts, sense of God's love in Christ, will support and keep life and vigour in the soul in the loss of outward peace, with whatever is desirable and valuable unto us on any account that relates to this world.

Now, there is no maintaining of this peace and rest in such a season, without the performance of this duty. So dealt Habakkuk, chap. iii. 16, "I trembled in myself, that I might rest in the day of trouble." That which God required of him in that season, *that* he brought up his soul unto, [in order] that he might have rest; and his endeavour had the glorious issue mentioned, verses 17, 18. Though spiritual peace may radically and virtually live under many sins and provocations, yet it will not flourish under them, or bring forth any refreshing fruit. To have the fruit and effect of peace under a continuance in any known sin, is impossible. Now, the omission of any known duty is a known sin; and that a peculiar pressing after eminency in universal holiness and godliness in such a season is a known duty, I have before evinced;—no maintaining of inward peace, rest in God, without it: and we shall be sure to be tried, whether it be in us of a truth or not. I discourse not what the carnal security of seared, blinded, hardened sinners will do; but I am sure the weak, tottering, uncertain peace of many believers, will not support them in such trials as it is not only possible that we may, but probable that we shall, meet withal. Would you now desire that your Master should find you unprepared,—that he should make his entrance whilst all things were in disorder? If the heavens should thunder over you, and the earth tremble under you, and the sword stand ready to devour;—oh! what sad thoughts must you have, if at the same time you should be forced to say, "O my soul! is not God mine enemy also? May not wrath, and hell, and judgment be at the end of this dispensation?" What is the reason that a very rumour, a noise oftentimes, is ready to fill many of our souls with such disturbances? Is it not because this peace doth not flourish in the inward man? And what shall we do in the day of trial itself? Let us, then, endeavour, as Peter exhorts, 2 Epist. iii. 14, to "be found of Christ in peace." And what may we do that we may be found of him in peace? "Why," saith he, "be 'without spot, and blameless.'" Let him come when he will, in what way he pleases, we shall be found in a way of peace, if we be found spotless and blameless, in a way of holiness. "And blessed is that servant whom his Master, when he cometh, shall find so doing." This will give light in a dungeon, as it did to Paul and Silas;—ease in the fire, in the furnace, as to Shadrach, Meshach, and Abednego;—contentment in the loss of all, as it did to Job;—satisfaction on the foresight of future trouble, as it did to David: "Although my house be not so with God, yet he hath made with me an everlasting covenant." Whatever sword be in the hand of Christ, whatever fire or tempest be before him and round about him, what vengeance soever he is to take on any or all of the sons of men,—this peace, kept up by the holiness he requires in such a season, will make a way to his bosom-love, and there repose the soul in rest and quietness.

[2.] As to others, what Paul saith to Timothy in another case, about preaching of the gospel, may in some sense be spoken in this. "Take heed," saith he, "to the doctrine; for thereby thou shalt save thyself, and them that hear thee." Who knows but that hereby we may save ourselves, and the nation wherein we live! The Lord Christ hath certainly a controversy with these nations; he hath begun to deal with them in his indignation; and we know that there are provocations enough amongst us to stir him up unto our ruin. Who knows, I say, but that by meeting him in a way of generation-holiness, we may divert deserved ruin; at least hinder, that it be not brought upon us for the provocations of his sons and daughters?

Now, there are several ways whereby this may have an influence into the safety and deliverance of the nations themselves:—

1*st.* By setting all things right between Christ and the saints, that he may have no need farther to shake the earth and dissolve the heavens of the nations, to awaken his own from their security, to loosen them from perishing things, or to accomplish any other glorious end towards them. Christ sometimes sifts nations, that his wheat may be separated from the chaff: he sets nations on fire, that they may be a furnace for the trial of his own; and when their dross is cleansed he will quench his fire. When there was but one saint in a ship, yet it was for his sake that a storm came on all the rest. It is not always for the sins of the wicked, that they may be destroyed, that he comes in a way of judgment; but for the sins of his people, that they may be cleansed. So "judgment," as Peter speaks, "begins at the house of God." It is not unlikely that our troubles were brought on these nations for the sins of the nations, in their persecution of Christ, his truths, and saints, against great light. Nor is it less likely that troubles are continued on these nations for the sins of the saints themselves,—such as those before insisted on. Now, what is it that in such trials Christ calls for, and which he will not cease calling for until he prevails? Is it not the work which we are in the pursuit of,—weanedness from the world, self-denial, zeal for truth, humbleness, fruitfulness, faithfulness, universal holiness? If here, then, lies the root of Christ's controversy with these nations, as most probably it doth; if this be the cause of our troubles (as to me questionless it is); an engagement into the pursuit of this work is the only remedy and cure of the evils that we either feel or fear in these nations. Other remedies have been tried, and all in vain. O that we had hearts, through the Holy Ghost, to make trial of this, which the great physician, Jesus Christ, hath prescribed unto us! Heaven and earth call for it at our hands; the nations groan under our sin;—if we regard not ourselves, yet let us make it our business to deliver England out of the hand of the Lord, Josh. xxii. 31.

2dly. In that it may be an effectual means for the reformation of the nation. Reformation is the great thing that we have been talking of many years; and this hath been our condition in our attempts after it,—the more that light for it hath broken forth amongst us, the more unreformed hath the body of the people been; yea, the more opposite, for the most part, unto reformation. And may not this, among other things, be one occasion, yea, the principal cause of it,—the light of truth hath been accompanied with so many scandals in some, with so little power and evidence in the most, that prejudices have been strengthened in the minds of men against all that hath been pretended or professed? I am persuaded that a design for generation-holiness, carried on according to the light that we have received, would have a greater influence on the minds of the men of the world to look after reformation, than any of our entreaties or exhortations have yet obtained. We are contemptible to the nation, in our pressing after reformation whilst we are divided amongst ourselves; conformable to the world, whilst we proclaim our unmortified lusts, pride, covetousness, ambition, revenge, self-seeking. Would all the people of God stir up themselves to show forth the power of that faith and life they have received, and so take away advantage from obdurate opposers of the gospel, and give an eminent example to others, who now abhor them on the account of many prejudices that they have taken, the nations would be more awakened unto their duty than now they are. Were we agreed and united on this principle, that we would jointly and severally make this our design,—what work might be wrought in families, councils, counties, cities! Now, reformation is acknowledged to be the means, the only means, of the preservation of a nation;—and this the only means of that.

3dly. This is the most effectual way of standing in the gap, to turn away the indignation of the Lord against the nation. Whatever is required thereunto is contained in this design of holiness: there is reformation, there is wrestling by prayer, sundry promises improving our interest in Christ,—all included in this duty. Now, this is the most common way of saving nations,—when wrath is ready to break forth, some Moses or Samuel stands up and pleads for a deliverance, and prevails. Says God, "Destroy not the cluster; there is a blessing in it." When the greatest and most dreadful judgment that God ever executed on sinners in this world was coming forth, had there been ten persons following after holiness, its accomplishment had been prevented. Here, then, we have a project to save three nations by; and without this, in vain shall they use any other remedies,—they shall not be healed.

[3.] Consider this thing, how it relates unto Christ and his glory. All the revenue of glory or honour that we bring unto Christ in this world, is by our obedience or holiness. He did not die for us that we might be great, or wise, or learned, or powerful in the world; but that he might purify us to be a peculiar people unto himself, zealous of good works. This was his design and aim,—that he might have a holy people, a faithful people in the world. He tells us that herein his Father is glorified, that we bear much fruit;—not that we be successful, that we rule and prevail, that we are in credit and reputation; but that we bring forth much fruit: and in the glory of the Father is the Son glorified also. It is this alone that adorns the doctrine of his gospel, and lifts up his name in the world; but especially is Christ glorified by the holiness of his saints in such a season; because,—

1*st.* Thereby we bear witness to the world that indeed we believe him to be come forth amongst us, and that the works that are on the wheel relate to his kingdom and interest. Let us talk of it whilst we please, unless we live and walk as those who have communion with Christ in the works he doth, the world will yet think that, whatever we profess, yet indeed we believe, as they do, that it is a common thing that hath befallen us. But when indeed they shall see that there is a real reverence of his person upon our spirits, and that we bestir ourselves in his ways, like servants in the presence of their master,—this carries a conviction along with it. To hear men talk of the coming of Christ, and the day of Christ, and the great and terrible things that Christ hath done in these days, and yet in the meantime to walk as the men of the world,—in a spirit of pride, selfishness, and wrath, in sensuality or pleasure, in neglect of prayer and humiliation, yea, of all gospel duties,—swearers and drunkards do not so dishonour Christ as such men do. But let men but see professors making it their business to be holy, humble, self-denying, useful in the world, condescending in love, resigning all to God,—they cannot but say, "Well, this is a great day to the saints; they verily believe that Christ is among them." This is a professing that brings conviction; words are but as speaking with tongues, that work not out the glory of Christ.

2*dly.* Thereby we bear witness unto what sort of kingdom it is that Christ hath in the world, and what a kind of king he is. I cannot but fear that our talking of the kingdom of Christ, and managing our notions of it (at least in the world's apprehensions) to carnal advantages, hath been a notable hinderance of the coming of it forth in beauty and glory amongst us. Every party talks of the kingdom of Christ, some more, some less,—all pretend unto it; but it is evident that many would set him on his throne with the petition of Zebedee's children in their mouths,—that they may sit on his right hand and his left. Hence the world doth really persuade itself, and is hardened every day in that persuasion, that, whatever is pretended of Christ, it is self-interest that carries all before it; and that men do entertain that notion for the promotion of self-ends. But now this design of abounding in real holiness sets up the pure, unmixed interest of Christ, and casts a conviction upon the world to that purpose. When the world may read in our lives that the kingdom we look for, though it be in this world, yet it is not indeed of this world, but is righteousness, and peace, and joy in the Holy Ghost,—this brings that honour to Christ wherein he is delighted, and the ignorance of foolish men is put to silence.

3dly. This brings honour unto Christ, and glorifies him in all the vengeance that he executes on his enemies, and all the care that he takes of his own. The world itself is hereby made to see that there is a real difference, indeed, in them between whom Christ puts a difference, and is convinced of the righteousness of his judgments. Every one may answer them when they inquire the reason of the dispensations amongst us, yea, they may answer themselves, "The LORD hath done great things for these, even these that serve him."

SERMON XIV.

THE SIN AND JUDGMENT OF SPIRITUAL BARRENNESS.

"But the miry places thereof, and the marshes thereof shall not be healed; they shall be given to salt."—EZEK. xlvii. 11.

THIS prophecy contains a vision of the glorious, holy, gospel state of the church, under the representation of a most glorious temple, incomparably excelling that built of old by Solomon; an exposition whereof we have, 2 Cor. iii. 6–8, etc.

The beginning of this chapter sets out the way and means of the calling and gathering of gospel churches, whose worship is to be so glorious; and this is under a vision of "waters issuing out of the sanctuary," to heal and quicken all places to which they come.

By the waters here mentioned is the preaching of the gospel intended. And we may observe of them, first, Their rise, which was from the *sanctuary;* secondly, Their progress,—they increased until they became a *river* that none could pass over; thirdly, Their effects or efficacy,—they healed all waters where they came, and quickened, or caused to live, the *fishes* that were in them.

I must not long insist on these particulars.

First. The house, or temple, from whence these waters issue, may be taken two ways:—

1. Mystically, to denote only the presence of God. God dwelt in his temple; thence come these waters—from his presence. He sends out the word of the gospel for the conversion and healing of the nations, Ps. cx. 2. Or,—

2. Figuratively; and that either for the place where the temple of old stood (that is, Jerusalem), as the preaching of the gospel was to go forth from Jerusalem, and the sound of it from thence to proceed unto all the world, as Isa. xli. 27, lii. 7; Acts i. 4, 8; or for the church of Christ and his apostles, the first glorious, spiritual temple unto God, whence these waters issued.

Secondly. Their progress; which is described by degrees, it being at first small,—few men preaching it, and to a few,—but afterward increasing until it filled the whole earth.

Thirdly. The effects mentioned or ascribed unto these waters are two,—quickening and healing; which I shall not in general speak farther unto, because I shall do it in the opening of my text.

In the words of the text you have the state and condition of those places whither the waters of the sanctuary do come, and the effects before ascribed unto them are not produced; for so the words are to be read,—they "shall not be healed."

We have here a description of some lands or places whereunto the holy waters do come. First, They are "miry and marshy places;" secondly, The event of the waters coming to them,—they are "not healed;" thirdly, The consequent of that event,—they are "given unto salt."

I shall in a few words lay open the allegory, or parable, unto you.

First. By the waters of the sanctuary, I told you, is meant the preaching of the gospel,—that quickening and healing word which the Lord sends out to gather his church unto himself all the world over, to call his saints to that glorious, gospel, spiritual worship, which is here described in this vision of a temple.

Secondly. The "miry and marshy places" where these waters come, are such where persons cleave inseparably and incurably to their lusts and sins, so that they are not healed by the word. The healing word of the gospel comes, but they receive it not; the water flows over them, they drink it not in,—are not quickened nor healed by it.

Thirdly. To be "given unto salt," is to be left unto barrenness, Deut. xxix. 23; Judges ix. 45; Jer. xvii. 6.

The figurative sense of the passage thus explained will afford us the following observations:—

Observation I. God is pleased oftentimes to send the waters of the sanctuary to "miry and marshy places," that "shall never be healed" by them, nor made fruitful;—or, God, in his infinite wisdom, is pleased to send the preaching of the word unto some places wherein it shall not put forth its quickening and sanctifying power and virtue upon the souls of them that hear it.

II. All places in the world are barren, unsound, and unhealthy, before the coming of the waters of the sanctuary upon them;—or, the souls of all men are spiritually dead and full of woful distempers, until they are quickened and healed by the dispensation of the gospel. The word must come and heal them.

III. The waters of the sanctuary are healing waters;—or, the word of the gospel is in its own nature a quickening, healing, sanctifying, saving word, to them who receive it.

IV. Where the waters of the sanctuary come, and the land is not healed, that land is given up of the Lord to salt or barrenness for ever;—or, where the word of the gospel is, by the infinitely wise disposal of God, preached unto a place or persons, and they receive it not so as to have their sinful distempers healed by it, they are usually, after a season, given up, by the righteous judgment of God, unto barrenness and everlasting ruin.

It is this last proposition, as that which is the direct design and scope of the place, that I intend to insist principally upon. But yet I shall speak somewhat to the former.

I. God is pleased oftentimes, in his infinite wisdom, to send the preaching of the word unto some places wherein it shall not put forth its quickening and sanctifying power and virtue upon the souls of them that hear it.

The whole Scripture, and whole story of the providence of God in sending the gospel abroad in the world, bears witness to this truth. It was his way from the foundation of the world, and continueth to this very day. Hence was that complaint of the prophet, Isa liii. 1, "Who hath believed our report? and to whom is the arm of the Lord revealed?"—the gospel is preached to them that believe not the report thereof;—and chap. xlix. 4, "Then I said, I have laboured in vain, I have spent my strength for nought." But we need no greater instance nor any other than that of our Saviour, who spent the greatest part of his ministry in preaching to them who were never healed,—never converted nor sanctified by his word. That account he gives of his work, Matt. xi. 21–24, "Woe unto thee, Chorazin! woe unto thee, Bethsaida!" etc.

Now, though there be no searching into the depths of the counsels of God, yet there appear many reasons wherein his wisdom in this dispensation doth shine forth; as,—

1. He doth it principally because, in those places where the word

is rejected by the generality of the people, yet there may be some secret, poor souls belonging to the election of grace, whom God will have gathered and called home to himself. So for their sakes, though in the world they are taken no notice of, the word shall be preached unto multitudes. Amos ix. 9, " I will sift the house of Israel among all nations, like as corn is sifted in a sieve, yet shall not the least grain fall upon the earth." The grains of Israel must be preserved through all the nations of the earth, that not one grain may be lost. Thus Paul preaches the gospel at Philippi, Acts xvi. 12, 13. And what entertainment meets it withal? He and his companion are taken and beaten, and cast into prison sore hurt and wounded; verses 22, 23. Why, then, was it that the gospel must be preached there? Why, there was a stranger come to that town, a poor woman, one Lydia, that dwelt at Thyatira, and she was to be converted, and brought home to God, verse 14. So at Athens, chap. xvii. 34. And the apostle affirms that he " endured all things for the elect's sakes," 2 Tim. ii. 10. Here and there a poor despised person is designed to be called.

2. God doth it for a testimony against them that receive it not, and to leave them inexcusable at the last day. Mark vi. 11, " Whosoever shall not receive you, nor hear you, when ye depart thence, shake off the dust under your feet for a testimony against them." The word is to be preached, and witness, as it were, is to be taken upon it that it was preached, that men may be left without excuse at the last day. As our Saviour pleads concerning his own preaching to the Pharisees, John xv. 22, " If I had not come and spoken unto them, they had not had sin; but now they have no cloak for their sin." God will cause men to be without excuse, by that tender of mercy which is made unto them in the gospel. It shall be for a testimony against them at the last day.

Use. Let not men boast themselves in the outward enjoyment of the word, nor rest themselves in it. It were well, indeed, if all were believers to whom the word is preached,—if all lands were healed where the waters of the sanctuary come; but the Holy Ghost tells us they are not so, Heb. iv. 2, " The word preached did not profit them." Capernaum was " exalted unto heaven," in the use of means; but " brought down to hell" for the neglect of them. Let men look to themselves; God hath various ends in sending the gospel. The Lord knows what will be the end of England's enjoying the gospel so long as it hath done. Sad symptoms appear of a tremendous issue. But I shall speak of this afterward.

II. The souls of all men are spiritually dead, and full of woful distempers, until they are quickened and healed by the dispensation of the gospel.

The waters of the sanctuary must come, to quicken them and heal them. They are distempered, therefore, and wofully disordered, before the coming of these waters. So the apostle informs us, Tit. iii. 3–5, "For we ourselves also were sometimes foolish, disobedient, deceived, serving divers lusts and pleasures, living in malice and envy, hateful, and hating one another. But after that the kindness and love of God our Saviour toward man appeared, not by works of righteousness which we have done, but according to his mercy he saved us, by the washing of regeneration, and renewing of the Holy Ghost." Before the gospel grace comes to heal and cleanse them, this is the state and condition of men; as it is more largely described by the apostle, Rom. i. 18 to the end.

I shall not stay to mention all the particular distempers that rage in some, and that rule and reign in all before the coming of the gospel; as darkness, blindness, ignorance, worldly-mindedness, sensuality, hatred of God, envy, and malice, which are fixed in the souls of men by presumption and self-righteousness. There is nothing in them of spiritual life or holiness, of purity or zeal,—nothing that is acceptable or pleasing unto God. But to set forth this to the utmost, were to describe the whole natural condition of men,—which is not my present work; and therefore I shall not farther insist on it.

III. The word of the gospel is in its own nature a quickening, healing, sanctifying, saving word, to them who receive it.

They [the waters of the sanctuary] bring Christ along with them, the great physician of souls, who alone is able to cure a sin-sick soul. They bring mercy with them to pardon sinners, that "the inhabitants of the land may no more say they are sick, having their sins forgiven them," Isa. xxxiii. 24. They bring grace with them to cure all the distempers of lusts, Isa. xi. 5–7; Tit. ii. 11, 12.

These things I have only touched upon, and proceed now to the fourth observation, on which I chiefly proposed to insist.

IV. Where the waters of the sanctuary come, and the land is not healed, that land is given up of the Lord to salt and barrenness for ever;—or, where the word of the gospel is preached unto a place or persons, and they receive it not so as to have their sinful distempers healed by it, they are given up by the righteous judgment of God unto barrenness and everlasting ruin.

To clear this proposition I shall show,—1. What I mean by the coming of the waters of the sanctuary, or the preaching of the gospel, to a place or persons; 2. What by healing their sinful distempers; 3. What by being given up to barrenness and ruin.

1. By the coming of the healing waters of the sanctuary, I intend not the occasional preaching of a sermon, although this be sufficient to justify God in the rejection of any person or people. In the first

preaching of the gospel, the refusal of one sermon lost many their souls unto all eternity. When the Lord Jesus sent out his disciples to preach the tidings of everlasting peace, he commanded them to pass through the towns, cities, and villages, and to offer them peace and mercy in the word of truth; which if they received not, they were to shake off the dust of their feet against them, Matt. x. 12–15; Luke x. 8–12. But O the unspeakable patience of Christ to many in the world, where the word is continued ofttimes for a very long season, and the salvation tendered therein despised! But this is that which I intend as the rule of the dispensation mentioned,—namely, when God by his providence doth cause the word to be preached for some continuance, and to the revelation of his whole counsel; as Paul affirmed himself to have done at Ephesus, Acts xx. 27, where he had abode above a year.

Nor do I mean any waters, but the waters of the sanctuary; not any preaching, but the preaching of the gospel of Jesus Christ: which Paul affirms to be his work, Eph. iii. 8. All waters are not the waters of the sanctuary; all preaching is not the preaching of the sanctuary. There is preaching in the world wherein God and the souls of men are no more concerned than in an oration of an ancient heathen. Many undertake to be preachers who never "stood in the counsel of God," as he complains, Jer. xxiii. 22, who never received of the Spirit of Christ, nor knew his mind,—blind leaders of the blind. The children of Zion are promised, under the gospel, that "they shall be all taught of God." And we have men undertaking to be teachers of them, who never learned any thing of Christ;—a wicked generation of soul-murderers, for which cursed work they every day invent new engines,—whom the Lord's soul abhors. See their condition and portion, Ezek. xxxiv. 3, 4, etc. I mean, therefore, a dispensation of the word according to the mind of Christ,—the due unfolding of the mystery of the gospel. This is the coming I intend.

2. What is meant by their sinful distempers not being healed? Look what the waters of the sanctuary come to do: if that be not effected, they are not healed.

Now, there are two effects here ascribed unto the waters of the sanctuary:—(1.) They quicken and give new life, verse 9. A natural life they had before, but these give them another life. (2.) Healing, as the waters of Jericho by Elisha, 2 Kings ii. 21. Where these effects are not produced, that is the condition described, that is the state of these "miry and marshy places,"—they are not healed:—

(1.) Men are not quickened; they receive not a new spiritual life; they are not so brought to the knowledge of God. It is not enough that men have their affections wrought upon, or their lives in some measure reformed;—unless they are quickened, unless they receive a new spiritual life by the word, they are as the unhealed places, over which the curse here mentioned hangs.

(2.) The healing of these quickened souls consists in the curing and mortifying of their sinful distempers. This follows the other. Where there is life, there will be healing. Let not men pretend that they live spiritually, if their lusts be not healed. If men are proud, worldly, sensual, they are dead also; there is no effect of the waters of the sanctuary upon them. If men are not made holy, humble, believing, zealous, if they receive not the spirit of prayer and faith, they are not healed.

This is the condition of the "miry and marshy places" here mentioned:—God, in his infinite wisdom and goodness, causeth the gospel to be dispensed among a people, to be preached, where they do, or may, and ought to attend unto it; but they are not converted by the word, not sanctified by it, but continue in their old state and condition. He that was filthy is filthy still; he that was unrighteous is so still;—he that was in the mire of the world and sin is so still.

3. What is the lot and portion of such persons? Why, "they shall be given to salt;" that is, as I have showed, to barrenness, fruitlessness, unprofitableness, and eternal ruin.

This is the meaning of the proposition; and it is a dreadful word, which yet is true, and will prove so at the last day. Woe to the "miry and marshy places" of the world! woe to the persons and places to whom [and to which] the waters of the sanctuary have come and they are not healed!

I shall not need to insist much on the proof of the proposition, the Scripture so abounds with testimonies of it. But I shall do these three things:—1. Name some places that plainly speak the same truth; 2. Show the degrees in which God proceeds usually in this great work, in giving up unprofitable hearers to ruin; and, 3. Give the grounds of it:—

1. For other Scriptures which assert the same truth, take Prov. i. 25–31, "But ye have set at nought all my counsel, and would none of my reproof: I also will laugh at your calamity; I will mock when your fear cometh; when your fear cometh as desolation, and your destruction cometh as a whirlwind; when distress and anguish cometh upon you. Then shall they call upon me, but I will not answer; they shall seek me early, but they shall not find me: for that they hated knowledge, and did not choose the fear of the LORD: they would none of my counsel: they despised all my reproof. Therefore shall they eat of the fruit of their own way, and be filled with their own devices;"—Prov. xxix. 1, "He that, being often reproved, hardeneth his neck, shall suddenly be destroyed, and that without remedy;"—Luke xiii. 6, "He spake also this parable; A certain man had a fig-

tree planted in his vineyard; and he came and sought fruit thereon, and found none," etc. So Heb. x. 28–30; 2 Cor. ii. 15, 16.

2. For the degrees of rejection, see Ezek. x. 18, xi. 23; Heb. vi. 8, "But that which beareth thorns and briers is rejected, and is nigh unto cursing; whose end is to be burned." They are first rejected, then cursed, and lastly burned. But,—

3. That which I shall principally insist upon, is to show the ways whereby God doth usually proceed in giving up such persons to barrenness, and so to everlasting ruin:—

(1.) He casts them out of his care;—he will be at no more charge nor cost with them, nor about them. So, Heb. vi. 8, the land is ἀδόκιμος,—"rejected;" the owner will take no more care or pains about such an unprofitable piece of land; he will till it no more, dress it no more, but leave it to its own barrenness. God is the great husbandman, John xv. 1. When a miry place is not healed, he will cast it out of his husbandry. So Ezek. xxiv. 13, They have had their time and season, and "are not purged;" therefore "they shall be purged no more." Jer. vi. 29, 30, "The bellows are burned, the lead is consumed of the fire; the founder melteth in vain: for the wicked are not plucked away. Reprobate silver shall men call them, because the LORD hath rejected them." This the Lord Christ declares to be his way of proceeding with them, Zech. xi. 8, 9, "My soul loathed them, and their soul also abhorred me. Then said I, I will not feed you: that that dieth, let it die; and that that is to be cut off, let it be cut off; and let the rest eat every one the flesh of another." A sad parting, the Lord knows! They give up Christ,—he gives up them; and their meeting will be infinitely more sad to them. Now, this the Lord doth several ways:—

[1.] He will sometimes utterly remove the gospel from them;—turn the stream of the waters of the sanctuary, that they shall come to them no more. So he threatened the church at Ephesus of old, Rev. ii. 5, "Remember therefore from whence thou art fallen," etc., "or else I will come unto thee quickly, and will remove thy candlestick out of his place." They shall have the light of the word no more; it shall be removed and taken from them. Ah! how many places lie under this woful judgment of God at this day,—this sentence of being given up to salt for ever! Places there are in the world that have enjoyed the word at God's appointed season, or, at least, the tender of it, and opportunity to enjoy it; but continuing unprofitable under it, what is now their state and condition? God hath left them to that sore judgment, that they themselves should be made instrumental to cast out the word from amongst them; like the foolish woman, pulling down the house with their own hands: and so [they] have got darkness for a vision, and they that would not rejoice in the truth, and in the light, do now, through the tremendous judgment of God, triumph in darkness, and in a thing of nought.

It is true, the gospel may be sometimes taken for a season from a people for their trial and exercise, and not penally;—it may be driven from them, and not absolutely sinned away. Now, as the Lord hath many glorious ends in such a dispensation, so it may easily be known whether people have lost the gospel only for a season, in a way of trial; or penally, as a beginning of their being given up to salt and barrenness. As,—

1*st*. They that are deprived for a season of gospel enjoyments for their trial and exercise, are sensible of the displeasure of God in that dispensation, and greatly humble themselves under his hand on that account. They say, as the church in Micah vii. 9, "I will bear the indignation of the LORD, because I have sinned against him, until he plead my cause, and execute judgment for me." They look on this as the greatest calamity and trial that can befall them; whereas they that lose it penally, are either very little concerned about it, or do greatly rejoice at it. The word tormented them, and they are glad they are freed from it. Rev. xi. 10, "And they that dwell upon the earth shall rejoice over them, and make merry, and shall send gifts one to another; because these two prophets tormented them that dwelt on the earth." Some never rejoice more than when they are got quit of the gospel; and others are like Gallio. Now, when such as these have the word taken from them, and are no way sensible of the displeasure of the Lord in it, nor do humble themselves before him on that account, it is a certain evidence that God is giving them up unto a state of salt; that is, barrenness and eternal ruin.

2*dly*. They that are deprived of it for a season in a way of trial have no rest, but are earnest with the Lord for the return of it. 1 Sam. vii. 2, The ark was gone; and though they had peace and plenty, and all things else in abundance, yet all will not satisfy them; the ark is absent, that pledge of God's presence, and they lamented after him. So is it with these;—let them have peace, or liberty, or prosperity, all is one; if they have not the ark,—if they have not the gospel and ordinances of God,—they can take no rest, but are still lamenting after the Lord, still longing after the enjoyment of his word. David doth excellently express this frame of heart, Ps. lxiii. 1, 2, "O God, thou art my God; early will I seek thee: my soul thirsteth for thee, my flesh longeth for thee in a dry and thirsty land, where no water is; to see thy power and thy glory, so as I have seen thee in the sanctuary." He was driven from the ordinances of God; the waters of the sanctuary came not to him. But now they from whom the word is taken penally are no way troubled about it, nor do long after it; they rejoice in what they have in the room of it,—are exceedingly well pleased without it. Let them have an increase of corn, and wine, and oil,—let them have their lusts and their sports, their formalities and follies,—they care not whether ever they hear of the word of the gospel any more. Such men are certainly entering into a condition of salt, of barrenness and ruin.

3dly. They who are deprived of the word for a season for their trial, have a high estimation and value of their mercy and privilege who enjoy it. They do not think the proud happy, nor envy at prosperous wickedness, nor bow in their hearts before the Hamans of the earth. But those they think blessed who enjoy the word, and the presence of God therein. This our Saviour teaches them to esteem, Luke xi. 28, "But he said, Yea, rather, blessed are they that hear the word of God, and keep it." David doth excellently set out this frame of heart, Ps. lxxxiv. 4, "Blessed are they that dwell in thy house; they will be still praising thee. Selah." "I am," saith he, "a poor outcast, deprived of thy word and ordinances. O the blessed condition of those who enjoy them! Let them be what they will as to their outward state, they are in a blessed condition if they may dwell in thy house,—enjoy the privileges of the spiritual house of God and his worship, in the gospel." This is the frame of such persons,—those only they esteem blessed who are refreshed with the waters of the sanctuary; but none are more despised by those from whom the gospel is judicially removed. It is the great, the mighty, the rich, the sensual, that they esteem blessed; for those others they esteem as the dirt or the mire.

Now, hence it is that God may at the same time remove his gospel from a place, judicially from some, and by a way of trial from others, whereby these contrary effects are produced:—Some are humbled under the hand of the Lord, mourn after his presence, and account them blessed who enjoy his ordinances;—others triumph and rejoice in their condition, look upon it as good and blessed; at least, are little concerned in the dispensation that God is dealing with them in. And as the Lord doth good to the former by this exercise, preparing them also for farther mercies, in a greater estimation of his word, and profiting under it when enjoyed; so to the other, this is the entrance of their ruin;—they are cast out of the care of God, and you never see such a people afterward obtain mercy.

[2.] God doth this sometimes though he causeth the word to be continued unto them,—by restraining the efficacy of it, that it shall not profit them. Men may have lived out their season that God hath given them to be healed in, and yet God have work to do in that place where they live; so that the word must be preached. Some poor souls amongst them are to be quickened or healed, called or edified; so that he will not turn away the course of these holy waters, but continue the dispensation of the gospel. But as for those who have withstood their season of healing, and are cast out of the care of God, God will so order things that the word shall have no power upon them. Now, though the righteous judgment of God have a hand in this matter, yet, by his permission, their own lusts are the immediate cause of it; as,—

1*st.* They shall have some prejudices against them by whom the gospel is dispensed in the power and purity of it, which shall keep them from attending unto or profiting by their message. So in the days of Ahab there were four hundred preachers that he had a mind to hear; but they were all false prophets, teachers of lies, idolatrous, and superstitious: only, there were two prophets of the Lord, Elijah the Tishbite, and Micaiah the son of Imlah; and both these he looked upon as his enemies, as persons not well affected unto him; so that he would believe nothing of what they preached. So of Elijah, 1 Kings xxi. 20; and of Micaiah, chap. xxii. 8. So shall it befall many whom God will leave to salt, because the season of their healing hath been withstood;—though the word be preached, they shall have prejudices against the dispensers of it, so that they shall not profit by them. And little do they think that these prejudices and hard thoughts are chains and fetters to keep them in unto the judgment of the great day. And of this nature also are other prejudices that men have.

2*dly.* He will suffer them to be unconquerably hardened in the love of some sin or lust, which shall keep off the power of the word from their hearts. So the ground here that is not healed is said to be "miry and marshy;"—such as hath a mixture of filth incorporated with it sufficient to repel all the virtue of the healing waters of the sanctuary. Thus we see men every day so furiously set upon their lusts, sports, and sensuality, that they hate, and are filled with madness and rage against, all that would persuade them to sobriety: much more doth the word of the gospel torment them, so that they rise with fury against it; and this keeps them from profiting by it. "They are given to salt."

3*dly.* God withdraws the efficacy of his Spirit in the dispensation of the word, that it shall not have that strength and power on them as upon others. God sends his word towards his own in a way of covenant; and then it is always accompanied with his Spirit, Isa. lix. 21. And where God dealeth with men in covenant mercy, these go together. But now when he casts men out of his care, though the word may be preached to their ear, because of some others whom he yet cares for, yet he hath said concerning them, that his Spirit shall strive with them no more. And thence it is that the word makes no impression on them,—its healing virtue is as to them withheld.

And this is the first thing the Lord doth to such poor creatures as he leaves to salt, to barrenness, and ruin, for despising the season and means of their healing,—he casts them out of his care, as to the dispensation of the word.

SERMON XV.

WE shall now proceed to the *uses.*

Use 1. Wonder not if you see a diversity of success in preaching of the word. Some receive it with joy; the most despise it as a thing of nought. Whence is this difference? Multitudes are rejected of God,—cast out of his care,—barren land; he will till them no more. A cursed state! Marvel not that many refuse to hear the word,—that they love lies; they are given up of God to their hearts' lusts. Marvel not that the word which they hear affects them no more;—the power of the Spirit is withheld from them. Multitudes are thus cast out of the care of God, and tokens of the plague are upon them. They like their condition, rejoice and triumph in it, think none so happy as themselves, and despise them that love the waters of the sanctuary: all which are tokens of this sore plague. Can they expel the gospel from any place? can they quench the light that is in it? can they triumph over the ways of God?—they suppose they have gotten a great victory. This is not an ordinary judgment: they are poor creatures, assuredly cast out of the care of God; "they are given to salt," and it is a miracle of mercy if ever any of them be healed.

Oh! it is a woful thing to look on a place or persons that give evidences of their withstanding the season of their healing, as so many in this nation do! How was our Saviour affected with it in reference to Jerusalem, Luke xix. 41, 42, "And when he was come near, he beheld the city, and wept over it, saying, If thou hadst known, even thou, at least in this thy day, the things which belong unto thy peace! but now they are hid from thine eyes." Oh! if we had but any measure of that pity and compassion which dwelt in his holy soul, how could we pass through towns and cities, and see and hear, and not mourn!

Use 2. Take that advice of the prophet, Jer. xiii. 16, "Give glory to the LORD your God, before he cause darkness, and before your feet stumble upon the dark mountains, and, while ye look for light, he turn it into the shadow of death, and make it gross darkness."

(2.) The second thing that God doth, in giving up an unhealed land unto barrenness, is his judicial hardening of them, or leaving them to hardness and impenitency, that so they may fill up the measure of their sins. Heb. vi. 8, "That which beareth thorns and briers is rejected, and is nigh unto cursing." When the care of God is once taken from them, they are nigh unto cursing. The next thing that God will do to them, is to curse them, as our Saviour did the barren fig-tree.

This woful judgment is at large set forth, Isa. vi. 9, 10, "And he said, Go and tell this people, Hear ye indeed, but understand not; and see ye indeed, but perceive not. Make the heart of this people fat, and make their ears heavy, and shut their eyes; lest they see with their eyes, and hear with their ears, and understand with their heart, and convert, and be healed." Isaiah was a gospel preacher; "Yet this," saith God, "shall be the effect of thy preaching towards them that have withstood their season, and have not been healed by the word." And John tells us that this very thing was accomplished when the gospel was preached by our Saviour himself, chap. xii. 40, 41. And surely their condition is most woful whom the preaching of the gospel hardeneth,—whom the only remedy destroys.

Now, there are four things in this spiritual judgment that God sends upon unhealed souls, that have outlived their season of healing, more or less:—

[1.] Blindness of mind and understanding. Their natural blindness and ignorance shall be increased and confirmed; and that by two ways:—

1*st.* God will send them a "spirit of slumber," Rom. xi. 8; that is, a great inadvertency and negligence as to the things of the gospel that are spoken of or preached unto them. As men that slumber take little notice of what is spoken to them or about them; they hear a noise, and sometimes discern a little what is spoken, but not to any use or purpose: so is it with these persons on whom God doth judicially send this spirit of slumber; they hear the sound of the word, and sometimes, it may be, take notice of some one thing or other that is spoken; but to receive and understand the design of it, to ponder it and improve it, that they cannot do;—they are under a spiritual slumber. We may see multitudes in this condition every day. The word hath no life nor vigour towards them; they perceive not the mind of God in it; they understand it not. God hath given them a "spirit of slumber," and they die under it.

2*dly.* God sends them a spirit of giddiness, causing them to err in their ways, Isa. xix. 14. We have a notable instance of this judgment of God, 2 Thess. ii. 10–12. The waters of the sanctuary came unto them, and they were not healed; the gospel was preached unto them, but they withstood their season. They received not the love of the truth; they did not believe and obey, that they might be saved;

—because they had pleasure in unrighteousness. How, then, doth God deal with them? Verse 11, He will send them a spirit of giddiness or delusion, that "they shall believe a lie,"—false doctrine, false worship, superstition, and idolatry. This they shall believe, and have pleasure in; which will have the fearful end mentioned, verse 12. And this judgment, as it is already come upon many, so it lies at the door, I fear, of the most. We see men every day that have for some years, it may be, enjoyed the preaching of the gospel; but not being healed, quickened, and sanctified by it, are now, with all greediness, given up to follow after fables on the one hand, or superstition on the other;—there is a spirit of giddiness from the Lord upon them. And by these means is the darkness of the minds of men increased when God is giving of them up to barrenness.

[2.] Obstinacy in the will, or hardness of heart properly so called, is in this judgment of God also. God will give up unhealed persons to hardness of heart. So is it in that place of Isaiah, chap. vi. 10: and it is the same with that which the apostle calls "a reprobate mind," Rom. i. 28; that is, a mind and heart that is good for nothing with regard to spiritual things,—profligate, and altogether insensible of them. And when this befalls any, they will openly despise the word, and cast it off, using one foolish pretence or other for their so doing; as Jer. xliv. 16, with xliii. 2. Such persons, whenever the word is preached unto them, and it lies cross to their carnal imaginations or sensual affections, lusts, or sports, rise up in their hearts with contempt, and rage against it. Sometimes they will colour their wickedness in their hearts by some pretence or other: "This is the way, the humour, the singularity, of the preacher." Or sometimes their rage will carry them directly out against the word, without any colour or pretence, but because it displeaseth them. Or if they fall not thus into pride and rage (which usually is occasioned by their temptations), they grow utterly senseless, and stupid, and unconcerned in the things of God. Let the word thunder from heaven against their sins, they regard it not; let the still small voice of the gospel persuade them unto reconciliation, they attend not unto it; let the judgments of God be abroad in the world, if they escape themselves they are not concerned about them. Do they reach their own persons, they have wrath, and anger, and vexation; but they cannot repent or turn to the Lord. This is, apparently, the condition of most in the world.

[3.] Sensuality of affections is in this judgment also, Rom. i. 26, "He gave them up to vile affections;" that is, to place their affections on vile, sensual things. Unhealed persons shall do so. Our streets, ale-houses, and many other places, are full of such whose affections are fixed with madness on vile things; and they please themselves in them, little thinking that this is part of the judgment whereunto they are given up of God for their unprofitableness under the word,—for their not being healed by the waters of the sanctuary.

[4.] Searedness of conscience. 1 Tim. iv. 2, "Having their conscience seared with a hot iron." Eph. iv. 19, "Being past feeling." Whatever sin they commit, or condition they fall into, conscience shall no more discharge its duty in them and towards them.

And this is the second thing that God will do towards such unhealed persons.

(3.) The third thing considerable is the event of this dealing of God with them, or what is meant by this land's becoming salt.

Two things, as I have showed before, are hereby intended:—[1.] Barrenness in this world; [2.] Eternal ruin in the world to come:—

[1.] Barrenness. They shall never bear any fruit to God. This was the curse that our Saviour gave to the fig-tree, "Never fruit grow on thee." Man was made to bear fruit unto God;—this is all he came into the world for. Now, when God shall say to any, "Go your ways; you shall never do any thing more for me whilst you live in this world; you shall never bear any fruit to me;"—what sorer judgment can any man possibly fall under? I might show you the misery of this condition in many particulars. "Israel is an empty vine," Hos. x. 1.

[2.] Eternal ruin, and that irreparable. Prov. xxix. 1, "He that, being often reproved, hardeneth his neck, shall suddenly be destroyed, and that without remedy." John xv. 6, "If a man abide not in me, he is cast forth as a branch, and is withered; and men gather them, and cast them into the fire, and they are burned." 2 Thess. ii. 12, "That they all might be damned who believed not the truth, but had pleasure in unrighteousness." Heb. vi. 8, "But that which beareth thorns and briers is rejected, and is nigh unto cursing; whose end is to be burned." This is the certain event of that land that is left unto salt, because not healed; and of those persons who, having passed over their season of quickening and sanctifying by the word, are given up to barrenness and ruin. It will do neither me nor you good to flatter you, and to put you into any better hope than your condition will admit of. See Ezek. xxxiii. 8, "When I say unto the wicked, O wicked man, thou shalt surely die; if thou dost not speak to warn the wicked from his way, that wicked man shall die in his iniquity, but his blood will I require at thine hand." This will be the end of the one and the other, when that course is taken. Did I not see the tokens of this judgment of God abroad in the world, I would not thus insist upon it as I do.

Use 1. Of exhortation. Make use of your season, that you fall not under this sore and inexpressible judgment. God gives men a season, a space to repent in, Rev. ii. 21. This space and season, as I have showed you before, is not ofttimes all the while that the gospel is preached unto you. The word may be preached, and yet its efficacy wholly restrained from you, and that because your time and season is gone. And so it comes to pass daily; and you know not how soon it may be your lot and portion, and you perceive it not. Therefore is the apostle so earnest in exhorting men to make use of their day, before their season be gone, Heb. iii. 12, 13, "Take heed, brethren, lest there be in any of you an evil heart of unbelief, in departing from the living God. But exhort one another daily, while it is called To-day; lest any of you be hardened through the deceitfulness of sin." As if he should say, "Take heed to yourselves; stir up yourselves: for if your day be once passed over, you are then gone for ever; it will then be too late for you to look out after mercy." And so again, 2 Cor. vi. 2, "Now is the day, now is the time." If you stand in need of any commodity that can be had but at one fair,—that day, that season you will not neglect. You stand in need, I am sure, of grace, mercy, pardon, Christ, life,—salvation; there is only this day, this season, for you to obtain it in. O that you would be persuaded to look out after it before it be hidden from you! See Heb. x. 31, "It is a fearful thing to fall into the hands of the living God." So the same apostle again, Heb. xii. 15, "Looking diligently lest any man fail of the grace of God." Use all diligence in this matter.

To excite you a little to this, consider,—

(1.) That if you are not healed during your season, you can never be healed. If the gospel cure you not, you must die in your sins. Men are greatly mistaken, when they flatter themselves that it can never be too late for them in this world,—there is time enough whilst they are alive. Alas! you have but your season; and that may be over with you many days before you leave the world, yea, many years. We have everywhere ground evidently "left to salt," though yet not burned up. Use your day.

(2.) You know not how your day is going away, nor when it will be over. The traveller on the road, that hath a journey to go, knows how to order his affairs. "It is," saith he, "so many hours to night, and I have time enough before me;"—so doth the labouring man also: but, alas! it is not so with you; you know not how soon your day may be over. I speak not of your lives, which, the Lord knows, are uncertain; but the day of the gospel may be over whilst the day of your lives continue. Nor can you be certain of the day of the preaching of the word; but your day, and your season in it, may come to an end this day, or this night, for aught that you or I know: so that your concernment is unspeakably great in the proposal that is made unto you. Remember the virgins that were shut out, and their cry at midnight!

You will say, then, "What shall we do to know when it is our season, that we may apply our hearts unto this exhortation?"

I answer, The Lord alone, who is the searcher of all hearts, knows how it is with you, and whether you have not any of you in particular outstood your opportunity. I can only tell you what is a gospel season; which you are to take care that you may have a share and interest in:—

[1.] It is required that the gospel be preached in the power and purity of it. This in general makes "the acceptable day, the time of salvation." And if there be nothing else concurring, this is enough to let a people or person know that the day of the Lord is come upon them,—that the waters of the sanctuary are come unto them. Now, consider with yourselves, whether the gospel be preached unto you or not, or whether you may not or might not have it so preached unto you, or enjoy the dispensation of it, did you but discharge your duty. If it be so, this is one evidence that it is yet your day.

[2.] It is a special season when providential calls do join in with and further gospel calls;—when God causes the gospel to be dispensed unto a people, and at the same time puts forth some acts of his providence, that are suited to awaken men to the consideration of their state and condition, then is the season of that people. I shall not go over the several providential calls that have been upon us to inquire after the ways of God. Are all the alterations that have been amongst us, discovering the great uncertainty of all things that are here below, no call? Was there no call in the great unseasonableness of the year?—no call in the danger of the loss of the gospel, which seems to stand ready for its flight from you?—the great uncertainty how long you may enjoy these waters of the sanctuary? It is certain, that if you have not neglected already your season, your day of grace, you are now under the time that you are to be tried in.

[3.] Then is the season, when God moves, [as he does] at some seasons, more effectually upon your hearts and spirits in the dispensation of the word than at other times. This you alone can give an account of;—you only know how it is with you. You can tell whether you have not been moved by the word more than formerly, or convinced by it; whether you have not had purposes of amendment and reformation wrought in you by it; whether you have not been caused to love it more than you have done formerly; whether it hath not begotten at times resolutions in you to try for life and immortality. If it have not, it is much to be feared lest the Lord is leaving of you to salt,—to an estate of perishing and everlasting ruin. But if you have had such effects wrought in you, know of a certain that the kingdom of God hath come unto you; and if you withstand your opportunity, you are gone and undone for ever, unless you make thorough work before this dispensation be overpast.

[4.] When you see others about you earnest after the word, this is God's call and ordinance unto you to look to your own condition.

If now, by any of these means, you come to know that the day of the Lord and the season of your healing is upon you, oh, that you would be prevailed with to be wise for your own souls, and to close with the word of the gospel before the things of your peace be hidden from your eyes!

I thought, in the next place, to have given you the signs of a departing gospel-day, and evidences of men's having outlived their season, and being given up to salt and barrenness; but for some reasons forbear.

Use 2. To discover the miserable condition of poor creatures that, having not in their season been healed by the waters of the sanctuary, are given up of the Lord to salt and barrenness. No heart can conceive, nor tongue express, the misery of such poor creatures. Let me only mention some particulars:—

(1.) They know not that they are so miserable. They perceive not, they understand not, the sore judgment that they are under. Do but their heads ache, or are they sick of an ague, they feel it presently, and seek out for remedies; but in this case the curse of God is upon them, and they do not at all perceive it, and so seek not out for relief. Hos. vii. 9, " Strangers have devoured his strength, and he knoweth it not; yea, grey hairs are here and there upon him, yet he knoweth not." They are nigh to ruin, to destruction, and perceive it not: they take no notice of the misery that is at hand ready to devour them; or if at any time they begin so to do, they shift off the thought of it, which is a great part of their misery.

(2.) They are pleased with the condition in which they are; " they cry, Peace and safety, when sudden destruction is at hand," 1 Thess. v. 3. They please themselves in their condition, when the vengeance of the Lord is ready to seize upon them. Is the gospel removed from them, and the streams of the sanctuary turned away?—They are so far from being troubled at it, that they rejoice in it, as hath been declared; they think they may now follow their lusts freely, and do whatever seems good unto themselves; they despise others and bless themselves, as if all were well with them. Or is the word yet continued, but they left to senselessness and salt under it?—They are pleased with their estate, wonder at those who are troubled under the word, and exceedingly despise them. All is well with themselves; and some of them are ready to deride all others that are under the work of the Lord. On this account it is that they do not, will not, look out for relief or healing.

(3.) No man can help or relieve them. Men may pity them, but they cannot help them. All the world cannot pull a poor creature out from under the curse of the great God.

(4.) Their eternal ruin is certain, as before proved.

(5.) This ruin is very sore on gospel despisers.

SERMON XVI.[1]

HUMAN POWER DEFEATED.

"The stout-hearted are spoiled, they have slept their sleep; and none of the men of might have found their hands.—Ps. lxxvi. 5.

THE common circumstances of this psalm, concerning the penman, title, and the like, I shall not at all inquire after. The time of its being given to the church is alone to us considerable; and yet all the knowledge thereof, also, is but conjectural. What particular time it was wherein it was given we know not; but that it was given for the use of all times, that we know. Probable it is, from verse 3, that it

[1] Dr Owen, according to Whitelocke in his "Memorials," p. 391, preached before the House of Commons on June 7, 1649. The following sermon was the one which he delivered on the occasion. It was a day of public thanksgiving for the defeat of the Levellers at Burford on May 18 of the same year. In times of political change and commotion, wild notions are frequently set afloat, incompatible with the restraints of law and the rights of property. A species of communism had sprung up in the Parliamentary forces. In 1647 Cromwell was obliged to resort to vigorous measures in order to restore discipline and subordination. The ringleaders were seized at a review of the troops,—tried by a court-martial on the spot, and condemned to be shot. The sentence was executed against one of them immediately, and the danger seemed to be gone; but disaffection was still cherished in the minds of many of the soldiers, and in 1649 broke out afresh in a more formidable shape. Many causes tended to foster this spirit of discontent. Some officers had taken offence at the way in which military honours had been distributed, and hence "the murmuring for pre-eminence" to which Owen in his sermon alludes. Evil principles, moreover, had been spread among the common soldiers. A party of them disturbed the worship of a congregation in the parish church of Walton-upon-Thames, and harangued the people in the churchyard on the necessity of abolishing the Sabbath, tithes, the ministry of the gospel, magistracy, and the Bible itself! Sympathy with these *levelling* views was evinced out of the army. At Cobham, one Everard, a disbanded soldier, gave himself out to be a prophet, and professed to have had a vision, in which he and his followers were commanded to arise and dig and plough the earth. Whitelocke (p. 384) supplies the interpretation of the vision. "They threaten," says he, "to pull down park pales, and to lay all open." Owen, too, in the course of his sermon, has a significant allusion to men, "heady, high-minded, *throwing up all bounds and fences.*" It was, accordingly, both a mutiny and an insurrection, and spread over several counties,—

was established as a monument of praise in the days of Hezekiah, when, by the immediate hand of God, Jerusalem was delivered from the army of Sennacherib. For a return of which mercy though good Hezekiah came short of the obligation laid on him, rendering not again according to the benefit done unto him, yet the Lord himself takes care for his own glory, setting forth this psalm as a monument of the praise due to his name unto all generations.

The deliverance of Jerusalem, then, from so great ruin as that impending over it from the threatening army of Sennacherib under their walls, being the occasion of penning this psalm, it cannot but yield us a meet foundation of making mention of the name of the Lord in a suitable work this day.

In general the whole is eucharistical, and hath two parts:—first, Narratory, concerning the work of God for his people; secondly, Laudatory, or the praise of his people for those works.

The first part hath three particulars:—1. An exordium, by way of exultation and rejoicing, verses 1, 2. 2. A special narration of the work of God, for which the praise of the whole is intended, verses 3, 5, 6. 3. An apostrophe to the Lord concerning the one and the other, verse 4.

The latter containeth,—1. A doctrinal observation for the use of the church, from the whole, verse 7. 2. The reasons and confirmation of the doctrine so laid down, taken from the power and righteousness of God in the actions recounted, verses 8, 9. 3. A threefold

Surrey, Oxford, Gloucester, Northampton, and so far north as Lancashire and the town of Newcastle. A small party of these Levellers came into contact with a detachment of the Parliamentary troops at Banbury, and were dispersed. The suppression of the whole movement, however, was intrusted to Cromwell, who accomplished the task with his characteristic energy. After an unsuccessful attempt on Oxford, the Levellers had taken up their position at Burford. Cromwell, by a rapid march of nearly fifty miles, took them by surprise *during the night*. Has the text of Owen's sermon any reference to the fact of this surprise? The poor Levellers, completely disconcerted by the vigour of their opponent, at once yielded when quarter was conceded to them. The mutiny was at an end; and, from the apparent ease and the rapidity with which it was suppressed, it is difficult now to understand the reason for all the alarm which it excited. Not a few of these Levellers, however, as Owen intimates in the sermon, and as their conduct showed, were brave and desperate men. Some of them, on being tried, confessed that one of their objects was the restoration of Prince Charles; and one passage in the sermon is evidently based on the belief in some such strange conjunction of interests. But for the activity of Cromwell, the movement might have been the beginning of disastrous anarchy throughout England. An extract from Whitelocke will show what estimate was formed by the Parliament of the threatened danger, the sense entertained of Cromwell's services on the occasion, and the importance attached to the event in regard to which Owen was called at this time to preach before the House of Commons. "Report by Lieutenant-General Cromwell of the suppressing of the Levellers: The House gave him their hearty thanks for that great service, and ordered one of their members to attend the General with the hearty thanks of the House for his great service in that business; and ordered a general day of thanksgiving for that great mercy," p. 389. The sermon of Owen is altogether remarkable for the skill and tact with which he suits himself to the occasion.—Ed.

use of the doctrine so confirmed:—of instruction, verse 10; of exhortation, verse 11; of establishment and consolation, verse 12.

The particulars preceding my text I shall a little touch upon, that the mind of the Holy Ghost therein may be the more clear unto you, and the doctrine from thence appear with the greater evidence:—

1. In the exordium, verses 1, 2, you have two things:—(1.) The names of the place wherein the work mentioned was wrought and the praise returned held forth;—and these are, Judah, Israel, Salem, Zion. (2.) The relation of God unto this place, which lies at the bottom of the work he did for them and the praise they returned unto him. He was known, his name was great amongst them; there was his tabernacle and his dwelling-place: which may be referred to two heads,—the knowledge of his will, verse 1; and the establishment of his worship, verse 2.

(1.) For the description of the place, by its several names and titles, I shall not insist upon it; they are all but various expressions of the same thing. It is the church of God that is adorned with all these titles and names of singular endearment:—Judah, that single tribe of which the Messiah was to come; Israel, a prevailing people, the posterity of him that prevailed with God; Salem, the place he chose above all the places of the earth to settle his name therein; and Zion, the choice ornament of that Salem,—a model wherein the beauty and excellency of all the other are contracted, whose gates were then so dear unto the Lord. Or perhaps you have the distribution of the whole into its several parts;—Judah, the governing tribe; Israel, the body of the people; Salem, the chief place of their residence and glory; and Zion, the presence of God in his worship amongst them all. Now, the mention of these titles of the church, so dear to the Lord, doth front the following narration, to afford us this observation:—

Observation. The care of Salem, of Zion, lies at the bottom of all God's powerful actings and workings among the sons of men. Every mighty work of God throughout the world may be prefaced with these two verses. The whole course of affairs in the world is steered by Providence in reference to the good of Salem. Zion hath been the rise and downfall of all the powers of the world; it is her deliverance or trial that is intended in their raising, and her recompense and vengeance in their ruin. God works not among the nations for their own sakes. When they are sifted with a sieve, they are but the chaff; Israel is the corn for whose sake it is done: whereof not the least grain shall fall to the ground, Amos ix. 9. She is precious in God's sight and honourable; he loves her: therefore he giveth men for her, and people for her life, Isa. xliii. 4. The men of the world are very apt to pride themselves in their thoughts, as though great were their share and interest in the glorious things that God is accomplishing; like a fly that sat on the chariot wheel, and cried, "What a dust have I raised round about!" The truth is, their names are written in the dust, and they are of no account in the eyes of the Lord in all he is accomplishing, but only to exalt his name in their miscarriage and destruction. Was it not in the thoughts of some lately amongst us, that their right hand had accomplished the work of the Lord, and that the end of it must be the satisfaction of their lusts? And hath not the Lord declared that they have neither part nor lot in this matter? It was Salem, not self,—Zion, not Babylon or confusion, that lay at the bottom of the whole.

(2.) There is a relation of God unto this place. His will was known there, verse 1; and his worship was established, verse 2. And these also have their particular mention.

Observation. In the deliverance of his people, God hath a special regard to the honour of his ordinances. Why so great things for Salem? Why, there his word is preached, whereby his will is known and his name made great;—there his tabernacle is fixed, and his dwelling-place established;—there he gives his presence in his worship and ordinances, wherein he is delighted. "Because of thy temple at Jerusalem shall kings bring presents unto thee," Ps. lxviii. 29. Here is the temple, Christ, and then, the worship of Christ: for their sake it shall be done. When vengeance is recompensed upon an opposing people, it is the vengeance of the temple, Jer. l. 28. And it is a voice from thence that rendereth recompense to his enemies, Isa. lxvi. 6. The great work which the Lord at this day is accomplishing in the world looks fully on this one thing. Wherefore is it that God shaketh the powers of this world, and causeth the towers to totter which they uphold? Is it not that the way of his worship may be vindicated from all their abominations, and vengeance taken upon them for their opposition thereunto? And there is no greater sign of God's care for a people, than when he shows a regard to his ordinances among that people. The defence he gives is of the glory of the assemblies of mount Zion, Isa. iv. 5. When the ark departs, you may call the children, "Ichabod." The taking away of his candlestick, the removal of his glory from the temple, is an assured prologue to the utter ruin of a people.

And hath not the Lord had a special eye this way in the late deliverance? It is his promise, that he will purge the rebels from amongst his people. And he hath done it. Were there not children of Edom amongst them, who cried, "Down with them, down with them even to the ground"? Hath not God magnified his despised word above all his name? Was it not as an offscouring to many particular persons among them in the late murmuring for pre-eminence against those whom the Lord hath chosen?—who, I suppose, have no other joy in their employment than Moses had in his, who once desired the Lord to slay him, that he might be freed from his burden. Only the will of the Lord and the good of a poor thankless people swayed their hearts unto it. And were there here any more discriminating rods cast in before the Lord, to have that bud and spring which he owned (as Numb. xvii.) than this one: Scripture, or no Scripture? solemn worship, or none at all? I speak only as to some particulars, and that I can upon my own experience. The Lord give their hearts a free discovery of his thoughts in this business! Doubtless he hath had respect to his tabernacle and dwelling-place. For my part, they are to me as the Theban shield; and, notwithstanding all my pressures, I would labour to say, as Mephibosheth, "Let all go, since I see the king in peace."

I might farther observe, from both these things together, that among the people of God alone is the residence of his glorious presence. This song is held out from Zion. "In his temple doth every one speak of his glory," Ps. xxix. 9. "Bless ye God in the congregations, the LORD, from the fountain of Israel," Ps. lxviii. 26. "Praise waiteth for thee, O God, in Sion," Ps. lxv. 1. As a lame leg, and as a thorn in the hand, ungraceful, painful, "so is a parable in the mouth of fools," Prov. xxvi. 7, 9. It is the saints who are bid to be joyful in the Lord; and the high praises of God must be in their moúths, Ps. cxlix. 5, 6. They are high things that beseem only those whom God doth magnify. If the Lord give us matter of praise, pray know from whom it will be acceptable,—whose praises they are he delighteth to inhabit. If you have some defiling lust, the sunshine of mercies will exhale nothing but the offensive steam of carnal affections. The sacrifices of wicked hearts are an abomination to the Lord. If your fleshly affections work this day, without the beatings of a pure heart, and the language of a pure lip, the Lord will reject your oblations. Would you have your praise as sweet to the Lord as a mercy is to you?—be assured that in Christ you are the Israel of God, and your prayers shall prevail, your praise shall be accepted.

2. The second particular, as I observed, is a special *narration* of the works of God, for which the whole is intended, verses 3, 5, 6. And therein you have these two things:—(1.) The place where these acts were wrought and are remembered, "There," verse 3; (2.) The acts themselves related; which refer,—[1.] To God the worker, verse 3, "He brake;" [2.] To the persons on whom they were wrought, verses 5, 6.

(1.) The place where these things were acted and the monuments of them erected,—that is, "There;" there, in Salem and Zion, Judah and Israel; there, not so much in those places, as with reference unto them.

Observation. All the mighty actings of God regard his church; and there are the monuments and trophies of his victories against his enemies erected. To the first part of this I spake before. A word for the latter:—God decketh and maketh Zion glorious with the spoils of his adversaries. There the glory of Pharaoh and all his host, drowned in the Red sea, is dedicated, Exod. xv.; there are the shields of all the mighty men in the host of Sennacherib, slain by an angel, hung up, Isa. xxxvii. 35, 36; there is the honour, the robes, the crown, and the reason of Nebuchadnezzar laid up, for the glory of Zion, Dan. iv. 33, 34, himself being changed into a beast; there is all the pomp and glory of Herod deposited, Acts xii. 23, when, as a reward of his pride and persecution, he was devoured of worms; there is the glory of all persecutors, with the blood of Julian in a special manner, who threw it into the air, and cried, "Vicisti Galilæe;" there Haman is visibly exalted upon the gallows by himself erected for the ruin of a prince of the people, Esth. vii. 10; there the peace and the joy of the church, their choice frame under the bloody massacres of the inhabitants of Zion, is set to show, for the glory of it; there all the rochets of popish prelates, the crowns, and glory, and thrones of the kings of the earth,—all set apart as monuments and trophies of God's victories in Zion; there is a place reserved for the man of sin, and all the kings of the earth who have committed fornication with the mother of harlots, whose destruction sleepeth not. God will at length certainly glorify Salem with the arrow of the bow, the shield, the sword, and all spoils of its oppressors.

(2.) There is what he did describe, both immediately in the actions themselves, verse 3, and with reference to the persons towards whom he so acted, verse 5. Now, because the former is fully contained in the latter, I shall not handle it apart, but descend immediately to the consideration of the words of my text, being a declaration of what the Lord hath done for his people in the day of their distress, with particular reference to the cause of that distress.

And here we shall look a little,—1. To the reading of the words; and, 2. To their explication:—

1. To the reading: The "stout-hearted;" or, the "strong in heart," the "mighty in heart," (so in the original;)—men of stout, stubborn, unpersuadable hearts and courage, whose epithet is, that they are "far from righteousness," Isa. xlvi. 12. The Septuagint have rendered it, *ἀσύνετοι τῇ καρδίᾳ*,[1]—"the foolish in heart." Stubborn-hearted men are

[1] So in the text (the Hebrew being אַבִּירֵי לֵב); as if the LXX. had read it, by mistake, אֲבֻדֵי לֵב—"who have lost their heart." In the parallel from Isaiah, they render it *ἀπολωλεκότες τὴν καρδίαν*. It is much better rendered by Symmachus, in the first instance, *ὑπερήφανοι τὴν καρδίαν*,—in the second, *σκληροκάρδιοι*. אַבִּיר sometimes signifies a *bull* (Ps. xxii. 13),—the symbol, when untamed, of stubbornness, Jer. xxxi. 18. It is an ingenious suggestion of Vitringa, adopted also by Parkhurst, that the original words correspond strikingly with the "*esprits forts*" of the French.—Ed.

foolish-hearted men: not to yield unto, is worse than not to understand, what is good. They "are spoiled,—אֶשְׁתּוֹלְלוּ, have yielded themselves to the spoil." So properly, and so rendered by most interpreters;[1] which sense I shall follow. "They have slept their sleep,"—נָמוּ, "dormitârunt," "They have slumbered their sleep." What it is "to slumber a sleep" we shall see afterward. The residue of the words are literally rendered, save only in the placing of the negation; for whereas we set it on the persons, "none of the men," in the original it is upon the act, "have not found;" affirming concerning the persons, "all the men of might have not,"—that is, "none of the men of might have:" a very frequent Hebraism, imitated by John, 1 Epist. iii. 15, Πᾶς ἀνθρωποκτόνος οὐκ ἔχει ζωὴν,—"Every man-slayer hath not life,"—that is, "none hath." And so you have the words, "The stout of heart have yielded themselves to the spoil, they have slumbered their sleep; and none of the men of might have found their hands."

2. The words thus read contain three general heads:—

(1.) A twofold description of the enemies of Salem:—

[1.] In respect of their internal affections: they were "stout of heart," men of high spirit and haughty courage, "cedere nescientes," not knowing how to yield to any thing but the dictates of their own proud spirits.

[2.] In respect of their power for outward acting: "Men of might;" strong of hand, as well as stout of heart. Courage without strength will but betray its possessor; and strength without courage is but "inutile pondus,"—a burdensome nothing: but when both meet,—a stout heart and strong hands,—who shall stand before them? Thus you have the enemies set out like Goliath, with his spear and helmet, defying the host of the living God.

(2.) You have a twofold issue of God's providence in dealing with them, suitably to this their double qualification:—

[1.] He opposeth himself to the stoutness of their hearts, and they "yield themselves to the spoil." Where observe, first, The act itself: they "yield themselves." Nothing in the world so contrary to a stout heart as to yield itself. To yield, is a thing of the greatest distance and contrariety to the principle of a stout heart in the world: it is far more reconcilable to death than yielding. But this God will effect. Secondly, The extent of this yielding: it was "to the spoil." This exceedingly heightens the mighty working of the Lord against them. Should they be brought to yield to reason, persuasion, and union, it were well; but that they should be so prevailed on as to yield to the spoil,—that is, to the mercy of those against whom they rose and opposed themselves,—this is "digitus Dei."

[1] See Isa. lix. 15, where the same word occurs again in the Hithpael form; and, as in the Targum and by Jerome, is rendered, "maketh himself a prey."—Ed.

[2.] He opposeth himself to their actual might: they "found not their hands." Hands are the instruments of acting the heart's resolution. The strength and power of a man is in his hands; if they be gone, all his hope is gone. If a man's sword be taken from him, he will do what he can with his hands; but if his hands be gone, he may go to sleep, for any disturbance he will work. For men not to find their hands, is not to have that power for the execution of their designs which formerly they had. In former days they had hands,—power for doing great things; but now, when they would use them against Salem, they could not find them. And why so?—God had taken them away; God took away their power,—their strength departed from them. Samson found not his strength when his locks were cut; though he thought to do as at other times, yet he was deceived, and taken. When God takes away men's power, they go forth, and think to do as in former days; but when they come to exercise it, all is gone: their hands are laid out of the way,—in allusion to one that seeketh.

(3.) There is the total issue of this whole dispensation, placed in the midst of both, as arising from both: "They have slumbered their sleep." When their hearts yielded, and their hands were lost, courage and power both taken away, what else should they do? Some take this for an expression of death, as it is sometimes used, Ps. xiii. 3, "Lighten mine eyes, lest I sleep the sleep of death." I rather conceive it to hold out that condition which God threateneth to bring upon the enemies of his people, when he sends them a "spirit of slumber," Rom. xi. 8. Now, in such a condition two things are eminent:—

[1.] Its weakness. A condition of slumber and sleep is a weak condition. A sleeping man is able to do nothing. Jael can destroy a drowsy Sisera.

[2.] Its vanity. Men in their sleep are apt to have foolish, vain fancies. This, then, is that which the Lord holds out concerning the enemies of his church, his people, his ways, when their hearts are gone and their hands gone:—they shall be brought to a condition of weakness in respect of others; they shall not be able to beat them: and of vanity in themselves; they shall feed themselves with vain thoughts, like the dream of a hungry man, Isa. xxix. 8, "He dreameth, and, behold, he eateth; he waketh, and, behold, he is empty." They please themselves for a little season with strong apprehensions of the accomplishment of their hearts' lusts and cobweb fancies; but the issue is shame and disappointment.

The words, being opened, will yield us these three observations:—I. Men of stout hearts and strong hands, of courage and power, are often engaged against the Lord. II. God suits the workings of providence for deliverance to the qualifications and actings of his opposers; their stout hearts shall yield, their strong hands be lost. III. Though men have courage, might, and success, yet when they engage themselves against the Lord, weakness and vanity shall be the issue thereof. In the brief handling whereof I hope you shall find the word of God and the works of God exceedingly suited.

I. Men of courage, power, and success, of eminent qualifications, are oftentimes engaged against the Lord, and the ways of the Lord.

I shall multiply neither testimonies nor instances of this truth; for that were but to set up a candle in the sun;—the experience of all ages has made it good. One or two places may suffice:—Ps. lxviii. 30, "Rebuke the company of spearmen, the multitude of the bulls, with the calves of the people." There are not only "calves of the people," easily deluded, sottish men; but also multitudes of "bulls," heady, high-minded, bearing down all before them, throwing up all bounds and fences, laying all common to their lusts, not easily to be resisted;—these also are amongst the adversaries of the ways of the Lord. The first open opposers of the ways of God were "giants," "mighty men," and "men of renown," Gen. vi. 4. At once "two hundred and fifty princes of the assembly, famous in the congregation, and men of renown," joined themselves in rebellion against the LORD, Numb. xvi. 2; and that,—

1. Because these very qualifications, of a stout heart, strong hands, and former success, are apt of themselves, if destitute of directing light and humbling grace, to puff up the spirits of men, and to engage them in ways of their own, contrary to the mind of the Lord. When men take advice of their stout hearts, strong hands, and former success, they are very evil counsellors. When Jeremiah advised the Jews from the Lord for their good, the proud men answered, they would not obey, Jer. xliii. 2. When Pharaoh is made stout for his ruin, he cries, "Who is the LORD, that I should obey his voice?" Exod. v. 2. And for success, God makes the Assyrian the rod of his anger, sends him against the people of his wrath, with charge "to take the spoil, and to take the prey, and to tread them down like the mire of the streets," Isa. x. 6. He goeth, accordingly, and prospereth. But when he hath so done, see what a conclusion he makes! He goes against Jerusalem, and cries, "'Let not your God deceive you. Have the gods of the nations delivered them?' and do you think so to be?" Isa. xxxvii. 10, 12. From the success he had from God, he concluded the success he should have against him;—like those of late amongst ourselves, who having been partners with others in former successes, whilst they went upon the command of God, doubtless received in their stout hearts establishment and strengthening to other undertakings; as if the God of the Parliament could not help. Amaziah, king of Judah, wages war with Edom, and they are destroyed before

him, 2 Kings xiv. 7. The war was of the Lord. Upon this he is lifted up, and causelessly provoketh Jehoash, king of Israel, verse 8, against the mind and will of God. Jehoash sends him word, that if the thistle pride itself against the cedar, the wild beast will tread it down, verse 9. But he had former success, and on he will go to his ruin. The stout-hearted men (for a delivery from whose fury and folly we desire this day to lift up the name of the Lord) having received help and assistance against Edom, will needs lift up the thistle against the cedar,—act out of their own sphere, turn subjection into dominion, to their shame and sorrow. But it were better their hearts should be filled with sorrow, than the nation, and especially the people of God in the nation, with blood and confusion, ending in bondage and tyranny. And this is the first account of it, why men of such qualifications are engaged against the Lord. The qualifications themselves do set up for it, if destitute of divine light and humbling grace. Such men will run upon God, and the thick bosses of his buckler.

2. God will have it so, that the greater may be his glory in the powerful protection and defence of his own, with the destruction, disappointment, and ruin of their enemies. If his enemies were all sottish, weak, foolish, childish, until he makes them so, where would be the praise of his great name? when would there be "Nodus Deo vindice dignus,"—work worthy of the appearance of the Most High? But when there is a great mountain before Zerubbabel (Zech. iv. 7), —a high, haughty, oppressing empire,—to level that to a plain is glorious. When God will get himself a name, he raises up, not a poor, effeminate Sardanapalus,—a poor, sensual, hypocritical wretch, as some have been; the Lord will not make an open contest by such a one, such as some of our sore oppressors have been: but he will raise up a Pharaoh, a crooked leviathan, a stout-hearted, cunning-headed, strong-handed oppressor; and he tells him (such a one as he), "For this cause have I raised thee up, for to show in thee my power; and that my name may be declared throughout all the earth," Exod. ix. 16. "Thou art a fit subject," saith he, "for me to exalt my glory in thy ruin." The beast is to make war with the Lamb; and he shall not do it alone: God will give him in assistance. And who shall these be?—women, and children, and weak ones? No; he will put it into the heart of the kings of the earth "to give their power and strength to the beast," Rev. xvii. 17, to break them in pieces. This will be glory indeed. All the opposers which formerly have risen, or at least most of them, have had the power to that height, as they have been exceedingly above all outwardly appearing means of being resisted. The breaking of the old monarchies and of papal power is a work meet for the Lord. And in this shall mainly consist the promised glory of the Church of Christ in after days; whose morning star, I

doubt not, is now upon us:—the Lord will more immediately and visibly break the high, stout, haughty ones of the earth, for the sake of his people, than in former times. Look upon all the glorious things that are spoken concerning Zion in the latter days, and you shall find them all interwoven with this still,—the shaking of heaven, the casting down of thrones, and dominions, and mighty ones. I mention this, because indeed I look upon this late mercy as the after-drops of a former refreshing shower,—as an appendix of good-will, for the confirming the former work which God had wrought. "Though," saith he, "'ye have lien among the pots,'—have been in a poor, defiled condition, a condition of bondage,—'yet shall ye be as the wings of a dove covered with silver, and her feathers with yellow gold,'—ye shall be made exceeding glorious." But how or when shall this be? Why, when the Almighty scattereth kings for her sake, then shall she be as white as snow in Salmon, Ps. lxviii. 13, 14. When God by his almighty power takes away so great opposers, then glory and beauty shall arise upon you. And this, in some degree, lies also at the bottom of the late dispensation of Providence,—men's hearts were full of fear of a storm; yea, a storm was necessary, that some evidence might be given of the Lord's continuing his presence amongst you, that if hereafter we be forsaken, it may appear that it was for our own unbelief, unthankfulness, and folly, and not for doing the work of the Lord. Now, how was this expected? "Why, this poor people, or that, unacquainted with the things of their peace, will rise and make opposition." "No," saith the Lord, "you shall not have so easy a trial; you shall have men of stout hearts and strong hands, with many former successes on their shoulders; that, when deliverance is given in, my name may be glorious indeed."

Use 1. Be not moved at the most formidable enemies that may arise against you in the ways of God. "It was told the house of David, saying, Syria is confederate with Ephraim. And his heart was moved, and the heart of his people, as the trees of the wood are moved with the wind," Isa. vii. 2. When strong combinations arise, how apt are we to shake and tremble before them, especially when they have some strangeness as well as strength! That Syria should come against Judah, is no wonder; but what, I pray, makes Ephraim too, their brother, and fellow in former afflictions? Besides, Syria and Ephraim were always at a mortal difference among themselves. But they who agree in nothing else usually consent in opposition to the ways of God. Then you shall have Edom, Ammon, Amalek, and Ashur altogether of one mind, Ps. lxxxiii. 6–8. And the kings of the west, that perpetually devour one another, yet have one mind in exalting the beast and opposing the Lamb, Rev. xvii. 14;—as, in our late troubles, there was a concurrence not only in the main of Syria and Ephraim, the two grand extremes, but also of innumerable particular fancies and designs; so that if a man should have met them, (like him in the fable, the lion, the ass, and the fox), he could not but wonder "Quo iter unâ facerent,"—whither they were travelling together. But, I say, when such combinations are made, how apt are we to shake and tremble! "They are stout men, valiant men; and perhaps Ahithophel is with them!" Why, if they were not such, I pray how should the Lord have any praise in the close of the dispensation? We would be delivered, but we care not that God should be glorified. If God's glory were dear to us, we should not care how high opposition did arise. Precious faith, where art thou fled? Had we but some few grains of it, we might see the rising of the greatest mountains to be but a means to make the name of God glorious, by removing them into the midst of the sea. Hath it not been thus in the days of old? The Lord humble us for our unbelief!

Use 2. Let men to whom the Lord hath given stout hearts, strong hands, and great success, watch carefully over their own spirits, lest they be led aside into any way against the mind of God. Great endowments are ofttimes great temptations. "The pride of thine heart hath deceived thee, thou that dwellest in the clefts of the rock, whose habitation is high; that saith in his heart, Who shall bring me down to the ground?" Obad. 3. Was it not the ruin of Amaziah, of whom notwithstanding it was said, "he did that which was right in the sight of the LORD?" 2 Chron. xxv. 2. He who is heightened against the king of terrors, if he hath not humility (one of the chief of graces), will quickly choose himself paths of his own. Alas, poor creatures! if hearts and hands be, and God be not, what will it avail? But of this afterward. I now proceed to the second observation.

II. God suits the workings and actings of providence for deliverance to the qualifications of the opposers.

Are they stout hearts?—they shall be made to yield themselves. Are they men of might?—they shall lose their power,—they shall not find their hands. To this I shall speak very little. This is the cutting off of Adonibezek's toes and thumbs. God countermines them in their actings, and blows them up in their own mine. "In the thing wherein they deal proudly, he is above them," Exod. xviii. 11. They shall not soar so high on the wings of their pride, but that still they shall find God uppermost. When they take counsel, and think to carry it by their advices, God saith, "I am wise also, and will bring evil," Isa. xxxi. 2. When they think to carry it by a high hand, his strength shall appear against them. When Herod owns the blasphemy of being called a god, he shall rot and be eaten of worms, Acts xii. 23. Pharaoh cries, "Come on, let us deal wisely against Israel," Exod. i. 10. He of all men shall play the fool, for his own ruin and the ruin of his people, Exod. xiv. 27, 28. If Sennacherib boasts of his mighty host, be sure he shall not find his hands. How evidently hath the Lord thus carried on his providence in the late dispensation! Were not many of the headless, heady undertakers, "robusti animo,"—mighty of heart? and were they not forced to yield themselves, yea, to "yield themselves to the spoil?" Were they not deep in their plotting? Doubtless they or their seducers had digged deep to lay their design; though of the generality of them it cannot be said, as was of Cæsar and his companions, "Accessere sobrii ad perdendum rempublicam." They were brought to act things in very folly and confusion. They were great men of might: whence is it they made no more opposition? The Lord laid their hands out of the way. Many reasons might be given of this; but I must pass to the last point.

III. Though men have courage, might, and former successes to accompany them, yet when they engage themselves against the Lord, or any way of his, vanity, weakness, and disappointment will be the issue thereof.

"Can your heart endure, or can your hands be strong, in the days that I shall deal with you?" saith the Lord, Ezek. xxii. 14. "Let the potsherds strive with the potsherds of the earth; woe unto him that contendeth with his Maker!" Isa. xlv. 9. "He is wise in heart, and mighty in strength: who hath hardened himself against him, and prospered?" Job ix. 4. "The LORD bringeth the counsel of the heathen to nought; but the counsel of the LORD standeth for ever. He maketh the devices of the people of none effect," Ps. xxxiii. 10, 11. Whoever riseth up without him, or against him, shall fall and come to nothing. This is a plain point, that we suppose ourselves exceedingly well versed in. But He who searcheth our spirits, and is acquainted with our inward parts, knows how great is our unbelief in this very thing; and therefore, in tender condescension, he hath carefully provided for our support herein. A man would think one word, once spoken, were enough to convince and persuade the whole world of this truth; but, the Lord knows, there must be line upon line, here a little, and there a little, to give his own people any establishment herein. And therefore it is that in so many places in his word he hath asserted and affirmed this one thing,—namely, let men be never so strong, powerful, and successful, if once they engage against him, they are utterly destroyed, unless he pluck them out of the snare. "Associate yourselves," etc., Isa. viii. 9.

But you will say, "Engage against the Lord! That is true; whoever engageth against him shall surely fall. But who is so mad as to do so? Very Rabshakeh himself affirms that he came not up to Jerusalem without the Lord, but that the Lord sent him to go up against the land to destroy it," Isa. xxxvi. 10. It is true he said so; and by this observation you have an answer to the Scripture. For though he said so, he lied before the Lord, and belied the Lord; his undertaking was against the Lord, and against his mind, as the sequel fully manifested. Many suppose they engage for God, when they engage against him. To engage against the Lord, is to engage against his mind and will. To undertake without the will of God, is enough to be the ruin of the best and stoutest; as we see in the case of Josiah; but to engage against him!—who can do it, and stand when he is provoked? This, then, is that which neither stout hearts nor strong hands shall ever be able to go through withal. For instance, to engage against that authority which God will own and defend, is successlessly to engage against the Lord. Now, because these are the days wherein the Lord will shake heaven and earth, beat the nations with a rod of iron, breaking much of the power of the world, it may be asked by some, how it shall be known that any authority is such as the Lord will not destroy and overturn, but own it as a way of his own? I answer, To omit the rule of reason, law, and common established principles amongst men, all which give a great light unto the rule of walking in this case, I shall give you six scriptural significations, "a posteriori," of such an authority as the Lord will make as a brasen wall, or a rock in the sea, against which the waves dash with noise and fury, but are themselves broken to pieces:—

1. If it be such as the Lord hath honoured with success and protection in great, hazardous, and difficult undertakings for himself. Thus was it with Moses. Never had a leader of a people more murmurings, revilings, and rebellions against him. The story is obvious unto all. He was envied, hated, reproached of all sorts, from the princes of the congregation to the mixed multitude. But Moses had travelled through the sea and the desert with the Lord, and was encompassed with success and protection; and therefore all attempts against him shall be birthless and fruitless. This is one; but it will never do alone, unless conjoined with those that follow.

2. If the persons enjoying that authority abide to act for God, and not for themselves, after such success and protection. Saul began to act for God, and he vexed all his enemies, which way soever he turned himself; but afterward, turning to himself, God left him to himself. Cyrus, how honoured, how anointed was he for his great undertaking against Babylon! but afterward, pursuing his own ambition, he was requited with blood for the blood he sought. The Lord is with them that are with him, and whilst they are so. The establishment of the house of Saul is far from the Lord: for "those that honour him, he will honour; and they that despise him shall be lightly esteemed," 1 Sam. ii. 30. There is no more certain sign in the world of persons devoted to ruin, or at least of their being divested of their authority, than that having followed God for a season in their enjoyment of

success and protection, they turn aside to pursue their own ends, like Jehu. I could give you an example of this, as yet not much above half a year old. But when men undertake with the Lord, and for him, and having known his assistance therein, shall continue to lay out themselves in his ways; the Lord will then build them a house like David, which shall not be prevailed against.

Here I must give one caution by the way;—that I am very far from countenancing any to move against just and righteous authority, who discern not these things: the Lord forbid. Let men look to the rule of their obedience, which I have nothing to do withal at this time. I only describe such as unto whom, if any dare to make opposition, in an ordinary dispensation of providence, it will prove fruitless and vain.

3. The third thing is, that they subject their power to the power of the Lord Christ, who is Lord of lords, and King of kings. The psalmist tells the rulers of the earth, that the reason of their spoiling is, that they do not "kiss the Son," Ps. ii. 12, or yield unfeigned obedience to the mighty King whom God hath set on his holy hill. God hath promised that he will give in the service of kings and nations to Christ in his kingdom; and therein shall be their security. When God puts it into the heart of rulers to rule according to the interest of Christ and his gospel, and to seek the advancement of his sceptre, they shall surely be as a fenced wall. I cannot stay to show what this interest of Christ is. In a word, it is the ordering, framing, carrying on of affairs as is most conducible to the unravelling and destruction of the mystery of iniquity.

4. If they are supported by the prayer of a chosen people, who seek their welfare, not for their own interest and advantage, but for the advantage of the gospel and the ways of Christ, by them asserted. If God's own people pray for them in authority, that under them they may enjoy some share of their own, and obtain some ends suited to any carnal interest of theirs, God will reject those prayers. But when they seek their welfare, because it is discovered to them that in their peace the gospel shall have peace and prosperity; surely the Lord will not cast out their prayers, nor shame the face of his poor supplicants.

5. If in sincerity, and with courage and zeal, they fulfil the work of their magistracy, in the administration of righteous judgment; especially in those great and unusual acts of justice, in breaking the jaws of the wicked and terrible, and delivering the spoil out of the teeth of the mighty, Job xxix. 17. Innumerable are the demonstrations of God's owning such persons.

6. If they have not the qualifications of that power which in these latter days God hath promised to destroy. Now these are two; I will but name them unto you. First, Drinking the cup of fornication that is in the hand of the harlot; that is, practising any false

worship and forms invented besides the word. Secondly, Giving their power to the beast, or engaging in any ways of persecution against any of the ways of God, or his saints in those ways. That the Lord is about to shake, break, and destroy all such powers as these, I did not long since, by his assistance, here demonstrate.

And so have I completed my instances that they who engage against such an authority as is attended with these qualifications, engage against the Lord. I could also give other instances, in other ways and institutions of God; but I chose these as most accommodated to the season. If now I should tell you, that, notwithstanding all clamours to the contrary, these things, for the main, are found in your assemblies, thousands in the world would (yet I hope your own consciences would not) return the lie for so saying. But yet, though the Lord seems to bear witness to some integrity in his late dispensations, I shall only pray that what is wanting may be supplied;—that you may never want the like protection in the like distress.

Come we now briefly to the reasons why those who oppose such authority shall not succeed. And it were an easy labour to multiply reasons hereof. The sovereignty, the power, all the attributes of God would furnish us with arguments. I shall omit them all; [and] only touch upon two that are couched in the text.

They shall have no better issue, because,—(1.) The Lord will take away their stout hearts, whereby they are supported; (2.) He will take away their strong hands, whereby they are confirmed: and when hearts and hands are gone, they also are gone.

(1.) He will take away their stout hearts, that they shall no more be able to carry them out to any success in their great undertakings. He will break that wheel at the very fountain, that it shall no more be the spring of their proceedings.

Now, this the Lord usually doth one or more of these four ways:—[1.] He fills them with fury and madness; so taking away their order. [2.] He fills them with folly and giddiness; so taking away their counsel. [3.] He fills them with terror and amazement; so depriving them of their courage. Or, [4.] with contrition and humility; so changing their spirits:—

[1.] He fills them with fury and madness, taking away their order, which is the tie and cement of all societies, in all undertakings. "'Though all the people of the earth,' saith the Lord, 'be gathered together against Jerusalem,' they shall not prosper." And why so? "I will smite every horse with astonishment, and his rider with madness," Zech. xii. 4. Madmen have often great strength, and with it great fury; but know not how to use it, except to their own ruin: when they think to do the greatest mischief, they cut and gash themselves. Thus the Lord threateneth those who in outward profession are his own people, when they walk contrary to him: "The LORD shall smite thee with madness of heart, and thou shalt not prosper in thy ways," Deut. xxviii. 28, 29. Because smitten with madness, therefore they shall not prosper. This is that untameable fury whereby men are carried out to sinful, destructive enterprises, as the horse rushes into the battle;—a judgment which some men vocally, as well as actually, at this day proclaim to be upon their spirits. They cry their blood boils, and their hearts rage for revenge; reviling those in authority, whereby to foment, Acts xix. Hence they stir up men for the engaging in such designs as, if accomplished, in the judgment of all men not mad like themselves, would certainly prove ruinous to themselves and others. And in this frame they delight, of it they boast; not once considering that it is a badge and character of men whom God will disappoint and destroy in their proceedings; it being nothing but the working of that evil spirit which came upon Saul, stirring him up to rage and fury, when once the meek, calming Spirit of the Lord departed from him.

[2.] He will fill them with folly and giddiness; so taking away their counsel. Foolish and giddy undertakers do but conceive chaff, and bring forth stubble. "The princes of Zoan are become fools, the princes of Noph are deceived; they have also seduced Egypt. The LORD hath mingled a perverse spirit in the midst thereof; and they have caused Egypt to err in every work thereof, as a drunken man staggereth in his vomit." Isa. xix. 13, 14. This he calls taking away the spirit of Egypt, and destroying the counsel thereof, verse 3. There is no means of ruin, destruction, and disappointment, that God doth more frequently threaten than this,—he will take wisdom from the wise, and then pour contempt upon the spirit of princes. When to their madness he adds blindness; to their fury, folly; to their rage, giddiness;—what can be the issue but such as is expressed: "They shall stagger like a drunken man in his vomit"? Stand before him, and he'll pour his filth upon you; let him alone, and he and it will quickly tumble to the ground. What, I pray, can be expected from mad, blind, furious, foolish, raging, giddy men? Should a man use these expressions of any, it would be said he railed; yet God hath spoken it, that all undertakers against him shall be so, and no otherwise. Now, hence ariseth upon the spirits of such men a twofold effect;—first, they shall not be able to advise rationally against others; nor, secondly, shall they be able to receive suitable advice from others. They shall be able neither to make out counsel to support them in the way wherein they are, nor to take in counsel for their reducing to better paths. If this were not evident in the late dispensation of the Lord towards poor creatures setting up themselves against the Lord, then never did any providence speak plain in any latter age.

[3.] He will fill them with fear and amazement; so taking away their courage. This God caused to fall upon a whole host at one time; [so] that, without seeing an enemy, they ran and fled, and lost all they had, and the spoil, 2 Kings vii. 6, 7. And he threatens that in such a condition he will make men like women,—they shall be afraid and fear, Isa. xix. 16. Yea, this is the way of God's usual dealing; first, he overcomes the spirit of his enemies, and then their armies or force: and the Lord is magnified therein; as is fully set out, Exod. xv. 14–16. The hearts and spirits of men are all in the hand of God; he can pluck them in, or let them out, as seems good unto him; make him that was mighty one day, the next day to be of no power: what is left of fury, folly shall devour; and what is left of folly, fear shall consume; and the purpose of the Lord shall be established.

[4.] If he have any favour for them, and so will not proceed in these ways of revenge against them, which would end in their speedy ruin; he will give them contrition and humility, so changing them. What a clear testimony of this did he give in the business of Jacob and Esau! Esau resolves and threatens his death upon the first opportunity, Gen. xxvii. 41; an opportunity is put into his hands by Jacob's return into Canaan, chap. xxxii.; means of revenge he is ready furnished withal, and comes out, accordingly, with a band of cut-throats for the purpose, in the same chapter. What should any man now rationally expect, but that poor Jacob must certainly be ruined, and the mother slain with the children? In an instant the Lord toucheth the heart of Esau, and all his menaces of revenge issue in tears and expressions of love and joy! chap. xxxiii. 4. It is to be rejoiced in, that the stout hearts of some men are changed upon their disappointment: and the issue of the mercy is no loss to you, to the nation, and themselves therein; though truly to them it had been an argument of greater love, had the Lord graciously bent their spirits unto it before. But by his infinite wisdom he hath accomplished his holy will.

Now, in one, more, or all of these ways, will the Lord proceed with the mighty of heart, that set up themselves against him, until he take away their hearts, and make them useless; that, either willingly or unwillingly, "they shall yield themselves" even "to the spoil."

(2.) He will not only take away their hearts, but also their hands; he will not only dispirit them, but he will also disarm them; he will take not only wisdom from their hearts, but the wheels from their chariots. He is the God of the power of men, as well as of the spirits of men. Will he continue power and strength unto men, to use it against him that gives it?

Use 1. To discover the ground of God's late dispensation, in taking away the hearts from the stout and hands from the mighty,—bringing them into a condition of weakness and vanity. Their undertakings were against the Lord, and their hearts could not endure, neither could their hands be strong.

I shall give some instances in their undertaking against the Lord:—

(1.) In their declared enmity to the ministry of the gospel;—not to the persons of ministers, because engaged in some faction in the state, wherein, perhaps, many may be opposed, and that from the Lord;—nor yet because of their persuasion for the administration of ordinances after this or that form; which often ariseth to very great animosities,—the Lord pardon them unto his people: but because in general they do administer ordinances. Now, certainly there is so much of God in that administration, that if they be opposed, not for other causes, or upon other pretences, but "eo nomine," as administrators of ordinances, that opposition is made to God himself. It was part of the end of Christ's ascension, that he might bestow those gifts upon them which they do enjoy, Eph. iv. 8. And shall the fury of men make the work of God, the purchase of Christ, of none effect? Doubtless in this respect God will make as many as are sincere "a fenced brasen wall," Jer. xv. 20. Men may batter their hands, and beat out their brains against them; but they shall not prevail. It is true, as many of them are pleased in these days to engage themselves in several parties; so, if they do close and act with them that are pernicious to the commonwealth, all inconvenience that lighteth upon them is from themselves,—their profession gives them no sanctuary from opposition: but when they are envied, "eo nomine," as administrators of ordinances, not in such or such a way, but as ordinances,—shall not the Lord plead for this thing? Now, that this was aimed at by some, I suppose none can doubt. The Lord open the eyes of them who in this deliverance have received deliverance, but will not see it! I fear some men had almost rather perish, than be delivered not in their own way. Envy in some men will outbalance safety. Alas! we are proud beggars, when we will refuse the mercy of God if we may not appoint the hand whereby it shall be bestowed.

(2.) Against the spiritual ordinances of God themselves. These are the carved work which they aimed to break down with their axes and hammers. Christ hath said, "I will build my church." Their voice was, "Down with it! down with it even to the ground!" Poor creatures! they dashed themselves against the rock. Is this a time, think you, to engage against all ordinances, when the Lord Jesus is joining battle with all the world for their abuse of them; and is vindicating them in order to more purity, beauty, lustre, power, efficacy, and peace, than ever yet he adorned them withal? You were not wise, poor souls, to discern the seasons. What! no time to pluck down, but when Christ himself is building! Ah! turn your weapons against Babylon; it will prove far the more thriving warfare. Let

Zion alone, if but for your own sakes. Jerusalem will prove a burdensome stone to all that take her up. You have received more loss in a week of days from Christ in this nation, than you would have done in a week of years from Antichrist in another. God will make them that shall go for Ireland sensible of this truth. See Ps. xlviii. 12–14.

(3.) Principally and immediately against magistracy; if not in the abstract, yet openly as established in the hands of those whom the Lord hath owned in the darkest day that ever this nation saw. It is the hope of my soul, that the Lord hath borne witness that they have the sixfold qualification before mentioned. And why would they have at once destroyed the Parliament and their own commander? Look upon the end of their common workmen: was it not that every one might have enjoyed their lust for a season? Of the more crafty: was it not to get themselves power to attempt their folly, and execute their fury? Look upon the end of the work: was it not to have wrapped us in confusion for a few months, and then to have given us up to the revengeful will of enraged enemies? So that, truly, there is but one thing wonderful to me in all this business, that God should take away the hearts and hands of these men in this enterprise; and that is, that he should do it in mercy for such an unthankful, unworthy, unbelieving people as we are. In this is he for ever to be admired and blessed. At thy rebuke, O God of Jacob, both the chariot and the horses have failed.

Use 2. If this be the cause why "they have slumbered their sleep," be instructed, ye that are rulers of this nation, in the ways of peace, protection, and safety;—be in the ways of God, and do the things of God, and no weapon that is formed against you shall ever prosper. Many protections and deliverances you have had in your actings for him. Hath he not deserved at your hands to be trusted and feared all your days, with all your power? As my heart hath always been towards the governors in Israel, who willingly offered themselves among the people; so truly my heart never more trembled over them than now. Oh! where shall we find hearts fit to receive so many mercies as have been given into our bosoms? Oh! where shall we have hearts large enough to receive all these mercies? The oil ceased when the vessel would hold no more. All my hope and confidence is, that God will work for his name's sake. I could exhort you to sundry particulars, and lay down several paths of God, walking wherein you shall be sure to find peace and safety; as especially, that you would regard that which God hath honoured, whereunto the opposition which he had resolved to make void was made.

Use 3. You that are men of courage, and might, and success, stout of heart and strong of hand, be watchful over yourselves, lest you should in any thing be engaged against the Lord. The ways of the

Lord are your locks;—step but out of them, they will be cut, and you will become like other men, and be made a prey and a mocking to the uncircumcised that are round about. These eminencies you have from God are eminent temptations to undertakings against God, if not seasoned with grace and watchfulness. Ah! how many baits have Satan and the world suited to these qualifications! Samson shook himself, and went out, saying, "I will do as at other times;" but he knew not that the Lord was departed from him. You may think, when you are walking in paths of your own, that you will do as at other times; but if your strength be departed away, what will be the end?

Use 4. Our last use should be of instruction in respect of God; that you may see both what he can do and trust him, and consider what he hath done and bless him. For the first;—weapons of all sorts, men of all sorts, judgments of all sorts, are at his command and disposal: see it in this psalm. And for what he hath done;—if there be any virtue in the presence of Christ in his ordinances,—if any worth in the gospel,—if any sweetness in carrying on the work of Christ's revenge against Babylon,—if any happiness in the establishment of the peace and liberty of a poor nation, purchased with so much blood and so long a contest,—if any content in the disappointment of the predictions and threats of God's enemies and his people's,—if any refreshment to our bowels that our necks are yet kept from the yoke of lawless lust, fury, and tyranny,—if any sweetness in a hope that a poor, distressed handful in Ireland may yet be relieved,—if any joy that God hath given yet another testimony of his presence amongst us,—if it be any way valuable that the instruments of our deliverance be not made the scorned object of men's revengeful violence,—if any happiness that the authority under which we enjoy all these mercies is not swallowed up,—is it not all in the womb of this deliverance? And who is he that hath given it into our bosom?

SERMON XVII.[1]

THE DIVINE POWER OF THE GOSPEL.

"For I am not ashamed of the gospel of Christ: for it is the power of God unto salvation, to every one that believeth; to the Jew first, and also to the Greek."—ROM. i. 16.

THE preceding verses of this chapter contain a declaration of the person who wrote this epistle, the apostolical authority wherewith it

[1] This sermon was preached May 19, 1670.

was wrote, and a gracious salutation of them to whom it was wrote. This verse makes an entrance upon the main subject-matter designed to be treated on in the whole epistle; so that it is the centre of this glorious part of the Scripture, wherein the first general part of it doth issue, and whereon the remaining part depends.

The church at Rome was planted some while before; but it is altogether uncertain by whom. The wisdom of God foreseeing what abuses would be made of the foundation of that church, hath hid it quite from us. There is nothing in Scripture, nothing in antiquity to intimate by whom the faith was there first preached. Probably it was by some believers of the Circumcision; whence those disputes arose and contentions about the observation of Judaical ceremonies, which the apostle handles and determines, chap. xiv., xv. of this epistle. Hearing of their faith, our apostle—upon whom, as he saith, "was the care of all the churches," and to whom "the ministry of the Uncircumcision was in an especial manner committed," Gal. ii. 7, 8—writes this epistle to them, to instruct them in the mystery of the gospel, and confirm them in the faith thereof, and in the worship of God required therein.

To give weight to what he wrote, and commend it to their consideration, he acquaints them with that love and care he had for them, answerable to his duty, from whence it did proceed; telling them, verses 14, 15, that "he was debtor both to the Greeks, and to the Barbarians; both to the wise, and to the unwise. So that as much as in him was, he was ready to preach the gospel to them that were at Rome also." And hereby he prevented a prejudice and jealousy that might possess their minds, and answers an objection they might make to him about his writing. For they might say in themselves, "What makes him, a stranger, at so great a distance, interpose in our concerns? Doth he not 'stretch himself beyond his measure,' or 'boast himself in another man's line?'"—which he affirms in another place he did not; for he was charged with such things. His zeal carrying him out to act for the gospel in a peculiar manner, he was charged to "exceed his measure," and "boast in another man's line." To obviate this, he tells them, "No; I do nothing but what becomes an honest man, discharging a debt the Lord Jesus Christ hath laid upon me by virtue of my call to my office, and my susception of it. 'I am debtor to the Greeks, and to the Barbarians; to the wise, and to the unwise.' I am called," saith he, "to preach the gospel to all sorts of people under heaven; my commission is to 'go into all the world, and preach the gospel to every creature,'" Mark xvi. 15,—that is, as expounded, Matt. xxviii. 19, "to all nations," persons of all nations,—"as I have opportunity." Our Lord Jesus Christ, out of his love and care unto them whom he had redeemed with his blood, that they might be saved, had given the apostles to be theirs,—"All things are yours; Paul is yours, Apollos is yours,"—and charged them to preach the gospel to them; so that, Acts xx. 26, 27, he saith, "Now I am free from the blood of all men." How doth he prove it? "I have not shunned to declare to them the whole counsel of God." He frees himself from any surmise that they might have that he had a design of his own, and sought some advantage to himself in thus interposing in the concerns of the gospel, by telling them he doth but discharge a debt. "I am a debtor," saith he. And it is truly and really the wisdom of those who, in their several spheres, have the dispensation of the gospel committed unto them, to let the people know that they need not absolutely, whatsoever they do consequentially, count themselves beholden to them for preaching the word; but that, indeed, our Lord Jesus Christ hath engaged us in a debt: which if in his name we pay and discharge, we are sure of a reward; if not, he will require it at our hands. We owe the preaching of the gospel to them that are willing to hear it; and if, upon any account, we withhold it from them, we do defraud them. "I am debtor," saith the apostle. And every one that receiveth the gift and call from Christ is a debtor, and so should esteem himself. "I have done nothing," saith he, "but engaged in the discharge of the debt which I owe to the souls of men."

But there might likewise arise another objection, "If he be so concerned in the publication of the gospel that he writes an epistle to Rome, the greatest theatre then upon the earth, the head of the empire, and most eminent place in the world, why did he not come himself and preach it?" He returns an answer thereunto, verse 15. "That," saith he, "is not at present in my power. I am not my own; I am disposed of by a call of Christ, and guidance of his Spirit. But 'I am ready to come to Rome;' I have a readiness to preach the gospel wheresoever God calls me."

Now, that he might not seem to have outbid himself, in speaking of going thither to preach the gospel, without considering what it might cost him, he gives them the reason and ground upon which he had so engaged himself to be ready to come to Rome, in the words of the text, "For I am not ashamed of the gospel of Christ: for it is the power of God unto salvation, to every one that believeth; to the Jew first, and also to the Greek."

In the words there are,—

First. A general assertion, laid down as the ground of what he had before affirmed; and that is in these words, "I am not ashamed of the gospel of Christ."

Secondly. He gives a reason of that assertion, what made him say so, "I am not ashamed, because the gospel is the power of God." To which reason he gives a threefold limitation:—First, As to the especial end of it, "The power of God." Whereunto?—for this or that end in the world? No; "It is the power of God for salvation." Secondly, He limits it in respect of the object, "The power of God unto salvation." To all? No; but "to every one that believeth,"—to all believers, consider them either antecedently to their being made believers, or consequentially, having received the word. To others it is "foolishness;" but to us that believe, it is "the power and the wisdom of God." Thirdly, It hath limits as to the manner of administration, "To the Jew first, and also to the Greek." The word "first" there, respects the order of dispensation, and not a priority of efficacy or excellency. The word was first to be preached to the Jews, as you know, in many places, and that for many ends not now to be insisted on. This is the design of the words.

I shall, for the opening of them, inquire into two things:—1. What is intended by the "gospel"? 2. What is it to be "ashamed of the gospel"? After which the great reason will ensue of the apostle's assertion, "Because it is the power of God unto salvation."

1. What is intended by the "gospel"? The gospel is taken two ways:—(1.) Absolutely, as it is in itself; (2.) Relatively, with reference unto our practice and observance of it:—

(1.) Absolutely, and in itself; and so also it is taken two ways:—

[1.] Strictly, according to the signification of the word "good tidings," for the good tidings of the accomplishment of the promise by the sending of Jesus Christ. The name is taken from Isa. lii. 7, "How beautiful upon the mountains are the feet of him that publisheth the good tidings of the gospel." And in this sense the apostle gives us a description of the gospel, Acts xiii. 32, 33, "We declare unto you glad tidings, how that the promise which was made unto the fathers, God hath fulfilled the same unto us their children, in that he hath raised up Jesus again;"—sent Christ according to the promise; the tidings of which is strictly the gospel.

[2.] The gospel is taken more largely for all things that were annexed to the accomplishment of the promise, the revelation of truths made there, with all the institutions and ordinances of worship that accompanied it,—the whole doctrine and worship of the gospel. The first is what God doth for us in giving Christ; the second is what God requireth of us, in faith and obedience, and in the whole worship of the gospel. And this is the common sense wherein this word "gospel" is taken.

(2.) The gospel may be considered relatively, with reference unto believers; and then it intends our profession of the gospel: which profession consists in the performance of all gospel duties, when and as they are to be performed by virtue of the command of Christ;—which

I would desire you to consider and remember; for I can assure you all your concerns in the gospel will be found to depend upon it.

It is in reference unto the gospel in both these senses that the apostle here speaks;—as it contains the promise of Christ, the doctrine of the gospel, the worship of God, the institutions therein, and every man's performance of his own duty, according to the rules and commands of Christ in the gospel. This is that which the apostle says he was "not ashamed" of.

2. What is it to be "ashamed of the gospel"? Shame in general is a grief, perturbation, and trouble of mind upon the account of things vile, foolish, or evil, rendering a man (as he thinks) liable to reproach and contempt, working a resolution in him to have no more to do with such things, if once delivered from them. As the prophet Jeremiah, chap. ii. 26, "A thief is ashamed when he is taken." Two things befall such a person:—fear, which respects his punishment; and shame, which respects the vileness and reproach of the thing that he is taken in. And shame doth particularly respect honour, esteem, and repute. Hence, if you can by any means take off the disrepute of a thing in men's judgment, they are no more ashamed of it. The world hath prevailed to take off among themselves, and within their own compass, the disrepute of as odious sins as can be committed in the world; and men cease thereupon to be ashamed of them. We meet with men that will not at all be ashamed of swearing, cursing, blaspheming, nay, of drunkenness,—scarce of uncleanness; the wickedness of the world hath taken off the disrepute of them within their own compass: yet take the same men in lying or theft, and it will fill them with shame; not but that the guilt and evil of other sins is as great, it may be greater than these, but these are under a disrepute, and therefore they are thus ashamed.

Now this shame may be considered two ways:—

(1.) Objectively, as to the things that in themselves are shameful, though men may be relieved against them, so as not to have any inward shame in their minds. So the apostle tells us, 1 Thess. ii. 2, that he was "shamefully entreated at Philippi;" he had all manner of shameful things done unto him. And, Acts v. 41, all the apostles together "rejoiced that they were counted worthy to suffer shame." "They suffered shame, but they were not ashamed," Heb. vi. 6. It is said those apostate backsliders "put the Son of God to open shame." They did those things unto him which in their own nature cast shame upon him; they deserted his worship and ways, as if he was not worthy to be followed. Now, our apostle was very far from thinking that nothing of this shame would befall him at Rome, that no shameful thing would befall him. He was led thither bound with a chain, and cast into prison. This is not the shame intended.

(2.) There is shame in the person. And this also may be considered two ways:—

[1.] As it merely respects the affections of the mind, before mentioned;—when persons have a trouble and confusion of mind upon them for any thing wherein they are concerned, as that which is dishonourable, base, vile, or foolish.

[2.] When there are the effects of shame;—when men act as though they were ashamed, and will have no more to do with those things wherein they have been engaged, but leave them as if ashamed. It is said of David's soldiers, who had done no shameful thing, but courageously acquitted themselves in the battle against Absalom, but because of David's carriage upon that business, "They went every one away as men ashamed, that fly in battle." It may be there is that light and conviction upon most concerning the gospel, that it is impossible for them to be brought into perfect trouble and confusion of mind about it, as though it were a shameful thing; but yet perhaps they will do like men that fly in battle and are ashamed. And in this sense the word is principally used; for saith Christ, Mark viii. 38, "Whosoever shall be ashamed of me, I will be ashamed of him." How is that? What will the Lord do? He will not own him; which is called being ashamed of him.

Now this is that which the apostle intends. "For the doctrine," saith he, "and worship of the gospel, and for my work in preaching and dispensing it, I have neither trouble of mind, nor will I desert it; 'I am not ashamed of the gospel of Christ.'"

But you will say, "What great matter is this? I am persuaded there is not one present but will be ready to think that they would be as forward as the apostle in this matter. Ashamed of the gospel of Christ! God forbid. What is there in it, that the apostle thus signally expresses it, that he would not be ashamed?" I answer, Pray consider these three things:—

1*st*. The apostle here expresses it with especial reference to his preaching and professing the gospel at Rome. "I will come to Rome also," saith he; "for I am not ashamed of the gospel of Christ." Now, there was at that time at Rome a collection of all the great, wise, and inquiring men of the world. And how did they look upon the gospel, and the profession of it? Our apostle tells you, 1 Cor. i. 23;—as a foolish, weak, contemptible thing. How did they look upon them that professed it?—as the filth and offscouring of all things, 1 Cor. iv. 13. Here is a collection of the rulers of the greatest empire of the world,—of all the wise and learned men and great philosophers, princes of the world,—all looking upon this gospel, obedience to it, and the worship of God in it, to be as foolish a thing as ever men engaged in,—fit for none but contemptible persons. But saith the apostle, notwithstanding this, "I am not ashamed of it."

And we may observe here, that there was not yet at Rome any actual persecution of the gospel, farther than shame and reproach. And the apostle declares by this word, that it is the duty of all men to gather up their spirits to confront present difficulties, whatsoever they be. It is loaded now with shame: "I am not ashamed." It will come to blood: "I will not fear my blood." He expresseth the whole in this which was his present duty. And for a person of those parts and that learning which he had, to come among all the wise men in the world, to be laughed at as a babbler, as one that came with a foolish thing in his mouth, and to say, "I am not ashamed;"—it was the presence of God with him, as well as a sense of duty, that enabled him hereunto.

2dly. To an ingenuous, gracious soul, in all sufferings nothing is more grievous than shame. Hence it is reckoned as a great part of the humiliation of Christ, that "he made himself of no reputation," Phil. ii. 7, 8. He forewent all the esteem he might have in the world as the Son of God. And Isa. l. 6, "He hid not himself from shame." So Heb. xii. 2, "He despised the shame." To be dealt withal as a vile person, as the offscouring of all things, as the "filth and dung of the city" (as the word signifies), to be carried before the face of scorners, makes a deeper impression upon gracious and ingenuous spirits than any thing else which can well be thought of. Therefore it is a great thing that the apostle saith,—"I am not ashamed of the gospel."

3dly. There is also a figure in the word, called Litotes,—wherein, by a negation of one, the contrary is affirmed, and that emphatically,—"I am not ashamed;" that is, "I am confident; it is a thing I glory in, that I make my boast of. I am ready to do and suffer any thing, according to the mind of God, for the gospel; willing to undergo whatsoever God calls me to, or to perform any thing he hath appointed, for the gospel."

The opening of these two things will give us ground for our observation from the words; which is this:—

Observation. Not to be ashamed of the gospel of Christ, but to own it, avow it, and profess it, as a thing holy and honourable, in all the duties it requires, against all reproaches and persecutions that are in the world, is the indispensable duty of every one who desires to be saved by the gospel.

I shall not produce many testimonies of Scripture to confirm this. But let us all be advised, in such a day as this, not to make darkness our refuge, and an unacquaintedness with our duty our relief; but let us search and see what Christ hath spoken concerning such a day, where there is the profession of the gospel.

I will give you one place, to which you may reduce all the rest: Luke ix. 26, "Whosoever shall be ashamed of me and of my words, of him shall the Son of man be ashamed, when he shall come in his own glory, and in his Father's, and of the holy angels." The whole sum of the gospel is comprised in this,—the person of Christ and the words of Christ. The person of Christ takes up the whole work of the promise; and the words take up all the commands and institutions of Christ. We have heard before what it is to be ashamed of them. And what shall be the end of such? The Son of man shall be ashamed of them, when he shall come in his own glory, and his Father's glory. There can be no greater weight put upon words, to strike awe and dread into the minds of men. The Son of man, who loved us, redeemed us, gave his life for us, shall come again, though now he be absent, and we think things are put off for a season; and then he will inquire into our deportment about the gospel: at which time he will appear in all his own glory, the glory given him upon the account of his doing his Father's will, and the glory of his Father and the holy angels. Certainly we should be extremely troubled then to hear Christ say, "I am ashamed of you." You have the same repeated, Mark viii. 38. Our apostle gives the same great rule, Rom. x. 10, "With the heart man believeth unto righteousness." "There is righteousness; let us rest there,—what need we do more?" Ay, but "with the mouth confession is made unto salvation;"—which confession comprises all the duties the gospel requires; and salvation as indispensably depends upon that as justification doth upon faith. We cannot be justified without faith, nor can we be saved without confession.

You will say, "How can this be?" To clear it to you, I shall do three things:—I. I shall show you what there is in the gospel that we are in danger to be ashamed of, if we look not well to it. II. How we may be ashamed of it. III. I shall give you the reasons why we ought not to be ashamed of it.

I. What is there in the gospel that we ought in an especial manner not to be ashamed of?

We ought not to be ashamed of whatever is in an especial manner exposed in the world to shame and contempt. The truth is, we do or have lived in days wherein it hath been so far from being a shame to be counted a Christian, that it hath been a shame for a man to be counted no Christian. It hath not been the especial duty of believers to profess the gospel in general, but the common custom of all. The profession of the gospel which many trust to in this world, is nothing but that conformity to the world which Christ curses. In this sense no man is ashamed of the gospel.

But there are some things that accompany the gospel which are exposed at all times to contempt and reproach, even where Christ and the gospel are publicly professed; and these we are to take heed not to be ashamed of. I will give you four instances:—1. The special truths of the gospel; 2. The special worship of the gospel; 3. The professors of the gospel; 4. The profession of the gospel according to godliness. These are things men are very apt to be ashamed of, as being all exposed to shame and contempt:—

1. There are some especial truths of the gospel that in all seasons are exposed to especial contempt and reproach. Peter (2 Epist. i. 12) calls it "The present truth;" which in the primitive times was twofold. The apostle had to do with Jews and Gentiles; and there were two especial truths exposed to contempt and reproach that he principally insisted upon, and would never forego. With the Gentiles, this was exposed to contempt, reproach, and persecution,—that there should be salvation by the cross, 1 Cor. i. 23. "It is foolishness to all the Gentiles," saith he, "that there should be salvation by the cross." What doth the apostle do?—let go this doctrine, and preach some other? No; he tells you, chap. ii. 2, "he determined to know nothing among them, but Christ, and him crucified." But when he had to do with Jews, where lay the difference? In addition of Judaical ceremonies unto the worship of God, and some place in justification. Thus, Gal. v. 11, "If I preach circumcision," says he, "why am I persecuted?"—that is, "If I preach circumcision as they do, they would persecute me no more." Will he do it, then? No; Gal. vi. 12: He will not give place; he will preach the cross of Christ, and nothing else; and preach against them, and encourage all to do so.

"How shall we know, then, what are the present truths of the gospel, that we may take care not to be ashamed of them?"

I answer, In two things:—

(1.) The first is, that we must shut our eyes very hard, or all the world will not suffer us to be unacquainted with them. A man must very much hide himself, if he will not know what the truths of the gospel are that meet with contempt and reproach in the world; for he may hear of them everywhere.

(2.) For a general rule, take this: Consider the ways and methods God hath proceeded in for the manifestation and declaration of himself, and we shall find whereabouts, in the general, the truths lie that we are not to be ashamed of, if we will continue our testimony to God:—

[1.] God made a revelation of himself principally in and as the person of the Father, the unity of the divine essence acting in the authority and power of the Father in the creation of the world, in the giving of the law, and the promise of sending Christ. What was the opposition the world made unto that declaration of God?—for the world doth never make conjunct opposition to the being of God, but unto the declaration that God makes of himself. While God made that declaration under the Old Testament, what was the opposition that the world made? It was plainly in idolatry and polytheism. They would have many gods, or make gods, till he was grown among them an unknown God. The testimony, then, which the people of God were to bear, and not be ashamed to give, was the unity of the divine essence.

[2.] In the fulness of time God sent his Son; and he was immediately declared and manifested in the love and work of the Son,—the second person. Where lay the opposition of the world? It lay directly and immediately against the person of Christ, and against his cross; it would not believe that he was the Messiah, but called him "a glutton, a wine-bibber, a friend of publicans and sinners." Wherein, then, consisted the testimony that believers were to give? Why, it was to the person of the Messiah, the Son of God incarnate, and to the work he had to do. God so revealing and glorifying himself in the incarnation and mediation of the Son,—the truths which concerned his person were those which men ought peculiarly not to be ashamed of, and which the world peculiarly opposed.

[3.] Where the gospel is preached, the whole work of glorifying God is committed to the Holy Ghost. Christ promised to send him to glorify him, to do the work of God in the world, and carry on all the concerns of the covenant. The Father laid the foundation of his own glory: the Son comes, and professes he came not to do his own will, but the will of him that sent him; and promises to send the Holy Ghost to do his will,—to accomplish all the concerns of the covenant of grace. Wherein, then, lay the opposition of the world to God? It lay in opposition unto the person, doctrine, graces, gifts, and office of the Holy Ghost, as he supplies the room of Christ, to carry on his kingdom in the world. The great opposition that is made in the world against God at this day is immediately against the work of the Holy Ghost, as carrying on the kingdom of Christ in the world. These are the objects of reproach and contempt.

By the way observe, that the opposition which was made by the heathens in their idolatry against the Deity, against God, and that made by the Jews against the person of Christ, and that which is now made against the work of the Holy Ghost, is all the same; the nature of the opposition is not changed, but only the object. The opposition that was in Cain, and the profession in Abel, is the same still: the one embraces the revelation of God, the other opposes it; and that principle that acts against the Holy Ghost would act against God, and set up idolatry in the world.

And hence we may see, that whereas God has, in the days wherein we live, given a great and illustrious testimony unto the gifts and graces of the Holy Ghost—it may be as great as in any age since the time he gave extraordinary gifts to the apostles,—and Satan had lost the advantage of managing an opposition by open blasphemies and reproaches of the Spirit, and being somewhat impatient till it returned into his hands again, he raises up another spirit, that should stand in competition with it, and do the same thing; a spirit which, like the unclean spirit that cast him into the fire and into the water in whom he was, threw those possessed by it into all difficulties, to manifest itself. But whatsoever glory it might have put upon it in some men, by enabling them to suffer and bear the rage of the world that was cast upon them, there are three things that will discover that it is not a spirit from God:—

1*st.* The place from whence it comes. It comes not from above,—it is not looked for, prayed for, to be the Spirit of Christ from heaven, which he hath promised; but is a mushroom that grows up in a night,—the gourd of a night, that springs up within themselves, and is called the light within them all. Now, the Spirit that doth the work of God is promised from above, is given by Christ, and is expected and received from thence.

2*dly.* It is known also by its company. The Spirit which beareth witness with Christ is always accompanied with the word. Isa. lix. 21, "This is my covenant with them, saith the LORD; My Spirit that is upon thee, and my words which I have put in thy mouth, shall not depart out of thy mouth," etc. Now, the work of this spirit is to cast the word of God out of the church,—to render it useless.

3*dly.* It is known by its work. The work of the Spirit of God is to glorify Christ; the work of this spirit is to glorify itself,—to resolve all into itself, for measure, rule, principle, and all abilities.

I could not but mention this by the way, because I put the great opposition that is made in the world in these days against the Spirit of God, his graces and gifts, and the worship which believers are enabled to perform by the Spirit, in this thing. And, therefore, let us try the spirits, and not believe every spirit that is gone forth.

This is the first thing we are not to be ashamed of,—namely, the truths of God that are reproached in the world, especially those concerning the Spirit, his graces and gifts, and the revelation of the mystery of the gospel, while a heathenish morality is advanced in their place. God forbid we should be ashamed of the gospel in this respect,—that every one of us should not bear his testimony, as God is pleased to call us!

2. There is the worship of the gospel, which is always exposed to reproach and contempt in the world in the due performance of it. I pray God to keep this always in our minds, that we have no other way to be ashamed of the gospel but by being ashamed of these things; and we have no other way to be ashamed of them than by neglecting

the due performance of them, as the gospel commands. Men are ashamed of the worship of the gospel,—(1.) Upon the account of the worshippers; and, (2.) Upon the account of the worship itself:—

(1.) Upon the account of the worshippers, who are for the most part poor and contemptible in the world; for "not many great, not many noble, not many wise and learned are called." Whatsoever work God hath to do by his, they are looked upon as the offscouring of all things,—such a company as those who are of gallant minds and spirits do despise. I wonder what thoughts they would have had of Christ himself, when followed by a company of fishermen, women, and children, crying "Hosanna;" and others, who said, "This people who knoweth not the law are cursed," John vii. 49. Now, is not a man apt to be ashamed of such abjects as follow Christ? Shall a man leave the society of great, and wise, and learned men, to join with them? Let those think of it who are upon any account lifted up in the world above their brethren. Do not be ashamed of them; they are such as you must accompany, if ever you intend to come to glory. We must keep company with them here, if we intend it hereafter. And, therefore, be not ashamed of the worship of Christ because of the worshippers, though they can do nothing but love Christ and worship him; notwithstanding the suffrage that lies against them by great and learned men, such as were at Rome when Paul was not ashamed of the gospel of Christ.

(2.) Upon the account of the worship itself. The world is, and ever was, in love with a gaudy worship, which some of them have called, being well painted, "The beauty of holiness." The Jews and Samaritans, take them in all,—the one was for the temple, the other for the mountain. The gospel comes and calls them from them both, to worship God in spirit and in truth;—to a worship that hath no beauty but what is given by the Spirit of Christ; nor order, but what is given by the word. This is greatly despised in the world; and not only despised, but persecuted;—I mean, sometimes it was so, I am sure, formerly. Therefore the apostle gives that caution, Heb. x. 25, "If you would not be ashamed, 'forsake not the assembling of yourselves together, as the manner of some is.'" There is a synecdoche in the word "assembling," and it is put for the whole worship of Christ, because worship was performed in their assemblies; and he that forsakes the assemblies, forsakes the worship of Christ: as some of them did when exposed to danger; and it is the manner of some still to do so. When a fair day comes, then they will go to the assemblies; but in a storm they will absent themselves, as did the Samaritans. But what should move them to forsake their assembling? He tells you, verses 33, 34, "Ye were made a gazing-stock, by reproaches and afflictions, and the spoiling of your goods. But ye know in yourselves that ye have in heaven a better and an enduring substance." This made some weary of assembling; but be not you ashamed of assembling, or of the worship of God. This is the second thing that is exposed to shame and reproach in the world; and which, in particular, we are bound by our profession not to be ashamed of.

SERMON XVIII.[1]

3. We are not to be ashamed of the professors of the gospel. Our Lord Christ hath laid it down as an everlasting rule, that in them he is honoured or dishonoured in the world. And it is the great rule whereby false professors will be tried at the last day,—men who pretend a profession of the name of Christ; as you may see, Matt. xxv. 40, 45, "What you have done unto them, you have done unto me," saith he; "and what you have omitted that ought to have been done to them, you have omitted the doing of it unto me." It is those alone in whom Christ may be honoured or despised in this world; for he is in himself, in his own person, in that condition that our goodness, our honour, extends not immediately unto him: and for the contempt and despising of men, he is not concerned in it. Hence this is reckoned as the great commendation of the faith of Moses, Heb. xi. 23–26, that he refused all the honours of the world, and all the reputation he might have had, to own and esteem the poor, reproached, despised, persecuted interest of Christ in the world; as he there calls it. He joined himself unto the professors of the faith, in opposition to all the world, and the greatness of it; which was his greatest commendation. And see the pathetical prayer of the apostle Paul for Onesiphorus upon the discharge of this duty, 2 Tim. i. 16–18, "The Lord," saith he, "give mercy to the house of Onesiphorus; for he oft refreshed me, and was not ashamed of my chain: but, when he was in Rome, he sought me out very diligently, and found me. The Lord grant unto him that he may find mercy of the Lord in that day." Onesiphorus was a man of some credit and repute in the world; poor Paul was a prisoner bound with a chain, that he might have been ashamed to own him: but, instead of that, he sought him out; he was not ashamed of his chain. To be ashamed of the poor professors of the gospel,—so in themselves, or made so by the power of oppressors,—is to be ashamed of the gospel of Christ, his truths, his worship, and his people.

[1] This sermon was preached May 26, 1670.

4. There is a special kind of profession, that, in its own nature, is exposed to reproach in the world. The apostle Paul tells us, 2 Tim. iii. 12, "They that will live godly in Christ Jesus shall suffer persecution." There is (John xv. 4, 5) a being in Christ by profession, and not living godly: for there are branches in the vine by profession, that bring forth no fruit;—men that have a profession wherewith they do not trouble the world, and for which the world will not trouble them;—that can go to that length in compliance with the world, and the ways of it, as that they shall not have one drop of the spirit of the witnesses of Christ, who torment the men of the earth. But "they that will live godly,"—that is, engage in a profession that shall, upon all occasions, and in all instances, manifest the power of it,—they "shall suffer persecution." We see many every day keep up a profession, but such a profession as will not provoke the world. Now, this is to be ashamed of the gospel,—to be ashamed of the power and glory of it,—to be ashamed of the Author of it. No man can put Jesus Christ to greater shame, than by professing the gospel without showing the power of it.

III.[1] I shall now give the reasons why we ought not in any thing to be ashamed of the gospel of Christ. I speak unto persons that are under a conviction that such and such things belong unto the gospel. If we are not, what makes us here this day? I do not go to persuade any that this or that worship, or this or that way, is according to the gospel; but I suppose a conviction thereof to be upon us: upon a supposition of which conviction and persuasion I shall offer these reasons why we ought not to be ashamed of the gospel. And,—

1. The first is this:—Because Christ, the captain of our salvation, and the great example of our obedience, was not ashamed of all that he had to undergo for us.

There are two things that greatly aggravate things shameful, and press, if possible, shame upon a person:—

(1.) The dignity of the person that is exposed to things shameful. It is more for a person honourable, noble, and in repute for wisdom in the world, to be exposed to indignities, reproaches, and things shameful, as the apostle speaks, than for beggars,—poor vile persons of no repute. Now, consider the person of Christ, who he was, and what he was. He was the eternal Son of God, the "first-born of the whole creation:" and as, in his divine nature, he was "the express" (the essential) "image of the Father;" so in his whole person, as incarnate, he was the glory of all the works of God. And the apostle,

[1] This sermon, according to the method announced, p. 224, is given under a threefold division. The second branch of the subject has either been omitted, or, what is more probable, to judge from the strain of the author's remarks, the illustration of the second is merged and contained in the first branch.—Ed.

when he would set out the great condescension of Christ in submitting unto things shameful, doth at the same time describe the greatness and glory of his person, Phil. ii. 6–8, "He made himself," says he, "of no reputation; he took upon him the form of a servant, and he was obedient unto the death of the cross;" which three things, as I could show you, are comprehensive of all that was shameful to Christ. But at the same time that he tells us what he did, how doth he describe him? When he did so, he was "in the form of God, and accounted it no robbery to be equal with God." He was the great God in his own person, and equal with the Father; yet then this honourable one condescended to all things shameful and reproachful in the world.

(2.) Shame is aggravated from the causes and matter of it There are various things that cause shame. Some are put to shame by reproaches, scandals, lies; some, by poverty; some, by imprisonment; and some, by death, made shameful by the ways, means, and preparations for it. By which of these was Christ now made an object of shame? By all of them, and inconceivably more than any heart is able to apprehend, or tongue to express. He was reproached as a wine-bibber and a glutton; as a seditious person and mover of sedition; as a fanatic, and one beside himself. He was in that state of poverty, that, during the whole course of his ministry, he had not where to lay his head, nor any thing to live upon, but what good people administered unto him of their substance. In the midst of this course he was taken praying; when, he told them, they might have taken him at any time. "I was," says he, "in the temple openly; I sat daily with you teaching in the temple, and ye laid no hold on me." He was taken by soldiers with swords and staves, as a thief and malefactor; apprehended, carried away, and hanged upon a tree (the shamefulest death then in the world), in the midst of Jews and Gentiles;—with both which sorts of men that kind of death was the most shameful. The Romans put none to that sort of death but slaves, thieves and robbers,—the worst malefactors: and among the Jews it was the only kind of death that was accursed, Deut. xxi. 23, "He that is hanged on the tree is accursed of God;"—which words our apostle repeats, and applies them to Christ, Gal. iii. 13. How did Christ behave himself now, as to all these shameful things that came upon him? Hear the prophet expressing of it in his name, Isa. l. 6, 7, "I gave my back to the smiters, and my cheeks to them that plucked off the hair" (the usual way of dealing with persons in such cases); "I hid not my face from shame and spitting. For the Lord GOD will help me; therefore shall I not be confounded: I know that I shall not be ashamed." Did he recoil, or go back from his work? did he repent of it? No; "'Thy law is written in my heart;' I am content 'to do thy will, O God.'" And in the issue of the whole, Heb. xii. 2, "He despised the shame, and endured the cross;" which made way for his glory.

Now, here lies the foundation of our reason:—If the Lord Jesus Christ, the Son of God,—being engaged purely out of his own love in a work for us poor, vile, sinful worms of the earth, whom he might have left justly to perish under the wrath of God, which we had deserved,—underwent all these shameful things, and never had a recoiling thought to draw back and leave us to ourselves; have we not an obligation of love, gratitude, and obedience, not to be ashamed of those few drops of this great storm that may possibly fall upon us in this world for the sake of our Lord Jesus Christ? Can we be disciples of Christ, and yet think in this matter to be above our Master? Can we be his servants, and think to be above our Lord? We are delicate and tender, and would fain have all men speak well of us; but we must come to another frame, if we intend to be the disciples of Christ. What would be the issue of our account at the last day, if he should inquire of us what we have done in reference to the profession of the gospel? whether we have observed all those duties that we have had a conviction upon our spirits and consciences we ought to observe and perform, in the assembling of ourselves, in the dispensation of the word, in the celebration of ordinances, in prayer, fasting, hearing the word, and all those things which the gospel requires of us? Should we make that answer, "Truly, Lord, we thought all very good; but were afraid, if we engaged in them, we should have been exposed to all the reproach, contempt, and trouble in the world: it would have brought trouble upon our persons, and the spoiling of our goods; it would have brought us into great distress." What would then be the reply, according to the rule of the gospel, but, "Stand upon your own bottom. That was my day, these were things I required of you: you were ashamed of me; I am now ashamed of you"? Certainly this would be a woful issue of it. But,—

2. The second reason is this:—That whatsoever state or condition we may be brought into, upon the account of the gospel, the Lord Jesus Christ will not be ashamed of us in that state and condition. I told you before, in the opening of the words, that shame principally respects dishonour and disreputation; that the things we are engaged in are vile, contemptible, exposed to reproach. Now if a man, in any thing he is called in question about, have those who are great and honourable to abide by him, and own the cause wherein he is engaged, whatever other affections he may have, it will take off his shame. Now, this great and honourable person will not be ashamed of us in any condition, Heb. ii. 11, "He is not ashamed to call them brethren." "But suppose they are poor, and have nothing left them in this world?"

It is all one. "Suppose they are in prison?" Christ will stand by them, and say, "These are my brethren." The word ἐπαισχύνεται, "ashamed," is there used peculiarly in respect to those shameful things that may befall us in this world. Notwithstanding all these sufferings, yet "he is not ashamed to call them brethren." "Doth he go no farther?" Yes: Heb. xi. 16, "Wherefore" (speaking directly to this cause in hand) "God is not ashamed to be called their God." What is the reason it is so expressed? The words are emphatical. Look upon the two parties that are in the world;—the one great, wise, glorious, powerful, and at liberty; the other poor, despised, contemned all the world over. God comes into the world and sees these two parties. Which, now, do you think he owns? Is it not a shame for the great and glorious God to own poor, despised, contemned, reproached, persecuted ones? No: God "is not ashamed to be called their God;" their God in particular, their God in covenant, one that owns them in opposition to all the world,—with whom they have to conflict. Oh, that we would persuade our hearts in every duty that this is our state,—that Jesus Christ stands by, and saith, "I am not ashamed of you!" God stands by, and saith, "I am not ashamed to be owned to be your God!" Is not this great encouragement?

3. The third reason is,—Because in the profession of the gospel we are called to nothing at all that is shameful in the judgment of any sober, wise, rational, judicious man. If the profession of the gospel called us unto any thing that is vile, dishonourable, unholy, of ill report among men, certainly we had reason to be extremely cautious of our practising of it. But is it any shame to own God to be our God, to own Jesus Christ to be our Lord and Master,—to profess we must yield obedience unto the commands of Christ? Is there any shame in praying, in hearing of the word of God, in preaching of it according to his mind and will? Is there any shame in fasting, in godly conference? Let all the world be judge whether there be any thing shameful in these things, which are good, useful, honourable to all mankind. The gospel calls to nothing that is shameful. Therefore the old heathens were so wise that they would not, against the light of nature, oppress the assemblies of Christians, where there was nothing shameful; and therefore they charged all shameful things upon them. The whole vogue of the world was, that they met together to further promiscuous lusts and seditions. They made that their pretence; they durst not disturb them merely upon the account of their profession. And it is so still. Men little know that we will not, dare not, cannot, take the name of our God in vain, and prostitute any ordinance of God, to give the least semblance to any seditious practice. Whatsoever violence may come upon the disciples of Christ, they had rather die than prostitute an ordinance of Christ, to

give the least countenance or semblance to any such thing. The gospel calls us to nothing that hath any reproach in it. If men will esteem the strict profession of the gospel—praying, hearing the word, abstinence from sin—to be shameful things; if they will count it strange that we run not out into the same excess of riot with themselves; shall we stand to the judgment of such sensualists, that live in a perpetual contradiction to themselves,—who profess that they honour Christ, and at the same time reproach every thing of Christ in the world? We have no reason, then, to be ashamed of the gospel, which requires no shameful thing at our hands,—nothing that is evil and hurtful to mankind; nothing but what is good, holy, beautiful, commendable, and useful unto all societies of mankind. And we dare not prostitute the least part of an ordinance to the encouraging any disorder in this world, and therein take the name of our God in vain.

4. The fourth reason is that which the apostle gives us, Heb. xii. 1, "We are compassed about with a cloud of witnesses," to this very end and purpose. In the preceding chapter he had given a catalogue of many under the Old Testament, patriarchs and prophets (time would have failed him to reckon up all), who signally manifested they were not ashamed of the gospel, and the promises of it, whatever difficulties did befall them. "And now," saith the apostle, "you have 'a cloud of witnesses,'—the great examples of those holy souls that are now at rest with God, enjoying the triumphs of Christ over all his adversaries. They were, as you are, conflicting in this world with reproaches, adversaries, persecution; and they had this issue by faith,—they made a conquest over all." And James says, "You have, my brethren, the prophets and apostles for your examples." The Lord help us, to take the example they have set us, Acts v. 41, when they went away triumphing that they were counted worthy to suffer shame and reproach for the name of Christ! The Lord help us, that we dishonour not the gospel by giving the world reason to say, that there is a race of professors risen up now who have no manner of conformity to them who went before them in the profession of the gospel!

5. The next reason I shall insist upon is taken out of the text, the particular reason the apostle here gives why he was not ashamed of it. "I am not ashamed," saith he, "of the gospel of Christ; for it is the power of God to salvation to all that believe." We talk of profession of the gospel. "What is it," say some, "but canting among yourselves,—speaking things unintelligible?" Such kind of expressions are cast upon it in the world. But, saith the apostle, "This gospel we profess is quite another thing than you dream or think of; and we profess it no other, nor ever will engage one day in the profession of the gospel any farther, than as it comes under this account, that 'it is the power of God unto salvation.'" Manifest to me that any way

or parcel of the gospel which we do profess, or practise, hath not the power of God in it and upon it, towards the furtherance of salvation, and I will throw off that profession.

But you will ask, perhaps, "In what sense is the gospel the power of God?" I answer, In a threefold sense:—

(1.) Negatively: there is not any other power in it. The world saw that there was a great efficacy in the gospel, and they knew not whence it was; but they charged it upon two things:—First, Upon the matter of it, that it was a cunningly-devised fable. So the apostle Peter tells us, 2 Epist. i. 16, "We have not followed cunningly-devised fables, when we made known unto you the power of Christ." The world charged it so, and thought that gave it its efficacy. Secondly, There was another thing to which they thought its efficacy was owing, and that was the eloquence and power of its preachers. "The preachers of it were surely eloquent, excellent men, that they could so prevail upon the people, and win them over to the gospel." No; saith the apostle, 1 Cor. ii. 4, 5, "My speech and preaching was not with enticing words of man's wisdom, but in demonstration of the Spirit, and of power; that your faith should not stand in the wisdom of men, but in the power of God." But let not men mistake; the efficacy of the gospel is owing to neither of these causes, but to the divine power that accompanies it.

(2.) It was the power of God declaratively; it made known the power of God. So our apostle declares in the very next words to the text. "For therein," saith he, "is the righteousness of God revealed." It hath made a revelation of the way whereby God will save men. It makes a revelation of that power which God puts forth for the salvation of men.

(3.) It is the power of God instrumentally. It is the instrument God puts forth to effect his great and mighty works in the world. Preaching is looked upon as a very foolish thing in the world. "We preach Christ crucified, to the Greeks foolishness," 1 Cor. i. 23. But God hath chosen this foolish thing to confound the wise. And though the preachers of it are very weak men, mere earthen vessels, God hath chosen this weak thing to bring to nought things that are strong and mighty,—the things of this world. Therefore (Acts xx. 32) it is called "The word of God's grace, which is able to build us up, and to give us an inheritance among all them which are sanctified." The plain preaching of it hath this power upon the souls of men,—to convince them, convert them, draw them home to God; to expose them to all troubles in this world; to make them let go their reputation and livelihood, and expose themselves even to death itself. It is the power of God to these ends and purposes; God hath made it his instrument for that end. If it were the power of God to give peace and prosperity unto a nation, or to heal the sick, there is no man need or ought to be ashamed of it; but to be the power of God for so excellent an end as the eternal salvation of the souls of men, makes it much more glorious. The gospel we profess,—all the parts of it, every thing wherein it is engaged,—is that whereby God puts forth his power to save our poor souls, and the souls of them who believe; and the Lord God never lay it to the charge of any who would hinder the dispensation of the gospel unto this end and purpose! It were sad for men to keep corn from the poor, physic from the sick, that lie a-dying; but to keep the word of God from the souls of men, that they might be saved, Lord, lay it not to the charge of any!

The Author of the gospel was not ashamed of his work he engaged in on our behalf; is not ashamed of us in any of our sufferings, in any of the shameful things we may undergo. The gospel requires no shameful thing at our hands,—puts us upon no duty that can justly expose us to shame; the things are good, useful, honourable to men. We have a cloud of witnesses about us; and if any man require of us what this gospel is which we profess, and an account whereupon we profess it, we can make this answer, "'It is the power of God unto salvation;' and for that end alone do we profess it."

I might speak to some farther reasons, to show why this duty is indispensably necessary; for, as I said, it is not only that we ought not to be ashamed, but the duty is indispensable. And I thought to have spoken to those two heads, which alone make a duty indispensable, that we may not upon any account be against it;—because it is necessary, as we say, "necessitate præcepti," and likewise "necessitate medii;" that is, both *upon the command of Christ*, and *upon the account of the order of the things themselves.*

It is necessary upon the command of Christ, because he hath required it at our hands; and under that condition, that if ever we intend to be owned by him at the last day, we should own his gospel in the profession of it. All the world, and all our own things, and all the injunctions of the sons of men, cannot give a dispensation to our souls to exempt them from under the authority of the commands of Christ. Let us look unto ourselves; we are under the commands of Christ, and there is no one particular duty to be avoided but what must be accommodated to this rule. And not only so,—

But it is necessary also from the order of things: Christ hath appointed it as a means for that great end of bringing our souls to salvation. As well may a man arrive to a city, and never come into the way that leads unto it, as we go to rest with Christ, and never come to the profession of the gospel, nor abide by it: this is the way that leads unto it.

I have done with what I thought to deliver upon this doctrine;

and among many uses that might be made, I shall only commend one unto you; without which it will be utterly impossible that any of us shall be able, at the long-run, to keep up to the profession of the gospel, or any duty of it. And that is this:—

Use. Get an experience of the power of the gospel, and all the ordinances of it, in and upon your own hearts, or all your profession is an expiring thing;—unless, I say, you find the power of God upon your own hearts in every ordinance, expect not any continuance in your profession. If the preaching of the word be not effectual unto the renewing of your souls, the illuminating of your minds, the endearing of your hearts to God,—if you do not find power in it, you will quickly reason with yourselves upon what account should you adventure trouble and reproach for it.

If you have an experience of this power upon your hearts, it will recover all your recoiling, wandering thoughts, when you find you cannot live without it. It is so as to every ordinance whatever; unless we can have some experience of the benefit of it, and of the power and efficacy of the grace of God in it, we can never expect to abide in our profession of it. What will you bear witness unto? an empty, bare profession, that neither honoureth God nor doth good to your own souls?

If you would, then, be established in this truth, of not being ashamed of the gospel, recall to your minds what benefit you have received by it. Have you received any advantage by hearing the word? hath it at any time restored your souls when you have been wandering? hath it comforted you when you have been cast down? hath it engaged your hearts unto God? Recall to mind what benefit and advantage you have had by it; and then ask what it hath done, that now you should forsake it. And in every ordinance that you are made partakers of, inquire diligently what power of God upon your own hearts goes forth in the dispensation of that ordinance. This will confirm and strengthen you; and without this all your profession is vain, and will signify nothing.

SERMON XIX.[1]

GOD THE SAINTS' ROCK.

"From the end of the earth will I cry unto thee, when my heart is overwhelmed: lead me to the rock that is higher than I."—Ps. lxi. 2.

THERE are two things in the words:—First, The state wherein the psalmist was. Secondly, The course that he steered in that state.

[1] This sermon was preached November 11, 1670.

His estate is doubly expressed:—1. From the place where he was,—"From the end of the earth;" and, 2. From the condition he was in,—"His heart was overwhelmed."

And in the course he steered there are two things also:—1. The manner of it,—"He cried unto the Lord." 2. The matter of that cry,—"Lead me to the rock that is higher than I."

First. There is the state wherein he was. And,—

1. The first description of it (for both parts are metaphorical) is from the place where he was,—"The end of the earth." Now, this may be taken two ways:—either naturally, and then it is an allusion to men that are far distant and remote from help, relief, and comfort; or, as I may say, ecclesiastically, with reference to the temple of God, which was "in medio terræ,"—"in the midst and heart of the land," where God manifested and gave tokens of his gracious presence and favour: as if he had said, "I am at the end of the earth; far from any tokens, pledges, or manifestations of the love and favour of God, as well as from outward help and assistance."

2. The second description of his state is, that "his heart was overwhelmed." Wherein we have two things:—

(1.) A confluence of calamities and distresses. (2.) The effect they had upon him;—his heart was overwhelmed, and fainted under them. As long as the heart will hold up, they may be borne,—"The spirit of a man will bear his infirmity;" but when "the spirit is wounded," and the heart faints, a confluence of calamities greatly oppresses.

What is meant by "overwhelmed," himself declares in another place, Ps. cii. The title of the psalm is, "A prayer of the afflicted, when he is overwhelmed." And he describes that condition in the psalm itself, verses 3, 4, etc., "My days are consumed like smoke, and my bones are burned as an hearth. My heart is smitten, and withered like grass; so that I forget to eat my bread. By reason of the voice of my groaning my bones cleave to my skin. I am like a pelican of the wilderness: I am like an owl of the desert. I watch, and am as a sparrow alone upon the house-top. Mine enemies reproach me all the day; and they that are mad against me are sworn against me. For I have eaten ashes like bread, and mingled my drink with weeping, because of thine indignation and thy wrath: for thou hast lifted me up, and cast me down." To be overwhelmed, is to be under a confluence of all manner of distressing calamities. Ps. cxlii. 3, 4, he describes again what it is to be overwhelmed: "When my spirit was overwhelmed within me, I looked on my right hand, and beheld, but there was no man that would know me: refuge failed me; no man cared for my soul." So that to have a confluence of manifold distresses, with an eye to the indignation of God as the spring of those distresses, until the spirit sink and faint under it, is to have the heart overwhelmed. This is his state and condition.

Secondly. The course he takes in this state, as we have already observed, is also doubly expressed:—

1. In the manner of it. "I cried," saith he, "unto thee." The word is frequently used in this case in Scripture; and it is naturally expressive of the principal actings of faith in a distressed condition.

There are four things that faith will do in a condition of distress in believers; and they are all of them comprised in this expression, "I cried:"—

(1.) It will make the heart sensible of the affliction. God abhors the proud and the stubborn, that think by their own spirits to bear up under their pressures. Isa. xlvi. 12, "Hearken unto me, ye stout-hearted, that are far from righteousness." Persons that think to bear themselves up, when God dealeth with them, by their stout heart, are such whom, of all others, God most despises and abhors: they are "far from righteousness." Now, crying doth include a sense of evils and pressures the soul is exercised withal, and that we do not despise God when we are chastened, as well as that we do not utterly faint, but cry unto the Lord.

(2.) The next act of faith is a holy complaint unto God in such a state and condition. So the psalmist tells us, Ps. cii., "A prayer of the afflicted, when he is overwhelmed, and poureth out his complaint before the LORD." He often mentions "his complaint, coming with his complaint unto the LORD." And God takes nothing more kindly than when we come to him with our complaints; not repining at them, but spreading them before the Lord, as from whom alone we expect relief: for it declares we believe God concerns himself in our state and condition. There is no man so foolish, whatsoever he suffers, as to go unto them with his complaints whom he supposes are not concerned in him, nor have any compassion for him. It is a professing unto God that we believe he is concerned in our condition, when we cry unto him, and pour out before him our complaints.

(3.) There is in it an endeavour to approach unto God; as you do when you cry after one whom you see at a distance, and are afraid he will go farther from you. It is the great work of faith to cry out after God at a distance, when you are afraid lest at the next turn he should be quite out of sight. Crying to the Lord, supposes him to be withdrawing or departing.

(4.) There is earnestness in it. It is expressive of the greatest earnestness of spirit we can use, when we cry out in any case.

Thus he behaves himself during the condition described:—He had a sense of his distress; he makes his complaint unto the Lord; he cries out after him, for fear he should withdraw himself, and that with earnestness, that God might come in to his help.

2. The matter of it is,—that God would "lead him to the rock;" that is, that God would give him an access unto himself by Jesus Christ, in whom God is our rock and our refuge in all our distresses; that he would but open a way through all his dark and overwhelming entanglements, that he might come unto himself, there to issue the troubles and perplexities that he was exercised withal.

That which I would speak to you, from the words thus opened, is this:—

Observation. In the most overwhelming, calamitous distresses that may befall a believing soul, faith still eyes a reserve in God, and delights to break through all to come unto him; though, at the same time, it looks upon God as the author of those calamities.

I have told you before, in the opening of the words, what I intend by these overwhelming distresses. They are of two sorts; inward and outward:—

First. Inward, in perplexities upon the soul and conscience about sin; when the soul is in darkness, and hath no apprehension of any ground upon which it may have acceptance with God; when it is pressed with the guilt of sin, and abides in darkness upon that account, and hath no light.

Secondly. Outward; and these are of two sorts:—

1. Private; in afflictions, losses, sickness, pains, poverty, either as to ourselves or those who are near unto us, and wherein we are concerned. These may sometimes have such an edge put upon them as to prove overwhelming.

2. Public, in reference unto the church of God; when that is in great distress, when there is no prospect of relief, no beam of light; when the summer is past, and the harvest ended,—expectations come to an issue, and no relief ensues. This is an overwhelming distress to them whose hearts are in the ways of God, and have a concern in his glory,—when Zion is in the dust, and the bones of the children of Zion lie scattered like wood upon the face of the earth.

These are the heads of overwhelming distresses. And I say, faith looks upon them as proceeding from God. Is the soul in distress upon the account of sin? They are God's rebukes, God's arrows;—it is God that hath caused this darkness. Is it troubled or pressed upon the account of afflictions or dangers? "Affliction," saith faith, "doth not spring out of the earth, or troubles from the ground;—these things are from God." Is it with respect unto the church of God? "Who gave Jacob for a spoil, and Israel to the robbers?" Is it not the Lord, he against whom we have sinned? It is, therefore, his wrath and indignation in all these things. Yet, notwithstanding this, faith will look through all, and make a reserve in God himself.

I shall,—I. Give some instances of this. II. Show the grounds of it. III. Come to that which I chiefly intend; namely, to discover what it is in God that in such an overwhelming condition faith can see and fix upon to give it support and relief. IV. Show how this differs from that general reserve which the nature of man is apt to take in his thoughts of God in distress.

I. I am to give some instances. And we have a very remarkable instance of this in Jonah, who tells us, chap. ii. 2, that he was in "the belly of hell." Hell in Scripture, when it is applied to the things of this world, doth intend the depth of temporal evils; as in Ps. xviii. 4, "The sorrows of hell compassed me," saith David, speaking of the time of his affliction and persecution under Saul. And "the belly of hell" must needs be the darkness and confusion of all those calamitous distresses. Where did Jonah (viewing himself in this condition) look for the cause from whence it did proceed? He tells us, verse 3, "For thou hast cast me into the deep." He knew the occasion of it was his own sinful frowardness; the instrumental cause,—the mariners, upon his own persuasion; but he refers it all to the principal cause, God himself: "Thou hast cast me into the deep." And how did this affect him? Verse 7, "My soul fainted within me." What relief then had he? Verses 5, 6, "The waters compassed me about, even to the soul; the depth closed me round about, the weeds were wrapped about my head. I went down to the bottom of the mountains; the earth with her bars was about me for ever." No manner of relief, support, or succour to be expected! What did he do in this case? He tells presently. "My prayer came in unto thee," saith he, looking upon God as him who had cast him into this condition; his eye was to him. David gives us several instances of it in himself. Once, I acknowledge, he was mistaken in his course. He tells us so. Ps. lv. 3–5, he had described the overwhelming condition wherein he was. And what course doth he take? Verse 6, "Oh that I had wings like a dove! for then would I fly away, and be at rest; I would wander far off, and be in the wilderness." "O that I was gone from the midst of all these perplexities,—that I was rid of those that are ready to overwhelm me!" But this was not a right course. I might give innumerable instances of the contrary. Ps. xxxi. 9, 10, etc., is a description of as sad a condition as any man can fall into, and which is accompanied with a great sense of God's displeasure, and of his own sin. Verse 10, "My strength faileth because of mine iniquity, and my bones are consumed." What course doth he then take? Verse 14, "But I trusted in thee, O Lord; I said, Thou art my God." "When my strength failed because of mine iniquities, and my bones were consumed; when there was nothing but distress round about me, and that from God, yet then 'I trusted in thee, and said, Thou art my God.'" And this is what God himself invites us unto. Isa. xl. 27, there is a complaint made by Jacob, "My way is hid from the LORD, and my judgment is passed over from my God." We have but two things wherein we are concerned in this world, as we are professors of the gospel; and they are,—our way, and our judgment. Our "way;" that is, the course of obedience and profession which, according to the truth, we are engaged in; as believing in Christ is called a "way." "My way of faith, my way of worship, my way of obedience, is hid from the Lord; God takes no notice of it;" which is as much as to say, "My all in the things of God is at a loss: God takes no notice of my way." Should that be our condition, really we should be of all men most miserable. But there is also our "judgment;" that is, the judgment that is to be passed upon our cause and way, which David doth so often pray about when he begs that God would "judge him in his righteousness." Now saith the church here, "God takes no notice of it, but hath put off the cause to the world. My judgment is passed over, determined for me no more; but he lets me suffer under the judgment of the world." And truly, when our way and judgment is passed over,—profession and obedience as it were hid from God,—God takes no notice of them. And when he puts off the judgment and determination of our cause, what have we more in the world? What doth God now propose to them for their relief? what promises, what encouragements, will he remind them of? Nothing but himself. Verse 28, "Hast thou not known? hast thou not heard, that the everlasting God, the LORD, the Creator of the ends of the earth, fainteth not, neither is weary? there is no searching of his understanding." God calls them to consider him in his own nature and being, with those glorious acts suited thereunto. He calls our faith to look for rest in himself alone. It is impossible thy way and thy judgment should thus pass over from him, because he is "the everlasting God, the LORD, the Creator."

II. I come now to the grounds of it,—whence it is that faith doth this. And that is upon a twofold account:—1. Because it knows how to distinguish between the nature of the covenant and the external administration of it. 2. Because it is natural to faith so to do; and that upon a double account, as we shall see presently:—

1. Faith doth this, because it is able to distinguish between the covenant itself, which is firm, stable, invariable; and the administration of the covenant, which is various and changeable,—I mean the outward administration of it. And this God teaches us, Ps. lxxxix. 30–34, "If his children"—the children of Jesus Christ—"forsake my law, and walk not in my judgments; if they break my statutes,

and keep not my commandments; then will I visit their transgression with the rod, and their iniquity with stripes. Nevertheless my loving-kindness will I not utterly take from him, nor suffer my faithfulness to fail. My covenant will I not break, nor alter the thing that is gone out of my lips." The covenant of God shall stand firm and unalterable, then, when the rod and the stripes of men are upon our backs. In the midst of all God's visiting for iniquity, whether by internal rebukes or outward chastisements, yet faith sees the covenant stable; and so makes unto God upon that account. David, when he comes to die, gives it as the sum of all his observation, that the covenant was immutable, but the outward administration various, 2 Sam. xxiii. 5, "Although my house be not so with God, yet he hath made with me an everlasting covenant, ordered in all things, and sure." "However God doth deal with my house, whatever misery is brought upon us, yet the covenant itself is everlasting; 'ordered in all things, and sure.'" Whatever misery and distress may fall upon a believing soul (and I pray God help me to believe it, as well as to say it),—whatever darkness or temptation he may be exercised withal upon the account of sin—whatever pressure, in afflictions, persecutions, dangers, may befall him—they all belong unto God's covenant dispensation in dealing with him. For God being his God in covenant, he acts according to the covenant in all things. Hence saith Hezekiah, Isa. xxxviii. 16, "O LORD, by these things men live, and in all these things is the life of my spirit." What are these things? Why, saith he, "I reckoned till morning, that, as a lion, so will he break all my bones; from day even to night wilt thou make an end of me. What shall I say? he hath both spoken unto me, and himself hath done it; I shall go softly all my years in the bitterness of my soul." One would think the next words would be, "By these things men die." No; but, "By these things believers live, and in all these things is the life of my soul:" because they are all administered from the invariable covenant for the good of the souls of them who are exercised with them. Now, as God is pleased to declare himself, so is the soul to think of God in these dispensations of the covenant. Doth God hide his face, and leave the soul to darkness?—in darkness it must be. Job xxxiv. 29, "When he giveth quietness, who then can make trouble? and when he hideth his face, who then can behold him?" Whether it be done against a nation, or against a man only,—be it against one person, or the whole church of God,—if he hides his face, and causeth darkness, none can behold him. When God chastens us, we cannot but look upon him as angry; when he gives us up into the hands of men, hard masters, we cannot but look upon it as a token of his displeasure. When God doth thus in his outward dispensation of the covenant, so that all things are dark, and show nothing but displeasure; and we are to look upon him as a God that hideth himself, and is displeased with us, and exercising anger towards us;—in such a day what shall the soul then do? Why, under all these outward tokens of God's displeasure, faith will, though but weak and faint, work through unto God himself, as invariable in his covenant; and there have a reserve in him beyond them all. Ps. xcvii. 2, "Clouds and darkness are round about him; but righteousness and judgment are the habitation of his throne." "I confess I have clouds and darkness round about me; but if I could but break through these clouds and darkness, that are the consequents of God's hiding his face, and come to his throne, there is righteousness and judgment,—that righteousness and judgment wherein he hath betrothed me unto himself in covenant," Hos. ii. 19. "Could I get through this darkness of mind, this pressure upon my spirit, this sense of guilt, and come unto his throne; there I should find him faithful and stable in his promises, and unalterable in his love." Now, suppose a person to have all these things upon him at once,—that God hath left him to a great sense of sin (for our troubles about sin are not according to the greatness of our sin, but to the sense God will let in upon us; and they are not to be reckoned the greatest sinners who are most troubled for their sin), and his troubles are very great; and at the same time the Lord, in his providential dispensation, is pleased to exercise him in sharp afflictions; and if at the same time his interest and concernment in the people of God is likewise in darkness and distress, that there is no relief in that neither,—to such a one there are clouds and darkness round about God. What then will faith do, in such a case? Why, true faith will secretly work through all to the throne of God, where there is righteousness, and judgment, and acceptance with him. So it is said, Isa. viii. 17, "I will wait upon the LORD, that hideth his face from the house of Jacob, and I will look for him." The face of God is his love in Christ, and the shining of his countenance in the promises of the covenant; for the way whereby God communicates his love unto our hearts, is by his promises. Now, when the soul is sensible of no communication of love, nor promise of it, then God is said to hide his face. What will faith do in such a case?—betake itself unto any thing else for relief? No; saith he, "I will wait upon God, that hideth his face." As a traveller, when the sky is filled with clouds and darkness, tempests and storms, that are ready to break upon him everywhere, yet remembers that these are but interpositions, and the sun is where it was; and if he can but shelter himself till the storm be over, the sun will shine out again, and its beams refresh him: so is it with the soul in this case; it remembers God is still where he was. "Though there are clouds within, and distresses without,—sorrow, and anguish, and fears round about us, and the enemy enters into the very soul; yet the sun is where it was still,—God will hide us where we may abide till this indignation be overpast, and the light of his countenance will yet shine upon me again." Faith considers God in the midst of all his various administrations; and so finds a way for relief.

2. Faith will naturally thus act, as it is the principle of the new nature in us, that came from God, and will tend unto him, whatever difficulties lie in the way.

Evangelical faith will have a secret double tendency to God:—

(1.) Upon that necessary respect which it indispensably and uncontrollably hath to Jesus Christ; for it being the purchase of Christ, and wrought in us by his Spirit, and being the product and travail of the soul of Christ, it hath a natural tendency unto him, 1 Pet. i. 21, "Who by him do believe in God,"—by Christ as mediator, as our surety, undertaking for us;—so that let what will overwhelm the soul, where there is but the least faith, it will have relief in this, that Christ was substituted in its room against all real indignation and wrath from God. The father of the faithful was once reduced to great distress,—when he had lifted up his knife to the throat of his only son: but when destruction lies so near at the door, a voice called to him from heaven, and stopped him; and he looked behind him, and saw a ram caught for a sacrifice to God. When many a poor soul hath the knife at the throat of all his consolations, ready to die away, he hears a voice behind him, that makes him look and see Christ provided for him, as a substituted sacrifice in his room.

(2.) The new creature is the child of God, whereof faith is the principle. It is begotten of God, of his own will; and so, against all interpositions and difficulties whatsoever, is tending to him.

III. I now proceed to show what it is that, in such an overwhelming condition as I have described, faith regards in God to give it a support and relief, that it be not utterly swallowed up and overwhelmed. And,—

1. The first thing faith considers, in such a condition, is, the nature of God himself and his excellencies. This is that which God, in the first place, proposes for our relief, Hos. xi. 9, "I will not execute the fierceness of mine anger, I will not return to destroy Ephraim." What reason doth he give to assure us that he will not? "For," saith he, "I am God, and not man; the Holy One in the midst of thee." He proposes his own nature to our faith, to confirm us that, whatever our expectations be, he will not execute the fierceness of his wrath; and he reproaches them who put their trust in any thing that is not God by nature. So Deut. xxxii. 21, "They have provoked me with that which is not God." And he curseth him "that trusteth in man, and maketh flesh his arm," Jer. xvii. 5. But he proposes himself for our trust,—one of infinite goodness, grace, bounty, and patience.

Now, there are two ways whereby God proposes his nature, and the consideration of it, for the relief of faith in overwhelming distresses:—

(1.) By his name. The name of God is God himself, Ps. ix. 10, "They that know thy name will put their trust in thee;" that is, "They that know thee." Whatsoever the word itself signifies, yet it is the nature of God that is declared by his name. And you know how he doth invite and encourage us to trust in the name of God: "The name of God is a strong tower; the righteous runneth into it, and is safe," Prov. xviii. 10. Isa. l. 10, "Let him trust in the name of the LORD, and stay upon his God." The name of the Lord, is what he declares himself to be, "The LORD God, merciful and gracious, long-suffering, and abundant in goodness and truth, forgiving iniquity, transgression, and sin," Exod. xxxiv. 6, 7. Here he reveals and declares his name. God proposes his name, and the declaration of it, against the working of unbelief; which apprehends that he is severe, wrathful,—that he watcheth for our halting, treasures up every failing and sin to be avenged of it, and that he will do it in fury. No: saith God, "Fury is not in me," Isa. xxvii. 4. The Lord is good and gracious, as appears by his name, especially as revealed in Christ; so that faith will find secret encouragement in it in all distresses.

By the way, hence you may observe, that God in former days, whilst revelation was under a progress, and he revealed himself by little and little, did still give out his name according as the state and condition of his church and people required; because he called them to trust in his name. How did he reveal himself unto Abraham? He tells you, Exod. vi. 3, "I revealed myself unto Abraham by the name of God Almighty." So, Gen. xvii. 1, he says to him, "I am the Almighty God." And he gives an explication of that name, Gen. xv. 1, "I am thy shield, and thy exceeding great reward." Abraham was in a state and condition wherein he wanted protection in the world; for he was a stranger, and wandered up and down among strange nations, that were stronger than he, and such as he might fear destruction from every day. "Fear not," saith God, "for 'I am God Almighty; I am thy shield.'" And in the faith of this did Abraham travel among the nations. And at that time he had no child. What end, then, should he have of all his labour and travel? Why, saith God, "I am thy reward." And Gen. xiv., where there is a discourse about the nations of the world, who began to fall into idolatry, Melchizedek is called "The priest of the most high God." God revealed himself to be a "high God," to cast contempt upon their dunghill gods. And when Abraham came to speak with the king of Sodom, he says, "I have sworn by the most high God." So when God came to bring the people out of the land of Egypt, he revealed himself unto them by his name Jehovah. "I did not reveal myself so before," saith God; " but now I reveal myself so, because I am come to give subsistence unto my promise." Thus God dealt with them, when he came to maintain his church, by gradual revelations. But now God reveals himself by his whole name; and we may take what suits our distress, especially that which is comprehensive of all the rest,—" The God and Father of our Lord Jesus Christ."

(2.) God doth this by comparing himself to such creatures as act out of natural kindness: " Can a woman forget her sucking child? Yet will I not forget."

Now, there are three reasons why it is necessary that faith, in an overwhelming condition, should have regard to the nature of God, and the essential properties of his nature, for its relief:—[1.] Because of the circumstances of our distresses; [2.] Because of the nature of them; and, [3.] Because of the nature of faith:—

[1.] Because of the circumstances of our distress. There are three or four circumstances that may befall us in our distress, that faith itself can get no relief against them, but from the essential properties of the nature of God:—

1*st*. The first is, place. Believers may be brought into distress in all places of the world;—in a lions' den, with Daniel,—in a dungeon with Jeremiah; they may be banished to the ends of the earth, as John to Patmos; or they may be driven into the wilderness, as the woman by the fury of the dragon. The whole church may be cast into places where no eye can see them, no hand relieve them,—where none knows whether they are among the living or the dead. Now, what can give relief against this circumstance of distress which may befall the people of God? Nothing but what Jeremiah tells us, chap. xxiii. 23, " Am I a God at hand, and not a God afar off, to the ends of the earth?" Ps. cxxxix. 7, " 'Whither shall I flee from thy presence?' to the utmost ends of the earth?" It is all in vain: the essential omnipresence of God can alone relieve the souls of believers against this great circumstance of various places, whither they may be driven to suffer distresses and be overwhelmed with them. If the world could cast us out where God is not, and hath nothing to do, how would it triumph! It was a part of their bondage and great difficulty of old, that the solemn worship of God was confined to one certain country and place; so that when the enemies of the church could cast them out from thence, they did, as it were, say unto them, " Go, serve other gods." God hath taken off that bondage; all the world cannot throw us out of a place where we cannot worship God. Wherever there is a holy people, there is a holy land, and we can be driven to no place but God is there; and if we should be compelled to leave our land, we have no ground to fear we shall leave our God behind us. God's essential omnipresence is a great relief against this circumstance of distress, especially to souls that are cast out where no eye can pity them. Should they be cast into dungeons, as Jeremiah was, yet they can say, "God is here."

2dly. It is so likewise with respect to time. The sufferings of the Church of God are not tied up to one age or generation. "We can see some little comfort and relief that may befall us in our own days; but what shall become of our posterity of future ages?" Why, God's immutability is the same throughout all generations; his "loving-kindness fails not," as the psalmist saith,—which is the only relief against this distress. Alas! if a man should take a prospect of the interest of Christ at this day in the world, and consider the coming on of wickedness like a flood in all parts of the earth, he would be ready to think, "What will God do for his great name? what will become of the gospel of Christ in another age?" But God is the same through all times and ages.

3dly. There is relief to be found in God, and only in himself, in the loss of all,—when nothing remains. Should a man lose his lands, if his house remains he hath something to relieve him; he knows where to repose his head under his cares. But when all is gone, what can relieve him? Nothing but God and his all-sufficiency. This was Habakkuk's comfort if all should fail him. "Yet," saith he, "I will rejoice in the LORD, and joy in the God of my salvation."

4thly. The last circumstance of distress is death. The way and manner whereby it may approach us, and how soon this will be, we know not. When all this state and frame of things shall vanish, and we prove to have an utter unconcernment in things below; when the curtain shall be turned aside, and we shall look into another world; the soul's relief lies in God's immutability,—that we shall find him the same to us in death as he was in life, and much more.

SERMON XX.[1]

"From the end of the earth will I cry unto thee, when my heart is overwhelmed: lead me to the rock that is higher than I."—Ps. lxi. 2.

IN my former discourse upon this text, I told you that there were three reasons why faith betakes itself to the nature of God for relief in overwhelming distresses. The first was taken from the circumstances of those distresses; the second from the nature of them; and the third from the nature of faith itself. I mentioned four circumstances in such distresses, that nothing can relieve the souls of men

[1] This sermon was preached November 25, 1670.

against, but the consideration of God's essential properties; which I shall not here repeat, but proceed to the second reason:—

[2.] There are some distresses that, in their own nature, refuse all relief that you can tender them, but only what is derived from the fountain itself,—the nature of God. Zion's distress did so, Isa. xlix. 14, "Zion said, The LORD hath forsaken me." And chap. xl. 27, "My way is hid from the LORD, and my judgment is passed over from my God." She was in that distress, that nothing but the nature of God could give her relief. God therefore proposeth that unto her, "Hast thou not known? hast thou not heard, that the everlasting God, the LORD, the Creator of the ends of the earth, fainteth not?" verse 28. A man would think, sometimes, it was no difficult thing to answer those objections which believing souls charge against themselves, even such as we are well and comfortably persuaded are believers. But it frequently falls out quite otherwise; and nothing will bring them to an issue, but the consideration of the infinite grace and goodness that is in God.

Nay, there may be temporal distresses that, in their own nature, will admit of no other relief;—as when the whole church of God is in extreme calamity in the world, which nothing can remove but infinite power, goodness, and wisdom. You know how Moses was put to it when God told him he would deliver Israel out of Egypt. He looked upon it as impossible, and raised objections till it came to that, Exod. iii. 13,—"If it must be so, tell me *thy name*." And God revealed his name: "I AM THAT I AM." Till God confirmed him with his name,—that is, with his nature,—Moses could see no way possible how the church should be delivered. And so it falls out with us as with Moses. When God did not appear, Moses thought he could have delivered them himself, and goes and kills the Egyptian; but when God appeared, he could not believe that God himself could do it, till he gave him his name.

But some may object, "When faith comes to approach unto God to find relief, as God proposes himself in his name, it will find other things in God besides his goodness, grace, and mercy. There is severity, justice, righteousness in God; which will give as much discouragement on the one hand as the other properties will give encouragement on the other. To come to God, and see him glorious in holiness, and infinite in severity and righteousness,—here will be discouragement."

I shall answer this briefly, and so pass on:—

1*st*. It is most true that God is so. He is no less infinitely holy than infinitely patient and condescending; no less infinitely righteous than infinitely merciful and gracious: but these properties of God's nature shall not be immediately glorified upon their persons who go unto him and make their addresses in faith; though he will be so to others. There is nothing but faith can take a proper view of God. Wicked men's thoughts of God are referred unto these two heads:—*First,* They think, wickedly, "that God is altogether such an one as themselves," Ps. l. 21. While under the power of their corruptions and temptations, while in pursuit of their lusts, they have no thoughts of God, but such as these. The meaning of which is,—that he is not much displeased with them in what they do; but hath the same care of them in the way of their sins, as of the holiest in the world. *Secondly,* Their other thoughts are (commonly when it is too late, and God lets his terrors into their souls) what the prophet saith in Isaiah, "Who of us shall dwell with eternal fire?"

2dly. God hath given believers assurance that he will not deal with them according to the strictness of his holiness and severity of his justice. So speaks Job, chap. xxiii. 3, 4, "Oh that I knew where I might find him! that I might come to his seat! I would order my cause before him, and fill my mouth with arguments." But doth he know of whom he speaks? and what this great and holy One will speak when he appears? Yes; verse 6, "Will he plead against me with his great power? No; but he will put strength in me." "God will not plead with me by his dread, and terror, and great severity; but he will put strength in me." Therefore, Isa. xxvii. 5, he bids them "lay hold on his arm." Who dare lay hold on God's arm? "Let them lay hold upon my arm, that they may have peace; and they shall have peace." Poor creatures are afraid to go to God, because of his power; but "Fury is not in me," saith God.

3dly. It is impossible for faith ever to consider the nature of God, but it hath a secret respect unto Jesus Christ, as the days-man or umpire between God and the soul, and as him by whom—as to all that concerns these properties of his nature—his severity and justice are already manifested and glorified.

[3.] There is one reason more why the soul will thus, in overwhelming distresses, betake itself unto the nature of God, as manifested by his name; and that is taken from the nature of faith itself. The formal reason of faith is the veracity of God's word. What we believe with divine faith, we believe upon this account,—that God hath revealed and spoken it. And the ultimate object of faith is God's all-sufficiency. And whatsoever you act faith immediately upon, it will not rest and be satisfied till it comes, as it were, to be immersed in the all-sufficiency of God; like the stream of a river that runs with great swiftness, and presses on till it comes to the ocean, where it is swallowed up. It is said, 1 Pet. i. 21, that "through Christ we believe in God." Christ is the immediate object of faith; but God in his all-sufficiency is the ultimate object of faith.

Again: faith acts thus, because it is the great principle of that divine nature which God hath inlaid in our souls, created in us, and whereof he is the Father; for "of his own will he hath begotten us, by the word of truth." Faith, therefore, as it is the child of God,—the new nature that God hath ingrafted in us,—has a natural tendency towards God; so that it is working in and through all to God himself, who is its Father. This is the first thing that the soul considers in God, that faith makes its application unto for relief.

2. In an overwhelming condition, faith finds relief in sovereign grace; that is, grace as it is absolutely free. What I mean by it, is that which is mentioned, Exod. xxxiii. 19, "I will be gracious unto whom I will be gracious, and I will show mercy upon whom I will show mercy." The things we stand in need of are grace and mercy; the principle from whence they flow, and are bestowed, is the sovereign will and pleasure of God. God refers the dispensation of all grace and mercy merely unto his own sovereign will and pleasure. Now, when the soul can find nothing in the promise, nothing in any evidence of the love of God, or in the experience that it hath formerly had, it betakes itself unto the sovereignty of grace. And in sovereign grace there are two things:—

(1.) That God is able to give relief in the state and condition wherein we are; whatever we stand in need of,—mercy, life, salvation,—God is able to give it: whatsoever he will do, he can do. And this in the Scripture is made a great encouragement of rest upon God. Thus, Dan. iii. 17, when Shadrach, Meshach, and Abednego were in that great and overwhelming distress, what did they relieve themselves withal? "If it be so," say they, "our God whom we serve is able to deliver us from the burning fiery furnace, and he will deliver us out of thine hand, O king. But if not, be it known unto thee, O king, that we will not serve thy gods, nor worship the golden image which thou hast set up." "If God will not:" it is not, "If God cannot;" for he can do what he will. If he had not been able, they would not have worshipped him. There is nothing for these sixteen hundred years that hath seemed harder to be effected, than the call of the Jews; but the apostle gives us this ground yet to fix our hopes upon, in the expectation of it:—"They may be graffed in; 'for God is able to graff them in again,'" Rom. xi. 23. The very power of God—that he is able to do whatever he pleases—is a foundation for faith to act upon, and relieve itself by. And therefore God pleads it emphatically, Isa. l. 2, 3, where he tells them that his hand is not shortened that it cannot save, but he is still able to do it. "Is my hand shortened at all," saith he, "that it cannot redeem? or have I no power to deliver? Behold, at my rebuke I dry up the sea: I make the rivers a wilderness: I clothe the heavens with blackness, and I make sackcloth their covering."

Now, there are four things that are included in this very apprehension of faith that God is able to do this, whatever our condition be:—

[1.] There is nothing contrary to his own nature in it. There are things that are contrary to the nature of God, and these things God cannot do. "God cannot lie," Tit. i. 2; Heb. vi. 18. It is one part of God's infinite perfection, that he can do nothing contrary unto his own nature. So that whatever I believe is of God's sovereign grace, which he is able to do, I believe there is nothing in it contrary unto the nature of God. Whatever apprehensions we have of pardon of sin, it includes an atonement; for without an atonement God is not able to pardon our sins: God cannot do it without satisfaction unto his justice. So that every soul that hath an apprehension that there is sovereign grace in God, whereby he is able to relieve and help him, he includes in that apprehension the belief of an atonement; without which God cannot do it. "He cannot deny himself." It is the judgment of God, that "they that commit sin are worthy of death."

[2.] If God be able, there is nothing in it contrary to any decree of God. There are many things that may be contrary to God's decree, that in themselves were not contrary unto his nature; for the decree of God is a free act of his will, which might have been, or not have been. But when the decree of God is engaged, if any thing be contrary unto it, God cannot do it; for he is not changeable.

Now, the decree of God may be taken two ways:—

1*st.* For his eternal purpose concerning this or that person or thing. But this I intend not.

2*dly.* The decree of God signifies "sententia lata," "a determinate sentence,' that God hath pronounced against any person or thing; contrary to which God will not proceed. So, Zeph. ii. 2, we are invited to "seek the LORD, before the decree bring forth;" that is, before God hath passed an absolute and determinate sentence in that matter and case. When Daniel would assure Nebuchadnezzar of his doom, he tells him it was "the decree of the Most High," chap. iv. 24. So in the case of Saul. "The LORD hath rejected thee," saith Samuel, 1 Sam. xv. 26. But will he not call it back? No; "The Strength of Israel will not lie," verse 29. The sentence is gone forth, and it shall stand. God rejected the house of Eli from the priesthood, 1 Sam. ii. But will he not return again? No; "The iniquity of the house of Eli shall not be purged with sacrifice nor offering for ever," chap. iii. 14. So it was with them of whom God "sware in his wrath they should never enter into his rest." Now, while there is faith in God's sovereignty, if there be no decree in the case, there is hope. But if God had decreed, and put forth his oath, he would not have raised my faith to look after sovereign grace;—which declares an ability in God, that he can do it.

[3.] It includes this, That there is nothing in it contrary unto the glory of God; for this is the measure of all that God doth in all his dealings with us,—he aims in all things at the manifestation of his glory. And we are not to desire any thing that is contrary to the glory of God. We are not to desire that God would not be holy and righteous because of us,—that we might be saved in our sins, and while we are obstinate in them. This is to desire that God would not be God, that we might live. But now, to save an humble, broken, contrite sinner,—a poor guilty creature, that lies at his feet for mercy,—to deliver poor distressed believers from ruin and oppression,—is not inconsistent with the glory of God. God can do this for the advancement of his glory. I have known it go well with some poor souls when they could come to believe this, that to save and pardon them was not contrary to God's nature, decree, and glory.

[4.] There is this in it also, That if there be need of power, God can put it forth,—that power which carried Abraham through all difficulties. Gen. xviii. 14, "Is any thing too hard for the LORD?" What is your difficulty? it may be an overwhelming guilt of sin? "Is any thing too hard for God?" What is your distress? a wicked, prevailing corruption? "Is any thing too hard for God?" In outward distresses that lie upon the church of God, there is this relief in sovereign grace: "Is any thing too hard for God?" Every thing is too hard for us; but nothing is too hard for God. This is the first thing in sovereign grace,—that God is able.

(2.) If it be so, then all that we have to do is resolved into the will of God; so that all I have to do in this world is but to go to God, as the leper did unto Christ: "Lord, if thou wilt, thou canst make me clean." If God will, he can pardon, sanctify, save me. And if God will, he can deliver his church and people. Here lies the whole question,—it is all resolved into his will.

Now, two things ensue after once a poor soul hath resolved all his concerns into the will of God:—

[1.] There will be an end put unto all other entangling disputes and dark thoughts, which overwhelm the mind: "For now," saith the soul, "it is come to this, that my whole condition depends upon God's sovereign pleasure." David somewhere makes his complaint, that he was in the mire. A poor creature is bemired; and the more he plungeth, the faster he sticks. When a soul is in this condition, saith God, "Be still, and know that I am God," Ps. xlvi. 10. And now all is rolled upon the will of God.

[2.] When once we can resolve our conditions absolutely, without farther dispute, into the will of God, innumerable arguments will arise to persuade the soul that God will be willing. I will name some of them:—

1*st.* One is taken from that goodness and graciousness of his nature which we have been before considering and proposing unto you, and doth now properly in this place occur unto us. Suppose any of us had a business with a man whom we believe to be a good man,—a man that hath something of the image of God upon him,—and the matter is to us of great importance (it may be, as much as our lives are worth), and he can easily do it, without any prejudice or disadvantage unto himself, with one word;—can we cast a greater reflection upon this man, than to think he will not be willing to do it?—that, merely to do us a mischief and spite, he will change his own nature, and act contrary to his own principles? Shall we, then, question the good-will of God? Shall we question, when all is resolved into his will, that he will not give us out grace and mercy in time of need? Our Saviour presses this argument, Luke xi. 11–13, and in other places, where he brings the issue as near as possible; telling us, it is not to be expected that a child, who finds nothing but his father's will to hinder, will mistrust his giving him bread. "And if ye, being evil," saith he, "know how to give good gifts unto your children, how much more shall your heavenly Father give the Holy Spirit to them that ask him?" And when we can bring the concerns of God's church and people merely to his will, his own nature will supply us with arguments enough to confirm our expectation that he will do it.

2*dly.* There is another great argument, when all is brought to the sovereignty of the will of God, which is mentioned, Rom. viii. 32, "He that spared not his own Son, but delivered him up unto death for us all, how shall he not with him also freely give us all things?" Shall I question whether God will do this thing or no, considering this great instance of his will? It was his will to send Jesus Christ to die for poor sinners. He did not send him to die in vain, and that his death should be lost. If God were not willing to give out grace and mercy to sinners, wherefore did he send Jesus Christ? why did he give his own Son out of his bosom? why did he not spare him, and cause our iniquities to meet upon ourselves? Can God give a greater sign of his readiness to spare sinners than his dealing with Jesus Christ? That is the second thing which faith considers, when it comes unto God for relief in an overwhelming condition,—sovereign grace, that God is able, all things are resolved into his will.

3*dly.* Faith in this matter takes into consideration that one particular property of the grace of God in Christ which is mentioned, Eph. iii. 8, "The unsearchable riches of Christ." Saith faith, "There is more grace and more mercy too in God (for these are God's riches that are here intended) than possibly I can see and look into. Will the mercy that hath been declared unto my faith, the promises that have been discovered and revealed unto me, give me satisfaction?

No, they will not. I cannot be satisfied with what I have received, with what discoveries have been made unto me of the grace of God." But, saith the soul, "There lie behind unsearchable riches of grace, which I can by no means conceive; which all the world, or all the angels in heaven cannot find out." This is a great relief in an overwhelming condition.

4thly. Once more: faith in such a condition learns to resolve former experiences, not into its own present condition, but into the unchangeableness of God. And this one thing being wisely managed, is enough to relieve our souls under many overwhelming distresses that do befall us. The psalmist doth so, Ps. lxxvii. He had experience of God, verse 6, "I call to remembrance my song in the night." Compare it with that in Job xxxv. 10, "Where is God my maker, who giveth songs in the night?" David intends some such intimation of the love and good-will of God as made him rejoice in the night season. But what is his state now? He tells you, verse 2, that it is the "day of his trouble;" that "his sores run in the night and cease not; his soul refuses to be comforted." And, verses 7, 8, etc., "Will the Lord cast off for ever? and will he be favourable no more? Is his mercy clean gone for ever? doth his promise fail for evermore? Hath God forgotten to be gracious? hath he in anger shut up his tender mercies?" In this grand and overwhelming distress where doth he find relief? He resolves his experience into the unchangeableness of God, verse 10, "This is my infirmity; but I will remember the years of the right hand of the Most High." "He that gave me that former song in the night season, though now I am nothing but darkness, and ready to fear his mercy is quite gone for ever; yet he is the same, and he will give in the like experience again: though I am changed, he is not."

3. I should go farther, to show what respect faith in such a condition hath unto the covenant of God; but I cannot now insist upon it.

IV. I thought to have shown you also, in the last place, the difference between the faith of the godly and that of unbelievers,—that which the worst of men will have in God in the time of their distresses, and that relief which true evangelical faith finds in an overwhelming condition; but I see it would take up too much time.

One word of use, and I have done.

Use. This is an overwhelming time,—a time wherein many are at the ends of the earth literally, and many metaphorically,—a time and season wherein most that fear the Lord are obnoxious to some overwhelming distress or other. Suppose that God hath not let forth upon many at this day an overwhelming sense of guilt,—that there are not many tempted, wounded, and troubled (though some there are, whom we meet with every day); yet I have great reason to fear that, if we were all rightly awakened, an overwhelming distress would come upon the minds of men, from the want of humility, holiness, fruitfulness, faith, and love; which ourselves have sometimes enjoyed, and are proposed unto us, and which the examples of them who are gone before us lead us to inquire after. Are none overwhelmed with the hardness of their hearts, instability of their spirits?—overgrown with careless, empty, light, worldly frames? Truly, more or less, we have all reason to be overwhelmed; and we have showed you a little where our relief lies in this state and condition.

Are we ready to be overwhelmed with the calamitous condition of the people of God all over the world, and as to ourselves, our goods, and personal concerns,—any thing that is near and dear unto us? I pray God make our hearts jealous over it, especially those that are at ease in their health and prosperity. When God throws others of his people into the furnace, such have great reason to be jealous lest he deal more severely with them than the poorest saint that wants a morsel of bread. Well, you see the way of relief in this case also. It is God alone unto whom we must make our application. He is willing to receive us, because of the goodness of his nature; and he is able to save us, because of the abundance of his grace and power.

SERMON XXI.[1]

GOSPEL CHARITY.

"And above all these things put on charity, which is the bond of perfectness."
COL. iii. 14.

THE word ἀγάπη, which we here translate "charity," is the only word used in the New Testament to signify "love." And I wish we had

[1] Joseph Caryl, so well known from his "Exposition of the Book of Job," was born in 1602. He studied at Oxford, and entered into holy orders in 1627. After preaching for some time in Oxford, he came to London, and preached with much acceptance before the Society of Lincoln's-Inn. He was a member of the Assembly of Divines in 1643; and in 1645 he was appointed to the charge of St Magnus', near London Bridge. Along with Dr Owen, he accompanied Cromwell to Scotland in 1650; and towards the close of 1653 he acted on the Commission of *Triers*, for removing ignorant and scandalous ministers. He attended the Conference at the Savoy in 1658, when several Independent divines endeavoured to agree on a Confession of Faith. He was again in Scotland with Major-General Whalley and Colonel Goffe, in order to confer with Monk on the state of public affairs. After the Restoration, he was ejected from St Magnus', in 1662; but continued to preach to a congregation of his former hearers till his death, which occurred in February 1672-3. The public duties to which he was often called be-

always rendered it so, because in our common use of speech, charity is restrained to one effect of love, in relieving the poor and afflicted; which is nowhere the sense of the word in Scripture. It is love, then, that is intended. "Above all these things put on love." There is no grace nor duty but the exercise and practice of it is commanded in the Scriptures, and most of them fall under particular commands, and are enjoined absolutely; but there is but this one, that I remember, which hath a preference given unto it in a command above other things, as here, Ἐπὶ πᾶσι δὲ τούτοις,—"Above all these things put on love." So 1 Pet. iv. 8, Πρὸ πάντων,—"Before all things, have fervent love among yourselves." And so in that of our apostle, 1 Cor. xii. 31. He had given them directions about the use and improvement of spiritual gifts for the edification of the church (and it is an excellent way to have the church edified, by the due and orderly exercise of the gifts of the Holy Ghost in the elders and members); but when he hath done, he adds, "Behold, I yet show you a more excellent way;" and that is this duty of love, as he shows in the next chapter. It is not only commanded, but it hath a special eminency and excellency put upon it, in reference to all other duties, for some certain end.

That which I shall at present discourse upon is this:—

Observation. Love, and its exercise, is the principal grace and duty that is required among, and expected from, the saints of God, especially as they are engaged in church-fellowship.

I shall not prove it in general, but speak to these three things:—I. I shall show you the nature of this love that is thus signalized in the gospel precept. II. Give you the reasons of the necessity and importance of it, by mentioning some of them the Scriptures give. III. Lay down some directions for its practice:—

I. Concerning the first we may observe, that the love here intended

speak his ability, and the confidence reposed in him by the leading men of his day. The savour of his piety yet remains in his works; which consist chiefly of sermons, and his bulky but precious commentary on Job. He had some share in the preparation of an English-Greek Lexicon for the New Testament; and his qualifications for the task must have been considerable, when they extorted from Anthony Wood the commendation of their author as "a learned and zealous Nonconformist."

Before his death, his congregation had been for some years worshipping in Leadenhall Street. The church under the care of Owen had been in the habit of assembling for worship at no great distance from them. About four months after the death of Caryl, the two churches united. It appears that, previously to the union, Owen's congregation consisted only of 36 members; in the Leadenhall Street congregation there were 136 communicants. In this small number, however, amounting only to 172, there were many whose names deserve to be held in remembrance for their rank in society and public services, and still more for their eminent Christian worth.—See "Life of Owen," vol. i. p. xc.

On the 5th of June 1673 the two congregations met together for the first time under the ministry of Owen; and it was in these circumstances he preached this sermon,—very suitable to the occasion, and rich in suggestions for the cultivation of Christian unity and love.—Ed.

is the second great duty that was brought to light by the gospel. There is nothing of it in the world, neither as to the degree nor as to the knowledge of it, but what proceeds from the gospel. The world neither hath it nor knows what it is. Variance, strife, wrath, entered by sin; for when we fell off from the love of God, and from his love to us, it is no wonder if we fell into all hatred and variance among ourselves. The love of God was originally, in the state of innocency, the bond of perfection: when that was broke, all the creation fell into disorder,—all mankind, in particular, into that state described by the apostle, Tit. iii. 3, "Living in malice and envy, hateful, and hating one another." There is carnal and natural love still in the world, that follows necessarily upon natural relations; and the same is in some degree in brutes themselves. There is also a love that arises from a society in sin, in pleasure,—from a suitableness of humour in conversation, or of design as to political ends; to which heads you may reduce all the love in the world: but all these are utter strangers from this evangelical love. And therefore, when it was brought to light by the gospel, there was nothing so much amazed the heathen world as to see this new love among Christians. It was even a proverb among them: "See how they love one another!" To see persons of different sorts, different nations, tempers, degrees, high and low, rich and poor, all knit together in love, was the great thing that amazed the heathen world. And I shall show you the grounds of it afterward.

You may likewise observe, that this love is the means of communion between all the members of the mystical body of Christ, as faith is the instrument of their communion with their head, Jesus Christ. And, therefore, our apostle doth seven or eight times in his epistles join faith and love together, as the entire means of the communion and fruitfulness of the mystical body of Christ. And in one place he hath so ordered his words, to show their inviolableness and indissolubleness, that you must make a distribution of them to gather their right sense. It is in Philemon, verse 5, "Hearing of thy love and faith, which thou hast toward the Lord Jesus, and toward all saints." A man would think that both the objects relate to both the duties,—faith and love towards Christ, and towards all the saints. But though Christ be the object of our love also, the saints are not the object of our faith; so that you must make a distribution of the words: "Hearing of thy faith towards the Lord Jesus Christ, and of thy love towards all the saints." But the apostle so places them to show how indissoluble these things are, that they must go together;—where the one is, there will be the other; and where the other is not, there that will not be. It is therefore the life, and soul, and quickening form[1] of all duties that are performed among believers toward one

[1] [Fire or power?]

another. Whatever duties you do perform, be they never so great and glorious, never so useful one to another, to any of the members of Christ; if they are not quickened and animated by this love, they are of no value to thy communion with Christ, and edification of the church. And men may perform many things that appear to be duties of love, without love. In the two verses before the text, saith the apostle, "Put on therefore, as the elect of God, bowels of mercies, kindness, humbleness of mind, meekness, long-suffering; forbearing one another, and forgiving one another, if any man have a quarrel against any: even as Christ forgave you, so also do ye. But above all these things put on love." So that all these things may be, yet not love. Those which seem to be the greatest and most effectual fruits of love whatever, yet they may be all without love. We may forbear without love, forgive without love, be kind to one another without love; and all this of no use, if above all these things, over and upon them, we do not superinduce love,—if we be not quickened and acted by love. The truth is, he that shall read over the New Testament, especially those things which we have most reason particularly to consider in it,—which are the special instructions and commands that Christ left unto his disciples when he was going out of this world,—would think this same love, whatever it be, is the sum and substance of all that Christ required of us; as indeed it is. And the apostle John, who lived long, and lived to see the Christian religion much propagated in the world, and very probably saw a decay of love, wrote his First Epistle almost to this very end and purpose,—to let us know, that there was neither truth of grace, nor evidence of the love of God to us, nor of our love to God, unless there was fervent and intense love towards the brethren. Whatsoever we think of our profession, if there be not an intense love unto the brethren, we have neither the truth of grace, nor evidence of God's love to us, or of our love to God.

But you will say, then, "What is this love?"

I answer briefly, It is a fruit of the Spirit of God, an effect of faith, whereby believers, being knit together by the strongest bonds of affection, upon the account of their interest in one head, Jesus Christ, and participating of one Spirit, do delight in, value, and esteem each other, and are in a constant readiness for all those regular duties whereby the temporal, spiritual, and eternal good of one another may be promoted.

I will a little open the description I have given of it, and so proceed:—

1. This love, concerning which I speak, is a fruit of the Spirit, Gal. v. 22, "The fruit of the Spirit is love." There may be, and is implanted in some natures, a great deal of love, kindness, and tender-

ness, in comparison of others that are froward; but that is not the love here intended. That which renders it peculiarly gospel love is its being the product of the Spirit of God in our hearts. Truly, I cannot turn aside to every particular, to show how we may know whether love be a fruit of the Spirit, or arising from our own natural inclination; but you must inquire into it upon those general rules that are given to discern and distinguish such things. This only I say, it is a fruit of the Spirit, a product of the Holy Ghost in us, or it belongs not to our work.

2. It is an effect of faith. So saith the apostle, " Faith worketh by love." How doth faith work by love? how doth faith set love on work? When it respects God's command requiring this love, his promise accepting it, and his glory, whereunto this love is directed,—then doth faith work by love. And it is not the love we aim at, which we design and press upon you, if it proceed upon any other account but this,—because Christ commands it, and promises to accept it, and because it lies in a tendency to his glory. Self may work by love sometimes,—flesh, interest, or reputation may work by love; that is, by the fruit of it: but it is that love which faith worketh by that we alone intend.

3. It is that love which doth knit together the hearts and souls of believers with entire affection one unto another. For the apostle tells us, Eph. iv. 16, speaking of that communion which the church hath by love, "The whole body is fitly joined together and compacted by that which every joint and part supplieth." Now, we can supply nothing to one another but by love; and from thence issues delight and esteem. "All my delight," saith he, "is in the saints," Ps. xvi. 3, "and in them that excel in the earth." And there is that valuation, that we ought to lay down our lives for the brethren; that is, to be willing to expose ourselves to difficulties and dangers, our lives to hazard, yea, to lay them down, if the edification of the church so require. The martyrs of old did not lay down their lives for Christ personally only, but for Christ mystical; they not only laid them down in faith, but in love,—love to the church. The apostle saith of all his afflictions, " I fill up the measure of the afflictions of Christ, for his body, which is the church." He bore his afflictions out of love to the church, as well as out of faith and love to Christ personally, that there might be no offence, scandal, or temptation befall the church. That their faith might be confirmed and strengthened was a great reason why the martyrs laid down their lives. And it should be so with us, if we come to be called thereunto. This is that love which the Scripture speaks of; and not that careless, negligent, carnally-influenced love which the world, I had almost said, nay, I will say it, which too many professors abound withal, and no more. And

it were a task, not for one sermon, but many discourses, to show what are the duties that his love requires of us, and will put us upon; how it will influence all our walkings, direct us in all our ways,—in our whole course and conversation, and all that we do.

It may be asked, seeing all believers are the objects of this love, "How are we to exercise it towards them, since there are few of them we know and are acquainted withal, and that we have a satisfaction in their state and condition that they are such,—few, that we know their occasions, straits, and necessities?"

I answer,—

(1.) The whole mystical body of Christ being the adequate object of gospel love, of love in and by the Holy Ghost, it is indispensably required of us that, radically and habitually, we have an equal love unto all believers, as such,—unto all the disciples of Christ throughout the world. But this is accompanied with some limitations:—

[1.] In the exercise of it, it will much answer the evidence that persons are interested in the mystical body of Christ. There are some whose vain opinions, and indeed corrupt practices, will exercise the most extensive charity to judge they belong unto the mystical body of Christ; yet according unto our evidence, so is our love to be.

[2.] There may be degrees in our love, especially as to delight and valuation, according as we see more or less of the image of Jesus Christ upon any believer; the likeness and image of Christ being the formal reason of this love.

[3.] The exercise of love must be determined by occasions and opportunities. But with these three qualifications a man may pronounce he is no believer who hath not, habitually and radically, a love to all the believers in the world, so as to be inwardly concerned in their good and evil, and to be influenced unto prayer, compassion, delight, and joy, according as their state and condition doth require.

(2.) There is required an inclination and readiness to all acts of love towards all believers, as opportunity shall be administered. If we turn away our face from our brother, and hide ourselves from him, how dwells the love of God in us? If there be a real love in any of us, of this kind, let it be but heightened and advantaged by an opportunity, it will break through difficulties, through reasonings, pleas of flesh and blood, to the exercise of itself. As they that know any thing in this world know that, as the first great opposition of hell, the world, and corrupt nature, is against faith to God by Christ; so the next great opposition made against us, is against our love. If we do not understand this, we are unwise, and have not considered the various states and conditions of things in this world; and how every moment things are presented unto us with a tendency to the weakening of love, upon one account or other. But,—

(3.) Our Lord Jesus Christ, in infinite wisdom, tenderness, and condescension, hath provided us a safe, suitable, constant, immediate object for the exercise of this love. Having given so great a command as that of love, and laid so great weight upon it, he will not leave us at an uncertainty, how, or where, or when we shall exercise it; but hath directed us to a particular way wherein he will make a trial of our obedience unto the command in general; and this is, by his institution of particular churches. There are two great ends why Christ did institute a particular church; and they were to express the two great graces and duties that he requires of us:—

[1.] The first end why Christ did institute a particular church was, that his saints together might jointly profess their faith in him, and obedience to him. And we have no other way of doing it: he hath tied us up to this. A blessed way! "You shall this way," saith he, "jointly profess your faith in me, and obedience to me, or no way."

[2.] The next great end why he did institute a particular church was, that we might have a direct exercise of his other great command, and of that other great duty, of love to believers. "I will try you here," saith Christ; "I require this of you indispensably,—to love all the saints, all believers, all my disciples. You shall not need to say you must go far, this way or that, for objects; I appoint you to such an order as wherein you shall have continual, immediate objects of all that love which I require of you." When God gives commands that great things turn upon, and [that] are general, he gives some particular instance wherein he will have our obedience tried to those commands. When he gave the great command at first in the state of innocency, he tried them in the tree of knowledge of good and evil, and the tree of life. The Lord Jesus Christ hath given us this great command of love, and hath plainly declared, that if we love not one another, we are not his disciples. "I will give you an instance whereby you may be tried," saith he;—"cast you into such a society, by my order and appointment, as wherein you may have immediate objects for the exercise of love to the utmost of what I do require." If we find a person that is orderly admitted into church society, he is as certain and evident an object of our love, as if we saw him lying in the arms of Christ. We walk by rule; he hath appointed us to do so. Let none, then, pretend that they love the brethren in general, and love the people of God, and love the saints, while their love is not fervently exercised towards those who are in the same church society with them. Christ hath given it you for a trial: he will try your love at the last day by your deportment in that church wherein you are. The apostle tells us, "He that loveth not his brother whom he hath seen, will never love God whom he hath not seen." I am sure I may say, he that exercises not love towards the brethren whom he doth see in that relation wherein Christ hath appointed him to exercise love, loves not the brethren whom he doth not see, and that he hath not that peculiar relation to and acquaintance withal. The great Lord and Guide of his church binds it upon all our spirits and consciences; it is our life, our being. I declare unto this congregation this day, I witness and testify unto you, that unless this evangelical love be found acted, not loosely and in general, but among ourselves mutually towards each other, we shall never give up our account with joy unto Jesus Christ, nor shall we ever carry on the great work of edification among ourselves. And if God be pleased but to give this spirit among you, I have nothing to fear but the mere weakness and pravity of my own heart and spirit. This is the great way Christ hath given us to exemplify our obedience unto that great and holy command of love to his disciples; and great weight is laid upon this duty.

II. The next thing I am to speak to is, to show you the grounds why this love is so necessary: "Before all these things have love. I show you a more excellent way; and that is love." There would be no end, if I should insist long upon the grounds and reasons of this duty. I will give you some of them that are of weight and importance unto me. Do but carry this along with you, that what I speak about love is to be exercised, first among ourselves, and then to have emanations, upon all opportunities and occasions, to the whole mystical body of Christ throughout the world:—

1. It is necessary, because it is the great way whereby we can give testimony to the power of the gospel, and our witness to the Messiah, the Christ that was sent of God. The great thing we have to do in tho world is, to bear witness unto God's sending Christ into the world for the work for which he came. How shall we do this? He himself shows us. John xvii. 21, "That they all may be one; as thou, Father, art in me, and I in thee, that they also may be one in us: that the world may believe that thou hast sent me." And again, verse 23, "I in them, and thou in me, that they may be made perfect in one; that the world may know that thou hast sent me." Jesus Christ lays the weight upon this,—that the world may be convinced that God hath sent him. How shall this be evidenced? Saith he, "If all believers are one it will be evidenced." There is, I acknowledge, another principle of the oneness of them that believe,—by a participation of that one Spirit of the Father and the Son, whereby we come to be one in the Father and the Son. But that is not the whole oneness; nay, I do not think it is at all the oneness here intended. And my reason is this, because it is perfectly invisible, and imperceptible unto the world; and he prays for such a oneness as may convince the world,—that the world may see that they are one, and so believe

that God had sent him. It is no oneness but that whereof love is the bond of perfection, the life, and soul, and spirit of it, that will give conviction unto the world that God hath sent Christ. And if this be not eminent in us, we do what lies in us to harden the world in their unbelief. Persons that profess the gospel, some way or other, have framed unity and uniformity to themselves; and neglecting this oneness of love under them hath been the greatest means of hardening the world in unbelief. "What great matter is there in this?" saith the world; "I can make such a union when I list; it is but making such and such laws about outward observations, and tie men to the observance of them." But the union of love, no man can give but Jesus Christ. And why will this convince the world that God hath sent Christ, when the disciples do so love one another? where lies the argument? From what topic do you argue to prove God hath sent Christ, because his disciples do so love one another? It lies in this, as I told you before:—when sin entered, the bond of all union and perfection among the creatures was quite broken, by the loss of love; the whole world was irrecoverably cast under envy, wrath,—"hateful, and hating one another." Nothing under heaven, no means in us, could retrieve men unto love again, to pure spiritual love. God sends Christ to retrieve this loss, to bring in a new creation, to bring things into order,—to renew the world and the face of things. That glorious part of the work wrought in the heart of man is invisible; that which is visible is love. The world sees here a new union brought forth among Christ's disciples, such as is not in the world, nor of the world,—such as the world doth not partake of. By this they know that God hath sent Christ to do this great work. The care, kindness, condescension, love, delight, and concernment we have in one another, as members of the mystical body of Christ, exemplified in our peculiar church relation, is the great testimony we give to the world that God hath sent Christ; and they will be forced to see, and say, at last, "A glorious work is done upon these persons, that 'were foolish and disobedient, living in divers lusts and pleasures, hateful, and hating one another;' a glorious work hath been done by the Son upon them: and we profess it is from Christ, from God's sending him for this end and purpose."

2. We have no evidence that we ourselves in particular are the disciples of Christ without it. John xiii. 34, 35, "A new commandment I give unto you, That ye love one another; as I have loved you, that ye also love one another. By this shall all men know that ye are my disciples, if ye have love one to another." I have a little inquired why this command of love is here and in other places called a new commandment. I told you before, when sin entered into the world, envy and hatred entered with it; and it is continued upon the

same account. "Whence come wars and fightings?" saith the apostle; "is it not from your lusts that war in your members?" In the first revelation God gave of himself in the law, he commanded love. Our Lord Jesus Christ tells us so,—that we are commanded to "love the Lord our God with all our heart, and our neighbour as ourselves." Whence, then, is this command so often called a new commandment? "A new commandment I give unto you, That ye love one another," saith he.

There are divers reasons of it:—

(1.) I judge one may be this,—That under the law God did indulge that carnal people in sundry things wherein they came short of the royal law of love, by reason of the hardness of their hearts. When Christ comes and gives this command in its full extent, it was a new command. Again,—

(2.) They were carnal, and did not see the spirituality of the command. And the truth of it is, you hear so little of it in the Old Testament, and so much of it in the New, that Christ may justly call it a new command. Besides,—

(3.) At the time when he came, there were cursed expositions of the law that went current in the whole church, which had overthrown the whole duty of love between the brethren and members of it; as you may see in our Saviour's vindicating of it, Matt. v. But Christ, coming to take off all indulgence to carnal men, by reason of the hardness of their hearts; and to take away the darkness that was upon their minds, whereby they could not see the spirituality of the command; and to remove those false expositions that were put upon the law, corrupting the command; he calls it a new commandment.

(4.) Above all these, there is one reason more for it, which lies here in the words I before read unto you: "A new commandment I give unto you, That ye love one another; as I have loved you, that ye love one another." The reason why it was a new commandment was, because there was no quickening, enlivening example of it, to express the power of love, under the Old Testament. This was reserved for Christ. He comes and gives that glorious instance of love, in his condescension in all that he did, and in all that he suffered. He shows that there was something in love that they never before had an instance of in the world. Whence the command for love lies thus: "Let the same mind be in you that was in Christ Jesus;"—"That ye love one another, as I have loved you." And then it is a new commandment indeed, which it was not before. "Hereby," saith he, "men shall know that ye are my disciples:—if the great example I have set you, the great command I have given you, and the great work I came into the world about, was to renew love; by love men will know that ye are my disciples, and not else." We have no other way to evidence ourselves to be disciples of Christ. Men's parts, gifts, wisdom, will not do it; if there be no love, the world has no reason to conclude that we are the disciples of Jesus Christ.

3. It is that wherein the communion of saints doth principally consist. There is great talk about communion of saints; and certainly it is a great thing. We may observe it had a place in all the ancient creeds of the church: where they profess to believe in God, in Christ, and in the Holy Ghost, they profess also to believe the communion of saints; which shows it to be a thing of great importance.

Wherein doth it consist? There are three things in it:—(1.) The fountain and spring of it; (2.) The profession and explanation of it; (3.) The formal reason and life of it:—

(1.) The fountain and spring of the communion of saints lies in their common participation of one Spirit from the one head, Jesus Christ. And you may as soon form a good society among dead men, as work a communion among professors, where it is not fundamentally laid in a common participation of the same Spirit with the head, Christ.

(2.) This communion is expressed principally in the participation of the same ordinances in the same church. This is the great expression of the communion of saints.

(3.) The life and formal reason of this communion, which derives strength from the fountain, and communicates it into that expression and profession, lies in love.

Truly, I have a little jealousy upon my spirit, that churches have been apt to place their communion too much, if not solely, in the participation of the same ordinances, depending upon the same pastor and teacher,—joining together in the celebration of the same sacred institutions. Friends, this is but the expression of our communion, and it may be without any real communion. There may be a communication in the same ordinances, without any communion of saints; you know it is too much [so] in the world. If we be not acted and influenced by this love in all we do, there is no communion. So far you are faithful unto your station in the church of God, so far you discharge your duty, and act as living members of the church, as you find love acting in you towards one another, and no farther. Your utmost diligence in attending unto order,—your constant attendance at the celebration of ordinances,—your dependence on the doctrine and instructions afforded in the church,—may all be without communion of saints. When you have all this, it is love makes this communion: that is the life and formal reason of it; as you may see in the place before quoted, Eph. iv. 15, 16, "But, speaking the truth in love, may grow up into him in all things, which is the head, even Christ: from whom the whole body fitly joined together and compacted by that which every joint supplieth, according to the effectual working in the measure of every part, maketh increase of the body unto the edifying of itself in love." It is the greatest and most glorious description of the communion of saints that we have in the Scripture. It begins in love,—"Speaking the truth in love;" and it ends in love, —"Edifying itself in love." And it is also carried on by love. There is the fountain and spring of this communion, that lies in the head,—in our relation unto, and dependence upon, Christ, the head. If we hold not the head, we can have no interest in this communion. But it is not enough there be a head; there must be a "growing up into him in all things, who is the head." We shall never carry on the work of communion unless we grow up into Christ, by express dependence on him; deriving life and strength from him, and returning all unto his praise and glory as our head: being thereby brought nearer, and made more like unto him. The exercise of faith in these things, is our growing up into Christ. Suppose, then, we go thus far in the business of communion:—we hold the head by faith; and by the exercise of faith and obedience grow up into the head; what is next? "From whom the whole body is fitly framed together." There will be such supplies from the head, Christ, being thus held and grown up into, as will communicate such variety of gifts and graces as shall suit the body, and every member one to another. But how are believers cast into church-union and order? I will not say how they are not: I know what attempts there are in the world. I will plainly tell you how they are. It is by the various communications of Christ, the head, unto them all, fitting and suiting them to one another. What do they, then, themselves herein? They are of two sorts; either joints or other parts. May be they are joints; that is, either officers or principal members, who, by reason of their gifts, yield a supply to the communication of the effects of those gifts and graces they have received, carrying on farther this supply that is received from the head. What shall become of the other members? Not only the joints, but every part doth so, according to the measure of each. The graces and gifts of Christ cast every member into what part it bears. Let none of us choose our own part in the house of God. The graces and gifts of Christ cast us into each part, or joint, and from thence do we supply, according to the measure of that part; and no more is required of us. But how shall we do this? Why, saith he, Ἀληθεύοντες δὲ ἐν ἀγάπῃ,—"Speaking the truth in love." The plain meaning of which is, that whatever we do, in declaring or obeying the truth,—in preaching, or in a way of duty,—we do it all in love. It is not merely speaking, or declaring; but it is a doing whatever we do in obedience to the truth. Whatever your concern is in the truths of the gospel, let love be acted in it; and that is the means whereby you convey your supplies from every joint and part unto the whole. Truth requires our pity, compassion, admonition, exhortation, forbearance, and the like. "Do it all in love," saith he. How then? "The body will be increased, and edify itself in love." It is all love. I have sometimes thought that ἐν ἀγάπῃ, "in love," may be taken for διὰ ἀγάπης, "by love,—"Shall edify itself by love." But take it as we have rendered it,—"Edify itself in love;" that is, love in the body shall be increased; and where love is increased, there the body is edified. A church full of love, is a church well built up. I had rather see a church filled with love a thousand times, than filled with the best, the highest, and most glorious gifts and parts that any men in this world may be made partakers of. Could they go beyond and exceed all we aim at or desire,—could they "speak with the tongues of men and angels,"—it is ten thousand times more for the glory of God and our own comfort, to be a company of poor saints, who are filled with love, than [to be] with those of the highest attainments without it. We neither give testimony unto the world that God sent Christ, nor evidence that we are his disciples, nor do we contribute any thing to the edification of the church, unless God give us to act this grace of love in an abundant measure. Whatever our gifts and parts are, and whatever our wisdom is, such things are apt to puff us up. If this love abound not in us, we shall be thorns in the sides of one another, and shall contribute nothing unto the real spiritual edification of the church. The apostle hath not only laid this down, but so disputed it, in the 12th and 13th chapters of the First Epistle to the Corinthians, that I shall not insist upon it. "Though I could," says he, "speak with the tongues of men and of angels, yet if I have not love, I am but as sounding brass, or a tinkling cymbal," that make a little pleasant noise that comes to nothing. I would wind up all arguments with this,—If we have not love, we have no grace. He that loves Him that begets, will love them that are begotten. If we love not the brethren, the love of God doth not dwell in us. It is not our outward order and form, nor our duties, nor any thing we do or can do, will evidence that we have any thing of the grace of God in us, if we want this grace of love.

III. Having spoken thus far of the nature of evangelical love, and of the reasons of its importance, I would willingly say something to press it upon your hearts and mine own.

The whole issue of this day's work which you have called us unto, under the care and kindness of Christ, depends wholly upon this one instance, of our discharging ourselves in this one duty of love. I know not how it comes to pass, but so it is, that professors have of late been wonderfully harassed with sharp invectives and bitter rebukes for their want of love; and yet I cannot observe there is any fruit of it, or any advantage made by it. And the reason of it seems to be, because all those invectives have been managed upon this principle,—"If you will do so and so,—if you will come up to such and such practices in things of religion,—if you will go thus far, and thus far,—if you will leave off these and those institutions and ways wherein ye walk,—then you have love; if not, you have none at all." And what hath been the fruit hereof? New divisions, new animosities, new rendings and tearings, without the least appearance of any improvement of love whatsoever. I should be very sorry that any man living should outgo me in desires that all that fear God throughout the world, especially in these nations, were of one way as well as of one heart. I know I desire it sincerely; but I do verily believe, that when God shall accomplish it, it will be the effect of love, and not the cause of love. It will proceed from love, before it brings forth love. There is not a greater vanity in the world, in my weak apprehensions, than to drive men into such and such a way, and then suppose that love will be the necessary consequence of that way;—to think that if, by sharp rebukes, by cutting, bitter expressions, they can but drive men into such and such practices, that then love will certainly ensue. We see the contrary all the world over,—that those who do most boast and glory in bringing all to uniformity of practice, have least love among them. You may see it in the papal church. They have obtained their end, in driving all into a uniformity in practice; and yet the members of it are fighting with and tearing one another. It is a vain supposition, to think to bring men to such a way whether they will or no, and then to love whether they will or no. I know not, truly, any way that any who fear God do walk in,—though some are nearer the truth than others,—which in itself is an obstruction of love. I profess, if I did, I would fly from that way as from a pest-house, or any thing that was mortally destructive; because I know the end of all Christ's institutions is to increase love. Some may be nearer the truth than others; some are so;—but if any way doth really in itself obstruct love, without farther consideration, without debating whether it was right or wrong, I would leave that way; for I know it is false. But for persons to reflect upon any institutions of Christ,—such as particular churches are, and will be proved to be,—as though they were hinderances of love, argues a great unskilfulness in the ways of God, if not ill-will towards them; nay, they are appointed of Christ for this end, that we may first exercise that love which he commands, immediately towards one another, that so we may learn to exercise it towards all believers throughout the world. Pray let us not be overtaken with any such apprehension, that we cannot exercise love until we come to such and such a way of agreement, and so put off the duty till we have no opportunity or ability to exercise it; but let us address ourselves to it in our present state and condition.

I shall close all with two or three cautions against things that may be hinderances in the diligent practice of this great duty I have been speaking of unto you:—

1. Let us take heed of a morose, sour, natural disposition. If it doth not hinder many fruits of love, yet it sullies the glory of its exercise extremely. Some good persons have so much of Nabal in them, that blasts the sweet fruit of love which comes from them; it is soured with something of an ill disposition, that hath no life or beauty in it. It is a great mistake, to believe that grace only subdues our carnal corruption, and doth not change our natural temper. I believe grace changes the natural temper, and ennobles it; it makes "the leopard to lie down with the kid," and "the bear to eat straw with the ox," as it is promised: it makes the froward meek; the passionate patient; and the morose benign and kind. And we are to applygrace to these ends and purposes; and not to humour and please ourselves, as though such things are our natural disposition. Grace comes to alter our natural dispositions, that are unsuited to love, and indispose us for it. We are apt to excuse ourselves and one another, and hope that Christ will do so too, because this or that is much from our natural temper. Pray let us not act thus; our natural tempers are to be cured by grace, or it hath not its perfect work upon us.

2. Take heed of such hinderances of love as may attend your peculiar state and condition. I would speak to them who have the advantage of riches, wealth, honour, reputation in the world; which encompass them with so many circumstances, that they know not how to break through them to that familiarity of love with the meanest member of the church which is required of them. Brethren, know the gospel leaves all your providential advantages entirely unto you; whatever you have by birth, education, inheritance, estate, titles, places, it leaves the entire enjoyment of them. But in things which purely concern your communion together, the gospel lays all level;—there is neither rich nor poor, free nor bond in Christ, but the new creature. Therefore we are so expressly commanded by the apostle James, chap. ii, that we should have no particular respect in the congregation to persons, upon the account of outward advantages. We all serve one common Master, the same Lord; and he is such a Lord, that when he was rich in all the glory of heaven, he became poor for our sakes. And let me beg of you that are rich to remember this common Lord and Master; and let not your outward advantages, therefore, keep you at a distance from the meanest, the poorest saint that belongs unto the congregation. If they do, your riches are your

temptation, and your place a disadvantage; which you must labour to break through.

Something also might be said to the poorest and lowest sort, who have their temptations, too, to keep them off from the exercise of love. But I shall waive it.

3. Lastly, Take heed of satisfying yourselves, all of you, with the duties of love, without looking after the entire working of the grace of love. You here, that are joined with us this day, have had for a long time so great a light and instructor, that I doubt not but you are acquainted with all the duties of love that are required of you in your especial relations wherein you stand, and that you have been found in the practice of them. I only mind you to take heed that you be spirited with the grace of love,—that which proceeds from faith, and is acted in you by the Holy Ghost,—that which gives you delight in, and a dear esteem and valuation of the saints, and creates a cheerfulness and readiness in you for the performance of all these duties.

I thought to have given you many other directions; but I must conclude. If God be pleased to imprint any thing from this word upon our hearts and spirits, we shall have cause to rejoice in it. However, remember thus much, that you were begged and entreated,—as you regard the glory of God, the honour of the gospel, and the edification of this church (which of two is now become one), concerning which you must all in your places give an account, as well as I in mine, and as you have any respect unto the ministry of him whom God hath set over you,—that all be wound up in this one duty of love; which if God please to increase, and make intense among us, I no way doubt but he will prosper this day's work of our union.

SERMON XXII.[1]

CHRIST'S PASTORAL CARE.

"Feed thy people with thy rod, the flock of thine heritage, which dwell solitarily in the wood, in the midst of Carmel: let them feed in Bashan and Gilead, as in the days of old."—MIC. vii. 14.

It is not much I shall offer unto you from these words; yet I cannot give you a right apprehension of the mind of God in them, and what I intend from them, without a little going over the chapter from

[1] This sermon was preached October 16, 1673.

the beginning. "Woe is me! for I am as when they have gathered the summer fruits," etc., verse 1. When the prophet says, "Woe is me," he speaks in the name of the earth, say some, as it was the seat of the church of God. I rather take it to be in the name of the church of God, of those who were truly so, in the midst of a profane but outwardly professing people. And this lamentation is with a prospect and view of the sin which was in the people, and of the misery which was coming upon them. They have both of them ever been matter of lamentation unto all that truly fear God. They cannot consider the sins and the miseries of an outwardly professing people, but every one of them ought to cry, "Woe is me! sorrow is to me; sadness of heart is to me." In respect of sin, David saith, Ps. cxix. 136, "Rivers of waters run down mine eyes, because men keep not thy law." And in respect of misery and judgments, Jeremiah expresses his sense thus, chap. ix. 1, "Oh that my head were waters, and mine eyes a fountain of tears, that I might weep day and night for the slain of the daughter of my people." The prophet foreseeing both these,—an overflowing of sin, and an overflowing of judgment,—had reason to cry, "Woe is me!"—"It is a lamentation unto me."

He gives an account of the state of the professing, visible church; which he looks upon to be like unto a field or a vineyard, after the harvest is past and the vintage over: "I am as when they have gathered the summer fruits, as the grape-gleanings of the vintage: there is no cluster to eat: my soul desireth the first ripe fruit." His prayer was, that they might be a fruitful vineyard unto God; but saith he, "We are just as when the vintage is over; there are some grapes, some clusters left under the leaves, but the principal are taken off:"—and not only so, but when a field is reaped, or a vineyard gathered, the owner leaves it for a season, takes down the fence, and the beasts come in and prey upon it, until the time of culture and tillage is come again. God never leaves a professing church to be a wilderness, unless upon the utmost apostasy; but he many times leaves them to be as a field after harvest, or a vineyard after the vintage. God will leave Babylon to be as a wilderness, that shall never be tilled any more,—shall have no rain, no fences, no tillage; but he will not leave his church so, unless the utmost apostasy come. In like manner, when a man hath gathered in his corn out of the field, you would think he had thrown off all his care about it; the fence is broken down, and the beasts come in; it lies in common,—men ride over it, and trample upon it, and he lets it alone: but when the time of culture is come again, the man makes up his fence, drives out the cattle, tills the ground again, and sows it with good seed, that it may bring forth good fruit. So God deals frequently with his church. He dealt so with them here. He takes down the hedge, he suffers the wild beasts to come in,—lets persons spoil at their pleasure; but there will come a time of culture again, when he will have fruit brought forth unto his praise.

In verse 2 the prophet refers the evil he complained of unto two heads:—first, That those who were good were very few; and, secondly, That those who were evil were very bad: "The good man is perished out of the earth, and there is none upright among men; they all lie in wait for blood; they hunt every man his brother with a net." This phrase, "The good man is perished out of the earth," is not that the good man perisheth, but that he is taken away, and the earth hath lost the benefit and advantage which it had by him. The same expression is used, Isa. lvii. 1, "The righteous perisheth, and no man layeth it to heart; and merciful men are taken away;" and Ps. xii. 1, "The godly man ceaseth; the faithful fail from among the children of men."

From hence, therefore, we may observe, that when the good are very few, and the bad are very bad, inevitable destruction lies at the door of that place or nation. If either of these be otherwise, there is yet hope. If there had been but ten good men in Sodom, it had been spared. If the sin of the Amorites had not been come to the full, they had not been ruined. If the good, therefore, are not very few, or the bad very bad, there is yet hope; but where both concur in a professing nation, as in this, which was the visible church of God, unavoidable destruction is at the door; there is neither hope nor recovery: and therefore, they that endeavour to make men good, to increase the number of the good, they do not only endeavour to save their own souls, but they endeavour to save the nation from ruin. And we will place our plea and our cause there,—wherein we are engaged in this world against the world and those that do reproach us,—that our design is to save the nation as far as we are able; for it is to increase the number of the good, to convert men unto God: the consequence of which is to preserve the nation. And it will at last be found, that they who are useful herein, do more for the preservation of the nation than armies or navies can do. But when the prophet says, "The good man perisheth, and there is none upright among men," it is an hyperbolical expression, intimating that there are but few that are either good or upright.

From the description of the other part of men, you may observe two things:—first, The instance of their sin; secondly, The manner of the prosecution of it. The instance of their sin was *blood;* which word comprises all violence, oppression, cruelty, and persecution: and the way of prosecuting this evil is, with much diligence and great endeavours: "They lie in wait for blood; and they hunt every man his brother;" or, as it is expressed, verse 3, "They do evil with both hands earnestly." And where men do lay out all their wisdom, and all their industry and strength in the pursuit of sin, there also destruction lies at the door. When men are slothful, careless, negligent,—sensual in all other things, but industrious only in doing evil,—this is another thing the prophet lays down as a certain sign of approaching destruction.

Having spoken this of the body of the people, he divides them into two parts; the rulers, and the residue of the people: and the rulers he also distributes into three sorts; *the prince, the judge*, and *the great man.* Thus saith he, "The prince asketh, and the judge asketh for a reward; and the great man uttereth his mischievous desire," verse 3. I shall not particularly open these words; but this is what the prophet would teach us,—That when there is, as it were, a conspiracy in all sorts of rulers to commit the same iniquity, and to *wrap up* the whole business by agreement among themselves; so that there is none to intercede, none to stand in the gap, none to do otherwise;—that lies in a tendency to those judgments which he will afterwards declare. And this was the state of affairs at that time: for this prophecy was given in the days of Ahaz; and there was a great agreement and conspiracy among all in power then to oppress, and to carry on their own covetous and "mischievous desires," as they could. They agreed together, and so *wrapped it up.*

In verse 4 he speaks as to the residue of the people. "The best of them," saith he, "is as a brier; the most upright is sharper than a thorn-hedge." The prophet, after he had laid so great a charge upon them, seems to reflect upon some that made a great pretence of friendliness to the Church of God, pretending they would be a hedge, a fence unto it; but saith he, "They prove 'briers and a thorn-hedge.'" "This hypocritical part of the nation, who speak so fair, and make such a mighty appearance of friendship, yet, when a man presses upon them, tear and rend him, and give him nothing but trouble and vexation. Whatever pretences they make, there is nothing to be expected from them but what you would look for from briers and thorns." And I observe, that the prophet, upon this occasion of dealing, with this hypocritical part of the people, doth insert a threatening as though the judgment should fall more upon them than those whose open wickedness he had before described. "Therefore 'the day of thy watchmen and thy visitation cometh;'" that is, the day which the watchmen had so often declared would come upon them, for their false and hypocritical dealing with God: "Now shall be their perplexity." When false professors make a specious pretence to relieve the church, but really neither design nor effect any thing for them but farther vexation and rending,—the day of the watchmen is then at hand.

In the 5th and 6th verses he showeth that this universal corruption that was among the people had extended itself to all sorts of relations,—that there was nothing of confidence left even among relations. "Trust ye not in a friend, put ye not confidence in a guide: keep the doors of thy mouth from her that lieth in thy bosom. For the son dishonoureth the father, the daughter riseth up against her mother, the daughter-in-law against her mother-in-law; a man's enemies are the men of his own house." It is a sign of extreme confusion, when disorder breaks in among relations, and all grounds of confidence between them are taken away. But this place is applied by our Saviour particularly unto the time of persecution for the gospel, Luke xii. 53; Matt. x. 35, 36. There is no wickedness doth so debauch the nature of man, and break off all confidence in the nearest and strongest relations, as an enmity to godliness, and persecution thereon. "When once they are engaged in this, then," saith our Saviour, "it shall be so and so."

This being the state and condition of the people of the land, the prophet makes, in the name of the church, a threefold application of himself:—*First,* To God, verse 7; *Secondly,* To her enemies, verses 8, 10; and *Thirdly,* To himself, verse 9.

First. Upon the prospect of this state and condition, he makes application to God: "Therefore I will look unto the LORD," saith he; "I will wait for the God of my salvation: my God will hear me," verse 7. When all things are in confusion and at a loss, the people of God are not discouraged from looking unto God; yea, they are encouraged thereunto; and it is made necessary for them so to do. And in such a season, not to be looking peculiarly unto God, is an evidence of a heart insensible of the state and condition of the church of God.

Secondly. The prophet, in the name of the church, applies himself unto her enemies: "Rejoice not against me, O mine enemy; when I fall, I shall arise; when I sit in darkness, the LORD shall be a light unto me. Then she that is mine enemy shall see it, and shame shall cover her which said unto me, Where is the LORD thy God? Mine eyes shall behold her; now shall she be trodden down as the mire of the streets," verses 8, 10.

We may observe here,—

1. Who this enemy is: "She that is mine enemy." Some say one thing, some another. Certainly it is some false church; it may be Babylon, or Samaria, or the false professors among themselves. But as Samaria was not yet carried captive, I take it most probably to be the false worshippers of Dan and Bethel, the false church that dwelt in the same land with them. There is no enemy to the true church of God like the false church.

2. Wherein this her enemy did show her enmity. He doth not speak of those enemies that outwardly wasted and destroyed them, but of that enemy which said unto her, "Where is now the LORD thy God?"—that enemy which reproached them with their profession of faith in God, their nearness unto God, and of God's accepting of them; which is the reproach of the false church continually. Others that are open heathens, do not think so much of it; but the false church's reproach usually is, "Where is the LORD thy God?"—"Where are your prayers and waitings upon God? where is your confidence in him?"

3. She intimates that there was some countenance in her present state and condition, through the providence of God, given to the enemy thus to reproach her, "Rejoice not against me, O mine enemy, when I fall." There is a fall that gives countenance to this enemy so to reproach her. But to all these reproaches she opposes her confidence in God: "My God will save me." And she comforts herself that the time was coming when God would certainly destroy this enemy of his church. This enemy; that is, any church of false worshippers who reproach the church of God, under their straits and difficulties, with former trusting and confidence in God.

Thirdly. He applies to himself, personating the church, verse 9, "I will bear the indignation of the LORD, because I have sinned against him," etc. Here is a very becoming frame under the present state of affliction,—a deep humiliation for sin, and a quiet submission to the corrections of God's hand; but, at the same time, here is expressed the firm resolution of faith to wait till God should plead her cause, and execute judgment on her enemies. There seems to be the utmost confidence in this case: "He will bring me forth to the light, and I shall behold his righteousness."

The issue of the whole of this prophecy is, the deliverance of the church, and that restoration which was accomplished in part in the deliverance of this people a long while after out of captivity. "In the day that thy walls are to be built, in that day shall the decree be far removed. In that day also he shall come even to thee from Assyria," etc. All the people that have been scattered about shall be gathered to Zion, to worship God in his temple, verses 11, 12. But when he had said this, he doth, as it were, correct himself. "Ay, but stay; that is not yet to come," verse 13. "Notwithstanding," saith he, "the land shall be desolate, because of them which dwell therein, for the fruit of their doings." As if he had said, "Notwithstanding all this, though God hath thoughts and a purpose of mercy for his own hidden, secret people, yet there is a time when he will by no means turn away the judgments that are due unto the provocations of the generality of professors. God will indeed do all these things for his church in the appointed time; but 'notwithstanding, the land shall be desolate;' there is no avoiding that. The description of things given before is such, that there is no issuing of it but in the desolation of the land, because of the wickedness of them that dwell therein, and for the fruit of their doings."

I have made these short observations upon this part of the chapter, to give you the state of things here represented. The land was full of sin, and of horrible provocations of God amongst all sorts of people, from the highest to the lowest. The people of God secretly complain hereof, and bear it as their burden, and tremble at the thoughts of judgments approaching. God had irrevocably, irrecoverably decreed desolation upon the whole land. Things were so stated, that whatever might be the mercy and goodness of God, and his thoughts towards his people, notwithstanding, the land was to be desolate.

In this state and condition, the prophet puts up this request: "Feed thy people with thy rod, the flock of thine heritage, which dwell solitarily in the wood, in the midst of Carmel: let them feed in Bashan and Gilead, as in the days of old."

The observation I shall make from the words is this:—

Observation. In the most calamitous season, in the greatest inundation of sin and judgment, under the unavoidableness of public judgments, there is yet ground for faith to plead with God for the preservation, safety, and deliverance of his people.

All these things are here laid down:—a calamitous season; an inundation of sin and judgment; and an irrecoverable purpose of God to destroy the land. Yet faith, I say, hath ground in this state and condition to plead with God for the preservation and protection of his own secret people. You will say, "This is no great matter. It may be we have heard arguments that God will preserve them and deliver them; and have heard the time computed when God will deliver them, and could say '*Amen*' to it. But it is to no purpose to go farther in teaching than in endeavours to raise up our faith and believing." I confess I can go no farther than this, that I have ground for duty; and to leave all the rest to God's sovereignty. If God should inevitably decree to destroy this nation, yet we have ground for faith to plead with God for the preservation and deliverance of his own inheritance.

I shall go no farther than the text to prove it; for the opening the text and the proof of the doctrine will be one and the same.

In the words we have,—I. What is prayed for, what the prophet pleads for; and that is, "Feed thy people with thy rod." II. There are the arguments of faith the prophet pleads in this condition, when God had inevitably decreed desolation to the whole land; and these are four:—1. That they were God's people: "Feed thy people." 2. That they were the flock of his heritage: "Feed thy people, the flock of thine heritage." 3. That they "dwelt solitarily in the wood, in the midst of Carmel." 4. That God had, in former days, "fed them in Bashan and Gilead."

I shall briefly handle these things, and both show you what is prayed for, and what in these arguments faith hath to plead in such a condition. For though God may say concerning a nation, "Plead no more for it," yet he never saith so concerning his own people.

I. We shall consider what the prophet here prays for; which is, that God would feed his people with his rod: "Feed thy people with thy rod." God is here compared to a shepherd; and it is a relation that he doth very frequently in Scripture take to himself; and you know what a large field I have to walk in, if I would insist upon the allusion. God is a shepherd, and Christ is a shepherd; therefore he saith, "Feed thy people with thy rod." The word שֵׁבֶט, here used, sometimes is put for a *sceptre*, wherewith kings rule; sometimes for a *staff;* and sometimes for a *rod*. It was the instrument, whatever it was, that shepherds used in those days. It is mentioned, Ps. xxiii., which is a great description of God as a shepherd, "Thy rod and thy staff;" the same word as here. God, as a shepherd, rules his people with a rod; which they used both for direction and correction. He will not strike his sheep with great and violent instruments, to break their bones, to destroy them; but he makes them know he hath a rod in his hand. But I take it, that this rod was principally for the direction of the flock; and he prays that God would "feed them with his rod." Truly, we have reason to consider what is in this word; because I think here is a rule of faith given us what we are to pray for the people of God in such a day as we have described. The great thing we are to pray for now is, that God would "feed them;" not that God would make them kings, and rulers, and great men, and give them the necks of their enemies to tread upon, and such kind of things. "But when things are thus," saith he, "your prayer should be, that God would 'feed them.'" There are three things in this feeding of God's people:—

1. That God would supply their spiritual and temporal wants, that they may be preserved from great distresses. This is in the word, Rev. xii. 6, "The woman fled into the wilderness; and God fed her there." While the woman was in the wilderness, she was preserved with such spiritual and temporal supplies as kept her from destroying distresses. This we may pray for, this we have a rule for, when we fear inevitable desolation is approaching upon a nation. God allows us to pray, and gives us a ground of faith to pray, that for his own

people he would provide spiritual and temporal supplies; so as they may be kept from great distress.

2. There is, in this feeding of them as a shepherd, that God, in that state which is coming upon them, would give them pledges, singular pledges, of his own tenderness and love. It is so said of Christ, under the like comparison, Isa. xl. 11, "He shall feed his flock like a shepherd." How is that? "He shall gather the lambs with his arm, and carry them in his bosom, and shall gently lead those that are with young." We have this in the rule of faith for prayer at this day,—that God would deal with all believers, of all sorts, according to their weakness, and according to their wants; that when the day of visitation and the day of perplexity comes upon the world, Christ, in a way of feeding, would suit himself to every one's condition. Some may be more able to be driven before; others must be carried in his arms and in his bosom. We must pray, therefore, that he will deal with every one of them according to their state and condition.

3. By feeding is intended, rule, protection, deliverance;—present rule, and protection and deliverance in God's appointed time. It is not for a shepherd merely to carry his flock into good pasture; but he is to take care to preserve them from all evil, whereunto they are exposed. David, that great shepherd, who was a type of Christ, gives this account of himself: "Thy servant kept his father's sheep, and there came a lion, and a bear, and took a lamb out of the flock: and I went out after him, and smote him, and delivered it out of his mouth: and when he rose against me, I caught him by his beard, and smote him, and slew him," 1 Sam. xvii. 34, 35. This was part of David's care as a shepherd over his sheep. Feeding is ruling, in the word here used; and chap. v. 4, it manifestly intends rule and protection: "He shall stand and feed," or rule, "in the strength of the LORD, in the majesty of the name of the LORD his God; and they shall abide." It is such a feeding of Christ, in the majesty and in the power of God, as his people shall be preserved by. We have, therefore, in our rule, particularly this comprised, thus far we may go:—necessary supplies of spiritual and temporal, inward and outward mercies; grace and mercy towards all, according as their state and condition doth require; to the weak, diseased, and those that are great with young, protection and powerful deliverance, in God's good time.

This is the first thing,—What it is we have a rule to pray for, even in the most calamitous season, and when inevitable destruction is decreed against a place or nation.

II. Let us now consider the arguments of faith to be pleaded in this case, which our text affords. And these, as I have said, are four.

I would only first observe of these arguments in general, that there is no one of them taken from any thing of worth, of desert, from any thing of good, nay, nor of grace, that is in the people themselves; but they are all taken from God himself, and the relation which they have to God, and what God had formerly done for them. Whatever pleadings or arguings, in such a day, we may have in our own spirits with God for safety and protection, if they are secretly influenced with thoughts that we are good, and better than others, there is nothing of faith in our arguings. God knows, all the graces and fruits of all believers and professors in this nation, considered in themselves, will not make up one argument. But to proceed:—

1. The first argument the prophet here uses is, That they were the people of God: "Feed thy people." They were the people of God upon a threefold account; each of which contains an argument:—

(1.) They are the people of God upon the account of election. Christ commands the apostle to abide preaching the gospel at Corinth with this argument, "I am with thee, and no man shall set on thee to hurt thee; for I have much people in this city," Acts xviii. 10. They were the people of God by election; God had eternally chosen them, and designed them to be converted by the gospel,—by the preaching of his ministry.

Will this afford any argument to plead with God? Yes: Luke xviii. 7, 8, "Shall not God avenge his own elect, which cry day and night unto him, though he tarry long? I tell you, he will avenge them speedily." The argument for vengeance is from his people's being his elect: "Shall he not avenge his elect?" There is something in God's decree of election and choosing his people that may be pleaded with him for the highest part of feeding; which is to avenge them of their enemies.

(2.) They are the people of God by purchase and acquisition. This was the great plea under the Old Testament: "The people of the LORD, whom thou hast redeemed with a high hand, and with a stretched-out arm;"—"whom thou hast taken out of the world, and planted for thyself." He made it his argument to plead with God, because they were his people by purchase and acquisition, "by a high hand, and by an out-stretched arm." And the argument is grown more strong under the gospel, because they are purchased by the blood of his Son. Rom. viii. 32, "If God spared not his own Son, but gave him up to death for us all, how shall he not with him also freely give us all things?" The people we plead for are God's elect people; and he will avenge his elect speedily: they are God's purchased people, and that purchased with the blood of his Son. And will he not together with him give them all things, all necessary things,—all things that pertain to life and godliness? Here is ground for faith to plead with God in such a case.

(3.) They are God's people by covenant. This is that which makes up their relation, which is prepared in election, acquisition, purchase, and redemption. But the formal denomination arises from the covenant: Jer. xxxii. 38–40, "I will make a covenant with them, and they shall be my people, and I will be their God." That completes the relation. Hosea, chap. ii. 23, speaks also to the same purpose.

What arguments arise from hence that they are the covenant people of God? The sum of all arguments that can be pleaded upon that head, and they are great and many, are all laid down, Luke i. 68, etc., "Blessed be the Lord God of Israel; for he hath visited and redeemed his people, and hath raised up an horn of salvation for us," etc.; "as he spake by the mouth of his holy prophets, which have been since the world began: that we should be saved from our enemies, and from the hand of all that hate us; to perform the mercy promised to our fathers, and to remember his holy covenant; the oath which he sware to our father Abraham, that he would grant unto us, that we being delivered out of the hands of our enemies might serve him without fear, in holiness and righteousness, all the days of our life." Here is all we have warrant to pray for,—all that is comprised in God's feeding of us. What is the plea and argument for it?—God will "remember his holy covenant, the oath which he hath sworn," whereby it is established; and hence he will establish us, that we may "serve him without fear, in holiness and righteousness, all the days of our life." A great argument, that those we plead for are God's covenant people! "'Lord, feed thy people,'—those that are thine by election, by acquisition and purchase; and those that are thine by covenant,—a people that have made a covenant with thee."

2. The next argument is, "Because they are 'the flock of thine heritage.'" There are two things in this argument that we may plead with God:—(1.) That they are "a flock;" (2.) That they are "the flock of God's heritage."

(1.) They are "a flock,"—that is, of sheep; wherein these three things are comprised, which are pleadable with God:—[1.] That they are helpless; [2.] Harmless; [3.] Useful. A flock of sheep is so:—

[1.] They are helpless. Sheep are poor, helpless creatures; the more of them there are, the more are they exposed unto all manner of rapine and destruction. When left unto themselves, they are poor, helpless creatures. And, truly, so are the people of God, unless Christ, their shepherd, be with them. They are, and have been, a poor, helpless people throughout the whole world. I confess, when Christ, their shepherd, goes before them, they will go through great difficulties; but of themselves they are altogether helpless.

[2.] They are harmless. So are sheep; and it is required of all the saints of God that they be so likewise, Phil. ii. 15, "Be harmless in the midst of a crooked and perverse generation." Let us do the world no harm, neither public nor private,—do them no wrong nor injury, —that we may have an argument from hence to plead with God.

[3.] Sheep are useful. And I will name three things (though I love not to pursue allegories) wherein the people of God are useful in the world:—1*st.* In the secret blessing that goes along with them; 2*dly.* In the good example they give; 3*dly*, In their industry in the world:—

1*st.* There is a secret blessing goes along with them; as you see here, chap. v. 7 of this prophecy, "The remnant of Jacob shall be in the midst" (or in the bowels) "of many people, as a dew from the LORD, as the showers upon the grass, that tarrieth not for man, nor waiteth for the sons of men." This poor remnant of Jacob, that lies in the bowels of the people, communicates secret blessings to them; this remnant is as the dew that makes them spring. All they have is from this remnant of Jacob in their bowels. But who sees it? "No," saith he, "it is not such a dew; 'it tarrieth not for man.'" None see the secret way whereby the dew falls; nor those secret ways whereby blessings are communicated to the whole nation from this secret remnant of Jacob, that lies in the bowels of them.

2*dly.* They are useful, from the good example they give; walking in the world as becomes creatures made to the glory of God. Tit. iii. 8, "This is a faithful saying, that they which have believed in God might be careful to maintain good works. These things are good and profitable unto men." Not only unto them who are relieved by them, but unto all mankind it is profitable. When professors are diligent and fruitful in good works, all mankind is profited by their example.

3*dly.* They are profitable and useful in the world, by their industry in it. Tit. iii. 14, "Let ours also learn to maintain good works," to profess honest trades, "for necessary uses, that they be not unfruitful;"—useful to the world by their "industry in their honest trades;" the words may be well rendered so, and it is so in the margin of your Bibles. Many others help only to consume the fruits of the earth in luxury and wantonness; but God gives these an industry in their honest callings. Here is argument in this, that this flock is helpless, harmless, fruitful, useful. But,—

(2.) The main of this argument lies upon the adjunct. Saith he, "Feed the flock of thine heritage." This flock is God's *heritage.* Deut. xxxii. 9, "The LORD's portion is his people; Jacob is the lot of his inheritance." Why "the lot of his inheritance"? When the people came to possess the land, it was divided to them all by lot. God hath his lot in the world. That which, if I may so say, is fallen to God's share is this flock; and Christ rejoices in it, Ps. xvi. 5, 6, "The lines are fallen unto me in pleasant places; yea, I have a goodly heritage." His lot was cast in Canaan,—in a good and fruitful place.

Christ takes a view of his church, and is satisfied with it. "I desire no more," saith he; "'the lines are fallen to me in a pleasant place,' this my lot is 'a goodly heritage.'"

And these things may be pleaded from this,—that they are "the flock of God's heritage:"—

[1.] It being God's heritage, if he take not care of it, nobody else will. Every man takes care of his own heritage,—that which belongs to him; and if God take not care of his, there is none else to care for them. It is frequently so expressed, that they are such as none care for. Why? It is not their heritage. It is not the heritage of princes and great men of the world,—of the Turk or the Pope. As, therefore, it is God's heritage, if he will not take care of it, it is in vain to expect it from any other.

[2.] It is the heritage of Him whom the whole world looks upon to be their greatest enemy. The whole world is at enmity against God: and you see the state of things in the world; every one's design is to destroy the heritage of his enemy. As long as the world continues in this enmity against God, its whole design is to destroy his heritage. Look upon the nations abroad in all their agitations;—their main design is to ruin this heritage, because it is God's; against whom they maintain enmity in their hearts, worship, and ways. If, therefore, God doth not take care of his own heritage, it will certainly be destroyed, because his.

[3.] This argument may also be pleaded:—If this flock be the lot of God's heritage, then take it away, and the whole world is hell. If God's lot be out, if this remnant be destroyed; let men make things as fine as they will, adorn their dungeons as much as they please,—it is all but hell.

These are the arguments that may be pleaded with God from this, "Feed thy people," and, "The flock of thy heritage:"—It is a poor, helpless, harmless flock; yet useful to the glory of God, and the good of men. It is God's heritage: if he minds it not, none will; and if it be taken out of the earth, it will presently become a hell. This is the second argument in the text for faith to plead with God.

3. The third argument is taken from their state and condition,—That they "dwell solitarily in the wood, in the midst of Carmel." The first argument pleads God's glory, his love, and faithfulness: "Thy people," in covenant. The second argument pleads God's interest: "The flock of thy heritage." This third argument pleads God's pity and compassion: "Which dwell solitarily in the wood, in the midst of Carmel." Every word hath argument in it to plead with God in this case:—

(1.) They "dwell solitarily;" that is, disconsolately. It is a poor, disconsolate flock that dwells separate from relief. This takes in two things:—inward disconsolation, from themselves, and their own fears and distresses; and outward helplessness. They are where none comes at them to relieve them. It is a great plea,—the solitariness of God's flock, with the compassion and mercy of God, for their relief. It may be, through our peace and plenty, and such things as we enjoy, we are not so sensible of the efficacy of this argument; but the Lord knows, and many of his understand, how strong a plea it is with God upon that account: "We are a poor solitary people; comfortless within, and helpless without."

(2.) As they "dwell solitarily," so "in the wood;" that is, in a dark and entangled condition. They are not only solitary, disconsolate, and helpless, but they are in the dark, see not their way, and so in danger to wander; and if they are out of the certain path, the wild beasts of the forest are ready to devour them. There is nothing harder with the people of God at this day, than that they are in the wood, where it is difficult to find their way. The Lord make them careful, and to see the steps of their Shepherd going before them, that they may not wander, and so be exposed to the wild beasts that are ready to devour them!

(3.) Another plea is from the place where this wood is; it is "in the midst of Carmel." Though there was a particular place so called, yet the word is a common name for a fruitful field for feeding. The country or nation where they lived was such. Some think this hath relation to Babylon, which was very fruitful unto the inhabitants of it; yet the poor remnant dwelt in the wood, in the midst of Carmel. The Jews did so. Nehemiah gives us a most pathetical description of their state, chap. ix. 36, 37, "Behold, we are servants this day; and for the land that thou gavest unto our fathers to eat the fruit thereof, and the good thereof, behold we are servants in it: and it yieldeth much increase unto the kings whom thou hast set over us, because of our sins: also, they have dominion over our bodies, and over our cattle, at their pleasure, and we are in great distress." This people "dwelt in the wood, in the midst of Carmel," a land good and pleasant; yet they were in a distressed condition.

(4.) There is yet another plea in it for mercy: That they are not only solitary for a little season, entered into the wood, but they *dwell* in this solitary condition,—have been long in it, and may continue long so. It signifies an abiding or continuing in that state. This argument, as I told you, respects the pity, the bowels of God, his compassion and tenderness, when his poor people shall dwell and abide long solitary, in an entangled, perplexed condition, as in a wood, in the midst of a fruitful land that God had given their fathers. It is so at this day with many of God's people; and it is a great plea for mercy and compassion.

4. There is one argument more in the words, which I shall but name, and I have done. "Let them feed," saith he, "in Bashan and Gilead, as in the days of old." Bashan and Gilead were places of very fruitful pasture. Whence the children of Reuben and Gad desired Moses that they might have their possession in Gilead, and in the kingdom of Bashan; "Because," say they, "it is a place for cattle, and thy servants have much cattle." It was a fruitful place, where their flocks were well fed and nourished.

Where lies the argument here? It is fetched from former experiences of what God had done,—it is from God's faithfulness, grounded upon former experience. "We have seen what God can do, how he hath brought his people out of straits, and carried them through difficulties, and delivered them out of troubles, and fed them in Bashan, and in the land of Gilead;"—which is made an argument that he would feed them so again.

I might press this argument farther, but I shall offer nothing more at present; and I think what I have said is not unseasonable. We have seen the state of things laid before us;—that we have a rule of faith what to pray for in such a day,—That God would "feed his people." We have showed you what is contained therein, and have gone over briefly those arguments that may be pleaded with God in such a case, reserving the time and season unto his own sovereignty.

SERMON XXIII.[1]

A CHRISTIAN, GOD'S TEMPLE.

"For ye are the temple of the living God; as God hath said, I will dwell in them, and walk in them; and I will be their God, and they shall be my people. Wherefore come out from among them, and be ye separate, saith the Lord, and touch not the unclean thing; and I will receive you, and will be a Father unto you, and ye shall be my sons and daughters, saith the Lord Almighty."—2 Cor. vi. 16–18.

There are three things in these words:—

First. The privilege of believers, especially as they are the church of God: They "are the temple of the living God, as God hath said."

Secondly. The duty which, by virtue of that privilege, is incumbent on all believers: "Wherefore," saith he, "come out from among them, and be ye separate, and touch not the unclean thing."

Thirdly. A promise made unto the due performance of the duty by virtue of that privilege: "And I will receive you, and will be a

[1] This sermon was preached March 27, 1674.

Father unto you, and ye shall be my sons and daughters, saith the Lord Almighty."

You may well think I shall not speak at large to these things. I intend only so far to touch upon them, as just to lead me to what I think is the present sin of this nation, and what are the causes of the judgments upon it.

In verse 16, believers are said to be dedicated, consecrated, and made holy to God, as his peculiar lot and portion. And then the use of it is to show the twofold sin for which judgment cometh upon this nation. The first is, That the nation deals not with them as God's consecrated lot and portion; that is the sin of the nation. The second is, That they behave not themselves as God's consecrated lot and portion; that is the sin of the people of God.

I shall spend some time in confirming my foundation. You have it, with the ground of it, Rev. v. 9, where the church speaks to Christ, "Thou wast slain, and hast redeemed us to God by thy blood out of every kindred, and tongue, and people, and nation; and hast made us unto our God kings and priests." Before the purchase of them by Christ, they lay in the common lot of mankind; they were in the people, and tongues, and kindreds, and nations of the earth. Christ makes a purchase of them. He did not die to redeem all, but to redeem some out of all the kindreds, and nations, and tongues under heaven. Upon Christ's making a purchase of them, they are no more their own. "Ye are bought with a price," saith the apostle; "ye are not your own." Whose, then, are they? They are Christ's, Rom. xiv. 9, "For this cause he both died and rose again, and revived, that he might be Lord both of the dead and living;" that is, of the whole church, alive and dead, that they might be his. He took them all into his disposal. And what did he do with them? When they were absolutely his own, and in his power to dispose of them as he saw good, he dedicates them to God. "He makes us kings and priests unto God," saith he. Christ might have disposed of his purchase another way; but this course he took,—he dedicates them unto God. Kings and priests were so, as I shall show you afterward. The apostle Peter tells us the same of all believers, 1 Pet. ii. 9, "But ye are a chosen generation, a royal priesthood, an holy nation, a peculiar" or purchased "people." The same is expressed again, Tit. ii. 14, and in sundry other places, which I shall not insist upon. But there is one expression of it which must be taken notice of; and that is, where they are called the "first-fruits unto God," James i. 18, "Of his own will begat he us with the word of truth, that we should be a kind of first-fruits of his creatures." And Rev. xiv. the expression occurs again,[1] "These are they which were not

[1] In the original edition the words are, "he expresses it again." As these

defiled with women, ... being the first-fruits unto God." When God gave and sanctified all things unto his church of old, he reserved the first-fruits unto himself. These were all to be dedicated to him, every one in his way whereof he was capable;—clean beasts by sacrifice; men by redemption; corn and wine by a meat-offering: but God retained all the first-fruits to himself. He laid it upon the land as a rent-charge, that he might keep up his title to the whole. So he tells them, Lev. xxv. 23, "The land is mine," saith he, "and ye are but strangers and sojourners with me." All the concernments of the Church of God are God's. He entertains us in his house, at his table, and sustains us with his ordinances. God took the first-fruits as an acknowledgment that they held all from him; and when he would take them no more, he destroyed the land.

Now God takes believers, that they may be a kind of first-fruits unto himself of the creatures. He satisfies himself with believers throughout the world, to be first-fruits of the whole creation. And if God should cease from taking these first-fruits, he would destroy the world. To what end should he maintain this fabric at such an expense of power, patience, forbearance, goodness, wisdom, if there came no revenue to him? Now, he never took any revenue but the first-fruits. And if any one (as I shall afterward show) do put forth his hands to this portion of God, he will be sure sorely to revenge it. For the most part this is the state of things among worldly men,—the more they have, the readier they are to lay their hands upon the portion of others. But I am sure the more men have throughout the world, the readier they are to lay their hands upon the portion of God. But saith he, Jer. ii. 3, "Israel was holiness unto the LORD, and the first-fruits of his increase: all that devour him shall offend; evil shall come upon them, saith the LORD;"—they shall contract guilt, and they shall have punishment fall upon them. "All that devour them shall offend." If that were all, they would not much care for it;—but, "Evil shall come upon them, saith the LORD."

Let us a little inquire how believers come to be dedicated, consecrated, and made holy unto God,—to be his temple, tabernacle, first-fruits, his lot and portion, as they are called.

Why, this notion is taken from the Old Testament, and it is spoken of in allusion to what was in use then, when both persons and things were dedicated to God.

By what way, then, were things dedicated and consecrated to God, made his portion, and became holy?

words are very ambiguous, and seemingly ascribe the language quoted from the Revelation of John to the apostle James, mentioned in the preceding sentence, we have ventured, in this instance, on a slight alteration of the text.—ED.

There were four ways whereby this was done:—I. By special call and legal constitution. II. By unction. III. By inhabitation. And, IV. By vow, and actual separation thereupon.

There is no other way whereby any thing was ever dedicated to God under the Old Testament. And we shall find [that] all these ways believers are dedicated and consecrated unto God.

I. There was a dedication to God by special call and law constitution. So Aaron was dedicated to God to be a priest, Exod. xxviii. 1, "Take to thee Aaron, and his sons with him, from among the children of Israel, that he may minister unto me in the priest's office." What was this? "No man," saith our apostle, "takes this honour to himself, unless called of God, as was Aaron." Aaron was called of God to be dedicated a peculiar priest unto him. And this was confirmed by the law of the priesthood. He "was made a priest after the law of a carnal commandment," saith he. And, Numb. i. 50, God took the Levites to the service of the tabernacle, whereby they became his portion; and, chap. iii. 3, 4, they are separated upon God's call.

This, then, is the first way whereby God takes any thing unto himself, and by which any one is separated and dedicated unto God;—it is by a solemn call, and legal constitution thereupon.

II. The second way whereby any thing was dedicated unto God, was by unction. So Aaron, after his call, to complete his dedication, chap. xxix., was anointed in his consecration; and so were his sons. In like manner Elisha was anointed to be a prophet in the room of Elijah; and David was anointed to be king over Israel. It was the great consummating ordinance whereby any were dedicated unto God. In Exod. xxx. 22, etc., you have the institution of the making of this oil. "Ye shall not," says God, "make any other like it, after the composition of it: it is holy, and it shall be holy unto you. Whosoever compoundeth any like it, shall be cut off from his people, or putteth any of it upon any stranger." What is the meaning hereof? Why, this anointing oil, wherewith the priests and all the holy utensils of the altar were anointed, was a type of the graces and gifts of the Spirit of God. And where God hath given the gifts and graces of his Spirit for holy ministrations,—for praying, for preaching the word, for administering the ordinances,—for any one to make an oil like it, by liturgies, homilies, and the like, is to act contrary to this command. All that is done in the whole liturgical, ceremonial course, is nothing but to make an oil like the oil God hath made for his sanctuary, which he doth so severely prohibit any man to put his hand unto; for this reason, because it was a type of the gifts and graces of the Holy Ghost that were to be poured out upon Christ, and believers under him.

This is the second way whereby any thing was consecrated unto God.

III. The third way whereby the temple (as believers are peculiarly said to be "God's temple," in the text and other places) and tabernacle were consecrated, was by inhabitation. God consecrated them unto himself by a glorious inhabitation, and dwelling in them. He came and dwelt in them. Thereby they became peculiarly his own. And this God did two ways:—1. By an extraordinary sign of taking first possession of his house, and entering into it, that all might take notice that this was his house. 2. By ordinary constant pledges of his presence:—

1. He did it by an extraordinary sign of his taking possession of his house. When the tabernacle was built, and ready to be set apart for service, the glory of the Lord filled it, Exod. xl. It was a dark cloud; for then God dwelt in thick darkness. And, 1 Kings viii. 10, when the temple was built, God came by a glorious sign, and took possession of it. The glory of the Lord filled the temple. And this also was a cloud. God took possession of those houses—the tabernacle and the temple—by a cloud, to signify those types and vails which the people were under, so that they could not see to the end of those houses; which were to denote the coming of the Son of God to fix his tabernacle among us, by taking human nature upon him.

2. God did it by a visible pledge of his abode and residence. Now, this was the ark, and the mercy-seat, encompassed with the cherubims, which had the direct form of a throne. The ark being supported to such a height, the mercy-seat placed upon that, and the cherubims shading it as arms, had the direct appearance of a throne. Hence the ark is sometimes called "The glory of God." It is called "The King of glory," Ps. xxiv., "Lift up your heads, ye everlasting doors, that the King of glory"—that is, the glorious ark, which was the type and representation of God's dwelling gloriously in the tabernacle and temple—"may come in." There are these two things required to inhabitation:—a glorious entrance by an extraordinary sign; and, a constant residence by an ordinary pledge: and both these were in the dedication of the temple and tabernacle. And two things ensued thereon:—

(1.) A special manifestation of God's glory. Where he dwells, there is a special manifestation of his glory. God is everywhere; but is not said to dwell everywhere. He fills heaven and earth by his omnipresence; but God's "dwelling" signifies something more;—not only his being, his essential, eternal being, but the manifestation of that being also. So, heaven is said to be his dwelling-place and throne, because God doth most gloriously manifest himself to those creatures of light, his holy saints and angels, that come to the enjoyment of him. In the tabernacle, and in the temple, there was such a manifestation of God's glorious presence continually. This made them holy. And hence it is, that if all the men in this world should agree together to build a glorious fabric for the worship of God,—suppose at Jerusalem,—and when they had done, dedicate it to God with all the power they have; they cannot make it holy, unless God come to take possession of it by a visible pledge of his presence, and appoint a token of his presence to be in the place. The very notion that some men have, though you may think there is little in it, that they can dedicate any thing to God, hath been the greatest ruin that ever befell religion in this world. It hath wholly cast out all apprehensions of God's portion from the minds of men, and erected another portion for God, which was never called, never anointed, never inhabited by God himself. And that hath occasioned men, who contract the guilt of persecuting God's only dedicated portion, to put the notion of sacrilege upon tithes and titles, and I know not what, that God never dedicated, nor put his name upon, nor ever took possession of. There is no dedication to God, but it must be by these means. And,—

(2.) The special worship of God must by God himself be confined unto it. And truly we have great reason—considering what conflicts and contests are befallen us in these latter days, which only divine wisdom could foresee—to bless our dear Lord Jesus Christ for that good word of liberty he gave us: "The day cometh that neither at Jerusalem, nor in this nor that mountain, men shall worship God; but he that worships God, let him worship him in spirit and in truth." This sets us at liberty from all ways, places, and forms of men's finding out and dedication.

That is the third way.

IV. There is one way more; and that is, by special vow of things that are in our power, giving them up to God according to his mind. So did Jacob, Gen. xxviii. 22, "Of all that thou shalt give me, I will surely give the tenth unto thee." Men are usually very tenacious of what they have got; they are loath to part with any portion of it,—no, not to God himself; therefore doth Jacob so well express it here, "Of all that thou shalt give me, I will give the tithe to thee." If ever Jacob had any thing God did not give him, that was all his own: and so he knew full well; for when he comes to call over this business again, he remembers, that "with his staff he went over Jordan, but God had now made him two bands." When men gave to God according to his mind, of things in their own power, they were, under the law, made holy unto the Lord.

Now, I say, believers are dedicated, consecrated to God, and become his portion by all these several ways:—

First. They are so by calling,—which was the first way; God calls them out of the world to be a peculiar portion unto himself, Rom. i. 7. They are "called to be saints," and separated unto God. So likewise, 1 Cor. i. 2. Now, though this calling doth also imply effectual internal vocation, whereby the heart and nature is really sanctified; yet it also includes an external separation and dedication unto God. Christ redeems us out of the world, and he calls us out of the world. An obediential compliance with that call of God for separation from the world makes us to be God's dedicated portion. "Come out from among them, and be separate," saith God. If we live in the world after the manner of the world,—if we are like the world in our ways and walk, in our affections and conversation,—we have no reason to look upon ourselves as the dedicated portion of God. He that is so, brethren, that is thus called to be God's, he endures the world, and doth his own duty in it; and that is all his concern;—I say, he endures the world. That which is the world, and properly so, hath nothing pleasing to him; only, he doth his own duty in it. If we intend to be at all interested in this great privilege here, let us secure ourselves that we are God's portion by calling,—that we have complied with his call to separate ourselves from the world. The people of God dwelt alone of old, and were not reckoned amongst the nations. Our mixtures in the world, our conformity to the world, our touching of the unclean thing, is the sin of professors at this day; whereby they are concerned in procuring all the judgments that God is pouring out upon the land.

Secondly. Believers are made God's peculiar portion, and are dedicated to him by unction. I will first show that they are anointed, and then how they are anointed:—

1. The apostle says, 2 Cor. i. 21, "He which stablisheth us with you in Christ, and hath anointed us, is God." And you know that place, 1 John ii. 20, 27, "Ye have an unction from the Holy One; and the anointing which ye received of him abideth in you." It is plain, therefore, that believers are anointed. God in his providence did suffer that name to go upon us, that we should be called Christians; which is in English, "Anointed ones." That is the name of God's people in the world. How well we answer that name, many of us may do well to consider.

2. We cannot know how we were anointed, how we became Christians, but by considering how our Head was anointed,—how Jesus became Christ. Christ was anointed, Isa. lxi. 1, "The Spirit of the Lord GOD is upon me; because the LORD hath anointed me." Heb. i. 9, "God, even thy God, hath anointed thee with the oil of gladness above thy fellows." Wherein consisted the unction of the Messiah, the anointing of the Most Holy? which was prophesied of, Dan. ix. 24. How did Jesus become Christ? Truly, I have elsewhere so largely

insisted upon the communication of the Spirit of God to the human nature of Christ,—how, and for what end,—that I shall not here speak to it again. In a word, it was the gift of the Spirit of God, with his gifts and graces, in an immeasurable manner, to the human nature of Christ: "For God giveth not the Spirit by measure unto him," John iii. 34. So he is, therefore, said to be "anointed with the oil of gladness above his fellows." How to his fellows? Eph. iv. 7, "To every one of us is given grace according to the measure of the gift of Christ." All believers have their measure. He had no measure. This anointing consists in the communication of the graces and gifts of the Holy Ghost to all believers. This is our unction,—thence we are called Christians. And those who despise the Spirit of God, and his graces and gifts, will find little relief in calling themselves Christians another day.

But how doth this anointing dedicate believers unto God? It doth it two ways:—

(1.) It gives a peculiar interest unto God in them, which is not in any others. Where there are the gifts and graces of the Spirit of God, there God hath something that is not in any part of the world beside. It is, indeed, the way whereby God takes possession of any soul; he comes and deposits this treasure there. "There is my treasure," saith God: "I lay it up there; and thereby I take possession of this soul to be mine."

(2.) Every thing dedicated to God was to be employed in the service of God. And this anointing makes us able to serve God according to his mind and will, when we can do so no otherwise. There is no serving of God without the graces and gifts of the Holy Ghost. God abhors all service proceeding from any thing else.

Thirdly. By inhabitation. The Spirit of God dwells in believers. I must say of this also, as I did of what went before,—I have shown so at large how the Spirit of God dwells in and inhabits in believers, and how they are his temple and tabernacle, that I shall not speak more to it now; but only apply to the case of believers what was said before,—that wherever God inhabits, he first takes possession in a cloud, and dwells in a visible pledge of his presence.

1. When God converts a soul, he comes into it with a cloud. I know nothing in this world that I would be more jealous of in my ministry, than of speaking any thing, on conversion or regeneration, that I had not experience of myself. I would not bind others by any experience of my own, unless it be confirmed by a general rule; for one man may have an experience that another hath not: and we ought to be wonderful tender in giving out any thing that should be found in persons, as to conversion and regeneration, if we have not a general rule for it as well as our own experience. But yet I think this I

can say, that God generally takes possession of souls in a cloud; that is, there is some darkness upon them: they cannot tell what their state is;—sometimes they have hopes, and sometimes fears; sometimes they think things are well, and sometimes they are cast down again. This is the way whereby God generally enters into all souls. These things may be in part where God doth not come; but seldom have I heard of any that have come unto God, but that God first took possession of them in a cloud.

2. God doth it by some visible pledge of his presence, when the cloud is over; for the cloud is but for a season, though it may continue upon some longer than upon others. I have shown before, that the pledge of God's visible presence in the temple and tabernacle was the ark and the mercy-seat, formed into the fashion of a throne with cherubims; which was a type of Jesus Christ. The ark had the law, and the mercy-seat was propitiatory, covering the law from the eye of justice; and so atonement was made. And this was a type of Christ.

How, then, doth God dwell in the hearts of believers by constant residence? When Christ is enthroned in the heart: and we can have no farther pledge of it. There may be a great deal of duty, careful and wary walking, and a great deal of profession; but if Christ be not upon the throne in the heart, there is no pledge of God's dwelling there. So God dedicates his people by inhabitation.

Fourthly. The last way whereby any thing was dedicated unto God was, by vow and covenant. Now, we are all of us under a two-fold dedication to God,—by vow and covenant: the one in general, whereof the token is baptism; and we are likewise under a particular vow and dedication as we are a church. What, I pray, is our engagement to walk with God in professed subjection to all the ordinances of Christ, but to give up ourselves to God by vow and covenant to be his, by a dedication of ourselves according to God's appointment and mind? God help us to look unto it, every one of us in our several places and stations;—there is more in these things than we are aware of.

Now, as there was never any other way whereby any thing could be dedicated to God, and believers being all these ways dedicated unto him, they become his peculiar portion. "They shall be mine," saith God. They are God's kings, priests, tabernacle, temple, sacrifice: "Yield your bodies a living sacrifice." And they are God's first-fruits, called so expressly.

There are two uses follow necessarily from hence:—

Use 1. If believers, especially as they are in church relation, which adds the last hand of dedication, by particular church vow and covenant to be God's; if believers, I say, are thus God's peculiar portion, dedicated unto him, it is not in my power to give warning unto the world to take heed how they meddle with this portion of God. They do not, they will not hear me; and if I could speak unto them, it would rather provoke them than cure them. But give me leave to say this, and to give glory and honour unto God therein, that among all the sins that so reign in the nation at this day, and have done so for a long season, that which hath peculiarly stirred up the displeasure of God against the nation,—so as to threaten us with spiritual judgments (the giving us up to Popery, which men are afraid of), and with temporal judgments of all sorts whatever,—hath been the violence that hath been done to God's portion all this nation over. Other sins are great and provoking, but God hath given the earth to the children of men. "He endures with much long-suffering the vessels of wrath, fitted for destruction." He will bear with men in all their abominations, leave them for many ages, in many places of the world, to sport themselves in the earth, like the leviathan in the waters; but when a nation comes (as it hath been the sin of this whole nation, from one end to the other) to put forth its hand against God's portion, tearing, rending, destroying, imprisoning, banishing, starving the remainder of God's heritage,—it is the cause (let it be spoke to the glory of God, and that which God will own at the last day) why wrath is gone out against us. This hath not been done in a corner, by some few, at some certain time. We have known the day when the whole nation, as one man, was on fire to consume the residue of God's heritage; it was the sin of the nation, from one end of it unto the other. Saith God, "All that devour her shall offend; evil shall come upon them." There hath been a great devouring of God's first-fruits; and truly in such a manner, that we have no greater cause to mourn this day, than that we have not been sensible of it as we ought to be, how these first-fruits of God have been devoured. But they shall offend, and evil shall come upon them. It is the very word that God speaks to the nation this day, if I understand any thing of the will of God in these matters. He speaks so again, Jer. xii. 14, "Thus saith the LORD against all mine evil neighbours, that touch the inheritance which I have caused my people Israel to inherit; Behold, I will pluck them out of their land, and pluck out the house of Judah from among them." What is the inheritance God hath caused us to inherit? It is his ordinances, his ways and worship; it is not the great things of this world. Let all take their portion and lot, as God in his providence directs. The inheritance which God causeth Israel to inherit, is his ways and worship, the purity of his ordinances, and their serving Christ in them. This is our inheritance. Saith God, "I will pluck up my evil neighbours, that will not leave my inheritance."—"Let them take what is their own; but they will not leave my inheritance."

That generation of vipers, those evil neighbours of God's inheritance everywhere, that have been devouring it, and taking of it away, their doom is read in the prophet, and will come upon them in God's appointed time. The great sin that is upon the nation, and which we ought to bewail, and be humbled for, is the violence they have done to God's portion. It hath not been done by this and that person;—no man hath cared for Zion, none hath pitied her; there have been none to plead her cause, none to relieve her, while her friends have died in prisons, been impoverished, banished, etc.

Use 2. There are sins with us, even with us also, against the Lord our God. And our great sin is this,—that notwithstanding all the violence that hath been showed us, all the fears, troubles, perplexities that we have undergone, yet we have not been willing to come out from among them, and be separate, but we have cleaved greatly to the unclean thing. There may be a time, and there hath been, when God calls his people to a local separation. So he did to his people in Babylon: "Come out of her, my people." And we can remember the day when God carried many of his people out of this nation into a wilderness, and there hid them for a season. They were under the call of God to a local separation. I see no ground for that now. God binds men down by his providence to their stations; relation and duty bind them down to bear a testimony to the ways of Christ against all those wicked oppositions that are made unto them. But to separate more in the holiness of our lives and conversations, to keep more from the uncleanness and vanities of the world, all the abominations of it;—God's call is upon us all for this. These two things being thus met together,—namely, violence upon the portion of Christ, upon God's separate ones; and neglect of duty in those separate ones, to separate themselves more and more from the world—who can save? who can deliver? and what can be our expectation while this frame doth abide? I wish I had a little more time to press this upon us, that if we intend to be made partakers of the last thing in my text,—which is the promise that God will "receive us, and be a Father to us," and use us as his sons and daughters,—if we would be made partakers of it, when an apprehension of an interest in it will be worth ten thousand times more than all this world can afford; then let us stir up ourselves to this great duty of farther and daily separation from the world in things moral and spiritual, in our minds, in our spirits, in our ways, in our whole course; that if it be the will of God, there may be some interposition for the saving of the land.

SERMON XXIV.[1]

GOD'S WITHDRAWING HIS PRESENCE, THE CORRECTION OF HIS CHURCH.

"O LORD, why hast thou made us to err from thy ways, and hardened our heart from thy fear? Return for thy servants' sake, the tribes of thine inheritance."—ISA. lxiii. 17.

THESE are words that carry a great deal of dread in them;—tremendous words, methinks, as any in the book of God. And, according as our concernment shall be found in them, they require very sad thoughts of heart. It is come now to the last; this is the last cast; if we miss in pursuing this great inquiry, we are undone for ever: "O LORD, why hast thou caused us to err from thy ways? why hast thou hardened our hearts from thy fear?" God is in this matter, whereof we have been complaining.

It is the true church of God that speaks these words. This is plain in the acting of faith as to the great interest and privilege of adoption, in the verse foregoing, where they say, "Doubtless thou art our Father;"—"However things are with us, 'doubtless thou art our Father.'" When all other evidences fail, faith will secretly maintain the soul with a persuasion of its relation unto God; as you see by the church in this place. They were "all as an unclean thing;" and their "holiness all faded away as a leaf," Isa. lxiv. 6. And yet faith maintains a sense of a relation to God; and therefore they cry, "Doubtless thou art our Father, though Abraham be ignorant of us, and Israel acknowledge us not: O LORD, thou art our Father, our Redeemer; thy name is from everlasting." And I am persuaded some of you have found it so,—that faith hath maintained an interest in a relation to God, when all particular evidences have failed. So it is in our head, Jesus Christ, when he cried, "My God, my God, why hast thou forsaken me?" When all particular evidences fail, he can still say, "My God, my God." So is it here with this miserable and distressed church and people of God;—all is lost and gone, and yet faith cries, "Doubtless thou art our Father." And if, in the matters of this day,

[1] This sermon was preached on a solemn day of fasting and prayer, March 21, 1675. For which occasion the Doctor had prepared another discourse; but by a special reason which then occurred, had his thoughts directed to this subject. [Such is the note appended to the sermon in the edition of 1721. It is to be regretted that it is not more full and explicit. We have not been able to discover what the circumstances were to which it makes allusion. Owen seems to have been unwell when the discourse was preached. See page 298.—ED.]

God would help us to maintain and not let go our interest in him as our Father, by faith, we should have a bottom and foundation to stand upon. If it be so with us as hath been confessed to God (and I fear it is worse), we shall be at a loss for our particular evidences, at one time or other; but yet it will be a great advantage, when faith can maintain its station, and we be enabled to say, "'Though Abraham be ignorant of us, and Israel will not own us,' such vile creatures; and though 'our righteousnesses are as filthy rags,' and our holiness 'fadeth away as a leaf,' and our adversaries have trodden upon us; 'yet doubtless thou art our Father.'" The Lord help us to say thus when we depart, and we shall yet have a foundation of hope.

I would observe here the condition of the church at that time. It was a state of affliction and *oppression;*—of *oppression* on the one hand, and of deep *conviction* of sin on the other. It is well when they go together.

First. It was a time of distress and *oppression;* as is declared, verse 18, "Our adversaries have trodden down thy sanctuary." The adversary had grievously oppressed them; but that which the church was most concerned in was, that they had trodden down the sanctuary,—disturbed the holy assemblies, and broken up the worship of God. And it is well, brethren, if, under all oppression and distresses that may befall us, we do really find our principal concern is for the treading down God's sanctuary. Whatever else lay upon them, this was that they complained of: "Our adversaries have trodden down thy sanctuary."

Secondly. It was also a time of deep *conviction* of sin with them. As the prayer is continued unto the end of the next chapter, you may see what a deep conviction of sin was fallen upon them, in verses 6, 7, "Behold, we are all as an unclean thing, and all our righteousnesses are as filthy rags; we all do fade as a leaf; and our iniquities, like the wind, have taken us away. And there is none that calleth upon thy name, that stirreth up himself to take hold of thee: for thou hast hid thy face from us, and melted us down, because of our iniquities."

Well, then, suppose it be a state of great oppression, and a state of great conviction of sin, what is the course that we should take? We may turn ourselves this way and that way; but the church, you see, is come to this,—to issue all in an inquiry after, and a sense of, God's displeasure, manifesting itself by spiritual judgments. And this, in truth, brethren, if I understand any thing of the state and condition of my own soul and yours, and of the generality of the churches of God in the world, is that which we are in particular called to, and where we are to issue all this business,—namely, to inquire into God's displeasure, and the reason of it, manifesting itself in spiritual judgments. "O LORD, why hast thou caused us to err from thy ways? and why hast thou hardened our hearts from thy fear?"

It is but a little I shall speak to you at this time; God, I hope, will give us other seasons to pursue the same design: my present distemper, and other occasions, will not suffer me now to enlarge. However, I will lay a foundation, if God help me, by opening the words unto you:—I. What is it to err from the ways of God? II. What is it to have our hearts hardened from the fear of God? III. What ways are there whereby God may cause us to err from his ways, and harden our hearts from his fear? IV. What may be the reasons why the Lord should deal thus severely with a poor people, after they have walked with him, it may be, many years,—that at length they should be brought to this complaint, "LORD, why hast thou caused us to err from thy ways, and hardened our hearts from thy fear?" And then, V. What is to be done for relief in this condition? what course is to be taken?

These are the things that should be first spoken to from the text; and then we should come to the last clause: "Return for thy servants' sake," etc. I shall proceed as far as I am able:—

I. What is it to err from the ways of God?

The ways of God are either God's ways towards us, or our ways towards him, that are of his appointment. God's ways towards us, are the ways of his providence: our ways towards God, are the ways of obedience and holiness. We may err in both.

I think in that place of the Hebrews, "They have always erred in heart, and have not known my ways," God principally intends his ways towards them; they did not know the ways of his providential workings, how mightily he had wrought for them. But the ways that God hath appointed for us to walk in towards him, are those here intended. Now, we may err from thence two ways:—1. In the inward principle. 2. In the outward order:—

1. We may err in the inward principle. When the principle of spiritual life in our hearts decays, when we "fade as a leaf," and wither, then is this our case.

2. We err as to outward order, when we fail in the performance of duty in our walking, and in the course of our obedience and holiness that God hath called us unto. These for the most part go together; but from the text, and the whole context, I judge the first here to be principally intended;—a failing in the principle, in our hearts, and in a lively power of walking in the ways of God, and of living unto him. So that to err from the ways of God is to have our hearts weakened, spiritually disenabled, often turned aside from the vigorous, effectual, powerful walking with God, which we are called unto.

II. What is it to have our hearts hardened from the fear of God?

There is a twofold hardening from God's fear:—1. There is a total hardening; and, 2. A partial hardening:—

1. There is a total hardening, like that mentioned, Isa. vi. 10, "Make the heart of this people fat, and make their ears heavy, and shut their eyes; lest they see with their eyes, and hear with their ears, and understand with their heart, and convert, and be healed." This was a total hardening that came upon the Jews when they rejected Christ. That is not the hardening here intended. Those that are given up to a total hardness will not thus humble themselves before God, nor plead with God. Blessed be God that he hath not given us up to a total hardening, that we should utterly and wickedly depart from his ways!

2. There is a partial hardening mentioned by the apostle, Heb. iii. 13, "Take heed, 'lest any of you be hardened through the deceitfulness of sin;' lest there come a hardness upon you that may be to your disadvantage." And it is this partial hardening that is here intended; and wherein it consists I shall speak a little afterward. It is this partial hardening that is intended in the text: "Thou hast hardened our hearts from thy fear."

III. How is God said to cause us to err from his ways, and to harden our hearts from his fear?

God is said to do it these several ways:—

1. God is said to do that (and it is not an uncommon form of speech in Scripture) whose contrary he doth not do, when it might be expected, as it were, from him. "If there be a prophet that doth prophesy so and so, 'I the Lord have deceived that prophet,'" Ezek. xiv. 9; that is, "I have not kept him from being deceived, but suffered him to follow the imaginations of his own heart, whereby he should be deceived." God may be said to cause us to err from his ways, and to harden our hearts from his fear merely negatively,—in that he hath not kept us up to his ways, nor kept our hearts humble and soft in them.

2. Again; God hardens men judicially, in a way of punishment. This is a total hardening; of which we spoke before. And there are these acts of it, which, I think, are as evident in the times wherein we live as the judgments of God have been in the plague, or burning of the city, inundations, or any thing else. Spiritual judgments of God, in hardening the hearts of men judicially and penally to their destruction, are as visible to every considering person as any of God's outward judgments whatsoever. This will appear if we consider the following things, wherein it consists:—

(1.) The first thing God doth, when he hardens men's hearts penally, is, to give them up to their own lusts. It is directly expressed, Rom. i. 24, "Wherefore God gave them up to their hearts' lusts."

When God leaves men, and gives them up to pursue their own lusts with delight and greediness, then he is hardening them. And this is a visible judgment of God at this day: he takes off shame, fear, all restraint and disadvantages, and gives men up to their hearts' lusts.

(2.) The second thing is, that God, in penal hardening, gives men up to Satan, to blind them, darken them, harden them; for he is "the god of this world, that blinds the eyes of men," and the great work of blinding and hardening men is committed unto him. And the principal way whereby he works at this day, is by being a lying spirit in the mouth of the false prophets, crying, "Peace, peace," when God hath not spoken a word of peace: as it was in the business of Ahab; when Satan went and catched at a commission to seduce Ahab to go up to Ramoth-gilead, he did it by being a lying spirit in the mouths of the false prophets. God is visibly at work in the world with this judgment, giving men up unto Satan, acting in the mouths of the false prophets, who cry, "Peace, peace," to all sorts of sinners, when God speaks not one word of peace.

(3.) The third way whereby God doth judicially give up men to hardness of heart is, by supplying them in his providence with opportunities to draw out their lusts. They shall have opportunity for them. It is commonly given for one of the darkest dispensations of divine providence towards men, when it orders things so that they shall have opportunities, to accomplish their lusts and go on in their ways, administered unto them.

(4.) Lastly; in pursuit of all these, God gives them over to a "reprobate mind," Rom. i.; that is, a mind that can neither judge nor approve of any thing that is good. Propose to men the most convincing things wherein their own interest and concern lies; show them that eternal ruin lies at the door;—it is all one; they having a mind that can judge of nothing that is good. And the world is full of evidences of this work of God.

3. God may be said to cause men to err from his ways, and to harden their hearts from his fear, by withholding, upon their provocation, some such supply of his Spirit and actings of his grace as they have formerly enjoyed, to keep up their hearts to the ways and in the fear of God. And that is the hardening here intended. The Lord had withheld, upon just provocations, those supplies of his grace and Spirit which formerly were enjoyed, and which had given them a vigorous spirit in the ways of God, and a tender heart in the fear of God, which now they have lost, or else they could never have been sensible of it.

From what has been said, we may make the following observations:—

Observation 1. Even true believers themselves may for a season so err from the ways of God as to have their hearts partially hardened from his fear; and may fall under this state and condition, to err from the ways of God, by a decay of the principle of grace: and so as to have their hearts hardened from his fear, that they know not where they are, what they are doing, how it is with them, which way to look for relief to supply themselves, or how to recover strength or heal themselves; but are forced to cry, "O LORD, why hast thou caused us to err from thy ways, and hardened our hearts from thy fear?"

Obs. 2. God himself hath a righteous hand in this frame of spirit that sometimes befalls believers.

Obs. 3. This frame is the most deplorable condition that can befall the Church of God at any time; which is manifest upon these two accounts,—that it both takes away all solid evidences of God's special love, and inevitably exposes us to outward distresses and ruin, if it be not remedied. And therefore it is a most deplorable condition, to be brought into such a state.

Let us now a little inquire, as we before proposed, what it is to have our hearts hardened thus partially from the fear of God.

The fear of God may be considered in several respects:—as it regards sin, and so is a fear of caution and humility; or as it regards judgments, and so is a fear of reverence, wisdom, and diligence to improve them; or, lastly, as it regards duty, and so becomes a fear of obedience and watchfulness. Now, the want of a due sense of sin, of judgments, or of a due attendance unto duties, is this partial hardening.

(1.) A partial hardening consists in the want of a due sense of sin. It is the fear of God alone that can give us a due sense of sin. Judgments will give dread, and convictions disquiet; but it is the fear of God alone that gives a due sense of sin. Therefore, when we want this, our hearts are in some measure hardened from the fear of God; which discovers itself in the following particulars:—[1.] A want of a due sense of secret sins; [2.] A want of a due sense of sin in an uncircumspect walking; [3.] A want of a due sense of surprisal into known sins; [4.] A want of a due sense of the sins of others. Where these things are, there is hardening from the fear of God.

[1.] This hardening consists in a want of a due sense of secret sins. And there is much in this. I shall but just name things unto you. The psalmist lays great weight on it, Ps. xix. 12, 13, "Cleanse thou me from secret faults;" also, "Keep back thy servant from presumptuous sins." In these two lie the life of a believer. And there is no more safety, if we are not cleansed from secret sins, than if we are not kept back from presumptuous sins. Every one will conclude, if they are not kept back from presumptuous sins, they are undone for ever; but the danger is the same if they are not cleansed and have not a due sense of secret sins.

If it be asked, "What are these secret sins?"—1*st.* They are the vain imaginations of the mind; 2*dly.* The corrupt actings of the affections of the heart; and, 3*dly.* A frame of soul suited unto them. These are the things I intend by secret sins:—

1*st.* The vain imaginations of the mind. The Holy Ghost tells us that by nature "all the imaginations of the heart of man are evil, and that continually." And God knows what remainders there are of this vanity of mind, and these vain imaginations, in all our hearts. I place it at the head of what I intend; whereof if we have not a due sense, we are under hardening from the fear of God. These vain imaginations of our mind are such as no eye sees, none knows, not the angels in heaven nor the devils; but are the special object of the eye, and sight, and knowledge of God.

2*dly.* The corrupt actings and desires of our affections, wherein lust conceiveth. Lust tempts and seduces in vain imaginations, but conceiveth in the corrupt desires and actings of our affections.

3*dly.* And both these, if indulged in any measure, will be continually pressing upon our nature;—both the vain imaginations of the mind, and the corrupt actings of the affections towards perishing, worldly, sensual things,—either to lawful objects in an undue manner, or to unlawful objects,—will both be pressing on the mind; and if, by solicitation, they take place upon it, then the mind is cast into a dead, lifeless, carnal, loose frame: which frame also I reckon among these secret sins.

Now, brethren, more or less these things are true in us, according to the several degrees of grace we have received, through the woful negligence we have been betrayed into. Have we a due sense of these things? or can we walk with boldness and confidence, peace and undisturbedness in our minds day and night, though these things be upon us? If so, we are in some measure hardened from the fear of God. The fear of God hath not its proper work upon us, which would keep us deeply sensible of these things, deeply afflict us for them, keep us in an abhorrence of them, and make us watchful against them night and day; and not suffer vain thoughts to come and go without spiritual conflicts; nor inordinate affections to the world, without wounds given to it by the Spirit of God. If it is not so with us, our hearts are hardened from the fear of God.

[2.] This partial hardening also contains in it a want of a due sense of an irregular course of walking. There is a course of walking that will please the world, satisfy the church, and which professors shall greatly approve of; and yet if a man come to examine his own heart by the rule, he shall find his course of walking judged: for though the world hath nothing to object against us, and though professors do well approve of us; yet when we come to the rule, that will discover our iniquity. We are bound to walk by rule. "God will have mercy on them that walk according to this rule." We are bound to walk circumspectly in all things: "Walk circumspectly, redeeming the time; worthy of God, worthy of the Lord;"—which extends to all duties of our walk in the whole course of our lives. If we satisfy ourselves that our walk is such as answers known duties that are required of us,—that none in the world can lay blame upon us, and professors will approve of,—but do not bring it to the rule, and judge it there, we err from the ways of God: and if we bring it to the rule, and judge it there, and have not a due sense, so as to be greatly humbled for it, our hearts are so far hardened from the fear of God; for if we were in the fear of God all the day long, as we ought to be, it would be so with us. Many men's boldness and confidence in the world, and many men's peace, will be resolved at length into a neglect of this duty,—that they have not proved their walk by this rule, and that light God hath set up in their own souls. We may, I say, brethren, have something of this partial hardness upon our hearts in these instances,—want of a deep sense as to secret sins, want of self-judging as to our irregular walking, wherein it comes short of the rule, the holy rule we are to attend unto. And who can say of his walk, that it is worthy of God and the Lord? which yet we are called unto. Alas! it is not worth the owning ourselves, and the profession we make:—how much less is it worthy of God!

[3.] This hardening, likewise, carries in it a want of a due sense of sin, upon surprisal into known sins. "There is no man that liveth and sinneth not;"—but this respects known sins; I do not mean sins that are known unto others, but sins we know in particular, wherein we have offended against God. And known sins are great sins,—sins against light, and for the most part against engagements and promises of watchfulness; and there is something, if we examine thoroughly, of wilfulness in them. And great sins should have great sorrow, and great humiliation. Truly, brethren, I am afraid (and I would be jealous over myself and you) that we are apt to put off even known sins upon slighter terms than the rule of the covenant doth admit of. We are apt to resolve them, in general, into the covenant of grace and mercy, or to pass them over with one or two confessions, or the like; and do not bring every known sin unto its proper issue in the blood of Christ, as we ought. If we do not do this, we are hardened thus partially from the fear of God. The true fear of God would keep us up to this, that no one known sin should ever pass us, without a particular issuing of it in the blood of Christ, and obtaining peace in it.

[4.] Want of a due sense of the sin of others is a great sign that we are partially hardened from God's fear; as it is a sign men are totally hardened, when they do not only commit sin themselves, but have pleasure in them that do it. We have before us the sins of professors, the sins of the world, the provoking sins of the nation in the generation wherein we live, and the sins of all sorts of men; and I think there is not in any one duty more spiritual wisdom required of believers, than how to deport themselves with a suitable frame of heart, in reference to the sins of other men. Some are ready to be contented that they should sin, and sometimes ready to make sport at their sins; and for the most part it is indifferent unto us at what rate men sin in the world, so it go well with us or the Church of Christ. We understand but little of that, "Rivers of waters run down mine eyes, because men keep not thy law," Ps. cxix. 136. I confess, I think there is little of this in the world,—that we can truly say, as he did, by the Spirit of God, that our eyes run down with water, because other men, all sorts of men, keep not God's law. There is a "sighing and mourning for all the abominations that are done among a people." What people? Truly, people that were idolaters, and false worshippers, and very wicked, as that people were at that time; yet God required there should be "sighing and mourning for all the abominations;" and took special notice of the working of grace that one way, above all other things. And the Lord help us, I am afraid we have very small concern for the sins of other men. And it is resolved into these two principles:—want of zeal for God's glory, and want of compassion to the souls of men; which would make us deeply concerned for the sins of other men. Sin in the world is grown a common thing to us; we do not rend our garments, when we hear of all the blasphemies and atheism in the world,—all the blood, uncleanness, profaneness, oaths. Every sin is grown common to us; nobody is affected. "None taketh hold upon God," saith the prophet. What will be the end of these things? Yet we speak of them as commonly as of our daily food. This is not to be under the power of the fear of the Lord. There is a partial hardness upon us from the fear of the Lord, in that general and almost universal unconcernedness that is upon us about the sins of other men.

I thought to have spoken to the remaining heads of this partial hardness of our hearts from God's fear;—the want of a due sense of God's judgments; and the want of a due attendance unto and walk with God in a way of duty: but I shall waive them, and proceed to the fourth thing proposed to be inquired into.

IV. Why doth the holy God deal thus with a professing people? What reason can we find in ourselves why it should be so, in making this complaint? that we neither charge God foolishly as the author and cause of sin, nor go about to extenuate our own sins, but aggravate and burden our consciences with a sense of them. Why doth the holy God thus deal with us?

The reasons are of two sorts:—1. What provokes God unto it, which are the procuring reasons; 2. What God aims at in it, which are the final reasons why it is thus with us.

1. What provokes God to it? I answer, three things:—

(1.) Unthankfulness for mercy received. Thus, in the chapter wherein is my text, it is said, verses 8–10, "Surely they are my people, children that will not lie: so he was their Saviour. In all their affliction he was afflicted, and the angel of his presence saved them: in his love and in his pity he redeemed them; and he bare them, and carried them all the days of old. But they rebelled, and vexed his holy Spirit: therefore he was turned to be their enemy, and he fought against them." God doth in this matter turn to be our enemy; he fights against us. Why doth he so? Because he hath redeemed us in his love,—because he hath borne us in his arms all the days of our lives,—because he hath manifested that in all our afflictions he was afflicted,—because he had been a Saviour and heard us; and under all these mercies received, we have rebelled and vexed his holy Spirit, have been unthankful and ungrateful: therefore he is become our enemy, and fights against us. I beg of you, brethren, that we may call over those innumerable mercies we have received from the Lord, spiritual mercies, temporal mercies, and consider whether these evils be not befallen us,—whether our unthankfulness for mercy hath not caused God to become our enemy, and to fight against us.

(2.) A second reason is,—inordinate cleaving to the things of the world at a most undue season. It may be it would not provoke God so much thus to fight against us, and harden our hearts from his fear, if the season of it was not undue. Do not we see with our eyes, and hear with our ears, that God is unsettling all things here below, and that all these things shall be dissolved? When God gives so many intimations that "all these things shall be dissolved, what manner of persons ought we to be in all holy conversation and godliness?" Cleaving inordinately to the things of the world at such a season, is that which provoketh God to deal thus: "For the iniquity of his covetousness was I wroth, and smote him; I hid me and was wroth, and he went on frowardly in the way of his heart." God smote them for the iniquity of their covetousness in such a woful, undue season. Let us, brethren, be at work. I may be under great mistakes and misapprehensions, but I must tell you what is upon my heart;—I cannot but think, that unless we are particularly at work, every one of us, we shall be overtaken with these dismal and dreadful effects, and God will appear against us, and fight against us.

(3.) The third reason is,—our unprofitableness, and unsuitableness to the means of grace we have enjoyed. O the barren land of England, upon which the rain hath often fallen, and [it] hath brought forth nothing but briers and thorns! We have had our proportion in it, brethren; you of this congregation can even make your boast of what you have enjoyed of this and that man's ministry for many years; but O the leanness and barrenness that is among us, now all is done!—our unsuitableness to the means we have enjoyed! We may repent one day that we ever had any among us who excelled others in gifts and graces, if we profit no more. We have not profited suitably to the means we have enjoyed; but every vain and foolish imagination hath turned us aside from keeping as we ought to the good and holy ways of God. We do not flourish in fruitfulness, in savouriness, and profitableness, answerable to what the dispensations of God have been towards us; for the dew of God hath been upon us from time to time.

Now, besides these things named, which are public causes, why God hath brought us under this dispensation, let us all search our hearts, and say, "Lord, why hast thou caused me thus far to err from thy ways, and hardened my heart from thy fear? Why have I not former faith, love, affection, zeal? Why do not I mourn more? Where are my tears and humiliation? those heart-breaking sighs and groans after God which my heart was once filled withal? O Lord, 'why is my heart thus hardened from thy fear?'" Let us inquire into the particular reasons, that at last we may come to cry, "Return, O LORD, for thy servants' sake, the tribes of thine inheritance."

2. What does God aim at in such a dispensation? We have mentioned the procuring reasons and causes; now, what are the final ends why God will thus deal with us?

There are two ends the holy God seems to have in these things:—

(1.) The first is, to awaken us unto the consideration of what an all-seeing God he is with whom we have to do. When we please the world and one another, and ourselves, in our walkings and conversations, God will have us know he is displeased. Though we please ourselves and cry, "Peace," and please the world and one another; yet God will so withdraw his Spirit and grace, that we shall be forced to say, "Why is God thus displeased with us?" He will have us glorify him, as one that is an all-seeing God,—as one that knows our inward frames, and tries us upon them.

(2.) God doth it to awaken us. If there be any thing of true grace in our hearts, a sense of spiritual judgments will awaken us, when all outward judgments in the world will not do it;—no, if thunder and lightning be round about us,—if ruin and the sword be before us, and the earth underneath be ready to swallow us up,—they will not work so kindly upon a believer's heart as a sense of spiritual judgments. I hope God hath a design of love to awaken us all by this dispensation to return unto him.

But to proceed to the last inquiry:—

V. What way shall we take now for retrieving our souls out of this state and condition?

One way is prescribed here:—It is by prayer, "Return, O LORD." It is to beg of God to return.

What arguments have we to plead with God to return? This being the case, the arguments here given are peculiar to the case; and we may plead them. They are two:—1. Sovereign mercy and compassion; and, 2. Faithfulness in covenant. They are both here pleaded:—

1. Sovereign mercy, verse 15, "Look down from heaven, and behold from the habitation of thy holiness and of thy glory: where is thy zeal and thy strength, the sounding of thy bowels and of thy mercies towards me? are they restrained?" Our great plea in this case is upon sovereign mercy and compassion. Plead the pity of God; beg mercy of God; come to God as those that stand in need of mercy, and of the sounding of his bowels.

2. The second argument is, God's faithfulness in the covenant, verse 16, "Doubtless thou art our Father; we are thine."

These are the two arguments. We are night and day to plead with God, for our recovery from the state and condition of erring from the ways of God, and of having our hearts hardened from his fear, sovereign mercy and covenant faithfulness. And this is all I shall speak to at this time.

SERMON XXV.[1]

THE BEAUTY AND STRENGTH OF ZION.

"Walk about Zion, and go round about her: tell the towers thereof. Mark ye well her bulwarks, consider her palaces; that ye may tell it to the generation following. For this God is our God for ever and ever; he will be our guide even unto death."—Ps. xlviii. 12–14.

MANY expositors think this psalm to be an ἐπινίκιον,—a triumphant song of thanksgiving after some great deliverance at Jerusalem.

[1] This sermon was preached April 22, 1675.

Some apply it to the times of Asa, when Zerah and the Ethiopians came with an army against Jerusalem of ten hundred thousand men; others apply it to the times of Jehoshaphat, when the Moabites, and Ammonites, and mount Seir (the Edomites), were gathered together against Judah; and others, again, to the days of Hezekiah, when Sennacherib and his army came against Jerusalem and were destroyed. They ground their interpretation upon verses 4–6, "Lo, the kings were assembled, they passed by together. They saw it" (but they could come no farther), "and so they marvelled; they were troubled, and hasted away. Fear took hold upon them there, and pain, as of a woman in travail:"—which is a description of some great consternation that befell the enemies of God, and the enemies of Jerusalem, when they drew near unto it. So the Jews do interpret these verses, "Walk about Zion, and go round about her: tell the towers thereof. Mark ye well her bulwarks, consider her palaces;"—that, notwithstanding this great and dreadful attempt, whether by the Ethiopians, or by the Moabites, or Sennacherib, there is not one tower broken down of Zion or of Jerusalem, but all things are safe and well. For my own part, I should rather judge this psalm to be composed by David, and purely mystical and prophetical. It is easy to manifest that all the foregoing psalms are so. And the close of the former psalm is the calling of the Gentiles, where he saith, "God reigneth over the heathen; God sitteth upon the throne of his holiness," verse 8. And in verse 9, you read, in the margin of your Bibles, better than in the text, "The voluntary of the people are gathered unto the people of the God of Abraham." The people were become a willing people in the day of his power. However, all conclude that these words are a graphical description of the defence that God will at all times give his church, which the psalmist doth set before our eyes.

Look upon it, and observe what a diligent view he requires to be taken of what he here proposes. He looks upon Zion as a well-fortified garrison, not like to be carried in haste by the enemy. And he would have you well consider, too, what the fortifications are; therefore he distributes his direction into so many particulars:—"Walk about Zion;" this is the way whereby you may come to see how Zion is fortified. It may be you have gone a little way in walking, and have seen much, but do not cease, "Go round about her;" see if you can find one weak place, where she is likely to be attacked by the enemy. "Tell the towers,"—cast up the number of them, and see that they are not few; which is what a man of judgment and understanding would do, if he were to take a view of a fortified place, and consider whether it would hold out against a strong enemy. "Mark ye well her bulwarks;" or, "Set your heart to her bulwarks;"

consider them,—do not take a general view of these fortifications of Zion, but ponder and consider whether they are likely to hold out or not, and whether you may put your trust in them. "Consider her palaces;" which were the great and eminent buildings in and about Zion, called in some place, "palaces of ivory," with which they were greatly adorned. So that here is this direction given, to take a very strict, sedate, considerate view of the fortifications of Zion; since it would certainly be attacked by great and powerful enemies. There are two things added:—One is, the particular end wherefore they should do so: "That ye may tell it to the generation following," since other ages of the church would have the use of it;—the other is, the ground why all this would be of benefit to them and the generations following: "For this God is our God in covenant, and that for ever and ever, and will be our guide unto death."

I shall make one observation from the words, and speak a little very briefly and plainly to it:—

Observation. A diligent search into, and consideration of, the means and causes of the preservation and protection of the church in the greatest dangers and difficulties, is a duty incumbent on us, for our own support against sinful fears, and to enable us to that testimony which is required for future generations, to encourage them to trust in the Lord.

Every age is to give over a good testimony of God's dealing with Zion to the age that comes after. And a diligent search and inquiry into the causes and means of the protection and preservation of the Church of God in the midst of imminent dangers and difficulties, is a duty incumbent upon us, that we may be fortified against sinful fears in ourselves, and encourage succeeding generations to trust in the Lord. As we have received the testimony of such who have gone before us, so we are to give our testimony to those who shall come after.

All that I shall do at present is to answer these five questions:—

I. What is to be understood by the preservation and protection of the church? so as we may look neither for less nor more than what we are like to meet with.

II. What is meant by searching into, and considering of, these causes and means of the church's preservation? "Walk about Zion, tell her towers, set your heart to her bulwarks, consider her palaces," etc.

III. What are those causes and means of the church's preservation, those towers and bulwarks which will not fail, whenever Zerah or Sennacherib comes, or whatever attempts are made upon Zion?

IV. What reason is there why we should thus search into and consider these causes of the church's preservation and protection?

V. What is the testimony which we have to give concerning this matter to the ensuing generation? "That ye may declare it to the generation to come."

I shall speak a little in answer to these five inquiries:—

I. What is that preservation and protection of Zion, the church of God, that we may expect,—whose causes and means we should inquire into?

This may be reduced unto three heads:—

1. The eternal salvation of the church of God. This is the goal and the prize that all this great running is about in the world. Satan is, in his own nature, as active and restless as he is malicious; and yet, I suppose, if this end was taken away, if this was not in his eye,—the eternal salvation of the church, of all that believe,—he would give himself much more leisure than he doth. All things here, evils, trials, persecutions, and the like, are but skirmishes; but where goes eternal bliss, there goes the victory. This, therefore, is part of that preservation and safety of Zion which we are to look after,—namely, as the apostle saith, "That all Israel shall be saved." You have a great security, that our Lord Jesus Christ gives of it, John x. 27, etc., "My sheep hear my voice, and I know them, and they follow me: and I give unto them eternal life; and they shall never perish, neither shall any man pluck them out of my hand. I and my Father are one."

This is the first thing in the church's preservation,—namely, that, let the conflict be never so great, never so severe, all true believers shall be eternally saved. And if we do not lay the principal weight in our thoughts upon this, our concern in other things will be of no moment unto us. There is one false opinion doth more mischief to the honour of God in the world in this matter than all the devils in hell are able to do; and that is, of the total and final apostasy of true believers: for if that be so, we have lost our very first principle of the preservation of Zion,—namely, that "all Israel shall be saved," and that none shall take believers out of the hands of Christ.

2. There is this in it also, that there shall be a church, a professing church, preserved in the world throughout all generations, in despite of all the oppositions of Satan and the world; that is, there shall be a called number, yielding obedience internally unto Christ, and openly professing that obedience, always preserved unto the end of the world. It is expressly included in that promise, Isa. ix. 7, "Of the increase of his government and peace there shall be no end, upon the throne of David, and upon his kingdom, to order it, and to establish it with judgment and with justice from henceforth even for ever. the zeal of the LORD of hosts will perform this." However it may fall out in particular places and nations, yet Zion will be preserved;

God will reserve for Jesus Christ a church visibly professing and yielding obedience unto him according to the gospel.

But you will say, perhaps, "Where was there such a church in the time of the antichristian apostasy? did not the visible church wholly fail?"

I answer,—Though I acknowledge all the churches in the world have greatly apostatized and fallen away, yet, in the first place, all did not fall away in the same length or manner with those in these parts of the world that were under the antichristian apostasy. There were churches in the east which, though very corrupt formerly, and now more so, yet might justly be esteemed a visible church. Besides, the church of God was then in Babylon until the Reformation. There was in the Roman church a number of persons that sincerely feared God, and belonged unto the Zion of Christ, who were preserved. Hence is that call, Rev. xviii. 4, "Come out of her, my people." Christ's people were in her until the time that God gave them a call to come out of her. And another part of them were in visible opposition all along to the growing apostasy of the Papacy. About four or five hundred years after Christ, the great composition was made between Christianity and Paganism, when the outward court was given to the Gentiles to be trodden down; that is, plainly, when those northern nations that divided and destroyed the Roman empire were brought in to be Christians. And, upon that composition, nations came in to a profession of Christianity with Pagan worship and manners; but yielded obedience unto Christian rulers,—bishops, priests, and the like. Now, from that very time, when all things sunk into Antichristianism, there was still a visible testimony given against it by the church of Christ; that is, by believers from one generation to another,—an eminent, blessed testimony, against all that cursed apostasy.

It is good to keep our faith and expectation within bounds,—that we do not look for more than is like to come to pass; and yet still to have our faith confirmed in those things that may be sure not to fail. "All ISRAEL shall be saved," and Christ will maintain his kingdom in the world against all opposition;—that is, the cause wherein we are engaged, whatsoever becomes of our persons, will be triumphant. Believers shall be saved, and a professing church shall be preserved; which is all the general cause wherein we are engaged. And God, it may be, hath placed us in this age to give over our testimony to the future generation.

3. There belongs to the preservation of the church, the protection and deliverance of the true church of God under persecution: this likewise comes within the compass of these fortifications. We are very apt to look after our own concerns, and, it may be, to imagine

we are more concerned in this third head than in both the former. But those that think so make a very wrong judgment; for the measure of all our concerns in present deliverance, or in the conflicts of the church, is to be taken from these two generals,—the eternal salvation of the church at last, and the preservation of the kingdom of Christ in the world. And if once we begin to measure them by our own advantages, peace, liberty, or friends, we shall take wrong measures of God's providence and our own expectation.

There are three seasons, or three ways, whereby churches, in particular times and places, are in danger of coming short of this protection, or seeming so to do:—(1.) When the power of Satan and the world are set upon them in a way of persecution. (2.) When the nations of the world among whom they live are so wicked that God will not forbear a general devastation and destruction. (3.) When themselves apostatize and decay, and provoke God to remove his candlestick from among them. In such seasons it comes to a trial, whether particular churches, or a church in any particular place, shall be preserved and protected in their present trial, or not. And I confess unto you that my thoughts are, that all three are upon us at present; which makes our case the more difficult and hard to be determined. But this, I bless God, I cannot but think, that what we most fear is least to be feared. It is plain we most fear the first; and I think I am certain that the first is least to be feared. I shall speak briefly to each of them:—

(1.) As to the first, there are two rules whereby to make a judgment of the preservation of the church in time of persecution. The one is that given by the prophet Hosea, chap xi. 12, "Ephraim compasseth me about with lies, and the house of Israel with deceit: but Judah yet ruleth with God, and is faithful with the saints." He prophesies the immediate destruction of Ephraim:—The Church of Israel shall wander to Assyria. But Judah shall yet abide. Why? "Judah yet ruleth with God;" that is, for God,—the ruling power of Judah is for God. I take that to be the meaning of the words; for if you will observe concerning Judah, all that ever were good among them was in the ruling power. In the very days of Josiah himself, Judah, that is, the body of the people, turned to God feignedly, and not with their whole heart, Jer. iii. 10. But yet the prophet foresaw a time would come that Judah should not be so. He shall rule, therefore, while he is faithful to God. Here, then, is your rule:—While the ruling power of a church or nation is for God, is faithful to God and his interest, walking with him, they are within these bulwarks. And truly, to speak what I believe in this matter (for in all things that are future, that we may not have clear and full evidence of, there is a reserve for sovereignty), wherever there are churches walking with God, ruling for God, and faithful to him, they shall never be prevailed against by outward persecution in any place; unless it be in subserviency to the hidden design of sovereign wisdom to remove the gospel wholly from such a place. This, then, is the second rule: and we can never fathom, and so must be in the dark, whether the church in this or that particular place shall be absolutely preserved; because, if God pleases, he can make the total scattering to be a means subservient to the spreading of the gospel. But so far as they walk with God, they are within this protection.

(2.) The church's danger lies in the destruction that may come upon places where they are, for national sins. There were in the days of Jehoiakim and Zedekiah, "good figs at Jerusalem, very good figs, even as the first ripe figs," Jer. xxiv. 2,—that is, there were many precious saints of God,—and there were also "evil figs, so evil that none could eat them;" and yet God puts all these figs into a basket, good and bad, and all must go into captivity. He could no longer forbear, for the provoking sins of the nation; the whole must go into captivity together. Now, if such a season may come upon any place, as hath upon many nations deservedly because of national sins, the good may suffer with the bad, and churches may receive a scattering.

(3.) The third danger is their own apostasy. There is not any thing in the world that we ought to be more afraid of than of a church's scattering in an apostatizing condition. Then we shall bear the burden of our guilt in our scattering, and be clean taken off from all means of retrieving it. But there is an interest of all particular churches walking with God in this preservation and protection that is here promised and described to be round about Zion; and it is an act of mere sovereignty where God dealeth otherwise with them. That is the preservation and protection of the church, in answer to the first inquiry.

II. The second question is,—What is it to search after and consider the causes and means of this preservation? Where shall we look for it?

To this I answer,—

1. Be sure to take off your search and consideration from those things which are not, and will not, prove to be the bulwarks of Zion. You know how they were blamed in such a case, Isa. xxii., in a time of great distress and invasion that was coming upon them. The prophet tells you what the people did, verse 8, etc., "He discovered the covering of Judah, and thou didst look in that day to the armour of the house of the forest. Ye have seen also the breaches of the city of David, that they are many; and ye gathered together the waters of the lower pool. And ye have numbered the houses of Jerusalem, and the houses have ye broken down to fortify the wall.

Ye made also a ditch between the two walls for the water of the old pool; but ye have not looked unto the Maker thereof, neither had respect unto him that fashioned it long ago." Looking unto carnal aids and helps in straits and difficulties hath been our folly. The first thing in this call to look to Zion, is, to "cease from man, whose breath is in his nostrils; for whereof is he to be accounted?"

2. Where shall we look for these bulwarks? We must look for the protection of the church where we look for the destruction of its adversaries. And where shall we look for that? The prophet tells us, Isa. xxxiv. 16, "Seek ye out of the book of the LORD, and read: no one of these shall fail, none shall want her mate: for my mouth it hath commanded, and his Spirit it hath gathered them." All the foregoing prophecy is concerning the utter destruction of Idumea in the type; but of Babylon, Rome, Antichrist, in the antitype. And the verses from 11 to 15 express the gathering of all the fowls of prey, dismal fowls, to dwell in the place. But how shall we know whether this will come to pass? Says the prophet, "Seek ye out of the book of the LORD, and read; no one of these shall fail:" that is, no one particular judgment that God hath threatened in his whole book against his adversaries shall ever fail; no, not in one circumstance: neither the cormorant nor the screech-owl shall want her mate. Seek it out of the book of the Lord; you will find it recorded in these prophecies: and nothing shall fail there; for the mouth of the Lord hath spoken it, and the Spirit of the Lord shall accomplish it. We are to look, therefore, and search for these defences, causes, and means of the protection of Zion, in the book of the Lord. This is "the tower of David, where hang a thousand shields, all shields of mighty men," Cant. iv. 4; where is recorded all the defence of the church and people of God. It is your duty to search in the book of God, and read, to see what are the causes and means of the protection and preservation of the church; and when you have found them out, you are then to consider them. Want of consideration weakens our faith greatly. If you can find, by reading in the book of God, that there are such and such defences and bulwarks of Zion; our duty is now to consider whether they will hold out against the greatest attacks and attempts of Satan and all our adversaries. I speak what is plain, but very fit for this day. When you have found out these defences, bring them to the shield of faith, and obedience to God, and consider whether they are like to hold out; consider each, and give judgment upon them. And if you judge they are so, then trust to them; drive all you have, all your concerns, within the compass of these fortifications, and trust to them. And this may suffice in answer to the second question,—Where are we to search for the preservation and protection of the church?

III. What are the causes and means of the preservation of Zion, and protection of the church, that we are to search out, and to consider, and trust unto?

It is but a little I can comply with the text in. I cannot go round about Zion, I cannot tell her towers; but we will consider some of her bulwarks, that will be a sure preservation against all opposition. And I will name four or five unto you:—

1. The designation and constitution of Jesus Christ to be king of the church, king of Zion, is the great bulwark of Zion. This is the fort-royal that never fails. Ps. ii., "Why do the heathen rage, and the people imagine a vain thing? The kings of the earth set themselves, and the rulers take counsel together, against the LORD, and against his Anointed, saying, Let us break their bands asunder, and cast away their cords from us. He that sitteth in the heavens shall laugh: the Lord shall have them in derision. Then shall he speak unto them in his wrath, and vex them in his sore displeasure. Yet have I set my king upon my holy hill of Zion."—"Notwithstanding all this tumult, conspiracy, and rage, all these counsels and advices, yet," saith he, "Zion must stand; for I have set my king, I have anointed Christ, my eternal Son, to be king upon my holy hill of Zion." But though Christ be made king, it doth not follow but he may give over reigning; and so there will be no security from hence. The truth is, he will do so, he will give over reigning as to his mediatory kingdom;[1] but not before he hath done with all his enemies, Ps. cx. 1, "Sit thou at my right hand, until I make thine enemies thy footstool." And the apostle, 1 Cor. xv., saith, "He must reign till he hath put all enemies under his feet." And when he shall have put down all power and authority, then he shall give up the kingdom. The great security of the church is from hence, that Christ is made king of Zion; and if he be a king he must have subjects. The word is his law; he rules by his Spirit: but rule and law together will not make a kingdom, unless there be subjects to yield obedience. If Christ be a king, if he sit upon Zion, the church must be preserved; for he must have a kingdom. There is but one way in the world that looks probable to put an end to Christ's reign; and that is, to cease being his enemies: for the express terms of his reign is, "Till all his enemies be made his footstool." How easy were it for me to dwell upon this, that this king of the church hath power to preserve it to all ends, and in all circumstances; power to preserve it to eternal salvation, in visible profession, or in particular trials! And what king is there

[1] On the subject of the continuance of Christ's mediatorial office in heaven, Dr Owen gives a detailed exhibition of his views in the last chapter of his "Treatise on the Person of Christ," published four years after this sermon was delivered, vol. i. p. 271.—ED.

among men that will not preserve his subjects in time of trial, when it is in his power so to do? The Lord Christ will preserve them. "I give unto them eternal life, and no man shall take them out of my hands." He is able to save them to the utmost, even all that come unto God by him; and he is given to be head over all things to the church,—to dispose of all as seems good unto him, for the end, use, and interest of the church.

This is the first bulwark and security we have for the preservation and protection of the church; and unless men can dethrone Jesus Christ, and cast him off from being king upon the holy hill of Zion, it is in vain to think of prevailing against Zion.

2. The second bulwark of Zion is the promises of God, which are innumerable. I will name but two of them. One is the foundation of the Old Testament, and the other of the New. One held it out for four thousand years, and was never impeached; and the other for these sixteen hundred years, and shall never be shaken.

The promise that was the foundation of the Old Testament, was the first promise of God, Gen. iii. 15, "I will put enmity between thee and the woman, and between thy seed and her seed; it shall bruise thy head, and thou shalt bruise his heel." There are these four things in that promise:—(1.) That there shall always be a two-fold seed in the world,—the seed of the serpent, and the seed of the woman; they shall never fail while this world stands. (2.) That these two seeds shall always be at enmity; there shall be an everlasting conflict, from the entrance of sin to the end of it. "I will put enmity," saith God, and such an enmity as shall be carried on by the highest and most severe warfare. The enmity is spiritual, but the warfare oftentimes is outward. The first manifestation of this enmity was in blood. Cain slew Abel. Why? Because he was of the evil one. And so it hath been carried on by blood from that day to this. (3.) That either seed hath a leader: there is "he and thou," "it and thou;" that is, Christ and Satan. Christ is the leader of the seed of the woman, the captain and head of it in this great conflict; and Satan, as he was the head of the apostasy from God, continues the head of his seed, the generation of vipers, to try out the contest with Christ unto the end. (4.) The victory shall always be to the seed of the woman. It is said, indeed, "Thou shalt bruise his heel,"—Christ's heel, in his sufferings, both in his own person and those of the church. But on the contrary, it is said likewise, "He shall bruise thy head;" —break thy power and strength,—conquer thee. Then Zion is safe. This was the foundation of the Old Testament: and though things oftentimes were brought to great distress,—sometimes by apostasy, and sometimes by persecution,—yet this promise carried it, and delivered over the church safe into the hand of Christ.

Now, when Christ takes the church, and goes to new-form it, and fashion it more for the glory of God, there is the foundation-promise made in the New Testament: "Upon this rock I will build my church, and the gates of hell shall not prevail against it," Matt. xvi. 18. If that obscure promise under the Old Testament did secure Zion, as to all those things before mentioned, four thousand years, shall not we trust to this promise of our Saviour for half the time? though it is, indeed, the continuance of the same promise; for "the gates of hell" is the seed of the serpent, and the "rock" is Christ. That is the second bulwark of Zion. We may be shaken in our faith and confidence, but we have the promise of God, that hath supported it thus far in the world, and will certainly preserve it to the end.

3. There is the watchful providence of God over the church. It is expressed, Deut. xi. 12, where the land of the church is said to be "a land which the LORD thy God careth for: the eyes of the LORD thy God are always upon it, from the beginning of the year unto the end of the year." That land which is the possession of the church, the seat of God's worship, the church itself, is what the Lord careth for. And it is expressed again to the same purpose, Isa. xxvii. 3, where this land is called God's vineyard, "I the LORD do keep it; I will water it every moment: lest any hurt it, I will keep it night and day." There is the watchful providence of God over the church, night and day preserving it; which providence, indeed, we live upon, though it is secret and invisible to us. There is power in it; but "God hides his power." We see little, we are not able to discern any thing to purpose, of the secret emanation of divine power and wisdom through the hearts and counsels of all mankind, to this end, that God may preserve his church, governing their affections, ruling their thoughts, turning and overturning their counsels;—things that will never appear nor come to light, what was their occasion and ends, till the great day when the thoughts of all hearts shall be discovered. The Lord will keep and preserve his church, that none may hurt it.

4. Another bulwark is God's special presence. God is in an especial manner present in his church. I have treated concerning the nature and special presence of God and Christ in the church, and proved it from many promises, and showed the effect of it; which I shall not now insist upon, but only show that this is a bulwark of the church. In Isa. viii. 9, 10, there is a gauntlet thrown out to all the adversaries of the people of God, and a challenge to do their worst: "Associate yourselves, O ye people, and ye shall be broken in pieces; and give ear, all ye of far countries: gird yourselves, and ye shall be broken in pieces. Take counsel together, and it shall come to nought; speak the word, and it shall not stand." What is the reason? "For

God is with us." The presence of God is with his church. Every thing of force, of counsel, of association and agreement,—all shall be broken and come to nought; they shall have no effect. And he gives this only reason, "Because God is with us." While God is with his church, it may be exercised with great trials, so that they may think they have lost the presence of God; as in Judges vi. 12, "The angel of the LORD appeared to Gideon, and said unto him, The LORD is with thee. Oh my Lord," saith he, "if the LORD be with us, why then is all this befallen us?"—"Whence is all this evil come upon us, that we should be under the power of the Midianites, oppressed and destroyed by them?" He could not believe that if God was with them, according to his promise, they could be so prevailed upon by their enemies. Great things of trouble may befall the church of God while God is present with them; so as they may be ready to say sometimes, "My way is hid from the LORD, and my judgment is passed over from my God: the LORD hath forsaken me, and my Lord hath forgotten me." "It cannot be," saith Gideon, "that God is with us, if we be thus ruined." But he will appear and manifest himself, for the protection of Zion.

5. The last bulwark, unto which all others may be reduced, is the covenant of God: "For this God is our God."—"That God who hath fortified Zion in all other generations, and wrought these deliverances, he is our God in covenant."

I shall not need to reckon any more than these five bulwarks of the church. Ponder and consider whether they are like to work out its preservation and protection. And if God gives us wisdom to single out these things, and consider them aright, we shall soon see what encouragement we have to pray for the preservation and protection of the church, however it may be attacked and attempted, even this day;—which is our present business.

IV. Why should we make this inquiry into these causes and means of the preservation and protection of the church?

The reason is, to deliver ourselves from our own sinful fears, and that by a discovery of the great mistake which all the adversaries of the church run upon. The reason why, the ground whereupon, they attempt the church, is that, and no other, which you have, Ezek. xxxviii. 10, 11, "Thus saith the Lord GOD; It shall also come to pass, that at the same time shall things come into thy mind, and thou shalt think an evil thought: and thou shalt say, I will go up to the land of unwalled villages; I will go to them that are at rest, that dwell safely, all of them dwelling without walls, and having neither bars nor gates." Here is the very ground of the undertaking of the world against the church in any age,—that they have no defence, are a poor people that dwell in unwalled villages, and have neither bars nor gates. It is a miserable disappointment, for men to go and undertake to destroy or oppress any place, thinking they are unprovided, and, when they come there, to find it quite otherwise. At this day there would not any move a tongue against the people of God, but upon this very account, that they have no defence, no protection. And sometimes they proceed so far as that they begin to discover the bulwarks of Zion,—if not in the causes, yet in the effects. The old world saw not God in the cause of what he did; but when the waters began to roll upon them, the psalmist tells us, "They saw it, and were afraid; and fearfulness took hold upon them."—"Is this the people that dwell in unwalled villages, that have neither bars nor gates? See their towers! behold their bulwarks! there is no attacking them." When once God makes them to see this, that the power of Christ is engaged for his people, they will then cry to the mountains and to the rocks to hide them from the day of his wrath; they will be surprised with fear.

Now, seeing the adversaries of the church of God are certainly upon this mistake attempting the church,—because, as they imagine, it hath no guard (and they will certainly find at last that they have a guard, which they saw not and were not acquainted with),—why should we be afraid in such a case? Nothing more encourages persons, than when they know their enemies do clearly mistake their condition. This is enough to make the veriest coward in the world valiant. Let us be sure to be found within this garrison and place of defence, and certain that we have to do in the concerns of Zion, and not of the world; and then shall we see the mountains all full of chariots and horses of fire round about us,—Christ reigning, the promise of Christ engaged, and the watchful eye of God upon the church continually. Our fears arise from the want of considering these things, and taking a carnal view and measure of things that are seen.

V. The last inquiry is,—What testimony are we to give over to the generation that is to come after us?

This testimony consists of two things:—

1. The exercise of faith and patience in all our own trials that may befall us, that there may be a remembrance of it in the generations that are to come. The martyrs that suffered here so long ago do still tell us in this generation, by their faith and patience, that Zion had walls and bulwarks round about her, and that God was her God and Guide. Had they not believed it, do you think they would have given up their bodies to the flames in this city and other parts of the nation? In like manner, that faith and patience which we shall exercise in any trial that may befall us in the behalf of Zion, is to tell the generations to come what God hath done, and how we have found it ourselves.

2. It is our duty to give it over by instruction to those that we bring up. Our fathers have told us what God did in their days; and we are to give in this testimony to God,—to tell our children what God hath done in our days:—"So long have we lived and been professors; so long have we walked in Zion; and we have found God faithful in his promise,—not one word or tittle hath failed that the mouth of the Lord hath spoken." Thus are we to instruct the generation that is growing up, that hath not seen those things which we have seen.

SERMON XXVI.[1]

PERILOUS TIMES.

"This know also, that in the last days perilous times shall come."—2 TIM. iii. 1.

YOU know, my way and manner upon these occasions is to speak as plainly and familiarly as I can unto what is of our present concernment; and so I design to do at this time, if it shall please God to help under infirmities.

The words contain a warning of imminent dangers. And there are four things in them:—First, The manner of the warning: "This know also." Secondly, The evil itself that they are warned of: "Perilous times." Thirdly, The way of their introduction: "They shall come." Fourthly, The time and season of it: "They shall come in the last days:"—

First. The manner of the warning: "This know also;"—"Thou Timothy, unto the other instructions which I have given thee how to behave thyself in the house of God, whereby thou mayest be set forth as a pattern unto all gospel ministers in future ages, I must also add this, 'This know also.' It belongs to thy duty and office to know and consider the impending judgments that are coming upon churches."

And so, as a justification of my present design, if God enable me unto it, I shall here premise, that it is the duty of the ministers of the gospel to foresee and take notice of the dangers which the churches are falling into. And the Lord help us, and all other ministers, to be awakened unto this part of our duty! You know how God sets it forth (Ezek. xxxiii.) in the parable of the watchman, to warn men of approaching dangers. And truly God hath given us this law:—If we

[1] This sermon was preached November 3, 1676, being a day set apart for solemn fasting and prayer.

warn the churches of their approaching dangers, we discharge our duty; if we do not, their blood will be required at our hands. The Spirit of God foresaw negligence apt to grow upon us in this matter; and therefore the Scripture only proposeth duty on the one hand, and on the other requires the people's blood at the hands of the watchmen, if they perform not their duty. So speaks the prophet Isaiah, chap. xxi. 8, "He cried, A lion: My lord, I stand continually upon the watch-tower." A lion is an emblem of approaching judgment. "The lion hath roared; who can but tremble?" saith the prophet Amos. It is the duty of ministers of the gospel to give warning of impending dangers.

Again; the apostle, in speaking unto Timothy, speaks unto us also, to us all, "This know ye also." It is the great concern of all professors and believers, of all churches, to have their hearts very much fixed upon present and approaching dangers. We have inquired so long about signs, tokens, and evidences of deliverance, and I know not what, that we have almost lost the benefit of all our trials, afflictions, and persecutions. The duty of all believers is, to be intent upon present and imminent dangers. "O Lord," say the disciples, Matt. xxiv., "what shall be the sign of thy coming?" They were fixed upon his coming. Our Saviour answers, "I will tell you: 1. There shall be an abounding of errors and false teachers: many shall say, 'Lo, here is Christ,' and, 'Lo, there is Christ.' 2. There shall be an apostasy from holiness: 'Iniquity shall abound, and the love of many shall wax cold.' 3. There shall be great distress of nations: 'Nation shall rise against nation, and kingdom against kingdom.' 4. There shall be great persecutions: 'And they shall persecute you, and bring you before rulers; and you shall be hated of all men for my name's sake.' 5. There shall be great tokens of God's wrath from heaven: 'Signs in the heavens, the sun, moon, and stars.'" The Lord Christ would acquaint believers how they should look for his coming; he tells them of all the dangers. Be intent upon these things. I know you are apt to overlook them; but these are the things that you are to be intent upon.

Not to be sensible of a present perilous season, is that security which the Scripture so condemns; and I will leave it with you, in short, under these three things:—1. It is that frame of heart which, of all others, God doth most detest and abhor. Nothing is more hateful to God than a secure frame in perilous days. 2. I will not fear to say this, and go with it, as to my sense, to the day of judgment: A secure person, in perilous seasons, is assuredly under the power of some predominant lust, whether it appears or not. 3. This secure, senseless frame is the certain presage of approaching ruin. This know, brethren, pray know this, I beg of you, for yours and my own soul, that you will be sensible of, and affected with, the perils of the season whereinto we are cast. What they are, if God help me, and give me a little strength, I shall show you by-and-by.

Secondly. There is the evil and danger itself thus forewarned of; and that is, καιροὶ χαλεποί,—hard times, perilous times, times of great difficulty, like those of public plagues, when death lies at every door; times that I am sure we shall not all escape, let it fall where it will. I will say no more of it now, because it is that which I shall principally speak to afterward.

Thirdly. The manner of their introduction, ἐνστήσονται,—" shall come." We have no word in our language that will express the force of ἐνίστημι. The Latins express it by " immineo, incido,"—the coming down of a fowl unto his prey. Now, our translators have given it the greatest force they could. They do not say, " Perilous times will come," as though they prognosticated future events; but, " Perilous times shall come." Here is a hand of God in this business; they shall so come, be so instant in their coming, that nothing shall keep them out; they shall instantly press themselves in, and prevail. Our great wisdom, then, will be, to eye the displeasure of God in perilous seasons; since there is a judicial hand of God in them, and we see in ourselves reason enough why they should come. But when shall they come?

Fourthly. They " shall come in the last days,"—ἐν ἐσχάταις ἡμέραις. The words " latter" or " last days" are taken three ways in Scripture;—sometimes for the times of the gospel, in opposition to the Judaical church-state; as in Heb. i. 2, " Hath in these last days spoken unto us by his Son;"—and elsewhere it may be taken (though I remember not the place) for days towards the consummation of all things and the end of the world;—and it is taken often for the latter days of churches; 1 Tim. iv. 1, " The Spirit speaketh expressly, that in the latter times some shall depart from the faith." And so the apostle John, 1 Epist. ii. 18, " Little children, it is the last time: and as ye have heard that antichrist shall come, even now are there many antichrists; whereby we know that it is the last time." And that is the season here intended. But yet you may take it in what sense you will: the last days, the days of the gospel; the last days, towards the consummation of all things and the end of the world; the last days, following the days of the profession of churches, those called Reformed Churches, or our own churches, in the ways wherein we walk; and the last days with many of us, with respect to our lives. In whatever sense the words are taken, it is time for us to look what shall come in these last days.

But the observation which at present I shall insist on from the text is this:—

Observation. When churches have been continued for a while in their profession, and begin to fall under decays therein, perilous seasons shall overtake them, which it will be hard for them to escape: " This know also, that perilous times shall come."

My design is only to dispose your minds a little to the work of the day: and all I shall do is, to show, in several instances, what are the things that make a season perilous; and what is our duty with reference unto such perilous seasons, both as to particular perils and perilous times in general. And it must not be said, as once it was of the prophet Ezekiel, " He prophesied of things a great way off." We do not prophesy of things a great way off; no, we shall speak of things that are even upon us,—what we see and know, and is as evident as if written with the beams of the sun.

I. The first thing that makes a season perilous is, when the profession of true religion is outwardly maintained under a visible predominancy of horrible lusts and wickedness. And the reason why I name it in the first place is, because it is what the apostle gives his instance in, in this place, " Perilous times shall come." Why? " ' For many shall be lovers of themselves, covetous, boasters, proud, blasphemers, disobedient to parents, unthankful, unholy, without natural affection, truce-breakers, false-accusers, incontinent, fierce, despisers of those that are good, traitors, heady, high-minded, lovers of pleasures more than lovers of God; having a form of godliness;'—maintaining their profession of the truth of religion under a predominancy, a visible, open predominancy, of vile lusts, and the practice of horrible sins." This rendered the season perilous. Whether this be such a season or not, do you judge. And I must say, by the way, we may and ought to witness against it, and mourn for the public sins of the days wherein we live. It is as glorious a thing to be a martyr for bearing testimony against the public sins of an age, as in bearing testimony unto any truth of the gospel whatsoever.

Now, where these things are, a season is perilous,—

1. Because of the infection. Churches and professors are apt to be infected with it. The historian[1] tells us of a plague at Athens, in the second and third years of the Peloponnesian war, whereof multitudes died; and of those that lived, few escaped but they lost a limb, or part of a limb,—some an eye, others an arm, and others a finger,—the infection was so great and terrible. And truly, brethren, where this plague comes,—of the visible practice of unclean lusts under an outward profession,—though men do not die, yet one loses an arm, another an eye, another a leg by it: the infection diffuses itself to the best of professors, more or less. This makes it a dangerous and perilous time.

2. It is dangerous, because of the effects; for when predominant

[1] Thucydides.

lusts have broken all bounds of divine light and rule, how long do you think that human rules will keep them in order? They break through all in such a season as the apostle describes. And if they come to break through all human restraints, as they have broken through divine, they will fill all things with ruin and confusion.

3. They are perilous in the consequence; which is, the judgments of God. When men do not receive the truth in the love of it, but have pleasure in unrighteousness, God will send them strong delusion, to believe a lie. So 2 Thess. ii. 10, 11, is a description how the Papacy came upon the world. Men professed the truth of religion, but did not love it,—they loved unrighteousness and ungodliness; and God sent them Popery. That is the interpretation of the place, according to the best divines. Will you profess the truth, and at the same time love unrighteousness? The consequence is, security under superstition and ungodliness. This is the end of such a perilous season; and the like may be said as to temporal judgments, which I need not mention.

Let us now consider what is our duty in such a perilous season:—

(1.) We ought greatly to mourn for the public abominations of the world, and of the land of our nativity wherein we live. I would only observe that place in Ezek. ix., God sends out his judgments, and destroys the city; but before, he sets a mark upon the foreheads of the men that sigh for all the abominations that are done in the midst thereof. You will find this passage referred in your books to Rev. vii. 3, "Hurt not the earth, neither the sea, nor the trees, till we have sealed the servants of our God in their foreheads." I would only observe this, that such only are the servants of God, let men profess what they will, "who mourn for the abominations that are done in the land." The mourners in the one place are the servants of God in the other. And truly, brethren, we are certainly to blame in this matter. We have been almost well contented that men should be as wicked as they would themselves, and we sit still and see what would come of it. Christ hath been dishonoured, the Spirit of God blasphemed, and God provoked against the land of our nativity; and yet we have not been affected with these things. I can truly say in sincerity, I bless God, I have sometimes laboured with my own heart about it. But I am afraid we all of us come exceeding short of our duty in this matter. "Rivers of waters," saith the psalmist, "run down mine eyes, because men keep not thy law." Horrible profanation of the name of God, horrible abominations, which our eyes have seen, and our ears heard, and yet our hearts been unaffected with them! Do you think this is a frame of heart God requireth of us in such a season,—to be regardless of all, and not to mourn for the public abominations of the land? The servants of God will mourn. I could speak, but am not free to speak, to those prejudices which keep us off from mourning for public abominations; but they may be easily suggested unto all your thoughts, and particularly what they are that have kept us off from attending more unto this duty of mourning for public abominations. And give me leave to say, that, according to the Scripture rule, there is no one of us can have any evidence that we shall escape outward judgments that God will bring for these abominations, if we have not been mourners for them; but that as smart a revenge, as to outward dispensations, may fall upon us as upon those that are most guilty of them, no Scripture evidence have we to the contrary. How God may deal with us, I know not.

This, then, is one part of the duty of this day,—that we should humble our souls for all the abominations that are committed in the land of our nativity; and, in particular, that we have no more mourned under them.

(2.) Our second duty, in reference to this perilous season is, to take care that we be not infected with the evils and sins of it. A man would think it were quite contrary; but really, to the best of my observation, this is, and hath been, the frame of things, unless upon some extraordinary dispensation of God's Spirit:—as some men's sins grow very high, other men's graces grow very low. Our Saviour hath told us, Matt. xxiv. 12, "Because iniquity shall abound, the love of many shall wax cold." A man would think the abounding of iniquity in the world should give great provocation to love one another. "No," saith our Saviour, "the contrary will be found true: as some men's sins grow high, other men's graces will grow low."

And there are these reasons for it:—

[1.] In such a season, we are apt to have light thoughts of great sins. The prophet looked upon it as a dreadful thing, that upon Jehoiakim's throwing the roll of Jeremiah's prophecy into the fire, till it was consumed, "yet they were not afraid, nor rent their garments, neither the king, nor any of his servants that heard all these words," Jer. xxxvi. 24. They were grown senseless, both of sin and judgment. And where men (be they in other respects never so wise) can grow senseless of sin, they will quickly grow senseless of judgments too. And I am afraid, the great reason why many of us have no impression upon our spirits of danger and perils in the days wherein we live, is because we are not sensible of sin.

[2.] Men are apt to countenance themselves in lesser evils, having their eyes fixed upon greater abominations of other men, that they behold every day; nay, there are those who pay their tribute to the devil,—walk in such and such abominations, and so countenance themselves in lesser evils. This is part of the public infection,—that they "do not run out into the same excess of riot that others do," though they live in the omission of duty, conformity to the world, and in many foolish, hurtful, and noisome lusts. They countenance themselves with this, that others are guilty of greater abominations.

[3.] Pray let such remember this, who have occasion for it (you may know it better than I; but yet I know it by rule, as much as you do by practice), that general converse in the world, in such a season, is full of danger and peril. Most professors are grown of the colour and complexion of those with whom they converse.

This is the first thing that makes a season perilous. I know not whether these things may be of concern and use unto you; they seem so to me, and I cannot but acquaint you with them.

II. A second perilous season, and that we shall hardly come off in, is, when men are prone to forsake the truth, and seducers abound to gather them up that are so; and you will have always these things go together. Do you see seducers abound? You may be sure there is a proneness in the minds of men to forsake the truth: and when there is such a proneness, they will never want seducers,—those that will lead off the minds of men from the truth; for there is both the hand of God and Satan in this business. God judicially leaves men, when he sees them grow weary of the truth, and prone to leave it; and Satan strikes in with the occasion, and stirs up seducers. This makes a season perilous. The apostle describes it, 1 Tim. iv. 1, "Now the Spirit speaketh expressly, that in the latter times" (these perilous days) "some shall depart from the faith, giving heed to seducing spirits, and doctrines of devils." And so Peter warns them to whom he writes, 2 Epist. ii. 1, 2, that "there shall come false teachers among them, who privily shall bring in damnable heresies, even denying the Lord that bought them, and bring upon themselves swift destruction: and many shall follow their pernicious ways." There shall come times full of peril, which shall draw men off from the truth into destruction.

If it be asked, how we may know whether there be a proneness in the minds of men in any season to depart from the truth? there are three ways whereby we may judge of it:—

1. The first is that mentioned, 2 Tim. iv. 3, "The time will come when they will not endure sound doctrine; but after their own lusts shall they heap to themselves teachers, having itching ears." When men grow weary of sound doctrine,—when it is too plain, too heavy, too dull, too common, too high, too mysterious, one thing or other that displeases them, and they would hear something new, something that may please,—it is a sign that there are in such an age many who are prone to forsake sound doctrine: and many such we know.

2. When men have lost the power of truth in their conversation, and are as prone and ready to part with the profession of it in their minds. Do you see a man retaining the profession of the truth under

a worldly conversation? He wants but baits from temptation, or a seducer, to take away his faith from him. An inclination to hearken after novelties, and loss of the power of truth in the conversation, is a sign of proneness unto this declension from the truth. Such a season, you see, is perilous. And why is it perilous? Because the souls of many are destroyed in it. The apostle tells us directly, 2 Pet. ii. 1, of "false prophets among the people, who privily bring in damnable heresies, even denying the Lord that bought them, and bring upon themselves swift destruction." Will it abide there? No: "And many shall follow their pernicious ways, by reason of whom the way of truth shall be evil spoken of." Brethren, while it is well with us, through the grace of God, and our own houses are not in flames, pray do not let us think the times are not perilous, when so many turn unto Popery and Quakerism, into pernicious errors, and fall into swift destruction. Will you say the time of the public plague was not perilous, because you are alive? No. Was the fire not dreadful, because your houses were not burned? No; you will, notwithstanding, say it was a dreadful plague, and a dreadful fire. And pray consider, is not this a perilous season, when multitudes have an inclination to depart from the truth, and God, in just judgment, hath permitted Satan to stir up seducers to draw them into pernicious ways, and their poor souls perish for ever.

Besides, there is a great aptness in such a season to work indifferency in the minds of those who do not intend utterly to forsake the truth. Little did I think I should ever have lived in this world to find the minds of professors grown altogether indifferent as to the doctrine of God's eternal election, the sovereign efficacy of grace in the conversion of sinners, justification by the imputation of the righteousness of Christ; but many are, as to all these things, grown to an indifferency: they know not whether they are so or not. I bless God I know something of the former generation, when professors would not hear of these things without the highest detestation; and now high professors begin to be leaders in it: and it is too much among the best of us. We are not so much concerned for the truth as our forefathers; I wish I could say we were as holy.

3. This proneness to depart from the truth is a perilous season, because it is the greatest evidence of the withdrawing of the Spirit of God from his church: for the Spirit of God is promised to this end, "to lead us into all truth;" and when the efficacy of truth begins to decay, it is the greatest evidence of the departing and withdrawing of the Spirit of God. And I think that this is a dangerous thing; for if the Spirit of God departs, then our glory and our life depart.

What, now, is our duty in reference to this perilous season? Forewarnings of perils are given us to instruct us in our duty.

(1.) The first is, not to be content with what you judge a sincere profession of truth; but to labour to be found in the exercise of all those graces which peculiarly respect the truth. There are graces that peculiarly respect the truth that we are to exercise; and if these are not found in our hearts, all our profession will issue in nothing. And these are,—

[1.] Love: "Because they loved not the truth." They made profession of the gospel; but they received not the truth in the love of it. There was want of love of the truth. Truth will do no man good where there is not the love of it. "Speaking the truth in love," is the substance of our Christian profession. Pray, brethren, let us labour to love the truth; and to take off all prejudices from our minds, that we may do so.

[2.] It is the great and only rule to preserve us in perilous times, —to labour to have the experience of the power of every truth in our hearts. If so be ye have learned the Lord Jesus. How? So as to "put off the old man, which is corrupt according to the deceitful lusts;" and to "put on the new man, which after God is created in righteousness and true holiness," Eph. iv. 22–24. This is to learn the truth. The great grace that is to be exercised with reference to truth in such a season as this, is to exemplify it in our hearts in the power of it. Labour for the experience of the power of every truth in your own hearts and lives.

[3.] Zeal for the truth. Truth is the most proper object for zeal. We ought to "contend earnestly for the truth once delivered to the saints;" to be willing, as God shall help us, to part with name and reputation, and to undergo scorn and contempt, all that this world can cast upon us, in giving testimony unto the truth. Every thing that this world counts dear and valuable is to be forsaken, rather than the truth. This was the great end for which Christ came into the world.

(2.) Cleave unto the means that God hath appointed and ordained for your preservation in the truth. I see some are ready to go to sleep, and think themselves not concerned in these things: the Lord awaken their hearts! Keep to the means of preservation in the truth, —the present ministry. Bless God for the remainder of a ministry valuing the truth, knowing the truth, sound in the faith;—cleave unto them. There is little influence upon the minds of men from this ordinance and institution of God, in the great business of the ministry. But know there is something more in it than that they seem to have better abilities to dispute than you; more knowledge, more light, better understandings than you. If you know no more in the ministry than this, you will never have benefit by it. They are God's ordinance; the name of God is upon them; God will be sanctified in them. They are God's ordinance for the preservation of the truth.

(3.) Let us carefully remember the faith of them who went before us in this nation, in the profession of the last age. I am apt to think there was not a more glorious profession for a thousand years upon the face of the earth, than was among the professors of the last age in this nation. And pray, what faith were they of? Were they half Arminian and half Socinian; half Papist and half I know not what? Remember how zealous they were for the truth; how little their holy souls would have borne with those public defections from the doctrine of truth which we see, and do not mourn over, but make nothing of, in the days wherein we live. God was with them; and they lived to his glory, and died in peace: "whose faith follow," and example pursue. And remember the faith they lived and died in: look round about, and see whether any of the new creeds have produced a new holiness to exceed theirs.

III. A third thing that makes a perilous season is, professors mixing themselves with the world, and learning their manners. And if the other perilous seasons are come upon us, this is come upon us also. This was the foundation and spring of the first perilous season that was in the world, that first brought in a deluge of sin and then a deluge of misery. It was the beginning of the first public apostasy of the church, which issued in the severest mark of God's displeasure. Gen. vi. 2, "The sons of God saw the daughters of men that they were fair; and they took them wives of all which they chose." This is but one instance of the church of God, the sons of God, professors, mixing themselves with the world. This was not all, that they took to themselves wives; but this was an instance the Holy Ghost gives that the church in those days did degenerate, and mix itself with the world. What is the end of mixing themselves in this manner with the world? Ps. cvi. 35, "They mingled themselves with the nations." And what then? "And learned their manners." If any thing under heaven will make a season perilous, this will do it,—when we mingle ourselves with the world, and learn their manners.

There are two things I shall speak to on this head:—1. Wherein professors do mingle themselves with the world. 2. The danger of it.

1. Professors mingle themselves with the world in that wherein it is the world, which is proper to the world. That which is more eminently and visibly of the devil, professors do not so soon mingle themselves withal; but in that wherein it is the world, in its own colours;—as in corrupt communication, which is the spirit of the world, the extract and fruit of vanity of mind,—that wherewith the world is corrupted, and doth corrupt. An evil, rotten kind of communication, whereby the manners of the world are corrupted,—this

comes from the spirit of the world. The devil hath his hand in all these things; but it is the world and the spirit of the world that is in corrupt communication. And how hath this spread itself among professors! Light, vain, foolish communication!—to spend a man's whole life therein; not upon this or that occasion, but almost always, and upon all occasions everywhere!—Vain habits and attire of the world is another instance. The habits and attire of the world are the things wherein the world doth design to show itself what it is. Men may read what the world is by evident characters, in the habits and attire that it wears. They are blind that cannot read vanity, folly, uncleanness, luxury, in the attire the world putteth upon itself. The declension of professors in imitating the ways of the world in their habits and garb, makes a season perilous: it is a mixture wherein we learn their manners; and the judgments of God will ensue upon it.—In this, likewise, we are grown like the world, that upon all occasions we are as regardless of the sins of the world, and as little troubled with them, as others are. Lot lived in Sodom, but "his righteous soul was vexed with their ungodly deeds and speeches." Live we where we will, when are our souls vexed, [so] that we do not pass through the things of the world, the greatest abominations, with the frame of spirit that the world itself doth? Not to speak of voluptuousness of living, and other things that attend this woful mixture with the world that professors have made in the days wherein we live,—corrupt communication, gaiety of attire, senselessness of the sins and abominations of the world round about us, are almost as much upon professors as upon the world. We have mixed ourselves with the people, and have learned their manners. But,—

2. Such a season is dangerous, because the sins of professors in it lie directly contrary to the whole design of the mediation of Christ in this world. Christ gave himself for us, that he might purge us from dead works, and purify us unto himself a peculiar people, Tit. ii. 14. "Ye are a royal nation, a peculiar people." Christ hath brought the hatred of the devil and all the world upon him and against him, for taking a people out of the world, and making them a peculiar people to himself; and their throwing themselves upon the world again is the greatest contempt that can be put upon Jesus Christ. He gave his life and shed his blood to recover us from the world, and we throw ourselves in again. How easy were it to show that this is an inlet to all other sins and abominations, and that for which I verily think the indignation and displeasure of God will soonest discover itself against professors and churches in this day! If we will not be differenced from the world in our ways, we shall not long be differenced from them in our privileges. If we are the same in our walkings, we shall be so in our worship, or have none at all.

As to our duty in such a perilous season, let me leave three cautions with you, and the Lord fix them upon your hearts:—

(1.) The profession of religion, and the performance of duties, under a world-like conversation, are nothing but a sophistical means to lead men blindfold into hell. We must not speak little things in such a great cause.

(2.) If you will be like the world, you must take the world's lot. It will go with you as it goes with the world. Inquire and see, in the whole book of God, how it will go with the world,—what God's thoughts are of the world,—whether it saith not, "If it lies in wickedness, it shall come to judgment," and that "the curse of God is upon it." If, therefore, you will be like the world, you must have the world's lot; God will not separate.

(3.) Lastly, consider we have by this means lost the most glorious cause of truth that ever was in the world. We do not know that there hath been a more glorious cause of truth since the apostles' days, than what God hath committed to his church and people in this nation, for the purity of the doctrine of the truth and ordinances; but we have lost all the beauty and glory of it by this mixture in the world. I verily think it is high time that the congregations in this city, by their elders and messengers, should consult together how to put a stop to this evil, that hath lost all the glory of our profession. It is a perilous time, when professors mix themselves so with the world.

There are other perilous seasons that I thought to have insisted on; but I will but name them.

IV. When there is great attendance on outward duties, but inward, spiritual decays. Now herein, my brethren, (most of this congregation are so in a peculiar manner, I hope, through the goodness of God,—in sincerity, though in much weakness, "Liberavi animam meam,") you know how long I have been treating of the causes and reasons of inward decays, and the means to be used for our recovery; I shall not, therefore, again insist upon them.

V. Times of persecution are also times of peril.

Now, I need not tell you whether these seasons are upon us or not; it is your duty to inquire into that. Whether there be not an outward retaining of the truth under a visible prevalency of abominable lusts in the world; whether there be not a proneness to forsake the truth, and seducers at work to draw men off; whether there be not a mingling ourselves with the world, and therein learning their manners; whether there be not inward decays, under the outward performance of duties; and whether many are not suffering under persecution and trouble, judge ye, and act accordingly.

One word of use, and I have done.

Use 1. Let us all be exhorted to endeavour to get our hearts affected with the perils of the day wherein we live. You have heard a poor, weak discourse concerning it, and perhaps it will be quickly forgotten. O that God would be pleased to give us this grace,—that we may find it our duty to endeavour to have our hearts affected with the perils of these seasons! It is not time to be asleep upon the top of a mast in a rough sea, when there are so many devouring dangers round about us. And the better to effect this,—

(1.) Consider the present things, and bring them to rule, and see what God's word says of them. We hear this and that story of horrible, prodigious wickedness; and bring it in the next opportunity of talk, and there slightly pass it over. We hear of the judgments of God abroad in the world; and bring them to the same standard of our own imaginations, and there is an end. And so we do with the distresses of others; we talk of them, and there is an end. But, brethren, when you observe any of these things, how it is with the world, if you would have your hearts affected, bring it to the word, and see what God saith of it: speak with God about it; ask and inquire at the mouth of God what God saith unto these prodigious wickednesses and judgments,—this coldness that is upon professors, and their mixtures with, and learning the manners of the world. You will never have your hearts affected with it, till you come and speak with God about it; and then you will find them represented in a glass that will make your hearts ache and tremble. And then,—

(2.) If you would be sensible of present perilous times, take heed of centring in self. While your greatest concern is self, or the world, all the angels in heaven cannot make you sensible of the peril of the days wherein you live. Whether you pursue riches or honours, while you centre there, nothing can make you sensible of the perils of the day. Therefore do not centre in self.

(3.) Pray that God would give us grace to be sensible of the perils of the day wherein we live. It may be we have had confidence, that though thousands fall at our right hand and at our left, yet we shall be able to carry it through. Believe me, it is great grace. Point your private, closet prayers, and your family prayers this way; and the Lord help us to point our public prayers to this thing, that God would make our hearts sensible of the perils of the time whereinto we are fallen in these last days!

Use 2. The next thing is this, that there are two things in a perilous season,—the sin of it, and the misery of it. Labour to be sensible of the former, or you will never be sensible of the latter. Though judgments lie at the door,—though the heavens be dark over us, and the earth shake under us at this day, and no wise man can see where he can build himself an abiding habitation,—we can talk of these things; and hear of other nations soaking in blood; and have tokens of God's displeasure,—warnings from heaven above and the earth beneath; and no man sensible of them! Why? Because they are not sensible of sin; nor ever will be, unless God make them so.

I shall range the sins that we should be sensible of under three heads:—the sins of the poor, wretched, perishing world, in the first place; the sins of professors in general, in the second place; and our own particular sins and decays, in the third place. And let us labour to have our hearts affected with these. It is to no purpose to tell you this and that judgment is approaching;—for your leaders, and those that are upon the watch-tower, to cry, "'A lion; my lord,' we see a lion." Unless God make our hearts sensible of sin, we shall not be sensible of judgments.

Use 3. Remember there is a special frame of spirit required in us all in such perilous seasons as these are. And what is that? It is a mourning frame of spirit. O that frame, that jolly frame of spirit that is upon us! The Lord forgive it, the Lord pardon it unto us; and keep us in a humble, broken, mournful frame of spirit: for it is a peculiar grace God looks for at such a time as this is. When he will pour out his Spirit, there will be great mourning, together and apart; but now we may say there is no mourning. The Lord help us, we have hard hearts and dry eyes under the consideration of all these perils that lie before us.

Use 4. Keep up church watch with diligence, and by the rule. When I say rule, I mean the life of it. I have no greater jealousy upon my heart, than that God should withdraw himself from his own institutions because of the sins of the people, and leave us only the carcase of outward rule and order. What doth God give them for? for their own sakes? No; but that they may be clothing for faith and love, meekness of spirit and bowels of compassion, watchfulness and diligence. Take away these, and farewell to all outward rule and order, whatever they are. Keep up a spirit that may live affected with it: get a spirit of church watch; which is not to lie at catch for faults, but diligently, out of pure love and compassion to the souls of men, to watch over them,—to wait to do them good, all we can. As it was with a poor man, who took a dead body and set it up, and it fell; and he set it up again, and it fell; upon which he cried out, "Oportet esse aliquid intus,"—"There wants something within," to enliven and quicken it;—so is it with church order and rule; set them up as often as you will, they will all fall, if there be not a love to one another, a delighting in the good of one another, "exhorting one another while it is called To-day, lest any be hardened through the deceitfulness of sin."

Use 5. Reckon upon it, that in such times as these are, all of us will not go free. You find no mention of a perilous season in Scripture, but it follows some shall have their faith overthrown, others shall follow pernicious ways, and others shall turn aside. Brethren and sisters, how do you know but you or I may fall? Let us double our watch, every one; for the season is come upon us wherein some of us may fall, and fall so as to smart for it. I do not say we shall perish eternally;—God deliver us from going into the pit! but some of us may so fall as to lose a limb, some member or other; and our works will be committed to the fire that shall burn them all. God hath kindled a fire in Zion that will try all our works; and we shall see in a short time what will become of us.

Use 6. Lastly, take that great rule which the apostle gives in such times as those wherewith we are concerned, "Nevertheless the foundation of God stands sure,"—O blessed be God for it!—"God knows who are his."

What, then, is required on our part? "Let him that nameth the name of Christ depart from evil." Your profession, your privileges, your light, will not secure you; you are gone, unless every one that nameth the name of Christ departs from all iniquity. What multitudes perish under a profession every day! O that our hearts could bleed to see poor souls in danger of perishing under the greatest profession!

Will you hear the sum of all? Perilous times and seasons are come upon us; many are wounded already; many have failed. The Lord help us! the crown is fallen from our head,—the glory of our profession is gone,—the time is short,—the Judge stands before the door. Take but this one word of counsel, my brethren: "Watch, therefore, that none of these things may come upon you, but that you may escape, and be accounted worthy to stand before the Son of God."

SERMON XXVII.[1]

THE CHRISTIAN'S WORK OF DYING DAILY.

"I protest by your rejoicing which I have in Christ Jesus our Lord, I die daily."
1 COR. xv. 31.

THESE words have a great vehemency and emphasis in them, and discover an uncommon earnestness upon the spirit of the apostle when he wrote them; and indeed they carry a greater appearance of

[1] This sermon was preached September 26, 1680.

such a vehemency in the original than in our translation. For the words we put in the last place, "I die daily," are the first in the original: Καθ' ἡμέραν ἀποθνήσκω, "I die daily;" Νὴ τὴν ὑμετέραν καύχησιν, ἣν ἔχω ἐν Χριστῷ Ἰησοῦ τῷ Κυρίῳ ἡμῶν,—"Yea, I do so by your rejoicing which I have in Christ Jesus our Lord." And there is no expression used by the apostle that hath a greater ardour of spirit in it than this hath.

The special reason of using it in this place is, to evidence the stability of his faith about the resurrection of the dead. That, you know, is the dispute he is upon. And he proves here that it was not an opinion that he had; but a firm-rooted faith, that carried him through all difficulties and sufferings. "Why stand we in jeopardy every hour? I protest by your rejoicing which I have in Christ Jesus our Lord, I die daily. If after the manner of men I have fought with beasts at Ephesus, what advantageth it me, if the dead rise not? let us eat and drink; for to-morrow we die." "I do evidence my faith," saith he, "of the resurrection, by my readiness to suffer all things in the confirmation of the truth of it." And it is the great duty of ministers to be ready at all times to evidence the stability of their own faith in the things which they preach to others, by a cheerful suffering for them.

There are two things in the words: An assertion; and the confirmation of it. The assertion is this, "I die daily." The confirmation of it, "I protest by your rejoicing which I have in Christ Jesus our Lord."

There are two or three difficulties in these words. I shall very little trouble you with conjectures, but give you what I think the sense of the Holy Ghost in them.

The one is from the ambiguous signification of the word καύχησις, which we render here "rejoicing." But in other places it is rendered sometimes by "confidence," sometimes by "boasting," and sometimes by "glorying." "Gloriation" is the word I would use, if our language would bear it. "And your gloriation;"—which is an exultation of joy.

There is another difficulty, in the transposition of the words, such as are not in the Scripture again. "I protest by your rejoicing which I have in Christ Jesus." This hath afforded variety of conjectures unto many; but plainly the sense of it is this, "By the rejoicing which you and I have in the Lord." And I could give instances of the like trajections in the Greek tongue, from one person to another, if it were to your edification.

There is yet a third difficulty. The particle νὴ here is a note of an oath, or swearing; as much as בְּ in the Hebrew tongue; or in our language, "by;" yet sometimes it is used as a note of strong asseveration. And we have chosen to express it by a middle word, "I protest." If it be a note of an oath, then the word is used to denote the object, "I swear by your rejoicing in the Lord;" that is, "by the Lord in whom you rejoice." As it is said expressly, "Jacob swore by the Fear of his father Isaac;" that is, "by Him whom his father Isaac feared." But I rather take it here as a note only of vehement asseveration; and so, says he, "It is as true as that you and I do glory in Christ, and rejoice in him, I die daily."

It may have a double sense, "I am every day, by reason of preaching the gospel, exposed to dangers and death." For he doth speak both before and after of the dangers he underwent in the work of preaching the gospel. "I die daily;" or, "'I die daily,' by continually preparing myself to die; I am always in a preparation to die; through the faith of the resurrection, I am always prepared to die cheerfully and comfortably, according to the will of God." And this is the sense I shall fix upon. And it being in a necessary duty, I may raise a general rule from a special instance, in this example of the apostle.

Observation. It is the duty of all believers to be preparing themselves every day to die cheerfully, comfortably, and, if it may be, triumphing in the Lord.

Observe only this, that there may be a dying safely, where there is not a dying cheerfully and comfortably. Every believer, whoever he be, shall die safely; but we see many believers do not die cheerfully and comfortably. I do not speak of the first, how all persons may come to die safely; but of the latter, how believers may die comfortably and cheerfully.

And there are two ways of dying cheerfully and comfortably:—

1. The one is in outward expressions, to the comfort of them that are about us. This depends much on the nature of the distemper whereof men may die, which may oppress the animal spirits, and cloud the mind; and therefore it falls not under rule, but is left to the providence of God.

2. But there is also a dying cheerfully and comfortably in persons' own souls; which, it may be, in their dying moments they cannot manifest, when they are thoroughly prepared for it.

Truly, brethren, all I can say is, that I am speaking to you of the things which I have considered on my own account, before ever I thought of considering them upon yours; and I cannot declare unto you what I have attained, which may be little or nothing; but only what I have aimed at, if it may be of use to us in this dying time, especially among good ministers, one or another [dying] almost every day.[1]

[1] At this time many eminent servants of Christ, who had been associated with Owen in the Christian ministry, and in important public duties, during the event-

I shall mention three things that, in my judgment, are requisite unto every believer who would die cheerfully, and come in a fit and full season into the presence of God:—

I. The constant exercise of faith, as to the resignation of a departing soul into the hand and sovereign will of God. "I die daily." How? Exercising faith constantly, in the resignation of a departing soul, when the time comes, unto the sovereign grace, good pleasure, power, and faithfulness of God. The soul is now taking its leave of all its concerns in this world; all that it sees, all that it knows by its senses, all its relations, everything it hath been acquainted withal, to have an eternal, absolute unconcern in them. It is entering into an invisible world, whereof it knows nothing but what it hath by faith. When Paul was taken up into the third heaven, 2 Cor. xii. 2, we should have been glad to have heard some tidings from the invisible world how things were there. He saw nothing; only he heard words. Why, blessed Paul, may we not hear those words? No; "They are not lawful to be uttered," saith he. God will not have us know any thing in the invisible world but what is revealed in the word, while we are here. Therefore the souls of them departed, who have died and lived again, as the soul of Lazarus, I doubt not but God supported in their being, but restrained all their operations. For if a separate soul had one natural, intuitive view of God, it would be the greatest misery in the world to send it back into a dying body. God will keep those things to be objects of faith. Lazarus could tell nothing of what was done in heaven; his soul was kept in its being, but all its operations were restrained. I bless God I have peculiarly exercised my thoughts, according to the conduct of the word, about the invisible world; whereof, in due time, you may hear something: but in the meantime, I know we have no notion of it but what is by pure revelation.

Whither now is the soul going? what will be the issue within a few moments? Is it annihilated? doth death not only separate the

ful times of the Protectorate, were passing into their eternal rest. In 1679, Thomas Goodwin, President of Magdalene College, a member of the Westminster Assembly, a happy expositor of Scripture, and, according to Anthony Wood, "one of the Atlases and Patriarchs of Independency,"—was removed from this world, and became, in the highest sense of his own phrase, "a child of light." It was but two months before this sermon was preached that Stephen Charnock died. He had been Senior Proctor in the University of Oxford during the Protectorate; and left behind him manuscripts, from which two large folios of posthumous works have been published,—works held in such estimation, that besides the detached issue of particular treatises, they have been, in their collected form, four times reprinted. Others might be mentioned who died about this period, such as Matthew Poole, author of the "Synopsis Criticorum;" and Theophilus Gale, author of "The Court of the Gentiles." Such facts may help to account for the touching and solemn tone of these discourses on preparation for death, as well as for the particular allusion in the paragraph above.—Ed.

body and soul, but destroy our being, so that we shall be no more to eternity? So some would have it; for it is their interest it should be so. Is the soul going into a state of wandering in the air, under the influence of more powerful spirits?—which was the opinion of the old pagan world, as that which caused appearances of the dead so frequently upon the earth.

And this persuasion was taken into purgatory by the Papists; from whence they concluded that there were great appearances of them that were departed continually. And you have a thousand stories of them, which we know to be all the actings and deceits of evil spirits. And such is our darkness as to the invisible world, that the greatest part of Christians have feigned a third state, that is not in it, but the fruit of superstition and idolatry. For this is superstition, to invent things in religion suited to men's natural affections, or to gratify their lusts for their own profit; both which were designed in this case. For when persons thought the souls of men that were gone into an eternal condition were lost, and that for ever,—"No, there is another venture for them," say they; and so they pacified them, that if they were the worst of men, yet there might be hope for them after death. Nor has it a less tendency to gratify men in their lusts, and encourage them to live at their pleasure. And the whole of this they turn to their own profit who invented it. This by the way,—only to manifest the darkness that mankind is in as to this invisible world. To proceed, therefore:—

Doth the soul go into a state wherein it is capable of no joy, no consolation? Brethren, let men pretend what they will, he that never received any joy or consolation in this world but by his senses, or his reason exercised about the objects of his senses, doth not know, nor can believe, the soul itself should be capable of any consolation in another world. He alone who hath received immediately into his soul spiritual comfort in this world, can believe that his soul is capable of it in another. But, however, this is certain, no man can undertake any thing about the conduct of his soul in another world.

What is your way, then, in this state and condition? what is your wisdom? Truly, to resign this departing soul unto the sovereign wisdom, pleasure, faithfulness, and power of God (which is the duty we have in hand), by the continual exercise of faith. So the apostle tells us, 2 Tim. i. 12. "For I know," saith he, "whom I have believed, and am persuaded that he is able to keep that which I have committed unto him against that day." It is a mighty thing to keep a separate soul to the day of the resurrection. Why, saith the apostle, "'I know whom I have trusted with it;' I trust it with almighty power." The Lord help us to believe that there shall be an act of almighty power put forth in the behalf of these poor souls of ours, when departed into the invisible world, to keep them to that day when body and soul shall be united, and come to enjoy God.

We have a glorious example for this duty and exercise of faith. Our Lord Jesus Christ died in the exercise of it. It was the last act of faith Christ put forth in this world, Luke xxiii. 46, "When Jesus had cried with a loud voice" (this was the voice of nature, but now he comes to the words of faith), "he said, Father, into thy hands I commend my spirit" (my departing soul): "and having said thus, he gave up the ghost." Here was the last exercise of the faith of our Lord Jesus Christ in this world,—the committing of his departing soul into the hands of God. And to what end did he do it? We are told, Ps. xvi. 8–11, "I have set the LORD always before me: because he is at my right hand, I shall not be moved. Therefore my heart is glad, and my glory rejoiceth: my flesh also shall rest in hope. For thou wilt not leave my soul in hell; neither wilt thou suffer thine Holy One to see corruption. Thou wilt show me the path of life: in thy presence is fulness of joy; at thy right hand there are pleasures for evermore." These are the words of David, which our Lord Jesus Christ made use of himself, when he said, "Into thy hands I commend my spirit." And the psalmist adds, "Thou hast redeemed me, O LORD God of truth," Ps. xxxi. 5. An experience of the work of redemption, communicated to us by the truth of the promise, is the greatest encouragement to commend a departing soul into the hands of God.

This, to me now (considering the vanishing of all these shadows and appearances, and the eternal dissolution of all relation to things below, and the subsisting of a soul in a separate condition, which we are not acquainted withal), is one of the first things we have to consider, if we will die cheerfully and comfortably,—namely, how we can resign a departing soul into the hand and sovereign disposal of God.

It is both a great and eminent act of faith, and is the last victorious act of faith, so to do:—

1. It is a great and eminent act of faith. [See] Heb. xi., where the mighty efficacy and great success of faith is spoken of. One of the particulars, and that wherein many of the rest did centre, is, "These all died in faith." It was a great thing to die in faith under the Old Testament, when they were encompassed with so many shadows, and so much darkness, and when their view into things invisible, within the vail, was exceeding much beneath what God hath communicated unto us. Nay, the state of things within the vail was not the same then as now; there was not Christ upon the throne, administering his office. Notwithstanding, faith carried them through all this darkness, and caused them to make a believing venture of their souls upon God, his faithfulness, mercy, and grace.

When it comes to this consideration, it lays all things in the balance:—in the one scale, our being, our walking, and life in this world; our sins, and their guilt; our fears, uncertainties, and darkness of a future state; our abhorrence of a dissolution, the consideration of all things that are round about us;—in the other, the power, faithfulness, and mercy of God, and his ability to receive, preserve, and keep us to that day, and to be better to us than all these things. "Here shall be my portion," saith faith; "all things in the other scale are of no value, of no weight to this exceeding weight of power and goodness of God." This is a glorious exercise of faith! Have you tried it, my brethren? Lay things on the one side and the other in the balance, and see which way the scale will draw,—what faith will do in such a case.

2. It is the last victorious act of faith, wherein it hath its final conquest over all its adversaries. Faith is the leading grace in all our spiritual warfare and conflict; but all along while we live, it hath faithful company that adheres to it, and helps it. Love works, and hope works, and all other graces,—self-denial, readiness to the cross,—they all work and help faith. But when we come to die, faith is left alone. Now, try what faith will do. The exercise of other graces ceases; only faith comes to a close conflict with its last adversary, wherein the whole is to be tried. And, by this one act of resigning all into the hand of God, faith triumphs over death, and cries, "'O death, where is thy sting? O grave, where is thy victory?' Come, give me an inlet into immortality and glory; the everlasting hand of God is ready to receive me!" This is the victory whereby we overcome all our spiritual enemies.

I thought to have made some use of what hath been said; to examine whether we do live in the exercise of this grace or no, and what benefit we have thereby: and I should have touched especially upon this one thing,—this alone will keep us from all surprisal of death. Not to be surprised with any thing is the substance of human wisdom; not to be surprised with death is a great part of the substance of our spiritual wisdom.

SERMON XXVIII.[1]

I MADE an entrance upon this portion of Scripture the last Lord's day, and I judged the subject very suitable, because of the warnings God hath variously given us to be exercising ourselves unto this

[1] This sermon was preached October 3, 1680.

duty. God hath since increased the seasonableness, by taking away a great and eminent servant[1] of his from among us; concerning whom I will say this one word, and no more:—

As far as I know by thirty years' acquaintance and friendship, and half that time in church-fellowship, it may be the age wherein he lived did not produce many more wise, more holy, more useful than he in his station, if any. And so I leave him at rest with God.

I proposed to insist upon those things which are necessary for us, to obtain a peaceable and comfortable departure out of this world. And I have spoken to one head; which was, the daily exercise of faith, in the resignation of a departing soul, to the sovereign power and will of God, to be treated and entertained by him according to the tenor of the covenant of grace.

I will not leave this point till I have made some use of it. And I shall take no other measure of my time but the strength God is pleased to give me.

Use 1. It may be worth our while to inquire into the especial nature of this duty which we are exhorted unto; for we may every day more and more understand the weakness of many, who think, it may be, they know something of it, when they know not what it means. We may, therefore, consider three things in it:—(1.) What is the special and immediate object of this exercise of faith; (2.) What is the form or special nature of it; and, (3.) What is the way and manner of its performance.

(1.) As to the especial and immediate object of this exercise of faith, and which must take with it a special motive,—that, I say, is God, under the consideration of his sovereignty, power, and faithfulness; and this upon the motive of some experience of his kindness and grace. So speaks the psalmist, Ps. xxxi. 5, "Into thine hand I commit my spirit." What was it that gave him confidence so to do? "Thou hast redeemed me," saith he, "O LORD God of truth." A sense of redeeming grace, conveyed by the truth of the promises, is required in all that would commit their spirits into the hand of God.

[1] The decease to which Dr Owen refers must have occurred between September 26 and October 3. Colonel Desborough, a member of his congregation, brother-in-law to Oliver Cromwell, and one of the heroes of the Commonwealth, died on the 10th September 1680. He refused to sit on the trial of Charles I.; and though so nearly related to Cromwell, opposed him when he sought to become king. But it is evident, from the dates, that the allusion cannot be to him. The quaint and pious Thomas Brooks, a preacher of distinguished pathos and usefulness, and author of some well-known treatises, such as "Heaven upon Earth," "The Unsearchable Riches of Christ," "Apples of Gold in Pictures of Silver," etc., died on the 27th of September 1680. The date would answer to the allusion in the discourse, if the terms of it did not leave an impression that Owen refers to a member of his own congregation. Brooks was a zealous Congregationalist; but this could hardly be all the "church-fellowship" to which Owen refers. In his work, "The Golden Key," he subscribes himself "late preacher of the word at Margaret's, New Fish Street."—ED.

And therefore, brethren, when you come to the exercise of this great duty, you must lay this foundation in some sense and experience of the grace and kindness of God, or you can never perform it in a due manner. And,—

[1.] Upon this motive, the first thing we consider in God, in the resignation of our souls to him, is his sovereignty. It is mentioned in two places in the Psalms, in both which this duty is proposed unto us. Ps. xvi. 1, 2, " Preserve me, O God: for in thee do I put my trust. O my soul, thou hast said unto the LORD" (thou hast said unto Jehovah), " Thou art my Lord." He doth not use the word יְהוָֹה again,—but אֲדֹנָי, " Thou art my Lord," (אֲדֹנָי אָתָּה,) " who hast the sovereign disposal of me. I am going to give up my spirit to thee; and I do it upon the consideration of thy sovereignty, that ' thou art my Lord.' " So Ps. xxxi. 14, 15, " I trusted in thee, O LORD." Why so? " I said, Thou art my God. My times are in thy hand."— " It is because of thy sovereignty. ' Thou art my God,' who hast the sovereign disposal of me; therefore I commit myself to thee." It follows those words, " Father, into thy hands I commend my spirit." Faith regards the glorious sovereignty of God, as the absolute free disposer of all things here, and unto eternity, without any reserve but his own pleasure, when it makes this resignation of the soul unto him.

[2.] It hath a peculiar respect unto the power of God, 2 Tim. i. 12, " I know whom I have believed, and am persuaded that he is able to keep that which I have committed to him against that day." It is common for persons to go through it in a customary manner. Die they must; but there is nothing can encourage them to yield up their souls to God, but an apprehension of such an infinite power that is able to preserve them in eternal being in the invisible world, especially to the day of the resurrection.

[3.] It respects the faithfulness of God, as one who hath promised that he will take care of us when we are gone out of this world, 1 Pet. iv. 19, " Wherefore, let them that suffer according to the will of God commit the keeping of their souls to him in well-doing, as unto a faithful Creator;" that is, as a God who is omnipotent, who made all things, and is faithful in the accomplishing of his promises.

So, then, this duty I exhort unto is an immediate address unto God, an exercise of faith upon him, with special respect unto his sovereignty, power, and faithfulness, upon an experience we have, in some measure, of his goodness and grace.

The seat before my eyes is very much changed in a short time, and I know not, brethren, how soon it may be the lot of any of you to stand in need of understanding this thing and bringing it into practice. You may, if you please, remember it, for it is of great importance to have immediate converse with God with respect unto those great and awful attributes of his sovereignty, power, and faithfulness. That is the first thing.

(2.) As to the special form of this duty, there are two words wherein it is expressed, and both of the same import: for in one place it is rendered, "commending;" in another, "committing," Luke xxiii. 46, and Ps. xxxi. 5. But it is a re-commending or committing, as men commit a trust. If a man lay a-dying, and had an only child, and an estate to leave him, with what solemnity would he commit him to the trust of his friend, to take care of him! "I commit this poor child, who is helpless and fatherless,—I commit him to your trust," saith he, "to your love, care, and power, to look after him." He doth it with great solemnity. The psalmist calls his soul his "darling," and "only one:" "Deliver 'my darling' from the dog, and 'my only one.'" And now when a person is about to leave this world, he is to commit his soul, and leave it in trust somewhere. Then this exercise of faith is a leaving in trust or committing our "darling," our "only one," that is departing out of this tabernacle, unto God, under the consideration of his sovereignty, power, and faithfulness. I do not yet speak unto the life of this duty; which consists in committing the trust of our souls unto God, to be dealt withal, not according to our choice, but according to the terms of the covenant of grace, let it fall where it will, to all eternity: that is the solemn committing.

(3.) As to the manner of it, it ought to be done expressly in words that we should say to God. I do not give instructions to them who are dying, but to them that live, that they may be prepared to die. We should say to God, "Lord, I have been thus long in this world; I have seen much variety in the outward dispensation of things in the world, but a thousand times more in the inward frame of my spirit; and I am now leaving the world upon thy call: I am to be here no more. O Lord, after all, being to enter into a new, eternal state, I commit my soul unto thee,—I leave it with thee,—I put all my trust and confidence in thy faithfulness, power, and sovereignty, to be dealt withal according to the terms of the covenant of grace. Now I can lie down in peace."

Use 2. What benefit shall we receive hereby, if we do thus exercise our souls? I answer, We shall receive these advantages:—

(1.) I know nothing that is more meet to keep our souls in a constant reverence of God; which is the very life and soul of holiness and obedience. And the best profession, where this is not, is of no value. Now, nothing is more suited to this than an immediate access unto God every day (frequently at least), under the consideration of his glorious sovereignty, power, and faithfulness, as if you were immediately going into his presence, and into his hands. The more you abound in it, the greater will your reverence of God be. We have deceitful hearts, and a very crafty adversary to deal withal. We are commanded to draw nigh, and to have our access unto God with boldness, Heb. x.;—to "come boldly to the throne of grace," Heb. iv. 16. And we should do it frequently. Now, nothing in this world is so suited to take off reverence, as boldness and frequency. Where men make bold, and where they [are] frequent,—as in a multitude of duties many are bold and frequent,—it works off the reverence of God. That is carnal boldness. But the more frequently you make your accesses unto God with spiritual boldness, the more will your hearts be filled with a reverence of God continually. And the more frequently you make your approaches unto God in outward duties without this holy and humble reverence, whatever your gifts be, reverence of God will decay. What poor, slight, withering things, have I seen some men grow to be, under a fair outward conversation, and multiplication of duties! And you may take this measure with you in all your duties;—if they increase a reverence of God, they are from grace; if they do not, they are from gifts, and no way sanctify the soul wherein they are.

(2.) It will support us under all our sufferings. The soul that is accustomed to this exercise of faith, will not be greatly moved in any of its sufferings. The Lord knows we are all moved and shaken,—and ready to be so, sometimes, very unhandsomely and unduly,—as the leaves of the forest; but it will keep us from being greatly moved. "I shall not be greatly moved," saith the psalmist. And elsewhere it is enjoined, "Let them that suffer according to the will of God, commit the keeping of their souls to God, as unto a faithful Creator." This will support you under all your sufferings. It is the very case and state in Ps. xxxi., from whence I have taken my principal testimony: "Have mercy upon me, O LORD, for I am in trouble: mine eye is consumed with grief, yea, my soul and my belly. For my life is spent with grief, and my years with sighing: my strength faileth because of mine iniquity, and my bones are consumed," etc. "For I have heard the slander of many; fear was on every side: while they took counsel together against me, they devised to take away my life." What course doth he then take in all these distresses, sufferings, and persecutions? Why, saith he, "I said, Thou art my God. My times are in thy hand." He makes a resignation of himself to the sovereignty of God, and so was at peace.

I have showed you now how you may exercise this duty; and I do reckon myself to be near my account, and speak as one that is sensible of it. Would I could prevail with you to bring it more or less into actual exercise, before you give rest to your eyes, or slumber to your eyelids!

Use 3. In the next place, who are they that do or can perform this duty as they ought, to live in this exercise of faith?

I am certain that they do not do so who live as if they were to live here for ever. But this is an evident proof of that distemper and confusion which is come upon the mind and soul of man. Truly, if a man of sobriety and reputation did come to such kind of men, who live in their sensuality and wickedness, as the world is full of them, and tell them, "Sirs! what do you do? I am persuaded that there is a death to come, and an eternal state of blessedness or woe near approaching: the way wherein you are will certainly engulf you in eternal destruction;"—they would say to him, "This is your opinion." Yet one would think a wise man should prevail with them to do something according to his opinion. But it is not so. They have convictions in their minds they must die; they will not only say it is mine or your opinion, but they themselves are convinced of a future state, and profess it. But will they do any thing from an influence of this conviction? Nothing at all; no more than if they were brute beasts. These are not able to come to the exercise of their duty.

Nor those who walk at all peradventure. They know they must die; but they are apt to think they have other things to do before they die, and it will be time enough hereafter, at one season or another, to be preparing to die. The apostle did "die daily" indeed; but they have something else to do. When death knocks at their neighbour's door, and they hear such a one is dead, and it comes to their own families, and takes away this or that person, then they have some thoughts for a little while; but they quickly wear off, and they return to their common frame of spirit again. "'Yet a little more slumber, a little more sleep, a little more folding of the hands to sleep;'—a little more secure converse in the world, attending unto our affairs." But death will come as an armed man, and they shall not be able to escape.

There are, therefore, two things required of every one that would be found in the exercise of this duty:—

(1.) That he lay the foundation of it in some comfortable persuasion of an interest in Christ; which alone will enable him to die safely: and having obtained that, he may labour after that which will enable him to die comfortably and cheerfully. Some men die safely; but, upon many considerations not now to be mentioned, they do not appear to die comfortably. And some men die very comfortably, to all outward appearance, that do not die safely. This, therefore, is necessary, that there be this foundation laid,—some comfortable persuasion of our interest in Christ, that we may die safely; or else it is to no purpose to expect to die comfortably.

(2.) Many think a few words at last will do it, and there is an end; but let me assure you, not only upon principles of Scripture truth, but of nature, there is no man can do it that hath not a view into the glory of spiritual and eternal things, outbalancing all his soul parts withal in this world. I hear men willing to die, and I find others do; but it is to go contrary to the principles of nature. No man under heaven (it implies a contradiction) can part with that which appears good to him, unless it be upon motives of a greater good. He must part with it; but he cannot willingly and cheerfully part with it. If you would be thus able willingly and cheerfully to resign a departing soul unto God, labour to have a view of those better things which are infinitely more great and glorious, which your souls shall come to the enjoyment of upon this departure.

The calls of God are great upon us, both public and private, and special to this congregation. God expects a special compliance with his calls from us; or else we shall yet be exercised with farther tokens of his displeasure.

SERMON XXIX.[1]

THAT which I have been treating upon from these words is, to declare the ways and duties whereby a believer may come to die, not only safely, which all believers shall, but also cheerfully and comfortably,—so as to have a free and abundant entrance into the kingdom of God in glory.

I have spoken but to one thing; which is, the exercise of faith in the resignation of a departing soul entering into the invisible world into the sovereign hand and pleasure of God, to be disposed of according to the tenor of the everlasting covenant.

There are two things yet remaining necessary to the same end,—at least I find them so; which, if God will, I shall despatch at this time.

II. There is required, unto this great end, a readiness and willingness to part with this body which we carry about us, and to lay it down in the dust. The soul's natural aversation to let go this body, is that which we call an unwillingness to die; that hath made some say, like him of old, "Mori nolo," etc.,—"I can be content to be dead, but I would not die."

There are two reasons why the soul hath a natural unwillingness to part with the body:—

1. Because it is, and hath been ever since it had a being, the only instrument of all the operations and actings of its faculties and powers.

[1] This sermon was first preached October 10, 1680.

The whole privilege of a being consists in its powers and acts. Now, from the first moment of its being, the soul hath had no instrument to act by but the body; and that not only in the outward actions that the body performs, but in all its internal, rational actings, it cannot act without the instrumentality of the body. Therefore we know a hurt in the body, as oftentimes in the head, hath utterly deprived the soul of the exercise of all its powers and faculties during life. It cannot act rational, internal actings but by the body, and how it can act without the body it knows not. This hath ingrafted a natural unwillingness in the soul to let go the body, whereby, from the first instant of its being, it hath constantly acted. This is but one reason of it; there is yet a greater.

2. The other reason is, that strict, near, unparalleled union and relation between the soul and the body. There is a near union between parents and children, a nearer between husband and wife; but they are nothing to this union between the soul and body. There is an ineffable, inconceivable union between the two natures, the divine and the human, in the person of the Son of God; but this union was eternally indissoluble from the first moment of it: when the body and soul of Christ were separated, yet they continued in their union with the person of the Son of God as much as before, or as now in heaven. But here is a union that is dissoluble between a heavenly spirit and an earthly, sensual body; that is, two essential parts of the same nature. Pray give me leave to speak a little to it. I have considered what it is to die, and examined whence ariseth the difficulty. Now, I say it ariseth from this peculiar constitution of our nature; there being no such thing in all the works of God, in heaven above, or in the earth beneath. The angels are pure, immaterial spirits; they have nothing in them that can die. God can annihilate an angel,—he that made all things out of nothing, can bring all things into nothing; but an angel cannot die, from the principles of his own constitution;—there is nothing in him that can die. A brute creature hath nothing in it that can live when death comes. "The spirit of a beast" Solomon speaks of as that which "goeth downward." It is not the object of almighty power to preserve it, because it is nothing but the act of the body in its temperature and constitution. But now man is "medium participationis;"—he hath an angelical nature from above that cannot die, and a nature from beneath that cannot always live, since the entrance of sin, though it might have done so before. And therefore, in the product of man there was a double act of creation, and but a single act in any other creature's. The creation of angels is not mentioned, unless in that, "Let there be light, and there was light;" but in all other things there was but one single act for its production. But when God came to make man,

there were two distinct acts of creation. "God made man of the dust of the earth." And what then? "And breathed into him the spirit of life." Here is something that is not in all God's creation beside. And now, upon this dissolution, all the actings of this nature, as it was one person, must cease unto the day of the resurrection. A wonderful change it is, that there shall be no more acting of the entire nature of man until the resurrection; only one part of this nature continues to act itself, according to its own powers. And one end of God's work upon us in the grave is, to free our bodies from all alliance, and relation, and likeness unto the bodies of beasts. So our Saviour tells us, Luke xx. "Do not mistake," saith he, "'you shall neither marry nor give in marriage,' nor have any one action common to brutes; but the whole man shall be *ἰσάγγελοι*,—'like unto the angels.'" This is the great privilege of our nature, as the wise man declares, Eccles. iii. 19, where he answers the objection of an epicure: "That which befalleth the sons of men befalleth beasts; even one thing befalleth them: as the one dieth, so dieth the other; yea, they have all one breath; so that a man hath no pre-eminence above a beast: all go unto one place; all are of the dust, and all turn to dust again." "As far as I can see it is so," saith the man. But what saith the wise man? "Who knoweth the spirit of man that goeth upward, and the spirit of the beast that goeth downward to the earth?" "Alas! you are mistaken: the difference doth not lie in this outward nature, wherein man and beast have a near alliance one to another; but in the spiritual, heavenly nature, that is from above;—and unless you know that, you will think all are as beasts indeed." This, then, is the foundation of the unalterable aversation in the mind and soul to part with the body,—this strange constitution of our nature, which has nothing like it in the whole work of God, nothing to give us any representation of it, but it is peculiar unto us. And then this dissolution is but once to be made. They observe of the old heroes, who would freely venture their lives, and cast them away in any great attempt, that when they came to die, when they had killed themselves, or were killed by others, their souls went away with groaning and indignation: they knew not how to bear the dissolution of the union.

And therefore this is in us all, brethren; it is our first desire, which we have upon a prospect that we cannot continue here, "to be clothed upon;" and, as the apostle says, "that mortality may be swallowed up of life,"—that the body and soul together may go into immortality and glory. But this is not God's way; this is that he will bring us to,—that we be ready and willing to part with these bodies of ours, notwithstanding this union, or we cannot die cheerfully and comfortably.

Upon what grounds, then, can a man be ready and willing to lay down his tabernacle in the dust?

I shall fix upon two reasons, both given us by the same apostle:—

(1.) The first is that which he gives us, Phil. i. 23, "Having a desire to depart, and to be with Christ." 'Επιθυμίαν ἔχω, "I have a strong bent and inclination of spirit." The word is that which in Scripture is used for "lust" and "concupiscence;" that is, always working with strong bent and inclination. "It is not a desire that sometimes befalls me, now and then, when in trouble, sickness, or pain; but I have an habitual, constant inclination." Unto what? 'Αναλῦσαι, "to depart," to leave this body. "It is usually translated in the passive; "I have a desire to be dissolved." But the plain meaning of the word is this, "I do desire that the contexture of my nature may be reduced unto its distinct principles,—may be analyzed." Now, analysis is the reducing of a speech from the present contexture into its proper, distinct principles. Then, here lies the difficulty. I told you the soul hath an aversation to this dissolution; and yet the apostle saith, "I have a continual, strong inclination to it." To what? Pray observe it,—"To be with Christ." I have no inclination to be dissolved as the end, but only as the means for another end, that without it I cannot be with Christ. There is my end. And so far with respect unto that end, that which is in itself no object of inclination becomes an object of desire. Brethren, I know no man dies willingly,—no man living can have an habitual inclination to close cheerfully with this dissolution,—but by looking upon it as a means to come to the enjoyment of Christ. I tell you, your bodies are better to you than all the world, than all your goods, or any thing else; but Christ is better to the soul than any thing: and therefore, unless it be for the enjoyment of Christ, let men pretend what they will, there is no man willing to part with the body,—to be dissolved. Grow in that desire of coming to Christ, and you will conquer the unwillingness of death.

(2.) The second reason is given us, Rom. viii. 10, "The body is dead because of sin; but the Spirit is life because of righteousness." The body is not only doomed to death by reason of original sin, as death entered upon all on that account; but the body must be brought to death, that sin may be rooted out of it. Sin hath taken such a close, inseparable habitation in the body, that nothing but the death of the body can make a separation. The body must be dead because of sin. Saith the sincere soul, "God knows that I have a thousand times attempted a thorough and absolute mortification of every sin, and God hath helped me to endeavour that it should abide no more in me. I have sometimes thought myself near an attainment, but I have found a disappointment; and I am perfectly satisfied in it, that as long as I have this body I shall never be without sin: it must be dead by reason of sin, or the fibres and roots of it will never be plucked up,—the nature of it can never be extinguished,—it can never be separated utterly from it." Here lies the great mystery of the grave under the covenant of grace, and by virtue of the death of Christ. What is it? worms and corruption? No; it is God's fining-pot, his way to purify: and there is no other way to make an eternal separation between sin and the body but by consuming of it in the grave. A secret virtue shall issue out from the death of Christ unto the body of a believer laid in the grave, that shall eternally purify it, at its resurrection, from every thing of sin. I will not say what apprehensions some have had concerning the state of souls upon the consumption of the body in the grave; because I will speak nothing unto you that is questionable.

This, then, is the second reason,—that all other attempts to eradicate sin have failed, and not had their issue; they have brought me to be ashamed of myself, in the frowardness, darkness, and unbelief of my nature; I will therefore be willing to part with my body. Such a one, then, will say, "This is that which God calls me unto. Go, then, thou poor, mortal, sinful flesh, 'Dust thou art, and unto dust thou shalt return.' I give thee up unto the doom of the Holy One, whose mouth hath spoken it, that thou must return to the dust. And there he will refine thee, and purify thee; [so] that notwithstanding this departure, 'my glory shall rejoice,' and thou, 'my flesh, shalt rest in hope;' for the time will come when 'he will have a desire to the work of his hands;' and 'will call, and thou shalt answer him' out of the dust;"—as Job xiv. 15, "Be not afraid to enter into darkness: as there is no sting in death, so there is no darkness in the grave, whither thou art going. It is but lying so long in the hands of the great Refiner, who will purge, purify, and restore thee. Therefore, lie down in the dust in peace."[1]

This is the second thing that is required in men that would die with their eyes open, that would die cheerfully and comfortably, according to the will of God,—to be willing to leave the body to God's disposal, to be laid up in the dust; because thereby it shall come to see Christ, and likewise shall have an end of sin.

I shall name but one thing more, and that very briefly; but it is the great thing that I would give in charge to my own soul: I pray God help me so to do; and it is this:—

[1] There is a similar strain of exhortation and reasoning, in which Christian faith and hope shine triumphant over the fears natural to all men in the prospect of dissolution, in the author's preface to his "Meditations on the Glory of Christ," vol. i., p. 280. The reader will find the paragraph to which this note is appended on p. 283, wrought up and refined, with the author's last touch and corrections, into a high degree of Christian eloquence.—Ed.

III. Let us take heed of being surprised with death.

This is that peculiar wisdom which God calls us all unto at this day. We know not how soon we may be called upon by death. It may not come in an ordinary course, by long sickness, and give us warning; nor when we have lived to the age of a man, which is "threescore years and ten," as the psalmist speaks; but we may be surprised with it when we look not for it. He that hath not learned it for himself from the dealings of God at this present in the world, and in this congregation, will not believe it if one should come from the dead and tell him so. Let this, then, be fixed upon our minds, that whatsoever be our state and condition, some are strong, young, and healthy, and some of us are old and feeble, going out of the world; but there are none of us but may be surprised with it. Take heed, therefore, that you be not surprised in an ill frame. I hope there are none of you but do understand that there is great variety in the frames of believers; sometimes they are in a good frame,—grace is active and quick,—they are ready to take impressions by the word and warnings, delighting in holy thoughts; and sometimes, again, it may be the world, temptations, or self-love, comes in, or over-valuation of our relations, and indisposes them again, and they are very unfit and lifeless for the performance of duties with delight and vigour of spirit; and these they lose, though they keep up to all their duties. I persuade myself you will confirm this with your own experience. There is no maintaining (though there may be impressions) of a quick, holy, lively frame, but by a sedulous contemplation and constant view of things that are above. Many will tell you, that when God hath been pleased to keep up their minds unto the thoughts of things above, and draw out their affections to cleave unto them, all things have gone well with them,—every prayer had life in it, and every sermon and duty, pleasure and joy; and their hearts have lain down and arisen in peace. But when they have lost their view of spiritual things, all other things continue, but there is a kind of deadness upon them. Why, then, our wisdom in this case is, to labour to keep up this spiritual view of eternal things, in a holy contemplation of and cleaving to them in our affections, or death will be surprising; come when it will, you will be surprised by it. But if this be our frame, what comes this messenger for? Death is a messenger sent of God; he knocks at the door, and what comes he for? To perfect the frame you are in, that you may see heavenly things more clearly. He is come to free you from that deadness you are burdened withal, that darkness you are entangled with, and to set you at perfect liberty in the enjoyment of those things your souls cleave unto. How, then, can your souls but bid this messenger welcome? Pray, then, that God would keep up your souls, by fresh supplies of his Spirit, unto a constant view of heavenly things. And you must do it by prayer, that God would give you fresh oil, to increase light in your minds and understandings. Some can tell you by experience, that, having made it their business with all their strength and study to live in that frame, they have found their own light decay, so that it would not be so fixed and constant towards heavenly things, nor so affect the heart as it had done before. Their light would work no more, until fresh supplies from the Holy Ghost gave quickness to it, and fresh oil to increase, to discern the beauty of spiritual and heavenly things. In plain terms, I speak to dying men, that know not how soon they may die. God advise my own heart of this thing, that I should labour and watch, that death might not find me out of the view of spiritual things! If it do,—if our bellies cleave unto the dust, and our eyes are turned to the ground,—if we are filled with other things, and death approaches,—do you think it will be an easy thing to gather in your minds and affections to a compliance with it? You will not find it so. When David was in a good frame, he could say, "Thou hast redeemed me, O LORD God of truth: O LORD, into thine hand I commit my spirit;"—"I am willing to come and lay down my tabernacle, and embrace this messenger. But David falls from his good frame, under some decays of spirit, Ps. xxxix., and there makes great complaint of it. Where is the readiness now of the good man, and where is his willingness of giving up his spirit into the hand of God? "Spare me a little, that I may recover my strength," verse 13. Not his outward strength, but a better frame, fit to die in. And if death overtake us in such a frame, the best of us will be found to cry so: "O spare me a little, to recover my strength."—"O the entanglements that have been brought upon me by this and that temptation, and diversion; by this coldness and decay! O Lord, spare me a little." There is mercy with God for persons in this frame; but if it were the will of God, I had rather it should be, "LORD, into thy hands I commend my spirit; for thou hast redeemed me, O LORD God of truth."

SERMON XXX.[1]

THE EVIL AND DANGER OF OFFENCES.

"Woe unto the world because of offences! for it must needs be that offences come; but woe to that man by whom the offence cometh!"—MATT. xviii. 7.

IT is very evident that our Lord Jesus Christ lays very great weight upon this matter of offences. He represents them like a two-edged

[1] This sermon was preached September 30, 1681.

sword, that cuts both ways: " Woe unto the world because of offences! woe to them by whom offences come!" He knits these two things together. It must needs be that there be offences; God hath appointed it, and it must be so. He doth not merely tell us, it will be; but, " it must be." God hath ordered that so it shall be.

I will speak a few things in reference to offences, that may be of use unto us, without looking into the depth of this great matter of offence and scandal; than which, I must needs say, I never yet saw any thing less inquired into, though there is no subject more written upon and spoken to. We should consider for ourselves the time wherein we may be sure offences will abound. It is necessary, from this wonderful caution of Christ here given, "Woe, woe!—it must be," that we should consider the times wherein it is likely offences will abound. And if all those times should prove to be upon us, certainly it is our duty to be wary.

First. The first is a time of persecution. Offences will abound in a time of persecution, to the ruin of many professors. So our Saviour tells us, Matt. xiii., " One received the seed of the word, and it sprang up; but when persecution for the word arose, immediately he was offended." " Woe unto him, he is gone!"

Secondly. A time of the abounding of great sins is a time of giving and taking great offence. This the Holy Spirit speaks expressly, that " in the latter days there shall be perilous times." All perils arise from offences. And why? Men's lusts shall abound. When there is an abounding of lusts, there will be an abounding of offences, that make the times perilous.

Thirdly. When there is a decay of churches, when they grow cold, and are under decays, it is a time of the abounding of offences: " Iniquity shall abound, and the love of many shall wax cold." That is a time when offences will abound; such as all the churches of Christ seem to be under at this day. All the virgins, wise and foolish, are asleep. It is what I have told you often, and I wish I could say I have told you with weeping, that we are under woful decays,—falling from our first faith, love, and works.

Now, if all these times should be upon us:—a time of persecution, as it is now throughout the world (saith the apostle, " Think it not strange concerning the fiery trial, or all that befalls you, brethren, in the world"); a time of the abounding of great sin in men (I need not enlarge upon this); and a time of great decays in all churches;—if it be thus with us, certainly it is very proper for us to look upon this warning of our Saviour, " Take heed of offences."

Offences are of two sorts:—I. Such as are taken only, and not given. II. Such as are given, and taken also:—

I. Such as are taken only, and not given. The great offence taken was at Jesus Christ himself. God appointed Christ to be the greatest offence in the world, Isa. viii. He had designed him to be a stumbling-block, and a rock of offence,—an insuperable offence. The poverty of Christ in the world and his cross were the rock of offence whereat both Jews and Gentiles stumbled and fell, and ruined themselves unto eternity. Now the apostle disputes, 1 Cor. i., that this was an offence taken, and not given. How does he prove it? Why, that wherein God puts forth his wisdom and his power is no offence given, but merely taken; but in Christ crucified God put forth his power (let him be as poor in the world as he will, let him be crucified, there is the wisdom and the power of God in it): and therefore, there can be no just offence.

This offence taken, and not given, is increased by the poverty of the church. "You see your calling, brethren;—not many great, not many wise, not many noble." In plain English, "You are a company of poor, weak, persecuted people." But saith the apostle, "This is no offence given; 'God chooses the things that are not, to bring to nought things that are.' These things are an offence taken, and not given."

II. There are offences given and taken:—

1. Offences given: and they are men's public sins, and the miscarriages of professors, that are under vows and obligations to honourable obedience. Men may give offence by errors and miscarriages in churches, and by immoralities in their lives. This was in the sin of David. God would pass by every thing but offence given: "'Because thou hast made my name to be blasphemed,' therefore I will deal so and so." What a talk did it occasion throughout the world! "There is your holy man, your godly man, your David!—a praying man! do you hear what a noise there is concerning him?"—"Thou hast made my name to be blasphemed," saith God; and this is a great provocation. So God speaks of the people of Israel: "These were my people; by reason of you my name is profaned among the Gentiles."—"These are the people of the Lord! see now, they are come into captivity! what a vile people they are!" Such things are an offence given.

2. Offences taken. Now offences are taken two ways:—(1.) As they occasion grief; and (2.) Sin. A given offence may be taken either of these ways:—

(1.) As they occasion grief. Rom. xiv., "See that by thy miscarriage 'thou grieve not thy brother.'" Men's offences who are professors are a grief, trouble, and burden, to those who are concerned in the same course of profession. But herein appears the wisdom of God,—when he doth, in his sovereignty, sometimes suffer persons to give offence, that may be sanctified unto the great advantage of the church. I am persuaded the church of Corinth was in so much disorder, that it had gone near to have been lost, if God had not suffered one among them to fall into a scandalous sin. But see what the end was! You find in the First Epistle the disorder they were in, and what a scandalous sin fell out among them; and in the Second Epistle, the sorrow upon it. When they knew it, they took offence, and were grieved at it: "For behold, that ye sorrowed after a godly sort, what carefulness it wrought in you, yea, what clearing of yourselves, yea, what indignation, yea, what fear, yea, what vehement desire, yea, what zeal, yea, what revenge! In all things," saith the apostle, "ye have approved yourselves to be clear in this matter." I look upon it to have been the greatest sanctified means that God appointed for the humiliation, recovery, and saving of that church, that he suffered, in his sovereign wisdom, such an offence to fall out among them. That is the first thing; and let us lay it up in our minds, that we may not be moved and shaken; for I speak with a prospect of what is to come, and not of what is come: "Offences will come;" and therefore let us remember that God can sanctify the greatest offences to our humiliation and recovery, and to the saving of our church. Such is his infinite wisdom.

(2.) Given offences occasion sin. There comes the woe, as to the world; for there is no woe from offences to them who are truly humbled for them, grieved at them, and made thereby watchful over themselves and their own ways. But now, when offences are made an occasion of sin, as in the world, the world takes no offence at all by their own sins, nor by the sins of one another. Let them be what they will, let their teachers be as scandalous in their lives as possible, they are not grieved nor concerned. And the reason is in that saying of David, 1 Sam. xxiv. 13, "As saith the proverb of the ancients" (it was a saying from the flood, if not from the beginning of the world), "Wickedness proceedeth from the wicked;"—"Look for nothing but wickedness from wicked men." So that it is no offence at all, to see wicked men do wicked things. They do not take offence at one another; nor doth the church of God take offence: for, as saith the proverb, they can do no otherwise. To show you how men are hardened in their prejudices against the truth, and confirmed in all their course by offences, would be too long a work for me to declare. But offences given are an occasion of sin, even among professors and believers themselves.

The worst way whereby a given offence is thus taken, is, when men countenance themselves in private sins by others' public sins; and go on in vices because they see such and such commit greater. Woe unto us if we so take offence! Again, a given offence is taken when our minds are provoked, exasperated, and carried off from a spirit of love and tenderness towards those that offend, and all others; and when we are discouraged, and despond, as though the ways of God would not carry us out. This is to take offence to our disadvantage.

Thus I have showed you the great weight and import that is to be laid upon this matter of offence, as being the greatest aggravation of sin.

I have showed you the times wherein offences will abound: a time of persecution; a time of the increase of abominable sins; and a time of the decay of churches,—such as are upon us.

I have likewise showed you, there are offences taken only, and not given: Christ and his cross, the poverty of the church, its persecution and distress in all places, and the hopes and fears of all mankind at present that it will be ruined;—these are offences taken only, and not given, being all suited to the wisdom, goodness, and righteousness of God. There are offences, also, that are given, by outward, known, public sins of persons who are under evangelical obligations to more honourable obedience. And under this head we might bring in every thing we see or hear; but some more gross than others. And these offences occasion either grief and sorrow; and then they prove a sanctified means in the hand of God for the church's good, making them more watchful and careful for the future: or they occasion sin, both by the world and by professors; and there comes the woe.

I shall give you a few rules from hence, and so conclude:—

Rule 1. The giving offence being a great aggravation of sin, let this rule lie continually in your hearts,—that the more public persons are, the more careful they ought to be that they "give no offence either to Jew or Gentile, or to the church of God." Why doth the apostle put Jew and Gentile before "the church of God?" Because more evil will ensue upon it, and more disadvantage, unto the souls of men. Let this be our rule in walking, especially those of us whose occasions do call us unto more converse in the world,—let us always endeavour to give no offence to Jew or Gentile, or to the church of God.

2. If what I have laid down be your first and your main rule (I doubt, where this is neglected, there is want of sincerity; but where it is your principal rule), there is nothing but hypocrisy. Men may walk by this rule, and have corrupt minds, and cherish wickedness in their hearts. If this be the principal rule that guides you,—that you will carry it so complyingly, that you will give no offence,—this is worse than neglecting the rule in the first case: that argues want of sincerity; this is a certain predominancy of hypocrisy. The principal rule commands conscience to God in all sincerity; and the second, to give no offence;—and if we make this our first rule, we are not upright with God. And therefore let none please themselves that they walk according to rule, if the internal power of God be not found in their souls.

3. Be not afraid of the great multiplication of offences at this day in the world. The truths of the gospel and holiness have broke through a thousand times more offences. They have broke through heresies and blasphemies, and poverty and persecution. God hath still preserved his people, who have broke through and got the conquest over the greatest offences;—over offences taken, in the cross of Christ, in the poverty of Christ, in persons that have preached the gospel, and in those who have professed it;—over offences given, in innumerable swarms of blasphemous heretics who have professed the name of Christ from the beginning; in false reports that have been cast upon Christians,—being reported generally throughout the world to be a vile generation of wicked persons. The truth and grace of God have conquered all these offences, and prevailed over them all, and will do so again, if we keep close unto truth and the power of religion.

4. Beg of God wisdom to manage yourselves under offences: and of all things take heed of that great evil which professors have been very apt to run into,—I mean, to receive and promote reports of offence among themselves, taking hold of the least colour or pretence to report such things as are matter of offence, and give advantage to the world. Take heed of this; it is the design of the devil to load professors with false reports. And if so, he is not a wise man, nor she a wise woman, that stand not upon their guard, when they see an engine the devil often makes use of;—who, when he hath raised false reports and wounded divers, is greatly pleased, and careth not if afterward they be discovered to be false, as knowing that he hath done his work; for hereby he hath drawn out and imbittered the spirits of men one against another. And therefore stand upon your guard, and know it is the devil's engine, though you see not his hand in the managing of it.

SEVERAL PRACTICAL

CASES OF CONSCIENCE RESOLVED.

DELIVERED IN SOME SHORT DISCOURSES AT CHURCH MEETINGS.

PREFATORY NOTE.

THESE brief Discourses are included in the folio edition of Owen's Sermons, published in 1721, and are there, for obvious reasons, made to occupy a place by themselves. They were delivered at church meetings for the purposes of devotion and conference among Christian brethren (see p. 403); and they relate to a particular department of Christian ethics. CASUISTRY—the science and doctrine of conscience—is designed, as the name denotes, to resolve *cases* of doubt and uncertainty in regard to points of subjective morality. As a branch of theological inquiry and discussion, it has in a great measure fallen into disrepute. It came to be regarded with suspicion and odium from the use made of it by the Jesuits in the fifteenth and sixteenth centuries, who converted it into an engine of successful villany. It was denounced as "the art of quibbling with God;" and it was partly the casuistical system of the Jesuits against which Pascal, in his "Provincial Letters," launched with scathing effect the bolts of his brilliant sarcasm.

But this science was for a time in great favour with the divines of the Reformation also; though studied and taught by them on different principles, and assuredly for very different ends. Mayer, a German theologian of the Lutheran Church (1650–1712), in his "Bibliotheca Biblica," has a list of the authors on Casuistry under three divisions, comprehending the Calvinistic, Lutheran, and Romish Churches. The science was at one time extensively cultivated in England, and by divines of eminent reputation. Sanderson, bishop of Lincoln after the Restoration, has two works on it,—"Casus Conscientiæ," and "De Obligatione Conscientiæ Prælectiones." The "Ductor Dubitantium" of Jeremy Taylor is widely known as one of the most learned and important works on this subject. Baxter's "Christian Directory" deserves also to be mentioned. Pike and Hayward's "Cases of Conscience" is a work that has been extensively circulated. There is a quarto volume in Latin entitled "Therapeutica Sacra," in which cases of conscience are discussed, by David Dickson, a Scotch divine, who, about 1650, was translated from the professorship of divinity in the University of Glasgow to the same chair in the University of Edinburgh. Four volumes of "The Morning Exercises" are occupied with the discussion and resolution of cases of conscience.

Casuistry is liable to abuse, and has often been abused. It tends to foster a morbid subjectivity, and to enervate principle. Every Christian pastor, however, in the course of his official duties, must sometimes be called to resolve the doubts and scruples which are apt to embarrass the tender conscience. As handled by the divines to whom we have last referred, it really embraces all questions of Christian obligation and practice; and on some points their discussions are among the best treatises on practical religion in the language. Nor can the divine entirely overlook casuistry, even in the strict sense of the term, seeing the apostle Paul was very careful to direct and enlighten the consciences of Christians in his day, who scrupled to eat "things offered in sacrifice unto idols."

It would be matter of regret, if the prejudice now entertained against a field of theological discussion cultivated to such an extent by divines of former generations, should prevent any reader from perusing the Discourses of our author which follow. Owen's was not the mind on any subject to be lost in obscure mysticism and refined subtilties, and to disport itself in a species of moral gymnastics, from which no overt and positive advantage could accrue to himself or to his hearers. These Discourses deal with momentous questions of religious experience, and are replete with suggestions and advices, which will be prized in proportion as the religion of the heart prevails, and so long as Christianity is not buried in formalism. The spirit which pervades all these brief but important Discourses, may be gathered from a weighty observation in one of them: "Suppose we should resolve with great earnestness, diligence, watchfulness, to abide in duties, in inward duties, to watch over our hearts,—which is required of us; yet if in our so doing we are taken off thereby from frequent actings of faith upon Christ, as the spring of our life, we shall decay, under all our endeavours, watchfulness, and multiplication of duties."—Ed.

DISCOURSE I.[1]

Question. *What conviction of a state of sin, and of the guilt of sin, is necessary to cause a soul sincerely to look after Christ?*

Answer. There is one thing only that I shall at present speak to, and that is this: What is the lowest condition that hath the nature of conviction in sincerity, so as that souls may not be discouraged from closing with Christ because they have had no greater convictions of sin? And I shall speak to it on this account,—because, although the things that have already been spoken by others are true, and such as those who have spoken them have found to be true by the word and their own experience; yet, it may be, others have not come up in their experience unto such a distinct observation of the work of conviction as hath been laid down, [so] that they may be discouraged. For, seeing conviction is so indispensably necessary, some may say, "It hath not been thus and thus with me,—according as hath been declared." Therefore, I would only show what I judge to be so necessary, as that without it a soul cannot be supposed sincerely to have closed with Christ. And we having all made our profession of choos-

[1] Delivered January 28, 1672.

ing and closing with Christ, as I would be loath to say any thing that might discourage any, lest they should have failed in the very necessary work of conviction; so I would not betray the truth of God, nor the souls of any.

Therefore, I shall place it upon this: What Jesus Christ doth indispensably call men unto, in order to believing in him, that is indispensably required of them. And this I shall manifest out of two or three places of Scripture:—Mark ii. 17, "I came not to call the righteous, but sinners to repentance." Now, this calling them unto repentance, is a calling them unto it by the faith which is in him. The apostle saith, 1 Tim. i. 15, "It is a faithful saying, and worthy of all acceptation, that Jesus Christ came into the world to save sinners." What kind of sinners doth Christ call? Whom he calls to repentance, he calls to faith; and whom he calls to faith, that they may truly believe, they are sinners,—opposed unto them that are righteous: "I came not to call the righteous, but sinners to repentance." "The righteous!" who are those righteous? The Scriptures tell us of these very men, that there were two sorts of them: First, Such as trusted in themselves that they were righteous, and despised other men. As long as a man trusteth in himself that he is righteous, Christ doth not call that man to believe. So long as a man is persuaded that his condition is good enough, he shall do well enough, that man hath no warrant to believe. Another description of these very persons, though upon another occasion, is given by the apostle Paul, Rom. x. 3, where he says, they were ignorant of the righteousness of God, and went about to establish their own righteousness. Though they did not come to trust in themselves for righteousness, yet sought righteousness as it were by the works of the law, and went about to establish their own righteousness;—Jesus Christ doth not call these men to believe: these righteous persons have no ground for believing. What is the conclusion? "Lost sinners," saith Christ, "this is that I require of you." So that this is what I assert to be indispensably necessary,—namely, that they are so far convinced that they are sinners as to state and course, that they are not righteous in themselves, and can have no righteousness in themselves. I say, therefore, when a person is not really convinced that he is not righteous, he is not under the call of Jesus Christ; and if he doth believe this, he is under a sovereign dispensation, and let not such despond.

Another direction of Christ is, "They that be whole need not a physician, but they that are sick," Matt. ix. 12. There are, in my apprehension, two things in a sick person that have need of a physician: First, He hath an uneasiness. A man who is sick, though he would shift it, yet his uneasiness will cause him to send for a physician. Saith Christ, "I come to such persons who say they can find no rest nor ease in their present condition." It may be they have often tried this and that, and see all will not do,—they are sick still; conscience reflects, and their hearts are burdened, and they must have relief, or they shall not be free. Secondly, There is a fear that it will end in death. This puts the sick person upon sending for a physician. When the soul is made uneasy in its state and condition, can find no rest nor ease, it thinks, "If I abide here, I shall be lost for ever." This soul doth Christ call; this man will be at the charge of a physician, cost what it will.

There is another word of Christ [which] very remarkably speaks just to the same purpose, Matt. xi. 28, "Come unto me, all ye that labour and are heavy laden, and I will give you rest,"—a soul finding itself under want, labouring after something whereby it may be accepted with God. I will not confine this to extraordinary instances, for sometimes he is found of them that sought him not; but the ordinary case of a labouring soul, before closing with Christ, is to abstain from sin, pray more or less, be found in duties, and under strong desires to be accepted with God. And what is the end of these labours and endeavours? They labour and are weary;—that is, they see their labour comes to no effect; they do not find rest, and peace, and acceptance with God. And here is the turning point; Isa. lvii. 10, "Thou art wearied in the greatness of thy way; yet saidst thou not, There is no hope." When the soul hath laboured for acceptance with God, and comes to be weary, saith Christ, "Come unto me." "No," saith the light of nature, "come unto me; trust unto your own endeavours." Saith the soul, "I will try what it will do; I will not say, 'There is no hope.'" Saith another, "I will not say so; I will go unto Christ:"—this is he whom Christ calls.

Now, these things I do account indispensably necessary, antecedently to believing, as to the substance of them. And this, I hope, hath been found in all our souls. And if we have obtained so far, we need not then question whether our closing with Christ be sincere or not. This is all that I dare assert to be absolutely and indispensably necessary. Many pretend to believe, though they never were convinced thoroughly that they were not righteous,—never were sick in their lives,—never had fears that they should die. These are contrary to the express rule Christ hath given, "I came not to call the righteous, but sinners;"—not those that say, "There is hope," but those that say, "There is no hope."

DISCOURSE II.[1]

QUESTION. *Seeing the act of closing with Christ is secret and hidden, and the special times and seasons of our conversion unto God are unknown unto most, what are the most certain evidences and pledges that we have cordially and sincerely received Christ, and returned unto God?*

ANSWER. I do acknowledge the inquiry is very large, and such as we may be straitened in, through the abundance of it. I shall only speak plainly some few things that to me are an evidence of a sincere closing with Christ, and receiving of Christ,—such as I know have been of use unto some.

First. When there is a permanency and abiding in the choice we have made of Christ, notwithstanding opposition against it that we shall be sure to meet withal. I do not speak to the nature of the choice, or the means of it,—how the mind is prepared for it; but I speak unto the poorest, the weakest of the flock, that may be inquiring whether they have made a sincere choice of Christ or not: I say, they may try it by the permanency and abiding in their choice against opposition.

And there are two sorts of oppositions that will try us and shake us, as to our choice, as I have found it, if I have had any experience of these things:—1. Opposition from charges of the guilt of sin and the law. 2. Opposition from temptations unto sin:—

1. There will, even after sincere believing and closing with Christ, be many a heavy charge brought against a soul from the law, and the guilt of sin in the conscience. Now, in such a case, the inquiry is, What the soul abides by when it is shaken? Why, truly, if a man go only upon mere convictions, on such shaking impressions of the guilt of sin, he will be very ready and inclined in his own mind to tack about to some other relief. He puts out fair for his voyage,—the storm arises,—the ship will not carry him;—he must tack about for another harbour. I have known it so with some; and experienced, when the wind hath set very strong that way with myself,—when the guilt of sin hath been charged with all its circumstances,—the soul hath been very hardly able to keep its hold, yet notwithstanding resolved, "I will trust to Christ:" but it hath been tacking about to self again,—"I must remedy this,—have relief for this from myself; I cannot abide by it, and live wholly upon Christ; and when the storm is over, then I will out to sea again." I say, this is no good sign to

[1] Delivered February 7, 1672.

me when things are so; but when a soul in all those charges that sometimes come upon it abides the issue,—"Here I will trust upon Christ, let the worst come upon me;"—this I call a permanency in our choice against opposition. I hope you have experience of it.

2. There must be a permanency in our choice of Christ against temptations unto sin, as well as against the charges from sin. Truly, the former—of abiding with Christ against the charges from sin—is our daily work: it is sometimes more high and pressing, but it is our daily work. But there are also temptations unto sin,—it may be to the neglect of our duty, or to a compliance in any evil way (which we are subject unto while in the body); and perhaps great sins. Here Joseph's reply, applied to Christ, is that which doth argue our choice of Christ to be sincere,—"How shall I do this great wickedness, and sin against God?" When the soul can draw a prevailing argument from that, "How shall I do this, and relinquish my Lord Christ?"—"I will not do this against him whom I have chosen,"—this is a good argument, if frequently reiterated, that our choice of Christ is sincere.

Secondly. Growing up in a love unto the person of Christ is a great evidence to me of a sincere choice of Christ. It is a blessed field that is before me, but I shall but hint things unto you. When the soul hath received Christ, it cannot but study Christ; and though it is no argument against the sincerity of a man's faith and grace, that he doth principally regard the offices and graces of Christ, and the benefits we have by him, yet it is an argument against the thrift and growth of it: for a thriving faith and grace will come to respect principally the person of Christ. I mean this;—when the soul studies the person of Christ,—the glory of God in him,—of his natures, the union of them in one person,—of his love, condescension and grace; and the heart is drawn out to love him, and cry, "Doubtless I count all things but loss and dung for the excellency of Christ Jesus my Lord." "What is thy beloved more than another beloved?" "My beloved is white and ruddy, the chiefest among ten thousand; he is altogether lovely." To see an excellency, a desirableness in the person of Christ, so as to grow in admiration and love of him, is to me an evidence that, when all fails besides, will greatly support the soul, and persuade it that its choice is true. Nay, it is one of the most spiritual evidences; for I much question whether an unregenerate man can love Christ for his own sake at all. But it is a good sign of growth, when our love to the person of Christ grows, when we meditate much upon it, and think much about it. I could show you wherein the beauty of Christ's person doth much consist; but I have not time now to do it.

Thirdly. Another evidence to me of the soul's having made a sincere choice of Christ is, when it continues to approve, judge well of, and every day more and more to see, the glory, the excellency, the holiness, the grace, which is in the way of salvation by Jesus Christ; approves of it as not only a necessary way,—a way it has betaken itself to, because it must unavoidably perish in any other way,—but when it approves of it to be a most excellent way, in pardoning sin freely through the atonement he hath made, and the imputation of his righteousness unto us,—while the righteousness, the holiness, and the grace of God in all this is glorified. Saith the soul, "What a blind, wretched creature was I, that I did not see an excellency in this way before! It is better than the way of the law and the old covenant. I approve of this way with all my heart. If all other ways were set before me, and made possible, I would choose this way, of going to God by Jesus Christ, as the best way,—that brings most glory to God and most satisfaction unto the creature, and is most suited to the desires of my heart. I would have no other way. 'I am the way, the truth, and the life,' says Christ; and this I will abide by, whatsoever becomes of me," replies the soul; "though I should perish, I will abide by it, since God hath given me such a discovery of the glory of saving sinners by Christ, that is inferior to nothing but the glory of heaven. I see that glory to God in it,—that exaltation to Christ, whom I would love,—that honour to the Holy Spirit, and safety to my own soul,—that I will abide by it." A growing in the approbation of this way gives some assurance that we have made a true and sincere choice of Christ.

Give me leave to add this one thing more:—

Fourthly. That a delight in obedience unto God by Christ, in the ways of his own appointment, is a great evidence that we have chosen Christ, and he us;—chosen him as our king, prophet, and priest. The ways of the worship of God in his church and ordinances, are the ways and worship of God in Christ, which he hath appointed. Take these things abstractedly and in themselves, and we should be apt to say of them, as was said of Christ, "There is no beauty in them, nor glory, that they should be desired." There is much more outward beauty and glory in other ways, that Christ hath not appointed. But if we love the ways Christ hath appointed, because he hath appointed them, then we choose those ways because we have chosen him to be our king; and that is it which gives them beauty and life. And when the ways of Christ's appointment grow heavy and burdensome to us, we are weary of them, and are willing to have our neck from under the yoke,—it is a sign we grow weary of him who is the author of them; and this is a great sign that we never made a right and sincere choice of him.

Many other things might be offered as evidences of sincere closing with Christ; but these are some which have been of use to me: and I hope they may be so unto some of you.

DISCOURSE III.

QUESTION. *What concern have we in the sins of the day wherein we live?*

ANSWER. All sins may be referred to two heads:—First, Irreligion. Secondly, Immorality.

First. Irreligion; and that may be reduced to two heads,—atheism and false worship: you may add, also, particularly, the contempt of all instituted worship. It takes up much of the sins against the first table; however, at present I shall only speak of the first of them:—

As to atheism, then, it may be no age can parallel that wherein we live, considering all the ways whereby the atheism of man's heart may discover itself. For, take it absolutely, and in the seat of it, it is found only in the heart of man; unless some one or other prodigious instance breaks out sometime, as we have had in our days: but otherwise, "The fool hath said in his heart, There is no God." The heart is the seat of atheism. But we consider the ways whereby this atheism may and doth manifest itself:—

(1.) By horrid, cursed, blasphemous swearing; which is a contempt of the name of God. And when did it ever more abound in this nation?

(2.) By reproaching of the Spirit of God. Perhaps this is the peculiar sin of the nation at this day; and that the like hath not been known or heard of in any nation under the sun.

(3.) By scoffing at all holy things;—at the Scriptures,—at every thing that carries a reverence and fear of God; so that a man who dares profess a fear of God in what he doth, makes himself a scorn.

(4.) Contempt of all God's providential warnings is another proof of atheism. Never had a nation more warnings from God's providence, nor ever were they more despised. These things, brethren, are not done in a corner; they are perpetrated in the face of the sun. The steam of them darkens the whole heaven, and they abound more and more every day.

Secondly. Shall we go to the other head,—namely, Immorality,—and see how it is there? It would be an endless thing, to go over the sins that reign among us: oppression, blood, uncleanness, sensuality, drunkenness,—all to the height, raging and reigning in the nation. I mention these things as a matter to be bewailed before the Lord by us this day; and we ought to be affected with the consideration of them.

Unto this great prevalency and predominancy of sin in the whole nation, there is added a strange and unspeakable security. The truth is, men were a little awakened one while in the nation. When the judgments of God—the pestilence, the fire, the sword, and, the year after, another warning from heaven—were upon us, then there was a little awakening, like a man out of a dead sleep, that lifts up his head, and rubs his eyes for a time. But I can say this, that it is now towards forty years since God enabled me to observe something in the world; and, to my knowledge, I never observed this nation in that state of security wherein it is at this day. For, even in former times, there were warnings continually that God had a controversy with the nation; and those that had any fear of God spake one to another about it; and we saw and found their warnings were not in vain. But here is now a general security. Men complain of straits, want, poverty, and the like; but as to any thing wherein God hath to do with the world, either my observation doth greatly deceive me, or I never saw, I think, so general a security as at this day in this nation. And this security hath reached us all,—even the churches of God themselves.

These things are matter of fact. The whole question is, Whether we are greatly to be concerned in these things or not? "They are the sins of wicked men, and they are the sins of the persecutors of God's people, and the like; and what have we to do with them?"

The psalmist of old said, that "rivers of waters ran down his eyes, because men did not keep the law of God." And you know that God doth set a special mark upon those, not that are free from the abominations of the age, but upon those that mourn for the abominations that are in the midst of us. It will not be enough for us, that we are free from those abominations, unless we are found to mourn for them. Brethren, our own hearts know we are guilty in this matter, and that we had need seek the face of God this day to give us a deeper sense of these things than we have obtained. The name of God is blasphemed, the Spirit of God reproached, a flood of iniquity spreads itself over the nation, the land of our nativity, over the inheritance of Christ, over a nation professing the reformed religion;—all things go backward,—every thing declines. Indeed, brethren, if you will not, I do acknowledge here before you, and to my own shame, I have great guilt upon me in this matter, that I have not been sensible of the abominations of the nation, so as to mourn for them and be humbled for them, as I ought to have been. And you will do well to search your hearts, and consider how it is with you;—whether indeed you have been affected with these things; or whether you have not thought all is well, while all hath been well with yourselves and families, and, it may be, with the church, that may have no trouble upon that account. The security that is upon the nation is dismal; and, I may say, I see no way or means whereby the nation should be freed from this security. The conduct of the ministry, which they are under generally, is not able to free them from this security; nor the dispensation of the word: [so] that it seems to be a security from God to lead on the nation to judgment; the means for the removal of it and the awakening of us being laid aside. And if it comes this way, or that way, any way, though we see not the morning of it, you will find yourselves concerned in it.—"Who may abide the day of his coming?"

We may do well, brethren, to consider the state of the church of God in the world, among ourselves, and our own condition. I need not tell you how it is in the world; but this I can say, that to my apprehensions, the interest of Christ and the gospel was never so fast going down in the world since it came into it, as at this day. I will give you my reason of what I say: When the gospel was first planted and brought into the world, the devil was not able to bring the church into its apostasy, under six, or seven, or eight hundred years, and that by degrees. Since the time of the Reformation, the church was progressive for about seventy years; it stood at a stay about the same proportion of time; and ever since, it hath been going backward, straitened in all places: the power of it decays, and the peace of it is taken away, and destruction everywhere seems to lie at the door. Many, indeed, are in great misery and distress: some I have heard of lately sold for slaves,[1] for the testimony of their conscience. How is it with the church of Christ in this nation? Truly, some [are] in great poverty, in great affliction, in great distress; and I am afraid we and others have not hearts to relieve them, as we ought to do, in a due manner: however, let us help them with our prayers. And that which is worst of all, there seems to me, I must acknowledge it, to be a very great decay in all churches of Christ in the nation, especially among those of us who have had most peace, most prosperity. That which we call zeal for God is almost quite lost among us. Some of us have almost forgot whether there be such a thing as the cause and interest of Christ in the world. We who have cried and prayed about it, and had it upon our hearts, have sat down in our narrow compass, and almost forgot there is such a thing as the interest of Christ in the world, so as to have an active zeal for the ordinances of

[1] No date is assigned to this discourse. It was about the time, however, in which these discourses seem to have been delivered, that many of the Scottish Covenanters were banished. They were crowded into vessels bound for the West Indies or North America; and, after enduring fearful sufferings on the passage, were sold, when they reached Jamaica or Carolina, to work as slaves on the plantations. By a refinement of cruelty, it was provided that this punishment should be reserved for "such rebels as were penitent"! From the language of Owen, it would seem that he alludes to some occurrences that had taken place at a distance, and not within the sphere of his own observation. It is probable, therefore, that he refers to the proceedings of the government in Scotland.—ED.

God according to rule, as God requires of us. Our primitive love,—how is it decayed! Value of the ordinances of Christ, and the society of his people for edification,—how cold are we grown in these things! How little is the church society upon our hearts, which some of us remember when it was the very joy of our souls! Truly we have reason to lift up our cry to God, that he would return and visit the churches, and pour out a new, fresh, reviving spirit upon them, that we fall not under the power of these decays till we come to formality, and God withdraws himself from us, and leaves us; which he seems to be at the very point of doing.

Then, brethren, let us remember our own church; that God would in an especial manner revive the spirit of life, power, and holiness among us; that he would be pleased to help the officers of the church to discharge their duty, and not suffer them to fall under any decay of grace or gifts, unfitting of them to the discharge of their office to the edification of the church; that he would give them also to beware and take heed of formality as to the exercise of gifts in their administration; and that he would take care of us, since we are apt to fall under these things. Let us pray that we may be acted by the Spirit of God, and enlivened by the grace of God, in all things we do.

Have any of us any particular occasions in reference to temptations, trials, and troubles?—we may bear it upon our hearts to the Lord this day. This is much better than by multiplying a company of formal bills. The Lord help us to know the plague of our own hearts, and to be enabled to plead with the Lord, upon this opportunity, for grace and mercy to help us in every time of need!

DISCOURSE IV.[1]

QUESTION. *How may we recover from a decay of the principle of grace?*

ANSWER. We have been speaking concerning the decay of the principle of grace; and I will now offer you some few thoughts that may be applied unto our recovery from the decay of this principle. In doing which, I shall tell you no more than I think I have found myself.

If we would recover spiritual life, we must come as near as we can unto, and abide as much as we are able at, the well-head of life.

[1] Delivered March 24, 1675–6.

Christ is the spring of our spiritual life; he is every way our life. It is in a derivation of life from Christ, and in conformity to him, that we must look for our spiritual life.

Before I mention how we should approach unto and lie at this well-head of life, let me observe to you this one thing,—that when there is a general contagious disease (the plague, or the like), every man will look to his health and safety with reference to other occasions, but will be most careful in regard to the general contagion. Now, if forsaking this spring of life be the plague of the age, and the plague of the place where we live, and the plague of Christians, we ought to be very careful lest this general contagion should reach us, more or less, one way or other. It is evident to me,—who have some advantage to consider things, as much as ordinary men,—that the apostasy, the cursed apostasy, that spreads itself over this nation, and whose fruits are in all ungodliness and uncleanness, consists in an apostasy from and forsaking the person of Christ. Some write of how little use the person of Christ is in religion;—none, but to declare the doctrine of the gospel to us. Consider the preaching and talk of men. You have much preaching and discourse about virtue and vice; so it was among the philosophers of old: but Jesus Christ is laid aside, quite as a thing forgotten; as if he was of no use, no consideration, in religion; as if men knew not at all how to make any use of him, as to living to God.

This being the general plague, as is evident, of the apostasy of the day wherein we live, if we are wise, we shall consider very carefully whether we ourselves are not influenced more or less with it; as where there is a general temptation, it doth more or less try all men, the best of believers, and prevail more or less upon their spirits. I am afraid we have not, some of us, that love for Christ, that delight in him, nor do make that constant abode with him, as we have done. We have very much lost out of our faith and our affections him who is the life and centre, the glory and the power, of all spiritual life, and of all we have to do with God,—Jesus Christ himself. I brought it in only to let us know, that if we would revive our spiritual life (and, believe it, if any of us are not concerned in our spiritual decays, these are sapless things, and will be heard with as much weariness as spoken), we are to abide more at the well-head of life. It is the direction of our Lord Jesus Christ, "Abide in me: unless ye abide in me, ye can bring forth no fruit. And every such branch shall be so and so purged."

But you will say, "How shall we do so? how shall we abide, more than we have done, at this well-head of life?"

1. We are to abide at the well-head of life by a frequency of the acts of faith upon the person of Christ. Faith is that grace, not only

whereby we are implanted into Christ, but whereby we also abide in him. If so, methinks the frequent actings of faith upon the person of Christ are a drawing near to the well-head of life. And though we are to put forth the vigour, the earnestness, the watchfulness of our hearts unto obedience; yet a ceasing to continue in the acting of faith upon the person of Christ, even under the vigour of our own endeavours by those general, outward desires of walking with God and living to him, will weaken us, and we shall find ourselves losers by it. Do you all understand me? I am not teaching the wise and more knowing of the flock; I would speak unto the meanest. I say, suppose we should resolve with great earnestness, diligence, watchfulness, to abide in duties, in inward duties, to watch over our hearts, which is required of us; yet, if in our so doing we are taken off thereby from frequent actings of faith upon Christ, as the spring of our life, we shall decay under all our endeavours, watchfulness, and multiplication of duties. Wherefore, my brethren, let me give you this advice,—that you would night and day, upon your beds, in your ways, upon all occasions, have the exercise of faith upon the person of Christ; faith working by a view of him as represented in the gospel, by trust in him, and by invocation of him,—that he may be continually nigh unto you. And you cannot have him nigh unto you, unless you make yourselves, by these actings of faith, through his grace, continually nigh unto him: so you will abide at the well-head.

I could show you those excellent advantages that we should have by continually being near to Christ, who is the overflowing spring of grace, and from whence it will issue out to us, if we abide with him, be nigh to him, and keep up to this well-head.

2. Abide with him in love. Oh, the warm affections for Christ which some of you can witness concerning yourselves,—that your hearts have been filled withal towards Christ, when you have been under his call to believe on him! And it is a marvellous way of abiding with Christ, to abide with him by love; which is called "cleaving to God and Christ:" it is the affection of adhesion, and gives a sense of union.

"How, then, shall we get our hearts to abide with Christ by love?"

This is a subject that if I were to preach upon, how many things would presently offer themselves to us, from the excellency of his person, from the excellency of his love, from our necessity of him, the advantages and benefits we have by him, and his kindness towards us! All these things, and many more, would quickly present themselves unto us.

But I will name but one thing, and I name it the rather, because I heard it mentioned in prayer since I came in: Labour to have your hearts filled with a love to Jesus Christ, as there is in him made a representation of all divine excellencies. This was God's glorious design. It is not to be separated from his design of glorifying himself in the work of redemption; for a great part of God's glorious design in the incarnation of Christ, was in him to represent himself unto us, "who is the image of the invisible God, the express image of his person." Now, if you do but consider Christ as God is gloriously represented unto you in him, you will find him the most proper object for divine love,—for that love which is wrought in your hearts by the Holy Ghost,—for that love that hath sweetness, complacency, satisfaction in it. Then, let us remember that we exercise our minds to consider Christ, as all the lovely properties of the divine nature and counsels of his will, as to love and grace, are manifested by Christ.

If we would abide at the well-head of life, we must abide in these things; and let love be excited to Christ under this especial consideration,—as he who represents the supreme object of your love, God himself, in all the glorious properties of his nature.

3. Add meditation hereunto; study Christ more, and all the things of Christ; delight more in the hearing and preaching of Christ. He is our best friend; let not the difficulties of the mystery of his person and grace deter you. There are wonderful things of the counsels of heaven, and of the glory of the holy God, in the person of Christ as the head of the church; if you would be found inquiring into them, an unsearchable treasure of divine wisdom, grace, and love is laid up in Christ: therefore meditate upon them more. Let me assure you this will prove the best expedient for the recovery of our spiritual life. And I will abide by this doctrine to eternity, that without it we shall never recover spiritual life to the glory of God in Christ.

4. And then, brethren, seeing we have, in the next place, felt decays in the midst of the performance of multiplied duties, labour to bring spirituality into your duties.

"What is that," you will say, "and wherein doth it consist?"

It is the due exercise of every grace that is required to the discharge of that duty. Let every such grace be in its due exercise, and that is to be spiritual in duty. As, for instance, would a man be spiritual in all his prayers?—let him, then, consider what grace and what exercise of grace is required to this duty. A due fear and reverence of the name of God; faith, love, and delight in him; an humble sense of his own wants, earnest desires of supply, dependence upon God for guidance, and the like;—we all know that these are the graces required to the discharge of this duty of praying by the Holy Ghost. And let these graces be in a due exercise, and then you are spiritual in this duty. Is the duty charity,—giving a supply to the poor? There is to be a ready mind, a compassionateness of heart, and obedience unto the command of Christ in that particular. These are the graces required to the discharge of that duty, and to watch against the contrary vices. So that if we would bring spirituality into duty, it is to exercise the graces that are required by the rule to the performance of that duty.

I shall only farther give you this one caution,—have a care that your head in notion and your tongue in talk do not too fast empty your hearts of truth. We are apt to lay it up in our heads by notions, and bring it forth in talk, and not let it be in our hearts; and this weakens spiritual life greatly. Ye hear the word preached; and it is of great concernment what account we shall give of the word that hath been preached unto you: for we that preach must give an account of our preaching, and so must you of what you hear; and many a good word is spoken, truly, and yet we see but little fruit of it. And the reason of this is, that some, when they hear it, take no farther regard of it, but "let it slip," as the apostle speaks, Heb. ii. 1. And if we complain of the treacherousness of our memories,—it is the most harmless way of the slipping out of the word. It is not the treachery of our memories, but of our hearts and affections, that makes the heart like a broken vessel,—that makes all the rents in it where the water runs out, as the comparison is. The word slips out by putting your affections into carnal exercise; and it quickly finds its way to depart from the heart that gives it no better entertainment. We talk away a sermon and the sense of it; which robs us both of the sermon and the fruit of it. A man hears a good word of truth, and, instead of taking the power of it into his heart, he takes the notion of it into his mind, and is satisfied therewith. But this is not the way to thrive. God grant that we may never preach to you any thing but what we may labour to have an experience of the power of it in our own hearts, and to profit ourselves by the word wherewith we design to profit others! And I pray God grant that you also may have some profit by the word dispensed to you,—that it slip not out through carnal affections, and be not drawn out through notions and talk, with a regardlessness to treasure it up in your hearts!

These things we are diligently to attend unto, if we would recover our spiritual losses that we are complaining of, and that not without just cause.

DISCOURSE V.[1]

QUESTION. *It was queried by some, how we may make our application unto Christ; not in general, but under what notion and apprehension of the person of Christ?*

ANSWER. Because some seem to apprehend there might be danger in terminating our worship upon the nature of Christ as a creature, I shall give you my thoughts and directions in it. And,—

First. You must observe we are to have no conceptions, in our acting of any duty, towards Christ or about him, but with respect unto his person as he is God and man in one person. It is not lawful for us to have any apprehensions of Christ, to make any application to him, as man only; nor is it lawful for us to have any apprehensions of him as God only: but all our apprehensions of Christ, and all our addresses unto him, must be as God and man in one person. So he is, and so he will be to all eternity. The union is inseparable and indissoluble; and for any man to make his application unto Christ either as God or as man, is to set up a false Christ. Christ is God and man in one person, and no other. So, in all our actings of faith upon him, and applications unto him, we ought to consider him as he was "the seed of David," and as "God over all, blessed for ever," in one person. This makes the great idolatry among the Papists;—in the image of Christ they represent the human nature of Christ separated from his Deity; for they can make no representation of one that is God and man in one person: hereby they become guilty of double idolatry, referring the mind unto one that is a man, and no more,—and doing it by means of an image.

Secondly. The person of Christ is the immediate and proper object of all divine worship. The worship of Christ is commanded in the first commandment. By worship, I intend faith, love, trust, subjection of soul, invocation on the name of Christ,—every act of the soul and mind whereby we ascribe infinite divine excellencies unto God; which is the worship of the mind. See John v. 23. It is the will of God "that all men should honour the Son, even as they honour the Father." How do we honour the Father? By divine faith, trust, love, and worship; making him our end and our reward. So the Son is to be honoured. And as to the divine person of the Son of God, being of the same nature, essence, and substance with the Father, there is no dispute of that among them by whom his Deity is acknowledged.

[1] Delivered April 7, 1676.

Thirdly. The divine person of the Son of God lost nothing of his glory and honour that was due unto him by the assumption of our human nature. Though thereby he became the Son of man as well as the Son of God,—a Lamb for sacrifice; yet he is still, in his whole and entire person, the object of all that worship I spake of before;—and the whole church of God agree together in giving that worship unto him, Rev. v. 8, 9, 11–13, "And when he had taken the book, the four beasts and four and twenty elders fell down before the Lamb, having every one of them harps, and golden vials full of odours, which are the prayers of saints. And they sung a new song, saying, Thou art worthy to take the book, and to open the seals thereof: for thou wast slain, and hast redeemed us to God by thy blood out of every kindred, and tongue, and people, and nation. And I beheld, and I heard the voice of many angels round about the throne and the beasts and the elders: and the number of them was ten thousand times ten thousand, and thousands of thousands; saying with a loud voice, Worthy is the Lamb that was slain to receive power, and riches, and wisdom, and strength, and honour, and glory, and blessing. And every creature which is in heaven, and on the earth, and under the earth, and such as are in the sea, and all that are in them, heard I saying, Blessing, and honour, and glory, and power, be unto him that sitteth upon the throne, and unto the Lamb for ever and ever." Jesus Christ is here distinguished from the Father. There is, "He that sitteth upon the throne," and "The Lamb;" and he is considered as incarnate,—as a Lamb slain: and yet there is all the glory, honour, praise, and worship, that is given to him that sitteth upon the throne, the Father, given to Jesus Christ, God and man, the Lamb slain, who hath redeemed us with his blood.

Fourthly. This person of Christ, God-man, must not be so much as severed by any conception of the mind. For distinction, as God and man, he may be considered two ways; either absolutely in himself, or in the discharge of his mediatory office. And this double consideration produceth a double kind of worship to the person of Christ.

1. Consider Christ absolutely in his own person, as the Son of God incarnate; and so he is the immediate and ultimate object of our faith, prayer, and invocation. So that a man may lawfully, under the guidance and conduct of the Spirit of God, direct his prayer immediately to the person of Christ. You have the example of Stephen in his last prayer. "Lord Jesus," saith he, "receive my spirit." These were the words of our Lord Jesus Christ when he died, "Father, into thy hands I commend my spirit." And Stephen, when he died, committed his spirit into the hands of Jesus Christ: "Lord Jesus," (for that is the name of the Son of God incarnate, "He shall be called Jesus, for he shall save his people from their sins,") "re-

ceive my spirit." So that a person may make an immediate address in his prayers and supplications unto the person of Christ, as God and man. I look upon it as the highest act of faith that a believer is called unto in this world,—to resign a departing soul into his hands, letting go all present things and future hopes; to resign, I say, a departing soul quietly and peaceably into the hands of Christ. Now, this Stephen did with respect unto Jesus: "Lord Jesus, receive my spirit." There he left himself by faith. So we may apply ourselves unto him upon any other account, in the acting of faith, upon any other occasion.

2. Consider Christ in the discharge of his mediatory office. And under that formal consideration, as discharging his mediatory office, he is not the ultimate object of our faith and invocation; but we call upon God, even the Father, in the name of Jesus Christ. "We through Christ have believed in God," saith Peter in one of his epistles. And it implies a contradiction to have it otherwise: for the calling him Mediator, showeth he is a means between God and us; and so it is contradictory to say our faith is terminated on his mediatory office. This he calls asking the Father in his name: "You shall ask the Father in my name;" that is, expressly plead the intervention of the mediation of Christ. And so the apostle tells us, in that grand rubric and directory of church worship, Eph. ii. 18, "By whom we have access by one Spirit unto the Father." The Father is proposed as the ultimate object of access in our worship; and the Spirit is the effecting cause, enabling us unto this worship; and the Son is the means whereby we approach unto God.

All that I shall add hereunto is this:—Seeing there is in Scripture a double worship of Christ that is immediate (for his person is considered absolutely, and as mediator between God and man), which of these ought we principally to apply ourselves unto?

I answer plainly,—

(1.) Our direction for solemn worship in the church generally respects Christ as mediator, in Scripture. The general worship that is to be performed unto God in the assemblies of the saints, doth look upon Christ as executing his mediatory office; and so our address is unto the throne of grace by him. By him we enter into the holy place,—through him and by him unto God. "I bow my knees unto (God) the Father of our Lord Jesus Christ," Eph. iii. 14. God, considered as the Father of our Lord Jesus Christ, is the proper, ultimate object of the solemn worship of the church.

(2.) In treating and dealing about our own souls, under the conduct of the Spirit of God, it is lawful and expedient for us in our prayers and supplications to make addresses to the person of Christ; as Stephen did.

DISCOURSE VI.[1]

QUESTION. *How may we make our addresses to Christ for the exercise of grace; that is, that we may have grace strengthened, and be ready for all exercise? or, How may we make application to Christ, that we may receive grace from him to recover from decays?*

ANSWER. I think the direction given by our Saviour himself is so plain, and doth so fall in with our experience, that we need not look much farther. Saith he, "Unless ye abide in me, ye cannot bear fruit." The business we aim at is fruit-bearing; which consists as much in the internal, vigorous actings of grace, as in the performance of outward duties,—to be faithful in our minds and souls, as well as in our lives. "The way for that," saith our Saviour, "is, 'Abide in me.'" And unless we do so, he tells us plainly, do we whatever we will else, we "cannot bring forth fruit." So that the whole of our fruitfulness depends upon our abiding in Christ. There cannot, then, be much more said unto this business, but to inquire a little what it is to abide in Christ.

Certainly, it is not a mere not going off from Christ; as we say, a man abides when he doth not go away. For I hope that, under all the decays we have complained of, and want of fruitfulness, yet we have not left Christ, and gone away from him. We have so far abode in him as the branch abideth in the root, from whence it hath its communication and supplies. Therefore there is something in particular included in this abiding in Christ, dwelling in Christ, and Christ dwelling in us.

And there seems to be this in it,—that to abide in Christ, is to be always nigh unto Christ, in the spiritual company of Christ, and in communication with Christ. It doth not lie in a naked, essential act of believing, whereby we are implanted into Christ, and will not go from him; but there is something of an especial, spiritual activity of soul in this abiding in Christ: it is abiding with him, and in his presence.

And as this abiding with Christ must be by some acts of our souls, let us consider what acts those are; which may give a little farther light into this matter. And, First, It must be, certainly, by some act of our minds. Secondly, By some act of our wills. Thirdly, By some act of our affections. And thus we abide with Christ; which is the way certainly to bring forth fruit.

[1] Delivered April 19, 1676.

First. There is an abiding with Christ in our minds. Now this, to me, is in contemplation and thoughts of him night and day,—"I sought him on my bed, in the night," saith the spouse;—to consider very much the person of Christ, to contemplate upon him as vested with his glorious office, and as intrusted and designed by the Father to this work. "We all," saith the apostle, "with open face beholding the glory of the Lord as in a glass, are changed into the same image from glory to glory, by the Spirit of the Lord." My brethren, that which you and I are aiming at is, to be "changed into the same image;" that is, into the image and likeness of the glory of God in Christ. I dare boldly say, by those of us who have reason to have daily apprehensions of our going out of the world, and leaving this state of things, that we have no greater desire, nor is there any thing more frequent in our minds, than this, that we may be more and more changed into that image before we go out of this world; for we are looking after perfection in likeness to Christ. Therefore aged Christians especially will bear witness, that there is nothing now we long for more than to be more and more changed into the image and likeness of Christ. How shall we get to this? Why, saith he, "The way is, by looking steadily upon Christ, as a man looks with an optic glass to an object at a great distance. We behold him," saith he, "by looking steadily upon Christ himself, and the glory of God in him." Now there is a wonderful large object for us to behold; for when you look upon the glory of God in Christ, you have what you please of Christ for the object of your eye and view;—the person of Christ, the office of Christ, the merit of Christ, the example of Christ, the death of Christ, and what you will, so you be much intent in your thoughts and minds, much in immediate contemplation about Christ. I do not know how you find it, brethren; but it is the advice I would give you who are aged Christians, and not likely to continue long in this world, to exercise yourselves in immediate contemplations upon Christ. All the teachings you have had from ministers, the principal end of them has been to enable you to this; and really, if I know any thing, we shall find them accompanied with a sweet transforming power, beyond what we have had experience of in other ways and duties. "We shall be changed into the same likeness."

Well, then, we abide with Christ in the acts of our mind, by immediate thoughtfulness and contemplation upon Christ in the night, and upon our beds, and in our walkings, and by the wayside, and in times we set apart for meditation. We are greatly to labour after an intuitive view of Christ; that is, a direct view in the contemplation of Christ.

Secondly. If you will abide with Christ, there must be an acting of your will in it also; and that is, in great diligence and carefulness about that obedience which Christ doth require, in all the instances of it. This is a great way of abiding with Christ, when we labour to have our wills in a readiness unto all the instances of obedience that Christ requireth at our hands. Let that be the question, whether it be the will of God that we should do thus, or not? And if it be so, pray let us be ready to show we do abide with Christ, by yielding cheerful and willing obedience to him in this instance and duty which he calleth us unto; and so in all other things. I would have every one of us think often of this matter,—what it is Christ requires of me personally, in a way of duty and obedience. And I would have us labour to have in great readiness all things which Christ requires of us. And especially, brethren, I would have this in a readiness, that Christ requires of me to walk very circumspectly and carefully,—to keep myself from spots and pollution, and defilements, by converse in the world. This Christ requires at all times, in all instances, and upon all occasions. What have we been preaching? what have former teachers been instructing us in? All that you are taught is, that you should come to the knowledge of all instances of duty, and the way of them, which Christ requires at your hands. And "if ye know these things, happy are ye if ye do them."

This is your fruit-bearing,—a direct contemplation upon Christ; wherein I would beg that both you and my own soul might be found more to abound, while we are in this world (and you will find Christ, in the discharge of this duty, will make very near approaches and frequent visits to your hearts,—more in the discharge of this duty than of any other); and to have our hearts in a readiness to comply with every instance of obedience Christ requires at our hands.

Thirdly. There is an abiding with Christ in point of affection. There may be love and delight in all these things; if there be not, very spiritual contemplations will be a bar. There is no duty that is required of any man in this world so spiritual, so heavenly, so evangelical, but, through want of love and delight, a man may be slothful in performing of it. I may tie myself to do so this hour or that hour, and have no benefit to my own soul, nor give any glory unto God, if there be not love and delight in it. They will sweeten the duty, and refresh the heart of God and man, Christ and us. So labour, brethren, and pray greatly for it, that you may abide with Christ with delight, that you may find a sweetness and refreshment in it, and that every season of retiring unto Christ may bring a kind of spiritual joy and gladness to your hearts. Now you have a great opportunity, having shaken off the occasions of life and other concernments, to dwell with Christ;—now it is a good time.

DISCOURSE VII.[1]

QUESTION. *When our own faith is weakened as to the hearing of our prayers—when we ourselves are hindered within ourselves from believing the answer of our prayers, have no ground to expect we should be heard, or no ground to believe we are heard—what are those things that greatly weaken our faith as to the answer of our prayers; that though we continue to pray, yet our faith is weakened as to the hearing of our prayers? and what are the grounds that weaken men's faith in such a state?*

ANSWER. If our hearts are not duly prepared to the consideration of the great and glorious properties, presence, and holiness of God, and duly affected with them in our preparation for prayer, it is certain we can have no faith for the hearing of our prayers.

It is also of great importance that we consider aright in what state the things we seek for are promised;—whether temporal things, that are left to God; or spiritual, that lie under a promise, and so we may press God immediately about them.

There are two things that are certainly great weakeners of our faith as to God's hearing our prayers:—

First. The one is, that intermixture of self which is apt to creep into our prayers, in public especially, in the congregation and assemblies. Self-reputation in the exercise of gifts, or whatever it be, weakens our faith as to the expectation of God's hearing our prayers.

Secondly. The other is, that we pray with earnestness and fervency, with noise and clamour of speech, but do not industriously pursue the things we pray for. Unless we watch and follow after these things, we shall not have ground of faith for the hearing of our prayers;—as, for instance, when the soul is burdened with a corruption, there is nothing we are more fervent in prayer unto God against; yet, when we have done this, we take no more care to get it mortified. Where is our faith that our prayers may be heard in this thing? We must pursue our prayers, or it will weaken our faith as to the hearing of them. We all pray; but do we believe that God will hear and answer our prayers?

I shall not speak unto the nature of that faith we exercise, or what assurance we may have of God's hearing our prayers; but I will tell you plainly what hinders in us the answer of our prayers:—

1. We are not clear that our persons are accepted. God had respect unto Abel and his offering, and not unto Cain and his offering.

[1] Delivered March 22, 1676.

We can have no more faith that our prayers are heard than we have faith that our persons are accepted. How many of us are dubious, and know not whether we believe or no! or are the children of God or no! According as our faith is as to the acceptance of our persons, so, ordinarily, our faith will be as to the hearing of our prayers. I do acknowledge that sometimes, under extraordinary darkness or temptation, whilst a person doth not at all know nor hath any assurance what is his own condition,—whether approved or rejected of God,—yet the Holy Spirit of God many times gives assurance of the hearing of that prayer which is poured out in the anguish of the soul. But let us bring things unto a good issue between God and our souls, and not complain that our prayers are not heard, when we are negligent to come unto the assurance of faith about the acceptance of our persons. We have had many days of prayer, and have not seen that return of our prayer that we designed. This evil lies at the bottom, —that we have been dubious as to our state of acceptance with God. Let us labour to amend it.

2. Another thing is this,—pray while you will, you will not believe your prayers are answered if you indulge any private lust, or do not vigorously endeavour the mortification of it, according to what the Scripture and duty require. If any lust ariseth in the soul, and we do not immediately engage to mortify it, as God requires, it will break out, and weaken our faith in all our prayers. Therefore, if you will be helped to believe the answer of your prayers, labour to search your hearts. Do not think that no corruption is indulged but such as break out into open sin. It may be you do not know the corruption you indulge; labour, therefore, to find it out, and you will find how your faith is weakened thereby.

3. Again; want of having treasured up former experiences of the hearing of prayer. We have not provided as we ought in this matter. If we had laid up manifold experiences of God's having heard our prayers, it would strengthen our faith that God doth hear them. It may be some have prayed all their days; God hath kept their souls alive, that they have not wickedly departed from God, and they have obtained particular mercies;—why, such ought to keep a constant record of God's hearing their prayers. Every discovery made of Christ that draws our souls more to love him, and engageth us to cleave unto him, is our experience of God's hearing our prayers.

4. I might add, when we ourselves are not sensible that we arise unto that fervency of prayer that is required of them that believe. If we pray in the congregation, in our closets, or families, and when we have done, are not sensible that we have risen up unto that fervency that is required, we cannot believe our prayers are answered.

It is the duty of all men to pray unto the Lord; but it is incumbent on none more than those who have really and sincerely given up themselves unto God, and yet in truth have no comfortable persuasion concerning their condition. That is a state wherein I am so far from discouraging prayer, that it is your season for prayer in the whole course of your lives. When Paul was first called, before such time as he had evidence of the pardon of his sins, it is said, "Behold, he prays." If they truly attend unto their state and condition, they may be sure to be the persons of whom also it will be said, "Behold, they pray." And even in these prayers they may exercise faith, when they have not faith to believe that their prayers are heard. But while in this condition, it will be hard to believe that their prayers are heard, when they cannot believe that their persons are accepted.

DISCOURSE VIII.

QUESTION. *When may any one sin, lust, or corruption, be esteemed habitually prevalent?*

ANSWER. I shall premise some few things before I come to answer the question:—

First. All lusts and corruptions whatsoever have their root and residence in our nature,—the worst of them. For, saith the apostle James, chap. i. 14, "Every man is tempted of his own lust." Every man hath his own lust, and every man hath all lust in him; for this lust, or corruption, is the depravation of our nature, and it is in all men And in the root and principle of it, it is in all men even after their conversion. So saith the apostle concerning believers, Gal. v. 17, "The flesh lusteth against the Spirit; so that ye" (believers) "cannot do the things that ye would." What doth the flesh lust unto? Why, it lusts unto the works of it. What are they? "Adultery, fornication, uncleanness, lasciviousness, idolatry, witchcraft, hatred, variance, emulations, wrath, strife, seditions, heresies, envyings, murders, drunkenness, revellings, and such like." The flesh lusteth unto all these things in believers,—the worst things that can be mentioned; whence is that [saying] of our Saviour, which yields to me a doctrine which is a sad truth, but so plain that nothing can be more. He foretells marvellous troubles, great desolations and destructions, that shall come upon the world, and befall all sorts of men, and says, "It is a day that 'as a snare shall come on all them that dwell on the face of the whole earth.'" Nothing makes me more believe that day, that terrible day of the Lord, is coming upon the face of the whole earth, than this, that it comes "as a snare." "Men do not take notice of it; do you, therefore, take heed to yourselves, you that are my disciples: believers, 'take heed to yourselves, lest at any time your hearts be overcharged with surfeiting, and drunkenness, and the cares of this life, and so that day come upon you at unawares.'" The doctrine I observe from thence is this,—that the best of men have need to be warned to take care of the worst of sins in the approach of the worst of times. Who would think, when such troubles, distresses, desolations, were coming upon a nation, in that place the disciples of Christ should be in danger of being overtaken with surfeiting, and drunkenness, and the cares of this life? Yet he who is the wisdom of God, knew how it would be with us. Nay, what if a man should say, from observation, that professors are never more in danger of sensual, provoking sins, than when destruction is lying nearest at the door? "In that day," saith he, "take care."

Secondly. Another thing I would premise is this,—that this root of sin abiding in us, as I have showed, will, upon its advantage, work unto all sorts of evils;—which should give us a godly jealousy over our souls, and over one another. Saith the apostle, Rom. vii. 8, "Sin wrought in me all manner of concupiscence."

Thirdly. If it be so, that sin doth thus always abide in us, and will upon occasions work to all its fruit, to all manner of concupiscence, then the mortification of sin is a continual duty, that we ought to be exercised in all our days. Col. iii. 3, "Ye are dead, and your life is hid with Christ in God." A blessed state and condition! I desire no better attainment in this world than this holds out. But what duty does the apostle infer from thence? "Therefore," saith he, "mortify your members which are upon the earth." What, I pray? "Fornication, uncleanness, inordinate affection, evil concupiscence, and covetousness, which is idolatry." The mortification of sin is a duty incumbent upon the best of saints.

Fourthly. The fourth thing I would premise is this,—that a particular sin doth not obtain a signal prevalency without it hath some signal advantage; for our corrupt nature is universally and equally corrupt; but a particular sin obtains prevalency by particular advantages.

It would be too long to speak of all those advantages. I shall name two, whereunto others may be reduced:—

1. The inclination of constitution gives particular advantages unto particular sins. Some may be very much inclined to envy; some to wrath and passion; and others to sensual sins,—gluttony, drunkenness, uncleanness,—to name the things which our Saviour names, and warns us of. It is with respect hereunto that David said he

"would keep himself from his iniquity," as some think. I have only this to say,—that it hath been much from the fallacy of the devil that men have been apt to plead constitution and the inclination of their constitution to the extenuation of their sin; when, indeed, it is an aggravation. "I am apt to be passionate in my nature," saith one; "I am sanguine," saith another, "and love company." They make their natural inclinations to be a cover and excuse for their sin. But this I must say, as my judgment,—that if grace does not cure constitution-sins, it hath cured none; and that we can have no trial of the efficacy of grace, if we have it not in curing constitution-sins. The great promise is, that it shall change the nature of the wolf and the lion, of the bear, the asp, the cockatrice, and that they shall become as lambs; which it can never do, if it doth not change it by an habitual counterworking of inclinations arising from constitution. If grace, being habitual, doth not change the very inclination of constitution, I know not what it doth. That is the first advantage whereby particular sins come to have signal advantage and prevalency.

2. Outward occasions; and I refer them unto two heads:—

(1.) To education. Particular sins get advantage by education. If we do even in education instruct our children to pride, by their fineries and deportment to themselves,—if we teach them to be proud, we heap dry fuel upon them, till such time as lust will flame. Let us take heed of this. It is an easy thing to bring forth a proud generation by such means.

(2.) Society in the world, according to occasion of life, is that which inflames particular corruptions. According as men delight in their converse, so corruption will be provoked and heightened by it.

I have spoke all these things previously, to show you where lies the nature and principle of the danger we are going to inquire into, and how it comes to that condition.

Now, I shall inquire a little into the question itself,—how we may know whether a particular corruption be habitually predominant or no?

Brethren, I take it for granted the vilest of those lusts which our Saviour and his apostles warn us against, to mortify and crucify, may be working in the hearts and minds of the best of us; and that a particular lust may be habitually prevalent, where, for particular reasons, it never brings forth outward effects: therefore, look to yourselves. I say, then, when the mind and soul is frequently and greatly, as there are occasions, urged upon and pressed with a particular lust and corruption, this doth not prove that particular lust and corruption to be habitually prevalent; for it may be a temptation. This may all proceed from the conjunction of temptation with indwelling sin; which will make it fight and war, and use force, and lead captive.

But suppose a person be in that condition, how shall he know whether it be a temptation in conjunction with indwelling sin in general, or whether it be an habitual prevalency of a particular corruption?

I answer,—

I. It is not from the prevalency of corruption these three ways:—

1. If the soul be more grieved with it than defiled by it, it is a temptation, and not a lust habitually prevalent. In this case, when a heart is so solicited with any sin, sin and grace are both at work, and have their contrary aims. The aim of grace is to humble the soul; and the aim of sin, to defile it. And the soul is so far defiled as, by the deceitfulness and solicitations of sin, consent is obtained. Defilement ariseth not from temptation as active upon the mind, but from temptation as admitted with consent: so far as it consents, whether by surprisal or long solicitations, so far it is defiled. It is otherwise if the soul be more grieved with it than defiled by it.

2. It is so, when the soul can truly, and doth, look upon that particular corruption as its greatest and most mortal enemy. "It is not soldiers who have ruined my estate, nor a disease that hath taken away my health, nor enemies who have ruined my name or opposed me; but this corruption, which is my great and mortal enemy." When the soul is truly under this apprehension, then it is to be hoped it is the power of temptation, and not the prevalency of lust or corruption.

3. It is so, also, when a man maintains his warfare and his conflict with it constantly, especially in those two great duties of private prayer and meditation; which if once the soul be beat off from, it is driven out of the field, and sin is conqueror. But so long as a man maintains the conflict in the exercise of grace in those duties, I look upon it as a temptation, and not an habitual, prevalent lust.

II. I shall now proceed to show when a corruption is habitually prevalent.

And here is a large field before me, but I shall only speak some few things:—

1. When a man doth choose, or willingly embrace, known occasions of his sin, that sin is habitually prevalent. There is no man that hath the common understanding of a Christian, and hath any corruption or lust working in him, but he knows what are the occasions that provoke it. No man, unless he is profligately wicked, can choose sin for sin's sake; but he who knows what are the occasions that stir up, excite, and draw forth, any particular corruption, and doth choose them, or willingly embrace them, there is the habitual prevalency of sin to a high degree in the mind of that man, whosoever he be: for sin is to be rejected in the occasion of it, or it will never be refused in the power of it.

2. Let a man fear it is so, when he finds arguments against it to lose their force. No man is under the power of particular corruption, but will have arguments suggested to his mind from fear, danger, shame, ruin, against continuing under that corruption. When a man begins to find these arguments abate in their force, and have not that prevalency upon his mind they have had, let him fear there is an habitual prevalency of his corruption.

3. When a man, upon conviction, is turned out of his course, but is not turned aside from his design,—when he traverseth his way like the wild ass, "In her occasion who shall turn her aside?"—if you meet her, or pursue her, you may turn her out of her way; but still she pursues her design. Men meet with strong convictions of sin, strong rebukes and reproofs; this a little puts them out of their way, but not from their design or inclination; the bent of their spirit lies that way still; and the secret language of their heart is, "that it were free with me to be as in former days!" Certainly a corruption is habitually prevalent, if it seldom or never fails to act itself under opportunities and temptations. If a man who trades cheats every time he is able to do so, he hath covetousness in his heart; or if a man whenever opportunity and occasion meet together to drink, doth it to excess,—this is a sign of an habitual corruption, if he be not able to hold out scarce at any time against a concurrence of temptation and opportunity.

4. When the soul, if it will examine itself, will find it is gone from under the conduct of renewing grace, and is, at the best, but under the evidence [influence?] of restraining grace. Believers are under the conduct of renewing grace; and I grant that sometimes, when, under the power of corruption and temptation, even they have broken the rule of renewing grace, God will keep them in order by restraining grace,—by fear of danger, shame, and infamy,—by outward considerations set home upon the mind by the Spirit of God, which keeps them off from sin: but this is but sometimes. But, if a man finds his heart wholly got from under the rule of renewing grace, and that he hath no leading or conduct but restraining grace, his sin hath got the perfect victory over him; that is, he would sin on to the end of his life, were it not for fear of shame, danger, death, and hell; he is no longer acted by renewing grace, which is faith and love,—faith working by love. A man who hath a spiritual understanding may examine himself, and find under what conduct he is.

4. Lastly, when there is a predominant will in sinning, then lust is habitually prevalent. Sin may entangle the mind and disorder the affections, and yet not be prevalent; but when it hath laid hold upon the will, it hath the mastery.

DISCOURSE IX.[1]

QUESTION. *Whether lust or corruption, habitually prevalent, be consistent with the truth of grace?*

ANSWER. This is a hard question; there are difficulties in it, and, it may be, it is not precisely to be determined. I am sure we should be wonderfully careful what we say upon such a question, which determines the present and eternal condition of the souls of men.

Supposing we retain something of what was spoken in stating a lust or corruption so habitually prevalent, because this is the foundation of our present inquiry, I shall bring what I have to say upon this question to a few heads, that they may be remembered.

I say, then,—

First. It is the duty of every believer to take care that this may never be his own case practically. We shall meet with straits enough, and fears enough, and doubts enough about our eternal condition, though we have no lust nor corruption habitually prevalent; therefore, I say, it is the duty of every believer to take care this may never be his case. David did so, Ps. xix. 12, 13, "Who can understand his errors?" saith he, "Cleanse thou me from secret faults. Keep back thy servant also from presumptuous sins: then shall I be upright, and I shall be innocent from the great transgression." He acknowledges his errors and sins, and prays for cleansing, purifying, pardon; but for presumptuous sins, sins with a high hand, and every habitual corruption, which hath something of presumption,—"Lord, keep back thy servant from them," saith he. The apostle's caution is to the same purpose, Heb. xii. 15, "Looking diligently lest any man fail of the grace of God; lest any root of bitterness spring up." There is the root of bitterness in every one; which I look upon as a corruption in some measure habitual, if it springs up unto great defilement. And I beseech you, brethren, beg of God, for your own souls and mine, that we may be careful this be never our case.

Secondly. The second thing I would observe is this,—whatever may be said concerning its consistency with grace, it is certainly inconsistent with peace. I wish we could remember what description was given before of this prevalent corruption, that we might consider the things now applied unto it. Here (though I would be as tender as of the apple of mine eye in these things) I will not fear to say this, that the peace which any one hath concurring with a prevalent corruption, is security, not peace. I know men may be at great peace

[1] Delivered April 19, 1677.

under prevalent corruptions, and live upon good hopes that they shall be accepted with God,—that it shall be well with them in the latter end; and that they shall have power one time or other against this corruption, and will leave it when it is seasonable, and strive against it more than they have done: but all such peace is but security. Under prevalent corruption there is a drawing back; for I would state the matter thus:—a person who is a professor, and hath kept up to duties and obedience till some lust hath gotten strength, by constitution, temptations, or occasions of life, and hath drawn him off from his former renovation in walking with God; there is then a drawing back. Now, saith the apostle, "If any man draw back, my soul shall have no pleasure in him," Heb. x. 38. And when God hath no pleasure according to the several degrees of backsliders (it may be that is meant of final apostasy), he doth not intimate any thing that is a ground of peace to that soul. So Isa. lvii. 17, "For the iniquity of his covetousness was I wroth, and hid myself from him." If there be an incurable iniquity of covetousness, or any other iniquity, whether manifest unto us or no, God is angry, and doth hide himself from us. I pray, brethren, let us examine our peace; and if we find we have a peace that can maintain its ground and station under prevalent corruption, trust no more to that peace,—it will not stand us in stead when it comes to a trial.

Thirdly. The third thing I would say is this,—that if a prevalent corruption be not inconsistent with the truth of grace, it is certainly inconsistent with the true exercise of grace. It is not, indeed, inconsistent with the performance of duties; but it is inconsistent with the true exercise of grace in the performance of duties. It is often seen and known, that persons under prevalent corruption will multiply duties, thereby to quiet conscience, and to compensate God for what they have done amiss. Persons may multiply prayers, follow preaching, and attend to other duties, when they use all these things, through the deceitfulness of sin, but as a cloak unto some prevailing corruption; but in all those duties there is no true exercise of grace.

The true determination of this question depends upon a right exposition of 1 John ii. 15. If we could understand that verse, it determines this point, "Love not the world, neither the things that are in the world. If any man love the world, the love of the Father is not in him." There is the question, whether prevalent corruption be inconsistent with true grace? I know the words may have this construction, "If any man do make the world his chiefest good, if any man put the world in the place of God, then the love of the Father is not in him; he hath either received no love from God, or he hath no love to God as a Father in Christ." But indeed the apostle, speaking unto believers, I am apt to think speaks not of the whole kind, but degrees,—if there be a prevalency of love of the world, there is no prevalency of the actings of the love of the Father,—that they do not concern the habitual principles of the love of the world, and of the love of the Father, but the prevailing actings of the one and the other. And, accordingly, it may be said of all other graces whatsoever, that where there is a prevalency of the acting of sin, there is a suspension of the exercise of grace. Brethren, if any of us have been under the power of prevalent corruption (I will be still tender, and speak what ought to be received and believed, whether people do or not), it is much to be feared we have lost all our prayers and hearing, because we have not had a true exercise of grace in them. Some exercise there may be, but a due and true exercise of grace will be laid asleep by prevalent corruption. And therefore let us take heed of prevalent corruption, as we would take heed of losing all things that we have wrought,—our praying, hearing, suffering, charity,—for want of a due exercise of grace in them.

Fourthly. I shall grant this, that spiritual life may be in a swoon, when the spiritual man is not dead. There is a kind of *deliquium* of the spirits, called swooning away, that may befall believers, which suspends all acts of life, when yet the man is not dead. So I say, though I should see a man, through the prevalency of corruption, have all the evidences of a spiritual life cast into a swoon, yet I will not presently conclude the spiritual man is dead. Take the case of David, from the time of his great fall and transgression in the matter of Uriah until the coming of Nathan the prophet. Persons are generally inclined to believe that the spiritual life was in a swoon, when the spiritual man was not dead. His fall, as an honest man said, beat the breath out of his body, and he lay a long time like a man dead, by reason of that power, which one signal sin left in his soul. And take that as a great instance that one sin, not immediately taken off by great humiliation, leaves great and even habitual inclinations in the soul to the same sin. So that some ascribed it unto the corruption of our nature. For it is a great and difficult question in divinity, how one particular sin, as the sin of Adam was, should bring in habitual corruption to our nature. To which some answer thus: That any one single moral act, performed with a high hand, hath great obliquity in it, disposing our whole nature to corruption. David, by that single act of flagrant wickedness, did continue in it for so long a space of time, till Nathan came and administered some good spirits to him, that relieved him out of his swoon. Wherefore I say that I will not judge a person to be spiritually dead, whom I have judged formerly to have had spiritual life, though I see him at present in a swoon as to all evidences of the spiritual life. And the reason why I will not judge so is this,—because if you judge a person dead, you neglect him, you leave him; but if you judge him in a swoon, though never so dangerous, you use all means for the retrieving of his life. So ought we to do to one another and our own souls.

Fifthly. There is a prevalency of sin that is inconsistent with true grace, which may befall those who have been professors. So the apostle doth plainly declare, Rom. vi. 16, " Know ye not, that to whom ye yield yourselves servants to obey, his servants ye are to whom ye obey; whether of sin unto death, or of obedience unto righteousness?" There is such a serving of sin as puts a man into a contrary state.

Sixthly. I shall add but one thing more, and that is this,—there may be a corruption, sin, or lust, habitually prevalent, as to whatsoever evidences the person in whom it is or others can discern; and yet the root of the matter, the root of spiritual life, be notwithstanding in the person.

Suppose, then, there be such a prevalency, that the soul judges to be habitual, how shall we know whether the root of the matter be in such a person or no?

If the soul hath any thing left of spiritual life, there will be something of vital operations in that soul. Now, the vital operations that give evidence the soul is not absolutely slain by prevalent corruption, are opposition and humiliation. So long as the soul, though it be never so much captivated, is conscious to itself of a sincerity in the opposition it makes, there is an evidence of a vital operation; as likewise where it is constant in its humiliation on that account.

But if it be farther inquired, how it may be known that this humiliation is sincere?

I answer, It cannot be known from its vigour and efficacy; for that overthrows the question. For if the opposition was vigorous and effectual, it would break the power of lust and corruption, so that it would be no more prevalent. But two ways it may be known.

1. By its constancy. If the root of the matter be still in us, there will be a constant opposition to every act of any prevailing corruption whatsoever. I do not speak about violent temptations, but ordinary cases; in which I know not whence we should conclude the root of the matter is in that man who doth not make a sincere opposition to every instance of the acting of prevalent corruption. If a man can pass over one and another instance of prevalent corruption without any humiliation for it, the holy, sovereign God show him grace and mercy! but it is to me " the way of a serpent upon a stone,"—I see it not, I know it not.

2. It is sincere, if it be from its proper spring; that is, if the opposition be not from conviction, light, or conscience only, but from

the will of the poor sinner. "I would do otherwise; I would have this sin destroyed,—I would have it rooted out, that it should be no more in me; my will lies against it, however it hath captivated my affections and disturbed my course."

This is all I dare say upon this question,—that there may be an habitual prevalency of corruption, which may seem so to them in whom it is, as also to those who converse with them, and yet the root of the matter be in them. We may know the root of the matter by the acting of spiritual life,—in opposition going before, and humiliation coming after. We may know the sincerity of these vital actings by their constancy, and by their spring,—if we are constant in them, and if they arise from our wills.

DISCOURSE X.[1]

QUESTION. *What shall a person do who finds himself under the power of a prevailing corruption, sin, or temptation?*

ANSWER. I shall premise only this one thing, and then inquire whether it belongs to us or no:—

This prevalency hath many degrees. It may be a prevalency to outward scandal, or to the utter loss of inward peace, or to the disquieting and divesting of us of that tranquillity of mind usually which Christ calleth us unto. Now, pray consider that I speak to it equally and in every degree. And perhaps there may be none of us but, at one time or other, after inquiry, will have had experience in one degree or other, either to disquietment, loss of peace, or scandal.

What shall such a person then do, who finds it so with him?

I answer,—

First. He should labour to affect his mind with the danger of it. It is not conceivable how subtle sin is to shift off an apprehension of the danger of it. "Notwithstanding this," says the man, "yet I hope I am in a state of grace, and shall be saved, and come to the issue of it at one time or other;" and so the mind keeps off a due sense of the danger of it. I beseech you, brethren and sisters, if this be your condition, labour to affect your minds that this state, as far as I know, will end in hell; and let not your minds be relieved from the apprehension that, upon due and good grounds of faith, these

[1] Delivered May 4, 1677.

ways go down to the chambers of death. Do not please yourselves, imagining you are members of the church, and have good hopes of salvation by Jesus Christ; but consider whither this tends, and affect your minds with it.

Secondly. When the person is affected with the danger of it, the next thing to be done is, to burden his conscience with the guilt of it. For the truth is, as our minds are, upon many pretences, slow to apprehend the danger of sin; so our consciences are very unwilling to take the weight of the burden of it as to its guilt. I speak not of men of seared consciences, that, lay what weight you will upon them, will feel none; but even of the consciences of renewed men, unless they use all the ways and means whereby conscience may be burdened,—as by apprehensions of the holiness of God, of the law, of the love of Christ, and of all those things whereby conscience must be made to feel the weight of its guilt. No sooner doth it begin to be made a little sick with a sense of the guilt of sin, but it takes a cordial presently. "Here this sin hath taken place, it hath contracted this and that guilt; I have been thus long negligent in this or that duty; I have thus long engaged in this and that folly, and been so given up unto the world: I must take to Christ by faith, or I am undone." It is afraid of making its load. But let conscience bear the burden, and not easily shift it off, unless it can, by true faith, guided by the word, load it upon Christ; which is not a thing of course to be done.

Thirdly. "What shall we do in case we have this apprehension of its danger, and can be thus burdened with its guilt?" Pray for deliverance. "How?" you will say. There is in the Scriptures mention of "roaring," Ps. xxxii. 3, "The voice of my roaring;" and likewise of "shouting," Lam. iii. 8, "I shouted and cried." This is a time to pray that God would not hide his face from our roaring, nor shut out our prayers when we shout unto him; that is, to cry out with all the vigour of our souls. Christ is able "to succour" and help them that "make an outcry" to him. The word signifies so;[1] and our word "succour," signifies a running in to help a man who is ready to be destroyed. These may seem hard things to us, but it is a great thing to save our souls, and to deliver ourselves from the snares of Satan.

Fourthly. Treasure up every warning, and every word that you are convinced was pointed against your particular corruption. There is none of you who may have the power of particular corruptions, but God, at one time or other, in his providence or word, gives particular warning, that the soul may say, "This is for me, I must comply with it;" but "it is like a man that sees his face in a glass, and goes away, and immediately forgets what manner of man he was,"—there is an

[1] Βοηθέω, (Βοὴ, θέω), to run in answer to a cry for help, Heb. ii. 18.—Ed.

end of it. But if God give you such warnings, set them down, treasure them up, lose them not; they must be accounted for. "He that, being often reproved, hardens his neck, shall suddenly be destroyed, and that without remedy."

Fifthly. I shall mind you of two rules, and so have done:—

1. In your perplexities as to the power of sin, exercise faith, that, notwithstanding all you see and find that you are almost lost and gone, there is a power in God, through Christ, for the subduing and conquering of it.

2. It is in vain for any to think to mortify a prevailing sin, who doth not at the same time endeavour to mortify all sin, and to be found in every duty. Here is a person troubled and perplexed with a temptation or corruption; both are the same in this case: he cries, "O that I were delivered! I had rather have deliverance than life! I will do my endeavour to watch against it." But it may be this person will not come up to a constancy in secret prayer;—he will go up and down, and wish himself free, but will not be brought up to such duties [as] wherein those lusts must be mortified. Therefore, take this rule along with you,—never hope to mortify any corruption whereby your hearts are grieved, unless you labour to mortify every corruption by which the Spirit of God is grieved; and be found in every duty, especially those under which grace thrives and flourishes.

DISCOURSE XI.

QUESTION. *What is our duty with respect to dark and difficult dispensations of God's providence in the world?*

ANSWER. In answer unto this question, three things are to be considered:—First. What are, in a Scripture sense, those things that make a season of providence dark and difficult? Secondly. What are the open signs of the coming and passing of such a season over us? And, Thirdly. What are our special duties in reference to our entering into, and passing through, such a season?

First. What are those things that make a season of providence dark and difficult?

I find four things in Scripture that make a dark season of providence; and, if I mistake not, they are all upon us:—

1. The long-continued prosperity of wicked men. This you are sensible is the most known case of all the Old Testament, Ps. lxxiii.;

Jer. xii. 1–3; Hab. i. 4, 13, and many other places. The holy men of old did confess themselves in great perplexity at the long-continued prosperity of wicked men, and their long-continued prosperity in ways of wickedness. Give but this one farther circumstance to it,—the long-continued prosperity of wicked men in their wickedness, when the light shines round about them to convince them of that wickedness, and God speaks in and by the light of his word against them; that is a trial. When all things were wrapped up in darkness and idolatry, it is no wonder at the patience of God; but when things come in any place to that state that many continue prosperous in wickedness when the day is upon them that judges them,—it is a difficulty.

2. It is a difficult season of providence, when the church is continued under persecution and distress in a time of prayer, when they give themselves to prayer. The difficulty seems mentioned, Ps. lxxx. 4, "O LORD, how long wilt thou smoke against the prayer of thy people?" This made it hard, that God should afflict his church, and keep her under distresses, and suffer the furrows to be made long upon her back, and continue her under oppression from one season to another. There may be evident reason for that. But saith God, "Call upon me in the time of trouble, and I will hear." God hath promised to hear the church: Will not God avenge the elect, that call upon him day and night? He will do it speedily. Now, when God seems to be angry with the prayers of his people, that is a difficult season: when they cry and shout, and God shuts out their prayers, that makes a dark providence.

As the other difficulty is evidently upon us, so I hope we have this difficulty to conflict withal, that the anger of God continues to smoke against the prayers of his people, as having stirred up many a blessed cry to himself; for there is a time when he will hear and answer their prayers.

3. It is a dark and difficult dispensation of providence, when the world and nations of the world are filled with confusion and blood, and no just reason appearing why it should be so. When our Saviour foretells a difficult season, Matt. xxiv. and Luke xxi., he says, "There shall be terrible times, such as never were; nation shall rise against nation, and kingdom against kingdom; and there shall be wars, bloodshed, and earthquakes; and the very elect shall hardly escape." Therefore God calls such a time, "a day of darkness," yea, of "thick darkness," Joel ii. 2, a dark, gloomy day. There is nothing to be seen in all the confusions that are in the world at this day, but that the frogs or unclean spirits are gone forth to stir up the lusts of men to make havoc of one another.

4. It adds greatly to the difficulty of a season, when we have no prospect whither things are tending, and what will be their issue.

There are two ways whereby we may have a prospect of things that are in being:—by the eye of God's providence, when we perceive which way that looks; and by Scripture rule. The truth is, we are in a time wherein no man can discern a fixed eye of providence looking this way or that way. What will be the issue of these things; whether it will be the deliverance of the church, or the desolation of the nation and straitening of the church; whether God will bring good out of them in this generation, or any other time, none knows: this makes it difficult. Ps. lxxiv. 9, "We see not our signs,"—have no tokens what God intends to do; "neither is there among us any to tell us how long."

There is none of these things but make a season difficult, and providence dark; but when all of them concur together, they cannot but greatly heighten it: and I think they are all upon us.

Secondly. What are the open signs of the coming and passing of such a season over us?

There are three tokens or outward evidences of a difficult season. It is so,—

1. When God's patience is abused. You know that place, Eccles. viii. 11, "Because sentence against an evil work is not executed speedily, therefore the heart of the sons of men is fully set in them to do evil." Things pass thus:—men fall into wickedness, great wickedness; their consciences fly in their faces, and they are afraid; the power of their lusts carries them into the same wickedness again, and their consciences begin to grow a little colder than they were: no evil comes of it, and judgment is not speedily executed; and so their hearts at last come to be wholly set to do evil. Hence others that look on say, "Here are men given up to all wickedness; surely judgment will speedily come upon these men." Judgment doth not come,—God is patient; and so they themselves turn as wicked as the former. Abusing of God's patience is an evident sign of a dispensation of the displeasure of God in his providence: and if ever it was upon any, it is upon us; and men learn it more and more every day. Every one talks of other men's sins; and seeing no judgment falls upon them, they give up themselves to the same sins.

2. It is so when God's warnings are despised: "When thine hand is lifted up, they will not see." That is a difficult season; for, saith God, "The fire of thine adversaries shall consume thee." Never had people more warnings than we have had;—warning in heaven above, and warning on the earth beneath; warnings by lesser judgments, and warnings by greater; and warnings by the word. God's hand hath been lifted up; but who takes notice of it? Some despise it, and others talk of it as a tale to be told; and there is an end of it. Who sanctifies the name of God in all the warnings that are given

us? "The LORD'S voice crieth unto the city," Mic. vi. 9; but it is only "the man of wisdom," of substance, that seeth the name of God in these his cries unto the city by his warnings from heaven and earth, signs and tokens, and great intimations of his displeasure.

3. An inclination in all sorts of people to security, and to take no notice of these things. I have spoken unto this business of security formerly, and I pray God warn you and myself of it; for I believe none of us are such strangers to our hearts, but we can say, that under all these warnings there is an inclination to security: if God did not prevent it, we should fall fast asleep under all the judgments that are round about us.

Any of these things shows that we are under a difficult dispensation of providence; but where all concur,—God be merciful to such a people!—it is the opening of the door to let out judgments to the uttermost.

Now if this be such a season, as I do verily believe we are all sensible it is, then,—

Thirdly, What shall we do? what are our special duties in reference to our entering into, and passing through, such a season?

I might speak unto the peculiar exercise of those graces which are required unto such a season; as faith, resignation to the will of God, readiness for his pleasure, waiting upon God, weanedness from the world, and the like; but I will only give you three or four duties, which are peculiarly hinted in such a season, and so have done:—

1. Our first duty is, that we should meet together, and confer about these things, Mal. iii. 16, 17. A good plan in difficult seasons, such as some of us have seen. The day of the Lord was coming that would burn as an oven: "Then they that feared the LORD spake often one to another: and the LORD hearkened, and heard it, and a book of remembrance was written before him for them that feared the LORD, and that thought upon his name. And they shall be mine, saith the LORD of hosts, in that day when I make up my jewels; and I will spare them, as a man spareth his own son that serveth him." When was this? In a time of great judgment, and great sin,—"when they called the proud happy, and they that wrought wickedness were set up, and they that tempted God were even delivered;" that is, "appeared to be delivered." It is the great duty of us all, as we have opportunity and occasion, to confer about these things; about the causes of them,—what ariseth from the profane, wicked world; what from a persecuting, idolatrous world; and (wherein we are more concerned) what from a professing generation; and see how we can sanctify the name of God in it. We might have as great advantages as any under the face of heaven for the discharge of this duty, if we did but make use of that "price" [Prov. xvii. 16] which

God hath put into our hands; but if we are "fools," and have no "heart" to improve it, the blame will be our own. You have opportunities for meeting and assembling: I fear there are cold affections in your private meetings; I wish there be not. It may be some thrive and grow; I hope so: and others are cold and backward; it is not a season for it. If God would help us to manage this church aright, and as we ought to do, there can be no greater advantage under such a season than we enjoy: but we want voluntary inspection; and the Lord lay it not to our charge we have deferred it so long. Much want of love might have been prevented, many duties furthered, and many evils removed, if we had come up to the light God hath given to us. But we are at a loss; and God knows we suffer under it, for want of discharging our duty.

That is the first thing,—to speak often one to another;—to sanctify the name of God by an humble, diligent inquiry into the causes of these dispensations, and preparation for these things.

2. The second duty in such a season is, for every one of us privately to inquire of Jesus Christ, in prayer and supplication, "What shall be the end of these things?" You have a great instance of it, Dan. viii. 13, 14, "Then I heard one saint speaking, and another saint said unto that certain saint which spake, How long shall be the vision concerning the daily sacrifice, and the transgression of desolation, to give both the sanctuary and the host to be trodden under foot? And he said unto me, Unto two thousand and three hundred days; then shall the sanctuary be cleansed." I suppose there is something of the ministry of angels in it; for this saint inquires, but the answer is made to Daniel, "One saint said unto another saint;"—"and he said unto me." But the speaking saint was Jesus Christ. There was the Holy One that spake, which he calls פַּלְמוֹנִי, "a certain saint;" but the derivation of the word is, "One that revealeth secrets."[1] There was application made unto Jesus Christ, who is the revealer of secrets, to know how long. And you will find in the Scriptures, in difficult dispensations, that is very many times the request of the saints to God, "How long?" Dan. xii. 6, 8, "How long shall it be to the end of these wonders?" and, "O my Lord, what shall be the end of these things?" There is an humble application by faith and prayer unto Jesus Christ, to know the mind of God in these things, that will bring satisfaction in to our souls. Do not leave yourselves to wander in your own thoughts and imaginations. It is impossible but we shall be debating things, and giving a rational account of them; but all will not bring us satisfaction. But let us go to Jesus Christ, and say to

[1] See this meaning supported in Willet on Daniel. The highest modern authorities consider the word as equivalent to two words combined,—viz., פְּלֹנִי—*an individual;* אַלְמֹנִי—*one who is nameless.*—Ed.

him, "O Lord, how long?" And he will give in secret satisfaction to our souls.

This is the second thing,—frequently confer about these things; and press Jesus Christ to give your souls satisfaction as to these dispensations And then,—

3. Another peculiar duty required in such a season is, to mourn for the sins that are in the world. That is recommended to us, Ezek. ix. When God had given commission unto the sword to slay both old and young, he spared only them that mourned for the abominations that were done in the land. We come short in our duty in that matter,—in [not] being affected with the sins of the worst of men. God being dishonoured, the Spirit of God blasphemed, the name of God reproached in them, we ought to mourn for their abominations. We mourn for the sins among God's people; but we ought also to mourn for those abominations others are guilty of,—for their idolatries, murders, bloodshed, uncleanness,—for all the abominations that the lands about us, as well as our own, are filled with. It is our duty, in such a season, to mourn for them, or we do not sanctify the name of God, and shall not be found prepared for those difficult dispensations of God's providence which are coming upon us.

4. The fourth and last peculiar duty which I shall mention is, to hide ourselves. And how shall we do that? The storm is coming; get an ark, as Noah did when the flood was coming upon the world: which is stated for a precedent of all judgments in future times. There are two things required to provide an ark,—fear and faith:—

(1.) Fear: "By faith Noah, being moved with fear, prepared an ark." If he had not been moved with the fear of God's judgments, he would never have provided an ark. It is a real complaint; we are not moved enough with the fear of God's judgments. We talk of [as] dreadful things as can befall human nature, and expect them every day; but yet we are not moved with fear. "Yet were they not afraid," saith Jeremiah, "nor rent their garments." Nor do we do so. Habakkuk, upon the view of God's judgments, was in another frame, chap. iii. 16, "When I heard," saith he, "my belly trembled; my lips quivered at the voice: rottenness entered into my bones, and I trembled in myself, that I might rest in the day of trouble." This is the way to find rest in the day of God's judgments. We are afraid of being esteemed cowards for fearing God's judgments; and then,—

(2.) We cannot well provide an ark for ourselves, unless we be guided by faith, as well as moved by fear. "By faith, Noah prepared an ark." How many things there are to encourage faith, you have heard;—the name, the properties of God, and the accomplishment of the promise of God. By virtue of all those properties, encourage faith in providing an ark.

But you will say, "We are yet at a loss what this providing of an ark and hiding of ourselves is. 'A prudent man foresees the evil, and hides himself.' God calls us to enter into the chamber of providence, and hide ourselves till the indignation be overpast. If we knew what this was, we should apply ourselves unto it." I will tell you what I think in one instance:—give no quiet to your minds, until, by some renewed act of faith, you have a strong and clear impression of the promises of God upon your hearts, and of your interest in them. If it be but one promise, it will prove an ark. If, under all these seasons, moved with fear, acted by faith, we can but get a renewed sense and pledge of our interest in any one promise of God, we have an ark over us that will endure, whatever the storm be. Think of it, and if nothing else occur to you, apply your minds to it, that you may not wander up and down at uncertainties; but endeavour to have a renewed pledge of your interest in some special promise of God, that it belongs unto you, and it will be an ark in every time of trouble that shall befall you.

DISCOURSE XII.[1]

I DID at two meetings inquire among ourselves what was required in the time of approaching judgments and calamities, that the world hath been, and is like to be, filled withal? And God was pleased to guide us to the discovery of the necessary exercise of many graces, and the necessary attendance unto many duties, for that end and purpose. And we did design to spend our time this day to beg that God would give us those graces, and stir them up by his Spirit unto a due exercise; and that he would help us unto such a performance of those duties, that when the Lord Christ shall come, by any holy dispensation of his providence, we may be found of him in peace. That was the especial occasion of allotting the present time unto this duty; no ways excluding the reasons, occasions, and matter of prayer, which at other times we attend to for ourselves, the church, and the nation.

I would offer a few words that may stir us up unto this duty:—

The Scripture doth everywhere, upon all such occasions, call expressly unto us for a special preparation, by the exercise of grace, in reformation and holiness: "Judgment must begin at the house of God;" and "what will be the end of them that obey not the gospel?" What, then, is our duty? Why, saith he, "Seeing that

[1] Delivered March 14, 1678.

all these things shall be dissolved" (all this outward frame of things), " what manner of persons ought we to be in all holy conversation and godliness?" Brethren, we ought at all times to attend unto " all holy conversation and godliness;" but saith the apostle, " The approach of judgment is a peculiar motive thereunto;—'seeing that all these things are to be dissolved.'" It is true, seeing Christ hath died for us, washed us in his blood, and given his Holy Spirit unto us, " What manner of persons ought we to be?" But the great motives are not exclusive of occasional exercises, but give an addition unto them. " Take heed that ye be not overtaken with surfeiting and drunkenness,"—with any excess in the use of the creature. What if it be so? " Then that day will come upon you at unawares;"—the day when all shall be dissolved,—the day of judgment,—the day of approaching calamities. " You ought at all times to take care of these things; but if your minds are not influenced in the consideration of the approach of that day, 'you are not my disciples.'" I do not at all speak unto what preparations are required.

I could also reflect on those places where God expresseth his great displeasure against such who did not labour for a peculiar preparation upon approaching calamities. Isa. xxii. 12–14, " 'I called for mourning, and fasting, and girding with sackcloth,' and you betook yourselves unto feasting on all occasions." "Surely, saith the LORD, this iniquity shall not be purged from you till ye die." And it is reckoned among the sins of the most profligate persons, that when God's hand is lifted up and ready to strike, they will not see, so as to learn righteousness, Isa. xxvi. 11.

Let us, therefore, beg for grace. Though God multiplieth warnings, makes appearances of mercy, and then writes death upon them, and entangles every thing in darkness, yet our work goes slowly on in preparation. Cry earnestly unto God for such supplies of his grace and Spirit that may effectually bring us unto him; that we may no longer abide in the frame wherein we are.

There are three things, and no more, that I know of (others may be named, but they may be reduced unto these three heads), that are required of us in reference unto approaching judgments; and there is not one of them through which we can pass, or which we can perform in a due manner, comfortably unto ourselves, and unto the glory of God, without we have some singular and eminent preparation for it. And they are these:—First. That we ourselves stand in the gap, to turn away the threatened judgments. Secondly. That we may be fit for deliverance, if it please the Lord graciously to give it unto us. Saith Christ, speaking of great calamities, " Lift up your heads; for your redemption draweth nigh." Thirdly. That we may cheerfully and comfortably go through the calamities, if they shall overtake us.

These three are comprehensive of all the threats of approaching judgments and darkness that encompass us at this day. Now, there is not one of them that we can be any way fit for, unless our hearts and lives are brought into an extraordinary preparation, according as God calls and requires. I do not know whether we believe these things or no, but they will be shortly found to be true.

First. Who dares among us to propose himself to stand in the gap, to divert judgments from the nation, otherwise than in a formal manner, who is not prepared by these things we have spoken of, and hath not some good and comfortable persuasion of his own personal interest in Christ, and hath not freed himself from those sins that have procured these judgments, and who lives not in a resignation of himself unto the will of God? who dares to do this? We shall provoke God, if we think to stand in the gap, and turn away judgments from the nation, when we see ourselves are concerned in procuring those judgments.

Secondly. We cannot be meet for deliverance, unless we are thus prepared. I have heard a notion preached and spoken upon other occasions,—which I confess I never liked, and the more I consider it, the more I dislike it; and that is, that God, in the deliverance of his people, works for his own name's sake, that he may have all the glory,—that it shall be seen merely to be of grace: and therefore he will oftentimes deliver his people, when they are in an unreformed and unreforming condition, that he may shame them and humble them by his mercy and grace afterward. I know no rule of Scripture upon which this notion may be grounded, nor one instance or example whereby it may be made out.

Here lies the truth of it,—when there are two things concurring in the deliverance of the church, God will deliver them, notwithstanding all their sins and unworthiness, without any previous humiliation in themselves:—first, When God hath fixed and limited a certain season in his word and promise for their deliverance; and, secondly, When, antecedent unto their deliverance, they want means for humiliation. God delivered the children of Israel out of Egypt when they were in a very bad condition,—an ignorant, stubborn, faithless generation; but both these things were concurring:—God was engaged, in point of his promise, that, at the end of four hundred and thirty years, he would visit and deliver them; and they were deprived of all ordinances of worship in Egypt: not a sacrifice could they offer while they were there; not a Sabbath, I believe, though it is not expressed in Scripture, could they observe;—the way of worship and knowledge of God was taken from them. So, when God delivered the children of Israel out of Babylon, they were in no very good condition; but God was engaged in point of promise as to that time, that at the end of seventy years they should be delivered; and in Babylon they had no means for instruction or reformation,—no temple, no sacrifice;—these were denied. But whenever God doth afford unto persons all the means of grace for humiliation, reformation, and turning unto himself,—it may be as good as ever they shall in this world, —that God did ever deliver that people out of their distresses, when they refused to be reformed, humbled, or to turn unto him, neither instances of Scripture nor God's dealing with his church will make this good. Therefore it is vain for us to expect any thing of this nature. If, indeed, for so many years we had been thrown into a wilderness condition, and had no preaching, no assemblies, no administration of ordinances, no warnings or charges from God, we might have expected the Lord would have given us deliverance; but to us, who have had all these things, and yet will not make use of what we have now at present, we have no ground to expect any such thing. Therefore I confess, neither by rule, instance, or example, do I expect deliverance, until God come in to work a thorough change and reformation in our hearts and lives; which makes it very necessary to be preparing to meet God in the way of his judgments.

Thirdly. The third thing that may lie before us is, how we may cheerfully go through the calamities which may overtake us. I will say no more unto that, because it is that which we did expressly insist upon in our former discourse. As to the best of us, who have been long in the ways of God, woful will be our surprisal when the days of calamity come, if we have lived in negligence of complying with the calls and warnings of God that we have had, to bring ourselves unto a more even and better frame. We shall find our strength to fail us, and have our comforts to seek, and be left to inward darkness when outward darkness increaseth, and not know whither to cause our sorrows to go.

These things, brethren, I thought fit to mention unto you, that, if it be the will of God, they may be of use to take us off from those false hopes and false expectations which we are wonderfully ready to feed ourselves withal in such a day as this is wherein we live. It is high time for us to be calling upon God for this end.

DISCOURSE XIII.

THE prophet Daniel tells us, when he understood by books—namely, the writings of the prophet Jeremiah—that the time wherein the great contest between Babylon and the church was to have its issue was come to a point, "Then," saith he, "I set my face to seek the LORD with prayer and supplications, and fasting." And if you will read his prayer, you will find nothing of confidence, nothing of self-ascription; but a deep acknowledgment of sin: "We, our kings, our princes, our fathers" (our church), "have all sinned;" so as that "to us belong shame and confusion of face." And never had such shame and confusion of face befallen the church as would have befallen them, if they had been disappointed in that trial. But he adds, "Unto thee belong mercies and forgivenesses." There he issues the whole business, upon "mercy and forgiveness," though he knew by books that the time was come.

Truly, brethren, we do not know by any Scripture revelation, as he did, that the time is come wherein the long contest and conflict between Babylon and the church will have its issue; but it looks like it in the book of providence, and so like it, that it is a plain duty we should give ourselves unto prayer and supplication, that it do not issue in shame and confusion of face; which belongeth unto us by reason of our sins. It is that contest which is now under consideration, and which seems to be coming to its issue, and all men are in expectation of it. It is the greatest, save one, that ever was; for the greatest contest that ever was in this world was between the person and the gospel of Christ on the one hand, and the devil and the pagan world on the other; and the next to that is the contest between Christ—in his offices and grace, in his gospel and worship—and Antichrist. And it is at this day upon its trial, in as signal an instance as ever it received. The question is, as to us and our posterity, Whether Christ or Antichrist? whether the worship of God or of idols? whether the effusion, and waiting for the effusion, of the Spirit of God in his worship, or all manner of superstitious impositions? This is the present contest; and, it may be, under heaven there never was a more signal instance of the issue of this contest than will be in these nations in these days;—I do not say presently or speedily; but this, you all know, is our state.

I mention it only to let you know that there is more than an ordinary earnestness and fervency of spirit and wrestling with God required of us at this day for the cause of Zion, the interest of Christ, and defeating of his adversaries. What way God will work we know not. If he be at work, he hath said, that when a flood was cast out of the mouth of the dragon, to swallow up the woman everywhere (and we have had a flood cast out of the mouth of the dragon to swallow up the whole interest of Christ in this nation), the earth lifted up herself and helped the woman, and turned aside the flood. Good old Eli's heart trembled for the ark of God. The interest of

God and the truths of Christ are yet among us, but hardly beset by the Philistines; and whether they may not take them I know not,—God only knows. But assuredly, brethren, our hearts ought now to tremble for the ark of God, that God would continue it among us, and not give his glory into the hands of the adversary.

I have mentioned these things only for this end,—that if God will, our hearts may be a little warmed, upon all occasions, in this great contest and conflict between Christ and Antichrist, to come in with our prayers to the help of the Lord, and of the ark of the Lord,—that we may see a blessed issue of this trial, and not be covered with that shame and confusion of face which belong unto us.

DISCOURSE XIV.[1]

THIS meeting is for conference, and I would ask you a few questions:—

First. Whether do you think there are extraordinary calls and warnings of God towards this nation at this time?

Secondly. If there be, what is the voice of these calls?

Thirdly. Whether any sort of men, believers, or churches, are exempted from attending unto and complying with these calls of God? For there lies a reserve in our hearts. The nation is very wicked (I shall not repeat the sins of the nation), the warning is general to the nation, the body of the people, and God testifies his displeasure against them. Now, the inquiry is, Whether there be any rule that we, who profess ourselves believers, and a church, should count ourselves exempted from a particular compliance with these extraordinary calls of God,—that they are for others, and not for us? "If the scourge slay suddenly, he will laugh at the trial of the innocent," Job ix. 23. And the good figs went first into captivity.

Fourthly. What have we done hitherto in order to it, that may evidence itself to be an answer to, a compliance with, these calls of God, which we have owned here before the Lord? We have been speaking of it, and it becomes me to judge that we have had good and sincere desires after it. And neither the church, nor any one in the church, shall have any reflections from me beyond evidence. It becomes me to judge that we have had in ourselves good intentions, and sincere endeavours after it, though they have been, it may be, no way suitable or proportionable to the present occasion; and there-

[1] Delivered February 15, 1680.

fore I must say, that, in an eminent and extraordinary manner, as yet we have done nothing. We have not consulted of it yet, what we should do, and "what it is" in particular "that the LORD our God requireth of us;" nor declared our designs and intentions for a universal compliance with these great calls of God for repentance and turning unto the Lord. I mourn over myself night and day; I mourn over you continually. I do not see that life and vigour in returning unto God, either in our persons or in our church relation, as I could desire. And give me leave to say, from an experience in my own heart, I am jealous over you. We may proceed to consider something of outward duties afterward; but as yet we are not at all come to it, but only to inquire into our hearts what we have done in compliance with these calls of God, in the reformation and change of our hearts, and vigour of spirit in walking with him. I speak it with all tenderness, that none might take offence; but I do acknowledge to you, that I have not myself attained, nor can I, though I am labouring to bring my heart to that frame which God requireth in us all at this time. I find many obstructions: if you have attained I shall rejoice in it with all my heart and soul; but if not, help them that are labouring after it. I intend no more at present but this,—to settle upon our souls a conviction that we have not as yet answered the calls of God in the heart: for if we have all apprehensions we have complied, the work is at an end.

I hope we may in due time go on to consider all the ways and instances whereby we may reform and return unto God; but in the meantime I offer this to you,—that unless the foundation of it be laid in a deep and broken sense of our past miscarriages and present frames, and I can see in the church some actings of a renewed spirit with vigour and earnestness to pursue our recovery and return to God, I shall much despond in this thing. But let us be persuaded that we are to lay this foundation (I desire we may agree upon this), that it is our duty to get a deep sense upon our hearts, as the first thing God aims at in his calls, of our past miscarriages, and of our present dead, wretched frame; in comparison of that vigour, liveliness, and activity of grace that ought to be found in us. Ought we not to lay the foundation here? If so, then we ought to apply ourselves unto it. It may be, though it be so with some, that they have such a lively, vigorous acting of faith in a deep and humble sense of their past miscarriages, yet it is not so with others; and we are looking for the edification of the whole. And therefore, brethren, do we judge it our present duty to labour to affect our hearts deeply with a sense of our present unanswerable frame unto the mind of God and Christ, and of our past miscarriages.

If it be so, let us every day pray that God would keep this thing in the imagination of the thoughts of our hearts; not only of ourselves, but of one another. Observe the phrase of the Holy Ghost: when you come to "the thoughts of the heart," you think you can go no farther; but saith David, "I pray, O LORD, preserve this 'in the imagination of the thoughts of the heart of thy people;'" that is, "in the first internal framing of our thoughts." There must be a frame acting and coining thoughts (if I may so say) continually in us to this purpose. But I recommend this to you,—that if this be a truth, and we are convinced it is our duty to labour to affect our hearts with a sense of the unanswerableness of our souls, and the frame of our minds unto the will of God and the holiness of Christ, who is coming to visit his churches,—"What manner of persons ought we to be?" Not such as we have been. We should labour for a deep sense of this, and I hope it may not be unsuitable unto you; for if any of us have any corruption, temptation, or disorder in our spirits and ways to conflict withal, in vain, believe me, shall we contend against it, unless we lay this foundation.

I know one great means for the beginning and carrying on of this work, is by earnest crying unto God,—by prayers and supplications, and humiliations. I am loath to issue it there; I have seen so many days of humiliation without reformation, that I dare not issue it there: we shall make use of them as God shall help us. I desire the church would do so, if they find in themselves a sense of duty, and a heart crying to God in sincerity and truth. I have now been very long, though very unprofitable, in the ministration of the word; and I have observed the beginning of churches, and wish I do not see the end of them in this their confidence of mere profession, and the observation of these duties of humiliation. God knows, I have thought often of this thing; and I say I dare not issue it there. Let us have as many as we have hearts for, and no more; and as many as shall end with reformation, but no more. But let us all begin among ourselves; and who knows but that God may give wisdom to this church? I am ready to faint, and give over, and to beg of the church they would think of some other person to conduct them in my room, without these disadvantages. The last day will discover I have nothing but a heart to lead you in the ways of God,—to the enjoyment of God.

POSTHUMOUS SERMONS.

PART III.

SERMONS PUBLISHED

M.DCC.LVI.

"He being dead yet speaketh."—HEB. xi. 4.

PREFATORY NOTE.

All the information needed in regard to the following thirteen Discourses is given in an advertisement prefixed to them when they were first published, in 1756. It is as follows:—

"To the Reader,—The following Discourses were preached by that truly venerable divine in the last century, Dr John Owen: and, in order to be fully satisfied they are genuine, Mrs Cooke of Stoke Newington, by this means informs the reader that her pious grandfather, Sir John Hartopp, Bart., wrote them in short-hand from the Doctor's own mouth, and then took the pains to transcribe them into long-hand; as thinking them worthy of being transmitted down to posterity. It is from his manuscripts this collection is now made public."

With the exception of the fourth and fifth, which are given in connection with the third, as these three Discourses relate to the origin, qualifications, and duties of the Christian minister, the rest of the Discourses under this division appear in chronological order. The division thus contains two Sermons on "the Everlasting Covenant the Believer's Support under Distress;" three Sermons preached at the ordination of ministers; four on "the Excellency of Christ;" and four on "the Use and Advantage of Faith."—Ed.

POSTHUMOUS SERMONS.

SERMON I.[1]

THE EVERLASTING COVENANT, THE BELIEVER'S SUPPORT UNDER DISTRESS.

"Although my house be not so with God; yet he hath made with me an everlasting covenant, ordered in all things, and sure: for this is all my salvation, and all my desire, although he make it not to grow."—2 SAM. xxiii. 5.

BEFORE I open these words, I shall read the whole context, from the 1st verse unto the end of the 7th: "Now these be the last words of David. David the son of Jesse said, and the man who was," etc.

"Now these be the last words of David;"—not absolutely, for you will find, both in the book of Samuel and also in the book of Chronicles, that David spake many words after these: but these were the last prophetical words of David; or this is the last prophecy of David. And he gives an account in this prophecy of all the faith and experience he had had in the world; and it comprises also the sum and substance of all he had prophesied of;—prophesied of as a king, the anointed of the God of Jacob; and prophesied of as a psalmist, as he was "The sweet psalmist of Israel."

Now there are three parts of this last prophecy of David:—

The first of them concerns the subject of all prophecy and promises that he had preached about and declared; and that is Christ himself, in the 3d and 4th verses; the second of them concerns himself, as he was a type of Christ, verse 5; and the third part concerns Satan and the enemies of the church, in opposition unto the kingdom of Jesus Christ.

The first part of his prophecy concerns Christ himself, verses 3, 4, "The God of Israel said, the Rock of Israel spake to me, He that ruleth over men must be just, ruling in the fear of God." So we have rendered the words; but if you look into the Bible, that "must be" is put into the text by the misunderstanding of them by interpreters.

[1] This sermon was preached June 27, 1669.

The words are, מוֹשֵׁל בָּאָדָם צַדִּיק;—"The ruler in or over men is the Just One;" which is Christ himself, who alone is this מוֹשֵׁל,—this "ruler." The word may be two ways interpreted (for to interpret it of a man that ruleth over men, the word will no way bear it, nor the prophecy);—the בָּאָדָם must be, either, "He that rules in the human nature is the Just One;" or, "He that rules over the human nature" (in all saints), "he is just," saith he; "and he rules in" or by "the fear of God." As, in Isa. xi. 3, it is prophesied of him, "He shall be of quick understanding in the fear of the LORD;" so here it is prophesied of him, that he shall rule in or by the fear of God;—that is the sceptre he shall have in the hearts of men,—that is the law he shall put upon the souls of his subjects: he shall rule them neither by outward violence nor force, nor any thing of that nature; but he shall rule them by the fear of God. Verse 4 declares, by sundry comparisons, what he shall be: Why, saith he, "He shall be as the light of the morning, when the sun riseth, even a morning without clouds; as the tender grass springing out of the earth by clear shining after rain." You know how often these things are applied unto Christ. He is called in Malachi, "The Sun of righteousness that ariseth," chap. iv. 2; he is called "The Day-spring from on high," Luke i. 78; and he is called "The bright and morning Star," Rev. xxii. 16. He is both a sun, and morning star, and day-spring. He shall be as the morning, that brings light, comfort, joy, refreshment to the church. "He shall be as a morning without clouds;"—there is no darkness in the kingdom of Christ. And "he shall be as the tender grass springing out of the earth by clear shining after rain;"—the same with that in Isaiah, "He shall spring up as the tender branch out of the earth." You know the reason of the allusion: when the grass hath been long dried, and there comes a great rain upon it, and clear shining upon that rain, how will the grass spring up! There was to be a great drought upon the church; but Christ comes, and he was as the rain, and as the sun shining upon the rain; then there was a springing up with great glory, and unto great fruitfulness.[1]

[1] It is a duty to apprize the reader, that the passage from which the text of Owen is selected has occasioned much embarrassment to critics. On the strength of a patient collation of old manuscripts, Kennicott has proposed important changes on the present rendering in our authorized version. The changes principally relate to the insertion of "Jehovah" in verse 4, the omission of the negative in the first clause of verse 5, and the connection of the last words of the same verse with the first words of the verse that follows. Michaelis affirms, "that, in the latter chapters of the Second Book of Samuel, the manuscripts have come down to us more disfigured with mistakes than in any other part of the Old Testament." The alterations proposed in the present instance serve to evince the prophetic character of the passage, as descriptive of the Messiah, and to strengthen the evidence of his divinity. The reader must be referred to the discussion of this passage by a master in Israel, Dr Pye Smith, in his profound and exhaustive work on "The Scripture Testimony to the Messiah," etc. We add his proposed version

I will at present overlook the 5th verse, to which I am to return; and only show that the 6th and 7th verses do contain a prophecy of the enemies of the church; as this does of Christ. "Belial shall be thrust away as thorns." We render it, "The sons of Belial;" but it is only Belial;—"Belial, all of it, the whole name of Belial." Sometimes the word is taken for wicked men, and sometimes for the prince of wicked men; as here for the devil and all his agents. And he follows on his allusion, that "they cannot be taken with hands;" Satan and his seed are so full of thorns and prickles against the church, that you can never seize them by the hand to bring them to any order. And the next verse gives caution how well we must be fenced if we touch them. This is the design of the prophecy.

I now return unto that part which I shall a little more distinctly open unto you, that concerns David himself, as he was chosen to be the great type of Christ. Saith he, "This Ruler of men, he shall be as the clear morning without clouds; although my house be not so with God."

There are two things in the words:—First, A supposition of a great disappointment and surprisal. Secondly, A relief against and under that disappointment and surprisal.

First. A great surprisal and disappointment: "Although my house be not so with God." "I have looked that it should be otherwise," saith he,—"that my house should have a great deal of glory, especially, that my house should be upright with God; but I begin to see it will be otherwise." You may observe, David's heart was exceedingly set

of the passage; which agrees substantially with the version proposed by Kennicott:—

4. "Ruling over man is a Righteous One,
Ruling in the fear of God:
Even as the light of the morning shall he arise,
Jehovah, the sun;
A morning without clouds for brightness,
[As] after rain the herbage from the earth.
5. Truly thus is my house with God;
For an everlasting covenant he hath fixed with me,
Ordered in every thing and secured;
For [this is] all my salvation, and all [my] desire:
6. But the wicked shall not grow."

Owen himself, as will be seen above, very properly corrects the authorized version in one point; and thus warrants our reference to subsequent discoveries, by which greater accuracy has been imparted to the original text in this part of Scripture. His own reasoning in the discourse principally depends upon the negative in the beginning of verse 5, which Kennicott would omit, on the slender authority, as it appears, of one manuscript dating from the close of the thirteenth century. It is a fair question, therefore, if the external evidence for the rejection of the negative be as strong as for the insertion of "Jehovah" in the preceding verse. Boothroyd, attaching an interrogative sense to the particle כִּי, throws the clause into the form of a question, and elicits the best meaning with the least violence to the text,—"Is not my house thus with God?"

It will be found, however, that the chief aim of Owen is to educe from the covenant of grace considerations fitted to sustain and console the minds of Christians under the grief of blighted hope. His argument is conclusive, whatever becomes of the mere criticism of his text.—Ed.

upon his house; therefore, whenever God spake to him concerning his house, it mightily wrought upon him; as 2 Sam. vii. 18, 19, "Who am I, O Lord GOD? and what is my house, that thou hast brought me hitherto? And this was yet a small thing in thy sight, O Lord GOD; but thou hast spoken also of thy servant's house for a great while to come. And is this the manner of man, O Lord GOD?" Verse 25, "And now, O LORD God, the word that thou hast spoken concerning thy servant, and concerning his house, establish it for ever, and do as thou hast said." I am sometimes afraid that David had (as under the Old Testament they generally had) some carnal apprehensions of those spiritual promises that God gave to David's house,—which were, principally, to bring Christ out of his loins, that should reign for ever: but David thought all things would come well out of his house also. How stands the case now? Now David sees that in his house Amnon had defiled Tamar, Absalom had slain Amnon for his sin, and he was cut off in his rebellion; and he foresaw, by a spirit of prophecy, that his whole house was like to perish and be cut down: and so comes to that now, "Although my house be not so with God." So that from hence we may take this observation,—

That the best of the saints of God do oftentimes meet with great surprisals and disappointments in the best of their earthly comforts: their houses are not so with God.

I will give you one or two places for this:—1 Chron. vii. 23, "Ephraim went in to his wife, and she conceived, and bare a son, and he called his name Beriah, because it went evil with his house." Ephraim had received a special blessing from God by Jacob, for the multiplying of his house: "He also shall be great, and his seed shall become a multitude of nations," Gen. xlviii. 19. Now, in Ephraim's old age, some of the chief of his sons are killed, 1 Chron. vii. 21, 22, "There were Zabad, and Shuthelah, and Ezer, and Elead, whom the men of Gath that were born in that land slew, because they came down to take away their cattle. And Ephraim their father mourned many days." And he called his other child Beriah, "because it went evil with his house." It was a great surprise unto him, because he had a promise for his house; though God afterwards retrieved it.

You know how great a surprisal befell Job. See what his thoughts were, Job xxix. 18. After, in all the foregoing part of the chapter, he had related the manifold blessings of God upon him in his prosperity, the uprightness of his own heart, his righteousness in his way, as he declares them to the utmost in the beginning of that chapter, he tells you his thoughts: "Then I said, I shall die in my nest, and I shall multiply my days as the sand." He expected, from the blessing of God, long life and peace. You know what surprisal befell him, and disappointment to all his comforts in this world,—that never man fell into greater; and he gives you an account how great his surprisal was throughout the next chapter.

The reasons hereof, why it may be thus, are,—

First. Because there is no promise of the covenant to the contrary; there is no promise of God secures absolutely unto us our outward comforts. Be they of what nature they will,—be they in our relations, in our enjoyments, in our persons,—of what kind they will, why, yet we may have a surprisal befall us in reference to them all; because there is no promise of God to secure the contrary, therefore it may be so.

Secondly. Sometimes it is needful it should be so, though we are apt to think the contrary;—and that for these three reasons:—

1. To keep continually upon our hearts a due awe of the judgments of God,—of the actings of God's providence in a way of judgment; which otherwise we should be apt to think ourselves freed from. David testified that this frame was in himself, Ps. cxix. 120, "My flesh," saith he, "trembleth for fear of thee; and I am afraid of thy judgments." There ought to be in our hearts an awe of the judgments of God; "for our God is a consuming fire:" and if we were secured from surprisals in our own concerns, so fleshly are we, so selfish and carnal, it would be impossible we should keep up a due awe and reverence of the judgments of God. But when these judgments of God may reach our nearest concerns,—our lives, and all we enjoy; then doth our flesh tremble in a due manner for fear of him: and we may be afraid of his judgments. A due fear of the judgments of God is a necessary balance upon the minds of the best of the saints.

2. It is needful, to keep us off from security in ourselves. There is such a treachery in our hearts, that we are able to build carnal security upon the spiritual dispensations of God's kindness and love. "I said, I shall never be moved," saith David;—an expression of carnal security. What was the ground? "Thou, LORD, hast made my rock so strong." He built up carnal security upon God's dispensations. It is needful, therefore, God should sometimes break in upon our concerns, that we may not turn a constant course of his kindness into a sinful security of our own.

3. They are sometimes actually needful, to awaken the soul out of such deep sleep of present satisfaction, or love of this world; which nothing else will do. Sometimes we so fall asleep in our own ways, either in our satisfaction or projects and desires, and are so earnest in the pursuit of them, that no ordinary jog will awaken us; it is necessary God should break in upon us in the best of our concerns, and make us put in an "although" in our course. "Although my children live not, and my house be not so with God;" "Although my house be destroyed," etc.

That which we should learn from hence, by way of use, is,—

1. Not to put too great a value upon any contentment, whatever we have in this world, lest God make us write an "although" upon it. David seems to have put too great a valuation upon his house, the carnal flourishing of his house; but in his last words he is forced to come to that, "Although my house be not so with God;" as if he had said, "What I placed all my hope and expectation upon, that I find is not so with God."

2. Let us be in an expectation of such changes of providence, that they may not be great surprisals unto us. When we are in peace, let us look for trouble; when we are at liberty, let us look for restraint; and when our children are about us, let us look for the removal of them; and be content to see all our comforts in their winding-sheet every day. It is impossible but our hearts will be too much upon them, unless we keep them in this frame.

The SECOND general observation is this:—

That the great reserve and relief for believers, under their surprisals and distresses, lies in betaking themselves to the covenant of God, or to God in his covenant. "'Although my house be not so with God,'—what shall I then do? what will become of me? Yet 'he hath made a covenant with me, an everlasting covenant, ordered in all things, and sure. This is all my desire, and all my salvation, although he make not my house to grow.'" I say, the great relief and only reserve of believers in their distresses and surprisals, such as may befall them in a very few days, is, to betake themselves to God in his covenant.

I will give you some instances of it:—Gen. xv. 1, 2. There God leads us to this I now mentioned. Abraham was in a perplexed condition; God comes to him in the 1st verse, and renews his covenant with him: "The word of the LORD came unto Abram in a vision, saying, Fear not, Abram: I am thy shield, and thy exceeding great reward." He minds him of the covenant, and bids him not fear. What is the matter, that God comes to Abraham with this, "Fear not, Abram"? The next verse discovers it: "And Abram said, Lord GOD, what wilt thou give me, seeing I go childless, and the steward of my house is this Eliezer of Damascus?" He was afraid that all the travail he had taken, in reference to the promise, would come to nothing; and he must leave it to Eliezer of Damascus. Now, God comes to give him relief, in minding him of his covenant.

Jacob also relieved his dying spirit with this, upon the foresight of great troubles in his blessing of Dan, Gen. xlix. 16–18, "Dan shall judge his people, as one of the tribes of Israel." He alludes to the name Dan, which signifies in Hebrew "to judge." When did Dan judge his people? Why, in Samson. This is matter of joy to Jacob. But what shall follow? "Dan shall be a serpent by the way, an adder in the path, that biteth the horse heels, so that his rider shall fall backward." "He shall be a serpent and an adder," saith he; that is, idolatry shall be set up in the tribe of Dan, and continue. The first idolatry that was set up in Israel (the work of the serpent), was in the tribe of Dan, Judges xviii. 30, when the Danites took away the graven image, etc., from Micah, and set it up, and made priests, until the day of the captivity of the land;—not the captivity by the Assyrians, but the captivity by the Philistines, when they overcame them and took away the ark; for then were all those things destroyed at Dan. And afterwards Jeroboam comes and sets up the calf in the same place, and that continued to the last captivity. With what, now, doth Jacob relieve himself? "I have waited for thy salvation, O LORD:" he betakes himself to the covenant, and therewith relieves himself against all the trouble which he foresaw was coming upon his posterity in that tribe; which, upon that account, when the other tribes were sealed in the Revelation, was left out, because idolatry first began and ended in Dan.

David expresseth the same course to the height, Ps. xxxi. 10–15. He describes a very sad condition upon all hands: "My life is spent with grief, and my years with sighing: my strength faileth because of mine iniquity, and my bones are consumed. I was a reproach among all mine enemies, but especially among my neighbours, and a fear to mine acquaintance," etc. Here is sin, and reproach, and contempt, and persecution, and danger of his life, all at once fallen upon him. What doth the man do? Why, in the 14th and 15th verses he tells you, "But I trusted in thee, O LORD: I said, Thou art my God. My times are in thy hand." He betakes himself to the covenant against all these troubles within doors and without doors, from sin, the world, wicked men, in reproach, contempt, persecution, that had almost slain him: he hath but this relief,—he goes to God and saith, "'Thou art my God;' thou shalt undertake for me against all these. I am not in the hand of sin, nor in the hand of my enemies; but my times of suffering, my time of life and death, are in thy hands." He betakes himself unto God's covenant, and there he finds rest. I might multiply instances.

Take one more, wherein the doctrine is plainly held out, Hab iii. 17, 18, "Although the fig-tree shall not blossom, neither shall fruit be in the vines; the labour of the olive shall fail, and the fields shall yield no meat; the flock shall be cut off from the fold, and there shall be no herd in the stalls: yet I will rejoice in the LORD, I will joy in the God of my salvation." "'Though my house be not so with God;' there is my family gone, the fruits of the earth gone, all is gone;—it is no matter," saith the believer, "'I will rejoice in the LORD, I will joy in the God of my salvation.'" Every word expresses the covenant of God. By these instances it doth appear that, in the most surprising trouble and disappointments, believers do, as David here doth, betake themselves unto God in covenant.

Why do they so? I will give no reason for it but what lies in the words:—

First. They do it because of the Author of the covenant. They consider who it is that makes it with us: "Because He hath made with me an everlasting covenant," saith David. There is a great emphasis upon that HE; who is that? Why, it is the Rock of Israel, the God of Israel,—HE hath made it. "It is not a covenant that man hath made with me, nor an angel; but it is a covenant that God hath made with me." And you may observe that God, whenever he would require our faith or obedience, doth signally preface his commands and promises with himself. You must know who it is that commands, and who it is that promises. So in the decalogue, the rule of commands, he prefaceth them with that, "I am the LORD thy God;" which influences the minds of men unto obedience, and brings them under his authority. And when he made this covenant that David speaks of here, he doth it thus, Gen. xvii. 1, "I am God Almighty." This David regards here, when he saith, "He hath made with me this covenant." He; who? "God Almighty, God All-sufficient; hither I retreat in all my wants and straits." Now, if we make a covenant one with another, we engage all that is in us to make good that covenant; we engage our power and ability, and reputation and faithfulness. If I have a covenant with any of you, I would reckon upon this covenant just according unto the esteem I have of your persons, your abilities, reputation, faithfulness; for when you engage in covenant, all you have is engaged. Now, God making this covenant, he engages according to his power, goodness, faithfulness; so that we have the reputation of God to secure us in the things of this covenant,—his all-sufficiency to assure us of the making good this covenant. So saith the soul, "I will retreat unto the covenant, because God hath made it, who is all-sufficient." This makes it a very honourable covenant,—it is a covenant made by God; and it makes it a very satisfactory covenant,—if all that is in God can give satisfaction unto the soul of a poor creature; and it makes it also a sure covenant, as we shall see afterwards.

This is the first reason why David makes his retreat in straits and difficulties unto this covenant,—because of the author of it, God himself, who made this covenant.

Secondly. The second reason is taken from the properties of the covenant,—what kind of one it is; and they are three:—It is an "everlasting" covenant; it is a covenant that is "ordered in all things;" and it is a covenant that is "sure:"—

1. It is the great relief of our souls, because it is "an everlasting covenant." The things we are troubled about, wherein our comforts consist in this world, are but temporal things; and an everlasting relief against temporal distresses will quite out-balance them.

How is this everlasting? It is everlasting in respect of the beginning of it; it is everlasting in respect of the end of it; and it is everlasting in respect of the matter of it:—

(1.) It is everlasting in respect of the beginning of it; it is a covenant that comes from everlasting love, Jer. xxxi. 3, "I have loved thee with an everlasting love." What then? "Therefore with loving-kindness have I drawn thee." This drawing with loving-kindness is the covenant here mentioned. And whence doth it proceed? From everlasting love. We had never had the drawing of the covenant, had not that been the spring. I will betake myself unto that covenant which hath its spring in eternity. This covenant had not its beginning when first I laid hold upon it; but it had its beginning in God's love from all eternity.

(2.) It is everlasting in respect of the end of it: it ceases not until it brings the whole person, soul and body, into everlasting glory. So our Saviour manifests, Matt. xxii. 32. There arose a question whether the dead should arise or no, and so the whole person be brought to God in glory; and the Sadducees came to Christ with a pitiful, sophistical question about a woman that had had seven husbands,—whose wife she should be in the resurrection? Christ answers them; but how doth he prove that there shall be a resurrection? No otherwise but by the words of the covenant, verse 32, "I am the God of Abraham, and the God of Isaac, and the God of Jacob: God is not the God of the dead, but of the living." They live unto God by virtue of the covenant unto this day; and by virtue of the covenant shall be raised again.

(3.) It is an everlasting covenant upon the account of the matter of it,—the things concerning which it is. It is not a covenant about corn, and wine, and oil,—about the growing of our houses, the increase of our families or selves in the world; but it is a covenant about everlasting things,—"things which are not seen," 2 Cor. iv. 18. Grace is eternal, mercy eternal, spiritual life, and joy, and comfort, are all eternal things. "This is life eternal, that they might know thee the only true God, and Jesus Christ, whom thou hast sent," John xvii. 3. Not only eternal glory, but the grace we have here by virtue of the covenant, is eternal. "It is not about the land of Canaan, thrones and kingdoms,—it is not about the prosperity of our families," saith he; "but about everlasting things."

Now, is there not here great ground for retreat unto this covenant in all our straits, that hath its rise in everlasting love, its end in everlasting rest, and the matter whereof are all everlasting things. This is the first property of it, and a reason why we ought to make it our relief,—because it is an everlasting covenant.

2. The second property of this covenant is,—that it is "ordered in all things." What is order? Order is the disposition of things into such a way,—such a relation one to another, and such a dependence one upon another,—as they may all be suited to attain their proper end. This is order. Now saith he, "This covenant is ordered." The truth is, order is the beauty of all things,—the glory of all things; and it is but a little, I acknowledge, that I am able to look into of the order of this covenant, which renders it exceeding beautiful and glorious; and much less that I shall now speak to you.

I would refer the order of the covenant to these three heads:—to its infinitely wise projection; to its solemn confirmation; and to its powerful execution. These three things give this covenant its order. Its infinitely wise projection, in the love and eternal wisdom of the Father; its solemn confirmation, in the blood and sacrifice of the Son; and its powerful execution, in the efficacy of the Holy Ghost, the Spirit of grace;—these are the heads of the glorious order of this covenant, that give it its life, beauty, and glory.

(1.) Its projection was in the wisdom and love of the Father. Whatsoever is spoken concerning the love, grace, and wisdom of the Father before the world was, was laid out in the projection of this covenant. Take it as it wraps Christ in it,—as it brings forth the forgiveness of sin,—as it is the centre of grace; and it compriseth the whole effect of divine wisdom, as far as the infinitely holy God ever manifested, or ever will manifest to eternity.

(2.) It had a solemn confirmation in the blood of the Son; hence the blood of Christ is called "The blood of the covenant." The covenant was solemnly confirmed in the blood of Christ. It is the design of the apostle, in the 10th chapter of the Hebrews, to prove the solemn confirmation of the new covenant in the blood of the Son of God. That makes it irrevocable and unchangeable.

(3.) But when all this is done, how shall this covenant be executed? Why, that is the work of the Holy Spirit. He hath undertaken two things:—[1.] To assure our souls of all things on the part of God;—to reveal the terms of the covenant, and make known unto us the end of God in it. And, [2.] To undertake on our part to give us hearts that we shall love him and fear him;—to write the terms of the covenant on our part in our souls, so that it shall have an infallible execution. If any thing had been wanting in this order, we could never have had benefit by this covenant.

There is an addition of order, in reference to the matter of it, here expressed. As it is "ordered," so it is "ordered in all things;"—it is ordered in all the things "of grace on the part of God;" it is ordered in all the things "of sin on our part." 1*st*, It is ordered in all the things "of grace on the part of God,"—that all grace whatsoever, that is needful for the covenanters, shall be given out unto them. If there were any needful grace that we should come short of, in reference unto the end of this covenant, it would not be "ordered in all things." If the covenant had been ordered but in some grace, in quickening grace, and not in persevering grace, we had never come to the end of the covenant: if in pardoning grace, and not renewing grace, we had never come to the end of the covenant; "for without holiness no man shall see the Lord." But whatsoever grace is needful to bring us to the enjoyment of God, it is ordered in all grace. The first covenant with Adam was ordered in grace, but not in all grace; it was ordered in righteousness, holiness, and innocency, but not ordered in the grace of perseverance: and failing in that grace, the whole covenant failed. But this covenant is "ordered in all things," with reference to believers. 2*d*, It is ordered in reference unto sin. There was a great deal of glory and beauty in the first covenant; but there was no order taken about sin: [so] that if any sin came in, the first covenant was gone and broken, and of no use any more. But this covenant hath taken order about sin; that there shall no sin befall believers but what the grace of the covenant will extend pardon unto. If a believer should fall into any one sin that would deprive him of the benefit of this covenant, it would not be "ordered in all things." There are sins that, if a believer should fall into, would break the covenant; but the covenant prevents such falls.

This is another motive to rely upon this covenant,—because it is "ordered in all things." What could God provide more for poor creatures?

3. The last property of this covenant is, that it is "sure." It is "ordered in all things, and sure." If it had not been sure, it would not have been a relief unto us. The springs of the security of this covenant are two:—(1.) The oath of God. (2.) The intercession of Christ.

God hath confirmed this covenant by his oath; and that gives surety in itself, and security unto us, Heb. vi. 17, 18.

And it is made sure by the interposition of Christ. He is made the surety of a better covenant, Heb. vii. 22. And he lives for ever to make intercession for them that come unto God by him, and so is able to save unto the uttermost, verse 25.

This is what I have to offer from the opening of the words, and the reasons contained in them, why they are the great relief and reserve of believers in all the surprisals, disappointments, and distresses, that may befall them; and we are marvellously unwise, if we do not live in a constant expectation of such surprisals. To say that we shall die in our nests, and our mountain is so strong that it shall not be moved,—this is carnal security.

I will answer one question, and I have done:—

How do believers betake themselves to this covenant for relief? or, What may we do that we may betake ourselves unto it for our relief in our surprisals and distresses?

I answer, first, The first way is, by faith to get a due and dear valuation of the things of the covenant, above all things we here enjoy in this world. We shall never have relief by it, until we value the things of it as we ought; and those who do so shall never want relief from it.

Secondly, We should seek unto God in covenant, for strength to support us under our surprisals and distresses. When Abraham was going to battle, he took with him Mamre, Eshcol, and Aner, who were the men of his covenant, Gen. xiv. 13. When our souls are engaged in battle with our sins, oppositions, and fears, let us take with us the men of our covenant; I mean, take God with us,—seek strength from the covenant: it is the way to support under soul-surprisals.

Thirdly and lastly, We must resolve, finally, to take up our rest in the covenant of God, and not in other things. In Isa. xxx. 15, God brings it to this, " Thus saith the Lord God, the Holy One of Israel; In returning and rest shall ye be saved; in quietness and in confidence shall be your strength." God, when he proposes the covenant unto us, doth it that we should take up our rest and confidence alone in that. " But ye would not, but said, We will flee upon horses; therefore shall ye flee." If we have other reserves, the covenant will never be a stable reserve unto us.

SERMON II.[1]

ON THE EVERLASTING COVENANT.

" Although my house be not so with God," etc.—2 Sam. xxiii. 5.

I do remember I have spoken in this place formerly from these words; and delivered somewhat concerning the covenant of God, so far as the exposition of the words did lead me.

I shall now add only one consideration, which is taken from the introduction of David's retreat unto, and assertion of, the everlasting

[1] This sermon was preached January 1, 1670.

covenant in this place; and that is in these words, "Although my house be not so with God."

David took a prospect now, in his latter days, of all the distresses and calamities that should assuredly come upon his family; and, it may be, he had regard unto those great and dreadful breaches that had before been made upon it, in the sins and judgments that ensued upon some of his children. This was enough to work in him a consternation of spirit and trouble of mind; and, in the view and prospect of it, he repairs for his relief unto the covenant of God: "Although my house be not so with God; yet he hath made with me an everlasting covenant, ordered in all things, and sure." What I would observe from it is this:—

Under present distresses and the saddest prospect of future troubles, it is the duty, and wisdom, and privilege of believers, to betake themselves for relief and support unto the covenant of God. Nothing can befall them, no case happen, for which there is no relief provided; and it is the greatest and best relief that can be provided, for any case whatsoever.

Having laid down this assertion, the substance of what I shall do at present is but to confirm it with some *Scripture instances*, and the *practice of believers* in former ages.

We have *one* instance in Gen. xxviii. 3, 4:—Isaac was sending away his son Jacob unto Padan-aram, to take him a wife; and he might easily know, and did, no doubt, what troubles, and distresses, and dangers, would befall Jacob in that great undertaking. And one would somewhat wonder why so great a man as Isaac was should send away his son with no better provision than Jacob was sent away with. He gives this account of it,—"I had nothing but my staff." "With my staff," saith he, "I went over Jordan." But it seems that temporal blessings being then a great token and evidence of God's covenant mercies, he would have Jacob work for himself, that he might have experience of God's blessing him in what he did. He should try God by his own experience. And what provision doth he give him, besides his staff, for this great undertaking? It is this, verses 3, 4, "God Almighty bless thee, and give thee the blessing of Abraham." Why does he say, "God Almighty"? Because that was the name whereby God revealed himself to Abraham when he entered into covenant with him, in Gen. xvii. 1, "I am the Almighty God." Isaac calls his son Jacob to renew his covenant interest with God, and to betake himself unto the blessing of the covenant, against that long and hazardous journey he was to go,—against the hard, false, oppressive, deceitful dealing he was to meet with,—against the dangers he was to encounter. He gives him the covenant for his security. And Jacob was not wanting to take the same course himself, Gen.

xxxii. 9, and so onward. He was in as great a distress, and under as just a fear, as ever man was in this world, or could be in; and so he expresses his fear unto God, verse 11, "Deliver me, I pray thee, from the hand of my brother, from the hand of Esau: for I fear him, lest he will come and smite me, and the mother with the children." He feared the universal destruction of himself and family, and so the failing of the promise he had received, and which he had pursued through so many difficulties and dangers. What course now doth Jacob take? Why, he appeals to the covenant, verse 9, "O God of my father Abraham, and God of my father Isaac;" which was the plea whereby they did plead the covenant that God entered solemnly into with them. Two things, it is evident, Jacob pleaded in this very great distress:—one was the covenant that God made with Abraham; that is, the covenant of grace: for so he doth, verse 9. He refers unto what blessing Isaac gave him when he went away;—"God Almighty bless thee, and give thee the blessing of Abraham." And, secondly, he appeals unto that particular covenant engagement which he himself had made unto God; for in chap. xxviii. 13, God comes unto him, and renews his covenant: "And, behold, the LORD stood above it, and said, I am the LORD God of Abraham thy father, and the God of Isaac;" and thereupon Jacob renews his covenant in particular with God, verse 20, "If God will be with me, and keep me in this way, then shall the LORD be my God." These two things doth Jacob in his great distress,—he minds the covenant in general, and the particular covenant engagement God had brought him into; for so he pleads, "Thou saidst unto me, Return unto thy country, and to thy kindred, and I will deal well with thee." Where did he say so? He said so in chap. xxxi. 13. When Jacob made his covenant with God, he pleaded these two things, in the greatest distress that could befall him in this world.

Shall I give you one instance more? David gives it us in his own person, Ps. xxxi. 9–13. He makes as sad a complaint of such a complication of distresses upon him as there is anywhere extant in the whole book of the Psalms. "Have mercy upon me, O LORD, for I am in trouble: mine eye is consumed with grief, yea, my soul and my belly," etc. I could easily manifest what a confluence of evil this holy man was now under. Within, iniquities prevailed, and the fear of them; and without, friends forsook him, and enemies took counsel to take away his life. Whereunto doth he retreat? what doth he seek for relief in? what is the contrivance of this man of wisdom, and courage, and interest in the world? See verse 14, "But I trusted in thee, O LORD: I said, Thou art my God;" and this put an end to all his difficulties. But this matter I have hinted in a former sermon.

It were an easy thing to multiply instances, both of particular persons and the church in general, who were taught this wisdom of God, and knew this to be their duty,—to let go all other vain contrivances, and to take up their relief only in the covenant of God; as David doth here in the text.

Let us see a little more into the nature of it, that it may give us encouragement to our duty. And,—

First. When a man betakes himself for relief unto God's covenant, "he doth put God in mind of it," wherewith he is greatly delighted; because therein he hath wrapped up his greatest glory in this world, and God is greatly delighted to be put in remembrance of that wherein he hath wrapped up the glory of his grace. It was Jacob's argument, when he wrestled with God, and prevailed; as signal an instance of the work of faith, and the deportment of a believer under great distresses, as the whole Old Testament affords us (and is given as an example to confirm our faith, Hos. xii. 4): "Thou saidst, I will surely do thee good," Gen. xxxii. 12. He put God in mind of what he had said to him when he made the covenant with him; and you know what a glorious issue it had. Jacob could not have done any thing more pleasing and acceptable unto God than to put him in remembrance of what, out of his goodness, grace, and bounty, he had promised; for he professes that "he was not worthy of the least of all the mercies and of all the truth which God had showed unto him." "I plead not any thing," says he, "of my own deservings; but, Lord, didst thou not say thou wouldst do me good?" God is greatly pleased with being remembered of the effects of his own grace, and wherein he hath wrapped so much of his own glory.

Secondly. As God would have us mind him of the covenant, "so his remembrance of it is still laid at the bottom of all the good he doth unto us," and of all the dispensations of his love and grace

God made a covenant with Noah, and with all the world in him; wherein he gave the preservation of the world from a universal destruction in covenant unto his saints; for the world is at this day, and to the last will be, preserved upon this account, that God hath given the preservation of it in covenant unto Noah, and to them that succeed in the faith of Noah. But how comes it to pass that God will destroy this world no more with a flood, when he had made this covenant? Saith God, "I will set my bow in the cloud, and it shall be for a token of the covenant; and the bow shall be in the cloud, and I will look upon it, that I may remember the everlasting covenant between God and every living creature." It is spoken after the manner of men, when they have made an engagement that they will do such a thing; it may be out of their mind, but if you remind them of it by a token, then they will recover their memory, and do according to their engagement. Now, saith God, "I will take it upon myself to remind myself." And when he remembers the covenant, what will he do? "Then I will restrain my wrath and indignation, and I will destroy the earth no more." The withholding of troubles, judgments, and desolations, is laid in God's remembering of the covenant. It is all comprised together, Luke i. 72–75, "To perform the mercy promised to our fathers, and to remember his holy covenant; the oath which he sware to our father Abraham, that he would grant unto us, that we being delivered out of the hand of our enemies might serve him without fear, in holiness and righteousness before him, all the days of our life." All deliverance from our enemies, of whom we are afraid; all communication of grace, and of spiritual strength, to enable us to serve God in holiness and righteousness; it all springs from this,—God's remembering of his covenant.

Now, he that retreats to God in his distresses, reminds God of his covenant: "Thou saidst thou wouldst do me good." And the bringing forth of God's word of promise is as good a token as his own bringing forth the bow in the cloud. And this is the foundation of all the good he doth *for* us, or *in* us.

Thirdly. What is there in the covenant, that God doth thus remember, that will give us relief in times of distress, and in our prospect of future calamities that may befall us? and what are we to have regard unto that may give us that relief? I answer,—

1. *God himself is in it;* there lies the nature of it. When he came to make it with Abraham, "I am God Almighty," saith he. He doth not speak a word there what he will do for Abraham; but, "I am God Almighty." He leaves it there; then requires his obedience: "Walk before me, and be thou perfect." Abraham shall rest in this, that God himself is in the covenant: "For the rest that is to be done, trust me with it; I take that upon myself." And saith he, Hos. ii. 23, "They shall be my people, and I will be their God." Here we have the eternal fountain and spring of all relief (if our houses are not so as we could desire),—that is, God himself. So that, if there be any thing in the nature of God, in his infinite, eternal excellency, that is suited to the relief of a soul, he hath made his covenant sufficient to convey it unto the souls of believers. And what we come short of is not for want of fulness in the fountain, and ability in the means of conveyance; but for want of faith to receive it.

2. *Christ* is in the covenant, Gal. iii. 16, "To Abraham and his seed were the promises made. He saith not, And to seeds, as of many; but as of one, And to thy seed, which is Christ." In all the promises made to Abraham, Christ, as the seed, was intended; so that Christ shall be theirs, with all his benefits. This is also in it. And,—

3. All the *promises* of God are in it; which are in unspeakable variety, as effects of infinite wisdom, suited unto the wants that may

befall us in this world: so as that it is utterly impossible that any believer should ever want any thing, that there is not grace in one promise or other suited unto that want. They all belong unto the covenant. Consider the *fountain* of it,—God himself, who is inexhaustible in stores of help and grace; consider the *means of procuring*,—Christ is in it, who hath purchased for us every thing that is needful; and, lastly, consider the *means of communication*,—which are the promises: so that there is nothing wanting for our relief.

Fourthly. If we would have relief in the covenant, let us consider our own entering into covenant with God, and what is comprised therein. Whosoever entereth into covenant with God, he doth accept God to be his God, for all the ends of the covenant whatever; and he that will retreat for relief unto the covenant, must stand to the covenant. And in this acceptance of God to be our God there are two things:—

1. An absolute *renunciation* of all expectation of any help for the ends of the covenant from any other thing whatsoever. For what we look for therein (and therein we look for all), there is to be an express renunciation of any expectation from any thing else to that end and purpose. So do they in Jer. iii. 22, 23, "Behold, we come unto thee; for thou art the LORD our God. Truly in vain is salvation hoped for from the hills, and from the multitude of mountains: truly in the LORD our God is the salvation of Israel." Things are called hills and mountains, because they make a great and goodly appearance of help and relief. The people here are directed to take up their relief in God alone: "We come unto thee; for thou art the LORD our God." What is required hereunto? Why, an absolute renunciation of all help and assistance from the hills and from the mountains. And one great reason why we are so slow in drinking in that relief, which God is so willing to give out unto us, is, because we are still casting our eyes towards the hills and mountains,—looking this way and that way for something that may give us relief. But it is in vain; there is an absolute renunciation of all other help included in accepting of God to be our God in covenant. So Hos. xiv. 3, "Asshur shall not save us; we will not ride upon horses: neither will we say any more to the work of our hands, Ye are our gods: for in thee the fatherless findeth mercy." And if there hath not been a solemn renunciation of other helps in our covenant with God, it is no wonder we do so halt as we do between God and the world, when we come to our straits and distresses. Where this hath been firm in the soul, and he is nakedly cast upon God as a poor, fatherless creature, to find mercy in him, and goes to him and saith, "Truly thou art our God, in thee is our help;"—that soul shall not fail of such supplies as shall be needful for him in his condition. This leads me to observe [that],—

2. The next thing to be done is, *an actual resting upon God*, or casting of ourselves upon him for all things.

Where these things are not, we do, in speaking of the covenant, but flatter God with our lips. There is no solemn covenant between God and us. This God required when he came to Abraham. Saith he, "Fear not, Abram." Why so? "I am thy shield, and exceeding great reward." Why so? Consider the condition of Abraham, and you will see what reason there was for God to give himself that title in this renewing of the covenant unto him. Abraham was in a wandering condition up and down the world,—exposed to dangers, injuries, distresses, from every hand. He knew not whether there was the fear of God in any place where he came. "Fear not, Abram," saith God; "I am thy shield;"—"Trust me for thy protection, trust me for thy deliverance out of danger." But saith Abraham, "I am engaged in a long and wearisome pilgrimage; 'and now, Lord GOD, what wilt thou give me, seeing I go childless?'" Men will labour and take pains for their posterity in an ordinary way. Abraham had not only that thought about his posterity, but also about the promise. Why, saith God, "I am thy reward,—a sufficient reward unto thee for all thy labour, and travel, and sufferings." We would be glad to be freed from danger, freed from trouble in our pilgrimage, which encompasses us on every hand; and there is none of us but would be glad to see some reward,—some prosperity of the church of God in this world, and deliverance from trouble. But if we truly enter into covenant with God, we are to take him as a full satisfaction for all our dangers, for all our labours, though we see not the fruit of them in this world. He that enters into covenant with God, takes God for his protection and reward, and him alone. Had we but the power of these things in our hearts, it would alleviate all our troubles, and ease us under all our dangers, fears, distresses, and disappointments.

Fifthly. If we would find relief in the covenant, we may do well to consider *upon what terms* we did enter into covenant with God. Now, entering into covenant with God is twofold:—

1. It may be explicit,—as when it comes to these express terms mentioned, Hos. iii. 3, "Thou shalt not be for another man: so will I also be for thee." Some persons have laid the foundation of their obedience in direct, express covenanting with God. And,—

2. Sometimes it is implicitly wrought; as where God, in the conversion of men, deals with them as he saith he will do with the church, Hos. ii. 14, "I will allure them into the wilderness, and there speak comfortably unto them." God, by little and little, various workings and reasonings of the Spirit by the word upon the heart and affections, doth allure them from their former state, draws them aside to

himself in the wilderness, there treats with them, and by little and little speaks comfort unto them; and so at length makes up the marriage covenant, which he mentions in verse 19, and "betroths them to himself for ever." So it is with many: God hath, as to this covenant with himself, allured them; though it would be useful, if not needful, for such persons solemnly and expressly, upon some occasions, to renew their covenant with God, as Jacob did.

Now, as to those whom God hath thus taken into covenant, whom he hath thus allured, there are always these two things upon their minds, in their thus entering into covenant with God, which we may do well to consider and remember,—

(1.) That they do surely accept God in Christ for himself, and make no conditions about peace, and prosperity, and freedom from trouble, in this world. Naaman made a reserve, that he would bow in the house of Rimmon; and that spoiled his whole covenant. Whoever hath in sincerity thus engaged in covenant with God, his own soul will bear him witness that he made no condition, had no reserve: and the proffer of any one condition to God or Christ whatever, is enough to ruin the whole marriage contract he tenders to us. Now, for a man to faint and sink under any thing that befalls him, let him retreat unto the covenant, and inquire there whether ever he made a condition against it,—against imprisonment, banishment, poverty, losses, troubles, distresses. Did he say, "If God would keep him from all these?" God made no such condition with him. What God hath actually engaged before in promise, that we may plead with him as a condition,—for Jacob did so, "If thou wilt be with me, and bless me." God had given him that promise, "Thou saidst, I will deal well with thee, and I will surely do thee good,"—but not else.

(2.) You may remember *with what affections* you engaged unto God. It is a marriage covenant, Jer. iii. 14, "I am married unto you," saith God; and Isa. liv. 5, "Thy Maker is thy husband; the LORD of hosts is his name." And there is nothing more eminent in the marriage covenant than a mighty prevalency of affection. I should much doubt whether I had really entered into covenant with God, if I had never found any thing of entire marriage affections towards God in Christ for himself. That soul that can, under his distresses, repair to some sense and experience of the prevalency of his affections in it formerly,—it will relieve him against all his troubles, and only make him cry out for such affections unto God again, that will fully satisfy, when they are drawn out unto him. The remembrance and calling over of these things will greatly relieve and support a soul, whatever its distress or perplexity may be.

Sixthly. I have one consideration more, which is the last I shall insist upon; and that is, to consider in this covenant, whereunto I make my retreat,—*who it is that hath made it with me.* And therein I would consider two things;—the one whereof will have the endearment of admiration, and the other will have full and plenary satisfaction.

Why, it is God that hath made this covenant with us: "HE hath made with me," saith David. If a great, a mighty king or prince of the earth, had made a covenant with us, and confirmed it solemnly by his oath, to take care of all our concerns; so carnal and so fleshy are we, that it would give us great relief against imminent danger and hazards. But who hath made this covenant with us? God hath made it; and two things are considerable in this:—1. His condescension in entering into this covenant. 2. His sufficiency to satisfy us in it.

1. His condescension. And we may consider the condescension of God, upon the account of his greatness, upon the account of his holiness, and upon the account of his self-sufficiency:—

(1.) Upon the account of his *greatness.* You may observe in sundry places, that where God doth mention his covenant, or the fruits of his covenant, he doth oftentimes mention his greatness with it. So, Isa. lvii. 15, "Thus saith the high and lofty One that inhabiteth eternity; I dwell with him also" (which is God's covenant) "that is of a contrite and humble spirit." The high and lofty One will condescend to dwell with the poor and humble. And Stephen, Acts vii. 2, mentioning God's calling of Abraham, saith, "The God of glory appeared unto our father Abraham." That the high and the lofty One, the great and the glorious God, should enter into this covenant with poor dust and ashes, worms of the earth as we are!—the Lord help us to understand it. Condescension is endearing and satisfying,—we find it so among men. If a man that is great in the world doth but condescend to respect and be familiar towards them that are poor, that are beggars, it is looked upon as a very great matter, and doth wonderfully engage such persons to them that thus condescend: but let that distance be what it will that is between the highest and greatest king and the meanest beggar, they are men still; and, upon some accounts, the meanest may be the better. But there is an infinite distance between God and us, between the high and the lofty One, the glorious God, the possessor of heaven and earth, and poor dust and ashes. That he should take us into covenant, and engage himself by oath for the accomplishment of it; and should accept of our answering of his covenant, and engaging of our hearts unto him, that he should be ours, and that we should be his;—no heart can fully conceive this condescension. But,—

(2.) There is greater condescension yet; and that is, his great condescension with respect unto his *holiness.* It is a great condescension of God, upon the account of his greatness, to enter into covenant with man; but it is a greater condescension for the holy God to enter into covenant with sinful man; and therefore, though there was great grace, and great excellency in the first covenant, wherein the Creator entered into covenant with the creature, yet the second covenant is far more excellent and mysterious, where the holy God entered into covenant with sinners. In the first covenant there was no need of a mediator; but when a covenant is made between the holy God and sinners, there comes in the person of Jesus Christ; which shows infinite condescension on the part of God.

(3.) Consider his condescension upon the account of his *self-sufficiency*. Though God be thus great, and though he be thus holy, yet may he not, however, have some use of poor man? may he not have some need of his service, as the greatest men upon earth have some need of their subjects and tenants? They have a revenue out of them; but God had no need of us at all, or of that service we tender him by virtue of this covenant. Ps. xvi. 2, " O my soul, thou hast said unto the LORD, Thou art my Lord." What, then, will he do for God? " My goodness extends not unto thee."—" It is true, thou art my God in a way of mere sovereign grace, but what I can do reaches not unto thee." So he saith, Job xxxv. 6–8, " If thou sinnest, what doest thou against him? or if thy transgressions be multiplied, what doest thou unto him? If thou be righteous, what givest thou him? or what receiveth he of thine hand? Thy wickedness may hurt a man as thou art; and thy righteousness may profit the son of man." God receives no profit, no advantage by it; so that it is an infinite condescension in God with respect to his self-sufficiency, and that upon two accounts:—[1.] Upon the absolute, eternal self-sufficiency of his own nature. All the creatures in the world add nothing to God's state of blessedness. He made them, not that he might have advantage by them, but that he might communicate of his own goodness unto them. He was no less infinitely, eternally blessed before a creature was made to contemplate his glory, than he is now. [2.] Suppose all those he takes into covenant should fail him, " he can out of stones raise up children unto Abraham;"—he can bring up another people that may serve him to his praise and glory.

That is the first thing that will greatly refresh our souls under distresses, if we consider God's gracious condescension in taking us into covenant with him, upon the account of his greatness, his holiness, and his self-sufficiency; and it is an endearing condescension. " What am I," said Elisabeth, " that the mother of my Lord should come unto me?" Much more may we say, " What are we, that the God and Father of our Lord Jesus Christ should thus come unto us, to take us into covenant with himself?"

2. It will be a relief, if we consider God's all-sufficiency to *satisfy our souls* in every state and condition. This he made the ground of his covenant with Abraham,—"I am God Almighty." And if there be any want in God, we are freed from the terms of the covenant;—that I may speak it to aggravate the sin of our instability, and the not taking up full satisfaction in him. "But is it so?" saith God, "Have I been a wilderness unto you, or a barren heath? as waters that fail?" Have we, at any time in our own experience, failed of any thing all our life long hitherto? have we wanted any thing? Our want arises because we will not admit, we will not receive; or we long after other things, which God is not pleased we should have. There is in God an all-sufficiency of grace and mercy to pardon us; there is an all-sufficiency of spiritual strength to support us and carry us through all our difficulties; there is an all-sufficiency of goodness and beauty to satisfy us; and there is an all-sufficiency of power and glory to reward us.

(1.) There is in God, to meet with our wants, an all-sufficiency of *grace and mercy to pardon us*, Tit. iii. 3, 4. The apostle having made a description of what we were before our conversion to God, and notwithstanding all the paint we put upon ourselves, has given us a character as black as hell: "We ourselves were foolish, disobedient, deceived, serving divers lusts and pleasures, living in malice and envy, hateful, and hating one another." How were we delivered? "The kindness and love of God our Saviour appeared." God, who is rich in grace, of his mercy wherewith he loved us in Christ, notwithstanding that cursed condition of ours, pardons, sanctifies, and saves us. There is an all-sufficiency of grace and mercy in God, I say, to pardon us. Where is there a believer that cannot say, he has found God all-sufficient to pardon sin?

(2.) There is an all-sufficiency of spiritual *strength in God to support us.* Here lies our great strait and perplexity,—the experience of our own weakness, of the unspeakable variety of temptations wherewith we are exercised, of oppositions that we meet withal, especially in such a time, wherein the floods lift up their voice, and rage. Who shall be able to go through all these difficulties,—these remaining trials, temptations, troubles of our pilgrimage? how shall we be able to withstand them? I know not how it is with others, but it is a wonder to myself that my soul is alive, considering what is come already: but "there is the residue of the Spirit with God." He tells you, Isa. xl. 28, to the end, that he will not faint in this work of giving out grace and spiritual strength, "He giveth power to the faint; and to them that have no might he increaseth strength." He is able to carry us through all, and cause us to sing, because of his majesty, in the very fire.

(3.) There is an all-sufficiency of goodness and beauty in God to *satisfy our souls.* We are scattering away our affections "upon every high hill, and under every green tree," Jer. ii. 20,—looking for, and seeking after satisfaction from, perishing things; but we find them all vanity and vexation of spirit: they will appear so unto us. But, "How great is his goodness, and how great is his beauty!" Zech. ix. 17. O the excellency and desirableness of God, to satisfy and fill all the affections of our hearts, in every state and condition!

(4.) And lastly, there is an all-sufficiency in God *to reward us* when we shall be here no more. The lion lies at the door,—death is ready to seize upon us;—let our condition be what it will, we are entering into eternity: but God hath engaged himself by covenant to be our God; he hath promised to carry us through the dark shade, and to crown our souls with glory. "Be thou faithful unto death, and I will give thee a crown of life."

SERMON III.[1]

"Wherefore he saith, When he ascended up on high, he led captivity captive, and gave gifts unto men."—EPH. iv. 8.

THE design of these words is to show that the gift of the ministry, and of ministers,—of the office, and persons to discharge that office,—is an eminent fruit of the exaltation of Christ, and a great expression and pledge of his care and love towards his church; and that is my doctrine, which I shall speak unto from them.

FIRST. It is a gift, Αὐτὸς ἔδωκε, verse 11, "He himself gave." The foundation of the ministry is in the gift of Christ. Let me answer that question which he put once to the Pharisees, "The baptism of John, is it from heaven? or is it of men?" In like manner, I say, The ministry, is it from heaven? or is it of men? The answer is in the text, "He gave;"—it is the gift of Christ. It is also the great promise that he would do so, Jer. iii. 15, "I will give you pastors according to mine heart, which shall feed you with knowledge and understanding." When shall that be? "When," saith he, "I shall take you one of a city, and two of a family, and bring you to Zion," as it is said in verse 14; or, "When I shall call you by the gospel, then I will give you pastors according to my own heart." And that this is a promise of the gospel, and so intended in that place of Jeremiah,

[1] This sermon was preached at the ordination of a minister, January 23, 1673.

you may see, chap. xxiii. 4, where the promise is repeated, " I will set up shepherds over them, which shall feed them." Verse 5, " When I raise unto David a righteous Branch, and a King shall reign and prosper." It is the great promise, that, under the gospel, Christ would give ministers to his church.

It may be said, " We know how Christ gave apostles when he was on earth; he called them, chose them, sent them: but how doth Christ now continue to give ministers to his church?" That we may not claim an interest in a gift, and a privilege that we have no right unto, I say, by four ways or means doth Christ continue to give ministers, in all ages, unto his church. The church is to consider them as that which is the bottom and foundation of the duties they perform and of the work undertaken this day.

First. He doth it " by the standing law, ordinance, and institution of the gospel," whereby he hath appointed this office of the ministry in the church, as the great Mediator of it. All the saints in the world, all the disciples of Christ, neither could nor ought (whatever necessity they could have thought they had seen of it,—whatever congruity from the light of nature) to have appointed teachers nor officers among them, neither could it ever have been blessed unto their advantage, if Christ had not, by a standing ordinance and law, appointed such an office. And if that law comes to an end,—if its obligation ceases,—the work of the ministry, and the whole office of it, must cease also; but if this ordinance be " as the ordinances of heaven," of the sun, moon, and stars, that change not, it shall never be altered in this world. It is plain, then, the neglect of the work and office of the ministry is so far a rebellion against the authority of Christ. " All power," saith he, Matt. xxviii. 18, 19, " is given unto me in heaven and in earth; therefore go preach the gospel: and, lo, I am with you alway, unto the end of the world." He is exalted, and he gives some to be pastors and some to be teachers, until all the elect of God are brought unto the unity of the faith, and unto a perfect man,—unto the measure of the stature of the fulness of Christ.

Secondly. The second thing he doth is, " the giving spiritual gifts" unto men, whereby they may be enabled unto the discharge of the office of the ministry, as to the edification of the church in all the ends of it. *Gifts make no man a minister; but all the world cannot make a minister of Christ without gifts.* If the Lord Jesus Christ should cease to give out spiritual gifts unto men for the work of the ministry, he need do no more to take away the ministry itself; it must cease also: and it is the very way the ministry ceases in apostatising churches,—Christ no more giving out unto them of the gifts of his Spirit; and all their outward forms and order, which they can continue, are of no signification in his sight.

Thirdly. Christ doth it by giving power unto his church to call persons to that office, by him appointed and prepared by the gifts to bestows. And you may observe three things concerning this power:—

1. That this power in the church is not despotical, lordly, and absolute. It is not from any authority of their own; but it consists in an absolute compliance with the command of Christ: it is but the doing what Christ hath commanded; and that gives virtue, efficacy, and power unto it. "Look not upon us as though, by our power and our virtue," may the church say, "we have made this man a minister this day. It is in the name and authority of Jesus Christ alone, by which we act; in obedience unto that, he is so constituted and appointed."

2. There is no power in any church to choose any one whom Christ hath not chosen before; that is, no church can make a man *formally* a minister, that Christ hath not made so *materially*, if I may so say. If Christ hath not pre-instructed and prefurnished him with gifts, it is not in the power of the church to choose or call him. And where these two things are,—where the law of Christ is the foundation, and where the gifts of Christ are the preparative,—thereupon the church calls, and persons are constituted elders by the Holy Ghost, and overseers of the flock; as in Acts xx. 28. Because he gave the law of the office, and because he gave these gifts to the officers, therefore are they constituted by the Holy Ghost. They were the ordinary elders of the church of Ephesus to whom the apostle gives in charge "to feed the flock of God, over which the Holy Ghost had made them overseers."

3. The way whereby the church doth call or constitute any person unto this office thus appointed, is, by giving themselves up unto him in the Lord; which they testify by their solemn choice and election by suffrage: the way, I say, is, by submitting themselves unto him in the Lord, witnessing it by their solemn suffrage in the choice of him. 2 Cor. viii. 5, "And this they did," saith the apostle (namely, the saints of Macedonia), "not as we hoped" (much beyond our expectation), "but first gave their ownselves to the Lord, and unto us by the will of God." It is the great work you have to do, let me tell you of this church, in your calling of an officer, to give up yourselves unto him by the will of God, to be led, guided, instructed, directed,—to have the work of the ministry fulfilled among you to your edification: and this submission wherein (as I could evince by arguments sufficient) the essence of the call doth consist, is to be testified by suffrage or by choice. When God ordered the Levites to be set apart unto the service of the tabernacle, in the name and on the behalf of the whole congregation, to show what weight he laid upon

the consent and suffrage of the people, he caused all the people to come together, and to lay their hands upon them, Numb. viii. 9, 10, "Thou shalt bring the Levites before the tabernacle of the congregation; and thou shalt gather the whole assembly of the children of Israel together" (all the church): "and thou shalt bring the Levites before the LORD; and the children of Israel shall put their hands upon the Levites:" namely, to testify their consent in their solemn dedication to the Lord to minister in the tabernacle in their name, and on their behalf.

We have, in the New Testament, thirteen times mentioned the setting apart of ministers unto their office; some of which I shall mention. The first account is in Acts i. 15, unto the end. It was while they were praying—upon a sermon of Peter's which he preached unto them—that they went about their work; "for every thing is sanctified by the word and prayer." There was an apostle to be called. But here God was to have a peculiar, sovereign interposition, and to give a special manifestation of his own divine choice; so that it could not be absolutely left unto the choice of the church. Yet thus far they went, that antecedently unto God's choice, "they appointed two," verse 23. This was the first church act that ever was performed in the New Testament. There was in it a pattern to be laid for after times and ages. Let the church proceed as far as possible with a reserve to the sovereignty of God. "They appointed two;" so far, I say, they went; and then God took his man. But still, to preserve the liberty of the church herein, it is added, when God had taken him, *συγκατεψηφίσθη*,—he was by common suffrage, as the word signifies, reckoned among the apostles. There was antecedently allowed them the choice of two; and, consequently, their common suffrage that he should be among the number of the apostles. The next call we have is in Acts vi., which is the "call of deacons;" where the whole matter is, by the assembly of apostles, referred unto the body of the church. One would wonder how such a forgetfulness should befall a world of men who call themselves Christians, to do all these things without them, as though the church had no concern in them, when the whole body of the apostles, being assembled together (who had all the power and authority in their hands Christ had committed unto any of the children of men), direct the church to use what power Christ had intrusted them with. "Brethren," say they, "look out from among yourselves," verse 3. "And the saying pleased the whole multitude," verse 5: "and they chose Stephen, a man full of the Holy Ghost;" and so the rest who were afterward set apart. If all the apostles were upon the earth together, where there was in truth a church of Christ, called according to his mind, they would not undertake to deprive the church of their liberty; which any man now, who is far from an apostle, you know, will take upon him at any time. A third Scripture where it is mentioned, is Acts xiv. 23, "And when they had ordained them elders in every church," etc. I confess I am not free to manage the argument now from this place, although it is the most cogent; because it depends merely and purely upon the signification of the original word. Only this I would *recommend* to you, that before *interest* had guided men in what they had to do, all the translations that were extant in English did read this text, "And ordained them elders by election," as the word doth signify: so you will find it in your old translations. But since, it was left out to serve a turn. We may freely say, there is no one instance to be found in the whole New Testament concerning the practical part of communicating an office unto any person, but it is peculiarly also declared that it was done by the election of the multitude, or the body of the church.

This is the third way whereby Christ continues to give these gifts unto men.

Fourthly. The fourth way is, by his law, ordinance, and institution, that the person so qualified, and so called, should be solemnly "set apart by fasting and prayer." So you have it, Acts xiv. 23, "And when they had ordained them elders" (chose them elders) "in every church, and had prayed with fasting, they commended them to the Lord." And upon the like occasion, when Paul and Barnabas were to be separated anew unto a special work, it is said, Acts xiii. 3, "When they had fasted and prayed, they sent them forth."

These, then, are the four ways to answer that great inquiry, How doth Christ continue to give ministers unto the church? He doth it by his law constituting the office,—the law in the gospel, which is an everlasting ordinance;—he doth it by his Spirit, communicating gifts unto persons;—he doth it by his church calling of them, and by a submission to them according to the will of God, and testifying that submission by their suffrage;—he doth it by his ordinance of solemnly setting them apart with fasting and prayer. And these, my brethren, are things that we are come together about this day. This is our faith, this is our warrant; wherein we do not pursue our own imaginations, nor the inventions of other men, nor follow cunningly-devised fables, but, from first to last, have our warrant from Christ. The good Lord pardon us wherein we come short of the preparation of the sanctuary, and accept us according to the desire of our hearts, to do the service of his house and tabernacle!

I will but speak a word or two of use to this part, and then we will proceed to that work which is your part this day; whereunto, if God give strength, I shall add some farther instructions, and then desire the help of our brethren present to carry it on.

First, then, if there be any office, let it be under never so glorious or so specious a title, if Christ hath not appointed that office by virtue of gospel ordinance and institution, there is a nullity in it,—it is no gift of Christ; let who will bear it and discharge it, with what formality soever they come unto it,—popes and cardinals, metropolitans and diocesans,—there is a nullity in the office, by reason there is no law, ordinance, or institution of Christ appointing of it. All the outward order and solemnity in the world, and all the holiness of persons, when engaging in such an office, cannot give it a right and title; because it wants the law of Christ for its foundation.

And where the office itself is appointed by Christ, if there be no communication of gifts unto the person, there is not a nullity in the office, absolutely; but there is a nullity as to the person. It is essential to the office, that Christ choose the person by communicating of gifts unto him. Where this is not, I will not say that there must always (for things are greatly varied with circumstances) be a nullity in all administrations; but there is a nullity in the person ministering before Christ.

Secondly. Let the church consider aright how they are to receive, and what apprehensions they have of, a minister that comes to them according to this law, order, and institution of Christ, which I have unfolded to you. He is a gift of Christ. It requires wisdom and prudence in a man to receive a gift (consider what he doth,—he takes an obligation upon himself); much more to receive a gift from a prince. But to receive a gift, and so great a gift, from Christ!—certainly there ought to be some particular preparation of our hearts for it. How great a mercy, how great a gift this is, I could easily demonstrate.

There are two things that I will but name:—1. Valuation and thankfulness. 2. Improvement. As soon as we are a church of God, these things are expected of us. When we receive so great a gift from Christ, he expects that it be valued, that it be thankfully received, and that it be duly improved.

And on the part of him, or of any of us who are called to the ministry, undoubtedly it is incumbent upon us so to behave ourselves, and so to approve ourselves, as that we may own ourselves to be a gift of Christ unto the church, and be owned by the church as a gift of Christ. I do not know, for my own part, a more trembling thought that a minister hath, or can have, in the consideration of his office, work, and duty, whereunto he is called, than this one, "How shall I approve myself, so as to be looked on as a gift from Christ given unto the church?"

There are three things that are required in every one who may be esteemed to be a gift given by Christ unto the church:—1. An imitation of Christ; 2. A representation of him; and, 3. Zeal for him:—

1. *An imitation of Christ*, as the great shepherd of the flock, in meekness, in care, in love, in tenderness towards the whole flock. So Christ is described, Isa. xl. 11, "He shall feed his flock like a shepherd; he shall gather the lambs with his arm, and carry them in his bosom, and shall gently lead those that are with young." Here is the great pattern, here is an example for all who are shepherds of the flock under Christ (who intend to give an account with comfort unto the great shepherd of the sheep, when he shall appear at the last day),— in meekness and condescension giving out help and assistance, bearing with all things, that cannot particularly be insisted upon; and especially conforming unto him who knows how to have compassion on the ignorant, and them that are out of the way.

2. There is required *a representation of Christ*, and that in all his offices:—

(1.) A representation of him in the rule and conduct of the church; that the church, under our rule and conduct, may be sensible that the government of Christ is spiritual and holy. What a woful representation of Christ is made by men who undertake to rule the church of God with rods and axes, with fire and fagot! Is this to represent the meek and holy King of the church, or rather a devouring tyrant, unto the world? It is our great work, in what interest Christ hath given us in the rule of the church, to represent him as spiritual, as holy, as meek,—as universally tending to edification, and not to destruction.

(2.) To represent Christ in his prophetical office. He was the great teacher of the church; and the principal work of ministers is, "to preach the word in season and out of season;"—by all means to carry on the church in the knowledge of God, and of our Lord and Saviour Jesus Christ. "I will give them 'pastors that shall feed them with knowledge and understanding.'" Those who take upon themselves to be pastors, and neglect this work of feeding the flock, may, at as cheap a rate, and with equal modesty, renounce Jesus Christ.

(3.) Christ is to be represented in the imitable part of his sacerdotal office; which is, to make continual prayers and intercession for the church,—and that church, in particular, whereunto we belong. So the apostle speaks, Col. iv. 12, "Epaphras, who is one of you" (that is, he was one of their elders and teachers), "a servant of Christ, saluteth you, always labouring fervently for you in prayers, that ye may stand perfect and complete in all the will of God." It is a great work thus, in all these things, to represent Christ in all his offices unto the church; and, indeed, who is sufficient for these things? I might add.

3. *Zeal for Christ.* He that comes as an ambassador from Christ, in Christ's stead, will have zeal for all the concerns of Christ in the church;—for his worship, for the purity of his ordinances, for the conversion of souls, and for the building up of the saints. This is required of them who are thus a gift from Christ.

This is the first thing that my text doth suggest unto me,—namely, that the ministry is the gift of Christ.

And having proceeded so far, I will here stay a little, and desire the church would attend to *their* work and duty. After which, if God give strength, I will speak somewhat more unto the eminency of this gift, according as it is set out in this text.

[Then the church assented to the election, by the lifting up of their hands; and the Doctor went on.]

I have showed you that the ministry and ministers are a gift that Christ himself gave the church. I shall now show you (which was the SECOND part of my proposition), *that it is a great and eminent gift*, or an eminent fruit of the exaltation and mediation of Christ:—

First. It appears to be so from the "great and glorious preparation" that was made for it. When did Christ give this gift? "When," saith he, "he ascended up on high, he led captivity captive, and gave gifts unto men." The words are taken out of Ps. lxviii. 17, 18, "The chariots of God are twenty thousand, even thousands of angels: the LORD is among them, as in Sinai, in the holy place. Thou hast ascended on high, thou hast led captivity captive: thou hast received gifts for men." The words, you see, in the first place are spoken of God himself, and applied by our apostle to Christ, upon these two grounds:—1. Because it was peculiarly the Son of God who appeared so to the fathers under the Old Testament. It was he who appeared to Abraham, and gave him the promise; and to Moses in the bush; it was he who gave the law at mount Sinai; and appeared to Joshua for the conquest of Canaan, where the church was to be set up;—so it was still the same person, though the articles were varied. 2. Because whatever was done in a way of solemnity under the Old Testament, was a representation, or a means of introducing of things that were to be done under the New. How did God lead "captivity captive," on the glorious giving of the law upon mount Sinai? That was the day wherein he made his people free. They had no rule, no order, no polity before that, but were under the relics of that captivity which they underwent in Egypt. God now had conquered Pharaoh, and triumphed gloriously over him in the Red sea,—over him and his host who had kept the people so long in bondage. He led captivity captive, and brought forth his people into liberty,—though it was but an initial liberty: it was a bondage in comparison of what was to ensue; but it was the beginning of liberty to them. And all this was to represent the glorious conquest at the ascension of Christ, expressed, Col. ii. 15, "And having spoiled principalities and powers, he made a show of them openly, triumphing over them in it," or in himself. When he spoiled Pharaoh, he triumphed over him gloriously,—"The horse and his rider hath he cast into the sea." It was the same divine person, who did that as a type of what he would do when he should spoil principalities and powers,—Satan, death, hell, sin, and all the spiritual adversaries of the church,—triumphing over them: then did he lead captivity captive. And therefore you may observe the change of the words, which all do who speak to this thing. In the Psalms, it is said, "Thou hast ascended on high, and led captivity captive, and received gifts for men." In my text it is said, "He ascended on high, and led captivity captive, and gave gifts unto men." Though Christ be spoken of as God in the 68th Psalm, wherein he was incapable of receiving gifts, yet it was in a mystery and prophecy that he should be in that state and condition wherein he should receive them, and receive them that he might give them; as in Acts ii. 32. When he was exalted on the right hand of God, and received the gift of the Spirit, he then gave it out unto men.

What is all this great preparation now for? what is it the apostle ushers in upon this theatre of glory? Nothing less than the giving of ministers unto the church. "He ascended up on high, and led captivity captive, and gave gifts unto men." What, I pray? Some to be pastors and teachers. *There is a greater glory in giving a minister to a poor congregation, than there is in the instalment and enthroning of all the popes, and cardinals, and metropolitans, that ever were in the world: let their glory be what it will, Christ is upon his theatre of glory in the communication of this office and these officers.*

Wherein, will you say, is this glory? You see no beauty, no comeliness in it: no more did the unbelieving world in the person of Christ, nor ways of Christ. Was there not a great deal of glory in the setting apart of Aaron unto his service, in all his glorious garments and ornaments, with all the solemnity of sacrifices that was used therein? doubtless there was. But saith our apostle, "It had no glory in comparison of the ministry of the Spirit. This is a glory that doth excel," 2 Cor. iii. 10. The reason why we see not the glory of it is, because we are carnal. It is a spiritual glory. God himself presides over the work of this day. "I will place my tabernacle with them, and I will walk with them, and be their God," Lev. xxvi. 11, 12. If we are the church and tabernacle of God, God walks among us this day; Christ is among us by his special presence. "Where two or three are gathered together in my name, there am I in the midst of them," Matt. xviii. 20. And much more may his presence be expected in so great a transaction of his authority as this we are now engaged in. The holy and elect angels are present with us, to give glory to the solemnity. Hence our apostle charges Timothy, chap. v. 21, "I charge thee before God, and the Lord Jesus Christ, and the elect angels, that thou observe these things." Why before the elect angels? Because they are present as *witnesses* in the collation of authority from Christ. Thou hast thousands of witnesses more than thou seest; there are more eyes upon thee than thou takest notice of;—God is present, Christ is present, the elect angels are present. These things are the true and faithful sayings of God. Here, then, is glory and beauty, in that it is not only a gift, but an eminent gift. That is the first thing in my text.

Secondly. It is glorious and eminent from *the foundation* and spring of it,—which is the humiliation and death of Christ. "Now that he ascended, what is it, but that he also descended into the lower parts of the earth?" Why doth the apostle mention here Christ's descending? Was it to take the advantage of a word? because having mentioned his ascension, will he mention also his descension? No; that is not the way of the Holy Ghost. There was no reason to mention it absolutely in this place: it must be with reference to the end that was under consideration. "There is something," saith he, "in Christ's descending into the lower part of the earth that doth contribute to this great gift of the ministry."

The lower part of the earth may have a double interpretation:—1. The earth may be spoken of with reference to the whole world. 2. Some part of the earth may be spoken of with reference to some other part.

1. If you take it in the first sense, Christ's descending into the lower part of the earth,—that is, into this lower part of the creation, which the earth is,—then it is the incarnation of Christ and his humiliation that he intends: which is so expressed, John iii. 13, "No man hath ascended up to heaven, but he that came down from heaven, even the Son of man," etc. Christ's descending and coming down, was by taking our nature upon him. So it may be here. "He descended into the lower parts of the earth," that is, "He came and assumed our nature, and was here in a state of humiliation."

Or, 2. The lower part of the earth intends a comparison between some part of the earth itself; and so may be taken for the *grave;*—"He descended into the grave." The burial of Christ, which was a great and evident testimony of his real death, is that which is intended; and so I look upon it in this place. The very descent of Christ into the grave, which is the lowest part of the earth that mankind descend into, is the apostle's meaning.

And observe from hence, that the death of Christ hath a great influence into this gift of the ministry. It is a branch that grew out of the grave of Christ: let it be esteemed as lightly as men please, had not Christ died for it, we had not had a ministry in the world.

And two ways the ministry relates to the death of Christ:—1. Because it was necessary unto his receiving of that power whereby alone he was able to give ministers. See that at large, Phil. ii. 6–11. It was his humbling himself unto the death, even the death of the cross, that was required to that exaltation whereby he had power to give ministers. The mediatorial authority of Christ, whereby he was enabled to give ministers to the church, was founded on his death. And, 2. It respects his death, because the very end of the ministry is, to preach that peace to mankind which was made by the death of Christ, Eph. ii. 14, "He is our peace,"—he hath made peace for us; and in verse 17, "Came and preached peace to you which were afar off, and to them that were nigh." How did Christ come and preach peace to the Gentiles,—to them that were afar off? It was no otherwise than by instituting the office of the ministry, and sending his ministers to preach peace to them. And we that are ministers may know the near relation of our office to the death of Christ, which will greatly direct us in the work we have to do; which is, I say, to preach that peace that was made with God by Christ. This is another thing in the text that sets forth the beauty, glory, and eminency of this great gift of Christ.

SERMON IV.[1]

"But all these worketh that one and the self-same Spirit, dividing to every man severally as he will."—1 COR. xii. 11.

YOU are a church of ancient standing, and therefore are acquainted both with the duty and practice of it. God hath guided you to call *them* to office over and among you who have been long experienced in the work of the ministry; so that I am sure neither they nor you stand in any need of my instruction, as to particular duties. Therefore I shall speak a word in general unto that which is the foundation of all our station, work, and duty, from these words, in 1 Cor. xii. 11, "But all these worketh," etc.

There is this disadvantage in preaching upon a particular occasion, especially for one who hath no more strength than I, that either we must omit insisting on the particular explication of the text, or be

[1] This sermon was preached at an ordination, April 3, 1678.

prevented in that which we aim at particularly from it. Both cannot be done; therefore I shall only give you the substance of the words, in that proposition which I intend to insist upon; namely,—

That it is the work of the Spirit of God, in all ages of the church, to communicate spiritual gifts and abilities to those who are called according unto his mind to the ministry of the church, to enable them unto all evangelical administrations, to his glory, and the edification of the church.

Had I time, I would inquire into these two things:—1. Whether the Holy Ghost doth indeed continue to communicate *spiritual gifts*, distinct from *natural* endowments and *acquired* abilities, to the discharge of the work of the ministry, to his glory, and the edification of the church. And, 2. Whether these spiritual gifts and abilities, so communicated, be not the material call to the work of the ministry, antecedently required to the formal call thereunto.

As to the first, it is opposed by them who say that these spiritual gifts we talk of are nothing, indeed, but men's natural and acquired abilities, with an ordinary blessing of God upon their ministry; and for other spiritual gifts there are none.

As to the second, it is denied that there is, or ought to be, an outward way and order for calling men to the office of the ministry; and that a compliance therewith makes their call good, valuable, and lawful, whether they have of these gifts we talk of or no. And in these two lie all the contests about church order and worship that we have in the world.

But I shall only speak in the general unto the above proposition,—namely, that it is the work of the Holy Spirit, in providing of an able ministry of the New Testament, for the use of the church to the end of the world, to communicate to them who are called according to his mind spiritual gifts and abilities, to enable them to the discharge of their duty in the administration of all ordinances, to the glory of Christ and the edification of the church. The proving of this one proposition, in which is the life of all gospel order, is all I shall do at this time.

And I shall do it in these following observations, principles, and deductions from it:—

First. Our Lord Jesus Christ hath faithfully promised, Matt. xxviii. 20, that he will be present with his church "unto the end of the world." It is his temple and habitation, "wherein he dwells, and in which he walks." And this is that which essentially and fundamentally differenceth his church from any other assembly or society of men whatever. Let men cast themselves into what order they please, and let it be the order that they apprehend prescribed unto them in the Scripture; or let them invent a better for themselves, as they think; and let them derive their title to power and authority whence they will; if Christ be not present with them, when they have done, they are *no gospel church.* They want a foundation; and where there is no foundation, the higher they raise the building, or the more glorious they make the appearance of it, the sooner it will tumble down and come to nothing. I shall not repeat those promises of Christ's presence now; they are known unto you: and this is the great interest of any church, to secure the promised presence of Christ with them. You have, I hope, under the conduct of the Holy Spirit of God, been guided in your choice of *such persons* as are able and faithful, to go before you in the work of the Lord: but your design ought to be, that thereby you might receive pledges of the presence of Christ with you; else all other things will be of no value. There are some who are little solicitous about these things. Do but build a house in such a frame, and say certain words, and suppose Christ is immured there; and there is a church built and made! But the observance of all outward rules and order, according to the gospel, will not constitute a church, unless Christ be taken into it. Moses built a tabernacle according to the mind of God; "according unto all that God commanded him, so did he," Exod. xl. 16;— but when he had framed it exactly, and set it up, and put every thing in its place, it was but an ordinary tabernacle, till the glory of God entered into it. And so it was with Solomon's temple; it was but an ordinary house, until the glory of God entered into it. And suppose we could frame our church societies according to the rule of the gospel, as Moses framed the tabernacle according to the pattern showed him in the mount; they would be no churches of Christ, unless *the glory of Christ* enter into them. Here is our difference and advantage:—the glory of God entered into the tabernacle and temple of old in clouds and darkness; but the glory of God enters into the gospel church, under the New Testament, in light. This is the first head,—Christ hath promised to be with his church to the end and consummation of all things.

Secondly. Christ is thus present with his church, principally and fundamentally, *by his Spirit.* There are three ways of the presence of Christ:—1. He is everywhere *essentially* present; present with all things by the immensity of his divine nature. Christ did not promise this, for it is not a subject for a promise. The promises are of *what may be,* and not of *what cannot but be.* This presence is necessary, and cannot be otherwise; neither doth it make any alteration. It doth not make a church; it doth not make one place heaven, another hell. I speak of the immense presence of the divine nature. Again, 2. Christ is, or may be, present in his *human nature:* this was that which brought a great entanglement on the spirits of his disciples. He told them he would never leave them; and where but two or three of them were assembled in his name, he would be among them, Matt. xviii. 20. At length he comes and tells them, "It is expedient for you that I go away," John xvi. 7. This filled their hearts with trouble; they knew not how to reconcile these things. Afterward, they were told that he was so gone from them as that they must not look for him till the day of judgment, Acts iii. 21. There must be, therefore, some other presence of Christ besides the essential presence of his divine nature, and besides the presence of his human nature; how else shall the promise be accomplished? Saith Christ, "I will tell you what that presence is; I will send you the Holy Ghost, to supply the presence of my human nature." It is the substance of the 14th, 15th, and 16th chapters of John, to declare this. "I will send you the Comforter to abide with you, to enable you to all church work. Therefore, though I am with you, and have instructed you, yet you can perform no church work at all, until the Holy Ghost comes. Abide at Jerusalem, till you have the promise of the Spirit." After the ascension of Christ, the apostles went about no church work till they had received the Holy Ghost. And Christ hath no vicar, but the Spirit. The truth is, the world grew weary of him, and took the work out of his hands for which he was promised; and he would have nothing to do in that which they call "the church." I need not prove this; it hath been the faith of the *catholic church*, from the first foundation of it, that the promised presence of Christ with his church was *by his Spirit*. Some begin to say in our days, that Christ is no otherwise present than by the outward ordinances of it,—his word and sacraments. I grant he is present with them, as pledges of his presence, and instruments wherewith, by his Spirit, he doth effectually work; but to make them the whole presence of Christ with us, I do not know what better church-state we have than the Jews, when they had the law of old.

Thirdly. This presence of the Spirit is promised and given unto the church by *an everlasting covenant*, Isa. lix. 21: "As for me, this is my covenant with them, saith the LORD; My Spirit that is upon thee, and my words which I have put in thy mouth, shall not depart out of thy mouth, nor out of the mouth of thy seed, nor out of the mouth of thy seed's seed, saith the LORD, from henceforth and for ever." To whom is this promise made? It is made unto the gospel church. In the verse foregoing, "The Redeemer shall come to Zion, and unto them that turn from transgression in Jacob, saith the LORD. As for me, this is my covenant with them." With whom? With them the Redeemer comes to in Zion, to redeem from iniquity. What is God's covenant with them? It is his word; *his word shall be in them*. Suppose *this* promise to cease, and God doth not continue his word to any people; will not their church-state cease, which is built upon the doctrine of the prophets and apostles, which is the word of God? Yes, take away the foundation, the state must fall. God's covenant is broken with a people, where he doth not continue his word. But how is it with the "Spirit of God?" He is also promised in the same covenant. Now, suppose there be not a continuance of this promise,—then I say, all covenant relation between God and a people must be dissolved; "For this is my covenant, saith the LORD," etc.;—as if he had said, "If I maintain a covenant with a people, I will give them my Spirit, to abide with them for ever." That covenant whereby you are joined, is dependent on this great promise; and if this be not made good, your church-state comes to an end, notwithstanding whatever outward order there may be among you. But he hath given his church a covenant which "shall abide for ever."

Fourthly. It is from hence that the ministry of the gospel is "the ministry of the Spirit," 2 Cor. iii. 6–8, "Who also hath made us able ministers of the new testament; not of the letter, but of the spirit." There were never but two ministrations, or two ministries, in the world, that were accepted of God; the one was "the ministration of the letter and of death;" the other was, and is, "the ministration of the Spirit, and of life:" and they were both glorious ministrations. That of the letter and death was glorious from its *institution*. You know what a glorious institution it had at mount Sinai, from the manner of its performance, in a glorious sanctuary or tabernacle, and temple. And from its *signification* it was glorious. "But the ministration of the Spirit is much more glorious." There never were but these two ministrations. If there be a ministration that is not a ministration of the letter and of death, nor a ministration of the Spirit and of life, it is Antichrist's. Now, the first it cannot be: the ministration of the letter and of death is the ministration of the law; and the ministration of the gospel is the ministration of the Spirit. But say some, "It is so, because the Spirit of God hath revealed all gospel dispensations; without which it had not been within the compass of the reason of man to have found them out." But, in answer to this, the Spirit of God revealed all the ordinances and ministrations of old, from first to last, even the little additions that David made after Moses' time. 1 Chron. xxviii. 12, 19, "All these things did the hand of God teach me by the Spirit." So that if it be the ministration of the Spirit, because the Spirit revealed them; so was the law the ministration of the Spirit, because the Spirit revealed that. The ministration of the Spirit must signify, either that the Spirit is the *efficient* of the ministration, or the effect of it. If the Spirit be the efficient of the ministration, then it is the Holy Spirit of God giving spiritual gifts and abilities to the ministers of the gospel, to enable them to administer all gospel ordinances to the glory of Christ and the edification of the church. Or the ministration of the Spirit may signify the communication of him, and so be the effect of the ministration. Gal. iii. 2, "Received ye the Spirit by the works of the law, or by the hearing of faith?"—that is, "Received ye the Spirit by the law, or by the gospel?" Then this follows, that so long as there is the preaching of the gospel, there is the communication of the Spirit. Take it which way you will, it is sufficient for my end. If you take the Spirit to be the efficient of the ministration of the church, enabling its ministers to perform their work, or for the effect of the ministration,—he is to abide with the church for ever. For the clearing of this, which is the hinge on which all gospel order turns, we have gone thus far,—that Christ hath promised the Spirit to be with the church; that it is neither the essential presence of his divine or human nature in particular; and that the Spirit is promised to be with the church by an everlasting and unchangeable covenant: from whence it is the gospel is the ministration of the Spirit and of life, and not of death.

Fifthly. Let us consider *the general end* why the Spirit is thus promised unto the church. God hath promised unto Jesus Christ, that he shall have a kingdom and church in the world while the sun and moon endure. Ps. lxxii. 17, "His name shall endure for ever: his name shall be continued as long as the sun;"—that is, to the end of the world. Isa. ix. 7, it is said, "Of the increase of his government," or church, "there shall be no end;"—he shall order it for ever. Matt. xvi. 18, "Upon this rock I will build my church,"—that is, upon himself,—"and the gates of hell shall not prevail against it." Now, this promise doth Christ require that we should mix with faith; which we cannot do, unless there be some ground for the infallible accomplishment of it. Whereon, then, doth depend the certain accomplishment of this great promise that God hath made unto Jesus Christ, concerning which we have as much reason to have our faith exercised at this day as ever? It must depend on some work of God or man. Suppose it depends on *some work of man*,—that is, upon the steadiness of the will of man in yielding obedience unto Jesus Christ, and so continuing his church and kingdom in the world, leaving the ordering of the things of the church according to God's institution of it,—and maintain, withal, that God doth not by effectual grace determine the will of man to obedience; and then God himself can only conjecture. Nor does this lay any ground for us to mix it with faith; but rather faith will depend on men's doing their duty in the world: which, indeed, can be no real ground of faith; for what happens in one place, in the same circumstances of things, may fall out in another: and we know some places where the gospel hath been embraced, and afterward hath come to nothing. Therefore, certainly, the accomplishment of this promise must depend upon *the work of God.* If you ask, "What work of God that is whereon the certainty of this promise doth depend?" I say, It is this work, and no other, of sending the Holy Spirit.

There are but two things to be considered therein,—its internal form, and its external form. Its *internal* form is union to Jesus Christ by saving grace; its *external* form and constitution is according to the law of the gospel, and its power: and this cannot be continued without the continued ministration of the Spirit of God in and with his church. To suppose the internal form, (that we may have union with Christ, or saving grace) without the effectual work of the Spirit, is at once to blot out all. Therefore, if God should cease to communicate the Spirit, as to an internal, saving work upon the hearts of the elect, the church would cease as to its internal form. No church would have a relation unto Jesus Christ as the mystical head, if God should cease to communicate the Spirit as to gifts. For the outward administration and form of the church, whatever order you bring into it, cannot be accounted a church of Christ, unless there be the presence of Christ in it. And no man can make confession "that Jesus Christ is the Lord, but by the Holy Ghost," 1 Cor. xii. 3. You can make no profession, continue no dispensation of ordinances, or any thing that is acceptable unto God, without the Holy Ghost. The sum of all you do this day is, your acknowledging Jesus Christ to be the Lord,—that you are in subjection unto his authority, that you are in the observation of his appointments, and that you recommend your consciences unto him who is "your Lord and your God." But you must have the Spirit of God and his presence, in order to this. The Holy Ghost is promised and given for the continuance and preservation of a church here below, and therein for the accomplishment of this promise which God hath made to us, to continue with the church to the end of all things. And *if he should cease* as to either of his operations,—either in working internal saving grace, or spiritual abilities for gospel administrations,—*the church must cease,* both in the internal and external form and power of it.

Having laid this foundation, I come, in the next place,—

Sixthly. To some particular *proof* of the proposition,—namely, that the Holy Ghost thus promised, thus sent, thus given, doth furnish the ministers of the gospel, according to his mind, with spiritual abilities in the discharge of their work; and without it they are no way fitted for nor able to it,—no way accepted with Christ in what they do, nor can give any faithful account of what they undertake. It is that which the Lord Jesus Christ intends to declare unto us,

Matt. xxv. 14–30. You have an account there given of the continuance of the church, the kingdom of Christ, in the world to the end of it. The great Lord is gone away, and intends to return again at the end of the world; in the meantime, he hath appointed servants to take care of the administration of the affairs of his house and kingdom: and for this end he gives them talents that they may trade with. He gives them variously, as he pleases;—to one, five; to another, two; and to another, but one; and he provides work for all their talents. Some men have grown so rich in the world that they care not to employ their stock; but it must not be so with us. We shall have trade for all our talents. None have so little but they may trade. He that had but one might have traded, as well as he that had five; and been as well accepted. It is agreed by all, that they are spiritual abilities that Christ gives his servants to trade with in the administration of gospel ordinances. And these three things are plainly held forth in the parable:—1. That wherever Jesus Christ calls and appoints a minister in his house, for the building work of it, he gives him spiritual abilities to do that work by the Holy Ghost. He set none at work in his house, when he went away, but he gave them talents. 2. For men to take upon them to serve Christ as officers in the work of his house, who have received none of these spiritual abilities to work with, is a high presumption, and casts reflection of dishonour on Jesus Christ; as if he called to work and gave no strength; as though he called to trade, and gave no stock; or required spiritual duties, and gave no spiritual abilities. Christ will say to such at the last day, "How came ye in hither?" 3. This is plain in the parable, also, that those who have received talents, or spiritual gifts and abilities of the Holy Ghost, they are to trade with them. And I do not know a warning that I judge more necessary to be given those who are called this day, than to charge them not to trade too much with their natural gifts, and abilities, and learning. These are talents in their kind; but it is the Spirit must manage all that learning they have, or it will prejudice them and you also. *I have known some good men have been so addicted to their study, that they have thought the last day of the week sufficient to prepare for their ministry, though they employ all the rest of the week in other studies.* But your great business is, to trade with your *spiritual* abilities.

There is another testimony given to this (to name one or two among many), in Rom. xii. 4–8, "For as we have many members in one body, and all members have not the same office; so we, being many, are one body in Christ, and every one members one of another. Having then gifts, differing according to the grace that is given to us, whether prophecy, let us prophesy according to the proportion of faith; or ministry, let us wait on our ministering; or he that teacheth, on teaching; or he that exhorteth, on exhortation," etc. It is not to my present concern whether offices or duties are intended in this place; but three things are plain to me in this text:—1. That this discourse and direction doth concern the ordinary state of the church in all ages. I profess to you I had rather a thousand times be of their opinion, bad as it is, who say that all church-state is ceased, than that there may be a church-state when these gifts and graces are not. If I did not see these graces and gifts continued to some, to keep up the ordinances of the church in some measure, I should believe it had ceased. 2. That gifts are the foundation of all church work, whether it be in office or out of office. "Having therefore gifts, let us," saith the apostle, do so and so. If there be no spiritual gifts, there is no spiritual work. Spiritual gifts are the foundation of office, which is the foundation of work in the church, and of all gospel administrations in a special manner, according to the gifts received. Truly, it may be you may think it lost labour to prove this; but there is nothing more despised or reproached in this world than this one apprehension, that there are spiritual gifts given unto persons, to enable them to perform all gospel administrations. 3. That not only the discharge of duty and work depends on the administration of gifts, but the measure of work depends upon the measure of gifts; it is according to the measure every one hath received: and there are many *measures*. As long as there is any measure of spiritual gifts, let it not be despised among you. The gifts of the Holy Ghost are not only for work, but, I say, for the measure of work, Eph. iv. 8–13. All these spiritual gifts the Holy Ghost doth bestow, to enable persons to perform their work.

Seventhly. As *spiritual gifts* are bestowed unto this end, so they are *necessary* for it. There can be no gospel administration without spiritual gifts; the ministration of the gospel being the ministration of the Spirit, and all gospel ministrations are spiritual ministrations. The truth is, one reason why they are called so, and are so, is, because they are no way to be administered to the glory of Christ but by the aid and help of these spiritual gifts. If the Lord Jesus Christ had appointed carnal ordinances, such as are suited to the reason and strength of a man, there had been no need for him to promise the assistance of the Spirit. The spirit of a man knows the things of a man, 1 Cor. ii. 11. All the things within the compass of a man, the spirit of a man will find them out, and give strength for the performance of them. Saith Christ, John vi. 63, "'My words, they are spirit,' and all my offices and ordinances are spiritual;'"—and thus there is a necessity of spiritual gifts for their administration: so that *spiritual gifts and spiritual administrations live and die together*. And the way whereby the world lost the spiritual ministrations of the gospel, was by the neglect and contempt of spiritual gifts; whereby alone they can be performed. This was the ground of the apostasy of the primitive church;—they grew weary of spiritual ministrations. It is the most difficult and laborious ministry. Men's hearts waxing carnal, they grew weary of spiritual things; they did not care to wait upon Christ for supplies of grace and the gifts of the Spirit; for these gifts are not grace, and in truth will flourish long in no other soil but where there is grace. As we should not have such a product of sin were it not for original corruption, whence it grows; so flourishing gifts will not long grow but in *the soil of the Spirit.* How many persons with gifts have flourished for a while, and then have withered, because they were planted in no good soil! It will be drudgery, for any man to keep up spiritual gifts where they have not a spiritual soil to grow in. The world grew weary of gospel ministrations, and would not keep up *that way.* What then? They found out imaginations suited to their inclinations; they will have prayer-books to read, ceremonies to perform, and a number of inventions to keep up a form of worship without those spiritual gifts. We have an instance in the church of Rome. What various extravagant things they have done to make an outward show, when they had lost spiritual gifts! All forms of worship are nothing but to keep an outward appearance. They did not like to retain these gifts in their minds, whereby alone spiritual worship is to be administered. The principle of the apostasy of all churches in the world is, from a weariness of serving God by the aid and assistance of the Spirit.

Eighthly. That there is a communication of spiritual gifts in all gospel ordinances, we plead *experience.* We know how this is derided by profane scoffers; but we plead the experience of those who are humble and holy, and have a spiritual acquaintance with these things. I hope I may plead against the world the experience of this congregation. Have you had no experience of those ministrations? Have you never found in the administrations of those whom God hath called to go before you, evidences of the presence of Christ by his Spirit, in the communication of gifts to them, to make them effectual to your edification and consolation? Have you not had a *proof of the Spirit of Christ speaking in them?* 2 Cor. xiii. 3.

It is intolerable presumption, for men to think of carrying on gospel administrations without the supplies of the Spirit; as you who are God's people can testify. And there is no congregation of Christ but can bear testimony to it, that " the Spirit divides to every man as he will;"—gives out as he pleases of his assistance. Let men, therefore, pretend never so much that they are able to be ministers of the New Testament, without any of those aids and assistances whereof we have been discoursing; let them please themselves with the applause they may receive from persons unacquainted with the mystery and glory of these things; let them despise and condemn whatever is testified to the contrary;—it is certain, where the gifts of the Spirit of God, as to the gospel ministrations of the church, are lost or neglected, Christ is so also, the Spirit of God is so also, and all the benefits of the gospel will be so too.

I have but one word to add, and that is of *exhortation,* unto those whom Christ hath called unto the work of the ministry, and whom you have called this day. I told you, at the beginning, I would not give them *instruction,*—but I may give them a word of *exhortation;* and that is, to attend unto the ministry whereunto God hath called them upon this foundation. And there are three motives I shall give them unto the work:—

First. It is *the most difficult ministration* of any that a person can be called unto;—as it is great, so it is difficult. Any way of administration is easy in comparison of this of spiritual gifts; easy to flesh and blood. What an easy ministration, with all their altars and services, hath the church of Rome provided for their ministers! so to read, and so to sing, come as they will, prepared or not prepared, having hearts and minds filled with what they will;—this is a ministry for them easier than any trade; and in this their natural endowments and abilities are employed. But if we intend the ministers by the gifts received from the Holy Ghost, the matter and root wherein alone they will grow must be carefully preserved. If grace decays in our hearts, a ministry in gifts will grow burdensome and unpleasing to ourselves, as well as useless to the congregation. We must look well unto the soil, or it will be of no advantage that we have this ministry committed to us. It is required there be no unuseful ministers. Hand and heart must be always filled with the work: "Meditate on these things," 1 Tim. iv. 15. If you have undertaken the work of the ministry, you must be meditating on it. Unless you are in these things continually, you will not make faithful dispensers of the word. A man may preach a very good sermon, who is otherwise himself; but he will never make *a good minister of Jesus Christ,* whose heart and mind is not always in the work. Spiritual gifts will require continual ruminating on the things of the gospel in our minds; which makes it a difficult ministry, that our hearts and minds may be cast into the mould and form of those things which we are to deliver to others. And it is surprising how a little necessary diversion will unfit the mind for this work.

Secondly. As it is a very difficult work to carry on to a right improvement of it, so it is *a glorious work,* let the world deride it as they will. The great design of the apostle, in 2 Cor. iii., is to show it is much more glorious than the old ministration was. Really, that was a very glorious ministration; but this ministry that is committed to us hath more glory in it, being "the ministration of the Spirit," whereby souls are converted by the power of grace, and holy converse with God kept up. It is much more glorious than beholding the high priest in Solomon's temple; being under the eye of the holy God, who is judge of these ministerial gifts: therefore do not divert from them by any means.

Thirdly. It is the *only* ministry that is indeed effectual unto the edification and building up of the church, Eph. iv. 8, etc. This is the great end for which gospel ministers are appointed,—"Till all are brought," by their ministry, "to the measure of the stature of the fulness of Christ." The Lord prosper it in your hands!

Give me leave to speak one word unto you that are *the church:*—Know what you are to do, in reference unto those you have called and made officers this day. Pray unto God for a fresh communication of gifts unto them;—they are capable of it. It is a renewed act of grace that prepares and opens the soul for receiving new communications of God's grace, for the administration of the holy things of Christ in the congregation. Pray much for them to that end and purpose.

SERMON V.[1]

"And I will give you pastors according to my heart, which shall feed you with knowledge and understanding."—JER. iii. 15.

ALL the names of the officers of the church under the New Testament have a double signification,—a *general* and more large signification, and a *special* signification. As, for instance, διάκονος, a "deacon," hath a general signification; it signifies any minister or servant: and it hath a special signification, when it denotes that *peculiar officer* which was instituted in the church to take care of the poor. And so the name of *a pastor* hath a more general and a more special signification. In general, it signifies any teacher or officer in the church, ordinary or extraordinary; in special, it signifies that peculiar officer in the church which, as such, is distinguished from a teacher, "He gave some to be pastors and teachers," Eph. iv. 11; for there is a distinction between pastor and teacher, *not as to degree, but as to order.* I do not use the distinction in the sense of those who make bishops and presbyters differ in degree, but not in order; but

[1] This sermon was preached at an ordination, September 8, 1682.

it is a distinction as to that beautiful order which Christ hath instituted in his church. Christ hath instituted a beautiful order in his church, if it were discovered and improved. And I have wished sometimes I could live to see it; but I do not think I shall. Yet this I would recommend to my brethren as the way to discover the order of Christ in the church:—there is no way to discover it but by the harmony that there is between gifts, office, and edification. The original of all church order and rule is in gifts; the exercise of those gifts is by office; the end of all those gifts and offices is, edification.

Now, I believe I can demonstrate that all ordinary spiritual gifts that Christ hath given to his church, are reducible to four heads: and all of them are for the exercise of these gifts; for they must all be exercised distinctly. Herein you will find out the beautiful order of Christ in the church, and not else. I say, all gifts may be reduced to four heads. The one head of these gifts is to be exercised by the *pastor;* one head by the *teacher;* one by the *ruler;* and one by the *deacon:* and all these gifts, exercised by all these officers, answer all ends for the edification of the church. For it is a vain opinion, that the rule and conduct of Christ's church is either in one or in all. There is nothing in what I have declared but what is the design of the apostle in Rom. xii. 6–8. Let us study that harmony more, and we shall find more of the beauty and glory of it.

I shall speak of those pastors mentioned here in the text; and I shall speak of them in general, as all teaching officers in the church,—which is the general signification of the word. And all that I shall speak of them is, to remind myself, and my brethren, and you, of somewhat of the duty of such a pastor;—what is incumbent on him,—what is expected from him. Now, I do not design to go through all the necessary duties of a pastor or teacher; I only design to give some instances.

First. The duty of such an officer of the church,[1]—a pastor, teacher, elder of the church,—is that mentioned in the text,—"to feed the church with knowledge and understanding." This feeding is by preaching of the gospel. He is no pastor who doth not feed his flock. It belongs essentially to the office; and that not now and then (according to the figure and image that is set up of the ministry in the world,—a dead idol) as occasion serves. But the apostle saith, Acts vi. 4, "We will give ourselves continually to the word." It is to "labour in the word and doctrine," 1 Tim. v. 17;—to make all things subservient to this work of preaching and instructing the church; to do it in that frame the apostle mentions in Col. i. 28. He speaks of

[1] It is proper to inform the reader, that several things in this sermon are to be found in Dr Owen's "True Nature of a Gospel Church," chap. v.

his preaching, and the design of his preaching: "Whom we preach, warning every man, and teaching every man in all wisdom; that we may present every man perfect in Christ Jesus." How doth he do it? Verse 29, "Whereunto I also labour, striving according to his working, which worketh in me mightily." There is not one word in our translation that answers the emphasis of the original words,—"Whereunto I labour,"—Εἰς ὃ καὶ κοπιῶ. Κοπιῶ is to labour with diligence and intention, with weariness and industry. "I labour 'usque ad fatigationem'—to the spending of myself. Striving (ἀγωνιζόμενος),—striving as a man that runs in a race, or striving as a man that wrestles for victory,"—as men did in their public contests. And how? Κατὰ τὴν ἐνέργειαν αὐτοῦ,—"According to the effectual in-working, or inward operation, of him (ἐνεργουμένην ἐν ἐμοί) who does effectually work in me." We cannot reach the emphasis by any words in our language. And how is all this? Ἐν δυνάμει,—"With mighty power." Here is the frame of the apostle's spirit (it should give dread to us in the consideration of it): "I labour diligently, I strive as in a race, I wrestle for victory,—by the mighty in-working power of Christ working in me; and that with great and exceeding power."

What I shall do is, to show you, in some instances, what is required unto this work of teaching or of feeding the congregation with knowledge and understanding, in this duty of preaching the word:—

1. There is *spiritual wisdom* in understanding the mysteries of the gospel, that we may be able to declare the whole counsel of God, and the riches and treasures of the grace of Christ, unto the souls of men. See Acts xx. 27; 1 Cor. ii. 1–4; Eph. iii. 7–9. Many in the church of God were, in those days of light, growing and thriving; they had a great insight into spiritual things, and into the mysteries of the gospel. The apostle prays that they might all have it, Eph. i. 17, 18, "That the God of our Lord Jesus Christ, the Father of glory, may give unto you the spirit of wisdom and revelation in the knowledge of him: the eyes of your understanding being enlightened; that ye may know what is the hope of his calling, and what the riches of the glory of his inheritance in the saints."

Really it is no easy thing for ministers to instruct to such kind of duties. If there be not some degree of eminency in themselves, how shall we lead on such persons as these to perfection? We must labour ourselves to have a thorough knowledge of these mysteries, or we shall be useless to a great part of the church. There is spiritual wisdom and understanding in the mysteries of the gospel required hereunto.

2. *Authority* is required. What is authority in a preaching ministry? It is a consequent of unction, and not of office. The scribes had an outward call to teach in the church; but they had no unction, no

anointing, that could evidence they had the Holy Ghost in his gifts and graces. Christ had no outward call; but he had an unction,—he had a full unction of the Holy Ghost in his gifts and graces, for the preaching of the gospel. Hereon there was a controversy about his authority. The scribes say unto him, Mark xi. 28, "By what authority doest thou these things? and who gave thee this authority?" The Holy Ghost determines the matter, Matt. vii. 29, "He preached as one having authority, and not as the scribes." They had the authority of office, but not of unction; Christ only had that. And preaching in the demonstration of the Spirit, which men quarrel so much about, is nothing less than the evidence in preaching of unction, in the communication of gifts and grace unto them, for the discharge of their office: for it is a vain thing for men to assume and personate authority. So much evidence as they have of unction from God in gifts and grace, so much authority they have, and no more, in preaching: and let every one, then, keep within his bounds.

3. Another thing required hereunto is, *experience* of the power of the things we preach to others. I think, truly, *that no man preaches that sermon well to others that doth not first preach it to his own heart.* He who doth not feed on, and digest, and thrive by, what he prepares for his people, he may give them poison, as far as he knows; for, unless he finds the power of it in his own heart, he cannot have any ground of confidence that it will have power in the hearts of others. *It is an easier thing to bring our heads to preach than our hearts to preach.* To bring our heads to preach, is but to fill our minds and memories with some notions of truth, of our own or other men, and speak them out to give satisfaction to ourselves and others: this is very easy. But to bring our hearts to preach, is to be transformed into the power of these truths; or to find the power of them, both before, in fashioning our minds and hearts, and in delivering of them, that we may have benefit; and to be acted with zeal for God and compassion to the souls of men. A man may preach every day in the week, and not have his heart engaged once. This hath lost us powerful preaching in the world, and set up, instead of it, quaint orations; for such men never seek after experience in their own hearts: and so it is come to pass, that some men's preaching, and some men's not preaching, have lost us the power of what we call the ministry; that though there be twenty or thirty thousand in orders, yet the nation perishes for want of knowledge, and is overwhelmed in all manner of sins, and not delivered from them unto this day.

4. *Skill* to divide the word aright. This skill to divide the word aright, is *practical wisdom* in considering the word of God,—to take out not only that which is substantial food for the souls of men, but what is meet food for them to whom we preach. And that,—

5. Requires *the knowledge* and consideration of the state of our flocks. He who hath not the state of his flock continually in his eye, and in his mind, in his work of preaching, fights uncertainly, as a man beating the air. If he doth not consider what is the state of his flock, with reference to temptations, in reference to their light or to their darkness, to their growth or to their decays, to their flourishing or to their withering, to the measure of their knowledge and attainments;—he who doth not duly consider these things, never preaches aright unto them.

6. There is required, too, that we be acted by *zeal* for the glory of God, and compassion to the souls of men.

Having spoken these few plain words, I may say, "Who is sufficient for these things?" There is required that spiritual wisdom which is necessary to understand the mysteries of the gospel, able to instruct and lead on to perfection the most grown in our congregations;—that authority which proceeds from unction, and is an evidence of an anointing with the graces and gifts of the Spirit; which alone gives authority in preaching;—that experience which conforms our whole souls into every sermon we preach, so as to feel the truth in the power of it;—that skill whereby to divide the word aright, etc. Hence we see we have great need to pray for ourselves, and that you should pray for us. Pray for your ministers. This, then, is the first duty required of gospel ministers.

Secondly. Another duty required is, *continual prayer* for the churches over which Christ hath made them overseers. I have not time to confirm these things by particular testimonies: you know how often the apostle expresses it of himself, and enjoins it unto others, continually to pray for the flock.

I will name four reasons why we ought to do so, and four things we ought to pray for:—

1. My first reason is,—because I believe that no man can have *any evidence* in his own soul that he doth conscientiously perform any ministerial duty towards his flock, who doth not *continually pray for them.* Let him preach as much as he will, visit as much as he will, speak as much as he will, unless God doth keep up in him *a spirit of prayer* in his closet and family for them, he can have no evidence that he doth perform any other ministerial duty in a due manner, or that what he doth is accepted with God. I speak to them who are wise, and understand these things.

2. This is the way whereby we may *bless* our congregations.

Authoritative blessing, as far as I know, is taken from us. There is only that which is euctical and declarative left to us. Pronouncing the blessing is only euctical[1] and declarative, and not authorita-

[1] *Euctical* (εὔχομαι, to desire earnestly, or to pray), expressive of desire.—Ed.

tive. Now there is no way whereby we can bless our flock by institution, but by *a continual praying* for a blessing upon them.

3. If men are but as they used to be, I do not believe any minister, any pastor in the world, can keep up a due love to his church, who doth not pray for them. He will meet with so many provocations, imprudences, and miscarriages, that nothing can keep up his heart with inflamed love towards them, but by praying for them continually. That will conquer all prejudices,—if he continues so doing. And,—

4. My last reason is this,—in our prayers for our people, *God will teach us what we shall preach* unto them. We cannot pray for them, but we must think on what it is we pray for, and that is the consideration of their condition; and therein God teaches the ministers of the gospel. If it be so with them, this is that they should teach them. The more we pray for our people, the better shall we be instructed what to preach to them. The apostles, to take us off from all other occasions, "gave themselves to prayer and the word," Acts. vi. 4. Prayer is in the first place. It is not personal, but ministerial prayer for the church, and the progress of the gospel.

What shall we pray for?

1. For *the success of the word* that we preach unto them. This falls in with the light of nature. We are to pray for the success of the word unto all the ends of it; and that is, for all the ends of living unto God,—for direction in duty, for instruction in the truth, for growth in grace, for all things whereby we may come to the enjoyment of God. We should pray that all these ends may be accomplished in our congregations, in the dispensation of the word, or else we sow seed at random, which will not succeed merely by our sowing; for let the husbandman break up the fallow ground, and harrow it, and cast in the seed,—unless showers come, he will have no crop; in like manner, after we have cast the seed of the gospel, though the hearts of men are prepared in some measure, unless there come the showers of the Spirit upon them, there will be no profiting. Therefore, let us pray that a blessing might be upon the word. The ministers of the word preach, and would be accepted with the people; take this "arcanum," [the secret] of it,—pray over it; and it is the only way to have it accepted in the hearts of the people: follow it on with prayer.

2. We are to pray *for the presence of Christ* in all our assemblies; for this is that whereon depends all the efficacy of the ordinances of the gospel. Christ hath given us many promises of it, and we are to act in faith concerning it, and to pray in faith for it in our assemblies; which is a great ministerial duty: and if we do it not, we are ignorant of our duty, and are willing to labour in the fire, where all must

perish; we fight at hazard, for all the efficacy of the ordinances of preaching and praying doth not depend upon any thing in ourselves,—on our gifts, notions, parts, fervency,—but it depends only upon the presence of Christ. Make this your business, to pray mightily for it in the congregation, to make all these effectual.

3. Our prayers should be with respect unto *the state and condition* of the church. It is supposed he that is a minister is satisfied he hath some measure of understanding and knowledge in the mysteries of the gospel; that he is able to conduct the best of the congregation unto salvation; that he knows their measure, their weakness, and their temptations; that he knows the times and seasons in which they are exercised and exposed, whether times of adversity or prosperity; and, as far as possible, knows how it is with their persons. And we ought to suit our prayers according to all we know concerning them, and be satisfied in it that Christ himself will come in to recover them who are fallen, to establish them who stand, to heal them who do backslide, to strengthen them who are tempted, to encourage them who are running and pressing forward to perfection, to relieve them who are disconsolate and in the dark: and we have of all these sorts in our churches. And our prayers should be for a communication of supplies unto them continually, in all these cases.

Thirdly. It is incumbent on men who are pastors and teachers of churches, *to preserve the truth* and doctrine of the gospel, that is committed to the church,—to keep it entire, and defend it against all opposition. See the weighty words wherewith the apostle gives this in charge unto Timothy, 1 Tim. vi. 20, " O Timothy, keep that which is committed to thy trust;" and 2 Tim. i. 14, " That good thing" (τὴν καλὴν παρακαταθήκην,—that good depositum, that good treasure) "that is committed to thee keep by the Holy Ghost, which dwelleth in us." This charge is given to all of us who are ministers, " *Keep the truth*, that good, that blessed thing." " It is," saith the apostle, " the glorious gospel of the blessed God, which was committed to my trust," 1 Tim. i. 11. And it is committed to *all* our trust; and we are to keep it against all opposition. The church is the ground and pillar of truth, to hold up and declare the truth, in and by its ministers. But is that all? No; the church " is like the tower of David builded for an armoury, whereon there hang a thousand bucklers, all shields of mighty men," Cant. iv. 4. The ministers of the gospel are shields and bucklers to defend the truth against all adversaries and opposers. The church hath had thousands of bucklers and shields of mighty men, or else the truth had been lost. They are not only to *declare* it in the preaching of the gospel; but to *defend* and preserve it against all opposition,—to hold up the shield and buckler of faith against all opposers.

But what is *required hereunto?*

1. There is required a *clear apprehension* in ourselves of those doctrines and truths which we are so to defend. Truth may be lost by weakness as well as by wickedness: if we have not a full apprehension of the truth, and that upon its own proper grounds and principles, we shall never be able to defend it. This is to be attained by all ways and means,—by the use, especially, of diligent prayer and study,—so that we may be able to stop the mouth of gainsayers.

2. There is required *love of the truth.* We shall never contend earnestly for the truth, we shall never "buy it and not sell it," whatever we know of it, unless our love and value of it arise from a sense and experience of it in our own souls. I fear there is much loss of truth, not for want of light, knowledge, and ability, but *for want of love.*

I have the advantage of most here present in this, that I know the contest we had for the truths of the gospel before our troubles began, and was an early person engaged in them; and knew those godly ministers that did contend for them as for their lives and souls, and that all the opposition that was made against them was never able to discourage them. What were these doctrines?—the doctrines of eternal predestination, effectual conversion to God, and the obduration of wicked reprobates by the providence of God. These truths are not lost for want of skill, but for want of love. We scarce hear one word of them; we are almost ashamed to mention them in the church; and he that doth it will be sure to expose himself to public obloquy and scorn: but we must not be ashamed of truth. Formerly we could not meet with a godly minister, but the error of Arminianism was looked upon by him as the ruin and poison of the souls of men: such did tremble at it,—wrote and disputed against it. But now it is not so; the doctrine of the gospel is owned still, though little taken notice of by some among ourselves, the love of it being greatly decayed,—the sense and the power of it almost lost. But we have got no ground by it; we are not more holy, more fruitful, than we were in the preaching those doctrines, and attending diligently unto them.

3. Let us take heed in ourselves of any inclination to *novel opinions,* especially in, or about, or against such points of faith as those wherein they who are gone before us and are fallen asleep found life, comfort, and power. Who would have thought that we should have come to an indifferency as to the doctrine of justification, and quarrel and dispute about the interest of works in justification; about general redemption, which takes off the efficacy of the redeeming work of Christ; and about the perseverance of the saints; when these were the soul and life of them who are gone before us, who found the power and comfort of them? We shall not maintain these truths,

unless we find the same comfort in them as they did. I have lived to see great alterations in the godly ministers of the nation, both as to zeal for and value of those important truths that were as the life of the Reformation; and the doctrine of free-will condemned in a prayer, bound up in the end of your Bibles. But now it is grown an indifferent thing; and the horrible corruptions we suffer to be introduced in the doctrine of justification have weakened all the vitals of religion. Let us, for the remainder of our days, " buy the truth, and sell it not;" and let us be zealous and watchful over any thing that should arise in our congregations.

Bring one man into the congregation who hath a by-opinion, and he shall make more stir about it than all the rest of the congregation in building up one another in their most holy faith. Take heed lest there be men arising from ourselves speaking perverse things; which is to make way for grievous wolves to break in and tear and rend the flock.

4. There is *skill and ability* required hereunto, to discover and be able to oppose and confound the cunning sophistry of the adversaries. Great prayer, watchfulness, and diligence are required, that we may be able to attend unto these things. And those who are less skilled may do well to advise with those who are more exercised in them, to give them help and assistance.

Lastly. I shall mention one duty more that is required of pastors and teachers in the church; and that is,—that *we labour diligently for the conversion of souls.* This work is committed to them. I should not mention this, but to rectify a mistake in some. The end of all particular churches is, the calling and edification of the catholic church. Christ hath not appointed his ministers to look unto themselves only; they are to be the means of calling and gathering the elect in all ages: and this they principally are to do by their ministry. I confess there are other outward ways and means whereby men have been, and may be, converted. I find, by long observation, that common light, in conjunction with afflictions, do begin the conversion of many, without this or that special word: and persons may be converted to God by religious conference. There may be many *occasional* conversions wrought by the instrumentality of men who have real spiritual gifts for the dispensation of the word, and are occasionally called thereunto. But principally this work is committed unto the pastors of churches, for the conversion of souls. Take this observation,—*the first object* of the word is *the world. Our work* is the same with the apostles'; the *method* directly contrary. The apostles had a work committed to them, and this was their method:—*The first work* committed to the apostles was the convincing and converting sinners to Christ among Jews and Gentiles,—to preach the gospel, to convert infidels;—this they accounted their chief work. Paul made nothing of administering the ordinance of baptism, in comparison of it. "Christ sent me not," saith he, "to baptize, but to preach the gospel," 1 Cor. i. 17. In comparison, I say, preaching was their chief work. And then, *their second work* was to teach those [who were] disciples to do and observe whatever Christ commanded them, and to bring them into church order. This was their method. Now the same work is committed unto the pastors of churches; but in a contrary method. The first object of our ministry is the church, —to build up and edify the church. But what then? Is the other part of the work taken away, that they should not preach to convert souls. God forbid. There be several ways whereby they who are pastors of churches do preach to the conversion of souls:—1. When other persons that are unconverted do come where they are preaching, to their own congregations (whereof we have experience every day), they are there converted to God by the pastoral discharge of their duty. "No," say some; "they preach to the church as *ministers*,—to others only as *spiritually gifted*." But no man can make this distinction in his own conscience. Suppose there be five hundred in this place, and a hundred of this church, can you make the distinction, that I am preaching in a *double* capacity,—to some as a minister, and to others not as a minister? Neither rule, nor reason, nor natural light, expresses any thing to that purpose. We preach *as ministers* to those to whom we preach, for the conversion of their souls 2. Ministers may preach for the conversion of souls, when they preach elsewhere occasionally. They preach as ministers wherever they preach. I know *the indelible character*[1] is a figment; but the pastor's office is not such a thing as men may leave at home when they go abroad. It is not in a minister's own power, unless lawfully dismissed or deposed, to hinder him from preaching as a minister. And it is the duty of particular churches (one end of their institution being the calling and gathering the catholic church) to part with their officers for a season, when called to preach in other places for the

[1] The "indelible character" is the dogma of the church of Rome;—that a man ordained to be a priest within its pale never can lose his priestly character; and though he even cease to be a Christian, cannot cease to be a Christian bishop, priest, or deacon, if he has previously held any of these offices in the church. The dogma can be traced no farther back than the days of the schoolmen. The Council of Nice decreed that certain bishops and presbyters, who had been ordained by Miletius, a deposed bishop, should be re-ordained before they could exercise their office. Dr Campbell, in his "Lectures on Ecclesiastical History," reviews at some length the discussions on the "indelible character." Speaking of those who argued for the unreiterable sacraments, to which ordination, according to the church of Rome, belongs, he remarks (lecture xi.), "The whole of what they agreed in amounts to this,—something, they know not what, is imprinted, they know not how, on something in the soul of the recipient, they know not where,— which never can be deleted."—ED.

converting souls to Christ. We had a glorious ministry in the last age,—wonderful instruments for the conversion of souls. Did they convert them *as gifted men*, and not *as ministers?* God forbid. I say, it may be done by them who have received gifts, and not [been] called to office; but I know no ground any man hath to give up himself to the constant exercise of ministerial gifts, and not say to the Lord in prayer, "Lord, here am I; send me."

Had I time and strength, I should tell you of the duty of pastors and teachers in administering of the seals, and what is required thereunto; and their duty in directing and comforting the consciences of all sorts of believers;—what prudence, purity, condescension, and patience are required in it, as a great part of our ministerial duty.

I should show you, also, their duty in the rule of the church. Not that ever Christ intended to commit the rule of the church to them alone,—to take them off from that great and important duty of preaching the gospel; but as time and occasions will allow them, to attend to the rule of the church.

And lastly, in exemplary conversation, and in assembling with other churches of their order, for the managing church communion.

"Who is sufficient for these things?" Pray, pray for us; and God strengthen us, and our brother, who hath been called this day to the work! It may not be unuseful to him and me, to be mindful of these things, and to beg the assistance of our brethren

---

SERMON VI.[1]

To the chief Musician upon Shoshannim, for the sons of Korah, Maschil, A Song of loves.

"My heart is inditing a good matter: I speak of the things which I have made touching the King; my tongue is the pen of a ready writer," etc.—Ps. xlv. 1–3.

THE whole Book of Psalms hath a peculiar respect unto Jesus Christ, either directly or in the person of David, who was his greatest personal type, next to Aaron and Melchizedeck; but there are some psalms that are altogether *directly* prophetical of him and of his offices,—namely, the 2d psalm is prophetical of his kingdom; the 16th psalm, of the work of his mediation and obedience to God therein; the 22d, of his priestly office, his sufferings, death, his resurrection, and intercession; the 40th, of his oblation and suffering;

[1] This sermon was preached June 7, 1674, at Stadham.

the 72d, of his kingly and prophetical power and glorious regard unto his people; the 68th, of his glorious exaltation; and this 45th psalm is a prophecy and description of his person, and his kingly office, and of the espousals of him and his church.

The title of the psalm is, " To the chief Musician upon Shoshannim, for the sons of Korah, Maschil, A Song of loves."

" To the chief musician;" so לַמְנַצֵּחַ is generally rendered,—"To him that excels." As נֵצַח signifies eternal, I have sometimes thought it might be as well rendered, " In perpetuam rei memoriam;"—" For an everlasting remembrance." But we may take it in the common acceptation,—that it was recommended unto him that did preside over the rest of the Levites in the worship of God in the temple, by singing on instruments of music.

" Upon Shoshannim." The word signifies *lilies;* whether it was a musical *instrument* or a certain *tune*, we know not, neither do the Jews.

" For the sons of Korah." Who these were we may see, 1 Chron. ix. 19, " The Korahites were over the work of the service, keepers of the gates of the tabernacle," etc. What were they else? Verse 33, " These are the singers, chief of the fathers of the Levites, who remaining in the chambers were free;" for they were employed in the work of singing the praises of God with instruments of music day and night.

David was the first who brought musical instruments into the solemn worship of God; not but that they did occasionally make use of timbrels and cymbals in the praises of God before, but he was the first that brought in a great number of musical instruments into the worship of God. And he speaks expressly, in 1 Chron. xxiii. 5, of praising God with instruments of music, " which," says he, " I made." He did it by the direction of the Spirit of God; otherwise he ought not to have done it: for so it is said, 1 Chron. xxviii. 12, when he had established all the ordinances of the temple,—*the pattern of all that he had by the Spirit.* And verse 19, " All this, said David, the LORD made me understand in writing by his hand upon me, even all the works of this pattern." It was all revealed unto him by the Holy Spirit, without which he could have introduced nothing at all into the worship of God. The Lord prepared him for this service while he was a shepherd; at which time he had attained great skill in singing on musical instruments.

And I cannot but observe, by the way, that it is a great mercy when God will engage the natural faculties and abilities of men, especially wherein they are excellent, in any way of his service. David had got an excellency in this faculty, and God engages it in his service. And those that had skill therein, and were not so engaged, are condemned in the prophet Amos, chap. vi. 5. What were they condemned for? Why, that they would invent *instruments of music like David.* David did it to serve the Lord; and they did it to serve their lusts. Where men have any peculiar faculty or ability, it is an unspeakable mercy to have it engaged for God; for otherwise it will certainly be engaged for the devil: and, to render the mercy more singular, I think it is evident the devil hath got the use and advantage of natural faculties and abilities above what is given up to God.

Again: this was David's special inclination; whence he is called "The sweet psalmist of Israel." The edge of his spirit lay to it. And we may observe, that it is an excellent mercy when the edge of our spirits, in special inclination, is engaged for the service of God. Prov. xxvii. 17, as "iron sharpeneth iron; so a man sharpeneth the countenance of his friend." Every man hath an edge; and there are several ways whereby it is sharpened. There is no man but *cuts* one way or other; and company and society is the great means whereby the edge is sharpened. One cuts to the world, another to pleasures, to lusts; and such company makes him more sharp. It is well when the edge of a man's spirit is set for the things of God, and he has some to sharpen that edge; for that way that a man's edge is set, *that way is he.* He may do something in the worship of God; but if his edge be to the world, that way is he; and if his edge be to lust and pleasure, that way is he. Now, here was David; the special inclination and edge of his spirit was set towards God, and so was employed of God.

There is a general title given to this psalm, "Maschil;" that is, a song to make wise, or to give instruction. They are the things of Christ that, in an especial manner, are suited to give instruction to the church of God.

The special matter of the psalm is, "A Song of loves." And why is it called "loves"? It may be upon three accounts:—1. Because the psalm mentions a *mutual* and *interchangeable* love. It is not only of the love of Christ to his church, nor only of the love of the church unto Christ,—but it is mutual, of the love of Christ to the church, and of the church to Christ; so that it is a song of loves. 2. It may be put in the plural number by way of *eminency,* which is frequent in the Hebrew; "of loves,"—that is, of *the most excellent love,* such as none other is to be compared unto it. 3. It may be called so, because of the *manifold fruits* of that one single love that is between Christ and his church. Though it be but a single love on each hand, yet various are the fruits of it; which will be described in the next verse.

I principally look upon it to be called so in the second sense, because it is more eminent than any other love in the world; the mystical, spiritual love that is between Christ and the church, is the most excellent love.

It is "A Song of loves." I shall not speak unto you of the nature of *songs*. "Let him that is merry," saith James, chap. v. 13 (or in a rejoicing, cheerful frame of heart and spirit), "sing psalms:" so that singing was a means appointed of God whereby men should express their joy in a way of thankfulness.

Thus this title of the psalm will yield us these two observations:—I. That the espousals of Christ and his church, or the *mutual love* that is between Christ and his church, is *a subject-matter for a song of great joy*. II. It is not a song of love, but it is a song of *loves*. I observe from thence, that there is no love like the love of Christ to his church in the day of espousals, and to every believing soul; it hath an eminency in it above all other love whatever.

I. This love of Christ and the church in their espousals is matter of great joy and rejoicing:—

1. It is so *to God himself*. He expresses the frame of his heart therein, Zeph. iii. 17, "He will rejoice over thee with joy; he will rest in his love, he will joy over thee with singing." The union of Christ and a believer (for it is spoken of there), is a matter of unspeakable joy to God himself. Not that God is subject to the like affections with us; but he expresses it to the height in Jer. xxxii. 41, that we may know how the heart of God approves it, "I will rejoice over them to do them good, with my whole heart and with my whole soul:" so that it is a song of loves to God himself. Also in Isa. lxii. 4, 5, "The LORD delighteth in thee, and thy land shall be married. For as a young man marrieth a virgin, so shall thy sons marry thee: and as the bridegroom rejoiceth over the bride, so shall thy God rejoice over thee." Many other places might be given to this purpose.

2. It is matter of joy *to Jesus Christ*. Cant. iii. 11, "Go forth, O ye daughters of Zion, and behold king Solomon with the crown wherewith his mother crowned him in the day of his espousals, and in the day of the gladness of his heart." This Solomon was a type of Christ; and the mother of Christ, that brought forth Christ as to his human nature, was the church: and in the espousals of the church to Christ set a crown upon his head; see Ps. xvi. 6, "The lines," saith Christ, in reference to his church, "are fallen unto me in pleasant places; yea, I have a goodly heritage;"—it is the approbation that Christ gives of his church when he is espoused unto it, in the day of the gladness of his heart.

3. It is matter of joy to *believers themselves*, 1 Pet. i. 8, "In whom, though now ye see him not, yet believing, ye rejoice with joy unspeakable, and full of glory." It is, I say, matter of joy and praise unto them.

Why are the loves of Christ and his church, or the espousals of Christ and a believing soul, matter of such joy as to be the subject of a song of loves to God himself, to Jesus Christ, and to believers?

(1.) Because, on the part of God, it is that wherein the glorious design and *purpose* of his grace is *accomplished,* and his goodness satisfied. God doth all things for "the praise of the glory of his grace," Eph. i. 6. Wherefore, when this grace of God is accomplished, and his goodness satisfied, it is matter of rejoicing unto God. When he had laid the foundation of *the old creation,* and all the sons of God shouted for joy, God himself looked upon all, and, "behold, it was very good;" he approved his whole work: and when he carried on the work of the *new creation,* whereof this I am speaking of is the greatest instance, even the espousal loves between Christ and a believing soul, having accomplished such a work of grace, and power, and goodness as this is, God himself doth approve of it; it is matter of joy unto him.

(2.) It is matter of joy to Jesus Christ, because "he sees of the travail of his soul, and is satisfied." This is that he laboured for, Isa. liii. 11, etc. It was matter of joy to Jacob, when he had obtained Rachel to be his wife, that he had got that he laboured for: "He served for a wife," saith the Holy Ghost, Hos. xii. 12. Why, the Lord Jesus Christ, when he hath united his church to himself (and in proportion, any believing soul), he hath that which he hath laboured for,—he sees of the travail of his soul. It cost him prayers and tears, blood and death; but now he sees what it is come unto: it hath produced this bride for him, or believing souls to be united to him; and he is satisfied. He fulfilled a hard service; but it was for his bride, in whom his soul delighted,—as he does in every believing soul, when he hath made them comely through his comeliness, or in and through the righteousness he puts upon them.

(3.) It is certainly matter of joy to all believers themselves, because *it instates them in those new relations,* and in that condition, which they, for their part, never ought to have expected or looked for, as to any thing that was in themselves. And therefore the prophet Isaiah, chap. liv. 5, calls upon the church to rejoice exceedingly, because "thy Maker is thine husband; the LORD of hosts is his name; and thy Redeemer the Holy One of Israel; The God of the whole earth shall he be called." All grace and privilege, all mercy, pardon, every thing else we enjoy in this world, and hope for in another, depends upon this, of relation unto Jesus Christ; therefore, certainly it is matter of joy and rejoicing to believers.

That which we may learn from hence, by way of *use,* is,—

1. The *infinite wisdom,* goodness, and condescension of God, in *disposing the way* of saving poor sinners so as that it shall be matter

of joy and rejoicing to him, to Jesus Christ, and to believers themselves. It was infinite wisdom and grace, that God would dispose any way for the salvation of his creatures. He gave out a way to Adam, whereby (by perfect obedience) he might have attained life, immortality, and glory. That was not a way that did issue in such great joy to God, to Christ, or to ourselves, as this doth, where God is glorified, Christ satisfied, and believers themselves are surprised. We were poor, desolate, forlorn, lost creatures; and that God should bring us into a way of saving us, so as that the heart of God and Christ, and our own hearts, should rejoice in it;—this calls for our admiration. I know it is hard for us to believe it; yet I know it is true, that God himself is rejoiced, and Christ rejoices in the taking of any one soul into espousals with himself. And, which may add more, all the angels in heaven rejoice too, Luke xv. 10, "There is joy in the presence of the angels of God over one sinner that repenteth;" because God is so glorified, and Christ so exalted. God hath put this way of converting and saving sinners into such a channel as will tend to his glory, and the glory of Christ, and so be matter of joy unto them.

2. Let us inquire whether we have found, or do find, this joy *in our own hearts.* Is the remembrance of the closing of our hearts with Christ a song of loves unto us? Truly, if our loves be earnest and intent upon *other* things, we find joy and refreshment *in them;* but are we not dead and cold to the thoughts of this great and excellent advantage, of being *espoused to Christ,* as all believers are? If so, it is but a sad evidence we are truly so espoused. Alas! if a poor beggar, a deformed creature, should be taken into the espousals of a great prince, would she not be sensible of it? We are poor, deformed, woful, sinful, polluted creatures; and for us to be taken into this relation with Jesus Christ!—*where are our hearts?* Why do not we rejoice in the Lord with joy unspeakable, and full of glory? Is it not because Christ hath not our whole hearts? because we are not so entirely with him and for him in our affections as becomes this relation? because the world hath too much hold upon us? Shall God rejoice, and Christ rejoice,—shall it be a song of loves to God and Christ that we are brought into this relation, and these dull hearts of ours be no farther affected with it? We ought to be ashamed to think how little we are concerned in this so great a privilege,—how little lifted up above the world, and alienated from the world; if, indeed, we are partakers of this mercy.

II. The second observation from its being a song of loves, is this,—that there is *no love like* to the love between Christ and the souls of believers. There are flaming loves in some to their lusts,—in others to the world, that even devour them; but yet I will say again, upon ten thousand accounts, there is no love like to the love between Christ and the souls of believers.

Should we go to speak now of the love of Christ, on the one side, it is an ocean,—we cannot fathom it. The best act of our souls towards Christ's love is *admiration*, astonishing admiration, till the heart is quite overwhelmed with it,—till our thoughts and understandings are, as it were, lost; the soul is taken out of itself, and laid in the dust as nothing, to be swallowed up in a holy contemplation of the unspeakable, inconceivable love of Jesus Christ.

I will name three heads of it, that may help us, in this admiration, to see that it is a love that is *inimitable:* the fiery loves of men, after this world and their lusts, are not to be named the same day with it:—

1. Consider it in its *condescension.* Now, I think we shall all confess that this love is inimitable, because nothing but infinite, divine power and wisdom could work such an effect as was the condescension of the Son of God,—out of his love to take our nature upon him, to become flesh as we are; and God never wrought it, nor will, *but in that instance*, to all eternity: and therefore, this love hath the pre-eminence above all other loves whatsoever. In Phil. ii. 6–8, it is there set forth, where he unites those things that are set at an infinite distance of being. He stoops so low, that he saith, Ps. xxii. 6, "I am a worm, and no man;" he comes to the lowest condition mankind can be reduced unto in this condescension: and surely this hath a pre-eminence above all other loves whatsoever.

2. The love of Christ was manifested *in his suffering* in that condition. You know what he suffered, and what he suffered for. He suffered to bear *the guilt* of our sins, so to take away the wrath of God; he suffered to wash away the filth of our sins, so to take away shame and confusion from our souls; he suffered to redeem us from the world, poor captive creatures as we were, that we might be his own: and therefore, God gives us the type of it in the prophet Hosea, chap. iii, by a harlot; and Christ bought us when we were harlots with the world (our hearts going after sin and Satan), that we might be his property. He suffered for us, so as to bear the guilt of our iniquities, that there may be no wrath from God upon us. "I will pay," saith Christ, "what I never took away." "For a good man," it is possible, "some would even dare to die," Rom. v. 7; but saith he, "Here is love, Christ died for us when we were sinners, when we were enemies." "He loved us, and washed us in his own blood," that we may be purified from the filth of our sins; he loved us, and redeemed us out of every kindred and nation in the world. Here lay all misery; —the guilt of sin, that rendered us obnoxious to the curse of God; and the filth of sin, that made us odious to God, and kept us under the

power of the world. This love hath suffered on purpose to redeem us from all this.

3. The care and *tenderness which the Lord Jesus Christ continues* to manifest towards us, now he is in heaven, while we are upon the earth, is *another fruit of this love.* Heb, v. 2, this high priest knows how to "have compassion on the ignorant, and them that are out of the way." Chap. iv. 15, He hath been "touched with the feeling of our infirmities," and "in all points tempted like as we;" and "he ever liveth to make intercession for us." In these things he expresses his love to, and care for, his people.

On the other side, I say, the love of believers to Christ is inexpressible, or beyond all other love whatsoever.

1. In a way *of value.* Matt. xiii. 45, when the merchant-man had found the precious pearl, he sells all he hath to buy it. Believers will part with all they have to obtain Christ; for they prefer him above all. What will they not part with, and what *do they not* part with and deny, for Christ? Whereby you may see it is a love that is transcendent to all other loves.

(1.) They part with their sin, lust, and corruption. There is not a believer in the world but hath naturally as great a love of, and adherence to, sin, lust, and corruption, as the highest debauched person upon the face of the earth; but a believer will part with them all, subdue them all, so that he might win Christ: which manifests it to be a transcendent love. And they that will not do this are not believers. If our hearts are not engaged to the mortifying of all sin, lust, and corruption, as he enables us, we are not married to Christ; for "they that are Christ's have crucified the flesh, with the affections and lusts," Gal. v. 24.

(2.) They will part with their *righteousness* for Christ. This was that the Jews would not give up, that they might obtain justification. They had a righteousness which was according to the law; and, saith the apostle, Rom. x. 3, "They will not submit to the righteousness of God, but go about to establish their own righteousness." All the righteousness which is in the world, that the men of the world value before Christ, while they are engaged in their lusts and pleasures, they will not part with it for Christ;—yea, even when they are wrought off their lusts and pleasures by conviction to some duties, yet they will not part with their own righteousness for Christ. But believers will part with theirs, and count it all as loss and dung.

If corruption be subdued, and righteousness be given up, what remains? Truly,—

(3.) *Self* remains. If a man denies not himself in lawful things, in any thing that will hinder his walking with God and living unto God, which will make him unfaithful in his place or unfruitful, to please God, he is not worthy of him. If he cannot deny his ease, liberty, peace, profit, or pleasure, he is not worthy of Jesus Christ. Now, that love which will carry a man out to deny all ungodliness and lust, to renounce all his own righteousness, to lose all he hath wrought in his own strength, to deny himself upon every instance wherein Christ requires him;—this is a transcendent love, above all other love whatsoever.

2. The love of believers manifests itself also *in suffering for Christ;* and O who can tell what the martyrs endured from love to the Lord Jesus!

So that this psalm, which treats of the espousals of Christ and believers, may well have this title,—" A Song of loves;" it being the most excellent love.

Two things, from hence, are incumbent upon us:—

First. To labour to *get a sense of this love of Christ* upon our hearts. If we are believers, all this love of Christ, who is " King of kings, and Lord of lords," is fixed upon every one of our souls; and it is our great duty to labour to let in a sense of this love of Christ into them. Out of his abundant love and grace, and for no other reason in the world, he loved us when we were strangers,—he reconciled us to himself when we were enemies, and engaged in enmity against him; give him, then, the glory of his sovereign grace with respect to your own souls. And,—

Secondly. Let us *examine ourselves* whether we have this transcendent love to Jesus Christ in our hearts. If we have, it will continually keep us up to the mortification of lust and corruption, to the renouncing of all self-righteousness, to the denying ourselves; and it will make us continually ready for all the service and suffering Christ shall call us unto.

SERMON VII.[1]

" My heart is inditing a good matter: I speak of the things which I have made touching the King; my tongue is the pen of a ready writer. Thou art fairer than the children of men; grace is poured into thy lips: therefore God hath blessed thee for ever. Gird thy sword upon thy thigh, O most Mighty, with thy glory and thy majesty."—Ps. xlv. 1–3.

THIS psalm hath three parts. The title of it is, " A Song of loves," which I have already spoken unto; the preface of it, in the 1st verse; and the song itself, from the 2d verse to the end.

[1] This sermon was preached at Stadham, June 7, 1674.

The 1st verse contains a preface to this song of loves:—" My heart is inditing a good matter: I speak of the things which I have made touching the King; my tongue is the pen of a ready writer."

I shall offer a few things from these words:—

Observe, in general, that he that lays a good foundation makes a good beginning of what he hath to say. It is from his heart. " My heart," saith he, " is inditing." If things do not begin at the heart, whatsoever we do about spiritual things, they are of no value, of no use. We may perform duties,—we may pray, and preach, and hear; but if these things do not spring from the heart (that is, from faith, and love, and delight working in the heart), all is lost. A sacrifice without a heart, a silly dove that has no heart, are things God abhors, Hos. vii. 11.

The heart of the psalmist was in this matter; and if our heart be in it, it will be a duty, in our measure and proportion, good and acceptable with God, as it was with him.

There are in the verse two things:—I. The subject-matter treated of in this song of loves. II. The manner of expressing it.

I. The subject treated of:—1. In general, that it is *a good matter*. It is not a song about vain, empty things; much less about wicked and sinful things, as the songs of the world are; neither is it only about things that are true, but have no goodness in them: but, saith he, " My heart is inditing a good matter."

2. What this good matter is, is declared: " I speak of the things which I have made touching the King." " The subject," saith he, " of this song of mine is the King; it is no ordinary person." It was the name whereby they called the Messiah, " Christ the Lord," under the Old Testament, who is, indeed, " The Lord of lords, and King of kings." " I have set my King upon my holy hill of Zion," Ps. ii. 6. He was principally prophesied of as " a prince, a ruler, a captain; being to deliver the people of God." He is the subject of the song. And it is limited to things touching or concerning him; as if he had said, " It is not for me, it is not for any mortal man, to conceive or express all the glories and excellencies of the great King, Jesus Christ; but," saith he, " *something touching*, something concerning him."

The best we can reach or attain unto in this world, is only something touching Christ. "We cannot yet behold the King in his glory; we cannot see his *uncreated excellencies* or beauties, nor those unspeakable glories of his person, natures, and works, as we shall one day contemplate and behold."

" I speak," saith he, " of the things I have made;" that is, " which I have prepared; I will mention only the things which I have composed concerning Christ."

So that the subject of this song is, in general, " a good matter;" in particular, things touching Christ, and such things as the psalmist, through the inspiration of the Holy Ghost, had composed.

II. There is the *manner* of their delivery, both as to their conception and as to outward expression. Their conception, it was in his heart; as to the outward delivery, it was by his tongue. And there is a peculiarity in both. It is not an ordinary conception of the heart,—it is not a common expression of the tongue. If you will look into the margin of your Bibles, you will find that what we have rendered here, "inditing," in the original signifies "boiling" or "bubbling up." The word refers to the bubbling up of water in a fountain or spring. The heart of the psalmist was so full of these things of Christ, things touching the King, that they did naturally overflow, as water rising out of a spring naturally flows into the stream, without any labour or difficulty. It was no hard thing to him to speak of the things of Christ; his heart was full of them. O that it was thus with us! It is promised it shall be so. In John iv. 14, Christ hath promised to give his people his Spirit, that "shall be in them as a well of water springing up into everlasting life."

"My tongue," saith he, "shall not only express it, but in a peculiar manner; 'my tongue is the pen of a ready writer.'"

"A ready writer,"—one speedy, steady, able to set down any thought or conception whatsoever. When we deal about the things of Christ, there is a peculiar manner required both in the conception of the heart and in the expression of the tongue.

Thus I have given you the sense of the words; and I shall now name some observations from them:—

First. That the things which concern Jesus Christ are a *good matter to believers.* They are not only true,—so as the mind may assent unto them and never be deceived,—but they have that in them which is the object of the soul's delight and valuation, and which the soul of a believer cleaves unto. The truth of it is, here lies the great difference between sincere believers and mere hypocrites:—hypocrites assent unto the doctrine of the gospel, things touching the King, *as true*, but they never embrace them *as good;* their hearts and affections do not *cleave* unto them, as finding a real sweetness, excellency, and suitableness unto their wants in them: for no man esteems that to be good which is not *suitable* unto him.

Jesus Christ, and the things of Christ, are a good matter unto believers; for,—

1. They are very *excellent in themselves.* Col. i. 18, "He hath in all things the pre-eminence." Whatsoever is good in any kind, it all centres in Christ. And what is in him is better than that which was in the state of nature; better than what was in the law; better than what is in self-righteousness; better than life itself: so that,

from their own nature, they are good things. Give me leave to say they are good things, because they are God's best things. As to temporal good things, take a king or a potentate;—his best things are peculiar treasures, gold and silver, and precious stones; but the things which concern Christ are the best things of the kingdom of heaven.

The things which concern God's only begotten Son, and which concern all the wisdom, grace, love, and power the holy God will exercise in the greatest work he ever set his hand to; surely they are good things. When the psalmist saith it is "a good matter," his meaning is, it is *the best matter* in the world.

2. They are a good matter to believers, because they have received the Spirit, whereby *they are able to discern the excellency of them.*

As to others, it is said, "He shall grow up as a tender plant, and as a root out of a dry ground: he hath no form nor comeliness; and when we shall see him, there is no beauty that we should desire him," Isa. liii. 2. Can we see no goodness, no excellency in Christ, in the grace of Christ, in his ways, in his people, why he should be desired? Believers can, 1 Cor. ii. 7–10. The Spirit of God discovers to them the excellent things of Christ, whereby they find them to be good; whereas to strangers from Christ they seem absurd and foolish things, and no way to be desired. Men of carnal wisdom, that have attained to the highest pitch of reason and ability in the world, they can see neither form nor comeliness in Christ, or the things of Christ; but when God opens the things of Christ by the Spirit, then they see that there is a goodness and an excellency in them.

By way of use.—Seeing the things of Christ are good things in themselves, and believers discern their goodness and their excellency; we may do well, then, to inquire whether the things of Christ are good things to us. Then they are good things to us, when we desire them above all other things whatsoever. Phil. iii. 8, "I count all things but loss for the excellency of the knowledge of Christ Jesus my Lord." He could make use of those things he had; but in comparison, his heart did really esteem them all as loss and dung,—when they stood in competition with Christ. And pray let us consider how the psalmist hath here stated it. Saith he, "My heart indites, and my tongue professes." It is easy to profess that the things of Christ are good things, and that we esteem all other things as loss and dung; but do our hearts so esteem them? otherwise we come short of what is here intended by the psalmist. Do our hearts really value the good things of Christ,—things concerning the glory of his person, his love to his church, the excellency of his kingdom and his rule? The things here treated of;—the glory of his person, "Fairer than the children of men;"—the glory of his kingdom, "In thy majesty ride prosperously;" "thy throne O God, is for ever and ever;"

—and his love to his church, "Hearken, O daughter, and consider and incline thine ear, forget also thine own people and thy father's house, so shall the King greatly desire thy beauty:"—do we value these things, I say, in our very hearts, so as to esteem all other things as loss and dung,—that we could freely forego them? Do we find satisfaction in the things of Christ, with and without all other things? *With* other things? It is the will of God, while he intrusts us with other things, that we should use them to his glory; but is our satisfaction in the good things of Christ so high that we can be satisfied *without* other things? Truly, I hope the Lord will help us, that if we come to lose all things for the good things of Christ (and how soon we may come to such a time we know not), we may do it cheerfully and willingly. This I can say, that the nearer some have been to the losing of all things, even life itself, the better Christ hath been unto them. And I would pray for you, that if God should reserve us for such a time as to deprive us of all other things, this may grow upon our hearts, that the things of Christ are better than ever you apprehended. This will carry us through all our darkness and trouble,—to be satisfied with them in the want of other things. And take it for your comfort, though you may tremble now at the parting with a hair of your head, as if it was the garment from your back, yet, if you are sincere believers, when you come to part with all, you will do it cheerfully. Christ will come in and enable you so to do. Examine, therefore, yourselves, whether you do not only give a naked assent to the gospel and the things of Christ, or whether you find a goodness in them, a suitableness and satisfaction in them,—that it is "a good matter" unto you.

Secondly. Observe from the words, that it is the duty of believers to be making things concerning Jesus Christ: "Things that I have made touching the King." Now, to be making things concerning Jesus Christ, is *to meditate upon him*,—to have firm and fixed meditations upon Christ, and upon the glory of his excellencies: this is it that here is called, "'The things I have made,' composed, framed in my mind." He did not make pictures of Christ, or frame such and such images of him; but he meditated upon Christ. It is called, "Beholding as in a glass the glory of the Lord," in 2 Cor. iii. 18. What is the glory of the Lord? Why, it is the glory of his person, the glory of his kingdom, the glory of his love. Where are these to be seen? They are all represented in the glass. What glass? The glass of the gospel. The gospel hath a reflection upon it of all these glories of Christ, and makes a representation of them unto us. What is our work and business? Why, it is to behold this glory; that is, to contemplate upon it by faith, to meditate upon it,—which is here called making "things touching the King." This is also called

"Christ's dwelling in us," Eph. iii. 17; and, "The word of Christ dwelling richly in us," Col. iii. 16;—which is, when the soul abounds in thoughts of Christ. I have had more advantage by private thoughts of Christ than by any thing in this world; and I think when a soul hath satisfying and exalting thoughts of Christ himself, his person and his glory, it is the way whereby Christ dwells in such a soul. If I have observed any thing by experience, it is this,—a man may take the measure of his growth and decay in grace according to his thoughts and meditations upon the person of Christ, and the glory of Christ's kingdom, and of his love. A heart that is inclined to converse with Christ as he is represented in the gospel, is a thriving heart; and if estranged from it and backward to it, it is under deadness and decays.

"Touching the King;"—the psalmist hath respect unto Christ as a king. Hence,—

Thirdly. Observe that there is a peculiar glory in the kingly office of Jesus Christ, that we should daily exercise our thoughts about. The comfort, joy, and refreshment of believers, in this world, lie in the kingly power of Christ. What a view is there taken of him in Isa. lxiii. 1, "Who is this that cometh from Edom, with dyed garments from Bozrah? this that is glorious in his apparel, travelling in the greatness of his strength? I that speak in righteousness, mighty to save;" and which refers us to but one part of his kingly office,—namely, to the power he will put forth in destroying his enemies. It is generally thought that Edom under the Old Testament shadows forth Rome under the New. This is a glorious description of Christ going forth in the greatness of his power, when the year of his redeemed is come, and the day of vengeance is in his heart. How dreadful will it be to the world! how glorious in the eyes of believers! when we shall see him glorious in his apparel, travelling in the greatness of his strength, till he hath destroyed all his stubborn adversaries.

There is a peculiar glory in the kingdom of Christ, that we ought much, for our relief, to meditate upon. If we could behold the internal and external workings of Christ; what he hath done, what he will do,—how that certainly he will save every believer, how that certainly he will destroy every enemy,—how infallible in his grace, and never-failing in his vengeance;—we should then see a peculiar glory in his kingdom.

Fourthly. Observe, that when a heart is full of love to Christ, it *will run over;* then men will be speaking of Christ, and of his glory. "We believe," saith the apostle, "and therefore speak," 2 Cor. iv. 13. If we do believe, we shall speak. And saith the apostle, Acts iv. 20, when they said, "Speak no more in this name," saith he, "'We cannot but speak the things which we have seen and heard;' we *cannot but* speak them." On the contrary, there is sad evidence how little there is of love in the hearts of men towards Christ. Alas! look about to the multitudes of them that are called Christians; when do you hear a word of him? when do you meet with a heart overflowing with love to Christ? Some speak of him to blaspheme him, some to the reproach of him; but for a natural readiness to speak for him, where do we find it? Yet if the heart be filled, it will boil over. There are some that pass for professors; you shall very seldom hear a word of Christ from them. If a man would make himself a reproach in the world, he cannot better do it than by owning Christ and his Spirit before men.

Fifthly, and lastly. That profession alone is acceptable to God, and useful in the church, *which proceeds from the fulness of the heart.* It is to no purpose to have our tongue "as the pen of a ready writer," if our hearts be not full. It must come from the boiling or meditation of our hearts, if our profession be good and acceptable.

This is the preface of the song.

SERMON VIII.[1]

"Thou art fairer than the children of men: grace is poured into thy lips: therefore God hath blessed thee for ever."—Ps. xlv. 2.

I HAVE given you an account of the general design and scope of this psalm already, and spoken something from the title of it, "To the chief Musician," etc.; and opened the 1st verse, and spoken something to that also,—which is the preface to the whole psalm.

I shall now speak something to you from the 2d verse: "Thou art fairer than the children of men: grace is poured into thy lips: therefore God hath blessed thee for ever." You know who it is that is intended in these words,—namely, our Lord Jesus Christ, the King, the Messiah; and this is a description of him, which the psalmist gives in prophecy.

There are three parts of the verse:—I. A description of *Christ's person,* "Thou art fairer than the children of men." II. An account of his endowments that were bestowed upon him to enable him to his work, "Grace is poured into thy lips." III. God's acceptance and approbation of him in his work, "Therefore God hath blessed thee for ever."

I. Here is a description of Christ's person, "Thou art fairer than the children of men."

[1] This sermon was preached at Stadham, June 14, 1674.

You may consider it,—1. Absolutely, that Christ is *fair*. 2. Comparatively, that he is *fairer* than the children of men.

1. Absolutely: Christ is *fair*. He ascribes beauty to him. There is mention of the beauty of God in Ps. xxvii. 4, "To behold the beauty of the LORD;"—that may concern his worship. But it is directly spoken of God himself, in Zech. ix. 17, "How great is his goodness, and how great is his beauty!" As beauty among men consists in the symmetry of parts, so in God it is the harmony of all the divine perfections. The infinite harmony, agreeableness, suitableness of all divine perfections, I say, is this beauty. Christ is called fair, to denote his glorious perfections.

2. Comparatively: "Thou art *fairer* than the children of men;" that is,—(1.) Than all worldly men. There is more excellency, more desirableness in Jesus Christ than in all the men of the world. (2.) More than in all those who were employed in the church, which is peculiarly here intended; more excellent than Moses and Aaron,—than any of the kings and prophets of old, who yet were so desirable. Aaron had his garments made for beauty and for glory. But saith he, "Christ is more beautiful, more fair, than any of the children of men."

I told you the design of the psalm was, to speak of the kingdom of Christ, and to set forth the mutual love that is between Christ and his church; but yet, in the first place, he lays down this description of his person as the foundation, "Thou art fairer than the children of men."

I say,—1. Absolutely, Christ is fair; and we may observe from hence, that, in the consideration of Jesus Christ, if we intend any interest in him, and any benefit by him, the first thing we ought to know and consider, is *his person*. So the psalmist here, when he had designed the description of his kingdom and benefits, begins with his person. And if we know not the person of Christ we have no interest in him. The apostle, in Phil. iii. 10, shows what our design should be, "That I may know him, and the power of his resurrection, and the fellowship of his sufferings," etc. First "know him," says he, before he speaks of the benefits of his mediation; which is consequential to the knowledge of himself. So he tells you, of the subject of his preaching, 1 Cor. ii. 2, "I determined not to know any thing among you, save Jesus Christ, and him crucified;"—first Christ, and then him crucified; first his person, and then his mediation.

The reasons are,—

(1.) Because Jesus Christ will be loved and preferred above all *for his own sake*. He tells his disciples, Matt. x. 37, "He that loveth father or mother more than me, is not worthy of me." If we intend to have any benefit by him, he must be valued above all for his own sake, or for the sake of what he is in himself He puts it as a mark upon them that followed him, "Because of the loaves," John vi. 26. And if, without the knowledge of Christ, without a due consideration of his person, we think to follow him only for his benefits, for the advantage which we hope to have by him (which is to follow him for the loaves), we shall be found strangers to him, when we think we are in a better state and condition.

(2.) Without this, no man can secure his love and faith *from being selfish*, or from beginning and ending in self. For if we regard only those things whereof we have advantage, so that we may have our sin pardoned, our iniquities done away, and our souls saved, we would not care whether there were a Christ to trust in or no. But as this tends not to the glory of God, so neither will it tend to the advantage of our own souls. So that if we intend any interest in Christ, we must begin with his person, and the knowledge of it: "Thou art fairer than the children of men."

The use of this point is,—

First, To show *how few real Christians* there be in the world,—seeing there are so few that have an acquaintance with, and a love unto, the person of Christ. Some deny him. We have a generation among ourselves that pretend to be Christians (I mean the Quakers), who deny the person of Christ,—leave him neither the perfection of the Deity, nor humanity, nor the union of his natures; and have framed to themselves a religion without Christ,—a carcase without a soul or life to quicken it, or enable it to be of any use. And there are others that evidence how little it is they value Christ. 1 Cor. ii. 8, "Had they known him, they would not have crucified the Lord of glory." Do ye think, if men knew Christ, whatsoever they pretend, they would so despise his ways, his ordinances, his worship?—prefer their own inventions and imaginations before them, and prosecute and persecute all that truly fear him, according to the power of their hand? Had they known him, they would not have done so. And the greatest part are perfectly sottish,—brutishly ignorant concerning the person of Christ: yea, many to whom he hath been preached, it is to them like the wind,—they hear a sound, but know not whence it comes, or what it means; perhaps they never had one serious thought in all their lives what Christ is, or who he is?—wherein his excellencies do consist, or what they expect from him. O how few labour to have a familiar intercourse with this Saviour! How few say to wisdom, "Thou art my sister, and call understanding their kinswoman," as in Prov. vii. 4, speaking of Christ, who is the wisdom of God. They that know Christ, will make him as near and familiar to their souls as they can.

Secondly. This shows what great cause *they* have to rejoice, unto whom God hath revealed Christ. Matt. xvi. 13, etc., "Whom do men say I am?" saith Christ to his disciples. "And they said, Some say thou art John the baptist; some, Elias; and others, Jeremias, or one of the prophets. He saith unto them, But whom say ye that I am? And Simon Peter answered and said, Thou art the Christ, the Son of the living God. And Jesus answered and said unto him, Blessed art thou, Simon Bar-jona: for flesh and blood hath not revealed it unto thee, but my Father which is in heaven." The world has very dark notions concerning Christ,—like the blind man, that saw men like trees walking: but as for those who have the knowledge of Christ, they are blessed; "for flesh and blood hath not revealed it." It is the greatest spiritual revelation, and the greatest evidence that we have received any spiritual revelation from God, when we know the person of Christ. Let us be thankful for any revelation God hath made of Christ unto our souls; that we behold his person, and know him; that he is not a stranger unto us, but that our souls have some holy acquaintance with him.

And if God hath thus revealed Christ unto us, let us be manifesting to all the world that we are Christ's, when others are ashamed of him. How? By our prizing, valuing, preferring him above all other things; above the world, and all the satisfactions and enjoyments of the world; above its ways, pleasures, converse: we have better satisfaction, better acquaintance to converse with and retire unto.

2. Observe from the words, that, in the knowledge of Christ, what we should chiefly consider are the things wherein he is fairer than the children of men, wherein he is more excellent, and to be preferred above all other persons and things whatsoever.

Now, wherein is Christ fairer than the children of men?

I answer, In three things:—(1.) In the dignity of his person; (2.) In the excellency of his work; and, (3.) In the power and heavenliness of his doctrine. Many other instances may be given, but things may be gathered to these three heads; whereby we may make answer unto the question, that is tacitly asked of us by nominal professors in the world, which was asked of the spouse by the daughters of Jerusalem, Cant. v. 9, "What is thy beloved more than another beloved?"—"What is there in Christ more than in other persons and things, that there is such a stir made about him?" I say, "He is fairer than the children of men."

(1.) In *the dignity of his person.* He is a more excellent person. Wherein consists the excellency of Christ's person? Truly, not at all in the outward appearance of his human nature, especially while here in the world. It is the foundation of all devotion among some, the making of glorious pictures of Christ; by which means to represent him fine and glorious. But what doth he speak of himself in Ps. xxii. 6?

"I am a worm, and no man." He was brought to that low condition that he was of no esteem, of no reputation. But if we could have had a sight of him, how comely would he have been! Why, "he had neither form nor comeliness," in his outward appearance, "that when we should see him we should desire him," Isa. liii. 2;—wherein, then, consists the dignity of his person? In two things:—[1.] In the glory of his divine nature. [2.] In the immeasurable fulness of his human nature with grace:—

[1.] In his *divine glory.* Phil. ii. 6, "Who being in the form of God, thought it not robbery to be equal with God." Here is his glory. Also in John i. 14, "We beheld his glory." Wherein consists that glory? "The glory of the only begotten of the Father."

If you ask us, "What is our beloved more than another beloved?" —"What is there in Christ, that our souls are sick of love for him, breathe and pant after the enjoyment of him, and that continually?" It is because we have seen his glory who is God blessed for ever.

[2.] It consists in the immeasurable, unspeakable *fulness of grace* that was given to his human nature. It is what I have as much thought of as any one thing, concerning the immeasurable fulness of grace which is in the human nature of Christ. So saith the apostle, John iii. 34, "God gave not the Spirit by measure unto him." How by measure? "To every one of us is given grace according to the measure of the gift of Christ," Eph. iv. 7. *We* have every one of us *a measure;* but it is given to him without a measure. There is an immeasurable fulness of grace in the human nature of Christ, which we are partakers of; "for of his fulness we all receive, and grace for grace." It is an infinity in the divine nature, transferred into the human nature of Christ, and through him communicated unto our souls. From the eternal fountain of the divine nature, through the human nature of Christ, which hath an immeasurable fulness, as the head of the church, it is, I say, transfused to all his members. In this he is "fairer than the children of men."

(2.) He is so in *the excellency of his work.* The work that Christ did was such as none ever did or could do, but only he himself. It is true, "The law was given by Moses," but "grace and truth came by Jesus Christ," John i. 17. Could not the law give grace, and do this business, so as to bring in an everlasting righteousness, pardon sin, save the soul, make us accepted with God? No; Rom. viii. 3, "What the law could not do, that God, sending his Son in the likeness of sinful flesh, did." But there were sacrifices of the law; when men had sinned, they could make atonement. No; "Sacrifice and burnt-offerings thou wouldest not. Then said I, Lo, I come to do thy will," Ps. xl. 7. But would there not be righteousness, if men observe the law, and follow after it? Alas! they could not obtain it; Rom. x. 3, 4,

"For Christ is the end of the law for righteousness to every one that believeth." So that neither the deeds of the law, nor the sacrifices of the law, nor the righteousness of the law, will do. "The redemption of our souls is precious," and would have ceased for ever, if Christ had not been found to undertake this work. When there was but a book to be opened of revelations for the church, none was found worthy to open it, until Christ prevailed, Rev. v. 2, etc. If there could be no new revelations made but only by Christ, much less could any in heaven or earth redeem the souls of men from death and hell, bring them into favour with God, and work out eternal redemption for them.

(3.) He is more excellent than all the sons of men, *in the revelation he has made of the will of God.* Christ has made such a revelation of the will, love, and grace of God, as none of the children of men ever saw before.

These are the things we ought to consider in Christ, as he is fairer than the children of men, in the dignity of his person, in the excellency of his work, and in the glory of his revelation.

You will say, "*Why* should we consider Christ in these his incomparable excellencies?" I answer,—

[1.] *That our hearts be not taken away* nor engrossed by the children of men, and what belongs unto them,—their glory, their honours, their lusts, their pleasures, their righteousness. If we would not have our hearts allured and drawn off with them, the way is, to exercise our faith upon the incomparable excellencies of the Lord Jesus Christ. Can the world be to us an all-sufficient God, and a great reward? Can the world pardon our sins, save our souls, deliver us from wrath to come, reveal to us the mystery of truth from the bosom of the Father? Can it make known the mind of God? communicate grace and love to us? If it cannot, then let us dwell in our thoughts on *him* who is fairer than the children of men.

[2.] *The consideration* of these excellencies in Christ is exceedingly *suited to increase faith and love in us.* They are the proper objects in Christ of these graces. What is it we believe and love? Do not we believe in Christ as the Son of God, as God-man in one person? do not we love him as he is so? do not we believe he hath made atonement for us? and do not we believe and love the excellency of his work? Then the exercise of our thoughts upon these things is the way to increase faith and love in us. And the great reason why we are so weak in our faith, and so cold in our love, is, because we exercise our souls no more to immediate, direct thoughts upon Christ and his excellencies. We live by *reflex* considerations upon the benefits of Christ; but if we could exercise our souls more *directly* in daily thoughts of Christ in faith and love, we should increase more in these graces, and be more transformed into his likeness. "Beholding as in a glass the glory of the Lord, we are changed into the same image," etc., 2 Cor. iii. 18. It is not such a cheap thing to be a Christian as most imagine. What wandering thoughts have the generality of Christians about Christ, and never once examine into their thoughts whether they have any spiritual acquaintance with him or no!

II. The second thing to consider in the words is,—*the endowment of Christ, in his human nature*, for the discharge of this great office and work, which is here ascribed unto him in this psalm, set forth by grace being poured into his lips.

And there are three things that may be observed:—1. The nature of this endowment; and that is, *grace*. 2. The manner of its communication, and that is, *poured;* it is not dropped, but poured. 3. The seat of it, being communicated; grace is poured into *his lips*.

1. The nature of this endowment; it is *grace*.

Grace in Scripture is taken two ways:—(1.) For *inherent* grace and holiness, or the graces of the Spirit. Things that are bestowed upon men, and wrought in them, they are called grace, the same as the principle of spiritual life. (2.) Grace is taken *externally* for favour and love. "Ye are saved by grace;" that is, by the free favour of God.

It is here taken in the first sense, for the internal principle of grace and holiness. This was poured into the lips of Christ. Grace in the second sense is also mentioned in the last clause of the verse, "Therefore God hath blessed thee for ever."

And we may observe, in reference to the seat of it, that it hath particular respect unto the prophetical office of Christ, whereby he discharged his duty in the revelation of the will of God. Christ did manifest and evidence grace in all he did and said in this world, as the lips are the way of manifesting the mind.

It is the first of these things I shall chiefly discourse on,—namely, the endowment that renders the human nature of Christ so exceedingly desirable and glorious, is *grace*.

That which rendered Christ so beautiful, so desirable, and glorious, was not secular wisdom, though there was in him the greatest fulness of all wisdom; it was not the pomp, the greatness, the glory of the world, outward ornaments, or any thing that men esteem: no, it was that which men hate and persecute that rendered Christ so beautiful and glorious. God did not endow Christ with riches; no, he was poor, so poor that he had not where to lay his head: nor with bodily appearance; for he was a worm, and no man. But saith God, "I will render him glorious." How? He shall be full of grace. "We beheld his glory, the glory as of the only begotten of the Father."

"We saw it," say they: "the world saw nothing but a poor man, whom they despised; but *we* saw his glory." And what was that glory? "He was full of grace," John i. 14. Even the glorv of Jesus Christ consists in grace.

And why doth this glory of Christ consist in grace? For these three ends:—

(1.) Because in this internal grace consists *the reparation of the image of God.* All the glory that God thought meet to communicate to his creature man (and it was unspeakable, and all he designed him for), was to make him in his own image and likeness. This was the glory God intended; every thing else doth but follow it. Now, we left this image, and became as like the devil as if we had been begotten by him. John viii. 44, We are the children of the devil, he is our father; we are a "generation of vipers,"—the seed of the serpent by nature. But it is grace that doth repair and renew this image of God. It is grace that makes a representation of God unto us; and therefore doth Christ's glory consist in grace. The apostle tells us so, 2 Cor. iv. 6, "We behold the glory of God in the face of Jesus Christ." How is that? Why, in that abounding grace that was in Christ there is made such a representation of God, that there we may see his likeness. It is the human nature of Christ that makes the great representation of God, because he hath all that which is the image and likeness of God—namely, grace in the fulness of it—in him.

(2.) This grace is the glory of Christ, because it is that *which inclines the heart of Jesus Christ* unto all that goodness and kindness that he hath showed unto us. Whence was it that Jesus Christ loved us so as to lay down his life for us? whence does he continue to have compassion on us, even when we were ignorant, and wandered out of the way? It is from that abounding, unspeakable, heavenly love that was in his heart and soul, that inclined him to it. The more grace we have, the more we have of love, compassion, and delight in doing the will of God. But there was that *abundance in Christ* that inclined him to do all this good for us,—to live, to die, to intercede for us. This makes Christ very beautiful and glorious to the eye of faith.

(3.) It is the glory of Christ, as he is the great *example* and pattern, whereunto we ought to labour after a conformity. When we had lost all, and wandered up and down, it was not enough that we should have a rule set us, but we must, moreover, have a pattern to follow; we must be like unto Christ. And there is an unconquerable desire implanted in the heart of every believer in the world to be like unto Jesus Christ; because God hath, in the way of an ordinance, appointed him to be our pattern. And we are but trifling Christians, and a dishonour to our profession, if we make not this the design of our souls continually,—that we may be in the world as Christ was,—that the same mind may be in us that was in him, Phil. ii. 5; the same meekness, humility, self-denial, faith, love, patience, that was in him.

To close in a way of use;—if this internal grace and holiness was that wherein Christ was fairer than the children of men, because grace was poured into his lips; then,—

1. Let us learn to *esteem* it above all other things. That which rendered Christ beautiful, will render us so: not in the eyes of the world;—no, it did not render Christ so to the world; the more he abounded in grace, the more they despised him;—but it renders us beautiful *in the sight of God* and all the holy angels, and in the judgment of all believers upon earth. If we be but like unto Christ in any measure, it will render us fair, beautiful, desirable in the eyes of all that have eyes to see and hearts to discern it.

2. Let us not value so much the lustre, the splendour, and glory that earthly men have in earthly things,—in their riches, power, honour, and the like. How apt are we to fret ourselves sometimes at the thoughts of these things; and think they have a peculiar happiness,—that they are so great and glorious as they appear and make a show of! But God knows there is nothing in them but what is the object of his contempt, and of all the saints and angels, and will be so to all eternity.

SERMON IX.[1]

"Gird thy sword upon thy thigh, O most Mighty, with thy glory and thy majesty."—Ps. xlv. 3.

In the 2d verse we have a description of the person of Christ, and of the ground of God's blessing and accepting of him in his work, the psalm having a double design;—first, To show the glory of Christ in his kingly office; secondly, To show the mutual love that is between Christ and his church.

This 3d verse sets forth his entering upon the first part of his work, and is spoken by the way of encouragement unto Christ, in the name of God the Father, to undertake his office, and to go through with it. "Gird thy sword," saith he, "upon thy thigh, O most Mighty, with thy glory and thy majesty."

There are three things in the words:—I. The *work* that is proposed unto Jesus Christ, or rather his *preparation* for his work: "Gird thy

[1] This sermon was preached at Stadham, June 21, 1674.

sword upon thy thigh." II. The *manner how* he should go through this work: "With thy glory and thy majesty." And (that which I shall particularly enlarge on) III. The *appellation* that is here given to Christ; which is, "Most Mighty." He is most mighty in the execution of his office which he is exalted unto:—

I. We have Christ's preparation for his work: "Gird thy sword on thy thigh." Consider two things:—1. What is the *sword* of Christ. 2. What is meant by *girding* this sword upon his thigh.

1. The sword of Christ is the word of God; so it is called, "The sword of the Spirit, which is the word of God," Eph. vi. 17. The Spirit being the great immediate agent whereby Christ administers his kingdom, that which is the sword of the Spirit is the sword of Christ: and therefore, where Christ is described in his kingdom, it is said that "he hath a sword proceeding out of his mouth," Rev. i. 16; which, in another place, is called "The rod of his mouth," Isa. xi. 4. It is the word of God, the great instrument of Christ in managing of his kingdom, that is called here his sword.

2. Concerning this it is said, "Gird thy sword upon thy thigh." The girding of the sword upon the thigh, is the putting of it into readiness for use. When David was going up against Nabal, he said unto his men, 1 Sam. xxv. 13, "Gird ye on every man his sword." Wherefore Christ's girding his sword upon his thigh, is the disposing of the word into the ordinances of the gospel, where it may be ready for use. It hath respect unto the time when he ascended on high, and sent forth his word for the setting up of his kingdom. Then he put his word in readiness to effect the great designs of his love and grace, when "he gave some apostles, and some prophets, and some evangelists, and some pastors and teachers," Eph. iv. 11. He furnished men with gifts and abilities to dispense this word unto the ends of his kingdom.

II. The *manner* of going through his work is, "With thy glory and thy majesty." The glory and majesty of Christ are his power and authority. And so it is prophesied of, as an encouragement unto the Lord Christ, that he should clothe his word with power and authority for the ends of setting up his kingdom,—the edification of his church and the preservation of it in the world.

These things I speak in a general way; I shall now more particularly address myself,—

III. To the appellation that is here given unto Christ,—"O most Mighty, גִּבּוֹר, from גָּבַר, one that prevails in every thing he takes in hand.

Observe from hence, that the Lord Jesus Christ, as king of the church, is endowed with a mighty power for the accomplishing of all the designs and ends of this rule and kingdom. It is said of him,

Ps. lxxxix. 19, God hath "laid help upon one that is mighty." It is spoken there primarily of David, "I have found David my servant." But what could poor David do? one taken from the sheepfold. It was not a laying help, therefore, upon David that was mighty, absolutely speaking; but a putting strength into him. But David was a type of Christ; and to him must the passage be referred;—he is the mighty One. Also Isaiah, chap. lxiii. 1, describing of Christ in his kingdom, saith, "It is 'I that speak in righteousness, mighty to save.'" And again, in Ps. xxiv. 7, etc., there is a description of his ascension into heaven; the gates and everlasting doors being lifted up, that he, the King of glory, may enter in. The question being asked, "Who is this King of glory?" saith he, "The LORD, strong and mighty." It is a property everywhere ascribed unto Jesus Christ, that he is mighty.

Here we may inquire,—1. *Whence* Christ is thus mighty for the execution of his kingly office? and, 2. *To what ends* he doth put forth this might and power?

1. *Whence* is Christ thus mighty? Christ is mighty upon two accounts:—

(1.) From the *omnipotent power* of his divine nature; which is the principle of his mighty operations in the union of his person. So the prophet declares, Isa. ix. 6, "Unto us a child is born, unto us a son is given." And how shall he be called? "Wonderful, Counsellor, THE MIGHTY GOD;"—"This child that is born unto us, this son that is given unto us, his name shall be (that is, he really is),—The mighty God." Why so? Because of the union of the divine nature with the human in the same person; whereby the same person becomes a child born, and also the mighty God.

(2.) He is mighty, from the *authority* and power that was *communicated* and given unto him *by the Father*, as mediator, for the accomplishing of his whole work. Two things concur to make one legally mighty to proper ends;—first, strength and power; secondly, authority. Where there is strength and power and no authority, it is force; and where there is authority, but no strength or power, that authority will be void. Christ had strength and power as the mighty God; and he hath authority too, as all power is communicated to him by God the Father; as may be seen in Matt. xxviii. 18; Eph. i. 20–22, and many other places.

But it will be objected, "If Christ be the mighty God *by nature*, how comes it to pass that he should have power and authority *given unto him?* God hath given unto him might and dominion, far above all principalities," etc.

I answer,—Christ, as his power is given to him, is considered not absolutely as God, nor absolutely as man; but as *God-man*,

Mediator,—one that mediates between God and man: and so his power to erect his kingdom is given him of his Father.

2. The second inquiry is,—*Unto what ends* doth the Lord Jesus put forth this mighty power wherewith he is endowed? I answer,—To these five ends:—(1.) Unto the erecting of his kingdom or church in the world; (2.) To the preservation of it; (3.) To the subduing of his enemies; (4.) To the raising of the dead; (5.) In the judging of all flesh, and distributing of eternal rewards and punishments: all which are acts of mighty power.

(1.) Jesus Christ puts forth this mighty power in *erecting and building of his church.* In Matt. xvi. 18, our Lord saith, "I will build my church;" and the apostle, in Heb. iii. 3, 4, shows that it was *an act of divine power* to build this church of God: "He that built all things is God." No one could build a church in all ages, but God himself. And if we were able to take a view how Jesus Christ first built his church in the world, we should learn not to distrust his power in any thing he had afterward to do. There was a combination of hell and of all the power of the world, against the interest of Christ and the gospel. The concurring suffrage of mankind, wise and unwise, learned and unlearned, Jew and Greek, influenced by their interest, by all that was dear unto them, set themselves in a combination against Christ's building of his kingdom. He employed against all this force a *few poor men*, unlearned, unskilful; and gives into their hands only the sword of the Spirit,—the word of God; furnishes them only with gifts and abilities for the dispensing of the word: which was "his girding of his sword upon his thigh." He set these poor men to work; and clothing them with his glory and majesty, they make havoc in the devil's kingdom, and destroy it by degrees, until they root it out of the earth. It was, then, an act of mighty power in Christ, to build his kingdom and church.

(2.) Christ puts forth this mighty power *in the preserving of his church*, being so founded and built on him. It is that which he expresses, Isa. xxvii. 3, "I the LORD do keep it; I will water it every moment: lest any hurt it, I will keep it night and day." The church being built, is not able to stand of itself; for unto the end of time the gates of hell and the power of the world shall be engaged against it. But saith he, "I will keep it, 'and the gates of hell shall not prevail against it.'" There is a carnal church in the world, or a worldly church; and how is *that* kept? By force,—laws and power of men who have wrapt up their secular interest in the preserving of it; and they will fight for their kingdom. On the contrary, the Lord Jesus Christ hath *a spiritual church*, of them that believe in him. They also are preserved; and by what means? By *a secret emanation* of mighty power from Jesus Christ. There hath not been any age in the world since the ascension of Christ, but there hath been an emanation, or putting forth of this mighty power of Christ in preserving of this church. He preserved a people under the whole apostasy of Antichrist. Had there been none left on the earth to fear him, and believe in him, all the promises of God to him had come to an end. But he did secretly, by his mighty power, preserve a people to himself in the midst of all the defection of Antichrist. And he doth so at this day, in the midst of the new defection made to Antichrist: for, in former days, the world fell off to Antichrist by superstition and idolatry; they are now falling off to him by profaneness and atheism: yet Jesus Christ, by his mighty power under both, or by a secret exertion of his power, preserves his church through all, and carries them as safe through the *new* opposition as he did through the *old.*

(3.) He puts forth his power for the *subduing* and conquering of his and his church's *enemies.*

What enemies has Christ? what enemies has the church? As many as there are devils in hell, and men and women in the world that are of the seed of the serpent. But I may reduce all the enmity to the interest of Christ upon earth to these four heads:—[1.] Satan; [2.] The world; [3.] Sin; [4.] Death. Christ is most mighty in conquering all these enemies:—

[1.] He puts forth his mighty power in conquering of *Satan.* This was the first word that was spoken of him in the world, in Gen. iii. 15, "I will put enmity between thee and the woman, and between thy seed and her seed: it shall bruise thy head, and thou shalt bruise his heel." The first discovery God made to his creatures concerning the incarnation of his Son was in this,—that he would destroy Satan; and so the Holy Ghost tells us he hath done, Col. ii. 15, "He spoiled principalities and powers, and made a show of them openly, triumphing over them in his cross." These words, "He spoiled principalities and powers," are an exposition of the former promise in Genesis, that "the seed of the woman" (Jesus Christ) "should bruise the serpent's head." How should he do it? Why, in spoiling principalities and powers, and triumphing over them openly in his cross. So he saith, in Heb. ii. 14, "That through death he might destroy him that had the power of death, that is, the devil." He did not destroy him as to his *being,* but as to his *power* and authority. Hence, first, The devil hath a limited power only remaining, such as shall never prejudice the eternal interest of the church; and, secondly, He is reserved unto eternal destruction by this mighty power of Christ.

[2.] The second enemy of Christ is the *world;* and that may be considered either in the men of it or in the power of it:—

In *the men* of it. The Lord Christ puts forth his mighty power to deal with and subdue all the men of the world that rise up in opposition against him. Whatever success they may seem to have, they are all made his footstool: "Thou shalt break them with a rod of iron; thou shalt dash them in pieces like a potter's vessel," Ps. ii. 9. And you have him twice or thrice described in the Revelation as going forth in his mighty power for the subduing of all his adversaries. See Rev. xix. 11–21.

And this *must* be; for he shall subdue all the *authority* in the world,—not only the *persons* of men, but all the *power* and all the authority which is set up against him, or exercised against his interest. 1 Cor. xv. 24, 25, "When he shall have put down all rule and all authority and power. For he must reign, till he hath put all enemies under his feet." There is a suspension of the issue of all things until Christ hath thus put down all that opposeth him and his interest. But there is an expectation in heaven, and in earth, in the whole creation: all are waiting, as if one single person, for the putting forth this mighty power of Christ for the subduing of all unto him; for the end will not be till then. Whatever we endure, we must be contented with it; whatsoever we suffer, the end must not be till all his enemies be made his footstool, and there be nothing to stand up against him who is most mighty.

[3.] *Sin* in his people is another *enemy of Christ.* Sin, as it is in men by nature, is that which gives life and efficacy to all the enmity that is acted against him; and, as it remains even in believers themselves, it doth act a great enmity against Christ. How come we, then, to be freed from it? how comes it to be subdued? The apostle, in Rom. vii., gives an account of the great contest and conflict that believers have with the remainder of sin in them, that makes them cry out for deliverance from it, verses 24, 25. It is a sudden breaking forth of the apostle there, when he was describing the law of sin; for he cries out, "O wretched man that I am! who shall deliver me?" etc. But he as suddenly takes up, "I thank God, through Jesus Christ our Lord;"—"Through the power of Christ this enemy, sin, shall be subdued." Therefore, chap. vi. 14, it is said, "Sin shall not have dominion over you: for ye are not under the law, but under grace;"—"If you come under grace, or under the rule of Christ, sin shall not have dominion over you." What is the reason of it? where is the consequence of the argument? Because sin is one great enemy of Christ, and he will certainly conquer it.

[4.] *Death* is another enemy. It is the last enemy, 1 Cor. xv. 25, 26, "He must reign, till he hath put all enemies under his feet. The last enemy that shall be destroyed is death." And, in verse 54, he tell us that "death is swallowed up in victory;" a conquest is obtained over it. It is the last enemy, because, until the consummation of all things, we shall be subject to its power; but *that* shall also come under the feet of Christ, when we shall die no more.

This is the third end wherefore Christ puts forth this mighty or exceeding greatness of his power,—namely, for the subduing of his enemies.

(4.) The fourth end for which Christ puts forth the greatness of his power is, for the *raising up all his church from the dead,* Phil. iii. 20, 21, " Our conversation is in heaven; from whence also we look for the Saviour, the Lord Jesus Christ: who shall change our vile body, that it may be fashioned like unto his glorious body, according to the working whereby he is able even to subdue all things unto himself." The mighty power of Christ reaches thus far, that the dead shall be raised thereby. Yes, our vile body shall,—the body of our humiliation; that is, the body as it is fallen into corruption, into a vile estate, though it come to worms and dust, yet he shall revive it by the exceeding greatness of his power. He shall raise the bodies of his people. The privilege of believers in that day will be, that they shall be first raised, and they shall be peculiarly raised by the power of Christ as mediator. Their bodies shall be raised in conformity to his glorious body, when others shall be raised after them by the mere divine power of Christ, and raised with all their own vileness upon them.

(5.) And lastly, to mention no more;—the mighty power of Christ is put forth in *judging of all the world,* and distributing to them rewards of bliss or woe that shall abide to all eternity, Matt. xxv. 31–46.

Thus you see why the Holy Ghost, by the psalmist, calls Christ here the Mighty One,—one that will mightily prevail in every thing. It is because of his divine power,—he is the mighty God. Because of his mediatorial authority there is committed unto him all power in heaven and in earth. He doth put forth this power for the erecting of his church, for its preservation, for the subduing of his enemies, in the raising of the dead, and distributing rewards and punishments.

SERMON X.[1]

THE USE AND ADVANTAGE OF FAITH IN A TIME OF PUBLIC CALAMITY.

" The just shall live by his faith."—HAB. ii. 4.

THIS is the first time these words are mentioned in the Scripture, but they are three times quoted by the apostle Paul: he preached,

[1] This sermon was preached April 9, 1680.

as it were, thrice upon them, Rom. i. 17; Gal. iii. 11; Heb. x. 38; for it is full of heavenly matter, and is made use of by the apostle to several purposes. I know no one text that hath been more preached upon, or more written upon by them who have treated of the life of faith;—how the just live the life of justification, and how they live the life of sanctification, the life of consolation, the life of peace, the life of joy, the life of obedience, etc. My design is quite of another nature, and is that which falls in with the design of the prophet in the first use of the words; as we shall presently see.

You know that, for many years, upon all these occasions, without failing, I have been warning of you continually of an approaching calamitous time, and considering the sins that have been the causes of it. The day is with the Lord,—the year and month I know not: but I have told you that "judgment will begin at the house of God;" that in the latter days of the church, "perilous times will come;" that God seems to have "hardened our hearts from his fear, and caused us to err from his ways;" and that none knows what "the power of his wrath" will be. In all these things I have foretold you of perilous, distressing, calamitous times; and in all men's apprehensions they now lie at the door, and are entering in upon us. Now I must change my design; and my present work will be, both upon this and, if I live, upon some other occasions, to show how we ought to deport ourselves in and under the approaches of distressing calamities that are coming upon us, and may reach, it may be, up to the very neck.

What this text teaches us is, that in the approaches of overwhelming calamities, and in the view of them, *we ought, in a peculiar manner, to live by faith.* That is the meaning of the place.

And that this is our duty appears from this passage and the context. For the prophet had received a vision, a dreadful vision, from God, of the coming in of the Chaldeans, and of the destruction they would bring upon the church and upon all the land, in the foregoing chapter. Having received this vision, he considers what is his own duty, and what is the duty of the church, in the approaches of this distressing, calamitous season. Why, saith he, verse 1, "I will stand upon my watch, and set me upon the tower, and will watch to see what he will say unto me, and what I shall answer when I am reproved."—"God will reprove me; there will be great arguings between God and my soul: I know my own guilt and sin, and I would be in a readiness to have something to answer God when I am reproved, —something to betake myself unto. The answer," saith he, "I will betake myself unto is this, 'The just shall live by his faith.'" Two things are here included:—

First. Saith he, "I will betake myself" (as the apostle makes use of it) "unto *Jesus Christ for righteousness.* I have nothing else to answer God when I am reproved."

Secondly. "I will pass through all these terrible and dreadful dispensations of providence that are coming upon me, by living the life of faith:" *a peculiar way of living,* as we shall presently see. When the flood was coming upon the world, Noah was "a preacher of righteousness," 2 Pet. ii. 5. What righteousness did Noah preach? Why, that righteousness whereof he himself was partaker; for he "became heir of the righteousness which is by faith," Heb. xi. 7. When the flood was coming, Noah preached the righteousness of faith to the world, that they might escape, if they would attend unto it; but it was rejected by them. Wherefore, I say, in the approach of a calamitous season, there is, in an especial way and manner, a living by faith required of us. But you will say, "What is a calamitous season?" or, "When do you esteem a season calamitous?"

I will give you two things for the description of such a season as I judge to be manifestly calamitous:—

1. When it *exceeds the bounds of affliction,* or when the dispensations of God's anger in it cannot be reduced to the head of affliction. Ezek. xxi. 9, 10, 13, "Son of man, prophesy, and say, Thus saith the LORD; say, A sword, a sword is sharpened, and also furbished: it is sharpened to make a sore slaughter; it is furbished that it may glitter: should we then make mirth? it contemneth the rod of my son, as every tree. Because it is a trial, and what if the sword contemn even the rod?" The *rod* comprises all affliction; but God will bring a *sword,*—a judgment that shall not be reducible to the head of affliction; it shall contemn it. Now, I say, let it be what it will, when a calamity doth befall a people, or the church of God, that cannot be reduced to the head of affliction, but that every one shall find there is *anger, judgment, wrath* in it; then it is a distressing time.

2. When judgments fall *promiscuously* upon all sorts of persons, and make no distinction, then I take it to be a distressing time; for they strip men of the comforts they cherish in their own minds. Job ix. 22, 23, "This is one thing, therefore I said it, He destroyeth the perfect and the wicked." "What! doth God always do so? doth he never make a distinction about judgments?" Yes, sometimes; but "if the scourge slay suddenly, he will laugh at the trial of the innocent." When God brings a scourge, or a sword that shall slay promiscuously, that shall seize upon, destroy, and devour the innocent, so that they shall not escape, he will be as one that standeth by *rejoicing* to see how they carry themselves under their trial.

Now, this is enough to give satisfaction as to what I intend by a distressing, calamitous time:—it cannot be reduced to the head of affliction; and it slayeth suddenly and promiscuously the perfect and the wicked; and, it may be, "the good figs shall go first into captivity." I am not much otherwise minded; and God may have mercy for them in that dispensation. I shall now show you these two things:— I. How we shall live by faith,—how we should deport ourselves; what faith will do in such a season,—what our duty is under the approach of these calamitous, distressing times that are coming upon us. II. I shall show you how faith doth and will carry it under other perplexities that we have upon us, that we either feel or fear:—

I. Faith will guide and act the soul, under the approach of these distressing calamities, in these following things:—

1. It will give the soul a *reverential fear of God* in his judgments. So it did unto the saints of old, Heb. xi. 7, "By faith Noah, being warned of God;" εὐλαβηθεὶς,—"moved with a reverential fear." There is no man that is not stout-hearted and far from righteousness, but is, upon God's warning, moved with a reverential fear of God in his judgments. It was so with David, Ps. cxix. 120, "My flesh trembleth for fear of thee; and I am afraid of thy judgments." He was not afraid as to outward judgments, but under them his flesh trembled with a reverential fear of God. And so was it with the prophet Habakkuk, upon the vision he had of the approach of the Chaldeans, chap. iii. 16, "When I heard, my belly trembled; my lips quivered at the voice: rottenness entered into my bones, and I trembled in myself, that I might rest in the day of trouble: when he cometh up unto the people, he will invade them with his troops." He had a reverential fear of God in his judgments working upon him. According to my best observation of things in this state wherein we are, the generality of people may be distributed under these three heads:—

(1) There are some that are, indeed, *really afraid* of approaching judgments; they do not know how soon they will reach unto themselves, their persons, their families, their relations, their estates,—all that they have laboured for, and exerted their utmost care and industry about in the world; the flood flies at the door, ready to carry all before it; they fear every day. Some men die, also, for fear of dying; they are poor for fear of poverty;—they will part with nothing, because they fear they must part with all. A strange contradiction of spirit! Now this is not the work of faith. So far as it prevails upon any of our spirits, God will rebuke us for it, Isa. li. 12, 13, "Who art thou, that thou shouldest be afraid of a man that shall die, and of the son of man which shall be made as grass; and forgettest the LORD thy maker, and hast feared continually every day because of the fury of the oppressor?" (chap. viii. 13,) "and hast not sanctified the LORD in thy heart, nor made him thy fear?" Who art thou? God hates this sinful fear; it is an abomination unto him. This is nothing but the fear of self; we will keep all warm about us,

while we are in this world, and are afraid of the besom of destruction.

(2.) There are others who *utterly despise* these things,—take no notice of them; who do not think any such distressing calamity shall come upon them: if it does, they shall deal well enough with it. Isa. xxviii. 14, 15, "They have made a covenant with death, and with hell are they at agreement;" and say, "When the overflowing scourge shall pass through, it shall not come unto us." They have a thousand ways to disinterest themselves from any thing of the most distressing calamity that is coming over the world. This swallows up the generality of mankind, and is that which the prophet doth so reflect upon, Isa. xxvi. 11, "When thy hand is lifted up, they will not see: but they shall see, and be ashamed for their envy at the people; yea, the fire of thine enemies shall devour them."

(3.) The other sort is mentioned in Judges v. 6, and may be called *way-side men*, idle, discoursive men, that have nothing else to do but to walk up and down and talk, and are not concerned with a reverence of God and his judgments; they talk of them as if there were no God in heaven to regard them, or as if they had no concernment with him. If we have the least true saving faith in exercise, it will cast this cursed frame out of our hearts, it will be daily working it out of our souls, and will bring us to that which I told you is its proper work "God," saith the psalmist, Ps. ix. 16, "is known by the judgment which he executeth." And what of God is principally known in the judgments which he executes in the world, is but little considered. That which God makes known of himself in a peculiar manner in these dreadful dispensations is, his majesty, his holiness, and his power.

God will appear to be awfully *majestic* and wonderfully *glorious* in such dispensations. He speaks of himself upon that occasion, Isa. ii. 20, 21, "In that day a man shall cast his idols of silver, and his idols of gold, to the moles and to the bats; to go into the clefts of the rocks, and into the tops of the ragged rocks, for fear of the LORD, and for the glory of his majesty, when he ariseth to shake terribly the earth." If we have the light of faith to let it in, we shall see a majesty and glory in God's actings, even in his public and distressing judgments,—such a greatness and a glory that the soul will be constrained to bow down before him.

God doth in his judgments also manifest his *holiness;* of which we shall speak afterward. So Rev. xv. 4, "Who shall not fear thee, O Lord, and glorify thy name? for thou only art holy." How doth this appear? "For thy judgments are made manifest." When God makes his judgments manifest, his holiness will appear. And so, when Habakkuk came to plead with God about that great judgment of the Chaldeans which gave occasion to my text, he cries out, "O LORD my God, my Holy One, thou art of purer eyes than to behold iniquity."

God in them also glorifies himself in his *power*. He sets up one, and pulleth down another, and doth whatsoever he pleases. Herein he manifestly shows his sovereign power.

Now, to live by faith, is to cast out all those cursed frames before mentioned, and to bring this frame into your hearts, as the foundation of all that follows,—namely, that you have a reverential fear of the majesty, the holiness, and the power of God, in all his judgments: and without this, we shall not please God in any thing we do. These are the true sayings of God. If there be another frame in us, this dispensation will pierce to the very soul before it be over: that is the first thing.

2. Where faith hath filled the soul with a reverential fear of God, its first work will be, to put the soul upon *preparing* and providing an ark for itself: so it was in the great example of our faith before mentioned. Noah, being moved by fear, "prepared an ark," wherein he saved himself and his family. Let men pretend what they will, unless they are under a strange, careless stupidity and security (which, I fear, is upon the generality of professors), they cannot, in such a season as this, but be preparing some reserve for themselves. "What shall we do when this comes upon us?" They have some predominant reserve. "The rich man's wealth is his strong city," Prov. xviii. 11;—he may lose a great deal, but he will save enough for himself: so the strong man trusts to his strength, the wise man to his wisdom: one thing or other men prepare for themselves, to be an ark against the storm comes; and those who do not so, they fluctuate up and down at uncertainties, hoping that by one way and means or another, that they know not of, they shall be carried above all, have a good issue,—that it shall not be as this or that prophet or minister foretells, but that some way they shall escape. This is not to prepare an ark; which is the work of faith to do. And here I shall inquire into two things:—(1.) What is this ark that is to be prepared; (2.) How we ought to enter into it, or how we are to make especial entrance into it, in reference to an approaching calamitous season. I say,—

(1.) *This ark is Jesus Christ.* Faith in him is necessary. In this chapter of my text, where inquiry is made what shall be answered unto God, and what course shall be taken upon the coming in of the overflowing flood of the Chaldeans; this is the course to be taken, "The just shall live by his faith." What is that? It is to seek for righteousness by Christ; to seek afresh for justification and life by Christ. There is no other way, no other ark; and he is described as this ark in that well known place, Isa. xxxii. 2, "And a man" (that is, Jesus Christ) "shall be as an hiding-place from the wind, and a covert from the tempest, as rivers of water in a dry place, as the shadow of a great rock in a weary land:" that is the ark. I know not how to describe [better] what I intend by securing ourselves in the ark, like the description the prophet here gives, though in terms metaphorical. Likewise in Mic. v. 5, having given a promise of Christ, he adds, "And this man shall be the peace, when the Assyrian shall come into our land." To betake ourselves to the ark, is to betake ourselves to the fountain of our peace. And so Ps. ii. 12, "If God's wrath be kindled but a little"—How then? "Blessed are all they that" betake themselves unto him—"trust in him." In whom? In the Son;—"Kiss the Son." And surely, my brethren, the wrath of God is now kindled, not a little, but a great deal, in all sorts and ways. The indications of the wrath of God are upon the spirits of men of all sorts,—of professors, of the world, in their own persons, in all societies and relations. Where are we, then, to betake ourselves, but unto Christ? "Blessed are all they that put their trust in him."

(2.) But now, it would not have advantaged either Noah or his sons to have an ark prepared for them, unless they had a door to the ark. "Make a door," saith God to them, "that ye may have entrance." To obtain an interest in Christ is the general work of faith all our days. But how shall we be able now to make *an especial entrance* into this ark, suitable unto the state and condition wherein we are, and to approach a calamitous season that is hastening upon us? I know but of one way for our making an especial entrance into this ark, Jesus Christ, in reference to such a season; which is, *the solemn renovation of our covenant with God.* This is the way that hath been used by the church from the foundation of the world, without any instance of the contrary;—that, when a storm was coming, if ever they were delivered from it, they entered into the ark, by the renovation of their covenant with God. And seeing the end is certain, we are *thus afresh* to enter into this ark, Jesus Christ. It is no wisdom in civil things to remove a means, unless we have a better to substitute in the room of it; and it is so in spirituals. I desire all that fear God would stir up their hearts and thoughts, and offer to us (if they can) a better way for this church, or any church, to enter into the ark in the approach of a storm than this, and it shall be embraced. This church hath done so; though I begin to fear some look upon it as a very dead, sluggish commodity, they know not how to trade with. But do not mistake, you have no such thing lies by you in the sight of God this day. Do not despond, the day is approaching "when others shall come" (as in Zech. viii. 23) "and lay hold upon your skirts, saying, We will go with you; for we have heard that God is with you." Some,—blessed be God, and let his holy name be exalted!—have far outgone us already, both in zeal and warmth and courage, under a sense of engagements that are upon them. I look for no safety, no deliverance, in the trials and afflictions that are coming upon the earth, but what is had in the way of believing. I value not those that are otherwise minded. Bless God, who hath provided for you this door of entrance before the flood comes and the rain falls; bless God, I say, for it, and make use of it, and be able to plead it with God: and let the Lord know that you have made your choice to be his, and are under his care, and not under the protection of the world. I will not say you shall be saved *temporally*, but you shall be saved *eternally;* I cannot say you shall have peace with *men*, but you shall have peace with *God;* I cannot say you shall not lose your *lives*, but I will say you shall not lose your *souls:* and these are our principal concernments. Make good your entrance. A door made into the ark will do you no good, unless you enter in and make good your entrance at the door. How shall we make good our entrance into the ark, that we may have safety therein? If we are not at this work, we have no faith. Why, stand to your engagements,—stand to the performance of those duties God requires at your hands; not only as there is no one thing required but what is a special duty of the new covenant, but stand to them now as those that have been your entrance into the ark, where God will give you all that rest that in this world you can be partakers of. This is another work of faith in the approach of a calamitous time.

3. If we live by faith in the approach of a calamitous season, this will *put us upon the search* and examination of our own hearts, what accession we have made to the sins that have procured these judgments. This is that which faith (where it is in any measure sincere) will assuredly put us upon; and it is that God doth now in an especial manner call for. Now, the sins which do and have procured these judgments are of two sorts:—(1.) The open and flagitious sins of the world. (2.) The sins of churches and professors.

(1.) The open and *flagitious sins of the world.* The apostle reckons them up together, 1 Cor. vi. 9, 10, "Be not deceived: neither fornicators, nor idolaters, nor adulterers, nor effeminate, nor abusers of themselves with mankind, nor thieves, nor covetous, nor drunkards, nor revilers, nor extortioners, shall inherit the kingdom of God." He doth it again in Eph. v. 5, 6, "For this ye know, that no whoremonger, nor unclean person, nor covetous man, who is an idolater, hath any inheritance in the kingdom of Christ; for because of these things cometh the wrath of God upon the children of disobedience." He reckons them up also in Gal. v. 19, etc., "The works of the flesh are manifest, which are these; Adultery, fornication, uncleanness, lasciviousness, idolatry, witchcraft, hatred, variance, emulations, wrath, strife, seditions, heresies, envyings, murders, drunkenness, and such like." There is a marvellous large copy written out of these texts in the nation at this day: every man may read an exposition of these things in the practice of multitudes. Some will say, they bless God they are free from these things; and so they hope they have had no hand in procuring the judgments of God that are coming upon the nation; let them fall upon them and their interest who are guilty of these provoking abominations, such as for which the wrath of God is revealed from heaven against their ungodliness. Why, it is well if they are not guilty of any of these sins; but the seed and foundation, even of all these sins, lie in *our nature*, if not in *our persons*, and what eruptions they have made towards the provoking the eyes of God's glory I know not. But suppose you have escaped these pollutions that are in the world through lust,—

(2.) There are other sins—*sins of churches*, and *of professors*—that, in reference to Christ's *mediatory* kingdom, have as great influence for the procuring of judgments as the worst sins of the world have for the procuring of judgments in his *providential* kingdom. I know a time when there was a storm, wherein a whole vessel, and all that were in it, were like to have been cast away; but one Jonah, that was in the ship, was the cause of the storm.

I shall just mention the judgment-procuring sins of churches and professors, which are reduced in Scripture to these four heads:—

[1.] *Lukewarmness;* which was the judgment-procuring sin of Laodicea.

[2.] *Contenting ourselves in outward order and freedom from scandal;* which was the judgment-procuring sin of Sardis, and will prove ruinous to the best churches in the world.

[3.] *Want of love* among ourselves, and division in churches.

[4.] *Earthly-mindedness,* and love of the world, and conformity to it, that is found among the generality of professors.

SERMON XI.[1]

THE USE OF FAITH UNDER REPROACHES AND PERSECUTIONS.

"The just shall live by his faith."—HAB. ii. 4.

YOU may remember, I spake occasionally from that of the psalmist, Ps. xcvii. 2, "Clouds and darkness are round about him: righteous-

[1] This sermon was preached April 30, 1680.

ness and judgment are the habitation of his throne;" and from thence took occasion to consider what is our especial duty when clouds and darkness are round about us, as they are at this day. And some of you know I have had a great persuasion that the clouds that are gathering will, at least in their first storm, fall upon the people of God. I must repeat it again and again; I have been warning you for some years, and telling you it would be so. The present frame wherewith I have to conflict in my own spirit, and that frame of spirit which I have observed in others, the state and condition of all churches and professors, so far as I know, is,—they are gone into a dreadful security. I speak my heart, and what I know with reference unto our present state and the cause of God; we are gone, I say, into a dismal security: which still confirms me that the storm will come upon us, and that it will not be long ere we feel it. My design is, therefore, to show you how we ought to behave ourselves under the perplexities and difficulties we are to conflict withal in this world. And I have not sat studying for things to speak, but only tell you the experience of my own heart, and what I am labouring after. I have already showed you what our duty is under the approach of these distressing, calamitous times that are coming upon us, and what faith will do in such a season.

II. I am now, in the second place, to show you how faith will carry it under other perplexities, that either are present or are coming upon us. And here I shall show you,—1. How we may live by faith, under all the reproaches and persecutions that do or may befall us, upon the account of that order and fellowship of the gospel, of that way of God's worship, which we do profess. 2. How we may live by faith, with reference unto the returning upon us of antichristian darkness and cruelty, if God shall suffer it so to be. 3. How we may live by faith under an apprehension of great and woful decays in churches, in church members, in professors of all sorts, and in the gradual withdrawings of the glory of God from us upon that account.

1. How may we live by faith, *with reference unto those reproaches,* that scorn and contempt, which are cast upon the ways of God which we profess, that worship of God wherein we are engaged, and that order of the gospel that we do observe, with the persecutions that will attend us upon the account thereof? Truly, I may say of it as the Jews said to Paul about Christianity, Acts xxviii. 22, "As for this sect, we know that everywhere it is spoken against." The whole world seems to be combined, that the name of Israel, in this way, may no more be had in remembrance. There are few that are concerned about these things while it is well with them, their families, their relations, estates, inheritances. Let the ways of God be reproached, what is that to them? they are not concerned in it. They

cannot say, as the psalmist doth, when he speaks in the person of Christ, Ps. lxix. 9, "The reproaches of them that reproached thee are fallen upon me." Perhaps some of us are more sensible than others (or, at least, have reason so to be) of those reproaches that are continually cast upon the ways of God, seeing they are more particularly upon us; but to those that are not concerned in this scorn and contempt, I would say three things:—

First. *What evidence have you that you have a concern in God's glory?* For these things are those whereby God is glorified in this world; and if you are not concerned when there are so many reflections thrown upon it, pray consider what evidence you have in yourselves of any concernment in the glory of God.

Secondly. *What evidence have you that you have a love to these things*, that can hear them reproached, scorned, contemned, and never be moved at it? An honest, good man, would find himself concerned if his wife or children were reproached with lies and shameful things, because of his interest in them; but for them that can hear the ways of God reproached every day, and, so long as it is well with them and theirs, are not concerned thereat,—they can have no evidence that they have a love unto them. Nehemiah cries out upon such an occasion, chap. iv. 4, "Hear, O our God; for we are despised: and turn their reproach upon their own head, and give them for a prey in the land of captivity." God hath made special promises to such as are thus concerned: Zeph. iii. 18, "I will gather them," saith he. Whom will he gather? "Them that are sorrowful for the solemn assembly, who are of thee, to whom the reproach of it was a burden." The solemn assemblies were reproached and mocked; and there were some of them (not all) to whom this reproach was a burden. "These," saith God, "I will gather;"—"gather them under my gracious protection."

Thirdly. To add one word more: If you are not concerned in the reproaches that are cast upon the ways of God, *persecution shall awaken you*, and either make you concerned or put an end unto all your profession.

Now, the inquiry is, how, under these difficulties that we have to conflict withal, we shall glorify God, and pass through them without loss,—unto our spiritual advantage?

The apostle, in the 10th chapter to the Hebrews, where he describes this very condition I have been speaking of, doth fully direct us. "Ye endured," saith he, "a great fight of afflictions; partly, whilst ye were made a gazingstock both by reproaches and afflictions; and partly, whilst ye became companions of them that were so used. For ye had compassion of me in my bonds, and took joyfully the spoiling of your goods," etc., verses 32–34. But how shall we carry ourselves under this condition here described? "Now," saith he, verse 38, "the just shall live by faith."

What is the work of faith in this condition, that we may glorify God, and carry it through to a good and comfortable issue to ourselves? Call your own hearts to an account, and see how faith will work to give you support and supply. I will tell you what I am labouring after in my own heart; and the Lord direct you to find out what will be more useful! What will faith do in such a case? I answer,—

(1.) *Faith will give us such an experience of the power*, efficacy, sweetness, and benefit of *gospel ordinances* and gospel worship, *as shall cause us to despise all that the world can do in opposition unto us.* Here I would cast my anchor, and exhort you not to be confident of yourselves; for nothing else will keep and preserve you. An opinion, a well-grounded opinion and judgment, will not preserve you; love to this or that man's ministry, will not preserve you; that you are able to dispute for your ways, will not preserve you (I can give you instances wherein they have all failed);—resolutions that, if all men should leave them, you would not, are insufficient. Nothing can preserve you but a sense and experience of the usefulness and sweetness of gospel administrations, according unto the mind of Jesus Christ. This faith alone can give you. "Desire," saith the apostle Peter, "the sincere milk of the word," 1 Epist. ii. 2;—"Desire, and labour to continue in, the ordinances of the gospel, and the worship of God under the administration of the word." How? "If so be ye have tasted that the Lord is gracious," verse 3; otherwise you will never desire it. I should hope that, through the grace of God (and otherwise I do not hope it), I might yet continue (if, indeed, I could keep alive) an experience that, in the dispensation of the word, I find a constant exercise of faith in God, delight in him, love to him;—if I find that I come to the word as expecting to receive from God a sense of his love and supply of his grace; I should then, I say, have good hope, through grace, that ten thousand difficulties should never shake me in my continuance in this way. But if it be otherwise, there will be no continuance nor abiding. I mention these things, because, to the best observation such a poor worm as I am can make, there is a mighty coldness and indifferency grown upon the spirits of men in attending to the worship of God. There is not that life, spirit, courage, and delight in it as hath been in times past; and if so, where it may end God only knows. This, I say, is the first thing that faith will do in this state, if we set it on work. If we would but labour to stir up faith to find those supplies of spiritual life and strength in the ways of his worship and ordinances,—if we would labour to overcome prejudices, and set ourselves against sloth and negligence,—we should find ourselves as other men, and greatly set at liberty as to what the world can do unto us. This is that which faith can do for us in such a state of things; and this is that I would be labouring to bring my own heart unto.

(2.) *Faith*, in such a season, *will bring the soul into such an experimental sense of the authority of Jesus Christ, as to make it despise all other things.* I profess, if it were not for the authority of Christ, I would renounce all your meetings; they would have neither form nor comeliness in them why they should be desired. But a deep respect unto the authority of Christ (unless our evil hearts are betrayed by unbelief and weakness) is that which will carry us through all that may befall us. Faith will work this double respect unto the authority of Christ:—

[1.] *As he is the great head and lawgiver of the church*, who alone hath received all power from the Father to institute all worship; and whoever imposes herein usurps his crown and dignity. All power to institute spiritual worship is given unto Christ in heaven and in earth. What then? "Go, therefore," saith he, "and teach men to observe all things whatsoever I have commanded you," Matt. xxviii. 18–20. Bring your souls to this exercise of faith, that those things we do are commanded us by Christ, who is the sovereign Lord of our consciences, who hath sovereign authority over our souls. We must all appear before his judgment-seat, who will require of us whether we have done and observed what he hath commanded us or no. Do not only say these things, but labour greatly by faith to *affect* your consciences with *this authority of Christ*, and you will find that all other *authorities will come to nothing*, however you may suffer for it.

[2.] Faith respects the authority of Christ, *as he is "Lord of lords, and King of kings;"* as he sits at the right hand of God, expecting all his enemies to become his footstool; as he hath not only a golden sceptre in his hand, "a sceptre of righteousness," wherewith he rules his church, but also an iron rod, to break all his enemies in pieces like a potter's vessel. If faith exercises itself upon this power and authority of Christ over his enemies, it will pour contempt upon all that the world can do. You cannot be carried before any magistrate, but Christ is there present, greater than them all,—who hath their breath in his hands, their lives and their ways at his disposal, and can do what he pleases with them. Faith will bring in the presence of Christ in such a season; when otherwise your hearts would fail for fear, and you would be left unto your own wisdom, which is folly, and your own strength, which is but weakness. But if you have but faith working in the sense of this authority, it will make you like those well-composed persons in the 3d of Daniel. Do not wonder at the greatness of their answer and the composure of their spirits when they looked on the fiery furnace on the one hand, and the fiery countenance of terrible majesty on the other. "Know, that God," say they, "whom we serve, is able to deliver us out of thy hand; but if not,—if God will not give us this present deliverance, be it known unto thee, O king, we will not serve thy gods, nor worship thy golden image," verses 17, 18. Faith will give us the same composure of spirit, and the same resolution; and with these things should we relieve ourselves under the worst that can befall us.

(3.) *Faith*, in such a case and condition, *will bring to mind*, and make effectual upon our souls, *the examples of them that have gone before us* in giving the same testimony that we do, and in the sufferings that they underwent upon that account. When the apostle had told the believing Hebrews, that through all their trials, tribulations, and sufferings, they must live by faith, Heb. x., "What encouragement," might they say, "shall we receive by faith?" Why, saith he, "Faith will bring to mind all the examples of them that have gone before you, that have suffered, and been afflicted, and distressed as you now are;"—which account takes up the whole 11th chapter, and a good part of the beginning of the 12th. It is a great thing when faith revives an example. Let us, then, by faith, carry in our minds the examples that are recorded in the Scripture. There is the example of Moses, the apostle gives it us; and it is an eminent instance: "He chose rather to suffer affliction with the people of God, than to enjoy the pleasures of sin for a season; esteeming the reproach of Christ greater riches than the treasures in Egypt." He, by the dark promise he had to live upon, endured the reproach of Christ. My brethren, take the prophets for an example of them that have suffered; and consider how the apostles have gone before us: but do not stop at them; for there is a greater than Moses, and the prophets, and apostles,—greater than even a cloud of witnesses; and that is no less a person than the Lord Jesus Christ. Heb. xii. 2, "Looking unto Jesus, the author and finisher of our faith; who for the joy that was set before him endured the cross, despising the shame." He underwent the contradiction of sinners against himself, "and is now set down at the right hand of God." Faith, calling to mind these great examples, would give us great support under all the trials we may be brought unto, and conflict with. Whither are we going? what do we hope for? We would be where Moses is, and where the prophets are; but how got they thither? They did not get thither through the increase of riches, and multiplying to themselves lordships in the world; but by sufferings and the cross. Through many tribulations they entered into the kingdom of heaven.

(4.) *Faith will receive in the supplies that Christ hath laid up for his people, in such a season.* Christ hath made peculiar provision for suffering saints. And it consists in two things:—First, In his special presence with them. He will be with them in the fire, and in the water. Secondly, In the communication of the sense of God's love unto them. Their "tribulation worketh patience, and patience experience, and experience hope; and then the love of God is shed abroad in our hearts by the Holy Ghost, which is given to us," Rom. v. 3–5. Faith will bring all these things into the soul. But your minds must be spiritual, or you cannot put forth one act of faith for the bringing in this special provision that is laid up for suffering saints;—and very few attain this spiritual frame, where faith fetches in these spiritual consolations Christ hath prepared for such souls. This is one way whereby we may live by faith in such a season. Search, therefore, and make inquiry in your entrance into troubles, what sense faith gives you of the love of God, to carry you through these difficulties.

(5.) *It is faith alone that can relieve us with respect unto the recompense of reward.* Moses "suffered affliction with the people of God; for he had respect to the recompense of reward," Heb. xi. 25, 26. The light and momentary affliction which we undergo in this world, "worketh for us a far more exceeding and eternal weight of glory," 2 Cor. iv. 17. Who knows, but in a few days some of us may be taken into that incomprehensible glory, where we shall eternally admire that ever we did put any manner of weight on things here below? Faith will fix your eye on the eternal recompense of reward. We have, indeed, a faith now at work, that fixes the minds of men upon this and that way of deliverance, and this and that strange accident; but we shall find that true faith will burn up all this as stubble.

(6.) And lastly, *faith will work by patience.* The apostle tells us "we have need of patience, that, after we have done the will of God, we might receive the promise;" and we are to be "followers of them who through faith and patience inherit the promises," Heb. x. 36, vi. 12.

This is something of what I had to offer unto you, and, I hope, both seasonable and useful. However, it is what I can attain unto in these times of reproach, scorn, and contempt, that are cast upon us, and persecutions approaching. I say, faith will discover to us that efficacy, sweetness, power, and advantage in spiritual ordinances, as to make us willing to undergo any thing for them. Faith will bring our souls into such subjection unto the authority of Christ, as Head of the church, and Lord over the whole creation, that we shall not be terrified with what man can do unto us. Faith will furnish us with examples of the saints of God, whom he hath helped and assisted to go through sufferings, and who are now crowned and at rest in heaven. Faith will help us to keep our eye fixed, not upon the things of this world, but upon the eternal recompense of another world, and glory therein. And faith will also work by patience, when difficulties shall be multiplied upon us.

SERMON XII.[1]

THE USE OF FAITH, IF POPERY SHOULD RETURN UPON US.

"The just shall live by his faith."—HAB. ii. 4.

OUR inquiry is, how we may live by faith, with reference unto those difficulties we have, or may have, to conflict with in the days wherein we live. The last head we spake to was, how we may live by faith in reference to all the reproaches and scornful contempt that are cast upon that way of worship, that order and fellowship of the gospel, which we cleave unto, and the persecutions which we may undergo upon that account. I now proceed:—

2. The second difficulty that we have, or may have, to conflict with, is, *the return of Popery into this land.* Half the talk of the world is upon this subject. I have nothing to say to some among ourselves; but I verily believe, that those who have the conduct of the papal, antichristian affairs throughout the world are endeavouring to bring it in upon us. I remember what holy Latimer said when he came to die, "Once I believed Popery would never return into England; but," said he, "I find it was not faith, but fancy." I wish it prove not so with many of us. Now, that which I am to speak unto is this,—how we should live by faith, both in the prospect of the danger of it, and if it should come upon us. I shall name unto you a few things which I exercise myself with. If you have more supporting thoughts, and a better guidance of light, I pray God confirm it unto you.

(1.) The first thing I would exercise my thoughts upon, and that my faith rests in, in this case, is this,—*that there is a fixed, determinate time* in the counsel of God, when Antichrist and Babylon, and idolatry and superstition, together with that profaneness of life which they have brought in, *shall be destroyed.* It is so fixed, that it shall not be altered: all the wisdom of men, all the sins of men, and all our unbelief, shall not hinder it a day; it shall assuredly come

[1] This sermon was preached May 7, 1680.

to pass in its appointed season. This time is reckoned up in Scripture by days, by months, by years;—not that we should know the *time* of it, but that we should know the *certainty* of it; for if it hath but so many days, but so many months and years, then it must have a certain period.

Under the Old Testament we see this all along. Saith God to Abraham, " Know of a surety that thy seed shall be a stranger in a land that is not theirs, and they shall afflict them four hundred years; and also that nation will I judge," Gen. xv. 13, 14. They knew not the beginning nor the ending of this four hundred years; but they knew that at the end of them it should be as God had said: and " the self-same day it came to pass," Exod. xii. 41. Likewise God threatens the Jews with a seventy-years captivity in Babylon: " And it shall come to pass," saith God, " when the seventy years are accomplished, that I will punish the king of Babylon, and that nation for their iniquity," Jer. xxv. 11, 12. The church knew not when they began, or when they would end; but this they knew, that the same day they were accomplished it should be as God had said. And so it was.

The fixing and computing of the time of the Man of Sin, of Antichrist, by days, and months, and years, is to secure our faith in the punctual determination of the season, but not to satisfy our curiosity when the season should be. But the consideration of this, that there is such a time, or a determinate season, is a great foundation of faith and patience. Isa. lx. 22, " A little one shall become a thousand, and a small one a strong nation: I the LORD will hasten it in his time." But if there be a fixed time for the accomplishment of this promise, you may ask, "How can it then be hastened?" Why, if you live in the exercise of faith and patience, it shall surprise you; it shall come when you do not think it will, nor expect it: " I will hasten it in his time;"—"I will not bring it before its time, be ye never so patient or impatient; but exercise faith and patience, and I will so order it, that it shall be a sweet surprisal unto you." And it is a means of patience, Hab. ii. 3, " If the vision" seem to "tarry, wait for it; for it will surely come." When we know it will come, when we know there is such a determinate time, and that it will surely come, it is a great ground of patience to wait for it. This is a great consideration with me, and I leave it with you. Here I can exercise faith, without fancy or conjecture, that there is a certain determinate time in the counsel of God wherein he will pour out all his judgments and plagues upon the antichristian world, until Antichristianism be destroyed and rooted out.

(2.) Another thing that comforts my heart is this,—it is *no less glorious* to suffer under the *beast* and the false prophet than it was to suffer under the *dragon*. The book of the Revelation is chiefly made up of these two things,—of the persecutions of the church; one by the dragon, and *he* is conquered; the other by the *beast and false prophet*, and *they* shall be conquered. The dragon was the heathen power of the Roman empire; and it was a glorious thing to suffer under that power. They that did so are described, Rev. vii. 14, 15, "These are they which came out of great tribulation, and have washed their robes, and made them white in the blood of the Lamb. Therefore are they before the throne of God, and serve him day and night in his temple: and he that sitteth on the throne shall dwell among them." And of those that suffered under the beast and the false prophet it is said, Rev. xii. 11, "They overcame him by the blood of the Lamb, and by the word of their testimony." We account them great and glorious persons who won the liberty of the gospel and the Christian religion by suffering against the pagan power, and who destroyed all idolatry by their blood, starving and "famishing all the gods of the earth," Zeph. ii. 11. Never were men more glorious than they. These made up the "Turba palmifera;" that is, the company who, with palms in their hands, and a new song in their mouths, give glory unto God, Rev. vii. 9–12. I say, it is not less glorious to suffer under the beast and false prophet, the second persecuting power,—that is, the papal, antichristian power,—than it was before under the pagan. This the church hath for many ages conflicted withal, and must continue to do so, until the time is come when they shall have a perfect and complete conquest over this also. It is a glorious thing, and I would have you reckon upon it as such. If a time of going into Smithfield should again come,—if God shall call us to that fiery trial or any other, whatever it may be,—remember that to suffer against Antichrist is as great and glorious as to suffer against Paganism.

(3.) Though our *persons* fall, our *cause* shall be as truly, certainly, and infallibly victorious, as that Christ sits at the right hand of God. Among the heathens, men of courage did not value their own lives, so their cause was carried on. Now, however your persons or my person may fall in this trial, yet the cause in which we are engaged shall as surely conquer as Christ is alive and shall prevail at last. Upon the first rise of the beast, it is said, Rev. xiii. 7, "He made war with the saints, and overcame them." The poor Waldenses looked upon themselves to be the people there prophesied of; and said, when they were under the butcheries of the papal power, "We are the conquered people of God; but there shall come forth conquerors." When going to die, they knew and believed their cause would conquer. And so, after Antichrist hath conquered and prevailed over persons for a season, at length it will come to a final issue. "They shall make war with the Lamb, and the Lamb shall overcome them; for they that are with him are called, and chosen, and faithful," Rev. xvii. 14. The gospel shall be victorious. This is the third thing that greatly comforts and refreshes me,—that if God should give me the honour, the strength, and grace to die in this cause, my cause shall be victorious, as sure as if I had the crown in my hand.

(4.) *The judgments of God shall come upon the antichristian world when they look not for them;* when the kings of the earth do not look for them; yea, when believers themselves do not look for them;—they shall come so suddenly. The Holy Ghost saith so expressly, Rev. xviii. 8, "Her plagues shall come in one day, death, and mourning, and famine; and she shall be utterly burned with fire." How is it possible that one that is in the state and condition wherein she is, should have her plagues come upon her in *one day?* The reason is added, "For strong is the Lord God who judgeth her." Almighty strength shall be put forth for the accomplishing of it. And if this be not enough, the 17th verse tells you that it shall come in "one hour." And I do verily believe that the destruction of this cursed antichristian state (of the head of it) will be brought about by none of those means we see or know of; but that the strong Lord God shall break in upon her and destroy her by ways unknown to us. It may be to-morrow; it may be not these hundred years. She herself, when it is done, shall look for no such thing. Verses 7, 8, "She hath glorified herself, and lived deliciously; for she saith in her heart, I sit a queen, and am no widow, and shall see no sorrow. Therefore shall her plagues come in one day." When she is boasting herself, destruction shall come;—when the kings of the earth shall have no expectation of it; for they shall cry, verse 16, "Alas, alas! that great city, Babylon, that mighty city; for in one hour so great riches is come to nought." And believers themselves will be such as the children of Israel in Egypt. When Moses came they could not believe, because of the cruel bondage they were under: it is like the day wherein God's judgments will come upon Antichrist, the old enemies of Jesus Christ.

(5.) I would consider very much with myself the greatness of *the indignation of God against those that shall in the least comply with Antichristianism* when it doth come upon us. In Rev. xiii. 11, there is mention of "a beast that had two horns like a lamb, and he spake as a dragon" (which, I think, is the pope), "and he exerciseth all the power of the first beast;" that is, he exercises a power answerable to the pagan power. And what then? Verse 16, "He caused all, both small and great, rich and poor, free and bond, to receive a mark in their right hand, or in their foreheads; and that no man might buy or sell, save he that had the mark." No matter what the mark is; but to receive any thing of him, is to receive his mark; either in our foreheads, where we shall show it unto all the world; or in our right hands, more privately, where it may be shown when opportunity serves. What then? Why, in chap. xiv. 6, 7, "I saw another angel fly in the midst of heaven, having the everlasting gospel to preach unto them that dwell on the earth, and to every nation, and kindred, and tongue, and people, saying with a loud voice, Fear God, and give glory to him; for the hour of his judgment is come: and worship him that made heaven and earth, and the sea, and the fountains of waters." When Antichrist would bring his mark on the foreheads of the people and into their hands, God, by his gospel, calls men from their false worship and idolatry. But what if they do not obey? The 9th and 10th verses tell us a "third angel followed, saying with a loud voice, If any man worship the beast and his image, and receive his mark in his forehead, or in his hand, the same shall drink of the wine of the wrath of God, which is poured out without mixture into the cup of his indignation; and he shall be tormented with fire and brimstone in the presence of the holy angels, and in the presence of the Lamb," etc. Some will be apt to say, "Let us make a fair composition, and use some compliance, to put an end to these disputes." No; do it at your peril. God saith you shall drink of the wine of his wrath, which is poured out without mixture into the cup of his indignation, and that for ever and ever. And I believe with all my heart and soul that this will be the portion of all the men and women in this nation that shall comply with any return of antichristian idolatry among us,—God shall pour out his indignation upon them.

(6.) Remember that *if the trial comes, it is a day of battle;* and it is not for you, when you should just engage in a battle, to be considering of this or that way or contrivance to escape. No; it is courage, and constancy, and faith alone, must be set on work, or you will not be preserved. All your wisdom and contrivances will not preserve you; but it being come to the issue between Christ and Antichrist, "it is the girding up the loins of your mind," and a "resisting unto blood against sin," and abiding in it, that is your duty, and must preserve you. Nothing will save you but faith, courage, and constancy.

(7.) There are in the Scripture *intimations*, that those who, in an especial manner, cleave unto God and his worship, with faith, love, and delight, shall be preserved and saved. I do not propose this unto you as an object of your faith; all the rest I do: but I say, there are intimations that give me some satisfaction; that they who with quick and lively spirits do act faith, and love, and delight in God and his worship, or that are worshippers in the inner court of the temple, shall be peculiarly secured at such a time. But I am afraid few of us shall have it; because I see so much coldness and deadness grown generally upon us and the churches of Christ. It makes me think exercises will come upon us all; for we have need of them.

To conclude,—

First. Let not your talk about *strange things* keep the thoughts of these things you have been hearing out of your hearts; for you will be tried with Antichristianism before you die. We talk of news, and great things we look for in the world, and that Antichrist shall be destroyed: and so he will; but I do believe he will try us sorely in the meantime.

Secondly. Take heed of *computations.* How wofully and wretchedly have we been mistaken by this! We know the time is determined,—its beginning and ending is known to God; and we must live by faith till the accomplishment.

Thirdly. So many of us as have afresh engaged ourselves in covenant unto God, let us remember that we have taken the "mark of God upon our foreheads;" and it will ill become us to set the mark of Antichrist by it.

This is all I have to offer unto you as to living by faith under the apprehensions of those difficulties we have to conflict withal, in reference to the coming in of profaneness and idolatry, wherewith we are threatened by hell and the world, which are at this day combining together to bring them again upon this nation.

SERMON XIII.[1]

THE USE OF FAITH IN A TIME OF GENERAL DECLENSION IN RELIGION.

"The just shall live by his faith."—HAB. ii. 4.

I AM now come to the last thing that was proposed to be spoken to, and with which I shall shut up the subject, namely,—

3. How we may live by faith, under an apprehension of great and woful decays in churches, in church-members, in professors of all sorts, and in the gradual withdrawing of the glory of God from us all on that account.

I would speak unto three things:—(1.) That this is such a time of decay among us, among churches, among church-members, and pro-

[1] This sermon was preached May 21, 1680.

fessors of all sorts and ways throughout this nation; yea, and other nations too, where there are any that fear God. (2.) That this is, and ought to be, a cause of great trouble and trial unto all that are true believers. And then,—(3.) I shall show you how we may live by faith in such a season,—what it is faith will do to support the soul at such a time.

(1.) That it is *now such a time of decay*, there are too many evidences of it. I will name a few things:—

[1.] A sense of it is impressed upon the minds of all the most judicious and diligent Christians, that do abound most in self-examination, or do take most notice of the ways of God. Multitudes have I heard testifying of it; complaints are received from many in this nation, and the neighbouring nations, that there is a great decay, as to the power of grace and life of faith, among all sorts of professors. And some of them will go farther in their evidence, and tell us that they find the effects of it in themselves; that they find it a matter of great difficulty, requiring great watchfulness and great diligence, in any measure to keep up themselves unto their former frames; and when they have done all, they do not attain their desire. And, to increase this evidence, we are all convinced of it, or else we are notorious hypocrites; for I know not how often I have heard it prayed over in this very place. So that there is sent forth from God a conviction upon the hearts and minds of spiritual, self-examining believers, that churches, church-members, professors, and themselves, are under spiritual decays. This is the first evidence; and therefore, in such a season, it was the best part of the church that made that sad complaint, Isa. lxiii. 17, "O LORD, why hast thou made us to err from thy ways, and hardened our heart from thy fear?" They were sensible that there was a judgment of the hand of God upon them.

[2.] The open *want of love* that is among churches, among church-members, among professors, is another evidence of decay. I will not speak of the want of love among churches one to another; but as to love among church-members, we have scarce the shadow of it remaining among us. Where men have relations, where they have acquaintance, where they have been old friends, where they agree in humour and converse,—there is an appearance of love; and where they agree in a party and faction, there is an appearance of love: but upon the *pure spiritual account* of Christianity and church-membership, we have, I say, scarce the shadow of it left among us. I remember how it was with us, when it was a joy of heart to behold the face of one another;—wherein there was love without dissimulation, in sincerity; love attended with pity, compassion, condescension; yea, love attended with delight. But it is dead in churches, dead among professors.

[3.] Another evidence of this decay is, *want of delight and dili-*

gence in the ordinances of gospel worship. These ordinances were wont to be a joy of heart unto all that feared God; but now there is so much deadness, coldness, and indifferency,—so much undervaluing of the word, self-fulness, pride, and so much an apprehension that we know every thing,—so little endeavour to tremble at every truth, by what means soever it be brought unto us,—as gives a manifest evidence of woful decays that are fallen upon us. Dead preachers! dead hearers!—all things now go down among the churches of God and professors in these nations. And this is attended with two desperate evils; one of which I heard of but lately (but upon inquiry, I find it to be a far greater evil than I took it to be), namely, men—under an apprehension that they do not see others enlivened nor quickened as they were wont to be by the ordinances of divine worship, and finding no such thing in their own hearts neither (in all probability finding themselves to grow dead and useless)—are fallen into an opinion that there is an end of them, and that they ought to attend unto them no more. And this doth befall some that have long walked soberly and with great diligence in the use of ordinances: some in this city, and in other places, are led by foolish delusions to it, because they do not find the spirit, and life, and power of the word and ordinances in themselves and, as they think, in others. A godly and learned minister, that showed me a discourse written upon this subject, in defence of ordinances, did acquaint me with so great a number falling into this abomination, that I did not think it had been possible. This is one of the evils.

The other evil that attends it is this,—that this deadness and indifferency unto ordinances, and want of bringing our necks to the yoke of Christ therein, against all disputings and arguings of flesh and blood, hath taken such place among us, and proceeded so far, that all ways of reformation are useless. Men may make divisions, and do I know not what; but this I know, there is no way of obtaining any reformation, but for men to engage their hearts to return unto God in more delight in his service than there hath been. Some utterly forsake the assemblies; some come with great indifferency,—using their liberty, off and on, at their pleasure. Are not these things evidences of great decays among us? To me they are. I speak not as to this congregation in particular, but as to the state of all churches that I know or can hear of in these nations.

[4.] The last evidence I shall mention of these decays among us, is *our worldly-mindedness,*—conformity to the world, and security. These things have been so often spoken to you, and no reformation hath ensued, that now they are looked upon as words of course; and I am discouraged from speaking of them any more. But assure yourselves, this conformity to the world, and this security that is yet found among us, is a great evidence that the glory of God is departing from us. Ministers preach against worldly-mindedness, security, etc., but it makes no impression upon the minds of men; for we can scarce give an instance of any, the least reformation. These things plainly demonstrate that we are all under great decays.

(2.) A sense of this general decay among churches, church-members, and professors, ought to be an exercise and concern unto our minds. If we think all is well with us, and are satisfied, while we are free from outward troubles, and [do] not concern ourselves about our decays, I will not say we are hypocrites, but, truly, we are poor, low, dead, carnal, unspiritual Christians. I thought to have spoken to these three heads, to show you,—

[1.] How God is dishonoured by this general decay;

[2.] How the world is offended and scandalized at it;

[3.] How the ruin of churches is hastened by it;—which will befall them assuredly, unless God recover us out of this bad state: but I shall waive these things, and proceed:—

(3.) Suppose it be thus (and we do complain of it to one another, not knowing what the issue will be, nor what it may come unto),—*how shall we live by faith under this consideration?* what is the work of faith in this state? If things are so (and I wish any one could evidence they are not; but suppose, for once, that they are so), and our souls are burdened with an apprehension that they are so,—then what will faith do to enable us to pass through this exercise, and to live to God?

I will tell you something of what *I find.* And if God help you not to better things, make use of these, and improve them, that you may give glory to God by believing under this condition also:—

[1.] Faith will mind the soul that notwithstanding this also, *yet Christ hath built his church upon that rock,* that it shall not be utterly prevailed against. "The promise," saith faith, "extends itself as well to the inbred adversaries of our own souls, unbelief, deadness, and all these things, as to our outward enemies." Matt. xvi. 18, "Upon this rock I will build my church; and the gates of hell shall not prevail against it." Though we were all dead, helpless, lifeless, poor creatures,—though we had retained almost nothing but outward order, and had lost the very vigour and essence of faith and obedience,—yet Christ's church shall abide and stand, and those that belong to him shall be preserved. "Such and such are turned apostates," saith the apostle, 2 Tim. ii. 19, "Nevertheless the foundation of God standeth sure, having this seal, The Lord knoweth them that are his." Here is my ground of hope, notwithstanding all this, though one falls after another, though one decays after another,—"Nevertheless the foundation of God standeth sure;" and it hath a seal upon it, "The Lord knoweth them that are his." Every one whom he hath effectually called, and built upon the rock, Jesus Christ, shall be preserved, whatever befalls the residue of the world. To see such a confluence of all manner of dangerous evils from without as are coming this day upon the church of God; and to see, in the meantime, so many evidences of a decaying spiritual state in believers themselves; it will put faith to exercise itself upon this promise of Christ,—"Upon this rock I will build my church; and the gates of hell shall not prevail against it." If you find your spirits at any time pressed with these things, if nothing better occurs at hand, exercise faith upon this promise of Christ, and upon the firm standing of the foundation of God,—that he knoweth who are his, and will carry them through all these difficulties, and land them safe in eternity.

[2.] Faith will also mind the soul that God hath yet *the fulness and residue of the Spirit*, and can pour it out when he pleases, to recover us from this woful state and condition, and to renew us to holy obedience unto himself. There are more promises of God's giving supplies of his Spirit to deliver us from inward decays, than there are for the putting forth the acts of his power to deliver us from our outward enemies. And God is as able to do the inward work,—to revive and renew a spirit of faith, love, and holiness, of meekness, humility, self-denial, and readiness for the cross: he is able, with one word and act of his grace, to renew it; as he is able, by one act of his power, to destroy all his enemies, and make them the footstool of Christ, when he pleases. Live in the faith of this.

The psalmist saith, in Ps. cxlvii. 16, 17, "He scattereth the hoarfrost;" and the issue is, the earth is frozen,—he brings a death upon it. But saith he, in Ps. civ. 30, "Thou sendest forth thy Spirit; and thou renewest the face of the earth." In like manner there is deadness upon all churches and professors, in some measure, at this time;—but God, who hath the fulness of the Spirit, can send him forth and renew the face of the soul,—can give professors and profession another face; not to trim and trick, as now so often is done; not so high and haughty, not so earthly and worldly, as is now so much seen; but humble, meek, holy, broken-hearted, and self-denying. God can send forth his Spirit when he pleases, and give all our churches and professors a new face, in the verdure and flourishing of his grace in them. When God will do this I know not: but I believe God can do this; he is able to do it,—able to renew all his churches, by sending out supplies of the Spirit, whose fulness is with him, to recover them in the due and appointed time. And more; I believe truly, that when God hath accomplished some ends upon us, and hath stained the glory of all flesh, he will renew the power and glory of religion among us again, even in this nation. I believe it truly, but not as I believe the other things I have mentioned unto you: for those I believe absolutely,—namely, that Christ hath built his church upon a rock, and that nothing shall ever finally prevail against it; and that God hath the fulness and the residue of the Spirit to renew us again to all the glory of profession and holy obedience. These I propose as truths that are infallible, that will not fail you, and upon which you may venture your souls to eternity. And if your faith in these things will not give you support and comfort, I know not what else will.

[3.] When your souls are perplexed within you about these things, your faith will say unto you, "O my soul, why art thou cast down? Are not all these things foretold thee,—1 Tim. iv. 1, 'That in the latter times some shall depart from the faith;' 2 Tim. iii. 1–5, 'That in the last days perilous times shall come;' because men should have 'a form of godliness, but deny the power?' Hath it not been foretold that churches shall decay, and lose their first faith and love, in examples that have been set before you?" "Why are you surprised?" saith our Saviour, John xvi. 4, "These things have I told you, that, when the time shall come, ye may remember that I told you of them." I was never nearer a surprisal than by this one thing, how it could possibly be, that after so many instructions,—after so many mercies, trials, fears,—after so many years carrying our lives in our hands, and so many glorious deliverances, there should yet be decays found amongst us, and such going backward. It is a great surprisal to one that considers it aright. But seeing it is foretold that so it shall be, "let us live by faith:" God hath some great end to accomplish out of it; and then all will be well. "When I have performed my whole work upon mount Zion," saith God, "then," etc., Isa. x. 12.

[4.] And lastly, *faith*, if it be in exercise, *will put every soul in whom it is upon an especial attendance unto those duties God calls him unto in such a season.* This accomplishes and completes our living by faith under such a trial as this is. If faith be in us, and in exercise, it will put us upon all these duties that God requires of us in such a season:—

1*st.* It will put us upon *self-examination*, how far we ourselves are engaged in these decays, and have contracted the guilt of them.

2*dly.* It will put us upon great *mourning*, by reason of God's withdrawing himself from us.

3*dly.* It will put us upon *watchfulness* over ourselves, and over one another, that we be not overtaken by the means and causes of these decays.

4*thly.* It will put us upon *zeal* for God and the honour of the gospel, that it may not suffer by reason of our miscarriages.

In one word, faith will do *something;* but for our parts, we do *little* or *nothing.* Faith will do something, I say, wherever it is, when it is stirred up to exercise; but as to these special duties, in reference to these decays that all professors are fallen under,—O how little is it we do in any kind whatever! Would we might advise with one another what to do under these decays,—to further one another in recovering ourselves from them! This, then, is what we are called to, and is required of us,—namely, faith in the faithfulness of Christ, who hath built his church upon the rock, [so] that, be things never so bad, it shall not be prevailed against;—faith in the fulness of the Spirit, and his promise to send him to renew the face of the church; faith in apprehending the truth of God, who hath foretold these things; and faith putting us upon those especial duties that God requires at our hands in such a season.

POSTHUMOUS SERMONS.

PART IV.

SERMONS PUBLISHED

M.DCC.LX.

PREFATORY NOTE.

The dedication and preface to these Sacramental Discourses sufficiently explain in what circumstances they were given to the world. The original publication of them was superintended by the Rev. Richard Winter, B.D., an excellent and useful minister in London, the co-pastor and successor of the Rev. Thomas Bradbury, in the Independent Church, New Court, Carey Street. An edition of them appeared in 1844, with a brief recommendatory preface by William Lindsay Alexander, D.D., of Edinburgh. We avail ourselves of an extract from it, as a just estimate of their character. Among works designed to promote the right observance of the Lord's Supper, these Discourses, he affirms, " by the venerated and learned John Owen, have long occupied a prominent place in the esteem of all competent judges. Though issued originally under the most unfavourable circumstances,—having been not only a posthumous publication, but derived from notes taken from the author's spoken addresses, which were never, in any shape, subjected to his subsequent revision,—they contain so much valuable instruction, profitable exhortation, and pious reflection, in a small compass, that even had they appeared under the sanction of a less illustrious name, it would not have been surprising that they should have gained an extensive and permanent reputation." He commends this work of Owen to all " not already acquainted with its excellencies, as, upon the whole, one of the most useful and instructive companions to the Lord's table with which the literature of our country can supply them."—Ed.

TO MRS COOKE OF STOKE NEWINGTON.

MADAM,—Four years ago the world was favoured, through your means, with a volume of Dr Owen's sermons which never before appeared in print; and it is at your instance that the following Sacramental Discourses of that same venerable divine are now made public. Hereby, madam, you at once express your high value and just esteem for the memory and works of that incomparable author, with your generous concern and prevailing desire of being serviceable to the cause of Christ;—a cause much more dear to you than all the worldly possessions with which the providence of God has blessed you.

With the greatest sincerity it may be said, your constant affection to the habitation of God's house,—your steady adherence to the peculiar doctrines of Christianity,—your kind regards to the faithful ministers of the gospel,—your extensive benevolence to the indigent and the distressed,—your affability to all you converse with,—and, in a word, your readiness to every good work, are so spread abroad, that, as the apostle says to the Thessalonians, "There is no need to speak any thing."

That the Lord would prolong your valuable life, daily refresh your soul with the dew of his grace, and enable you, when the hour of death approaches, to rejoice in the full prospect of eternal life through our Lord Jesus Christ, is the prayer,

Madam,

Of your affectionate and obedient servant,

RICHARD WINTER.

TOOKE'S COURT, CURSITOR STREET,
March 4, 1760.

PREFACE.

The preceding dedication is sufficient to acquaint the public that these Sacramental Discourses are the genuine productions of that great man of God, Dr John Owen, who was for some time, in the last age, vice-chancellor of Oxford. They enter the world through the same channel as his Thirteen Sermons on various occasions, published four years since,—namely, they were at first taken in short-hand from the Doctor's mouth, and, by the late Sir John Hartopp, baronet, Mrs Cooke's pious grandfather, were transcribed into long-hand.

Mr Matthew Henry has this note in his annotations on 2 Kings ii.,—"There are remains of great and good men, which, like Elijah's mantle, ought to be gathered up, and preserved by the survivors,—their sayings, their writings, their examples; that as their works follow them in the reward of them, they may stay behind in the benefit of them." Not that our faith is to stand in the wisdom of men;—the Bible alone is the standard of truth; and there we are bid to go by the footsteps of the flock, and to keep the paths of the righteous. There is a strange itch in the minds of men after novelties; and it is too common a case, that they who are for striking out something new in divinity, are ready to pour contempt on the valuable writings of those who are gone before them; and even the most learned, peaceable, and pious men, shall not escape their unrighteous censures. This is notorious in the conduct of those who embrace the new scheme.

If we inquire of the former age, we shall find there flourished in it some of the greatest and best of men; for whose printed works many acknowledge they have abundant cause to bless God to eternity. Among these, the writings of Dr Owen shine with a peculiar lustre, in the judgment of judicious Christians; and I am persuaded they who peruse them with the spirit of love and of a sound mind, will be as far from asserting that, in his manner of maintaining the doctrine of faith, his right arm appeared to be weakened, as from saying that his right eye was darkened, and unable to discern the object of it.

As to the following Discourses, which the Doctor calls "Familiar Exercises," they are now printed in hopes they will be made useful, through the divine blessing, to assist the meditations of Christians of all denominations in their approaches to the Lord's table, seeing they are so well adapted to answer that sacred purpose.

POSTHUMOUS SERMONS.

DISCOURSE I.[1]

"For he hath made him to be sin for us, who knew no sin; that we might be made the righteousness of God in him."—2 Cor. v. 21.

I SHALL not enter into the opening of this Scripture, but only propose some few things that may be a suitable subject for your present meditation.

There are three things concerning *God the Father*, three things *concerning the Son*, and three things *concerning ourselves*, all in these words that I have mentioned, and all suitable for us to be acting faith upon.

I. I would remember, if the Lord help me, the *sovereignty* of God the Father, his *justice*, and his *grace*:—His sovereignty, "He made him,"—God the Father made him; his justice, "He made him to be sin,"—a sacrifice and an offering for sin; and his grace, "That we might be made the righteousness of God in Christ:"—

1. The *sovereignty* of God. I could mention that this sovereignty of God extends itself to all persons chosen, and show for whom Christ should be made sin; for he was not made sin for all, but for them who became "the righteousness of God in him:" also, the sovereignty of God over things, dispensing with the law so far, that He suffered for sin "who knew no sin;" and we, who had sinned, were let go free;—the sovereignty of God in appointing the Son to this work, "He made him;" for none else could,—he was the servant of the Father. So that the whole foundation of this great transaction lies in the sovereignty of God over persons and things, in reference unto Christ. Let us, then, remember to bow down to the sovereignty of God in this ordinance of the Lord's supper.

2. There is the *justice* of God. "He made him to be sin,"—imputed sin unto him, reckoned unto him all the sins of the elect, caused all our sins to meet upon him, made him a sin-offering, a sacrifice for sin, laid all the punishment of our sins upon him. To this end he sent him forth to be a propitiation for sin, to declare his

[1] Delivered October 10, 1669.

righteousness. The Lord help us to remember that his righteousness is in a special manner exalted by the death of Christ. He would not save us any other way but by making him sin.

3. There is *the grace* of God, [which] manifests itself in the aim and design of God in all this matter. What did God aim at? It was "that we might become the righteousness of God in him,"—that we might be made righteous, and freed from sin.

II. There are three things that lie clear in the words, that we may call to remembrance, concerning the Son. There is his *innocency*, his *purity;* he "knew no sin." There is his *sufferings;* he was "made to be sin." And there is *his merit;* it was "that we might become the righteousness of God in him." Here is another object for faith to meditate upon:—

1. There are many things in Scripture that direct us to thoughts of the spotless *purity*, righteousness, and holiness of Christ, when we think of his sufferings. A "Lamb of God, without spot." He "did no sin, nor had any guile in his mouth." He was "holy, harmless, undefiled, separate from sinners." Faith should call this to mind in the sufferings of Christ, that he "knew no sin." That expression sets sin at the greatest distance from Jesus Christ.

2. The *sufferings* of Christ. "He was made sin;"—a comprehensive word, that sets out his whole sufferings. Look, whatever the justice of God, the law of God, whatever the threatenings of God did require to be inflicted as a punishment for sin, Christ underwent it all. They are dreadful apprehensions that we ourselves have, or can take in, concerning the issue and effect of sin, from the wrath of God, when under convictions, and not relieved by the promises of the gospel; but we see not the thousandth part of the evil of sin, that follows inseparably from the righteousness and holiness of God. The effects of God's justice for sin will no more enter into our hearts fully to apprehend, than the effects of his grace and glory will; yet, whatever it was, Christ underwent it all.

3. Then there is the *merit* of Christ; which is another object of faith that we should call over in the celebration of this ordinance. Why was "he made sin"? It was "that we might become the righteousness of God in him." It is answerable to that other expression in Gal. iii. 13, 14, He hath borne the curse,—"was made a curse for us." To what end? That "the blessing of faithful Abraham might come upon us;" or, that we might be completely made righteous. The design of our assembling together, is to remember how we come to be made righteous. It is, by Christ's being made sin.

III. We may see three things concerning ourselves:—

1. Our own *sin* and *guilt:* he was made sin "for us." If Christ was made sin for us, then we were sinners.

2. We may remember our *deliverance*,—how we were delivered from sin, and all the evils of it. It was not by a word of command or power, or by the interposition of saints or angels, or by our own endeavours; but by the sufferings of the Son of God. And,—

3. God would have us remember and call to mind the *state whereinto we are brought*,—which is a state of righteousness; that we may bless him for that which in this world will issue in our righteousness, and in the world to come, eternal glory.

These things we may call over for our faith to meditate upon. Our minds are apt to be distracted; the ordinance is to fix them: and if we act faith in an especial manner in this ordinance, God will be glorified.

DISCOURSE II.

"The cup of blessing which we bless, is it not the communion of the blood of Christ? The bread which we break, is it not the communion of the body of Christ?"—1 COR. x. 16.

THERE is, in the ordinance of the Lord's supper, an especial and peculiar communion with Christ, in his body and blood, to be obtained. One reason why we so little value the ordinance, and profit so little by it, may be, because we understand so little of the nature of that special communion with Christ which we have therein.

We have this special communion upon the account of the special object that faith is exercised upon in this ordinance, and the special acts that it puts forth in reference to that or those objects: for the acts follow the special nature of their objects. Now,—

1. The special *object of faith*, as acted in this ordinance, is not the *object of faith*, as *faith;* that is, the most general object of it, which is the divine veracity: "He that hath received his testimony, hath set to his seal that God is true," John iii. 33. The divine veracity, or the truth of God, *that* is the formal object of faith, as faith; and makes our faith to be divine faith. But now this is not the special object of faith in this ordinance, but something that doth suppose that.

2. The special object of faith, *as justifying*, is not the special object of faith in this ordinance. The special object of faith, as justifying, is the promise, and Christ in the promise, in general, as "the Saviour of sinners:" so when the apostle called men "to repent and believe," he tells them, "The promise is unto you," Acts ii. 39. And I suppose

[1] Delivered November 26, 1669.

I need not insist upon the proof of this, that the promise, and Christ in the promise as Saviour and Redeemer, is the object of faith, as it is justifying. But this also is supposed in the actings of faith in this ordinance; which is peculiar, and gives us peculiar communion with Christ. Therefore,—

3. The special and peculiar object of faith, the *immediate* object of it in this ordinance, in its largest extent is,—

(1.) The *human nature of Christ,* as the subject wherein mediation and redemption was wrought. Christ is considered to come as a sacrifice; that is laid down as the foundation of it, Ps. xl. 6; Heb. x. 5, "A body hast thou prepared me;" which is synecdochically taken for the whole human nature. Faith, when it would lead itself unto the sacrifice of Christ, which is here represented, doth in an especial manner consider the human nature of Christ; that God prepared him a body for that end. This we are to have peculiar regard unto when we come to the administration or participation of this ordinance. For that end we now celebrate it. Nay,—

(2.) Faith goes farther, and doth not consider merely the human nature of Christ, but considers it as *distinguished into its integral parts,—into body and blood;* both which have a price, value, and virtue given unto them by their union with his human soul: for both the body of Christ and the blood of Christ, upon which the work of our redemption is put in Scripture, have their value and worth from their relation unto his soul; as soul and body, making the human nature, had its value and worth from its relation unto the Son of God: otherwise, he saith of his body, "Handle it, it is but flesh and bones." But where the body of Christ is mentioned, and the blood of Christ is mentioned, there is a distribution of the human nature into its integral parts, each part retaining its relation to his soul; and from thence is its value and excellency. This is the second peculiar in the object of faith in this ordinance.

(3.) There is more than this: they are not only considered as *distinguished,* but as *separate* also;—the blood separate from the body, the body left without the blood. This truth our apostle, in this chapter and the next, doth most signally insist upon; namely, the distinct parts of this ordinance,—one to represent the body, and the other to represent the blood,—that faith may consider them as separate.

The Papists, we know, do sacrilegiously take away the cup from the people; they will give them the bread, but they will not give them the cup: and as it always falls out that one error must be covered with another, or else it will keep no man dry under it, they have invented the doctrine of *concomitance,*—that there is a concomitance; that is, whole Christ is in every kind,—in the bread, and in the wine,—the one doth accompany the other: which is directly to overthrow the ordinance upon another account,—as it is to represent Christ's body and blood as separated one from the other. Our Lord Jesus blessed the bread and the cup, and said, "This is my body;" ["This is my blood;"]—which cannot be spoken distinctly, unless supposed to be separate.

Here, then, is a threefold limitation of the act of faith, even in this ordinance, in a peculiar manner restraining it to a special communion with God in Christ:—that it hath a special regard to the human nature of Christ; to his human nature as consisting of body and blood; and as it respects them as separated, body and blood. Yea,—

(4.) It respects them as *separate in that manner*. You all along know that I do not intend these objects of faith as the ultimate object,—for it is *the person of Christ* that faith rests in,—but those immediate objects that faith is exercised about, to bring it to rest in God. It is exercised about the manner of this separation; that is, the blood of Christ comes to be distinct by being shed, and the body of Christ comes to be separate by being bruised and broken. All the instituted sacrifices of old did signify this,—a violent separation of body and blood: the blood was let out with the hand of violence, and so separated; and then sprinkled upon the altar, and then towards the holy place; and then the body was burned distinct by itself. So, the apostle tells us, it is "the cup which we bless, and the bread which we break;" the cup is poured out, as well as the bread broken, to remind faith of the violent separation of the body and blood of Christ. From this last consideration, of faith acting itself upon the separation of the body and blood of Christ by way of violence, it is led to a peculiar acting of itself upon all the causes of it,—whence it was that this body and this blood of Christ were represented thus separate: and by inquiring into the causes of it, it finds a moving cause, a procuring cause, an efficient cause, and a final cause; which it ought to exercise itself peculiarly upon always in this ordinance.

[1.] A *moving* cause; and that is, the eternal love of God in giving Christ in this manner, to have his body bruised, and his blood shed. The apostle, going to express the love of God towards us, tells you it was in this, that "he spared not his own Son," Rom. viii. 32. One would have thought that the love of God might have wrought in sending his Son into the world; but it also wrought in not sparing of him. Thus faith is called in this ordinance to exercise itself upon that love which gives out Christ not to be spared.

[2.] It reflects upon the *procuring* cause;—whence it is, or what it is, that hath procured it, that there should be this representation of the separated body and blood of Christ; and this is even our own sin. "He was delivered for our offences,"—given for our transgressions,—died to make reconciliation and atonement for our sins: they were the procuring cause of it, upon such considerations of union and covenant which I shall not now insist upon. It leads faith, I say, upon a special respect to sin, as the procuring cause of the death of Christ. A natural conscience, on the breach of the law, leads the soul to the consideration of sin, as that which exposes itself alone to the wrath of God and eternal damnation, but in this ordinance we consider sin as that which exposed Christ to death: which is a peculiar consideration of the nature of sin.

[3.] There is the *efficient* cause;—whence it was that the body and blood of Christ were thus separated; and that is threefold:—principal, instrumental, and adjuvant.

What is the *principal* efficient cause of the sufferings of Christ? Why, the justice and righteousness of God. "God hath set him forth to be a propitiation, to declare his righteousness," Rom. iii. 25. Whence it is said, "He spared him not." He caused all our sins to meet upon him: "The chastisement of our peace was upon him."

Again, there is the *instrumental* cause; and that is the law of God. Whence did that separation, which is here represented unto us, ensue and flow? It came from the sentence of the law, whereby he was hanged upon the tree.

Moreover, the *adjuvant* cause was those outward instruments, the wrath and malice of men: "For of a truth against thy holy child Jesus, whom thou hast anointed, both Herod, and Pontius Pilate, with the Gentiles, and the people of Israel, were gathered together," Acts iv. 27.

Faith considers the cause whence it was that Christ was thus given up, the eternal love of God; the procuring cause was our own sins: and if once faith takes a view of sin as that which hath nailed Christ to the cross, it will have a blessed effect on the soul. And it considers the efficient cause; which is the justice and righteousness of God: the law of God was the instrument in the hand of righteousness, which was holpen on by those outward instruments who had a hand in his suffering, but none in his sacrifice.

[4.] Faith considers in this matter the *end of this separation* of the body and blood of Christ which is thus represented; and that is, ultimately and absolutely, the glory of God. He "set him forth to declare his righteousness," Rom. iii. 25, Eph. i. 6. God aimed at the glorifying of himself. I could easily manifest unto you how all the glorious properties of his nature are advanced, exalted, and will be so to eternity, in this suffering of Christ. The subordinate ends are two; I mean the subordinate ends of this very peculiar act of separation of the body and blood:—1*st*. It was to *confirm the covenant*. Every covenant of old was to be ratified and confirmed by sacrifice; and in confirming the covenant by sacrifice, they divided the sacrifice into two parts, and passed between them before they were offered; and then took it upon themselves that they would stand to the covenant which was so confirmed. Jesus Christ being to confirm the covenant, Heb. ix. 16, the body and blood of Christ, this sacrifice, was to be parted, that this covenant might be confirmed. And,—

2dly. A special end of it was, for the confirming and *strengthening of our faith.* God gives out unto us the object of our faith in parcels. We are not able to take this great mysterious fruit of God's love in gross, in the lump; and therefore he gives it out, I say, in parcels. We shall have the body broken to be considered; and the blood shed is likewise to be considered. This is the peculiar communion which we have with Christ in this ordinance; because there are peculiar objects for faith to act itself upon in this ordinance above others.

The very nature of the ordinance itself gives us a peculiar communion; and there are four things that attend the nature of this ordinance that are peculiar:—It is commemorative, professional, eucharistical, and federal:—

1. The ordinance is *commemorative:* "Do this in remembrance of me." And there is no greater joy to the heart of sinners, and a man knows not how to give greater glory to God, than to call the atonement of sin unto remembrance. It is observed in the offering for jealousy, Numb. v. 15, if a man was jealous, and caused an offering to be brought to God, God allowed neither oil nor frankincense; and the reason is, because it was to bring sin to remembrance. But how sweet is that offering that brings to our remembrance the atonement made for all our sins! That is pleasing and acceptable unto God, and sweet unto the souls of sinners.

2. It has a peculiar *profession* attending it. Saith the apostle, "Doing this, 'ye show forth the Lord's death till he come;' you make a profession and manifestation of it." And, give me leave to say it, they that look towards Christ, and do not put themselves in a way of partaking of this ordinance, they refuse the principal part of that profession which God calls them unto in this world. The truth is, we have been apt to content ourselves with a profession of moral obedience; but it is a profession of Christ's institution by which alone we glorify him in this world. "I will have my death shown forth," saith Christ, "and not only remembered." The use of this ordinance is to show forth the death of Christ. As Christ requires of us to show forth his death, so, surely, he hath deserved it by his death.

3. It is peculiarly *eucharistical.* There is a peculiar thanksgiving that ought to attend this ordinance. It is called "The cup of blessing," or "The cup of thanksgiving;"—the word εὐλογία is used promiscuously for "blessing" and "thanksgiving." It is called "The cup of blessing," because of the institution, and prayer for the blessing of

God upon it; and it is called "The cup of thanksgiving," because we do in a peculiar manner give thanks to God for Christ, and for his love in him.

4. It is a *federal* ordinance, wherein God confirms the covenant unto us, and wherein he calls us to make a recognition of the covenant unto God. The covenant is once made; but we know that we stand in need that it should be often transacted in our souls,—that God should often testify his covenant unto us, and that we should often actually renew our covenant engagements unto him. God never fails nor breaks his promises; so that he hath no need to renew them, but testify them anew: we break and fail in ours; so that we have need actually to renew them. And that is it which we are called unto in this ordinance; which is the ordinance of the great seal of the covenant in the blood of Christ.

Upon all these accounts have we special communion with Christ in this ordinance. There is none of them but I might easily enlarge upon, but I name these heads: and my design is, to help my own faith and yours from roving in the administration of this ordinance, or from a general acting of itself,—to fix it to that which is its particular duty; that we may find no weariness nor heaviness in the administration. Here in these things is there enough to entertain us for ever, and to make them new and fresh to us. But while we come with uncertain thoughts, and know not what to direct our faith to act particularly upon, we lose the benefit of the ordinance.

For the use, it is,—

1. To *bless* God for his institution of his church; which is the seat of the administration of this ordinance, wherein we have such peculiar and intimate communion with Christ. There is not one instance of those which I have named, but, if God would help us to act faith upon Christ in a peculiar manner through it, would give new strength and life to our souls. Now, in the church we have all this treasure. We lose it, I confess, by our unbelief and disesteem of it; but it will be found to be an inestimable treasure to those that use it, and improve it in a due manner.

2. Doth God give us this favour and privilege, that we should be invited to this special communion with Christ in this ordinance? *Let us prepare our hearts for it in the authority of its institution;* let us lay our souls and consciences in subjection to the authority of Christ, who hath commanded these things, and who did it in a signal manner the same night wherein he was betrayed: so that there is a special command of Christ lies upon us; and if we will yield obedience to any of the commands of Christ, then let us yield obedience to this. Prepare your souls for special communion with him, then, by subjugating them thoroughly to the authority of Christ in this ordinance.

3. It will be good for us all to be in *a gradual exercising of our faith* unto these special things, wherein we have communion with Christ. You have heard sundry particulars: here is an object of your faith, that is given to be represented unto you in this ordinance,—that God hath prepared Christ a body, that he might be a sacrifice for you; and that this body was afterward distinguished into his body, strictly so taken, and his blood separated from it; and this in a design of love from God, as procuring the pardon of our sins, as tending to the glory of God, and the establishing of the covenant. Train up a young faith in the way it should go, and it will not depart from it when old. And new things will be found herein every day to strengthen your faith, and you will find much sweetness in the ordinance itself.

DISCOURSE III.[1]

"The cup of blessing which we bless, is it not the communion of the blood of Christ? The bread which we break, is it not the communion of the body of Christ?"—1 COR. x. 16.

I HAVE been treating somewhat about the special communion which believers have with Christ in the ordinance of the Lord's supper. There remains yet something farther to be spoken unto, for our direction in this great work and duty; and this is taken from *the immediate ends* of this ordinance. I spake, as I remember, the last day to the specialty of our communion, from the consideration of the immediate ends of the death of Christ: now I shall speak to it in reference unto the immediate ends of this ordinance; and they are two,—one whereof respects our faith and our love, and the other respects our profession: which two make up the whole of what is required of us; for, as the apostle speaks, Rom. x. 10, "With the heart man believeth unto righteousness, and with the mouth confession is made unto salvation." Both these ends—that which respects our faith and love, and that which respects our profession—are mentioned by our apostle in the next chapter. Verse 24, there is mention of that end of this ordinance which respects our faith. Now, that is recognition. Recognition is a calling over or a commemoration of the death of Christ. "This do," says he, "in remembrance of me." That which respects our profession is a representation and declaration of the Lord's death. Verse 26, "As often as ye eat this bread, and drink this cup, ye do show"—ye

[1] Delivered December 10, 1669.

declare, ye manifest—"the Lord's death till he come." These are the two immediate great ends of this ordinance:—a recognition of the death of Christ, which respects our faith and love; and a representation of it, which respects our profession. Both are required of us.

I. There is that which respects our *faith.* The great work of faith is to make things that are absent, present to a soul, in regard to their sweetness, power, and efficacy; whence it is said to be "the evidence of things not seen:" and it looks backward unto the causes of things, and it looks forward unto the effects of things,—to what hath wrought out grace, and to what grace is wrought out; and makes them, in their efficacy, comfort, and power, to meet and centre in the believing soul.

Now, there are three things in reference unto the death of Christ that faith in this ordinance doth recognise, call over, and commemorate. The first is, the faith of Christ in and for his work; the second is, the obedience of Christ; and the third is, the work itself:—

1. Faith calls over the *faith of Christ.* Christ had a double faith in reference to his death:—one with respect unto himself, and his own interest in God; and the other in respect to the cause whose management he had undertaken, and the success of it. He had faith for both these.

(1.) The Lord Christ had faith in reference to *his own person* and to his own interest in God. The apostle, declaring (Heb. ii. 14) that because "the children were partakers of flesh and blood, Christ also did partake of the same," that so he might die to deliver us from death, brings that text of Scripture, verse 13, in confirmation of it, which is taken out of Ps. xviii. 2, "And again," saith he, "I will put my trust in him." How doth this confirm what the apostle produces it for? Why, from hence, that in that great and difficult work that Christ did undertake, to deliver and redeem the children, he was all along carried through it by faith and trust in God. "He trusted in God," saith he; and that made him undertake it. And he gives a great instance of his faith when he was departing out of the world. There are three things that stick very close to a departing soul:—the giving up of itself; the state wherein it shall be when it is given up; and the final issue of that estate. Our Lord Jesus Christ expressed his faith as to all three of them. As to his departure, Luke xxiii. 46, "He cried with a loud voice, Father, into thy hands I commend my spirit: and having said thus, he gave up the ghost." What was his faith as to what would become of him afterwards? That also he expresses, Ps. xvi. 10, "For thou wilt not leave my soul in hell; neither wilt thou suffer thine Holy One to see corruption,"—"My soul shall not be left under the state of the dead, whereunto it is going; nor my body see corruption." What was his faith as to the future issue of things? That he expresses, verse 11, "Thou wilt show me the path of life" (which is his faith for his rising again): "in thy presence is fulness of joy; at thy right hand there are pleasures for evermore;" —where he was to be exalted. And these words, "Father, into thy hands I commend my spirit," were the first breaking forth of the faith of Christ towards a conquest. He looked through all the clouds of darkness round about him towards the rising sun,—through all storms, to the harbour,—when he cried those words with a loud voice, and gave up the ghost. And, by the way, it is the highest act of faith upon a stable bottom and foundation, such as will not fail, to give up a departing soul into the hands of God; which Jesus Christ here did for our example. Some die upon presumptions,—some in the dark; but faith can go no higher than, upon a sure and stable ground, to give up a departing soul into the hands of God: and that for these reasons, to show the faith of Christ in this matter:—

[1.] Because the soul is then entering into a *new state*, whereof there are these two properties that will try it to the utmost:—that it is *invisible;* and that it is *unchangeable.* I say, there are two properties that make this a great act of faith:—

1*st.* The state is *invisible.* The soul is going into a condition of things that "eye hath not seen, nor ear heard;"—that nothing can take any prospect into but faith alone. However men may talk of the invisible state of things which our souls are departing into, it is all but talk and conjecture, besides what we have by faith. So that to give up a soul cheerfully and comfortably into that state, is a pure act of faith.

2*dly.* It is *unchangeable.* It is a state wherein there is no alteration, and though all alterations should prove for the worse, yet it is in the nature of man to hope good from them; but here is no more alteration left: the soul enters into an unchangeable state. And,—

[2.] The second reason is,—because *the total sum of a man's life is now cast up,* and he sees what it will come to. While men are trading in the world, though they meet with some straits and difficulties, yet they have that going on which will bring in something, this way or that way;—but when it comes to this, that they can go no farther, then see how things stand with a departing soul; the whole sum is cast up, there is no more venture to be made, no more advantage to be gained,—he must stand as he is. And when a man takes a view of what he is to come to, he needs faith to obtain a comfortable passage out of it. And,—

[3.] Even *death itself brings a terror with it, that nothing can conquer but faith;* I mean, conquer duly. He is not crowned, that doth not overcome by faith. It is only to be done through the death of Christ. "He delivered them who through fear of death were all their lifetime subject to bondage." There is no deliverance that is true and real, from a bondage-frame of spirit [with reference] to death, but by faith in Christ.

I touch on this by the way, to manifest the glorious success the faith of Christ had; who, in his dying moments, cried out, "Father, into thy hands I commend my spirit." And this is that we are to call over in the remembering of his death. It is a very great argument the apostle uses to confirm our faith, when, speaking of the patriarchs of old, he says, "These all died in faith." But that "all" is nothing to this argument, that Jesus Christ, our head and representative, who went before us, "He died in faith." And this is the principal inlet into life, immortality, and glory,—the consideration of the death of Christ, dying in that faith that he gave up his soul into the hands of God, and was persuaded "God would not leave his soul in hell, nor suffer his Holy One to see corruption;" but that he would show him the "path of life," and bring him to his "right hand, where there are pleasures for evermore."

(2.) Christ had a faith for *the cause wherein he was engaged.* He was engaged in a glorious cause, a great undertaking;—to deliver all the elect of God from death, hell, Satan, and sin; to answer the law, to undergo the curse, and to bring his many children unto glory. And dreadful oppositions lay against him in this his undertaking. See what faith he had for his cause, Isa. l. 7–9, "The Lord GOD will help me; therefore shall I not be confounded: therefore have I set my face like a flint, and I know that I shall not be ashamed. He is near that justifieth me; who will contend with me? who is mine adversary? let him come near to me. Behold, the Lord GOD will help me; who is he that shall condemn me?"—"Who is mine adversary?" or (as in the Hebrew), "Who is the master of my cause? I have a cause to plead, who is the master of it?" "I am engaged in a great cause," saith he, "and I am greatly opposed; they seek to make me ashamed, to confound me, to condemn me." But here is faith for his cause: "The Lord GOD will justify me," saith he. It was with Christ as it would have been with us under the covenant of works: man ought to have believed he should be justified of God, though not by Jesus Christ; so here, he had faith that he should be justified. "God will justify me; I shall not be condemned in this cause that I have undertaken."

It is matter of great comfort and support, to consider that when the Lord Jesus Christ had in his eye all the sins of all the elect upon the one hand, and the whole curse of the law and the wrath of God on the other, yet he cried, "I shall not be confounded;"—"I shall go through it, I shall see an end of this business, and make an end of sin, and bring in everlasting righteousness; and God will justify me in it." We are in an especial manner to call to remembrance the faith that Christ had for his cause; and we ought to have the same faith for it now, for this great conquest of overcoming the devil, sin, death, hell, and the saving of our souls. He hath given us an example for it.

There is one objection lies against all this, and that is this: "But did not Christ despond in his great agony in the garden, when he cried three times, 'Father, if it be possible, let this cup pass from me?' and in that dreadful outcry upon the cross, which he took from the 22d Psalm, a prophecy of him, 'My God, my God, why hast thou forsaken me?' Doth not Christ seem to repent here, and to despond?"

I answer, In this difficult inquiry two things are to be stated:—first, in reference *to his person*, That it was impossible Christ should have the indissolubility of his personal union utterly hid from him. He knew the union of his human nature unto the Son of God could not be utterly dissolved,—that could not be utterly hid from him; so that there could not be despair, properly so called, in Christ. And, secondly, this is certain also, That *the contract* he had with the Father, and the promises he had given him of being successful, could never utterly be hid from him. So that his faith, either as to his person or cause, could not possibly be utterly ruined. But there was a severe and terrible conflict in the human nature, arising from these four things:—

First. From the view which he was exalted to take of *the nature of the curse that was then upon him.* For the curse was upon him, Gal. iii. 13, "He was made a curse for us: for it is written, Cursed is every one that hangeth on a tree." Give me leave to say, Jesus Christ saw more into the nature of the curse of God for sin than all the damned in hell are able to see; which caused a dreadful conflict in his human soul upon that prospect.

Secondly. It arose from hence, that *the comforting influences of the union with the divine nature were restrained.* Jesus Christ was in himself "a man of sorrows, and acquainted with grief;" but yet, all the while, there were the influences of light and glory from the divine nature to the human, by virtue of their union;—and now they are restrained, and instead of that, was horrible darkness, and trembling, and the curse, and sin, and Satan, round about him; all presenting themselves unto him: which gave occasion to that part of his prayer, Ps. xxii. 12–21, "Deliver my soul from the sword; my darling from the power of the dog. Save me from the lion's mouth," etc. There was the sword in the curse of the law, and the dog and the lion, or Satan, as it were, gaping upon him, as if ready to devour him; for it was the hour and power of darkness, dread and terror. Besides, there were cruel men, which he compares to "the bulls of Bashan," which rent him. This caused that terrible conflict.

Thirdly. It was from *the penal desertion of God.* That he was under a penal desertion from God is plain: "My God, my God, why hast thou forsaken me?" And when I say so, I know little of what I say;—I mean, what it is to be under such penal desertion. For the great punishment of hell, is an everlasting penal desertion from God.

Fourthly. It was from the unspeakable *extremity of the things that he suffered;*—not merely as to the things themselves which outwardly fell upon his body, but as unto that "sword of God which was awakened against him," and which had pierced him to the very soul. The advantage which he had in his sufferings by his divine union, was that which supported and bore him up under that weight, which would have sunk any mere creature to nothing. His heart was enlarged to receive in those pains, that dread and terror, that otherwise he could not have received. And notwithstanding all this, as I showed before, Christ kept up his faith in reference to his person, and kept up his faith in reference to his cause; and a great example he hath given unto us, that though the dog and the lion should encompass us, though we should have desertion from God and pressures more than nature is able to bear, yet there is a way of keeping up faith, trust, and confidence through all, and not to let go our hold of God.

Now, this is the first thing we are to call over in remembrance of Christ, in reference to his death;—that faith he had, both for his person and his cause, in his death. For if you remember any of the martyrs that died, you will stick upon these two things, more than upon the flames that consumed them:—they expressed great faith of their interest in Christ, and in reference to the cause they died for. They are things you will remember. And this you are to be remembering of him who was the head of the martyrs,—our Lord Jesus Christ's faith.

2. We are to call over *his obedience in his death.* The apostle doth propose it unto us, Phil. ii. 5, 6, etc., "Let this mind be in you, which was also in Christ Jesus: who, being in the form of God, thought it not robbery to be equal with God: but made himself of no reputation, and took upon him the form of a servant, and became obedient unto death, even the death of the cross." We are to call over the mind of Christ in suffering. And the following things the Scripture doth peculiarly direct us to consider in the obedience of Christ unto death:—The principle of it, which was love; readiness to and for it; submission under it; his patience during it. They are things the Scripture minds us of concerning the obedience of Christ in his death:—

(1.) Consider *his love,* which is one of the principal things to be regarded in this obedience of Christ;—the love wherewith it was principled. Gal. ii. 20, "He loved me," saith the apostle, "and gave himself for me." 1 John iii. 16, "Hereby perceive we the love of God, because he laid down his life for us." It was his love did it. Rev. i. 5, "Who loved us, and washed us from our sins in his own blood." This gives life to the whole sufferings of Christ, and to our faith too. It was a high act of obedience to God, that he laid down his life; but that obedience was principled with love to us.

And now I pray God to enable me to consider this with my own soul, what that love would stick at, that did not stick at this kind of death we have been speaking of. If Jesus Christ had reserved the greatest thing he was to do for us unto the last, we had not known but his love might have stuck when it came to that,—I mean, when it came to the curse of the law,—though he had done other things. But having done this, he that would not withdraw, nor take off from that, because he loved us, what will he stick at for the future? Our hearts are apt to be full of unkind and unthankful thoughts towards him; as though, upon every dark and black temptation and trial, he would desert us, whose love was such as he would not do it when himself was to be deserted and made a curse. Call over, then, the love of Christ in this obedience. "Yes; but love prevails sometimes," you will say, "with many, to do things that they have no great mind to: we come very difficultly to do some things, when yet, out of love, we will not deny them." But it was not so with Christ; his love was such that he had,—

(2.) An eternal *readiness unto his work.* There are two texts of Scripture inform us of it: Prov. viii. 30, 31, where the Holy Ghost describes the prospect that the Wisdom of God—that is, the Son of God—took of the world and the children of men, in reference to the time he was to come among them. "I was," saith he, "daily his delight, rejoicing always before him; rejoicing in the habitable part of his earth; and my delights were with the sons of men." He considered what work he had to do for the sons of men, and delighted in it. The 40th Psalm expounds this, verses 6–8, "Sacrifice and offering thou didst not desire; mine ears hast thou opened: burnt-offering and sin-offering hast thou not required. Then said I, Lo, I come: in the volume of the book it is written of me," etc. "Sacrifice and burnt-offering will not take away sin," saith he; "then, lo, I come." But doth he come willingly? Yes; "I delight," saith he, "to do thy will, O my God: yea, thy law is within my heart." What part of the will of God was it? The apostle tells you, Heb. x. 10, "Offering the body of Jesus Christ once for all; by the which will we are sanctified." He came not only willingly, but with delight. The baptism he was to be baptized with, he was straitened till it was accomplished. The love he had unto the souls of men, that great design and project he had for the glory of God, gave him delight in his undertaking, notwithstanding all the difficulties he was to meet with.

(3.) We are to remember *his submission to the great work* he was called unto. This he expresses, Isa. l. 5, 6, "The Lord God," saith he, "hath opened mine ear, and I was not rebellious, neither turned away back. I gave my back to the smiters, and my cheeks to them that plucked off the hair: I hid not my face from shame and spitting." The Lord God called him to it, and he was not rebellious, but submitted unto it.

There is one objection arises against this submission; and that is the prayer of Christ in the garden: "Father, if it be possible, let this cup pass from me."

I answer, That was an expression of the horror which was upon the human nature, which we mentioned before. But there were two things that Christ immediately closed upon, which gave evidence to this submission,—that he did not draw back, nor rebel, nor hide himself, nor turn away his face from shame and spitting;—one was this, "Father, thy will be done," saith he; and the other was this, that he refused that aid to deliver him which he might have had: "Know ye not that I could pray the Father, and he would give me more than twelve legions of angels?" He then suffered under the Roman power, and their power was reduced to twelve legions. Saith he, "I could have more than these;" which argues his full submission unto the will of God.

(4.) We are to call over *his patience under his sufferings, in his obedience*, Isa. liii. 7, "He was oppressed, and he was afflicted; yet he opened not his mouth: he is brought as a lamb to the slaughter, and as a sheep before her shearers is dumb, so he openeth not his mouth;"—the highest expressions of an absolute, complete, and perfect patience. Though he was afflicted, and though he had all manner of provocations, "though he was reviled, he reviled not again." The apostle tells us, Heb. xii. 2, "He endured the cross" (that is, he patiently endured it, as the word signifies), "and despised the shame, that he might sit down at the right hand of God."

You see, then, the end of this ordinance of the Lord's supper, is to stir us up to call over the obedience of Christ, both as to his love in it, as to his readiness for it, submission to the will of God in it, and patience under it.

3. Faith is to call over *the work itself;* and that was the *death of Christ.* I shall not now be able to manifest under what consideration in this ordinance faith calls over the death of Christ; but these are the heads I shall speak unto:—It calls it over as a sacrifice, in that it was bloody; it calls it over as shameful, in that it was under

the curse; it calls it over as bitter and dreadful, in that it was penal. It was a bloody, shameful, and penal death: as bloody, a sacrifice; as cursed, shameful; and as it was penal, it was bitter. In the work of faith's calling over these things, there is a peculiar work of love also. Saith our Saviour, "This do in remembrance of me." These are the words we would use unto a friend, when we give him a token or pledge, "Remember me." What is the meaning of it? "Remember my love to you, my kindness for you; remember my person." There is a remembrance of love towards Christ to be acted in this ordinance, as well as a remembrance of faith: and as the next object of faith is the benefits of Christ, and thereby to his person; so the next object of love is the person of Christ, and thereby to his benefits;—I mean, as represented in this ordinance. "Remember me," saith he; that is, "with a heart full of love towards me." And there are three things wherein this remembrance of Christ by love, in the celebration of this ordinance, doth consist:—delight in him, thankfulness unto him, and the keeping of his word. He that remembers Christ with love, hath these three affections in his heart:—

(1.) He *delights in him.* The thoughts of Christ are sweet unto him, as of an absent friend; but only in spiritual things we have this great advantage, we can make an absent Christ present to us. This we cannot in natural things. We can converse with friends only by imagination; but by faith we make Christ present with us, and delight in him.

(2.) There is *thanksgiving towards him.* That love which is fixed upon the person of Christ will break forth in great thankfulness; which is one peculiar act of this ordinance: "The cup which we bless," or give thanks for.

(3.) It *will greatly incline the heart to keep his word.* "If ye are my disciples, 'if ye love me, keep my commandments.'" Every act of love fixed upon the person of Christ, gives a new spring of obedience to all the ordinances of Christ: and the truth is, there is no keeping up our hearts unto obedience to ordinances, but by renewed acts of obedience upon the person of Christ;—this will make the soul cry, "When shall I be in an actual observation of Christ's ordinance, who hath thus loved me, and washed me with his own blood,—that hath done such great things for me?"

This is the end of the death of Christ which concerns our faith and love,—the end of *commemoration,* or calling to remembrance.

II. There is an end of *profession* also; which is, to "show the Lord's death till he come." But this must be spoken to at some other time. If we come to the practice of these things, we shall find them great things to call over,—namely, the whole frame of the heart of Christ in his death, and his death itself, and our own concern therein, and the great example he hath set unto us. Some of them, I hope, may abide upon our hearts and spirits for our use.

DISCOURSE IV.[1]

"As often as ye eat this bread, and drink this cup, ye do show the Lord's death till he come."—1 COR. xi. 26.

ONE end, you see, of this great ordinance, is to show the Lord's death,—to declare it, to represent it, to show it forth, hold it forth; the word is thus variously rendered. And in the especial ends of this ordinance it is that we have special communion with our Lord Jesus Christ.

Now, there are two ways whereby we show forth the Lord's death; the one is the way of *representation* to ourselves; and the other is a way of *profession* unto others:—

I. The way of *representation to ourselves.* The work of representing Christ aright to the soul is a great work. God and men are agreed in it; and therefore God, when he represents Christ, his design is to represent him to the *faith* of men. Men that have not faith, have a great desire to have Christ represented to their *fancy* and *imagination;* and, therefore, when the way of representing Christ to the faith of men was lost among them, the greatest part of their religion was taken up in representing Christ to their fancy. They would make pictures and images of his cross, resurrection, ascension, and every thing he did.

There are three ways whereby God represents Christ to the faith of believers:—the one is, by the word of the gospel itself as *written;* the second is by the *ministry* of the gospel and preaching of the word; and the third, in particular, is by this *sacrament*, wherein we represent the Lord's death to the faith of our own souls:—

1. God doth it by the *word* itself. Hence are those descriptions that are given of Christ in Scripture to represent him desirable to the souls of men. The great design of the book of Canticles consists, for the most part, in this,—in a mystical, allegorical description of the graces and excellencies of the person of Christ, to render him desirable to the souls of believers; as in the 5th chapter, from the 9th verse to the end, there is nothing but that one subject. And it was a great promise made to them of old, Isa. xxxiii. 17, "Thine eyes shall see

[1] Delivered December 24, 1669.

the King in his beauty." The promises of the Old Testament are much spent in representing the person of Christ as beautiful, desirable, and lovely to the faith of believers. And you will see, in 2 Cor. iii. 18, what is the end of the gospel: "We all with open face beholding as in a glass the glory of the Lord, are changed into the same image from glory to glory, even as by the Spirit of the Lord." The gospel is the glass here intended; and looking into the glass, there is an image appears in it: not our own; but the representation the gospel makes of Jesus Christ is the image that appears in the glass. The work and design of the gospel is, to make a representation of Christ unto us, as Christ makes a representation of the Father; and therefore he is called his image,—"The image of the invisible God." Why so? Because all the glorious properties of the invisible God are represented to us in Christ; and we looking upon the image of Christ in this glass,—that is, the representation made of him in the gospel,—it is the effectual means whereby the Spirit of God transforms us into his image.

This is the first way whereby God doth this great work of representing Christ unto the faith of men; which men having lost, have made it their whole religion to represent Christ unto their fancy.

2. The second way is, by *the ministry of the word.* The great work of the ministry of the word is to represent Jesus Christ. The apostle Paul tells us, Gal. iii. 1, "O foolish Galatians, who hath bewitched you, that ye should not obey the truth, before whose eyes Jesus Christ hath been evidently set forth, crucified among you?" He is "depictus crucifixus,"—crucified before their eyes. How was this? Not before their bodily eyes; but the apostle had in his preaching made such a lively representation unto their faith of the death of Christ, that he was as one painted before them. One said well, on this text, "Of old the apostles did not preach Christ by painting, but they painted him by preaching;" they did in so lively a manner represent him.

Abraham's servant (in the 24th chapter of Genesis), that was sent to take a wife for his son Isaac, is by all granted to be, if not a type, yet a resemblance of the ministers of the gospel, that go forth to prepare a bride for Christ. And what does he do? Truly he is a great example. When he came to the opportunity, though he had many things to divert him, yet he would not be diverted. There was set meat before him to eat; but he said, "I will not eat, till I have told my errand." Nothing should divert the ministers of the gospel,—no, not their necessary meat,—when they have an opportunity of dealing with souls on behalf of Christ. What course does Abraham's servant take? He saith, "I am Abraham's servant; and the LORD hath blessed my master greatly; and he is become great: and he hath given him flocks, and herds, and silver, and gold, and men-servants, and maid-servants, and camels, and asses." What is all this to Isaac? —he was to take a wife for Isaac, not for Abraham. He goes on: "And Sarah my master's wife bare a son to my master when she was old: and unto him hath he given all that he hath." The way to procure this wife for Isaac was, to let them know that this great man, Abraham, had given all he had to Isaac; and it is the work of ministers of the gospel to let the people know that God the Father hath given all things into the hands of his Son. They are to represent Christ as Abraham's servant does here his master Isaac,—as one who inherited all the goods of Abraham; so Christ is the appointed heir of all things, of the kingdom of heaven,—the whole household of God. They are to represent him thus to the souls of men, to make him desirable to them. This is the great work of ministers, who are ambassadors of God; they are sent from God to take a wife for Christ, or to make ready a bride for him, from among the children of men.

3. The special way whereby we represent Christ unto our souls through faith, is in the *administration of this ordinance;* which I will speak to upon the great end of showing forth the death of the Lord.

Now, the former representations were general, this is particular; and I cannot at this time go over particulars. I bless the Lord, my soul hath many times admired the wisdom and goodness of God in the institution of this one ordinance; that he took bread and wine for that end and purpose, merely arbitrary, of his own choice, and might have taken any thing else,—what he had pleased; that he should fix on the cream of the creation: which is an endless storehouse, if pursued, of representing the mysteries of Christ. When the folly of men goes about to invent ceremonies that they would have significant; when they have found them out, they cannot well tell what they signify. But, though I do acknowledge that all the significancy of this ordinance depends upon the institution, yet there is great wisdom in the fitting of it; the thing was fitted and suited to be made use of to that end and purpose.

One end of the ordinance itself is, to represent the death of Christ unto us; and it represents Christ with reference to these five things:— 1. It represents him with reference to God's *setting him forth.* 2. In reference to his own *passion.* 3. In reference to his *exhibition in the promise.* 4. To our *participation* of him by believing. And, 5. To his *incorporation* with us in union.

1. The great end of God in reference to Christ, as to his death, was, his *setting of him forth,* Rom. iii. 25, "Whom God hath set forth to be a propitiation." And in the very setting forth of the elements in this ordinance there is a representation of God's setting forth his

Son,—of giving him out for this work, of giving him up unto it, to be a propitiation.

2. There is a plain representation of his *passion*, of his suffering and death, and the manner of it. This, with all the concerns of it, I treated of the last Lord's day, under the head of Recognition, or calling over the death of Christ, "This do in remembrance of me;" and so I shall not again insist upon it.

3. There is a representation of Christ in it as to the *exhibition* and tender of him in the promise. Many promises are expressed in invitations, "Ho, every one that thirsteth, come;"—"Take, eat:" there is a promise in it. And in the tender that is made even of the sacramental elements, there is the exhibition of Christ in the promise represented to the soul. I told you before, God hath carefully provided to represent Christ unto our faith, and not to our fancy; and, therefore, there is no outward similitude and figure. We can say concerning this ordinance, with all its representations, as God said concerning his appearing to Moses upon mount Horeb, "Thou sawest no similitude." God hath taken care there shall be no natural figure, that all representations made may stand upon institution. *Now, there is this tender with an invitation.* The very elements of the ordinance are a great representation of the proposal of Christ to a believing soul. God holds out Christ as willing to be received, with an invitation. So we show forth the Lord's death.

4. There is in this ordinance a representation of Christ as to our *reception* of him; for hereon depends the whole of the matter. God might make a feast of fat things, and propose it to men; but if they do not come to eat, they will not be nourished by it. If you make a tender of payment to a man, if he doth not receive it, the thing remains at a distance, as before. Christ being tendered to a soul, if that soul doth not receive him, he hath no benefit by it. All these steps you may go:—there may be God's exhibition of Christ, and setting of him forth; there may be his own oblation and suffering, laying the foundation of all that is to come; there may be an exhibition of him in the promise, tender, and invitation: and yet, if not received, we have no profit by all these things. What a great representation of this receiving is there in the administration of this ordinance, when every one takes the representation of it to himself, or doth receive it!

5. It gives us a representation of our *incorporation* in Christ; the allusion whereto, from the nature of the elements' incorporation with us, and being the strength of our lives, might easily be pursued. This is the first way of showing forth the Lord's death.

II. I shall now speak a few words to the *profession* of it among ourselves, and to others.

Let me take one or two observations, to make way for it:—

1. That *visible profession is a matter of more importance than most men make of it;* as the apostle saith, Rom. x. 10, "With the heart man believeth unto righteousness; and with the mouth confession is made unto salvation." Look how indispensably necessary believing is unto righteousness, to justification;—no less indispensably necessary is confession or profession unto salvation. There is no man that doth believe with his heart unto righteousness, but he will with his mouth (which is there taken, by a synecdoche, for the whole of our profession) make confession unto salvation. This is that which brings glory to God. The apostle tells us, 2 Cor. ix. 13, that men, "by the experiment of this ministration, glorify God for your professed subjection unto the gospel of Christ." Glory doth not arise out of obedience so much as by your profession of it;—by the giving them experiment both of your faith and the reality of it, and that by this fruit of your profession.

Now profession consists in these two things:—(1.) *In an abstinence from all things, with reference to God and his worship, which Christ has not appinted.* (2.) *In the observation and performance of all things that Christ has appointed.*

Men are apt to think that *abstinence* from the pollutions that are in the world through lust, the keeping themselves from the sins and defilements of the world, and inclining to that party that is not of the world, is profession. These things are good; but our profession consists in the observation of Christ's commands, what he requires of us. "Go, teach them." What to do? "Whatsoever I have commanded you; and, lo, I am with you alway, unto the end of the world." There is an expression, John xiv. 24, wherein our Saviour puts a trial of our love to him upon the keeping of his sayings: "He that loveth me not keepeth not my sayings." To keep the sayings of Christ, is to observe the commands of Christ; which is the perfect trial of our love to him.

2. There is in this ordinance a *special profession* of Christ. There is a profession of him against the shame of the world; a profession of him against the curse of the law; and a profession of him against the power of the devil. All our profession doth much centre, or is mightily acted, in this ordinance.

(1.) The death of our Lord Jesus Christ was in the world a *shameful death,* and that with which Christians were constantly reproached, and which hardly went down with the world. It is a known story, that when the Jesuits preached the gospel, as they call it, in China, they never let them know of the death of Christ, till the Congregation "De Propagandâ Fide" commanded it; for the world is mightily scandalized at the shameful death of the cross.

Now, in this ordinance, we profess the death of Christ, wherein he was crucified as a malefactor, against all the contempt of the world. It was a great part of the confession of the Christians of old, and there is something in it still: here we come solemnly before God and all the world, and profess that we expect all our life and salvation from the death of this crucified Saviour.

(2.) In our profession we *show forth the death of the Lord*, in the celebration of this ordinance, in opposition "to the curse of the law;"—that whereas the curse of the law doth lay claim to us because we are sinners, here we profess that God hath transferred the curse of the law to another, who underwent it. So they did with the sacrifices of old: when they had confessed all the sins and iniquities of the people over the head of the goat, then they sent him away into destruction. So it is in this ordinance: here we confess all our sins and iniquities over the head of this great sacrifice, and profess to the law, and all its accusations, that there our sins are charged. "Who shall lay any thing to our charge? and who shall condemn? It is Christ that died." We confront the claim of the law, shake off its authority, as to its curse, and profess to it that its charge is satisfied.

(3.) We make a profession *against the power of Satan;* for the great trial of the power and interest of the devil in, unto, and over the souls of men, was in the cross of Jesus Christ. He put his kingdom to a trial, staked his all upon it, and mustered up all the strength he had got,—all the aids that the guilt of sin and the rage of the world could furnish him with. "Now," saith Christ, "is your hour, and the power of darkness;"—"He comes to try what he can do." And what was the issue of the death of Christ? Why, saith the apostle, "He spoiled principalities and powers, and triumphed over them in his cross:" so that, in our celebration of the death of Christ, we do profess against Satan, that his power is broken, that he is conquered,—tied to the chariot wheels of Christ, who has disarmed him.

This is the profession we make, when we show forth the Lord's death, against the shame of the world, against the curse of the law, and the power of hell. This is the second general end of this ordinance; and another means it is whereby we have especial communion with Christ in it: which was the thing I aimed at from the words I had chosen. And now I have gone through all I intend upon this subject.

A word or two of use, and I have done:—

1. It is a very *great honour and privilege*, to be called of God unto this great work of showing forth the death of Christ. I think it is as great and glorious a work as any of the children of men can be engaged in, in this world. I have showed you formerly, how all the acts of the glorious properties of God's nature centre themselves in

this infinite, wise, holy product of them, the death of Christ; and [how] that God should call us to represent and show forth this death. The Lord forgive us where we have not longed to perform this work as we ought; for we have suffered carnal fears and affections, and any thing else, to keep us off from employing ourselves in this great and glorious work. The grace and mercy of God, in this matter, is ever to be acknowledged, in that he has called us to this great and glorious work.

2. Then, surely, it is our duty *to answer the mind of God* in this work, and not to attend to it in a cold, careless, and transient manner. But, methinks, we might rejoice in our hearts when we have thoughts of it, and say within ourselves, "Come, we will go and show forth the Lord's death." The world, the law, and Satan, are conquered by it: blessed be God, that has given us an opportunity to profess this! O that our hearts may long after the season for it! and say, "When shall the time come?"

3. We may do well to remember what was spoken before concerning the great duty of representing God to our souls, that we may know how to attend to it. I would speak unto the meanest of the flock, to guide our hearts and thoughts, which are too ready to wander, and are so unprofitable, for want of spiritual fixation. We would fain trust to our affections rather than to our faith; and would rather have them moved, than faith graciously to act itself. And when we fail therein, we are apt to think we fail in our end of the ordinance, because our affections were not moved. Set faith genuinely at work, and we have the end of the ordinance. Let it represent Christ to our souls, as exhibited of God, and given out unto us; as suffering, as tendered to us, and as received and incorporated with us.

DISCOURSE V.[1]

"But let a man examine himself, and so let him eat of that bread, and drink of that cup."—1 COR. xi. 28.

I HAVE been treating of that special communion which believers have with Christ, in the administration of the ordinance of the supper of the Lord; and thought I should have treated no more of that subject, having gone through all the particulars of it which were practical, such as might be reduced to present practice. But I re-

[1] Delivered January 7, 1669–70.

member I said nothing concerning *preparation for it,* which yet is a needful duty; and therefore I shall a little speak to that also,—not what may *doctrinally be* delivered upon it, but those things, or some of them at least, in which every soul will find *a practical concern* that intends to be a partaker of that ordinance to benefit and advantage, —and I have taken these words of the apostle for my groundwork: " But let a man examine himself, and so let him eat of that bread, and drink of that cup."

There were many disorders fallen in this church at Corinth, and that various ways,—in schisms and divisions, in neglect of discipline, in false opinions, and particularly in a great abuse of the administration of this great ordinance of the supper of the Lord. And though I do not, I dare not, I ought not, to bless God for their sin, yet I bless God for his providence. Had it not been for their disorders, we had all of us been much in darkness as to all church way. The correction of their disorders contains the principal rule for church communion and the administration of this sacrament that we have in the whole Scripture; which might have been hid from us, but that God suffered them to fall into them on purpose that, through their fall, in them and by them he might instruct his church in all ages to the end of the world.

The apostle is here rectifying abuses about the administration of the Lord's supper, which were many; and he applies particular directions to all their particular miscarriages, not now to be insisted on; and he gathers up all directions into this one general rule that I have here read, " Let a man examine himself, and so let him eat," etc. Now, this self-examination extends itself unto the whole due preparation of the souls of men for the actual participation of this ordinance. And I shall endeavour, by plain instances out of the Scripture (which is my way in these familiar exercises), to manifest that there is a preparation necessary for the celebration or observance of all solemn ordinances; and I shall show you what that preparation is, and wherein it doth consist; and then I shall deduce from thence what is that particular preparation which is incumbent upon us, in reference unto this special ordinance, that is superadded unto the general preparation that is required unto all ordinances.

I. I shall manifest that there is *a preparation necessary for the celebration of solemn worship.* We have an early instance of it in Gen. xxxv. 1–5. In the 1st verse, " God said unto Jacob, Arise, go up to Bethel, and make there an altar unto God." It was a solemn ordinance Jacob was called unto,—to build an altar unto God, and to offer sacrifice. What course did he take? You may see, verses 2, 3, " Then Jacob said unto his household, and to all that were with him, Put away the strange gods that are among you, and be clean, and change your garments: and let us arise, and go up to Bethel; and I will make there an altar unto God." "I will not engage," saith he, "in this great duty without a preparation for it; and," saith he, "the preparation shall be suitable." Peculiar, special preparation (to observe that by the way) for any ordinance, consists in the removal of that from us which stands in peculiar opposition to that ordinance, whatever it be. "I am to build an altar unto God; put away the strange gods:" and accordingly he did so

When God came to treat with the people in that great ordinance of giving the law, which was the foundation of all following ordinances, Exod. xix. 10, 11, "The LORD said unto Moses, Go unto the people, and sanctify them to-day and to-morrow, and let them wash their clothes, and be ready against the third day: for the third day the LORD will come down upon mount Sinai." I will not insist on these typical preparations, but only say, it sufficiently proves the general thesis, that there ought to be such a preparation for any meeting with God, in any of his ordinances. Saith he, "Sanctify yourselves," etc., "and on the third day I will come." God is a great God, with whom we have to do. It is not good to have carnal boldness in our accesses and approaches to him; and therefore he teaches us that there is a preparation due. And what weight God lays upon this, you may see, 2 Chron. xxx. 18–20. A multitude of people came to the sacrifice of the passover; but, saith he, "They had not cleansed themselves,"—there was not due preparation: but "Hezekiah prayed for them, saying, The good LORD pardon every one that prepareth his heart to seek God, the LORD God of his fathers, though he be not cleansed according to the purification of the sanctuary. And the LORD hearkened to Hezekiah, and healed the people." Perhaps the people might have thought it enough that they had their personal qualification,—that they were believers,—that they had prepared their hearts to seek the Lord God of their fathers,—a thing most persons trust unto in this matter. No; saith the king, in praying for them, "They did prepare their hearts for the Lord God of their fathers; but they were not prepared according to the purification of the sanctuary." There is *an instituted preparation* as well as *a personal disposition;* which, if not observed, God will smite them. God had smote the people,—given them some token of his displeasure: they come with great willingness and desire to be partakers of this holy ordinance; yet because they were not prepared according to the purification of the sanctuary, God smites them.

It was an ordinance of God that Paul had to perform, and we would have thought it a thing that he might easily have done without any great forethought; but it had that weight upon his spirit, Rom. xv. 30, 31, that, with all earnestness, he begs the prayers of others, that he might be carried through the performance of it: "Now I beseech you, brethren, for the Lord Jesus Christ's sake, and for the love of the Spirit, that ye strive together with me in your prayers to God for me; that my service which I have for Jerusalem may be accepted of the saints." He had a service to do at Jerusalem. He was gathering the contributions of the saints (an ordinance of God), to carry them up to the poor of Jerusalem; and it was upon his heart that this his service might find acceptance with them; therefore he begs with all his soul, "I beseech you, brethren," etc.: so great weight did he lay upon the performance of an ordinance that one would think might be easily passed over without any great regard.

The caution we have, Eccles. v. 1, is to the same purpose: "Keep thy foot when thou goest into the house of God, and be more ready to hear, than to give the sacrifice of fools: for they consider not that they do evil." I shall not stand upon the particular exposition of any of these expressions; but it is a plain caution of diligent consideration of ourselves in all things we have to do in the house of God. A bold venturing upon an ordinance is but "the sacrifice of fools." "Keep thy foot,"—look to thy affections; "be more ready to hear," saith he,—that is, to attend unto the command, what God requires from thee, and the way and manner of it,—"than merely to run upon a sacrifice, or the performance of the duty itself."

I will name one place more, Ps. xxvi. 6, "I will wash mine hands in innocency: so will I compass thine altar, O Lord."

I have a little confirmed this general proposition, that all take for granted; and I fear we content ourselves for the most part with the state and condition of those mentioned, who prepared their hearts to meet the Lord God of their fathers, not considering how they may be prepared "according to the purification of the sanctuary." You will ask, "What is that preparation?"

This question brings me to,—

II. The second general head I propounded to speak unto: I answer, that the general preparation that respects all ordinances hath reference *unto God, to ourselves*, to the *ordinance itself*:—

1. It *hath respect unto God.* This is the first thing to be considered; for this he lays down as the great law of his ordinances, "I will be sanctified in them that come nigh me," Lev. x. 3. God is, in the first place, to be considered in all our drawings nigh unto him; as that is the general name of all ordinances,—a drawing nigh, an access unto God. "I will be sanctified," etc. Now God is to be considered three ways, that he may be sanctified in any ordinance,—as the author, as the object, as the end of it. I shall speak only to those things that lie practically before us, and are indispensably required of us in waiting upon God in any and every ordinance:—

(1.) Our preparation, in reference unto God, consists in due consideration *of God as the author of any ordinance wherein we draw nigh unto him.* For this is the foundation of all ordinances, Rom. xiv. 11, "As I live, saith the Lord, every knee shall bow to me, and every tongue shall confess to God." A practical sense of the authority of God in every ordinance, is that which is required in the very first place for our preparation. I know full well how that the mind of man is [apt] to be influenced by general convictions and particular customs. Particular usages, built upon general convictions, carry most people through their duties; but that is no preparation of heart. There is to be an immediate sense of the authority and command of God.

(2.) We are to consider God in Christ as *the immediate object of that worship which in every ordinance we do perform.* You will ask, "What special apprehensions concerning God are particularly necessary to this duty of preparation for communion with God in an ordinance?" I answer, Two are particularly necessary, that should be practically upon our thoughts in every ordinance,—the presence of God, and the holiness of God. As God is the object of our worship, these two properties of God are principally to be considered in all our preparations:—

[1.] The *presence* of God. When Elijah (1 Kings xviii. 27) derided the worshippers of Baal, the chief part of his derision was, "He is in a journey;"—"You have a god that is absent," saith Elijah. And the end of all idolatry in the world, is to feign the presence of an absent Deity. All images and idols are set up for no other end but to feign the presence of what really is absent. Our God is present, and in all his ordinances. I beg of God I may have a double sense of his presence,—

1*st.* A *special sense* of his omnipresence. God requires that we should put in all ordinances a specialty of faith upon his general attributes. Gen. xxviii. 16, Jacob, when God appeared unto him, though but in a dream, awaked out of sleep, and said, "Surely the LORD is in this place; and I knew it not." I would say so concerning every ordinance whereunto I go;—the Lord is in that place. I speak now only concerning his real presence; for if idolaters adorn all their places of worship with pictures, images, and idols, that they might feign the presence of a god, I ought to act faith particularly upon the real presence of the immense and omnipresent God. He bids us consider it in the business of his worship, Jer. xxiii. 23, "Am I a God at hand, saith the LORD, and not a God afar off?"—"Consider my glorious presence is everywhere." As we ought always, wherever we are, and whatever we do, to carry a sense with us of the presence of God, to say, "God is here," that we may not be surprised in our journeys, or in any thing that may befall us,—suppose a broken leg or a broken arm, then we may say, "God is in this place, and I knew it not;"—so, particularly, where we have to do in his ordinances, let there be an antecedent remembrance that God is in that place.

2*dly.* We are to remember *the gracious presence of God.* There was a twofold presence of God of old;—the one, temporary, by an extraordinary appearance; the other, standing, by a continued institution. Wherever God made an extraordinary appearance, there he required of his people to look upon him to have a special presence. It was but temporary when God appeared to Moses in the bush. "Draw not nigh hither," saith God; "put off thy shoes from off thy feet, for the place whereon thou standest is holy ground," because of God's special appearance: but the next day, as far as I know, sheep fed upon that holy ground. It was no longer holy than God's appearance made it so. So he said to Joshua, when he was by Jericho, "Loose thy shoe from off thy foot; for the place whereon thou standest is holy," Josh. v. 15. It was a temporary appearance of God; there was his special presence. It was so on the institution of the tabernacle and temple; God instituted them, and gave his special presence to them by virtue of his institution. Our Saviour tells us all this is departed under the gospel, John iv. 21, "You shall no longer worship God," saith he, "neither in this mountain, nor yet at Jerusalem; but he that worshippeth God must worship him in spirit and in truth." Is there no special presence of God remains, then? Yea, there is a special presence of God in all his ordinances and institutions. "In all places where I record my name" (as the name of God is upon all his institutions), "I will come unto thee, and I will bless thee," saith God in Exod. xx. 24. Let us exercise our thoughts, then, to this especial promised presence of God in every ordinance and institution; it belongs greatly to our preparation for an ordinance. It was no hard thing for them, you may think, of old, where God had put his presence in a place, to go thither, and expect the presence of God. Things that are absent are hard; things that are present are not so. But it is no harder matter for us to go and expect God's presence in his instituted ordinances now than for them to go to the temple; considering [that] God, as the object of our worship, is no less present with us.

[2.] The second property which is principally to be considered in God in his ordinances, as he is the object of them, is *his holiness.* This is the general rule that God gives in all ordinances, "Be ye holy, for I the LORD your God am holy." And Joshua, chap. xxiv. 19 tells the people what they were principally to consider in serving the Lord. "We will serve the LORD," say the people. Saith Joshua,

"Ye cannot serve the LORD; for he is an holy God:" intimating that they were to have due apprehensions of his holiness; and without it there is no approaching unto him in his service. The apostle gives a great and plain rule to this purpose, Heb. xii. 28, 29, "Let us have grace," saith he, "whereby we may serve God acceptably with reverence and godly fear." What doth he propose, now, as the principal reason why he requires this preparation? "For," saith he, "our God is a consuming fire." What property of God is expressed by this word, "consuming fire?" It is the holiness of God, the purity of God's nature, that can bear no corrupt nor defiled thing. It is set forth by that metaphorical expression, "a consuming fire." "As fire is the most pure and unmixed element, and so powerful of itself as that it will consume and destroy every thing that is not perfectly of its own nature, so is God," saith he, "'a consuming fire;' and in all your serving of him, and approaches unto him, labour to obtain a frame of spirit that becomes them who have to do with that God who is so pure and holy."

I do but choose out these things, which, in the way of ordinances, I *would* say are (I *may* say, [I] desire should be) most upon my heart and spirit: I might easily enlarge it to other considerations; but let these two considerations dwell upon our minds, as our preparation for our access unto God,—thoughts of his glorious and gracious presence, and of his holiness. Ps. xciii. 5, "Holiness becometh thine house, O LORD, for ever." That is the second thing with respect to God as the object of all the ordinances of our worship.

(3.) Our preparation respects God as he is *the end of ordinances;* and that to these three purposes, if I could insist upon them:—he is the end of them, as we aim in them to "give glory unto him;" he is the end of them, as we aim in them "to be accepted with him;" he is the end of them, as we aim in them "to be blessed by him." These are the three things that are our end in all ordinances that we celebrate.

[1.] The first is, *the general end* of all that we do in this world; we are to do all to the glory of God: it is the immediate end of all our worship. "If I am a father," saith he, "where is mine honour?"—"where is my glory?" Mal. i. 6. "Do you come to worship? you are to give me honour, as to a father; glory, as to a master, as to a lord." We come to own him as our Father, acknowledge our dependence upon him as a Father, our submission to him as our Lord and Master; and thus give glory to him. He hath never taken one step to the preparing of his heart according to the preparation of the sanctuary, in the celebration of ordinances, who hath not designed in them to give glory unto God.

[2.] Another end is, *to be accepted with him;* according to that great promise which you have, Ezek. xliii. 27, "You shall make your burnt-offerings upon the altar; and I will accept you, saith the Lord GOD." It is a promise of gospel times; for it is in the description of the new glorious temple. We come to God to have our persons and offerings accepted by Jesus Christ. And,—

[3.] To *be blessed according to his promise,*—that "God will bless us out of Zion." What the particular blessings are we look for in particular ordinances, in due time, God assisting, I shall acquaint you with, when we come to the special and particular preparation for that ordinance we aim at; but this is necessary to all, and so to that.

2. This preparation *respects ourselves.* There are three things which I desire my heart may be prepared by, in reference to the ordinances of God:—

(1.) The first is indispensably necessary, laid down in that great rule, Ps. lxvi. 18, "If I regard iniquity in my heart, the Lord will not hear me;"—that I bring a heart to ordinances without regard to any particular iniquity. We have the dreadful instance of Judas, who came to that great ordinance of the passover with regard to iniquity in his heart,—which particular iniquity was covetousness,—and went away with the devil in his whole mind and soul.

Ezek. xiv. 4 is another place to this purpose, "Therefore speak unto them, and say unto them, Thus saith the Lord GOD; Every man of the house of Israel that setteth up his idols in his heart, and putteth the stumbling-block of his iniquity before his face, and cometh to the prophet; I the LORD will answer him that cometh, according to the multitude of his idols." There is no more effectual course in the world to make poor souls incorrigible, than to come to ordinances, and to be able to digest under them a regard to iniquity in our hearts. If we have idols, God will answer us according to our idols. What is the answering of men according to their idols? Why, plainly, it is this, allotting them peace while they have their idols: "You shall have peace with regard to iniquity; you come for peace, take peace;—which is the saddest condition any soul can be left under: you shall have peace and your idols together." Whenever we prepare ourselves, if this part of our preparation be wanting,—if we do not all of us cast out the idols of our hearts, and cease regarding of iniquity,—all is lost.

(2.) The second head of preparation on our own part is *self-abasement,* out of a deep sense of the infinite distance that is between God and us, whom we go to meet. "I have taken upon myself to speak to the great possessor of heaven and earth, who am but dust and ashes." Nothing brings God and man so near together as a due sense of our infinite distance. Isa. lvii. 15, "Thus saith the high and lofty One that inhabiteth eternity, whose name is Holy; I dwell in the high and holy place, with him also that is of a contrite and humble spirit."

(3.) *A heart filled with love to ordinances* is a great preparation for an ordinance. How doth David, in the 84th Psalm, pant and long and breathe after the ordinances of God! To love prayer, to love the word, is a great preparation for both. To love the presence of Christ in the supper, is a great preparation for it,—to keep an habitual frame of love in the heart for ordinances.

I would not load your memories with particulars. I mention plain practical things unto those for whose spiritual welfare I am more particularly concerned; that we may retain them for our use, and know them for ourselves: and they are such as I know, more or less (though, perhaps, not so distinctly), all our hearts work after: and in these things our souls do live.

3. Our preparation in reference *unto any ordinance itself;* which consists in two things:—

(1.) A satisfactory *persuasion of the institution of the ordinance itself,* that it is that which God hath appointed. If God should meet us, and say, "Who hath required these things at your hand?" and Christ should come and tell us, "Every plant that my heavenly Father hath not planted shall be plucked up;" or, "In vain do ye worship me; teaching for doctrines the commandments of men;"—how would such words fill the hearts of poor creatures with confusion, if engaged in such ways that God hath not required! We must be careful, then, that, for the substance of the duty, it be appointed of God.

(2.) That it be performed in *a due manner.* One failure herein, what a disturbance did it bring upon poor David! It is observed by many, that, search the whole course of David's life, that which he was most eminent in, which God did so bless him for and own him in, was his love to the ordinances of God. And I cannot but think with what a full heart David went to bring home the ark; with what longings after God; with what rejoicings in him; with what promises to himself, what glorious things there would be after he had the ark of God to be with him;—and yet, when he went to do this, you know what a breach God made upon him,—dashed all his hopes and all the good frame in him. God made a breach upon Uzzah; and it is said the thing God did displeased David,—it quite unframed him, and threw a damp on his joy and delight for the present. But he afterward gathers it up, 1 Chron. xv. 12, 13, "He spake to the Levites: Sanctify yourselves, both ye and your brethren, that ye may bring up the ark of the LORD God of Israel unto the place that I have prepared for it. For because ye did it not at the first, the LORD our

God made a breach upon us, for that we sought him not after the due order." We sought him, saith he, but "not after the due order." And what that due order was he shows in the next verses, where he declares that the Levites carried the ark upon their own shoulders, with the staves thereon, as Moses commanded, according to the word of the Lord; whereas, before, they carried it in a cart, which was not for that service. It is a great thing to have the administration of an ordinance in the due order. God lays great weight upon it, and we ought to take care that the order be observed.

This is what we have to offer to you concerning the two general propositions:—that there is a preparation required of us for the observance of all solemn ordinances; and that this preparation consists in a due regard to God, to ourselves, and to the ordinance, whatever it be;—to God, as the author, as the object, and as the end of ordinances; to ourselves, to remove that which would hinder,—not to regard iniquity,—to be self-abased in our hearts with respect to the infinite distance that there is between God and us, and with a love unto ordinances; with respect unto the ordinance itself, that it be of God's appointment for the matter and manner. These things may help us to a due consideration whether we have failed in any of them or not.

I have mentioned nothing but what is plain and evident from the Scripture, and what is practicable; nothing but what is really required of us; such things as we ought not to esteem a burden, but an advantage: and wherein soever we have been wanting, we should do well to labour to have our hearts affected with it; for it hath been one cause why so many of us have laboured in the fire under ordinances, and have had no profit nor benefit by them. As I said before, conviction is the foundation. Custom is the building of most in their observation of ordinances. Some grow weary of them; some wear them on their necks as a burden; some seek relief from them, and do not find it;—and is it any wonder if this great duty be wanting, having neither considered God nor ourselves in what we go about? And, above all things, take heed of that deceit I mentioned (which is certainly very apt to impose itself upon us), that *where there is a disposition in the person there needs no preparation for the duty.* There was a preparation in those whom God broke out upon because they were not prepared according to the preparation of the sanctuary; that is, in that way and manner of preparation,—they had not gone through those cleansings which were instituted under the law.

DISCOURSE VI.[1]

"But let a man examine himself, and so let him eat of that bread, and drink of that cup."—1 COR. xi. 28.

I HAVE been treating, in sundry of these familiar exercises, about communion with Jesus Christ in that great ordinance of the Lord's supper, intending principally, if not solely, the instruction of those who have, it may be, been least exercised in such duties. I have spoke something of preparation for it; and on the last opportunity of this kind, I did insist upon these two things:—that there is a preparation required unto the due observance of every solemn ordinance; and I did manifest what in general was required to that preparation. I have nothing to do at present but to consider the application of those general rules to the special ordinance of the supper of the Lord; for the special preparation for an ordinance consists in the special respect which we have to that ordinance in our general preparation: and I shall speak to it plainly, so as that the weakest who are concerned may see their interest in it, and have some guidance to their practice.

And there are two things which may be considered to this purpose:—the *time* wherein this duty is to be performed; and the *duty* of preparation itself.

I. The *time* of the performance of the duty; for that, indeed, regards as well what hath been said concerning preparation in general as what shall now be farther added concerning preparation in particular, with respect to this ordinance.

Time hath a double respect unto the worship of God, as a part of it (so it is when it is separated by the appointment of God himself), and as a necessary adjunct of those actions whereby the worship of God is performed; for there is nothing can be done but it must be done in time,—the inseparable adjunct of all actions.

And therefore, having proved that a preparation is necessary, I shall prove that there is a time necessary; for there can be no duty performed but it must be performed, as I said, in some time.

For the right stating of that, therefore, I shall give you these rules:—

1. That there is a time *antecedent* to the celebration of this ordinance to be set apart for preparation unto it. The very nature of the duty, which we call *preparation*, doth inevitably include this, that the time for it must be antecedent to the great duty of observing the

[1] Delivered January 21, 1669–70.

ordinance itself. So, Matt. xxvii. 62, the evening before the passover is called "The preparation of the passover,"—time set apart for the preparation of it.

2. The second rule is this,—*That there is no particular, set time*, neither as to the day or season of the day, as to the beginning or ending of it, that is *determined for this duty* in the Scripture; but the duty itself being commanded, the time is left unto our own prudence, to be regulated according to what duty doth require: so that you are not to expect that I should precisely determine this or that time, this or that day, this or that hour, so long or so short; for God hath left these things to our liberty, to be regulated by our own duty and necessity.

3. There are three things that will greatly guide a man in the determination of the time which is thus left unto his own judgment, according to the apprehension of his duty:—

(1.) That *he choose a time wherein the preparation of it may probably influence his mind and spirit in and unto the ordinance itself.* Persons may choose a time for preparation when there may be such an interposition of worldly thoughts and business between the preparation and the ordinance, that their minds may be no way influenced by it in the performance and observation of the duty. The time ought to be so fixed, that the duty may leave a savour upon the soul unto the time of the celebration of the ordinance itself. Whether it be the preceding day, or whether it be the same day, the work is lost unless a man endeavours to keep up a sense of those impressions which he received in that work.

(2.) Providential *occurrences and intimations are great rules for the choosing of time and season for duties.* Paul comes to Athens, Acts xvii., and in all probability he intended not to preach immediately upon his journey;—he intended to take some time for his refreshment. But observing the wickedness of the place, verse 16, "that they were wholly given to idolatry," and observing their altar to "the unknown God," verse 23, he laid hold of that hint of providence, that intimation given him by God's providence from these things, and immediately fell upon his work; which God blessed with great success. There be a thousand ways, if I may so say, wherein an observing Christian may find God hinting and intimating duties unto him. The sins of other men, their graces, mercies, dangers, may be all unto us intimations of a season for duty. Were none of us ever sent to God by the outrageous wickedness of others? by the very observation of it? And it is a sign of a good spirit, to turn providential intimations into duties. The psalmist speaks to that purpose, Ps. xxxii. 8, 9, "I will guide thee with mine eye," saith he. The next words are, "Be ye not as the horse, or as the mule, which have no understanding: whose mouth must be held in with bit and bridle." God loves a pliable spirit, that upon every look of his eye will be guided to a duty. But those who are like horses and mules, that must be held with a strong rein, that will not be turned till God puts great strength to it, are possessed with such a frame of spirit as God approves not. You are left at liberty to choose a time; but observe any intimation of providence that may direct to that time.

(3.) Be sure to *improve surprisals with gracious dispositions;* I mean, in the approach of solemn ordinances. Sometimes the soul is surprised with a gracious disposition, as in Cant. vi. 12, "Or ever I was aware, my soul made me like the chariots of Amminadib." "I knew it not," saith the church, "I was not aware of it; but I found my soul in a special willing manner drawn forth to communion with Christ." Is God pleased at any time to give us such gracious surprisals, with a holy disposition to be dealing with him?—it will be the best season; let it not be omitted.

These things will a little direct us in the determination of the time for preparation; which is left unto our own liberty.

4. Take care that *the time designed and allotted does neither too much intrench upon the occasions of the outward man, nor upon the weakness of the inward man.* If it doth, they will be too hard for us. I confess, in this general observation which professors are fallen into, and that custom which is in the observation of duties, there is little need to give this rule. But we are not to accommodate our rule unto our corruptions, but unto our duties: and so there is a double rule in Scripture fortifies this rule. The one is that great rule of our Saviour, that "God will have mercy, and not sacrifice." Where these duties of observing sacrifices do sensibly intrench upon duties of mercy, God doth not require it; which hath a great regard even unto our outward occasions. And the other rule is this,—that bodily exercise profits little. When we assign so long a time as wearies out our spirits, and observe the time because of the time, it is bodily exercise, when the vigour of our spirits is gone; which is a sacrifice God delights not in. As Jacob told Esau, if the cattle were driven beyond their pace they would die; so we find by experience, that though with strong resolutions we may engage unto duties in such a manner as may intrench upon these outward occasions or those weaknesses, they will return, and be too hard for us, and instead of getting ground, they will drive us off from ours: so that there is prudence to be required therein.

5. Let not *the time allotted be so short as to be unmeet for the going through with the duty effectually.* Men may be ready to turn their private prayers into a few ejaculations, and going in or out of a room may serve them for preparation for the most solemn ordinance. This hath lost us the power, the glory, the beauty of our profession.

Never was profession held up to more glory and beauty, than when persons were most exact in their preparation for the duties of their profession; nothing will serve their turn, but their souls having real and suitable converse with God as unto the duty that lies before them.

6. The *time of preparation is to be extended and made more solemn upon extraordinary occasions.* The intervention of extraordinary occasions must add a solemnity to the time of preparation, if we intend to walk with God in a due manner. These extraordinary occasions may be referred to three heads:—particular sins; particular mercies; particular duties:—

(1.) Is there *an interveniency upon the conscience of any special sin,* that either the soul hath been really overtaken with, or that God is pleased to set home afresh upon the spirit?—there is then an addition to be made unto the time of our preparation, to bring things to that issue between God and our souls that we may attend upon the ordinance, to hearken what God the Lord will now speak; and then he will speak peace. This is the first, principal, extraordinary interveniency that must make an addition to the time of preparation for this ordinance.

(2.) The *interveniences of mercies.* The ordinance hath the nature of a thank-offering, and is the great medium or means of our returning praise unto God that we can make use of in this world. And then are we truly thankful for a temporal mercy, when it engages our hearts to thank God for Christ, by whom all mercies are blessed to us. Hath God cast in any special mercy?—add unto the special preparation, that the heart may be fit to bless God for him who is the fountain and cause of all mercies.

(3.) Special *duties require the like.* For it being the solemn time of our renewing covenant with God, we stand in need of a renewal of strength from God, if we intend to perform special duties; and in our renewing covenant with God, we receive that especial strength for these special duties.

These rules I have offered you concerning the time of this great duty of preparation which I am speaking unto; and I shall add one more, without which you will easily grant that all the rest will fall to the ground, and with which God will teach you all the rest; and that is, *be sure you set apart some time.* I am greatly afraid of customariness in this matter. Persons complain that, in waiting upon God in that ordinance, they do not receive that entertainment at the hand of God, that refreshment, which they looked for. They have more reason to wonder that they were not cast out, as those who came without a "wedding garment." That is not only required of us, that we come with our wedding garment, which every believer hath, but that we come decked with this garment. A man may have a garment that may fit very ill, very unhandsomely about him. The bride decks herself with her garments for the bridegroom. We are to do so for the meeting with Christ in this ordinance,—to stir up all the graces God hath bestowed upon us, that we may be decked for Christ. There lies the unprofitableness under that ordinance,—that though God has given us the wedding garment, we are not cast out, yet we take not care to deck ourselves, that God and Christ may give us refreshing entertainment when we come into his presence. Our failing herein evidently and apparently witnesses to the faces of most professors that this is the ground of their unprofitableness under that ordinance. So much for the time.

II. I shall now speak a little to *the duty itself of preparation for that ordinance;* remembering what I spake before of preparation in general unto all solemn ordinances, which must still be supposed.

Now, the duty may be reduced to these four heads:—meditation; examination; supplication; expectation. And, if I mistake not, they are all given us in one verse; and though not directly applied to this ordinance, yet to this, among other ways, of our intimate communion with Christ, Zech. xii. 10, "I will pour upon the house of David, and upon the inhabitants of Jerusalem, the spirit of grace and of supplications: and they shall look upon me whom they have pierced, and they shall mourn for him, as one mourneth for his only son, and shall be in bitterness for him, as one that is in bitterness for his first-born." There is,—1. Meditation: "They shall look upon him;" this is no otherwise to be performed but by the meditation of faith. Our looking upon Christ is by believing meditation. Looking argues the fixing of the sight; and meditation is the fixing of faith in its actings. Looking is a fixing of the eye; faith is the eye of the soul: and to look, is to fix faith in meditation. And there is,—2. Examination; which produceth the mourning here mentioned. For though it is said, "They shall mourn for him," it was not to mourn for his sufferings,—for so he said, "Weep not for me,"—but to mourn upon the account of those things wherein they were concerned in his sufferings. It brings to repentance, which is the principal design of this examination. 3. There is supplication; for there shall be poured out a spirit of grace and supplication. And, 4. There is expectation; which is included also in that of looking unto Christ.

1. The first part of this duty of preparation consists in *meditation;* and meditation is a duty that, by reason of the vanity of our own minds, and the variety of objects which they are apt to fix upon, even believers themselves do find as great a difficulty therein as any.

I shall only mention those special objects which our thoughts are to be fixed upon in this preparatory duty; and you may reduce them to the following heads:—

(1.) The principal object of meditation, in our preparation for this ordinance, is *the horrible guilt and provocation that is in sin.* There is a representation of the guilt of sin made in the cross of Christ. There was a great representation of it in the punishment of angels; a great representation of it is made in the destruction of Sodom and Gomorrah; and both these are proposed unto us in a special manner, 2 Pet. ii. 4–6, to set forth the heinous nature of the guilt of sin: but they come very short,—nay, give me leave to say, that hell itself comes short,—of representing the guilt of sin, in comparison of the cross of Christ. And the Holy Ghost would have us mind it, where he saith, "He hath made him sin for us," 2 Cor. v. 21. "See what comes of sin," saith he, "what demerit, what provocation there is in it." To see the Son of God praying, crying, trembling, bleeding, dying; God hiding his face from him; the earth trembling under him; darkness round about him;—how can the soul but cry out, "O Lord, is this the effect of sin? is all this in sin?" Here, then, take a view of sin. Others look on it in its pleasures and the advantages of it, and cry, "Is it not a little one?" as Lot of Zoar; but look on it in the cross of Christ, and there it appears in another hue. "All this is from my sin," saith the contrite soul.

(2.) The *purity*, the *holiness*, and the *severity* of God, that would not pass by sin, when it was charged upon his Son. "He set him forth," Rom. iii. 25, "to declare his righteousness." As there was a representation of the guilt of sin, so there was an everlasting representation of the holiness and righteousness of God in the cross of Jesus Christ. "He spared him not." And may [not] the soul say, "Is God thus holy in his nature, thus severe in the execution of his wrath, so to punish and so to revenge sin, when his Son undertook to answer for it? How dreadful is this God! How glorious! What a consuming fire!" It is that which will make sinners in Zion cry, "Who among us shall dwell with the devouring fire? who among us shall dwell with everlasting burnings?" Isa. xxxiii. 14. Consider the holiness and the severity of God in the cross of Christ, and it will make the soul look about him, how to appear in the presence of that God.

(3.) Would you have another object of your meditation in this matter?—let it be *the infinite wisdom and the infinite love of God, that found out this way of glorifying his holiness and justice*, and dealing with sin according to its demerit. "God so loved the world," John iii. 16, "that he gave his only begotten Son." And, "Herein is love,"—love indeed! 1 John iv. 10, "that God sent his Son to be the propitiation for our sins." And the apostle, Eph. iii. 10, lays it upon "the manifold wisdom of God." Bring forth your faith; be your faith never so weak, never so little a reality, do but realize it, and do not let common thoughts and notions take up and possess your spirits.

Here is a glorious object for it to work upon,—to consider the infinite wisdom and love that found out this way. It was out of love unsearchable. And now, what may not my poor, sinful soul expect from this love? what difficulties can I be entangled in, but this wisdom can disentangle me? and what distempers can I be under, but this love may heal and recover? "There is hope, then," saith the soul, in preparation for these things.

(4.) Let the *infinite love of Jesus Christ himself* be also at such a season had in remembrance. Gal. ii. 20, "Who loved me, and gave himself for me." Rev. i. 5, "Who loved us, and washed us from our sins in his own blood." Phil. ii. 6–8, "Who, being in the form of God, thought it not robbery to be equal with God, but humbled himself, and became obedient unto death, even the death of the cross." 2 Cor. viii. 9, This was "the grace of our Lord Jesus Christ, that though he was rich, yet for your sakes he became poor, that ye through his poverty might be rich." The all-conquering and all-endearing love of Christ is a blessed preparative meditation for this great ordinance.

(5.) There is the *end*, what all this came to. This guilt of sin, this holiness of God, this wisdom of grace, this love of Christ; what did all this come to? Why, the apostle tells us, Col. i. 20, "He hath made peace through the blood of his cross." The end of it all was to make peace between God and us: and this undertaking issued in his blood; that was able to do it, and nothing else,—yea, that hath done it. It is a very hard thing for a soul to believe that there is peace made with God for him and for his sin; but really trace it through these steps, and it will give a great deal of strength to faith. Derive it from the lowest, the deepest pit of the guilt of sin, carry it into the presence of the severity of God, and so bring it to the love of Christ; and the issue which the Scriptures testify of all these things was,—to make peace and reconciliation.

Some may say, that they would willingly meditate upon these things, but they cannot remember them, they cannot retain them, and it would be long work to go through and think of them all, and such as they have not strength and season for.

I answer,—First. My intention is *not to burden your memory* or your practice, but to help your faith. I do not prescribe these things, as all of them necessary to be gone through in every duty of preparation; but you all know they are such as may be used, every one of them, singly in the duty; though they that would go through them all again and again would be no losers by it, but will find something that will be food and refreshment for their souls. But,—

Secondly. Let your *peculiar meditation* be regulated by your *peculiar present condition.* Suppose, for instance, the soul is pressed with a sense of the guilt of any sin, or of many sins, let the preparative meditation be fixed upon the grace of God, and upon the love of Jesus Christ, that are suited to give relief unto the soul in such a condition. Is the soul burdened with senselessness of sin? doth it not find itself so sensible of sin as it would be, but rather, that it can entertain slight thoughts of sin?—let meditation be principally directed unto the great guilt of sin, as represented in the death and cross of Christ, and to the severity of God as there represented. Other things may lay hold upon our carnal affections, but if this lay not hold upon faith, nothing will.

I have one rule more in these meditations:—Doth any thing fall in that doth peculiarly affect your spirits, as to that regard which you have to God?—set it down. Most Christians are poor in experience,—they have no stock; they have not laid up any thing for a dear year or a hard time,—though they may have had many tokens for good, yet they have forgot them. When your hearts are raised by intercourse between God and yourselves in the performance of this duty, be at pains *to set this down* for your own use; if any thing do immediately affect your spirits, you will be no loser by it: it is as easy a way to grow rich in spiritual experiences as any I know. This is the first part of this duty of preparation; which, with the rules given, may be constantly so observed as to be no way burdensome nor wearisome to you, but very much to your advantage. The other duties I shall but name, and so have done.

2. There is *examination*. Examination is the word of my text, and that duty which most have commonly spoke unto, that have treated any thing about preparation for this ordinance. It respects principally two things,—namely, repentance and faith.

(1.) Our examination *as to repentance*, as far as it concerns preparation unto this duty, may be referred to three heads:—

[1.] To call ourselves to account *whether indeed we have habitually that mourning frame* of spirit upon us which is required in them who converse with God in the cross of Jesus Christ. "They shall look upon me whom they have pierced, and mourn." There is an habitual mourning frame of spirit required in us; and we may do well to search ourselves about it, whether it is maintained and kept up or no,—whether worldly security and carnal joys do not devour it; for spiritual joys will not do it. Spiritual joys will take off nothing from spiritual mourning; but worldly security and carnal joy and pleasures will devour that frame of spirit.

[2.] Our examination as to repentance respects *actual sins*, especially as for those who have the privilege and advantage of frequent and ordinary participation of this ordinance. It respects the surprisals that have befallen us (as there is no man that doeth good, and sinneth not) since we received the last pledge of the love of God in the administration of that ordinance. Friends, let us not be afraid of calling ourselves to a strict account. We have to do with Him "that is greater than we, and knoweth all things." Let us not be afraid to look into *the book of conscience and conversation*, to look over our surprisals, our neglects, our sinful failings and miscarriages. These things belong to this preparation,—to look over them, and mourn over them also. I would not be thought to myself or you to prescribe a hard burden in this duty of preparation. It is nothing but what God expects from us, and what we must do if we intend any communion with him in this ordinance. I may add,—

[3.] Whether *we have kept alive our last received pledges of the love of God.* It may be, at an ordinance we have received some special intimations of the good-will of God. It is our duty to keep them alive in our spirits; and let us never be afraid we shall have no room for more. The keeping of them makes way for what farther is to come. Have we lost such sensible impressions?—there is then matter for repentance and humiliation.

(2.) Examination *also concerns faith;* and that in general and in particular. In general:—Is not my heart hypocritical? or do I really do what in this ordinance I profess? which is, placing all my faith and hope in Jesus Christ, for life, mercy, salvation, and for peace with God. And in particular:—Do I stir up and act faith to meet Christ in this ordinance? I shall not enlarge upon these things, that are commonly spoken unto.

3. The third part of our preparation is *supplication;* that is, adding prayer to this meditation and examination. Add prayer, which may inlay and digest all the rest in the soul. Pray over what we have thought on, what we have conceived, what we have apprehended, what we desire, and what we fear; gather all up into supplications to God.

4. There belongs unto this duty *expectation* also; that is, to expect that God will answer his promise, and meet us according to the desire of our hearts. We should look to meet God, because he hath promised to meet us there, and we go upon his promise of grace, expecting he will answer his word, and meet us: not going at all adventures, as not knowing whether we shall find him or not. God may, indeed, then surprise us; as he did Jacob, when he appeared unto him, and made him say, "God is in this place, and I knew it not,"—but we go where we know God is. He hath placed his name upon his ordinances, and there he is. Go to them with expectation, and rise from the rest of the duties with this expectation.

This is the substance of what might be of use to some in reference unto this duty of preparation for this great and solemn ordinance, which God hath graciously given unto any of you the privilege to be made partakers of.

Have we failed in these things, or in things of a like nature?—let us admire the infinite patience of God, that hath borne with us all this while,—that he hath not cast us out of his house,—that he hath not deprived us of these enjoyments; which he might justly have done, when we have so undervalued them as far as lay in us, and despised them,—when we have had so little care to make entertainment for the receiving of the great God and our Lord Jesus Christ, who comes to visit us in this ordinance. We may be ready to complain of what outward concerns in and about the worship of God some have been deprived of; we have infinite more reason to admire that there is any thing left unto us,—any name, any place, any nail, any remembrance in the house of God, considering the regardlessness which hath been upon our spirits in our communion with him. "Go away, and sin no more, lest a worse thing befall us." If there be in any that have not risen up in a due manner in this duty, any conviction of the necessity and usefulness of it, God forbid we should be found sinning against this conviction.

DISCOURSE VII.[1]

"He said, ... Take, eat."—1 COR. xi. 24.

I SHALL show briefly what it is to obtain a sacramental part of Jesus Christ in this ordinance of the Lord's supper.

It is a great mystery, and great wisdom and exercise of faith lie in it, how to obtain a participation of Christ. When the world had lost an understanding of this mystery, for want of spiritual sight, they contrived a means to make it up, that should be *easy* on the part of them that did partake, and very *prodigious* on the part of them that administered. The priest, with a few words, turned the bread into the body of Christ; and the people have no more to do but to put it into their mouths, and so Christ is partaken of. It was the loss of the mystery of faith in the real participation of Christ that put them on that invention.

Neither is there in this ordinance a *naked figure*,—a naked representation: there is something in the figure, something in the representation; but there is not all in it. When the bread is broken, it is a figure, a representation that the body of Christ was broken for us; and the pouring out of the wine is a figure and representation of the pouring of the blood of Christ, or the pouring forth of his soul unto death. And there are useful meditations that may arise from thence;

[1] Delivered July 7, 1673.

but in this ordinance there is a real exhibition of Christ unto every believing soul.

I shall a little inquire into it, to lead your faith into a due exercise in it, under the administration of this ordinance:—

First. *The exhibition and tender of Christ in this ordinance is distinct from the tender of Christ in the promise of the gospel.* As in many other things, so it is in this:—in the promise of the gospel, the person of the Father is principally looked upon as proposing and tendering Christ unto us; in this ordinance Christ tenders himself. "This is my body," saith he; "this do in remembrance of me." He makes an immediate tender of himself unto a believing soul; and calls our faith unto a respect to his grace, to his love,—to his readiness to unite and spiritually to incorporate with us. Again,—

Secondly. It is a tender of Christ and an exhibition of Christ under an especial consideration;—not in general, but under this consideration, as he is, as it were, "newly" (so the word is) "sacrificed;"[1] as he is a new and fresh sacrifice in the great work of reconciling, making peace with God, making an end of sin, doing all that was to be done between God and sinners, that they might be at peace.

Christ makes a double representation of himself, as the great Mediator, upon his death and the oblation and sacrifice which he accomplished thereby.

He presents himself unto God in heaven, there to do whatever remains to be done with God on our behalf, by his intercession. The intercession of Christ is nothing but the presentation of himself unto God, upon his oblation and sacrifice.

He presents himself unto God, to do with him what remains to be done on our part,—to procure mercy and grace for us.

He presents himself unto us in this ordinance, to do with us what remains to be done on the part of God; and this answers to his intercession above, which is the counterpart of his present mediation, to do with us what remains on the part of God,—to give out peace and mercy in the seal of the covenant unto our souls.

There is this special exhibition of Jesus Christ; and it is given directly for this special exercise of faith, that we may know how to receive him in this ordinance.

1. *We receive him as one that hath actually accomplished the great work* (so he tenders himself) of making peace with God for

[1] The reference is to Heb. x. 20, *πρόσφατον*, new (*πρὸς, φάω*), *newly killed.* "The blood of other sacrifices was always to be used *immediately* upon its effusion; for if it were cold or congealed, it was of no use to be offered, or to be sprinkled, Lev. xvii. 11. But the blood of Christ is always hot and warm. . . . . Hence the way of approach which we have to God thereby is said to be *ζῶσα καὶ πρόσφατος*,—always *living*, and yet always as *newly slain*."—See Owen on the Holy Spirit, book iv. chap. v.—Ed.

us,—for the blotting out of sins, and for the bringing in everlasting righteousness. He doth not tender himself as one that *can* do these things (it is a relief when we have an apprehension that Christ *can* do all this for us); nor doth he tender himself as one that *will* do these things upon any such or such conditions as shall be prescribed unto us: but he tenders himself unto our faith as one that hath done these things; and as such are we to receive him, if we intend to glorify him in this ordinance as one that hath actually done this, actually made peace for us,—actually blotted out our sins, and purchased eternal redemption for us.

Brethren, can we receive Christ thus? are we willing to receive him thus? If so, we may go away and be no more sorrowful. If we come short herein, we come short of that faith which is required of us in this ordinance. Pray let us endeavour to consider how Jesus Christ doth hereby make a tender of himself unto us,—as one that hath actually taken away all our sins, and all our iniquities, that none of them shall ever be laid unto our charge; and to receive him as such, is to give glory unto him.

2. He *tenders himself as one that hath done this work by his death;* for it is the remembrance of his death in a peculiar manner that we celebrate. What there is of love, what there is of efficacy, of power and comfort in that, what there is of security, I may have occasion another time to speak unto you. At present this is all I would offer:—that for the doing of these great things, for the doing the greatest, the hardest things that our faith is exercised about,—which are, the pardon of our sins, and the acceptation of our persons with God,—for the accomplishment hereof he died an accursed death; and that death had no power over him, but the bands of it were loosed,—he rose from under it, and was acquitted. Let us act faith on Jesus Christ as one that brings with him mercy and pardon, as that which was procured by his death; against which lies no exception. I could show you that nothing was too hard for it, that nothing was left to be done by it which we are to receive.

3. To *be made partakers of him in this sacramental tender, by submitting unto his authority in his institutions,* by assenting unto the truth of his word in the promise that he will be present with us and give himself unto us, and by approving of that glorious way of making peace for us which he hath trodden and gone in, in his sufferings and [death] in our stead;—to get a view of Christ as tendering himself unto every one of our souls in this ordinance of his own institution, as him who hath perfectly made an end of all differences between God and us, and who brings along with him all the mercy and grace that is in the heart of God and in his covenant;—to have such a view of him, and so to receive him by faith that it shall be life unto our

souls, is the way to give glory unto God, and to have peace and rest in our own bosoms.

4. And lastly, in one word, faith is so to receive him as to enable us to sit down at God's table as those that are the Lord's friends,—as those that are invited to feast upon the sacrifice. The sacrifice is offered; Christ is the sacrifice,—God's passover; God makes a feast upon it, and invites his friends to sit down at his table, there being now no difference between him and us. Let us pray that he would help us to exercise faith to this purpose.

DISCOURSE VIII.[1]

"Christ also hath once suffered for sins, the just for the unjust, that he might bring us to God; being put to death in the flesh, but quickened by the Spirit."—1 PET. iii. 18.

YOU know I usually speak a few words to prepare us for this ordinance. You know it is an ordinance of calling to remembrance: "This do in remembrance of me." There was, under the Old Testament, but one sacrifice to call any thing to remembrance; and God puts a mark upon that sacrifice, as that which was not, as it were, well-pleasing unto him, but only what necessity did require, and that was "the sacrifice of jealousy," Numb. v. 15. Saith God, "There shall be no oil in it" (a token of peace); "there shall be no frankincense" (that should yield a sweet savour), "for it is an offering to bring iniquity to remembrance." This great ordinance of the Lord's supper is not to call iniquity to remembrance; but it is to call to remembrance the putting an end to iniquity: God will make an end of sin, and this ordinance is our solemn remembrance of it.

Now, there are sundry things that we are to call to remembrance. I have done my endeavour to help you to call the love of Christ to remembrance. The Lord, I trust, hath guided my thoughts now to direct you to call the sufferings of Christ unto remembrance. I know it may be a suitable meditation to take up your minds and mine in and under this ordinance. It is our duty, in this holy ordinance, solemnly to call to remembrance the sufferings of Christ.

It is said of the preaching of the gospel, that Jesus Christ is therein "evidently set forth crucified before our eyes," Gal. iii. 1. And if Christ be evidently crucified before our eyes in the preaching of the gospel, Christ is much more evidently crucified before our eyes in the administration of this ordinance, which is instituted for that very end.

[1] Delivered November 2, 1673.

And certainly, when Christ is crucified before our eyes, we ought deeply to consider his sufferings. It would be a great sign of a hard and senseless heart in us, if we were not willing, in some measure, to consider his sufferings upon such an occasion. We are, therefore, solemnly to remember them.

Well, shall I a little mind myself and you how we may and how we ought to call to remembrance the sufferings of Christ?

Let us remember that *we* ourselves were obnoxious unto these sufferings. The curse lay doubly upon *us*. The original curse, "In the day that thou eatest thereof, thou shalt surely die," lay upon us all. The consequent curse, "Cursed be every one who continueth not in all things that are written in the book of the law to do them," that also lay upon us all: we were under both the original and the consequent curse. We know what is in the curse, even all the anger and wrath that a displeased holy God can and will inflict upon sinful creatures to all eternity. In this state and condition, then, all lay upon us, and all must lie upon us: unless we come to have an interest in the sufferings of Christ, there is no relief for us. I will not insist upon calling to your mind that heaven and earth, and all God's creation combining together, could not have procured relief for one of our souls. Christ, the Son of God, offered himself, and said, "Lo, I come." Indeed, it was a good saying of David, it was nobly said, when he saw the angel of the Lord destroying the people with a pestilence; "Lord," saith he, "it is I and my father's house that have sinned; but as for these sheep," these poor people, "what have they done?" It was otherwise with Christ; he came in the place of sinners, and said, "Let not these poor sheep die." If God would, by faith, give your souls and mine a view of the voluntary substitution of Jesus Christ in his person in our room and on our behalf, it would comfort and refresh us. When the curse of God was ready to break forth upon us, God accepted of this tender, of this offer of Christ, "Lo, I come to do thy will," to be a sacrifice. And what did he do? Why this God did. Saith he, "Then if he will come, if he will do it, let him plainly know how the case stands: the curse is upon them, wrath is upon them,—punishment must be undergone; my holiness, faithfulness, righteousness, and truth, are all engaged." Yet saith Christ, "Lo, I come." Well, what doth God do? He tells you, Isa. liii. 6, "All we like sheep have gone astray; we have turned every one to his own way; and the LORD hath made the iniquity of us all to meet on him." God so far relaxed his own law that the sentence shall not fall upon their persons, but upon their substitute, one that hath put himself in their place and stead. "Be it so; all their iniquities be upon thee." "All the iniquities of this congregation," saith God, "be upon my Son Jesus Christ."

Well, what then did he *suffer?* He suffered that which answered the justice of God; he suffered that which answered the law of God; he suffered that which fully repaired the glory of God. Brethren, let us encourage ourselves in the Lord. If there be any demands to be made of you or me, it must be upon the account of the righteousness and justice of God, or upon the account of the law of God, or upon the account of the loss that God suffered in his glory by us. If the Lord Jesus hath come in and answered all these, we have a good plea to make in the presence of the holy God:—

1. He *suffered all that the justice of God did require.* Hence it is said that "God set him forth to be a propitiation through faith in his blood, to declare his righteousness for the forgiveness of sins," Rom. iii. 25. And you may observe, that the apostle uses the very same words in respect of Christ's sufferings that he uses in respect of the sufferings of the damned angels, Rom. viii. 32, "God spared him not." And when he would speak of the righteousness of God in inflicting punishment upon the sinning angels, he doth it by that very word, "God spared them not." So that whatever the righteousness of God did require against sinners, Christ therein was not spared at all. What God required against your sins and mine, and all his elect, God spared him nothing, but he paid the utmost farthing.

2. The *sufferings of Christ did answer the law of God.* That makes the next demand of us. The law is that which requires our poor guilty souls to punishment, in the name of the justice of God. Why, saith the apostle, "He hath redeemed us from the curse of the law, being made a curse for us," Gal. iii. 13. By undergoing and suffering the curse of the law, he redeemed us from it.

3. He *suffered every thing that was required to repair and make up the glory of God.* Better you and I, and all the world, should perish, than God should be endamaged in his glory. It is a truth, and I hope God will bring all our hearts to say, "Christ hath suffered to make up that." The obedience that was in the sufferings of Christ brought more glory to God than the disobedience of Adam, who was the original of the apostasy of the whole creation from God, brought dishonour unto him. That which seemed to reflect great dishonour upon God was, that all his creatures should, as one man, fall off by apostasy from him. God will have his honour repaired; and it is done by the obedience of Christ much more. There cometh, I say, more glory to God by the obedience of Christ and his sufferings, than there did dishonour by the disobedience of Adam;—and so there comes more glory by Christ's sufferings and obedience upon the cross than by the sufferings of the damned for ever. God loses no glory by setting believers free from suffering, because of the sufferings of the Son of God. This was a fruit of eternal wisdom.

Now, having thus touched a little upon the sufferings of Christ what shall we do in a way of duty?

(1.) Let us *by faith consider* truly and really this great *substitution of Jesus Christ* (*the just suffering for the unjust*) in our stead, in our room,—undergoing what we should have undergone. The Lord help us to admire the infinite holiness, righteousness, and truth, that is in it. We are not able to comprehend these things in it; but if God enables us to exercise faith upon it, we shall admire it. Whence is it that the Son of God should be substituted in our place? Pray remember that we are now representing this infinite effect of divine wisdom in substituting Jesus Christ in our room, to undergo the wrath and curse of God for us.

(2.) Let us learn from the cross of Christ *what indeed is in our sins;* that when Christ, the Son of God, in whom he was always well pleased, that did the whole will of God, was in his bosom from all eternity, came and substituted himself in our room, "God spared him not." Let not any sinner under heaven, that is estranged from Christ, ever think to be spared. If God would have spared any, he would have spared *his only Son.* But if he will be a mediator of the covenant, God will not spare him, *though his own Son.* We may acquaint you hereafter what it cost Christ to stand in the room of sinners. The Lord from thence give our hearts some sense of that great provocation that is in sin, that we may mourn before him, when we look upon *him* whom our sins have pierced.

(3.) Will God help us to *take a view of the issue of all this;*—of the substitution of Jesus Christ, placing him in our stead, putting his soul in the place of our souls, his person in the place of our persons;—of the commutation of punishment, in which the righteousness, holiness, and wisdom of God laid that on him which was due unto us? What is the issue of all this? It is to *bring us unto God,*—to peace with God, and acquitment from all our sins; and to make us acceptable with the righteous, holy, and faithful God; to give us boldness before him;—this is the issue. Let us consider this issue of the sufferings of Christ, and be thankful.

DISCOURSE IX.[1]

"They worshipped him; but some doubted."—MATT. xxviii. 17.

IT is the table of the Lord that we are invited to draw nigh unto. Our Lord hath a large heart and bountiful hand,—hath made plenti-

[1] Delivered February 22, 1673-4.

ful provision for our souls at this table; and he saith unto us, by his Spirit in his word, "Eat, O my friends, yea, drink abundantly." It is that feast that God hath provided for *sinners.* And there are *three sorts of sinners* that I would speak a word unto, to stir them up unto a due exercise of faith in this ordinance, according as their condition doth require. There are such as are *not sensible* of their sins so as they ought to be,—they know they are not; they are not able to get their hearts affected with their sins as they desire. There are some that are *so burdened* and overpressed with the sense of their sins, that they are scarce able to hold up under the weight of them,—under the doubts and fears wherewith they are distressed. And there are sinners who are in *enjoyment of a sense of the pardon of sin,* and do desire to have hearts to improve it in thankfulness and fruitfulness.

Something of these several frames may be in us all; yet it may be one is predominant, one is chief,—one in one, another in another: and therefore I will speak a few words distinctly to them all:—

1. There are sinners who are believers, *who cannot get their hearts and spirits affected with sin so as they ought,* and so as they desire. There is not a sadder complaint of the church, as I know, in the whole book of God, than that, Isa. lxiii. 17, "Why hast thou hardened our heart from thy fear?" Poor creatures may come unto that perplexity, through an apprehension of the want of a due sense of the guilt of sin, as to be ready thus to cry out, "Why is it thus with me? why am I so senseless under the guilt of all the sins that I have contracted?" I have a word of direction unto such persons. Are there such among us? It is a direction unto faith to be acting in this ordinance. It is that which we have, Zech. xii. 10, "They shall look unto him whom they have pierced, and mourn." Why, brethren, Christ is represented unto us in this ordinance as he was pierced,—as his precious blood was poured out for us. Let us act faith, if God help us, in two things:—

(1.) Upon *the dolorous sufferings of Christ,* which are represented here unto us. Let us take a view of the Son of God under the curse of God.

(2.) Remember that all these sufferings were *for us:* "They shall look upon me whom they have pierced," and then "mourn." The acting of faith upon the sufferings of Christ, as one that suffered *for us,* is the great means, in this ordinance, to bring our hearts to mourn for sin indeed. Therefore, pray let us beg of God, whoever of us are in any measure under this frame, that our insensibleness of the guilt and burden of sin may be our great burden. Let us try the power of faith in this ordinance, by getting our hearts affected with the sufferings of Christ in our behalf. Let us bind it to our hearts and consciences; and may the Lord give a blessing!

2. There are others who, it may be, *are pressed under the weight of their sins,* walk mournfully, walk disconsolately. I know there are some so,—in the condition expressed by the psalmist, Ps. xl. 12, "Innumerable evils have compassed me about: mine iniquities have taken hold upon me, so that I am not able to look up; they are more than the hairs of mine head; therefore my heart faileth me." Some may be in that condition that their hearts are ready to fail them, through the multitude of their iniquities taking hold upon them. What would you direct such unto in this ordinance? Truly, that which is given, John iii. 14, 15, "As Moses lifted up the serpent in the wilderness, even so must the Son of man be lifted up: that whosoever believeth in him should not perish, but have eternal life." The Lord Jesus Christ was lifted up, as *Moses* lifted up the serpent in the wilderness; and here he is lifted up, as bearing all our sins in his own body upon the tree. Here is a representation made unto poor sinners whose hearts are most burdened,—here is Jesus Christ lifted up with all our sins upon the tree. Let such a soul labour to have a view of Christ as bearing all our iniquities, that believing on him we should not perish, but have life everlasting. God hath appointed him to be crucified evidently before our eyes, that every poor soul that is stung with sin, ready to die by sin, should look up unto him, and be healed. And virtue will go forth, if we look upon him; for "by his stripes we are healed."

3. There may be *some that live in full satisfaction of the pardon of their sins,* and are solicitous how their hearts may be drawn forth unto thankfulness and fruitfulness. Remember that place, Rev. i. 5, 6, "Unto him that loved us, and washed us from our sins in his own blood; to him be glory and dominion for ever and ever." Remember this, that whatever your state and condition be, you have here a proper object for faith to exercise itself upon; only be not wanting unto your own comfort and advantage.

DISCOURSE X.[1]

"Teaching them to observe all things whatsoever I have commanded you: and, lo, I am with you alway, even unto the end of the world."—MATT. xxviii. 20.

BY "the end of the world" we are to understand the consummation of all things; when all church work is done, and all church duties are over; when the time comes that we shall pray no more,

[1] Delivered May 17, 1674.

hear no more, no more administer ordinances. "But till then;" saith Christ, "take this for your life and for your comfort,—Do what I command you, and you shall have my presence with you."

There are three things whereby Christ makes good this promise, and is with his church to the end of the world:—

First. By *his Spirit.* "Where," saith he, "two or three are gathered together in my name, there am I in the midst of them," Matt. xviii. 20;—by his quickening, guiding, directing Spirit, as a Spirit of grace and supplication, as a Spirit of light and holiness, and as a Spirit of comfort.

Secondly. Christ is present with us *by his word.* Saith the apostle, Col. iii. 16, "Let the word of Christ dwell in you richly," or plentifully. And how then? "Then," saith he, Eph. iii. 17, "Christ dwelleth in your hearts by faith." The word dwelleth in us plentifully, if mixed with faith; and Christ dwelleth in us,—he is present with us by his word.

Thirdly. Christ is present with us *in an especial manner in this ordinance.* One of the greatest engines that ever the devil made use of to overthrow the faith of the church was, by forging *such a presence of Christ* as is not truly in this ordinance, to drive us off from looking after that great presence which is *true.* I look upon it as one of the greatest engines that ever hell set on work. It is not a *corporeal* presence; there are innumerable arguments against *that.* Every thing that is in sense, reason, and the faith of a man, overthrows that corporeal presence. But I will remind you of one or two texts wherewith it is inconsistent. The first is that in John xvi. 7, "Nevertheless," saith our Saviour, "it is expedient for you that I go away: for if I go not away, the Comforter will not come unto you." The corporeal presence of Christ, and the evangelical presence of the Holy Ghost as the Comforter, in the New Testament, are inconsistent. "I must go away, or the Comforter will not come." But he *so* went away as to his presence as to come again with his bodily presence as often as the priests call! No; saith Peter, Acts iii. 21, "The heaven must receive him." For how long? "Till the time of the restitution of all things."—"I go away as to my bodily presence, or the Comforter will not come." And when he is gone away, the heaven must receive him until the time of the restitution of all things. We must not, therefore, look after *such* a presence.

I will give you a word or two what is the presence of Christ with us in this ordinance, what is our duty, and how we may meet with Christ when he is thus present with us; which is the work I have in hand. Christ is present in this ordinance in an especial manner three ways:—I. By *representation;* II. By *exhibition;* III. By *obsignation* or sealing.

I. He is present here by *representation.* So in a low, shadowy way God was present in the tabernacle, in the temple, in the ark and mercy-seat; they had a representation of his glory. But Christ here hath given us a more eminent and clear representation of himself. I will name but two things:—

1. *A representation of himself, as he is the food of our souls.*
2. *A representation of himself, as he suffered for our sins.*

These are two great ways whereby Christ is represented as the food of our souls in the *matter* of the ordinance; and Christ as suffering for our sins, is represented in the *manner* of the ordinance; both by his own appointment. The apostle saith, Gal. iii. 1, "Jesus Christ was evidently crucified before their eyes." "Evidently crucified" doth not intend particularly this ordinance, but the preaching of the gospel, which gave a delineation, a picture, and image of the crucifixion of Christ unto the faith of believers. But of all things that belong unto the gospel, he is most evidently crucified before our eyes in this ordinance; and it is agreed on all hands that Christ is represented unto the soul in this ordinance. How shall we do this? shall we do it by crucifixes, pictures, and images? No; they are all cursed of that God who said, "Thou shalt not make unto thee any graven image." But *that way* by which God himself, and Christ himself, hath appointed to represent these things unto us,—*that* he blesses and makes effectual. This way, as I have often showed, is the way that was chosen by the wisdom and goodness of Jesus Christ; the name of God is upon it; it is blessed unto us, and will be effectual, if we are not wanting to ourselves.

II. Christ is present with us by way of *exhibition;* that is, he doth really tender and exhibit himself unto the souls of believers in this ordinance; which the world hath lost, and knows not what to make of it. They [the symbols] exhibit that which they do not contain. This bread doth *not contain* the body of Christ, or the flesh of Christ; the cup doth *not contain* the blood of Christ: but they *exhibit* them; both do as really exhibit them to believers as they partake of the outward signs. Certainly we believe that our Lord Jesus Christ doth not invite us unto this table for the *bread that perishes,* for outward food: it is to feed *our souls.* What do we think, then? doth he invite us unto an empty, painted feast? do we deal so with our friends? Here is something really exhibited by Jesus Christ unto us to receive, besides the outward pledges of bread and wine. We must not think the Lord Jesus Christ deludes our souls with empty shows and appearances. That which is exhibited is himself; it is "his flesh as meat indeed, and his blood as drink indeed;" it is himself as broken and crucified that he exhibits unto us. And it is the fault and sin of every one of us, if we do not receive him *this day,* when an exhibition and tender is made unto us, as here, by way of food. To what end do we receive it? Truly, we receive it for these two ends:—for *incorporation;* for *nourishment:*—

1. We receive our food that it may *incorporate* and turn into blood and spirits,—that it may become one with us; and when we have so done,—

2. Our end and design is, that we may be *nourished,* nature strengthened, comforted, and supported, and we enabled for the duties of life.

Christ doth exhibit himself unto our souls, if we are not wanting unto ourselves, for these two things:—*incorporation and nourishment;* to be received into union, and to give strength unto our souls.

III. Christ is present in this ordinance by way of *obsignation:* he comes here to seal the covenant; and therefore the cup is called "The new testament in the blood of Christ." How in the blood of Christ? It is the new covenant that was sealed, ratified, confirmed, and made so stable, as you have heard, by the blood of Jesus Christ. For, from the foundation of the world, no covenant was ever intended to be established, but it was confirmed *by blood;* and this covenant is confirmed by *the blood of Christ;* and he comes and seals the covenant with his own blood in the administration of this ordinance.

Well, if Jesus Christ be thus present by way of *representation, exhibition,* and *obsignation,* what is required of us, that we may meet him, and be present with him? For it is not our mere coming hither that is a meeting with Christ; it is a work of faith: and there are three *acts of faith* whereby we may be present with Christ, who is thus present with us:—

1. The first is by *recognition,* answering his *representation.* As Christ in this ordinance doth represent his death unto us, so we are to remember it and call it over. Pray consider how things were done formerly in reference unto it. The paschal lamb was an ordinance *for remembrance:* "It is a night to be had in remembrance;" and this they should do for a remembrance. And it was to be eaten with bitter herbs. There was once a-year a feast, wherein all the sins, iniquities, and transgressions of the children of Israel were called to remembrance; and it was to be done by greatly afflicting of their souls. If we intend to call to remembrance the death of Christ, we may do well to do it with some *bitter herbs;* there should be some *remembrance of sin* with it, some *brokenness of heart* for sin, with respect to him who was pierced and broken for us. Our work is to call over and show forth the death of Christ. Pray, brethren, let us a little consider whether our hearts be suitably affected with respect to our sins, which were upon Jesus Christ when he died for us, or no; lest

we draw nigh unto him with the outward bodily presence, when our hearts are far from him.

2. If Christ be present with us by way of *exhibition,* we ought to be present by way of *admission.* It will not advantage you or me that Christ tenders himself unto us, unless *we receive him.* This is the great work; herein lies the main work upon all the members of the church. When we are to dispense the word, the first work lies upon *ministers;* and when the work is sufficiently discharged, they will be a good savour unto God in them that believe, and in them that perish: but in this ordinance, the main work lies upon *yourselves.* If in the name of Christ we make a tender of him unto you, and he be not actually received, there is but half the work done; so that you are in a peculiar manner to stir up yourselves, as having a more especial interest in this duty, than in any other duty of the church whatsoever; and you may take a better measure of yourselves by your acting in this duty, than of us by our acting in the ministry. Let Christ be received into your hearts by faith and love, upon this particular tender that he assuredly makes in this ordinance of himself unto you; for, as I said, he hath not invited you unto an empty, painted feast or table.

3. Know what you come to meet him for; which is, *to seal the covenant,*—solemnly to take upon yourselves again the *performance of your part of the covenant.* I hope I speak in a deep sense of the thing itself, and that which I have much thought of. This is that which ruins the world,—the hearing that God hath made a covenant of grace and mercy; it is preached to them, and declared unto them, and they think to be saved by this covenant, though they themselves do not perform what the covenant requires on their part. What great and glorious words do we speak in the covenant,—that God gives himself over unto us, to be our God! Brethren, there is *our giving ourselves unto God* (to answer this) universally and absolutely. If we give ourselves unto the world, and to our lusts, and to self, we are not to expect any benefit by God's covenant of grace. If it be not made up by *our sealing* of the covenant of grace, or by a universal resignation of ourselves, in all that we are and do, unto him, we do not meet Jesus Christ; we disappoint him when he comes to seal the covenant. "Where is this people," saith Christ, "that would enter into covenant with me?" Let it be in our hearts to see him seal the covenant of grace as represented in this ordinance; and to take upon ourselves the performance of what is required of us, by a universal giving up ourselves unto God.

DISCOURSE XI.[1]

I SHALL now produce some few places of Scripture, one especially, that may administer occasion unto you for the exercise of faith, the great duty required of us at this time. You may do well to think of these words of the prophet concerning Jesus Christ, concerning his sufferings and death, which we are here gathered together in his name to remember. They are,—

"He shall see of the travail of his soul, and shall be satisfied."—ISA. liii. 11.

There are two things that the Holy Ghost minds us of in these words:—First. That Jesus Christ was in *a great travail of soul* to bring forth the redemption and salvation of the church. Secondly. He minds us that Jesus Christ *was satisfied*, and much rejoiced in the consideration of the effects and fruits of the travail of his soul. I shall speak a word to both, and a word to show you how both these things are called over in this ordinance,—both the travail of the soul of Christ and his satisfaction in the fruit of that travail.

First. Christ was in *a great travail of soul to bring forth the redemption and salvation of the church.* It was a great work that Christ had to do. It is usually said, "We are not saved as the world was made,—*by a word*," but there was *travail* in it: it is the word whereby the bringing forth of children into the world is expressed,—the travail of a woman. And there are three things in that travail:—an *agony of mind, outcrying for help*, and *sense of pain:* all these things were in the travail of the soul of Christ. I will name the Scriptures, to call them to your remembrance:—

1. He was "in an agony," Luke xxii. 44. An agony is an inexpressible conflict of mind about things dreadful and terrible. So it was with Christ. No heart can conceive, much less can tongue express, the conflict that was in the soul of Jesus Christ with the wrath of God, the curse of the law, the pains of hell and death, that stood before him in this work of our redemption. There was an agony.

2. There was *an outcrying for help*, Heb. v. 7, "Who in the days of his flesh offered up prayers and supplications, with strong crying and tears unto him that was able to save him." Such is the outcry of a person in travail, crying out unto them that are able to save them. So it was with Jesus Christ when he was in the travail of his soul about our salvation. He made these strong cries unto God,—to him that was able to save him.

3. There was *pain in it, which is the last thing in travail;* so that

[1] Delivered August 9, 1674.

he complained that "the pains of hell had taken hold upon him." Whatever pain there was in the curse of the law, in the wrath of God,—whatever the justice of God did ever design to inflict upon sinners, was then upon the soul of Jesus Christ; so that he was in travail. That is the first thing I would mind you of,—that in the bringing forth the work of our redemption and salvation, the Lord Jesus was in travail.

Secondly. It was a *satisfaction*, a rejoicing unto the Lord Jesus Christ, to consider the fruits and effects of this travail of his soul, which God had promised he should see. He was satisfied in the prospect he had of the fruit of the travail of his soul. So the apostle tells us, Heb. xii. 2, that, "for the joy that was set before him,"—which was the joy of bringing us unto God, of being the captain of salvation unto them that should obey him,—he "endured the cross, despising the shame." He went through all with a prospect he had of the fruit of his travail. There would joy come out of it; the joy that was set before him, as he speaks, Ps. xvi. 6, where God presents unto him what he shall have by this travail, what he shall get by it. Saith he, "The lines are fallen unto me in a pleasant place; yea, I have a goodly heritage." It is the satisfaction that Jesus Christ (who is there spoken of *only* in that psalm) takes in the fruit of the travail of his soul; he is contented with it. He doth not do as Hiram; who when Solomon gave him the twenty cities in the land of Galilee, calls them, "Cabul;" they were dirty, and they displeased him, 1 Kings ix. 11, etc. No; but, "The lines are fallen unto me in a pleasant place;" he *rejoiced* in his travail. It is expressed, in my apprehension, to the height in Jer. xxxi. 25, 26, "I have satiated the weary soul, and I have replenished every sorrowful soul." What follows? "Upon this I awaked, and beheld; and my sleep was sweet unto me." They are the words of Jesus Christ; and he speaks concerning his death, wherein he was as asleep in the grave. Now, consider what was the effect and fruit of it? It was sweet unto Jesus Christ, after all the travail of his soul, that he had "satiated the weary soul," and "replenished every sorrowful soul."

In one word, both these things—the travail of the soul of Christ, and the satisfaction he took in the fruit of his travail—are represented unto us in this ordinance.

There is the travail of the soul of Christ to us, in the manner of the participation of this ordinance,—in the breaking of the bread, and in the pouring out of the wine, representing unto us the breaking of the body of Christ, the shedding of his blood, and the separation of the one from the other; which was the cause of his death. Now, though these were outward things in Christ (because the travail of his soul cannot be represented by any outward things, wherein the great work of our redemption lay), we are in this ordinance to be led through these outward things to the travail of the soul of Christ: we are not to rest in the mere outward act or acts of the breaking of the body of Christ, and pouring out of his blood, the separation of the one from the other, and of his death thereby; but through all them we are to inquire what is *under them.* There was Christ's making his soul an offering for sin; there was Christ's being made a curse under them,—Christ's travail of soul, in an agony to bring forth the redemption and salvation of the church.

Brethren, let us be able by faith, not only to look through these outward signs to that which makes the representation itself unto us,—the body and blood of Christ; but even with them and through them to the travail of the soul of Christ,—the work that he was doing between God and himself for the redemption of the church.

And here is also a representation made unto us of that *satisfaction* the soul of Christ received in the fruit of his travail, having appointed it in a particular manner to be done in remembrance of him. No man will appoint a remembrance of that which he doth not delight in. When Job had no more delight in his life, he desired that the time of his birth might never be remembered. When God brought the children of Israel out of Egypt, whereby he exalted his glory, he appointed a *passover*, and said, "It is a day greatly to be remembered." Because the people had a great deliverance, and God received great glory and great satisfaction; therefore it was greatly to be remembered. We are to celebrate this ordinance in remembrance of Christ; and therefore there is a representation of that satisfaction which Jesus Christ did receive in the travail of his soul: so that he never repented him of one groan, of one sigh, of one tear, of one prayer, of one wrestling with the wrath of God. It is matter of rejoicing, and to be remembered; and do you rejoice in the remembrance of it.

Again; it is apparent from hence, because this ordinance is in an especial manner *an ordinance of thanksgiving:*—the bread that is blessed, or which we give thanks for; the cup which is blessed;—Christ gave thanks. Now, if hereby we give thanks, it is to call to remembrance, not merely the travail of Christ's soul, but the success of that travail; [that] hereby all differences were made up between God and us; hereby grace and glory were purchased for us, and he became the captain of salvation unto us.

To shut up all; here is, by Christ's institution, bread and wine provided for us; but it is bread broken, and wine poured out. There are two things in it:—there is the *weak part*, that is Christ's; there is the *nourishing part*, that is given unto us. The Lord Christ hath chosen by this ordinance to represent himself by these things that are the staff of our lives; they comprise the whole nourishment and sustenance of our bodies. He hath so chosen to represent them by breaking and pouring out, that they shall signify his sufferings. Here are both. As the bread is broken, and as the wine is poured out, there is the representation of the travail of the soul of Christ to us; as bread is received, and the cup, which is the means of the nourishment of man's life, here is the fruit of Christ's death exhibited unto us, and his sufferings. The Lord help us to look into the satisfaction that Christ received from this, that we may be partakers of the one and the other!

DISCOURSE XII.[1]

We are met here to remember, to celebrate, and set forth the death of Christ,—to profess and plead our interest therein. And there are two things that we should principally consider in reference to ourselves, and our duty, and the death of Christ. The first is, the *benefits* of it, and our *participation* of them; and the second is, *our conformity* unto it. Both are mentioned together by the apostle in

PHIL. iii. 10,—"That I may know him, and the power of his resurrection, and the fellowship of his sufferings, being made conformable unto his death."

I shall speak a word or two (upon this occasion of remembering the death of Christ) unto the latter clause,—of our "being made conformable unto his death,"—wherein a very great part of our due preparation unto this ordinance doth consist; and for the furtherance whereof we do in an especial manner wait upon God in this part of his worship. Therefore I shall in a few words mind you wherein we ought to be conformable unto the death of Christ, and how we are advantaged therein by this ordinance.

We are to be conformable unto the death of Christ in the *internal, moral cause* of it, and in the *external means* of it.

The *cause* of the death of Christ was *sin;* the *means* of the death of Christ was *suffering.* Our being conformable unto the death of Christ must respect sin and suffering.

The procuring cause of the death of Christ was *sin.* He died for sin; he died for our sin; our iniquities were upon him, and were the cause of all the punishment that befell him.

Wherein can we be conformable unto the death of Christ with respect unto sin? We cannot die for sin. Our hope and faith is, in and through him, that we shall never die for sin. No mortal man

[1] Delivered February 21, 1674–5.

can be made like unto Christ in suffering for sin. Those that undergo what he underwent, because they were unlike him, must go to hell and be made more unlike him to eternity. Therefore the apostle tells us that our conformity unto the death of Christ with respect unto sin lies in this,—that as he died *for* sin, so we should die *unto* sin,—that that sin which he died for should die in us. He tells us so, Rom. vi. 5, "We are planted together in the likeness of his death;"—"We are made conformable unto the death of Christ, planted into him, so as to have a likeness to him in his death." Wherein? "Knowing that our old man is crucified with him," saith he, verse 6. It is the crucifixion of the old man, the crucifying of the body of sin, the mortifying of sin, that makes us conformable unto the death of Christ; as to the internal moral cause of it, that procures it. See another apostle tells us, 1 Pet. iv. 1, 2, "Forasmuch then as Christ hath suffered for us in the flesh, arm yourselves likewise with the same mind: for he that hath suffered in the flesh hath ceased from sin; that he no longer should live the rest of his time in the flesh to the lusts of men, but to the will of God." Here is our conformity to Christ, as he suffered in the flesh,—that we should no longer live to our lusts, nor unto the will of man, but unto the will of God. And, brethren, let me tell you, he who approacheth unto this remembrance of the death of Christ, that hath not laboured, that doth not labour, for conformity to his death in the universal mortification of all sin, runs a hazard to his soul, and puts an affront upon Jesus Christ. O let none of us come in a way of thankfulness to remember the death of Jesus Christ, and bring along with us the murderer whereby he was slain! To harbour with us, and bring along with us to the death of Christ, unmortified lusts and corruptions, such as we do not continually and sincerely endeavour to kill and mortify, is to come and upbraid Christ with his murderer, instead of obtaining any spiritual advantage. What can such poor souls expect?

To be conformable unto the death of Christ as to *the outward* means, is to be conformable unto him *in suffering.* We here remember Christ's sufferings. And I am persuaded, and hope I have considered it, that he who is unready to be conformable unto Christ in suffering, was never upright and sincere in endeavouring to be conformable unto Christ in the killing of sin; for we are called as much to the one as to the other. Christ hath suffered for us, "leaving us an example," that we should also suffer when we are called thereunto. And our unwillingness to suffer like unto Christ arises from some unmortified corruption in our hearts, which we have not endeavoured to subdue, that we may be like unto Christ in the mortification and death of sin.

There are four things required, that we may be conformable unto the death of Christ in suffering; for we may suffer, and yet not be like unto Christ in it, nor by it:—

1. The first is, that we *suffer for Christ*, 1 Pet. iv. 15, 16, "Let none suffer as a murderer, or as a thief, or as an evil-doer," etc.; "yet if any man suffer as a Christian, let him not be ashamed." To suffer *as a Christian* is to suffer *for Christ*,—for the name of Christ, for the truths of Christ, for the ways of Christ, for the worship of Christ.

2. It is required that we suffer *in the strength of Christ;*—that we do not suffer in the strength of our own will, our own reason, our own resolutions; but that we suffer, I say, in the strength of Christ. When we suffer aright, "it is given unto us in the behalf of Christ, not only to believe on him, but to suffer for him." As all other graces are to be derived from Christ, as our head and root, stock and foundation; so, in particular, that grace which enables us to suffer for Christ must be from him. And we do well to consider whether it be so or no; for if it be not, all our sufferings are lost, and not acceptable to him. It is a sacrifice without *salt*, yea, without *a heart*, that will not be accepted.

3. It is required that we suffer *in imitation of Christ*, as making him *our example*. We are not to take up the cross but with design to follow Christ. "Take up the cross," is but half the command; "Take up the cross, and follow me," is the whole command: and we are to suffer willingly and cheerfully, or we are the most unlike Jesus Christ in our sufferings of any persons in the world. Christ was willing and cheerful: "Lo, I come to do thy will. I have a baptism to be baptized with, and how am I straitened till it be accomplished," saith he. And,

4. We are to suffer *to the glory of Christ*.

These are things wherein we ought to endeavour conformity to the death of Christ, that we now remember. I pray, let none of us trust to the outward ordinance, the performance of the outward duty. If these things be not in us, we do not remember the Lord's death in a right manner.

How may we attain the strength and ability from this ordinance, to be made conformable to his death? that we may not come and remember the death of Christ, and go away and be more unlike him than formerly?

There is power to this end communicated to us, *doctrinally*, *morally*, and *spiritually*.

There is no such sermon to teach *mortification of sin*, as the commemoration of the death of Christ. It is the greatest outward instruction unto this duty that God hath left unto his church; and, I am persuaded, which he doth most bless to them who are sincere. Do we see Christ evidently crucified before our eyes, his body broken, his blood shed for sin? and is it not of powerful instruction to us to go on to mortify sin? He that hath not learned this, never learned any thing aright from this ordinance, nor did he ever receive any benefit from it. There is a constraining power in this instruction, to put us upon the mortification of sin; God grant we may see the fruit of it! It hath *a teaching efficacy;* it teaches, as it is peculiarly blessed of God to this end and purpose. And I hope many a soul can say that they have received that encouragement and that strength by it, as that they have been enabled to more steadiness and constancy in fighting against sin, and have received more success afterward.

There is a *moral* way whereby it communicates strength to us; because it is our duty now to engage ourselves unto this very work. Meeting at the death of Christ, it is our duty to engage ourselves unto God; and that gives strength. And I would beg of you all, brethren, that not one of us would pass through or go over this ordinance, this representation of the death of Christ, without a fresh obligation to God to abide more constant and vigorous in the mortification of sin: we all need it.

And lastly; *a spiritually beholding of Christ by faith is the means to change us into the image and likeness of Christ.* Beholding the death of Christ by faith, as represented to us in this ordinance, is the means to change us into his image and likeness, and make us conformable unto his death, in the death of sin in us.

(1.) Take this instruction from the ordinance:—as you believe in Christ, as you love him, as you desire to remember him, *sin ought to be mortified,* that we may be conformed unto him in his death.

(2.) That we do every one of us bring our souls under *an engagement so to do;* which is required of us in the very nature of the duty.

(3.) That we labour by faith *so* to behold a dying Christ, that strength *may thence issue forth* for the death of sin in our souls.

DISCOURSE XIII.[1]

I HAVE generally, *on this occasion,* fixed on something particular that may draw forth and guide present meditation; but I shall at present enter on what may be farther carried on, and speak a little to you about *the nature and use of the ordinance itself,* in which, it may be, some of us (for there are of all degrees and sizes of know-

[1] Delivered April 18, 1675.

ledge in the church) may not be so well instructed. God has taught us, that the using of an ordinance will not be of advantage to us, unless we understand the institution, and the nature and the ends of it. It was so under the Old Testament, when their worship was more carnal; yet God would have them to know the nature and the reason of that great ordinance of *the passover*, as you may see in Exod. xii. 24–27, "And ye shall observe this thing for an ordinance to thee and to thy sons for ever. And it shall come to pass, when ye be come to the land which the LORD will give you, according as he hath promised, that ye shall keep this service. And it shall come to pass, when your children shall say unto you, What mean ye by this service? that ye shall say, It is the sacrifice of the LORD's passover," etc. Carry along with you the *institution;* it is *the ordinance of God,* "You shall keep this service." Then you must have *the meaning* of it, which is this, "It is the LORD's passover." And *the occasion* of the institution was this, "The LORD passed over our houses when he smote the Egyptians, and delivered us out of Egypt." There is a great mystery in that word, "It is the sacrifice of the LORD'S passover." Their deliverance was by *the blood of a sacrifice;* it was a sacrifice which made them look to the great sacrifice, "Christ our passover, who was sacrificed for us." And there is a mystical instruction: "It is the LORD's passover," says he. It was a pledge and sign of the Lord's passing over and sparing the Israelites, for it was not *itself* the Lord's passover. Christ says, "*This is my body;*" that is, a pledge and token of it. Under the Old Testament, God would not have his people to observe this great service and ordinance, but they should know *the reason* of it, and the *end* and *rise* of it, that it might be a service of faith.

All these things are clearly comprised, in reference unto this ordinance of the Lord's supper, in those words of the apostle:—

> "For I have received of the Lord that which also I delivered unto you, That the Lord Jesus, the same night in which he was betrayed, took bread: and, when he had given thanks, he brake it, and said, Take, eat; this is my body, which is broken for you: this do in remembrance of me. After the same manner also he took the cup, when he had supped, saying, This cup is the new testament in my blood: this do ye, as oft as ye drink it, in remembrance of me. For as often as ye eat this bread, and drink this cup, ye do show the Lord's death till he come."—1 COR. xi. 23–26.

You have both the institution and the nature, the use and ends of this ordinance in these words; and I shall speak so briefly to them, and under such short heads, as those who are young and less experienced may do well to retain:—

First. There is the *institution* of it: "I received," said he, "of the Lord;" and he received it on this account, that the *Lord appointed it:* and if you would come in faith unto this ordinance, you are to consider two things in this institution:—

1. The *authority of Christ.* It was *the Lord,*—the Lord, the head and king of the church. Our Lord, our lawgiver, our ruler, he has appointed this service; and if you would have your performance of it an act of obedience, acceptable to God, you must get your conscience influenced with the authority of Christ, that we can give this reason in the presence of God why we come together to perform this service, "It is because Jesus Christ, *our Lord,* has *appointed* it; he hath required it of us." And what is done in obedience to his command, that is a part of our reasonable service; and therein we are accepted with God.

2. In the institution of it there is also *his love;* which is manifested in the *time* of its appointment: "The Lord Jesus, the same night in which he was betrayed." One would think that our Lord Jesus Christ, who knew all the troubles, the distresses, the anguish, the sufferings, the derelictions of God, which were coming upon him, and into which he was just now entering, would have had something else to think of besides this provision for his church. But his heart was filled with love to his people; and that love which carried him to all that darkness and difficulty that he was to go through,—that love at the same time did move him to institute this ordinance, for the benefit and advantage of his church. And this I shall only say, that that heart which is made spiritually sensible of the love of Jesus Christ in the institution of this ordinance, and in what this ordinance doth represent, is truly prepared for communion with Christ in this ordinance. O let us all labour for this in particular, if possible, that through the power of the Spirit of God, we may have some impressions of the love of Christ on our hearts! Brethren, if we have not brought it with us, if we do not yet find it in us, I pray let us be careful to endeavour that we do not go away without it. Thus you have what is to be observed in the institution itself,—the *authority* and the *love* of Christ.

Secondly. I shall speak to the *use* and *ends of this ordinance;* and they are three:—1. *Recognition;* 2. *Exhibition;* 3. *Profession.*

1. *Recognition;* that is, the solemn calling over and remembrance of what is intended in this ordinance.

There is an *habitual* remembrance of Christ; what all believers ought continually to carry about them. And here lies the difference between those that are spiritual and those that are carnal:—They all agree that Christians ought to have a continual remembrance of Christ; but what way shall we obtain it? Why, set up images and pictures of him in every corner of the house and chapel; that is to bring Christ to remembrance. That way carnal men take for this purpose. But the way believers have to bring Christ to remembrance, is by the Spirit of Christ working through the word. We have no image of Christ but *the word;* and the Spirit represents Christ to us thereby, wherein he is evidently crucified before our eyes. But this recognition I speak of is a solemn remembrance *in the way of an ordinance,* wherein, unto the internal actings of our minds, there is added the external representation of the signs that God has appointed, "This do in remembrance of me." It is twice mentioned, in verses 24, 25.

Concerning this remembrance, we may consider two things:—(1.) What is the *object* of this remembrance or recognition; and, (2.) What is *the act* of it;—what we are to remember, and what is that act of remembrance that is acceptable to God in this ordinance.

(1.) What is the *object* of this remembrance. The object of this remembrance principally is Christ; but it is not Christ *absolutely* considered, it is Christ *in those circumstances* wherein he then was. "Do it in remembrance of me," saith he; "as I am sent of God, designed to be a sacrifice for the sins of the elect, and as I am now going to die for that end and purpose, so do it in remembrance of me." Wherefore, there are these four things that we are to remember of Christ as proposed in those circumstances wherein he will be remembered; and I will be careful not to mention any thing but what the meanest of us may bring into present exercise at the ordinance:—

[1.] Remember the *grace and love of God, even the Father, in sending Christ, in setting him forth, and proposing him to us.* This is everywhere mentioned in Scripture. We are minded of this in Scripture, whenever we are called to thoughts of the death of Christ:— John iii. 16, "God so loved the world, that he gave his only begotten Son;" Rom. iii. 25, "God set him forth to be a propitiation through faith in his blood;" Rom. v. 8, "God commendeth his love toward us, in that, while we were yet sinners, Christ died for us." Remember, I pray you, the unspeakable grace and love of God in sending, giving, and setting forth Jesus Christ to be the propitiation.

Now, how does this ordinance guide us in calling this love and grace of God to remembrance? Why, in this, in that it is in the way of a furnished table provided for us. So God has expressed his love in this matter, Isa. xxv. 6, "In this mountain shall the LORD of hosts make unto all people a feast of fat things, a feast of wines on the lees; of fat things full of marrow, of wines on the lees well refined." The preparation of the table here is to mind us to call to remembrance the love and grace of God, in sending and exhibiting his Son Jesus Christ to be a ransom and propitiation for us. That is the first thing.

[2.] Remember, in particular, the *love of Jesus Christ, as God-man, in giving himself for us.* This love is frequently proposed to us with what he did for us; and it is represented peculiarly in this ordinance. "Who loved me, and gave himself for me," says the apostle. Faith will never be able to live upon the last expression,—"Gave himself for me," unless it can rise up to the first, "Who loved me;" Rev. i. 5, 6, "Who loved us, and washed us from our sins in his own blood," etc.

I think we are all satisfied in this, that in calling Christ to remembrance, we should in an especial manner call *the love* of Christ to remembrance. And that soul in whom God shall work a sense of the love of Christ in any measure (for it is past comprehension, and our minds and souls are apt to lose themselves in it, when we attempt to fix our thoughts upon it),—that he who is God-man should do thus for us, [will find that] it is too great for any thing but faith; which can rest in that which it can no way comprehend, if it go to try the depth, and breadth, and length of it, to fathom its dimensions, and consider it with reason: for it is past all understanding; but faith can *rest* in what it cannot *comprehend.* So should we remember the love of Christ, of him who is God-man, who gave himself for us, and will be remembered in this ordinance.

[3.] We shall not manage our spirits aright as to this first part of the duty (the end of the ordinance in *recognition*), unless we call over and remember what was *the ground upon which the profit and benefit of the sufferings of Christ doth redound to us.*

Let us remember that this is no other but that *eternal covenant* and compact that was between the Father and the Son, that Christ should undertake for sinners, and that what he did in that undertaking should be done on their behalf, should be reckoned to them and accounted as theirs. So our Saviour speaks, Ps. xl. 6, 7, "Sacrifice and offering thou didst not desire; mine ears hast thou opened: burnt-offering and sin-offering hast thou not required. Then said I, Lo, I come: in the volume of the book it is written of me," etc.

Christ does that in our behalf which sacrifice and burnt-offerings could not perform. We have this covenant declared at large, Isa. liii. 10, 11, "Yet it pleased the LORD to bruise him; he hath put him to grief: when thou shalt make his soul an offering for sin, he shall see his seed," etc. Pray, brethren, be wise and understanding in this matter, and not children in calling over and remembering Christ in this ordinance. Remember the counsel of peace that was between them both; when it was agreed on the part of Christ to undertake and answer for what we had done; and upon the part of God the Father, that upon his so doing, righteousness, life, and salvation, should be given to sinners.

[4.] Remember *the sufferings of Christ;* this is a main thing. Now the sufferings of Christ may be considered three ways:—1*st.* The sufferings *in his soul;* 2*dly.* The sufferings in his body; 3*dly.* The sufferings *of his person* in the dissolution of his human nature, soul and body, by death itself.

1*st.* Remember *the sufferings in his soul;* and they were of two sorts:—(1*st.*) *Privative,* his sufferings in the desertion and dereliction of God his Father; and, (2*dly.*) *Positive,* in the emission of the sense of God's wrath and the curse of the law on his soul.

(1*st.*) The head of Christ's sufferings was in *the divine desertion,* whence he cried out, "My God, my God, why hast thou forsaken me?" It is certain Christ was forsaken of God; he had not else so complained,—forsaken of God in his soul. How? The divine nature in the *second person* did not forsake the human; nor did the divine nature in the *third person* forsake the human, as to the whole work of sanctification and holiness, but kept alive in Christ all grace whatsoever,—all grace in that fulness whereof he had ever been partaker: but the desertion was as to *all influence of comfort* and *all evidence* of love from God the Father (who is the fountain of love and comfort), administered by the Holy Ghost. Hence some of our divines have not spared to say, that Christ did *despair* in that great cry, "My God, my God," etc. Now, *despair* signifies two things:—a *total want of the evidence of faith* as to acceptance with God; and *a resolution in the soul to seek no farther after it,* and not to wait for it from that fountain. In the first way Christ *did despair,*—that is *penal only;* in the latter he *did not,*—that is *sinful also.* There was a total interception of *all evidence* of love from God, but *not a ceasing* in him to wait upon God for the manifestation of that love in his appointed time. Remember, Christ was thus forsaken that his people might never be forsaken.

(2*dly.*) There were *sufferings positive* in his soul, when he was made sin and a curse for us, and had *a sense of the wrath* and anger of God on his soul. This brought those expressions concerning him and from him: "He began to be sore amazed, and said, My soul is exceeding sorrowful, even unto death." He was "in an agony." I desire no more for my soul everlastingly to confute that *blasphemy, that Christ died only as a martyr, to confirm the truth he had preached,* but the consideration of this one thing: for courage, resolution, and cheerfulness, are the principal virtues and graces in him who dies *only as a martyr;* but for him who had the weight of the wrath of God and the curse of the law upon his soul, it *became him to be in an agony,—to sweat great drops of blood,*—to cry out, "My God, my God, why hast thou forsaken me?" which,[1] had he been called to for

[1] The close of this sentence is obscure, and hardly develops and completes the author's argument. If it were not too great a liberty with the text, the following alteration might have been made, and seems to elicit the meaning designed to be conveyed:—"[whereas] had he been called to [die] for nothing else but barely to confirm the truth he had preached, he would have done [it] without much trouble or shaking of mind." It must be borne in mind that these discourses were not only posthumous, but printed from notes taken by the hearers of Owen.—ED.

nothing else but barely to confirm the truth he had preached, he would have done without much trouble or shaking of mind.

I shall not now speak of *the sufferings in his body*, which I am afraid we do not consider enough. Some poor souls are apt to consider *nothing but* the sufferings of his body; and some do not *enough* consider them. We may call this over some other time, as also the sufferings of his person in the dissolution of his human nature, by a separation of the soul from the body; which was also comprised in the curse.

"This do in remembrance of me." What are we to remember? These are things of no great research; they are not hard and difficult, but such as we all may come up to the practice of in the administration of this very ordinance. Remember the unspeakable grace and love of God, in setting forth Christ to be a propitiation. Remember the love of Christ, who gave himself for us notwithstanding he knew all that would befall him on our account. Remember the compact and agreement between the Father and the Son, that what was due to us he should undergo, and the benefit of what he did should redound to us. Remember the greatness of the work he undertook for these ends, in the sufferings of his whole person, when he would redeem his church with his own blood.

(2.) One word for *the act of remembrance*, and I have done. How shall we remember? Remembrance in itself is a solemn calling over of what is true and past: and there are two things required in our remembrance; the first is *faith*, and the second is *thankfulness*.

[1.] *Faith;* so to call it over as to believe it. But who does not believe it? Why, truly, brethren, *many believe the story of it, or the fact*, who do not believe it *to that advantage for themselves* they ought to do. In a word, we are *so to believe it as to put our trust for life and salvation* in those things that we call to remembrance. *Trust and confidence belong to the essence of saving faith.* So remember these things as to place your trust in them. Shall I gather up your workings of faith into one expression?—the apostle calls it, Rom. v. 11, the "receiving the atonement." If God help us afresh to receive the atonement at this time, we have discharged our duty in this ordinance; for here is the atonement proposed, from the love of God, and from the love of Christ, by virtue of the compact between the Father and the Son, through the sufferings and sacrifice of Christ, in his whole person, soul and body. Here is an atonement with God proposed unto us: the working of our faith is to receive it, or to believe it *so as to approve of it* as an excellent way, full of wisdom, goodness, holiness; to embrace it, and trust in it.

[2.] Remember, that among the offerings of old which were appointed to shadow out the death of Christ, there was a *thank-offering;*

for there was *a burning of the fat upon the altar of thank-offering*, to signify there was thankfulness to God always, as part of the remembrance of the sacrifice that Christ made for us. Receive the atonement, and be thankful. The Lord lead us into the practice of these things!

DISCOURSE XIV.

"For I have received of the Lord," etc.—1 COR. xi. 23–26.

THE last time I spake to you on this occasion, I told you that the grace of God and our duty in this ordinance might be drawn under the three heads of *recognition* or calling over, of *exhibition*, and of *profession*. The first of these I then spake unto, and showed you what we are to recognise or call over therein.

2. The second thing is *exhibition and reception,—exhibition on the part of Christ, reception on our part;* wherein the essence of this ordinance doth consist. I shall briefly explain it to you, rather now to stir up faith unto exercise than to instruct in the doctrine. And that we may exercise our faith aright, we may consider,—(1.) Who it is that makes an exhibition, that offers, proposes, and gives something to us at this time in this ordinance; (2.) What it is that is exhibited, proposed, and communicated in this ordinance; and, (3.) How or in what manner we receive it:—

(1.) Who *is it that makes an exhibition?* It is *Christ himself.* When Christ was given for us, God the Father gave him, and set him forth to be a propitiation; but in this exhibition it is *Christ himself*, I say, that is the *immediate exhibiter.* The tender that is made, of whatever it be, it is made by Christ. And as our faith stands in need of directions and boundaries to be given to it in this holy duty, it will direct our faith to consider Jesus Christ present among us, *by his Spirit* and *by his word*, making this tender or this exhibition unto us. It is Christ that does it; which calls out our faith unto an immediate exercise *on his person.*

(2.) What *is it Christ does exhibit and propose to us?*

[1.] Not *empty and outward signs.* God never instituted such things in his church. From the foundation of the world he never designed to feed his people with such outward symbols. Those under the Old Testament were not empty, though they had not a fulness like those under the New. They had not a fulness, because they had respect to what was yet to come and could not be filled with that light, that grace, that evidence of the things themselves, as the present signs are, which are accomplished. Christ doth not give us empty signs. Nor,—

[2.] *Does Christ give us his flesh and blood, taken in a carnal sense.* If men would believe him, he has told us a long time ago, when that doubt arose upon that declaration of his [about] eating his flesh and drinking his blood, John vi. 52 (though he *did not then speak of the sacrament*, but of that which was the essence and life of it), "How can this man give us his flesh to eat?" He told us, that eating his flesh profited nothing, in that way they thought of eating it; for they apprehended, as the Papists do now, that they were to eat flesh,—body, bones, and all. Why, says he, "'The flesh profiteth nothing; it is the Spirit that quickeneth;' that power that is to be communicated to you is by the Spirit." So that Christ does not give us his flesh and blood in a carnal manner, as the men at Capernaum thought, and others look for. This would not feed our souls.

But then, what is it that Christ does exhibit, that we may exercise our faith upon? I say, it is *himself* as immediately discharging his great office of a *priest*, being sacrificed for us. It is himself, as accompanied with all the benefits of that great part of his mediation, in dying for us. May the Lord stir up our hearts to believe that the tender Christ makes unto us is originally and principally of himself; because all the benefits of his mediation arise from that fountain and spring, when God purchased the church with his own blood. A way this is which the Lord Jesus Christ, who is the wisdom of God, has found out and appointed, to make a special tender of his person to our souls, to be received by us. And he tenders himself, in the discharge of his mediation, in the most amiable and most glorious representation of himself to the soul of a sinner. Christ is glorious in himself, in all his offices, and in all the representations that are made of him in the Scripture unto our faith; but Christ is most amiable, most beautiful, most glorious to the soul of a believing sinner, when he is represented as dying,—making atonement for sin, making peace for sinners, as bearing our iniquities, satisfying the wrath of God and curse of the law, to draw out our hearts unto faith and love. Christ in this ordinance makes such a representation of himself, as bleeding for us, making atonement for our sins, and sealing the everlasting covenant: and he proposes himself unto us with all the benefits of his death, of that redemption he wrought out for us,—peace with God, making an end of sin, bringing in everlasting righteousness, and the like. I intend only to remind you of these things; for we are at a loss sometimes as to the exercise of faith in and under this duty.

3. There remains to be considered, *reception;* for unless it be received, there is nothing done to any saving purpose. Notwithstand-

ing all this tender that is made, the issue of all the benefit and consolation lies upon receiving.

There are two ways whereby we do receive Christ:—(1.) We receive him *sacramentally*, by obedience in church-order; and, (2.) We receive him *spiritually* and really by faith, or believing in him.

(1.) We receive him *sacramentally*. This consists in the due and orderly performance of what he has appointed in his word for this end and purpose, that therein and thereby he may exhibit himself to our souls. It doth not consist (as some have thought) *in partaking of the elements;* that is but one part of it, and but one small part. Our sacramental reception consists in the due observation of the whole order of the institution according to the mind of Christ.

(2.) We receive him by faith *spiritually;* and if we could rightly understand that special *act of faith* which we are to exercise in the reception of Christ, when he does thus exhibit himself to us, then should we glorify God,—then should we bring in advantage to our own souls.

I have but a word to say; and that is this,—it is that acting of faith which is now required of us which draws nearest unto *spiritual, sensible experience.* Faith has *many degrees*, and *many acts;*—some at a kind of distance from the object, in *mere reliance and recumbency;* and many other acts of faith make very near approaches to the object, and rise up to *sensible experience.* It should be (if God would help us) such an act of faith as rises up nearest to a sensible experience. It is that which the Holy Ghost would teach us by this ordinance, when we receive it by eating and drinking, which are things of sense; and things of sense are chosen to express faith wrought up to an experience. And they who had some apprehension hereof, —that it must be a peculiar acting of faith and rising up to a spiritual experience,—but finding nothing of the light and power of it in their own souls, gave birth to *transubstantiation;* that they might do that with their mouths and teeth which they could not do with their souls.

Faith should rise up to an experience in two things,—[1.] In *representation;* [2.] In *incorporation:*—

[1.] The thing we are to aim at, to be carried unto by faith in this ordinance, is, that there may be *a near and evident representation* of Christ in his tender unto our souls,—faith being satisfied in it; faith being in this matter the evidence of things not seen, making it exist in the soul, making Christ more present to the soul than he would be to our bodily eyes if he were among us,—more assuredly so. Faith should rise up to evidence in that near and close representation it makes of Christ in this exhibition of himself. And,—

[2.] *Faith is to answer the end of eating and drinking, which is incorporation.* We are so to receive Christ as to receive him into a spiritual incorporation,—that the flesh and blood of Christ, as communicated in this ordinance, through faith, may be turned and changed in our hearts into *spiritual, vital principles*, and unto growth and satisfaction. These are the three things we receive by nourishment, and wherein incorporation does consist:—there is an increase and quickening of vital principles, there is growth, and there is satisfaction, in receiving suitable food and nourishment. Faith, I say, should rise up to these three things in its acts. I mention these things to direct the actings of our faith in this holy administration.

DISCOURSE XV.[1]

I SHALL offer a few words to direct you in the present exercise of faith in this ordinance. I design no more but to give occasion to that particular exercise of faith which is now required of us, whereby we may sanctify the name of God in a due manner, give glory to him by believing, and receive establishment unto our own souls: and I would do it by minding you of that word of our Lord Jesus Christ in

JOHN xii. 32,—" And I, if I be lifted up from the earth, will draw all men unto me."

What he means by his *lifting up*, the evangelist expounds in the next words, which are these, " This he said, signifying what death he should die." So that the lifting up of *Christ on the cross*, is that which he lays as the foundation of *his drawing sinners unto him.* No sinner will come near to Christ unless he be drawn; and to be drawn, is to be *made willing* to come unto him, and to follow him in chains of love. Christ draws none to him whether they will or no; but he casts on their minds, hearts, and wills the cords of his grace and love, working in them powerfully, working on them kindly, to cause them to choose him, to come to him, and to follow him. "Draw me; we will run after thee." The great principle and fountain from whence the drawing efficacy and power of grace doth proceed, is from the lifting up of Christ. Drawing grace is manifested in, and drawing love proceeds from, the sufferings of Jesus Christ on the cross.

But that which I would just mind you of at present is this, that the *look of faith* unto Christ as lifted up is the only means of bringing our souls near to him. Our faith is often expressed by *looking unto Christ:* Isa. xlv. 22, " Look unto me," says he, " and be ye saved, all the ends of the earth." The conclusion is, that those who so look unto him shall be justified and saved: Isa. lxv. 1, " Behold me, behold me."

[1] Delivered September 5, 1675.

And it is the great promise of the efficacy of the Spirit poured out upon us, that "we shall look upon him whom we have pierced," Zech. xii. 10. God calls us to look off from all other things; look off from the law, look off from self, look off from sin,—look *only* unto Christ. Is Christ said to be lifted up in his death, and to die that manner of death wherein he was lifted up on the cross?—so it was expressed in the type; the brasen serpent was lifted up on a pole, that those who were smote with the fiery serpents might look to it. If the soul can but turn an eye of faith unto Jesus Christ as thus lifted up, it will receive healing, though the sight of one be not so clear as the sight of another. All had not *a like sharpness of sight* that looked to the brasen serpent, nor have all *the like vigour of faith* to look to Christ: but one sincere look to Christ is pleasing to him; so as he says, Cant. iv. 9, "Thou hast ravished my heart, my sister, my spouse; thou hast ravished my heart with one of thine eyes." A soul sensible of guilt and sin, that casts but one look of faith to Christ as lifted up, it even raises the heart of Christ himself; and such a soul shall not go away unrefreshed, unrelieved.

Now, brethren, the end of this ordinance is, to lift up Christ *in representation:* as he was lifted up really on the cross, and as in the whole preaching of the gospel Christ is evidently crucified before our eyes, so more especially in the administration of this ordinance. Do we see, then, wherein the special acting of faith in this ordinance does consist? God forbid we should neglect the stirring up our hearts unto the particular acting of faith in Jesus Christ, who herein is lifted up before us. That which we are to endeavour in this ordinance is, to get a view by faith,—faith working by thoughts, by meditation, acting by love,—a view of Christ as lifted up; that is, as bearing our iniquities in his own body on the tree. What did Christ do on the tree? what was he lifted up for, if it was not to bear our sins? Out of his love and zeal to the glory of God, and out of compassion to the souls of men, Christ bore the guilt and punishment of sin, and made expiation for it. O that God in this ordinance would give our souls a view of him! I shall give it to myself and to you in charge at this time,—if we have a view of Christ by faith as lifted up, our hearts will be drawn nearer to him. If we find not our hearts in any manner drawn nearer to him, it is much to be feared we have not had a view of him as bearing our iniquities. Take, therefore, this one remembrance as to the acting of faith in the administration of this ordinance,—labour to have it fixed upon Christ as bearing sin, making atonement for it, with his heart full of love to accomplish a cause in righteousness and truth.

DISCOURSE XVI.[1]

To whet our minds, and lead us to a particular exercise of faith and love in this duty, I shall add a few words from that Scripture which I have already spoken something to upon this occasion, namely,—

JOHN xii. 32,—"And I, if I be lifted up from the earth, will draw all men unto me."

This lifting up, as I said before, was the lifting up of Christ on the cross, when, as the apostle Peter tells us, "he bore," or, as the word is, he carried up, "our sins in his own body on the tree." Christ died for three ends:—1. *To answer an institution;* 2. *To fulfil a type;* and, 3. *To be a moral representation of the work of God in his death.*

1. It was to answer *the institution,* that *he who was hanged on a tree was accursed of God,* Deut. xxi. 23. There were many other ways appointed of God to put malefactors to death among the Jews. Some were stoned; in some cases they were burned with fire; but it is only by God appointed that *he that was hanged on a tree was accursed of God:* and Christ died that death, to show that it was he who underwent the curse of God; as the apostle shows, Gal. iii. 13, "He was made a curse for us; for it is written, Cursed is every one that hangeth on a tree."

2. Christ died that death to *fulfil a type.* For it was a bloody and most painful death, yet it was a death wherein a bone of him was not broken; typified of him in the *paschal lamb,* of which a bone was not to be broken. Christ was lifted up on the cross to fulfil that type: so that though his death was bitter, lingering, painful, shameful, yet not a bone was broke; that every one might have *a whole Christ, an entire Saviour,* notwithstanding all his suffering and rending on our behalf.

3. He was so lifted up that it might be a *moral representation unto all;* to answer that other *type,* also, of the serpent lifted up in the wilderness: so that he was the person that might say, "Behold me, behold me." He was lifted up between heaven and earth, that all creatures might see God had set him forth to be a propitiation.

"And I, when I am lifted up,"—what will he then do? "When I have answered the curse, when I have fulfilled the types, when I have complied with the will of God in being a propitiation, 'I will draw all men unto me.'" It is placed upon *Christ's lifting up.* Now that is actually past; nor was it done merely while Christ was hanging on the cross. There are two ways whereby there is a representation made of Christ being lifted up to draw men unto him:—

[1] Delivered October 31, 1675.

1. By *the preaching of the word.* So the apostle tells us, Gal. iii. 1, that "Jesus Christ was evidently set forth crucified among them, before their eyes." The great end of preaching the word is, to represent evidently Christ crucified;—it is to lift up Christ, that he may draw sinners unto him. And,—

2. It is represented *in this ordinance of the Lord's supper,* wherein we show forth his death. Christ is peculiarly and eminently lifted up in this ordinance, because it is a peculiar and eminent representation of his death.

Now there are *two ways* of Christ's drawing persons to himself:—1. His way of drawing *sinners* to him by *faith and repentance.* 2. His way of drawing *believers* to him, as to *actual communion* with him.

Christ draws sinners to him by faith and repentance, as he is lifted up in the preaching of the word; and he draws believers to him, as unto actual communion, as by the word, so in an especial manner by this ordinance. I shall only speak a word on the latter,—how Christ is lifted up in this ordinance that represents his death unto us; or, how he draws us into *actual communion* with him.

1. He does it *by his love.* The principal thing that is always to be considered, in the lifting up of Christ, is his love. "Who loved me," says the apostle, "and gave himself for me;" and, "Who loved us, and washed us from our sins in his own blood." I could show you that love is attractive, that it is encouraging and constraining. I will only leave this with you:—whatever apprehensions God in this ordinance shall give you of the love of Christ, you have therein an experience of Christ's drawing you, as he is lifted up, unto actual communion with him. It is of great concernment to you. Christ is never so lovely unto the soul of a sinner as when he is considered as lifted up; that is, as undergoing the curse of God, that a blessing might come upon us. O that he who has loved us, and because he has loved us, would draw us with the cords of his loving-kindness! as God says he does, Jer. xxxi. 3, "Yea, I have loved thee with an everlasting love; therefore with loving-kindness have I drawn thee."

2. The *sufferings of Christ in soul and body* are attractive of, and do draw the souls of believers to him. "They shall look on me whom they have pierced, and mourn." It is a look to Christ as pierced for sin, under his sufferings, that is attractive to the souls of believers in this ordinance; because these sufferings were for us. Call to mind, brethren, some of these texts of Scripture; see what God will give you out of them:—"He was made sin for us, who knew no sin, that we might be made the righteousness of God in him." "He was made a curse for us;" and "he bore our sins in his own body on the tree;" and "died, the just for the unjust, that he might bring us unto God." If Jesus Christ be pleased to let in a sense of his suffer-

ings for us, by these Scriptures, upon our souls, then we have another experience of his drawing us as he is lifted up.

3. Christ draws us as he is *lifted up*, by *the effects* of it. What was he lifted up for? It was to make peace with God through his blood: "God was in Christ reconciling the world unto himself." When? When "he made him to be sin for us, who knew no sin." It is the sacrifice of atonement; it is the sacrifice wherewith the covenant between God and us was sealed. This is one notion of the supper of our Lord. Covenants were confirmed *with sacrifice*. Isaac made a covenant with Abimelech, and confirmed it with sacrifice; so it was with Jacob and Laban: and in both places, when they had confirmed the covenant with a sacrifice, they had a *feast upon the sacrifice*. Christ by his sacrifice has ratified the covenant between God and us, and invites us in this ordinance to a participation of it. He draws us by it to faith in him, as he has made an atonement by his sacrifice.

These are some of the ways whereby Christ draws the souls of believers unto communion with him in this ordinance, that represents him as lifted up:—by expressing his love, by representing his sufferings, and tendering the sealing of the covenant as confirmed with a sacrifice, inviting us to feed on the remainder of the sacrifice that is left to us, for the nourishment of our souls. O that he would cast some of these cords of love upon our souls! for if he should be lifted up, and we should not come, if we should find no cords of love cast upon us to draw us into actual communion, we should have no advantage by this ordinance.

How shall we come in actual communion unto Christ in this ordinance, upon his drawing? what is required of us? Why,—

1. We are to come by faith, to "receive the atonement," Rom. v. 11. We come to a due communion with Christ in this ordinance, if we come to receive the atonement made by his death, as full of divine wisdom, grace, and love; and, as the truth and faithfulness of God is confirmed in it, to receive and lay hold on this atonement, that we may have peace with God. Isa. xxvii. 5, "Let him take hold of my strength; and he shall be at peace with me." Brethren, here is the arm of God, Christ the power of God, Christ lifted up. We ourselves have sinned, and provoked God. What shall we do? shall we set briers and thorns in battle array against God? No; says he, "I will pass through and devour such persons." What then? "Let him take hold of my strength," of my arm, "and be at peace." God speaks this to every soul of us, in this lifting up of Christ. Now, receive the atonement as full of infinite wisdom, holiness, and truth.

2. Faith comes and brings the soul to Christ as he is thus lifted up; but it is always *accompanied with love*, whereby the soul *adheres to Christ* when it is come.

Doth faith bring us to Christ, on his drawing, to receive the atonement?—set love at work to cleave unto him, to take him into our hearts and souls, and to abide with him.

3. It is to come *with mourning and godly sorrow,* because of our own sins. "Look unto him whom we have pierced, and mourn." These things are very consistent. Do not think we speak things at random: they are consistent in experience,—that we should receive Christ as making an atonement, and have peace with God in the pardon of our sins, and nevertheless mourn for our own iniquities. The Lord give experience of them in your hearts!

Let us now pray that some of these cords wherewith he draws the souls of believers may be on our souls in this ordinance.

DISCOURSE XVII.

WHEN we have opportunity of speaking to you on these occasions, it is for the direction of the exercise of your faith in this ordinance in a due manner. Here is a representation of the death of Christ; and there is in the word a representation of that which we should principally consider, and act faith with respect unto, in the representation that is made in this ordinance; and that is, of a blessed change and commutation that is made between Christ and believers, *in the imputation of their sins unto him, and in the imputation of his righteousness unto them:* and the principal part of the life and exercise of faith consists in a due consideration and improvement thereof. God taught this to the church of the Old Testament in the type of the offering of the *scape-goat:*—

> "And Aaron shall lay both his hands upon the head of the live goat, and confess over him all the iniquities of the children of Israel, and all their transgressions in all their sins, putting them upon the head of the goat," etc.—LEV. xvi. 21.

Aaron was not only *to confess* all the sins and iniquities of the people over the head of the goat, but he was *to put all their sins* upon him. Here is a double act:—*the confession of sin,* which is, as it were, the gathering of all their sins together; and *the putting of them on the goat,* to give a lively representation of it unto faith. So God did instruct Aaron to the putting of the guilt of our iniquities *typically* upon the sacrifice, *really* upon Jesus Christ.

He doth not say, "He shall bear the *punishment;*" but, "He shall take the *sin itself*" (that is, as to the *guilt* of it), "and carry it quite away." And therefore in the sacrifice appointed in Deut. xxi. for expiation of an uncertain murder,—when a man was killed, and none knew who killed him, so none was liable to punishment, but there was guilt *upon the land;*—then the elders of the city that was nearest the place where the murder was committed, to take away the guilt, were to cut off the neck of a heifer, by God's appointment; and that took away the guilt. Thus did God instruct the church under the Old Testament in this great, sovereign act of his wisdom and righteousness, in transferring the guilt of sin from the church unto Christ. Therefore the prophet says, Isa. liii. 5, 6, "The LORD hath laid on him the iniquity of us all." What then? "By his stripes we are healed." The stripes were all due to us; but they were due to us for our iniquities, and for no other cause. Now, our iniquities being transferred to Christ, all the stripes came to be his, and the healing came to be ours. To the same purpose the apostle says, "He was made sin for us, who knew no sin, that we might be made the righteousness of God in him." As we are made the righteousness of God in him, so he is made sin for us. We are made the righteousness of God in him by the *imputation* of his righteousness unto us; for our apostle is to be believed, that righteousness is by imputation: "God imputes righteousness," says he. We have no righteousness before God but by imputation; and when we are made righteous,—the righteousness of God, which God ordains, approves, and accepts, it is the righteousness of Christ *imputed to us.* And how is he made sin for us? Because our sin is *imputed to him.* Some will say, "He was made sin for us; that is, a sacrifice for sin." Be it so; but nothing could be made an expiatory sacrifice, but it had first the sin imputed to it. Aaron shall put his hands on the goat, confessing all their sins over his head;—be their sins on the head of the goat, or the expiatory sacrifice was nothing.

The same exchange you have again in Gal. iii. 13, 14, "He was made a curse for us." The curse was due to us, and this Christ was made for us. And to confirm our faith, God did institute a visible pledge long beforehand, to let us know he was made a curse for us. He had made it a sign of the curse, for one to be hanged on a tree; as it is written, "Cursed is every one that hangeth on a tree." What, then, comes to us? Why, "the blessing of faithful Abraham." What is that? "Abraham believed God, and it was accounted to him for righteousness." Justification and acceptance with God is the blessing of faithful Abraham. Here is the great exchange represented to us in Scripture in these things,—that all our sins are transferred upon Christ by imputation, and the righteousness of Christ transferred to us by imputation. Both these are acts of God, and not our acts. It is God who imputes our sin to Christ: "He hath made him to be sin for us." And it is God who imputes the righteousness of Christ to us: "It is God that justifieth." He who made Christ to be "sin," he also makes us to be "righteousness." These acts of God we ought to go over in our minds by faith; which is that I now call you to.

The way to apply the benefits and advantage of this great commutation to our souls, is in our minds, by faith, to [put our] seal to these acts of God. Christ in the gospel, and especially in this ordinance, is "evidently crucified before our eyes," Gal. iii. 1. God hath set him forth to be a propitiation; so he is declared in this ordinance. And Christ at the same time calls us to him: "Come unto me: look unto me, all the ends of the earth;"—"Come with your burdens; come you that are heavy laden with the guilt of sin." What God has done in a way of righteous *imputation*, that we are to do in this ordinance in a way of *believing*. We are, by the divine help, to lay our sins by faith on Jesus Christ, by closing with that act of God which is represented to us in the word,—that God has imputed all our sins to Jesus Christ. Let you and I, and all of us, say "Amen," by faith; "So be it, O Lord,—let the guilt of all our sins be on the head of Jesus Christ:" and therein admire the goodness, the grace, the love, the holiness, the infinite wisdom of God in this matter. If we were able to say Amen to this great truth, we should have the comfort of it in our souls,—to acquiesce in it, to find power and reality in it.

Then the other act of God is, the imputation of the righteousness of Christ to us. It is not enough to us that *our sins* are all carried away into a land not inhabited; we stand in need of *a righteousness* whereby we may be accepted before God. He makes us to be the righteousness of God; we do not make ourselves so, but are made so by the imputation of the righteousness of Christ.

Our second act of faith, that God may stir us up unto in this ordinance, is, to "receive the atonement." So the apostle expresses it, Rom. v. 11. We receive together with it *all the fruits* of the atonement.

Now, if the Lord will be pleased to stir up our hearts from under their deadness,—to gather them in from their wanderings, to make us sensible of our concern, to give us the acting of faith in this matter, that truly and really the holy God has laid all our iniquities upon Christ, and tenders to us life, righteousness, justification, and mercy by him,—we shall then have the fruit of this administration.

DISCOURSE XVIII.[1]

I SHALL offer a few words, with a view to prepare our minds to the exercise of faith and communion with God in this ordinance: and because we ought to be in the highest exercise of faith in this ordinance, I shall take occasion from those words, which express as high an acting of faith, I think, as any is in the Scripture; I mean those words of the apostle in

GAL. ii. 20,—"I am crucified with Christ: nevertheless I live; yet not I, but Christ liveth in me: and the life which I now live in the flesh I live by the faith of the Son of God, who loved me, and gave himself for me."

Our inquiry now is, How we may act faith? It acts two ways:—

1. By *way of adherence*,—cleaving to, trusting and acquiescing in, God in Christ, as declaring his love, grace, and good-will in his promises. This is the faith whereby *we live*, whereby we are justified,—the faith without which this ordinance will not profit, but disadvantage us; for without this faith we cannot discern the Lord's body,—we cannot discern him as crucified for us. This is that we are in an especial manner to examine ourselves about in reference to a participation of this ordinance; for *self-examination* is a gospel institution proper for this ordinance. And this is the faith whereby we are in Christ; without which a participation of the outward signs and pledges of Christ will not avail us. So, then, with faith thus acting, we are to be qualified and prepared unto a participation of this ordinance.

2. Another way by which faith ought to act in this ordinance, is that of *special application*. "Who loved me, and gave himself for me;"—this is faith acting by particular application. I hope the Lord has given us that faith whereby we may be prepared for this ordinance. And now I am to inquire and direct you a little in that faith which you may act in this ordinance. I say, it is this faith of special application to our own souls that God now requires we should act; and I prove it thus:—It is because in this ordinance there is a proposition, tender, and communication of Christ to *every one in particular*. In the promise of the gospel Christ is proposed *indefinitely*, to all that believe; and so the faith I mentioned before (of acquiescence in him) answers what is required of us by virtue of the promise in the gospel: but in this ordinance, by God's institution, Christ is tendered and given to me and to thee,—to every one in particular; for it is by his institution that the elements in this ordinance are

[1] Delivered April 16, 1676.

distributed to every particular person, to show that there is a tender and communication of Christ to particular persons. Now, such a particular communication is to be received by this particular faith, the faith of application, to receive him to our own souls.

And then, moreover, one great end of the ordinance is, manifestly, that it requires the acting of faith in a particular way of application to every one of us. It is for a farther incorporation of Christ in our souls; it is for receiving Christ as nourishment,—as the bread that came down from heaven,—as giving his body and blood for spiritual food. Now every one knows, that whatever feasts be prepared in the world, unless every one in particular takes his own portion, and eats and digests it, it will not turn to nourishment unto him. This particular act of application answers that eating, drinking, and digesting, which the nature of the ordinance does require. So, brethren, this is that I aim at,—that it is our duty, in this ordinance, to act a particular faith as to the application of Christ and all his benefits, each one to his own soul.

You will say, then, "What is *the special object* of this special faith?" Truly that which the apostle tells us here;—it is *special love*, in the first place; and it is *the special design* of the death of Christ, in the next place: "Who loved me, and gave himself for me." The object you ought to fix upon, in the exercise of this faith of application to your own souls, is the special love of Christ,—that Christ had a special love, not only to the church in general, but the truth is, Christ had a special love *for me* in particular. It will be a very hard thing for you or me to rise up to an act of faith that Christ hath a love for us in particular, unless we can answer this question, *Why should Christ love you or me in particular?* What answer can I give hereto, when I know he does not love *all the world?* I can give but this answer to it, *Even because he would.* I know nothing in me, or in any of you, that can deserve his love. Was there ever such a thing heard of,—that Christ should have a particular love for such as we are? would ever any person go and fix his love on a creature who was all over leprous? is this the manner of man? Truly, Christ would never have fixed his love upon any of our poor, defiled, leprous souls, but upon this one consideration, *I know I can cleanse them, and I will.* He loved us.

But what will he do with such deformed, polluted creatures as we are? Why, "he loved the church, and gave himself for it, that he might wash and purify it, and present it to himself a glorious church, not having spot or wrinkle, or any such thing." Though we are altogether deformed and defiled,—though no example, no instance can be given, in things below, or among the creatures, of any fixing love on such as we are, yet Christ has done it out of sovereign grace; with this resolution, that he would cleanse us with his own blood, to make us fit for himself.

O that God would help you and me to some firm, unshaken acts of faith, that Jesus Christ did, out of sovereign grace, love us in particular; and that in pursuit of this love he has washed us in his blood, to make us lovely and meet for himself! This is love to be adored and celebrated in time and to eternity.

This special love of Christ is not only to be considered by us, in this special acting of faith, as *free* and undeserved, but it is to be considered as *invincible*,—that would break through all oppositions, or whatever stood in the way,—that nothing should hinder or turn him aside in his design of doing good to our souls. It is a glorious pitch that the spouse rises to in Cant. viii. 7, "Many waters cannot quench love, neither can the floods drown it: if a man would give all the substance of his house for love, it would utterly be contemned;" speaking of her own love to Christ: nothing could quench, nothing could drown it, nothing could make a purchase of it from her; but her love was invincible, and would carry her through all difficulties. O how much more was the love of Christ! for our love being once fixed on Christ, meets with no difficulties of that nature that the love of Christ met withal when it was fixed on us. What did the love of Christ meet with, when it was fixed on us? *That* we must take along with us,—namely, "the curse of the law" was the first thing that presented itself to him: "The soul that sinneth, it shall die;"—"Cursed is every one that continueth not in all things written in the book of the law, to do them." That he was to make "his soul an offering for sin," was presented to him. We are to look on this love of Christ as sovereign and free, and with a design of making our souls lovely; so invincible, also, that it broke up the eternal obstacles,—that nothing could stand before it until it had accomplished his whole work and design: "Who loved me, and gave himself for me."

I speak on this manner, and of these things, to encourage and direct the weakest and most unskilful in the mysteries of the gospel,—to instruct them in the exercise of faith in this ordinance: and therefore I say, that as this special faith (which I proved to you to be our duty in this ordinance) is to respect the love of Christ; so it is to respect more especially the *peculiar acting* of the love of Christ, whereby he gave himself *for us*. Gave himself! how is that? Truly thus, brethren,—the Lord help me to believe it!—that I stood before the judgment-seat of God, charged with my original apostasy from him, and with all the sins of my life, multiplied above the hairs of my head, and being ready to perish, to have the sentence pronounced against me; then Christ came and stood in my place, putting the sinner aside, and undertaking to answer this matter: "Let the poor sinner stand aside a while. Come, enter into rest; abide here in the cleft of the rock; I will undertake thy cause, and plead it out at God's judgment-seat." In this undertaking God spared him not; as if God should say, "If you will stand in the place of the sinner, and undertake his cause, then it must go with you as with him; I will not spare." "Lo, I come," says Christ, notwithstanding this, "to do thy will, O God;"—"Whatever thou dost require to make good this cause I have espoused, lo, I come to do it."

So Christ loved me, and gave himself for me. Everlasting rest and peace will dwell upon our souls, if the Lord will be pleased to help us to exercise faith on Christ's love in this ordinance, wherein all these things are represented to us.

DISCOURSE XIX.[1]

"I am crucified with Christ: nevertheless I live; yet not I, but Christ liveth in me: and the life which I now live in the flesh I live by the faith of the Son of God, who loved me, and gave himself for me."—GAL. ii. 20.

THE apostle in this place is expressing the *vigour*, and indeed the *triumph*, of the life of faith: "Nevertheless I live." To show the excellency of that life, says he, "Yet not I, but Christ liveth in me," etc. That which I would to our purpose observe from these words is this, that the exercise of faith *on the death of Christ*—"Who loved me, and gave himself for me"—is *the very life* of faith. This is that we are now called to,—to the exercise of faith on the death of Christ. And I cannot more recommend it to you than by this observation, to show that the life of faith does greatly consist in this peculiar exercise of it upon the death of Christ. And that,—

1. *Because Christ in his death, as the ordinance of God for the salvation of believing sinners, is the proper and peculiar object of faith as it justifies and saves.* Now, when faith is in its exercise upon its direct, immediate, proper object, it is like a person that is feeding on his proper food, which gives refreshment, spirits, and strength; for faith and its object are in Scripture set out as an appetite and food; and especially it is so represented to us *in this ordinance*, where the spiritual food of our souls is conveyed to our faith under the symbol and representation of food to our bodies, which we eat and drink. Therefore, brethren, our faith is in its proper place, it is about its proper work, it is directing the soul to its special food, when it is exercised about the death of Christ as the ordinance of God for the salvation of sinners.

2. As the death of Christ is thus the immediate and direct object

[1] Delivered June 11, 1676.

of our faith,—for "God hath set him forth as a propitiation for sin, through faith in his blood," which is the proper object of faith, as it justifies,—so the ultimate and supreme object of our faith is, *the properties of God, as manifested and glorified in the death of Christ;* so that you shall see how faith has its plain and full work in coming to this, "Who loved me, and gave himself for me." The properties of God are God *himself;* the properties of God, as manifested and glorified, are God's *name;* and God himself and his name are the supreme and ultimate object of our faith and trust. All the inquiry, then, is, what special properties of the nature of God, God did design to manifest and glorify in the death of Christ, so as we should make them the special, ultimate object of our faith,—that which faith will find rest and satisfaction in, and wherein it will give glory to God. For the reason why God has made faith the *alone* instrument (and no other grace) of justification, and so of salvation, it is not because it is so fitted and suited to receive in us, as that it is the only grace whereby we give glory to God, and can do so.

Now let us see, that we may know how to exercise faith therein, what are those properties of the divine nature which God designs to manifest and glorify in the death of Christ; that our faith may stand in and be fixed upon them. I find several things that God distinctly proposes of his divine excellency for our faith to fix upon in the death of Christ:—

(1.) His *righteousness:* Rom. iii. 25, "Whom God hath set forth to be a propitiation through faith in his blood, to declare his righteousness." I shall not now show how or wherein; but, to me, this it is that manifests his righteousness in granting forgiveness of sin in the death of Christ,—in that he caused all our iniquities to meet upon him. Remember, brethren, we are here to give God the glory he designed to himself in sending Christ to die for us; and he tells us plainly what it was: and therefore it is expected of us that we should give glory to him. Let us labour to be in the actual exercise of faith, whereby we may declare the righteousness of God in this thing.

(2.) God designed *to glorify his love.* This is more particularly insisted on than any property of God in this matter. "God so loved the world, that he gave his only begotten Son." "God commendeth his love toward us, in that, while we were yet sinners, Christ died for us." "Herein is love, not that we loved God, but that he loved us, and sent his Son to be the propitiation for our sins." There is no property of the nature of God which he doth so eminently design to glorify in the death of Christ as his love. That we may know that God is love, that the Father himself loves us, he has sent Jesus Christ, out of his eternal love, to save sinners; and if we have not due apprehensions of these things, it is not our appearing in this place that will give glory to God.

(3.) God does design *to glorify his grace or pardoning mercy.* Eph. i. 6, "He hath made us accepted in the Beloved, to the praise of the glory of his grace." This God purposed, to make his grace in pardoning sinners very glorious by giving Christ to die for us.

(4.) God designed *to glorify his wisdom.* Eph. i. 8, "He has abounded towards us in all wisdom and prudence." Eph. iii. 10, There appeared "the manifold wisdom of God." 1 Cor. i. 24, "Christ the power of God, and the wisdom of God."

Now, let us gather up these things:—The special, ultimate object of faith, whereby we are justified, are those divine properties of God's nature which he designed to manifest in the death of Christ,—his righteousness, his love, his grace, his wisdom.

The reason, therefore, why the life of faith does consist in its exercise on the death of Christ, is, because the death of Christ is the immediate, proper object of faith, as the ordinance of God for the salvation of sinners; and because the glorious properties of the nature of God, which are manifested in the death of Christ, are the ultimate object of our faith, wherein we give glory to him, and find rest to our own souls.

Let us, then, be called on and be stirred up to this exercise of faith upon this present occasion. And to that end,—

1. We might consider *the deplorable condition of all our souls without this blessed provision* and ordinance of God for our deliverance by the death of Christ. We had been in a deplorable condition, the wrath of God abiding on us, had not God made this a blessed way for our deliverance.

2. If you would be found acting faith in this matter, labour to come up to a *firm, vigorous assent of your minds,* not only that these things are true, but that this is *the way wherein God will be glorified to eternity.* The truth of it is, that person who is firmly satisfied and heartily pleased that this way of the death of Christ for the salvation of sinners, by the forgiveness of sin, is the way whereby God is and will be glorified; I say, that person is a true believer. Now, let not your assent be only to this thing,—that it is true that Christ came into the world to save sinners; but to this,—that this is the way whereby God is and will be glorified. He will be glorified in pardoning such guilty creatures as we are, in imputing righteousness to such sinners as we are. He is glorified in laying all our iniquities on Christ. By this way, his righteousness, his love, grace, and wisdom, are all manifested; this is God's being glorified. If our souls come up to a free close with these things, that all these properties are manifested in this way,—that is an act of faith; and may the Lord help us unto it!

3. Let us *gather up our minds to this institution,* whereby these

things are represented to us. Here is represented the death of Christ, the immediate object of our faith, as God's ordinance. If the Lord help us to see it so represented to us, as that divine righteousness and wisdom, love and grace do all centre therein, and appear eminently to our souls, we shall have communion with God in this ordinance.

DISCOURSE XX.[1]

You have been minded of, and instructed in, the nature and benefit of our love to God; and I shall take occasion thence a little to mind you of the love of Christ unto us, the love, in an especial manner, which he showed in dying for us; which is that we are here gathered together to remember and celebrate; not barely the death of Christ, but that which is *the life of that death,*—the love of Christ in his death. And I would ground it on that which the apostle speaks in

Rom. v. 5,—"The love of God is shed abroad in our hearts by the Holy Ghost, which is given unto us."

This is that which I know you all long for, and prize above life: "The loving-kindness of God is better than life." Why so? "For," says he, "when we were yet without strength, in due time Christ died for the ungodly."

An apprehension of the love of Christ, as dying for us ungodly creatures, is that which is shed abroad in our hearts by the Holy Ghost. Do not let your minds go upon uncertainties. When the Holy Ghost gives you a due apprehension of Christ's love in dying for ungodly sinners, as we are, then is this love shed abroad in our hearts. The apostle there proceeds to show how *great* this love was, in that Christ died. He died, not for *good* men, and *righteous* men, and for *friends;* but he died for the *ungodly*, for *sinners*, and for *enemies.* This was great love, indeed. We are here to remember that love of Christ wherewith he gave himself to death for us when we were enemies, and would have continued so to eternity, had he not loved us, and given himself for us.

Brethren, if we barely remember the love of Christ in the way of an ordinance, and our hearts be not powerfully affected with it, we are in danger of being disadvantaged by our attendance. Pray remember it; you know how plainly I use to speak on these occasions: I say, we have frequent opportunities of remembering the love of

[1] Delivered September 3, 1676.

Christ in dying for us, in this ordinance representing of it; but if our hearts be not powerfully influenced and affected by it, we shall be losers by the frequency of ordinances.

I will add one word more. According as our hearts are affected with the love of Christ, so will be our love to Christ, and no otherwise. And truly, even that faith which discovers too much selfishness is very dangerous. If we come here to act faith, to look for no other effect of it but what evidence and sense we have of the pardon of our own sins,—how our consciences may be quieted and cleared,—faith ends *in self;* it is dangerous, lest it should be only a branch from, and commensurate with, convictions. True faith, acting itself on Christ in this ordinance, will work by love unto Christ: I would not say, principally, or in the first place,—I know poor creatures are apt to look after themselves, and their own relief; but it will so work also. And truly, brethren, this it will not do, we shall not have faith working by love towards him, unless we have some sense of the love of Christ on our hearts.

How shall we know whether our hearts are under the powerful influence of the love of Christ in dying for us? Why, the love of Christ in dying for us has three properties with it, which will have an influence on our souls, if we are affected with it:—

1. It has a *transforming* power, property, and efficacy with it. They are plain truths I am speaking, but of great concern to our souls, to know whether we are affected with the love of Christ or not. If we are rightly affected with it, I say, it will transform and change our whole souls in some measure into the likeness of Christ. How so? I will tell you in the most familiar manner I am able:—If you are affected with the love of Christ, it lays hold upon and possesses your *affections;* the affections being possessed, stir up many *thoughts;* thoughts are the very image of the soul, represent it, to show you what the soul is: and those things concerning which your thoughts do most abound, they carry *the frame of the soul.* Let a man profess what he will, if his thoughts are generally conversant about earthly and worldly things, he has an earthly and worldly mind; and if [his] thoughts are conversant about sensual things, he has a sensual and carnal mind: for, whatever he may outwardly say, *as he thinks, so is he;*—there is the image and likeness of the soul.

Now, if we are affected with the love of Christ, it will beget in our souls many thoughts of Christ,—in our lying down and in our rising up, in our beds, in our ways, on our occasions, as well as in ordinances. If, indeed, our hearts are affected with the love of Christ, our thoughts of Christ will abound; and those thoughts will work again on our affections, and conform our souls more and more unto the image of Jesus Christ. That man who thinks much of the earth, because affected with it, his soul is like the earth; and that man who thinks much on the love of Christ, because he is affected with it, his soul is like Christ.

If it has been thus with us, brethren, in our preparation for this ordinance, or at any time, that thoughts of Christ have not abounded, verily there has been a failing in us. Let us strive for the future to amend it, that we may find the love of Christ begetting in us many thoughts of him, working upon our affections, and, with a transforming power, changing the frame of our souls into his own likeness.

Again: 2. The love of Christ, if we are affected with it, has an *attractive* power: John xii. 32, "And I, if I be lifted up from the earth, will draw all men unto me." I cannot stay to show you the drawing power and efficacy there is in the love of Christ, when dying on the cross; but this I will say, it is that which converted the world of all that did believe. It was the love of Christ, set forth in his death as one crucified for them, that drew all men unto him. "When I am lifted up,—when I have accomplished, manifested, and evidenced the unspeakable love which I have for the sinful sons of men, in being lifted up for them,—I will draw them unto me." If you have a true sense, brethren, of the love of Christ in dying for you, it will draw your souls unto him. Cant. i. 4, "Draw me, we will run after thee." I do not now speak to you about the *first drawing* of Christ, which is as unto believing (I hope Christ has so drawn all our souls); but the *following efficacy* of the love of Christ to draw souls that do believe *nearer* unto him. Whoever is sensible of this attractive power of the death of Christ, it will have this efficacy upon him,—it will have adherence and delight,—it will cause him more to cleave to Christ. The soul will cleave to Christ with delight, that is affected with the attractive, drawing power of his loving-kindness in his death. There is a great deal in that word, "Cleave unto Christ with love and delight," with the best of our affections and dearest of our valuations; to cleave to him with trust, and to him alone. I do but remind you of what you know, that you may reduce it into practice. Pray, in this ordinance, labour to have such a sense of the drawing power of the love of Christ in his death, that you may resolve to cleave unto him with full purpose of heart, to cleave unto this Christ who has thus loved us.

3. Whenever we are affected with the love of Christ, it is accompanied with a *constraining* power, 2 Cor. v. 14, "The love of Christ constraineth us;" and that constraint is unto obedience: it constrains us to judge that we ought to live to him who died for us. It is a blessed thing, brethren, to walk in our obedience under a sense of the constraining efficacy of the love of Christ. Take but this one word, to discover to you whether you walk in your obedience under

a sense of the constraining power of Christ, it comprehends all others, 1 John v. 3, "His commandments are not grievous." When a soul works out of love, what it doth is "not grievous." And the inward and outward commands of Christ will be grievous to all that are not under the constraining power and efficacy of his love.

I have no more to say, but only to tell you that we should labour to have our hearts affected with the love of Christ in this ordinance. I have showed you the danger if it be otherwise; and given you some ways to examine your hearts, whether they are so affected or not. The Lord grant that where they are, it may be increased; and where they are not, that God would renew it by his Spirit in us.

DISCOURSE XXI.[1]

We have had, through the providence of God, so good and so seasonable a word unto the present occasion, that there is no need, as well as but little time, to offer any thing farther unto you; yet a few words, in compliance with what we have heard, may not be altogether unseasonable or unuseful.

Our business and duty is, to set forth the sufferings and death of our Lord Jesus Christ, and therein principally to call to mind his love. What you have heard may very well occasion us to think of that passage of the apostle wherein he earnestly prays for them,—

Eph. iii. 19,—"And to know the love of Christ, which passeth knowledge."

This is a *peculiar* kind of expression. The meaning is, that we may know that *experimentally*, which we cannot know *comprehensively;* —that we may know *that* in its *power* and *effects*, which we cannot comprehend in its *nature* and *depths.* A weary person may receive refreshment from a spring, who cannot fathom the depths of the ocean from whence it doth proceed. And if we would have our hearts, in this ordinance, and at other times, affected with the love of Christ, which is the thing we are to aim at (to know his love, and to experience the power of it), it is of great advantage to us to consider that it is such a love as passes knowledge; that our faith concerning it must issue in *admiration*, not *comprehension.*

I shall name two or three things that may give a little sense of this love as it passes knowledge.

1. The *love of Christ is the fountain and spring of all the glory*

[1] Delivered October 29, 1676.

that is in heaven, or shall be there unto all eternity. God's eternal glory is eternally the same, "From everlasting to everlasting thou art God;" but all the created glory that is in heaven, or that ever shall be there, springs out of the love of Christ. It is true, the angels were not *redeemed* by him; but they were *confirmed* by him. They were not recovered out of a lost estate by him; but they were continued in their first estate by him. Hence it is that God gathered all things in heaven and earth unto a head in him, Eph. i. 10. And there is a great deal to the same purpose in that expression of the apostle, when he had mentioned "principalities and powers," Col. i. 17, "By him all things consist;" they have their consistence in him. All would dissolve and fall to nothing, if they had not their consistence in Jesus Christ. Certainly this is a love that passes knowledge, that is the fountain and spring of all the glory that is in heaven. If God help us by faith to look within the vail, and to take a view of all those glories wherewith the holy God is encompassed, we shall see that this love is the fountain and spring of them. The interposition of Christ saved the creation, and brought in that everlasting glory that shall dwell in heaven. God knows this love,—God understands the way of it; but as to us, it passes knowledge.

Again: 2. This *love of Christ passes the comprehension and knowledge of angels;* and therefore Peter tells us, 1 Epist. i. 12, speaking of the sufferings of Christ, and the glory that followed, "Which things," says he, "the angels desire to" bow down and "look into."[1] The angels in heaven live in an admiration of the love of Christ unto sinners; that is, that love he expressed in suffering, and in the glory that did ensue. And, oh! what thoughts ought *we* to have of this love, who have all the benefits of it? The angels had no benefit by the sufferings of Christ; but their benefit and advantage ensued on the assumption of the human nature to bring the creation into a consistence, and in his interposition between God and all his creatures. They admire and adore it. What ought such poor creatures as we are to do? It may well be said to pass *our* knowledge, for it passes the knowledge of *all the angels* in heaven.

3. It passes knowledge, in that *the effects of it in Christ himself pass all our knowledge and comprehension.*

To give but two instances:—(1.) His *condescension to assume our human nature passes all our comprehension.* No man can fully understand the mystery of the assumption of our nature into the personal subsistence of the Son of God. Some dispute whether we shall *understand* the *mystery* of the incarnation *in heaven; here we believe* it. It is love which passes knowledge, that the eternal Son of God

[1] Owen seems desirous, by this paraphrase, to express the full meaning of the original word, παρακύψαι.—Ed.

should take our nature into personal union with himself: it is that we may admire, and ought to admire; and God help us, we are such poor earthly creatures, that we cannot admire it as we ought, though it be much in our nature to admire what we cannot comprehend.

(2.) We *cannot fully understand his passion and sufferings.* God alone knows what is in the curse of the law; we do not know it. God alone knows what is *the true desert of sin;* it cannot be fully understood by any but himself. They who undergo it must suffer to eternity; there is no end,—they never see, never know, what sin deserved. How do we know, then, what Christ suffered, when the punishment due to our sin, when all our iniquities met upon him, with the curse of the law? God only knows what is in these things. The *fruits and effects* of this love in himself, in his incarnation and passion, are past our knowledge; therefore *the love itself* surpasses our knowledge.

4. Give me leave to say, *the very fruits of it in ourselves do pass knowledge.* No man that lives knows what there is in these three general heads of the fruits of Christ's love,—in *justification* and pardon of sin,—in the *renovation* and sanctification of our natures, and in the *inhabitation* and consolations of the Holy Spirit. No man living can find out these things to perfection. None of us fully understands and comprehends what it is to be justified in the sight of God, to have sin pardoned, to have our natures renewed and transformed into the likeness of God, and to have the Holy Ghost dwell in us. The love of Christ, therefore, passes all knowledge; for the very fruits of it in ourselves are beyond what we can comprehend,—there is a greatness in them we cannot reach unto. Why, then, my brethren, let us labour to have our hearts affected with this love. If God would be pleased to give unto every one of us some sense and impression of the greatness of this love of Christ, glance it into our hearts, beam it upon us in this ordinance,—we should have cause to bless him all the days of our lives. The faith and light of it issue in admiration; the light of glory will bring us to comprehension. Let us have such a sense as may cause us to admire what we cannot now comprehend.

(1.) I could speak something, but I will not now, to *the actings of faith* in admiration; it being the proper nature of faith to issue itself in the admiration of that which is infinite. If we can get our souls up to a holy admiration of this love, we have some gracious sense of it upon our hearts, if we can go no farther.

(2.) Let us learn to *run up all the mercies* we are partakers of, whatsoever it be we value, *to the proper spring:* "Who loved me, and gave himself for me." If we have any relief, or supply, or refreshment of soul, in a sense of pardon of sin, in spiritual light or consolation, pray let us exercise ourselves to run up all these things to the fountain:—it is all from the love of Christ, that unspeakable love which passes knowledge.

(3.) *In this let us be ashamed,* [that] seeing the love of Christ to us is such as passes our knowledge, our love to him is so weak, that *sometimes we know not whether we have any or not.* For this let us be greatly humbled. This is not the way to answer that love which passes knowledge, to know not whether we love Christ again or not. Let us be ashamed for our want of love.

And lastly, *let us abound in praise and thanksgiving for his love,* and all the fruits of it.

For my part, I do not know whether that vision in Rev. v. 9 does express the rejoicing of the *church above,* or the duty of the *church below;* but both, I am sure, are of so near affinity, that apply it to which you will, you do not miss it. And what do they there? Why, it is said, "They sung a new song, saying, Thou art worthy to take the book, and to open the seals thereof: for thou wast slain, and hast redeemed us to God by thy blood, out of every kindred, and tongue, and people, and nation; and hast made us unto our God kings and priests," etc. And it is said again, "Worthy is the Lamb that was slain to receive power, and riches, and wisdom, and strength, and honour, and glory, and blessing;" and again he repeats it in verse 13. I say, I know not whether this be a representation of the rejoicing of the church above, or a representation of the duty of the church below; but I can conclude from it, that the enjoyment of the one and the duty of the other consist greatly in continual giving praise and thanks to Christ for his unspeakable love in our redemption.

DISCOURSE XXII.[1]

"And lo a voice from heaven, saying, This is my beloved Son, in whom I am well pleased."—MATT. iii. 17.

WE are met here to remember the death of Christ, in the way and by the means that he himself hath appointed; and in remembering *the death of Christ* we are principally to remember *the love of Christ:* "Who loved us, and washed us from our sins in his own blood." And that which on our part is required herein is *faith in Christ,* who died for us; and *love to Christ,* who loved us so as to give himself an offering and a sacrifice to God for us.

1. That which I would now observe is this (to make way for the stirring up of our love), that *the person of Christ is the adequate, complete object of the love of God, and of the whole creation that*

[1] Delivered February 18, 1676.

bears the image of God;—I mean, the church of God above, the angels and saints; and the church of God below, in believers: which are the creation that has the image of God upon it.

The person of Christ is the first complete object of the love of God the Father. A great part (if I may so speak, and I must so speak) of the essential blessedness of the holy Trinity consists in the mutual love of the Father and the Son, by the Holy Ghost; which is the love of them both.

That which I would now take notice of, I say, as the foundation of all, is this,—that the *divine nature* in the person of the Son is the only full, resting, complete object of the love of God the Father. I will give you a place or two of Scripture for it, and so go on to another instance: Prov. viii. 30, "Then," saith he (that is, from everlasting), "I was by him, as one brought up with him: and I was daily his delight, rejoicing always before him;" that is, as the special object of his love,—as among you men, one that is brought up with you, as your child is. The delight of the Father from all eternity was in the Son. The ineffable love and mutual delight of the Father and the Son by the Spirit is that which is the least notion we have of the blessedness of the eternal God. John i. 18, "The only begotten Son, which is in the bosom of the Father." Pray observe it, that I speak yet only of the divine person of Christ *antecedent* unto his incarnation, and the ineffable mutual love of the blessed persons in the holy Trinity; which Jesus Christ wonderfully sets out in John xvii. There is his relation unto God; he is "the only begotten Son," by eternal generation. What follows? He is "in the bosom of the Father,"—is in the Father's eternal, infinite love. Herein is God's love; and every thing else of love is but a free act of the will of God,—a free emanation from this eternal love between the Father and the Son. God never did any thing *without himself*, but the end of it was to manifest what is *in himself*. The old and new creation that God hath wrought was to manifest what was in himself. God made this world to manifest his power and wisdom;—God made the new world by Jesus Christ to manifest his grace, his love, goodness, etc.

The sole reason why there is such a thing as love in the world among the creatures, angels or men,—that God ever implanted it in the nature of rational creatures,—was, that it might shadow and represent the ineffable, eternal love that the Father had unto the Son, and the Son unto the Father, by the Spirit.

Contemplative men of old did always admire love; wherein they would have the life, lustre, and glory of all things to consist: but they could never see the *rise* of it; and they traced some things to this,—that God necessarily loved himself. And it is true, it cannot otherwise be; but God's loving of himself absolutely as God, is nothing but his eternal blessed acquiescence in the holy, self-sufficing properties of his nature. This they had some reach after; but of this eternal, ineffable love "of the Father to the Son, and of the Son to the Father, by the Spirit," that they had no conjecture of. Yet this is the fountain and spring-head; and all such things as love in the old and new creation, as I said, is but to resemble and shadow out this great prototype of divine love. I acknowledge there is little discerned of these things, by reason of the weakness of our understandings; but the Scripture has so directly declared to us the mutual love of the Father and the Son (which, truly, is of such singular use, that I would fix persons upon it in conceiving of the doctrine of the Trinity), that it is matter of admiration and thankfulness to us. Here lies the foundation of all love, whereunto we hope to reduce our love unto Christ,—namely, in the unchangeable love of the Father to the Son.

2. The person of Christ, *as vested with our nature*, and undertaking the work of mediation, is the first object of the Father's love wherein there is any mixture of any thing *without himself.*

The first love of God the Father to the Son is that which we call *ad intra*, where the divine persons are objects of one another's actings;—the Father knows the Son, and the Son knows the Father; the Father loves the Son, and the Son loves the Father; and so, consequently, of the Holy Ghost, the medium of all these actings.

But now, I say, the first act of the love of God the Father wherein there is any thing *ad extra*, or *without the divine essence*, is the person of Christ considered as invested with our nature. And had not the love of God been fixed in the first place in all things upon the person of Christ, there would have been no redundancy to us, nor communication of love unto us. From the first eternal love of God proceeds all love that was in the first creation; and from this second love of God, to the person of Christ as incarnate, proceeds all the love in the second creation. See how God expresses it in a prospect of what he should be, Isa. xlii. 1, "Behold my servant, whom I uphold; mine elect, in whom my soul delighteth." And this is singular in the whole Scripture, that God spake the same words twice from heaven immediately; and they were these, "This is my beloved Son, in whom I am well pleased,"—at his baptism, Matt. iii. 17, and at his entrance on his sufferings, Matt. xvii. 5;—which was the voice which came from "The excellent glory." I would observe this unto you, because I think it is what God would have us take notice of, the emphasis in the words, "Behold my servant, mine elect, my Son, my beloved Son!" What of him?—"In whom I rest, in whom I am well pleased and delighted." All of them emphatical words. Saith God. "Let the sons of men (I speak it from heaven again and again) take notice of this, that the infinite love of my whole soul is fixed on the person of Jesus Christ as incarnate." And you will find the Lord Jesus Christ pleading this as the ground of that trust committed unto him, and all that he received, John iii. 35, "The Father loveth the Son, and hath given all things into his hand." John v. 20, "The Father loveth the Son, and showeth him all things that himself doeth: and he will show him greater works than these." He lays the foundation of all the trust that God the Father committed unto him in the peculiar love of the Father to him, as the Son incarnate.

Truly, I shall not go beyond this foundation to manifest to you that the person of Christ is the complete, adequate object of the love of the Father. The great satisfaction of the soul of God, wherein he rests and delights, consists in love to Christ as incarnate.

I will make but this one inference from it:—proportionable to the renovation of the image and likeness of God upon any of our souls, is our love to Jesus Christ. He that knows Jesus Christ most, is most like unto God; for there the soul of God rests,—there is the complacency of God: and if we would be like to God, have pledges in ourselves of the renovation of this image upon us, it must be in the gracious exercise of our love to the person of Jesus Christ. And pray let me observe it to you, the world, that is full of enmity to God, doth not exercise its enmity against God *immediately* under the first notion of God, but exerciseth its enmity against God *in Christ:* and if we return to God by the renovation of his image, we do not exercise our love to God immediately as God, but our love to God by and in Christ: "That ye through him might believe in God." Here is a trial, brethren, of our return to God, and of the renovation of his image in us,—namely, in our love to Jesus Christ. There God and man do meet,—there God and his church above and below centre. The Lord grant that this ordinance may be the means to stir up our hearts more to the exercise of this grace!

DISCOURSE XXIII.[1]

I SHALL speak to them who have a mind to be found performing their duty, but, it may be, it doth not occur to them what is particularly required of them. They are such as are least acquainted with this mystery that I would have most respect unto, that nothing of God's provision in his house may be lost to his children for want of understanding aright to come to his table, where he makes this provision.

[1] Delivered July 8, 1677.

I pray you, brethren, exercise your thoughts unto the *institution* of this ordinance, wherein you exercise your obedience; unto the *proposition* of Christ in this ordinance, wherein consists the peculiar acting of your faith; and unto the *exhibition* of Christ in this ordinance, which is the ground of your thankfulness.

What shall I do that I may please God now, please Jesus Christ, and benefit my own soul, in the administration of this ordinance?

Why,—1. Consider the *institution* of it, wherein we have the authority of Jesus Christ put forth and acting towards our souls: "This do in remembrance of me." Labour, therefore, to bring your hearts into an actual obedience to the authority of Jesus Christ in what we are about. This the Lord Jesus doth require at our hands. We do not come here in a customary manner, to satisfy our convictions, because we ought to come; we do not come here merely to make use of our privilege; but our hearts are to *bow to the authority of Jesus Christ.* Consider, I pray you, the institution of this ordinance, and labour to bring your souls into actual obedience to Jesus Christ. We do it because Christ has required it of us. If our hearts are in that frame, that we are here upon the command of Christ, to do what he has appointed, and we can recommend our consciences unto him, that it is in obedience to his command that we are here, then our obedience is in exercise.

2. Consider the *proposition* that is made of Jesus Christ in this ordinance to us, that our faith may be in its proper exercise.

The Lord take off our hearts from the consideration of the outward signs merely! Christ in his love, Christ in his bloodshed, agony, and prayer, Christ in his death, is here proposed before us. "Ye do show the Lord's death." Who proposes it? He that hath appointed these things proposes it. And there is the engagement of the faithfulness of God and Christ in this proposition and tender that is made of Jesus Christ; and it is a peculiar way, and, as I could prove, full of love, that God hath found out a way to propound Christ as dying, and crucified, to all our souls. Therefore stir up your hearts to this. To every one of you there is, by the grace and faithfulness of God, a proposal of Jesus Christ in his death, and all the benefits of it, unto your souls. The whole question is, whether you will stir up your hearts to a new and fresh receiving of Jesus Christ, who is thus proposed and tendered unto you, evidently crucified before your eyes, offered to you by the love and faithfulness of God? But if we do not endeavour, every one of us, in the participation of this ordinance, a fresh acceptance of Jesus Christ, we do what we can to make God a liar, as though he was not tendered unto us. The especial exercise of your faith in this ordinance is upon the love, grace, and faithfulness of God, proposing and tendering of Christ unto you,—the death of Christ, and the benefits of Christ, in this way which he has chosen. Submit unto it, and embrace it.

3. As your obedience is required with respect to the institution (we give this account before God, angels, and men, that we are here in obedience to the command of our Lord Jesus Christ), and as faith is required with respect to the proposition of Christ, whereby he is evidently proposed and tendered by God unto us; so in this ordinance, to them that believe, there is an *exhibition* of Christ. Christ is really exhibited and communicated to the souls of men who exercise faith upon him in this ordinance,—really exhibited, with all the benefits of his death. And want of receiving by faith in particular Christ as exhibited and communicated in this ordinance, is the great ground of our want of profiting by it, and thriving under it,—of our want of receiving strength, joy, and life by it; because we do not exercise ourselves to the receiving of Christ as he is exhibited, as God doth really give him out and communicate him to them that do believe.

That there is such an exhibition of Christ, appears,—(1.) By *the sacramental relation* there is between the *outward elements* and the *thing signified.* "This is my body," says Christ,—"this bread is so;" and, "This is my blood." It is the body of Christ and the blood of Christ that we are invited to the participation of. If there was no more in this ordinance exhibited but only the outward elements, and not, by virtue of sacramental relation upon God's institution, the body and blood of Christ, his life, and death, and merits, exhibited unto us, we should come to the Lord's table like men in a dream, eating and drinking, and be quite empty when we have done; for this bread and wine will not satisfy *our souls.*

(2.) As it is plain, from the sign and the thing signified, that there is a grant or a real communication of Jesus Christ unto the souls of them that do believe; so it is evident *from the nature of the exercise of faith* in this ordinance. It is by *eating and drinking.* Can you eat and drink, unless something be really communicated? You are called to eat the flesh and drink the blood of the Son of man; unless *really communicated,* we cannot eat it nor drink it. We may have other apprehensions of these things, but our faith cannot be exercised in eating and drinking; which is a receiving of what is really exhibited and communicated. As truly, my brethren, as we do eat of this bread, and drink of this cup, which is really communicated to us; so every true believer doth receive Christ, his body and blood, in all the benefits of it, that are really exhibited by God unto the soul in this ordinance: and it is a means of communicating to faith.

We come to receive a crucified Christ, come to be made partakers of the body and blood of the Lord,—to have the Lord Jesus really united to our hearts more and more. The Lord open our hearts to embrace the tender, receive the exhibition, take in Jesus Christ as food; that he may be incorporated in our hearts by faith, that he may dwell in us plentifully more and more,—that we may go away refreshed by this heavenly food, this glorious feast of fat things, which the Lord has made in his mount for his people! The whole of our comfort depends on our particular receiving of Christ by faith, and carrying him away by believing.

DISCOURSE XXIV.[1]

We are met together again, by the patience and kindness of God, for the celebration of this great ordinance; and therein to show forth the death of the Lord.

I have often spoken to you on this occasion concerning the nature of this ordinance, the expression of the love of God and Christ that is in it, and the especial acts of faith and love that are required of us in this ordinance.

I have one word now, somewhat of another nature, but yet such as I judge not unseasonable; and it is to this purpose,—that we, who so frequently enjoy the privilege of the representation of the death of Christ unto us, ought to be very diligent in inquiring after *an experience of the power of the death of Christ in us.* Without this, our privilege will not be to our advantage.

The power and efficacy of the death of Christ, which we now remember in a peculiar manner, is twofold:—

1. Towards *God*, as the consummation of the sacrifice of atonement. This we have often spoke to.

2. Towards *our own souls* and towards the *church;* and that is, to be an example, a precedent, a pattern of what is to be wrought in us. In this sense the power of the death of Christ, is its efficacy to [produce] conformity with Christ in his death. It is to be "crucified with Christ," as the apostle speaks, Gal. ii. 20. Power comes forth from the death of Christ, if received by faith in a due manner, to render us conformable to him in the death of sin in us. The apostle has a great and glorious word concerning himself, 2 Cor. iv. 10, "Always bearing about in the body the dying of the Lord Jesus." I acknowledge, the words are usually applied to the representation of the sufferings of Christ in the sufferings of the ministers of the gospel, concerning which the apostle there discourses; but the antithesis in the following

[1] Delivered September 30, 1677.

words, "That the life of Jesus might be manifest in our body," does certainly lead to a larger sense. Then, brethren, we may have an experience of the power of Christ in us, when we can say we always carry about with us the dying of the Lord Jesus,—carry it in our meditation, carry it in our conversation, carry it in our constant, universal endeavours for conformity to it; and without this we have not experience of the power of his death in us, and it will not avail us to have the nature of his death represented to us.

1. We are always to carry about the dying of Jesus Christ in *our thoughts and meditations.* O that our thoughts were much fixed upon it! I verily believe that the life of faith doth answer in proportion to our thoughts about the dying of Jesus. The dying of Jesus compriseth the love from whence he died, the death itself he died, and the end for which he died. Let us carry about us always thoughts hereof, for his sake who loved us, and who died for us. Meditate more on these things.

2. In our *conversation.* It is not a time to reflect upon any, unless I did it upon myself. But truly, brethren, I am afraid we do not carry about and manifest to all the dying of the Lord Jesus in our conversation; or perform all things so as it may appear and be made manifest to ourselves and others that our hearts are set upon his dying love, and that we have not such quick, such active and vigorous affections to the world and the things of the world, nor that fury of diligence after them and in them, as other men have, and we have had; *we* cannot do it,—the dying of the Lord Jesus crucifies our hearts. These are hard words, I know;—how far from our practice! But if we live not in an endeavour after it, in all things to manifest that our hearts are full of the dying of the Lord Jesus, we have not experience of the power of it in our souls. These things depend on one another. If we dwelt more upon this subject in our meditations, we should manifest it, and carry it about and represent it more in our conversation.

3. Carry it about, in *a constant endeavour for conformity to Jesus Christ in all things in his death.* Did CHRIST die, and shall *sin* live? Was he crucified in the world, and shall we have quick and lively affections to the world? O where is the temper and spirit of that apostle who, by "the cross of Christ, was crucified to the world, and the world crucified to him"? If there be any among us that should be indulgent to the life of any one lust or corruption, that soul can have no experience of the power of the death of Christ in himself,—cannot carry about him the dying of Christ. Endeavour to destroy sin, that we may be like unto Christ.

I will not make particular application of these things to all the concerns of our walk, but leave it with you with this word; begging of you and my own heart, and of God for us all, that, having these blessed representations of the death of Christ to us, we may have no rest in our spirits but when we have experience of the power of the death of Christ in us.

DISCOURSE XXV.[1]

It is a common, received notion among Christians, and it is true, that there is a peculiar communion with Christ in this ordinance, which we have in no other ordinance; that there is a peculiar acting of faith in this ordinance, which is in no other ordinance. This is the faith of the whole church of Christ, and has been so in all ages. This is the greatest mystery of all the *practicals* of our Christian religion,—a way of receiving Christ by *eating and drinking*,—something peculiar, that is not in prayer, that is not in the hearing of the word, nor in any other part of divine worship whatsoever,—a peculiar participation of Christ, a peculiar acting of faith towards Christ. This participation of Christ is not *carnal*, but *spiritual*. In the beginning of the ministry of our Lord Jesus Christ, when he began to instruct them in the communication of himself and the benefit of his mediation to believers, because it was a new thing, he expresses it by eating his flesh, and drinking his blood, John vi. 53, "Except ye eat the flesh of the Son of man, and drink his blood, ye have no life in you." This offended and amazed them. They thought he taught them to eat his natural flesh and blood. "How can this man give us his flesh to eat?" They thought he instructed them to be cannibals. Whereupon he gives that everlasting rule for the guidance of the church, which the church forsook, and thereby ruined itself;—saith he, "It is the Spirit that quickeneth; the flesh profiteth nothing: the words that I speak unto you, they are spirit, and they are life." "It is a spiritual communication," saith he, "of myself unto you; but it is as intimate, and gives as real an incorporation, as if you did eat my flesh and drink my blood." The church, forsaking this rule of a spiritual interpretation, ruined itself, and set up a monster instead of this blessed, mysterious ordinance.

We may inquire, therefore, how faith doth peculiarly act itself towards Christ in this ordinance, whereby we have a distinct participation of Christ, otherwise than we have by and in any other ordinance whatsoever. And I would mention four things unto you, which you may make use of:—

[1] Delivered September 20, 1682.

1. That faith hath a peculiar respect to the *sole authority of Christ* in the institution of this ordinance.

All other ordinances draw upon the *light of nature* and upon the *moral law*, as prayer, preaching the word, and singing of psalms to the praise of God; but *this*, that we should receive Jesus by eating of bread and drinking of wine, it has no respect to the light of nature or the moral law at all: and we should as soon choose to honour God by sacrifices and eating the flesh of them, if it were not for the authority of Jesus Christ. Herein doth faith give honour to Christ in his *kingly office*. This is the most direct profession of the subjection of our souls and consciences to the authority of Christ in all our religion. We can give no other reason, we can take no allusion from things, but merely this,—Christ would have it so.

2. Faith hath a peculiar respect *to the love of Christ in dying for us*, making the atonement for us by his blood, and therein the glorifying of the wisdom, love, and grace of God the Father. Faith is led into special communion with Christ as dying for us to make the atonement; and therein we give glory to Christ in *his priestly office* in a peculiar manner in this ordinance, it respecting the sacrifice of Christ, whereby he made atonement for us.

3. Faith hath respect *to this special manner of the exhibition of Christ to the souls of believers*, under the outward signs and symbols of bread and wine, by his institution making such a sacramental union between the thing signified and the sign, that the signs remaining to be what they are in themselves, they are unto us the thing that is signified, by virtue of the sacramental union that Christ hath appointed between his body and blood and the benefits of it: and this bread and wine, though not changed at all in themselves, yet they become to us, by faith, not what they are in themselves, but what is signified by them,—the body and blood of Christ. Herein we give glory to Christ in his *prophetical office*. It is he who has revealed, taught, and instructed his church in this truth, which depends on the sacramental union which follows by his institution. That is the third thing wherein faith peculiarly acts itself in this ordinance.

4. The fourth thing is, the *mysteriousness;* which I leave to your *experience*, for it is beyond expression,—*the mysterious reception* of Christ in this peculiar way of exhibition. There is a reception of Christ as tendered in the *promise of the gospel;* but here is a *peculiar way* of his exhibition under outward signs, and a mysterious reception of him in them, really, so as to come to a real substantial incorporation in our souls. This is that which believers ought to labour after an experience of in themselves,—to find that indeed, under these four considerations, they submit to the authority of Jesus Christ in a peculiar manner, giving him the glory of his *kingly office;*

mixing faith with him as dying and making atonement by his blood, so giving him the glory and honour of his *priestly office;* much considering the sacramental union that is, by his institution, between the outward signs and the thing signified, thus glorifying him in his *prophetical office;* and raising up their souls to a mysterious reception and incorporation of him,—receiving him to dwell in them, warming, cherishing, comforting, and strengthening their hearts.

I have mentioned these things as those which lie in your practice, and to obviate that (if I may mention it) which you may be tried with. There is but one plausible pretence that our adversaries, who design to oppress us, have in this business: "If," say they, "there be not a *real presence* and a real substantial transmutation of the elements into the substance of the body and blood of Christ, show you a way whereby you may have a peculiar communion with Christ, any more than in the word preached." We say, we have in these things *experience of a peculiar communion* with Christ, in a way made proper to this ordinance, which is not to be found in any other ordinance.

END OF VOL. IX.